1964	1965	1966	1967	1968	1969	1970	1971					1976	1977
31.6	34.2	37.3	40.4	44.0	48.0	50.6	55.1	61.6	70.5	82.2	95.0	108.1	120.6
10.0	12.2	13.9	13.1	13.9	16.3	15.9	17.9	20.4	26.3	33.9	36.7	42.4	45.0
10.5	11.8	13.9	15.8	17.5	19.4	22.1	24.6	27.1	30.3	37.0	44.6	50.2	56.7
10.1	10.8	12.6	14.2	16.2	17.8	20.1	21.1	23.8	29.9	37.8	39.0	44.3	51.2
9.5	10.8	12.6	13.5	15.2	17.7	17.8	19.5	22.8	28.1	37.5	42.0	45.7	51.6
52.7	58.1	64.9	69.8	76.3	84.0	90.4	98.6	110.1	129.2	154.3	173.9	200.3	221.4
26.6	29.6	33.5	37.1	40.3	45.1	48.9	53.6	60.1	69.2	82.6	96.3	111.4	123.4
1.7	1.9	2.1	2.4	2.8	3.2	3.5	4.0	4.7	5.8	8.6	10.4	13.0	15.5
6.4	7.0	7.5	7.7	8.6	9.3	8.9	9.9	12.1	16.9	22.0	21.4	22.7	24.1
5.4	5.6	6.4	5.9	6.5	7.0	7.1	7.6	7.9	9.9	10.9	11.9	12.2	12.6
40.1	44.1	49.5	53.1	58.2	64.6	68.4	75.1	84.8	101.8	124.1	140.0	159.3	175.6
6.4	7.1	8.0	8.7	9.4	10.0	11.7	12.4	13.1	13.1	13.0	14.3	18.6	20.9
6.2	6.7	7.4	8.1	8.7	9.5	10.3	11.2	12.2	14.2	17.2	19.7	22.5	24.9
52.7	58.1	64.9	69.8	76.3	84.0	90.4	98.6	110.1	129.2	154.3	173.9	200.3	221.4
289.5	307.4	326.1	337.2	354.9	375.0	384.7	404.1	426.7	458.2	476.2	487.1	513.6	530.9
7.1	6.2	6.1	3.4	5.2	5.7	2.6	5.0	5.6	7.4	3.9	2.3	5.4	3.4
19.3	19.6	20.0	20.4	20.7	21.0	21.3	22.0	22.2	22.5	22.8	23.1	23.4	23.7
6.9	7.1	7.5	7.7	8.0	8.2	8.4	8.6	8.9	9.3	9.6	10.0	10.5	10.8
6.6	6.9	7.2	7.5	7.6	7.8	7.9	8.1	8.3	8.8	9.1	9.3	9.8	9.9
0.3	0.3	0.3	0.3	0.4	0.4	0.5	0.5	0.6	0.5	0.5	0.7	0.7	0.9
54.1	54.4	55.1	55.5	55.5	55.8	57.8	58.1	58.6	59.7	60.5	61.1	61.5	61.8
4.7	3.9	3.3	3.8	4.5	4.4	5.7	6.2	6.2	5.6	5.3	6.9	7.0	8.0
15,000	15,684	16,305	16,529	17,145	17,857	18,061	18,368	19,221	20,364	20,886	21,087	21,949	22,401
4.9	4.6	4.0	1.4	3.7	4.2	1.1	1.7	4.6	5.9	2.6	1.0	4.1	2.1
–	–	–	–	32.2	35.7	38.9	43.8	49.8	58.1	70.1	81.5	94.6	110.7
18.2	18.9	19.9	20.7	21.5	22.4	23.5	24.4	25.8	28.2	32.4	35.7	39.0	41.7
2.2	3.8	5.3	4.0	3.9	4.2	4.9	3.8	5.7	9.3	14.9	10.2	9.2	6.9
19.6	20.0	20.8	21.5	22.4	23.4	24.2	24.9	26.1	28.1	31.1	34.5	37.1	40.0
2.1	2.0	4.0	3.4	4.2	4.5	3.4	2.9	4.8	7.7	10.7	10.9	7.5	7.8
−0.5	−1.8	−1.7	−1.4	−1.1	−2.1	0.5	−1.0	−2.4	−2.1	−4.5	−8.3	−7.5	−7.4
3.8	4.0	5.0	4.6	6.3	7.2	6.0	3.5	3.6	5.5	7.8	7.4	8.9	7.3
5.1	5.3	5.7	6.0	6.7	7.6	7.9	7.0	7.2	7.6	8.9	9.0	9.2	8.7

FOUNDATIONS *of* MACROECONOMICS

T he challenge and thrill of learning a new subject is like the task of the explorers who first charted Canada's lakes and rivers. When we set out, we are unsure of the direction to take. Along the way, we often feel lost. But as we progress forward, we see ever more clearly the path we're taking, even the parts where we felt lost, and we see how our path fits into a bigger and broader picture.

Students, like explorers, benefit enormously from the experience of those who have explored before them and from the maps that these earlier explorers have made. They also benefit from retracing their path. And they gain perspective by pausing on the way and looking back at where they've been.

Our aims in *Foundations of Macroeconomics* are to travel with you on a journey of discovery, to support you every step of the way so that you are never disoriented or lost, and to help you understand and appreciate the economic landscape that surrounds you.

The cover of this text symbolizes our aims. The lake is the terrain of economics that we're going to cover, understand, and appreciate. The rising sun and *Foundations* icon are our light sources and map— the clearest and most sharply focused explanations and illustrations of economic principles and ideas. The icon also emphasizes the idea of building blocks that fit one on top of another but that stand on a firm foundation. Each block is a small and easily handled object that can be understood on its own and then more keenly appreciated as part of a larger picture.

FOUNDATIONS *of* MACROECONOMICS

ROBIN BADE   **MICHAEL PARKIN**   **BRIAN LYONS**

University of   *Sheridan College*
Western Ontario

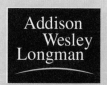

Addison
Wesley
Longman

Toronto

National Library of Canada Cataloguing in Publication Data

Bade, Robin
    Foundations of macroeconomics

Canadian ed.
Includes index.
ISBN 0-201-79334-2

1. Macroeconomics. 1. Parkin, Michael, 1939–   . II. Lyons, Brian. III. Title.

HB172.5.B32 2003   339   C2001-903215-3

0-201-79334-2

Vice President, Editorial Director: Michael J. Young
Executive Editor: Dave Ward
Projects Manager: Andrew Winton
Marketing Manager: Deborah Meredith
Developmental Editor: Madhu Ranadive
Production Editor: Marisa D'Andrea
Copy Editor: Gail Marsden
Production Coordinator: Deborah Starks
Photo Research: Lisa Brant
Page Layout: Anthony Leung
Illustrator: Richard Parkin
Art Director: Mary Opper
Cover Design: Anthony Leung
Cover Image: Firstlight.ca

1 2 3 4 5   05 04 03 02 01

Printed and bound in U.S.A.

Statistics Canada information is used with the permission of the Minister of Industry, as Minister responsible for Statistics Canada. Information on the availability of the wide range of data from Statistics Canada can be obtained from Statistics Canada's Regional Offices, its World Wide Web site at http://www.statcan.ca, and its toll-free access number 1-800-263-1136.

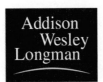

Text and photo credits appear on page C-1, which constitutes a continuation of the copyright page.

To Erin, Tessa, Jack,

and Abby;

and to Amber, Marnie,

Brent, Dylan, and Liam

About the Authors

Robin Bade was an undergraduate at the University of Queensland, Australia, where she earned degrees in mathematics and economics. After a spell teaching high school math and physics, she enrolled in the Ph.D. program at the Australian National University, from which she graduated in 1970. She has held faculty appointments at the University of Edinburgh in Scotland, at Bond University in Australia, and at the Universities of Manitoba, Toronto, and Western Ontario in Canada. Her research on international capital flows appears in the *International Economic Review* and the *Economic Record*. Robin first taught the principles of economics course in 1970 and has taught it most years since then. She developed many of the ideas found in this text while conducting tutorials with her students at the University of Western Ontario. Her other textbooks (with Michael Parkin) include *Macroeconomics* (Prentice-Hall), *Modern Macroeconomics* (Pearson Education Canada), and *Economics: Canada in the Global Environment*, the Canadian adaptation of Parkin, *Economics* (Addison-Wesley).

Michael Parkin studied economics in England and began his university teaching career immediately after graduating with a B.A. from the University of Leicester. He learned the subject on the job at the University of Essex, England's most exciting new university of the 1960s, and at the age of 30 became one of the youngest full professors. He is a past president of the Canadian Economics Association and has served on the editorial boards of the *American Economic Review* and the *Journal of Monetary Economics*. His research on macroeconomics, monetary economics, and international economics has resulted in more than 160 publications in journals and edited volumes, including the *American Economic Review*, the *Journal of Political Economy*, the *Review of Economic Studies*, the *Journal of Monetary Economics*, and the *Journal of Money, Credit, and Banking*.

Brian Lyons studied at the University of Toronto, where he earned a degree in commerce and finance before completing a Master's degree in economics. He was a member of the founding faculty at Sheridan College in Brampton, Ontario, where he teaches in the School of Business. In addition to macroeconomics, he also teaches introductory microeconomics, business policy, and business strategy across all three years of the school's business administration programs, as well as economics in its e-commerce management program. He is the author of *Canadian Macroeconomics: Problems and Policies* and *Canadian Microeconomics: Problems and Policies* (Pearson Education Canada), which are now in their sixth edition. He finds that teaching is a constantly changing, energizing, and rejuvenating challenge, which is fortunate in view of the fact that he now has to try to keep up with two young grandsons.

Macroeconomics

Brief Contents

Contents

PART 2 MONITORING THE MACROECONOMY 105

PART 6   THE GLOBAL MACROECONOMY

Preface

Why?

With Parkin and Bade's *Economics: Canada in the Global Environment* (now in its fourth edition) and Lyons's *Canadian Macroeconomics: Problems and Policies* and *Canadian Microeconomics: Problems and Policies* (now in its sixth edition) established, best-selling principles of economics textbooks, why have we combined our forces and written *Foundations of Macroeconomics* and its companion *Foundations of Microeconomics*? Is this rational behaviour?

We think so. We have been driven to write *Foundations* by what our own students and our fellow economists in colleges and universities across Canada have repeatedly told us. Economics is a core competency for the responsible citizen and is a foundation tool for every type of career. But the challenges of learning and teaching economics are formidable. Our students have diverse backgrounds and learning styles. We must fit an entire course in macroeconomics into too few weeks. And we must meet the challenge of using new technologies in our classrooms.

As we contemplated these challenges, it became clear to us that to meet them, we needed to rethink the way we teach our subject and to create a new learning system for our students.

LOWERING THE BARRIERS TO ENTRY

Most economics professors and instructors want to teach a serious, analytical course that explains the core principles of our subject and helps students apply these principles in their lives and jobs. No one wants to teach "dumbed-down" economics. But most students drown rather than learn to swim when thrown into the deep end of the pool. In this book and its accompanying learning tools, we make painstaking efforts to lower the barriers to learning and to reach out to the beginning student.

We focus on core concepts. We steer a steady path between an overload of detail that swamps the students and a minimalist approach that leaves the student dangling with too much unsaid. We explain tough concepts with the simplest, most straightforward language possible, and we reinforce them with clear, fully explained graphs. And we offer students a rich array of active learning tools that provide alternate ways of accessing and mastering the material.

■ Focus on Core Concepts

Each chapter of *Foundations* concentrates on a manageable number of main ideas (most commonly three or four) and reinforces each idea several times throughout the chapter. This patient, confidence-building approach guides students through unfamiliar terrain and helps them to focus their efforts on the most important tools and concepts of our discipline.

■ Diagrams That Tell the Whole Story

We developed the style of our diagrams with extensive feedback from faculty focus group participants and student reviewers. All figures make consistent use of colour to show the direction of shifts and contain detailed, numbered captions designed to direct students' attention step by step through the action. Because beginning students of economics are often apprehensive about working with graphs, we have made a special effort to present material in as many as three ways—with graphs, words, and tables—in the same figure. And in an innovation that seems necessary but is to our knowledge unmatched, nearly all of the information supporting a figure appears on the same page as the figure itself. No more flipping pages back and forth!

■ Many Learning Tools for Many Learning Styles

Our text and its integrated print and electronic learning package recognize that our students have a variety of learning styles. Some learn easily by reading the textbook; others benefit from audio and visual reinforcement. All students can profit from an active learning approach. Your students' textbooks come with access to a suite of innovative learning tools, including tutorial software, an eText featuring animated graphs with audio voiceovers, interactive quizzing, and more.

PRACTICE MAKES PERFECT

Everyone agrees that the only way to learn economics is to do it! Reading and remembering doesn't work. Active involvement, working problems, repeated self-testing: These are the ingredients to success in this subject. We have structured this text and its accompanying electronic and print tools to encourage learning by doing. The central device that accomplishes this goal is a tightly knit learning system based on our innovative *Checklist-Checkpoints* structure.

■ Checklists

Each chapter opens with a *Chapter Checklist*—a list of (usually) three or four tasks the student will be able to perform after completing the chapter. Each item in the Checklist corresponds to a major section of the chapter that engages the student with a conversational writing style, well-chosen examples, and rich and carefully designed illustrations.

■ Checkpoints

A full-page *Checkpoint*—containing a Practice Problem with solution and a parallel Exercise—immediately follows each chapter section. The Checkpoints serve as stopping points and encourage students to review the concept and to practise using it before moving on to new ideas. Diagrams and tables bring added clarity to the Checkpoint problems and solutions.

Each Checkpoint also contains an exact page reference to corresponding material in the Study Guide as well as a reference to the corresponding section of *e*Foundations, our online learning environment. We describe these learning tools more fully below.

■ Chapter Checkpoints

At the end of each chapter, a *Chapter Checkpoint* summarizes what the student has just learned with a set of key points, a list of key terms, and a set of exercises, many of which send the student to our Web site for further information or data.

■ Conveying the Excitement

Students learn best when they can see the point of what they are studying. We show the point in a series of *Eye On …* features and in *Economics in the News*. Current and recent events appear in *Eye on the Canadian Economy* boxes. We place our present experience in global and historical perspective with *Eye on the Global Economy* and *Eye on the Past* boxes. All three types of *Eye On …* boxes connect theory with reality.

Economics in the News, which appears once each chapter, is a brief news item with questions for discussion or assignment. A Web link provides access to a more complete version of the news item, together with links to other relevant information. The Instructor's Manual contains answers to the questions, and a set of PowerPoint presentations enables the news story to be discussed and illustrated in the classroom.

ORGANIZATION

Our text focuses on core topics with maximum flexibility. We cover all the standard topics of the principles of macroeconomics curriculum. And we do so in the order that is increasingly finding favour in the principles course. We believe that a powerful case can be made for teaching the subject in the order in which we present it here. The organizing device is the idea that at full employment, the real economy is influenced by only real variables and the price level is proportional to the quantity of money. This idea has been incredibly productive in advancing our understanding of both the full employment economy and the business cycle. By having a firm understanding of the fundamental forces that determine potential GDP, the student better appreciates the more complex inter-actions of real and monetary factors that bring economic fluctuations. Further, the student sees that the long-term trends in our economy play a larger role in determining our standard of living and cost of living than do the fluctuations around the trends.

Deciding the order in which to teach the components of macroeconomics involves a balancing act that trades off the cumulative nature of the material against the desire to cover topics that are in the news early in the course. There is little disagreement that the place to begin is with production possibilities and demand and supply, followed by the definitions and measurement of the key macroeconomic variables. We provide a carefully paced and thoroughly modern treatment of these topics.

The text then divides naturally into three parts. The first part provides a quick overview of macroeconomics in the form of the *AS-AD* model and then focuses on explaining the real economy at full employment (potential GDP, investment, saving, the real interest rate, and economic growth, including poli-cies for achieving faster growth). The second part explains the money economy (determining the interest rate in the short run and price level and inflation in the long run). The third part explains economic fluctuations (interactions between the real and monetary sectors and stabilization policy issues).

Extensive reviewing suggests that most teachers agree with our view on how to organize the text. But we recognize that there is a range of opinion about sequencing course topics, and we have structured our text so that it works equally well if other sequences are preferred. Some teachers want to follow the measurement material with the aggregate expenditure (fixed price level) model and aggregate demand and aggregate supply. Money and economic fluctuations come next. And the influences on potential GDP and economic growth either come last or are omitted. Our text fully supports this sequence. After Chapter 7, it is possible to jump to Chapter 14 (Expenditure Multipliers) or, if an instructor wishes to skip the Aggregate Expenditures model, directly to Chapter 15 (Aggregate Supply and Aggregate Demand). The money chapters (Chapters 11, 12, and 13) can be covered next followed by stabilization policy (Chapters 16, 17, and 18).

A RICH ARRAY OF SUPPORT MATERIALS FOR THE STUDENT

Foundations of Macroeconomics is accompanied by the most comprehensive set of learning tools ever assembled. All the components of our package are organized by Checkpoint topic so that the student may move easily between the textbook, the Study Guide, eText, interactive tutorial, and online quiz, while mastering a single core concept.

The variety of tools that we provide enables students to select the path through the material that best suits their individual learning styles. The package is technology enabled, *not* technology dependent. Active learners will make extensive use of the *Foundations Interactive* software tutorial and the animated graphics of eText, our online version of the textbook. Reflective learners may follow a print-only path if they prefer.

Study Guide

Jeannie Shearer-Gillmore of the University of Western Ontario has prepared a Study Guide that is available in both print and electronic formats. The Study Guide provides an expanded Chapter Checklist that enables the student to break the learning tasks down into smaller, bite-sized pieces; self-test materials; expanded explanations of the solutions to the practice problems in the text; and additional practice problems. To ensure consistency across the entire package, the same author wrote both the self-test questions in the Study Guide and the Test Bank questions.

■ Foundations Interactive

Robin and Michael have created *Foundations Interactive*, a Java and JavaScript tutorial software program that runs in a Web browser. *Foundations Interactive* contains electronic interactive versions of most of the textbook figures. The student manipulates the figures by changing the conditions that lie behind them and observes how the economy responds to events. Quizzes that use five question types: fill-in-the-blank, true-or-false, multiple-choice, numeric, and complete-the-graph can be worked with (or optionally without) detailed feedback. *Foundations Interactive* is available through the Web site and on CD-ROM.

 eFoundations

The *e*Foundations icons found throughout the textbook refer students to the Foundations Web site, a powerful online learning environment and self-assessment tool. On the Web site, students will find:

- The textbook—the *entire textbook in HTML* with hyperlinks and animated figures, more than 100 of which are accompanied by audio explanations
- *Foundations Interactive*—tutorials, quizzes, and graph tools that with a click of the mouse make curves shift and graphs come to life
- The Study Guide—the entire study guide, free, online—with online quizzes
- Economics in the News updated daily during the school year
- Online "Office Hours"—ask your question via email and one of us will answer you within 24 hours!
- Economic links—links to sites that keep you up to date with what's going on in the economy and that enable you to work end-of-chapter Web-based exercises

The power of *e*Foundations lies not just in the breadth and depth of learning tools available, but also in the way that we have linked the tools together. For example, suppose that a student logs on to *e*Foundations to take a multiple-choice quiz from the *e*Study Guide. When the quiz is submitted for a grade, the student receives a scorecard with an explanation of why each answer is correct or incorrect *and a hyperlink to the part of the eText that the student should read to better understand the concept.* The student is thus able to navigate easily through the site and to maximize the payoff from her or his study efforts.

■ Economist.com Edition

The premier online source of economic news analysis, Economist.com provides your students with insight and opinion on current economic events. Through an agreement between Pearson Education Canada and *The Economist*, your students can receive a low-cost subscription to this premium Web site for 3 months, including the complete text of the current issue of *The Economist* and access to *The Economist*'s searchable archives. Other features include Web-only weekly articles, news feeds with current world and business news, and stock market and currency data. Professors who adopt this special edition will receive a complimentary one-year subscription to *The Economist* and Economist.com.

■ Financial Times Edition

Featuring international news and analysis from FT journalists in more than 50 countries, the *Financial Times* will provide your students with insights and perspectives on economic developments around the world. The *Financial Times Edition* provides your students with a 15-week subscription to one of the world's leading business publications. Adopting professors will receive a complimentary one-year subscription to the *Financial Times* as well as access to the Online Edition at FT.com.

A QUALITY-ASSURED SUPPORT SYSTEM FOR THE INSTRUCTOR

Our instructor resource tools are the most comprehensive, carefully developed, and accurate materials ever made available. We recognize and respect the desire of every instructor to use a text and package that contains no nasty surprises—that is safe. This text and package are safe! *Foundations Interactive*, the Study Guide, the Web site, *and the Test Banks* all key off the Checkpoints in the textbook. The entire package has a tight integrity. We are the authors of *Foundations Interactive* and the Web site and we've played a key role in reviewing and revising the Study Guide, Instructor's Manual, and Test Banks to ensure that every element of the package achieves the level of coherence that students and teachers need.

■ Instructor's Manual

Brian prepared the Instructor's Manual, which contains chapter outlines and road maps, answers to in-text exercises and Economics in the News questions, additional exercises with solutions, and a virtual encyclopedia of suggestions on how to enrich class presentation and use class time efficiently.

■ Test Bank

John Cavaliere, of Sault College, prepared our Test Bank, which contains more than 3,500 questions in multiple-choice, true-false, numerical, fill-in-the-blank, short-answer, and essay formats. We have been especially careful to ensure that the Test Bank questions are similar in style and coverage to those in the Study Guide and on the Web site.

■ PowerPoint Resources

Robin and Michael created the PowerPoint tools. Every figure and table—every single one, even those used in Checkpoint questions and solutions—is included in the PowerPoint lecture notes, many of them animated so that you can build them gradually in the classroom. We have created these figures and determined the optimal build sequence for those that are animated. They are all produced with the same degree of clarity and precision as the figures in the text.

For instructors who prefer to make up their own PowerPoint notes and who want larger versions of the figures, we've also provided a set of full-screen figures that can be used alone or be cut and pasted into the instructor's own PowerPoint presentations.

■ eFoundations

All of the same resources as for students, but with the addition of PowerPoint lecture notes, classroom experiments resources, and an online "Consult the Authors" feature—ask your questions and make your suggestions via email, and one of use will answer you within 24 hours!

■ Instructor's Resource Disk with Computerized Test Banks

This CD-ROM contains Computerized Test Bank files, Instructor's Manual files in Microsoft Word, and PowerPoint files. The Test Bank is available in Test Generator Software (TestGen-EQ with QuizMaster-EQ). Fully networkable, it is available for Windows and Macintosh. TestGen-EQ's graphical interface enables instructors to view, edit, and add questions; transfer questions to tests; and print different forms of tests. Tests can be formatted by varying fonts and styles, margins, and headers and footers, as in any word-processing document. Search and sort features let the instructor quickly locate questions and arrange them in a preferred order. QuizMaster-EQ, working with your school's computer network, automatically grades the exams, stores the results on disk, and allows the instructor to view and print a variety of reports.

■ Course Management System

Pearson Education Canada has created an interactive online course with flexible tools and rich content resources that enable instructors to easily and effectively customize online course materials to suite their needs. Now instructors can track and analyze student performance on an array of economic activities. Available in WebCT, Blackboard, and CourseCompass formats. Ask your Pearson Education Canada representative for more details.

■ Guide to Instructor's Technology

Cheryl Jenkins, of John Abbott College, has prepared a detailed tutorial guide to all of the components of the technology for the instructor. This guide is available on the Instructor's Resource Disk and on the Instructor's section of the Foundations Web site. The guide provides valuable information on how to use each of the technology components in the classroom and a step-by-step guide to integrating the course management system into your course.

ACKNOWLEDGMENTS

Working on a project such as this generates many debts that can never be repaid. But they can be acknowledged, and it is a special pleasure to be able to do so here and to express our heartfelt thanks to each and every one of the following long list, without whose contributions we would have had a lesser product.

The ideas that ultimately became *Foundations* began to form over dinner with two outstanding editors, Denise Clinton and Sylvia Mallory. We gratefully acknowledge their role in conceiving this text and in bringing its U.S. counterpart to completion.

Our executive editor, Dave Ward, has steered this project forward and has coordinated its many elements. We are enormously indebted to him for his skill in keeping us focused and for his ability to find creative solutions to the problems we have posed.

Madhu Ranadive, our development editor, rounded up an outstanding group of reviewers and steered the project along through its successive drafts, redrafts, and polishes; and Susanne Marshall, associate editor, worked hard to keep the reviewers on schedule throughout the developmental process.

Andrew Winton, our projects manager, played a key leadership role in every aspect of the development and production of both the print and electronic supplements. He directed the creation of the Web site to ensure its high standard of design and accuracy. And he reviewed the supplements to ensure their accuracy and consistency with each other and with the text.

Deborah Starks, production manager, directed the production process, and Marisa D'Andrea, our production editor, worked tirelessly, cheerfully, and efficiently to ensure that all the elements of the text eventually came together to bring our book out on schedule. Designer and electronic formatter, Anthony Leung, worked extremely quickly, turned pages around very efficiently, and performed his magic to make our pages look beautiful and come out on time.

Our marketing manager, Deborah Meredith, has added value, not only by being acutely intelligent and having a sensitive understanding of the market, but also by sharpening our vision of our text and package.

Lisa Brant provided outstanding photo research, and Gail Marsden, copy editor, and Karen Bennett, proofreader, gave our work a thorough review and helpful polish.

Richard Parkin, our technical illustrator, created the figures in the text, the dynamic figures in the online version of the text, the illustrations in *Foundations Interactive*, and the animated versions of the figures in the PowerPoint presentations and contributed many ideas to improve the clarity of our illustrations. Laurel Davies created and edited the *Foundations Interactive* database and acted as its accuracy checker and reviewer.

Jeannie Shearer-Gillmore, our personal assistant, worked closely with us creating *Foundations Interactive* and served as a meticulous accuracy checker. Cheryl Jenkins served as a technology coordinator and wrote the technology guide. Kit Pasula of Okanagan University College also provided a careful accuracy review. Jane McAndrew, economics librarian at the University of Western Ontario, went the extra mile on many occasions to help us track down the data and references we needed. Ann Parkin came to our rescue in the closing weeks of this project and helped with a final accuracy check of the pages, table of contents, glossary, and index.

Finally, our reviewers, whose names appear on the following page, have made an enormous contribution to this text. In the many texts that we've now written, we've never seen reviewing of the quality that we enjoyed in this project. It has been a pleasure (if at times a challenge) to respond constructively to their many excellent suggestions.

Robin Bade, Michael Parkin, Brian Lyons
December 2001

Reviewers

Ather Akbari, St. Mary's University
Rene Blais, Southern Alberta Institute of Technology (SAIT)
Wilson Brown, University of Winnipeg
Norman Cameron, University of Manitoba
Ricardo A. Carreras, Memorial University of Newfoundland
John Cavaliere, Sault College of Applied Arts and Technology
Scott Cawfield, Centennial College
Wendy Cornwall, Mount Saint Vincent University
Veronique Flambard, Grant MacEwan College
Zuzana Fromm, British Columbia Institute of Technology (BCIT)
Tom Fulton , Langara College
Barbara Gardner, Southern Alberta Institute of Technology (SAIT)
Brenda Gayle, Seneca College
George Gekas, Algoma College
Carl Graham, Assiniboine Community College
Dan Haggerty, Sir Sandford Fleming College
Bruce Hammond, Fanshawe College
David Harrison, Certified General Accountants Association of Canada
Ibrahim Hayani, Seneca College
Matlub Hussain, Dawson College
Robert Jeacock, Malaspina University College
Ron Kessler, British Columbia Institute of Technology (BCIT)
Peter J. MacDonald, Cambrian College
Chris McDonnell, Malaspina University College
Dennis McGuire, Okanagan University College
Miroslav Misina, Concordia University
Martin Moy, University College of Cape Breton
Alfred Nimarko, Vanier College
Kit Pasula, Okanagan University College
Bill Rice, Fairview College
Charlene Richter, British Columbia Institute of Technology (BCIT)
June Riley, John Abbott College
Lance Shandler, Kwantlen College
Barbara Smith, Niagara College
Joe Vieira, Confederation College
Claus Westerman, Northern College
Ian Wilson, St. Lawrence College
Vic de Witt, Red River College
Don Woolridge, College of the North Atlantic
Emmanuel Yiridoe, Nova Scotia Agricultural College

Introduction

Getting Started

CHAPTER CHECKLIST

When you have completed your study of this chapter,
you will be able to:

1 Define economics, distinguish between microeconomics and
macroeconomics, and explain the questions of macroeconomics.

2 Describe what economists do and some of the problems they
encounter.

3 Explain four core ideas that define the way economists think about
macroeconomic questions.

4 Explain why economics is worth studying.

You are studying macroeconomics at a time of
enormous change. New businesses such as
Amazon.com are bringing e-commerce into our
homes and transforming the way we shop. MP3
music and DVD movies are transforming the way
we play. But inequality is increasing: the less educated are falling behind. Of the world's 6 billion
people, more than a billion survive on $1 a day
or less. Disturbed by the combination of increasing wealth
and persistent poverty, some people are pointing to global-
ization as the source of growing inequality.

You've just glimpsed at some of the macroeconomic
issues in today's world. Your course in macroeconomics will
help you to understand the powerful forces that are shaping
this world. Our goal throughout this text and its accompanying study guide, CD, and Web site is to help you to learn
macroeconomics and use it to interpret the macroeconomic
events that affect your life and work.

1.1 DEFINITIONS AND QUESTIONS

All economic questions and problems arise because human wants exceed the resources available to satisfy them. We want good health and long lives. We want good schools, colleges, and universities. We want well-run day-care facilities. We want a peaceful and secure world. We want spacious and comfortable homes. We want a huge range of sports and recreational equipment from running shoes to snowboards. We want the time to enjoy our favourite sports, video games, novels, music, movies, travel to exotic places, and just hanging out with friends.

In the everyday world of politics and the media, it is easy to get carried away with the idea that we can have it all. A random sample of news headlines might include these:

Everyone must get the best health care.

There must be a computer in every classroom.

We cannot afford to stop exploring space.

We must stop polluting our lakes and rivers.

Most people would agree that each headline expresses a desirable goal. But we might not be able to achieve them all. The ability of each of us to satisfy our wants is limited by time and by the incomes we earn and the prices we pay for the things we buy. These limits mean that everyone ends up with some unsatisfied wants. Our ability as a society to satisfy our wants is limited by the productive resources that exist. These resources include the gifts of nature, our own labour and ingenuity, and tools and equipment that we have produced.

Scarcity
The condition that arises because the available resources are insufficient to satisfy wants.

Our inability to satisfy all our wants is called **scarcity**. The poor and the rich alike face scarcity. A child wants a $1.00 can of pop and two 50¢ packs of gum but has only $1.00 in his pocket. He faces scarcity. A millionaire wants to spend the weekend playing golf *and* spend the same weekend at the office attending a business strategy meeting. She faces scarcity. A society wants to provide vastly improved health care, install a computer in every classroom, explore space, clean polluted lakes and rivers, and so on. Society also faces scarcity.

Not only do I want a cracker—we all want a cracker!

Faced with scarcity, we must make choices. We must *choose* among the available alternatives. The child must *choose* the pop *or* the gum. The millionaire must choose the golf game *or* the meeting. As a society, we must *choose* among health care, computers, highways, the environment, and so on.

Economics is the social science that studies the choices that individuals, businesses, government, and entire societies make as they cope with scarcity. The subject divides into two main parts:

- Microeconomics
- Macroeconomics

Economics
The social science that studies the choices that individuals, businesses, governments, and entire societies make as they cope with scarcity.

◼ Microeconomics

Microeconomics is the study of the choices that individuals and businesses make, the way these choices interact, and the influence that governments exert on these choices. Some microeconomic questions are: Why are more people buying SUVs and fewer people buying minivans? Why, when Sony Corporation launched its new PlayStation 2, did it ship too small a quantity to its eagerly awaiting customers? How would a tax on e-commerce affect the growth of the Internet?

Microeconomics
The study of the choices that individuals and businesses make, the interaction of these choices, and the influence that governments exert on these choices.

◼ Macroeconomics

Macroeconomics is the study of the aggregate (or total) effects on the national economy and the global economy of the choices that individuals, businesses, and governments make. Some macroeconomic questions are: Why does the number of Canadians who are unemployed fluctuate? Why did production expand so rapidly in Canada in 2000? Why has Japan had a long period of economic stagnation? Why does the Bank of Canada raise and lower interest rates?

Macroeconomics
The study of the aggregate (or total) effects on the national economy and the global economy of the choices that individuals, businesses, and governments make.

The distinction between microeconomics and macroeconomics is similar to the distinction between two views of a display of national flags in an Olympic stadium. The micro view is of a single participant and the actions he or she is taking (on the left). The macro view is the patterns formed by the joint actions of all the people participating in the entire display (on the right).

■ Macroeconomic Questions

The three big issues that macroeconomics tries to understand are:

- The standard of living
- The cost of living
- Economic fluctuations—recessions and expansions

The Standard of Living

Standard of living
The level of consumption of goods and services that people enjoy on the average; it is measured by average income per person.

Goods and services
The objects that people value and produce to satisfy human wants. Goods are physical objects, and services are work done for people.

The **standard of living** is the level of consumption of goods and services that people enjoy, on the average, and is measured by average income per person. **Goods and services** are the objects that people value and produce to satisfy human wants. Goods are tangible objects such as golf balls. Services are intangible objects such as haircuts. The nation's farms, factories, construction sites, shops, and offices produce a dazzling array of goods and services that range from necessities such as food, houses and apartments, and health-care services to leisure items such as ocean cruises, SUVs, and DVD players.

In 2000, the quantity of goods and services produced by the nation's farms, factories, shops, and offices, measured by their value in today's prices, was more than 20 times greater than in 1900. But over that same 100 years, the population of Canada has increased to not quite six times its 1900 level. Because we now produce more goods and services per person, we have a much higher standard of living than our grandparents had.

For most of us, achieving a high standard of living means finding a good job. And if we lose our job, it means spending some time being unemployed while we search for the right new job. **Unemployment** is the state of being available and willing to work but unable to find suitable work. In Canada during 2000, 61 percent of adults had jobs and only 7 percent of people who think of themselves as being in the labour force were looking for jobs but unable to find them. Some other countries, for example, Spain, experience much higher unemployment than does Canada; and other countries, for example, the United States and Japan, experience lower unemployment than does Canada.

Unemployment
The state of being available and willing to work but unable to find suitable work.

Will the standard of living continue to rise? Will your world and the world of your children be more prosperous than today's? What kind of job will you find when you graduate? Will you have lots of choice, or will you face a labour market with a high level of unemployment in which jobs are hard to find?

Your study of macroeconomics will help you to understand the progress that economists have made in seeking answers to questions like these.

The Cost of Living

The **cost of living** is the number of dollars it takes to buy the goods and services that a typical family consumes. A rising cost of living, which is called **inflation**, means a shrinking value of the dollar. A falling cost of living, which is called *deflation*, means a rising value of the dollar.

Has the cost of living increased or decreased? If we look back over the past 100 years, we see that it has increased and the value of the dollar has shrunk. In your great-grandparent's youth, when the electric light bulb was the latest big thing, the average Canadian earned less than $1 a day. But five cents in 1901 would buy what you need a dollar to buy today—the dollar of 2001 is worth only one-twentieth of the dollar of 1901. If the dollar continues to shrink in value at its average rate of loss since 1901, by the time you retire (sure, that's a long time in the future), you'll need almost $5 to buy what $1 buys today. The dollar of 2051 will be worth about one-fifth of the value of the dollar of 2001.

You've seen that over the years, our standard of living has increased. Why doesn't a rising *cost* of living mean that people must constantly cut back on their spending and endure a falling *standard* of living? Although the cost of living has increased steadily, incomes have increased more quickly. And because incomes have increased faster than the cost of living, the standard of living has increased.

During the past few years, the cost of living has increased slowly. Can we count on it rising slowly in the future? What will the dollar buy next year? What will it buy in 10 years when you are paying off your student loan? And what will it buy in 50 years when you are spending your life's savings in retirement?

In your study of macroeconomics, you will learn what economists have discovered about the answers to questions like these.

Economic Fluctuations—Recessions and Expansions

Over long periods, both the standard of living and the cost of living have increased. But these increases have not been smooth and continuous. Our economy fluctuates in a **business cycle**, a periodic but irregular up-and-down movement in production and jobs.

Cost of living
The number of dollars it takes to buy the goods and services that achieve a given standard of living.

Inflation
A situation in which the cost of living is rising and the value of money is shrinking.

Business cycle
A periodic but irregular up-and-down movement in production and jobs.

"Three hundred dollars' of regular."

FIGURE 1.1
Business Cycle Phases and Turning Points

In a business cycle expansion, production and jobs increase more rapidly than normal. In a recession, production and jobs shrink. An expansion ends at a peak, and a recession ends at a trough.

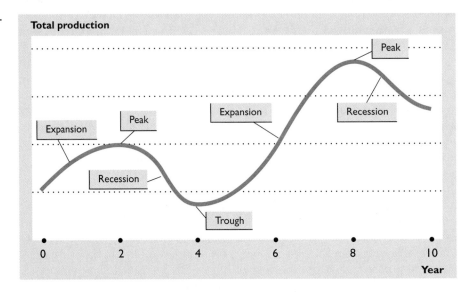

When production and jobs increase, the economy is in a business cycle *expansion*. When production and jobs shrink, the economy is in a *recession*.

Figure 1.1 illustrates the phases and turning points of a business cycle. The economy in this figure has a recession from year 2 to year 4, then an expansion through year 8, followed by another recession through year 10. An expansion ends at a peak, and a recession ends at a trough.

The last recession in Canada occurred in 1990–1991. During 2001, the Canadian economy was in an expansion that began at the trough of the 1991 recession. This expansion has been an unusually long one but signs that it might soon end were emerging during 2001.

Great Depression
A period during the 1930s in which the economy experienced its worst-ever recession.

The worst recession ever experienced occurred during the 1930s in an episode called the **Great Depression**. During this period, production in Canada shrank by 28 percent.

When a recession occurs, unemployment increases. During the Great Depression, almost 20 percent of the Canadian labour force was unable to find work. During the 1990s recession, more than 11 percent couldn't find work.

CHECKPOINT 1.1

1   **Define economics, distinguish between microeconomics and macroeconomics, and explain the questions of macroeconomics.**

Study Guide pp. 2–5

*e*Foundations 1.1

Practice Problems 1.1

1.   Economics studies choices that arise from one fact. What is that fact?

2.   Sort the following headlines into those that deal with (i) the standard of living, (ii) the cost of living, and (iii) unemployment and the business cycle:
   a.   Production per worker has grown for the tenth straight year.
   b.   Another price hike for consumers?
   c.   Firms lay off more workers as orders decline.
   d.   The government pays more unemployment benefits.
   e.   New robots boost production across a wide range of industries.
   f.   Money doesn't buy what it used to.

Exercises 1.1

1.   Every day, we make many choices. Can't we avoid having to make choices?

2.   Check your local news media for headlines that examine each of the three questions of macroeconomics.

3.   Which of the following media headlines anticipates a recession and which anticipates an expansion:
   a.   Jobless claims rose again last month.
   b.   The Bank of Canada forecasts rising prices.
   c.   Housing starts rise.
   d.   Firms recall workers.
   e.   Auto-makers worried as car sales plummet.

Solutions to Practice Problems 1.1

1.   Choices arise because our wants exceed the resources available to satisfy them. In deciding which wants will be satisfied, we must make choices. We cannot have everything we want.

2a.   Deals with the standard of living because when production per worker increases, consumption per person, which measures the standard of living, increases.

2b.   Deals with the cost of living because as the prices consumers have to pay for goods and services increases, the cost of living increases.

2c.   Deals with unemployment and the business cycle because as orders decline, production decreases and more workers become unemployed.

2d.   Deals with unemployment and the business cycle because during a recession, more people are unemployed and qualify for benefits.

2e.   Deals with the standard of living because robots that increase production across a wide range of industries increases production per worker.

2f.   Deals with the cost of living because the value of money has fallen. The value of money falls when the prices of goods and services increase, which increases the cost of living.

1.2 ECONOMICS: A SOCIAL SCIENCE

We've defined economics as the *social science* that studies the choices that individuals and societies make as they cope with scarcity. We're now going to look at the way economists go about their work as social scientists and at some of the problems they encounter.

The major goal of economists is to discover how the economic world works. In pursuit of this goal, economists (like all scientists) distinguish between two types of statements:

- What *is*
- What *ought to be*

Statements about what *is* are called *positive* statements. They say what is currently believed about the way the world operates. A positive statement might be right or wrong. And we can test a positive statement by checking it against the data. When a chemist does an experiment in her laboratory, she is attempting to check a positive statement against the facts.

Statements about what *ought to be* are called *normative* statements. These statements depend on opinions and cannot be tested. When Parliament debates a motion, it is ultimately trying to decide what ought to be. It is making a normative statement.

To see the distinction between positive and normative statements, consider the controversy about global warming. Some scientists believe that 200 years of industrial activity and the large quantities of coal and oil that we burn are increasing the carbon dioxide content of the earth's atmosphere with devastating consequences for life on this planet. Other scientists disagree. The statement, "Our planet is warming because of a carbon dioxide buildup in the atmosphere" is a positive statement. It can (in principle and with sufficient data) be tested. In contrast, the statement, "We ought to cut back on our use of carbon-based fuels such as coal and oil" is a normative statement. You may agree with or disagree with this statement, but you can't test it. It is based on values. Health-care reform provides an economic example of the distinction. "Universal health care cuts the amount of work time lost to illness" is a positive statement. "Every Canadian should have equal access to health care" is a normative statement.

The task of economic science is to discover and catalogue positive statements that are consistent with what we observe in the world and that enable us to understand how the economic world works. This task is a large one that can be broken into three steps:

- Observing and measuring
- Model building
- Testing

■ Observing and Measuring

The first step towards understanding how the economic world works is to observe and measure it. Economists keep track of huge amounts of economic data. Some examples are the amounts and locations of natural and human resources; wages and work hours; the prices and quantities of the different things produced; taxes and government spending; and the volume of international trade.

■ Model Building

The second step is to build models. An **economic model** is a description of some aspect of the economic world that includes only those features of the world that are needed for the purpose at hand. A model is simpler than the reality it describes. What a model includes and what it leaves out result from *assumptions* about what is essential and what are inessential details.

You can see how ignoring details is useful—even essential—to our understanding by thinking about a model that you see every day, the TV weather map. The weather map is a model that helps to predict the temperature, wind speed and direction, and precipitation over a future period. The weather map shows lines called isobars—lines of equal barometric pressure. The weather map doesn't show the highways. The reason is that we think the location of the highways has no influence on the weather but the air pressure patterns do have an influence.

An economic model is similar to a weather map. It tells us how a number of variables are determined by a number of other variables. For example, an economic model of Toronto's bid for the 2008 Olympic Games might tell us the effects of the Games on the sporting facilities, housing, transit system, and jobs in Toronto and the surrounding areas.

Economists use a variety of methods to describe their economic models. Most commonly, the method is mathematical. If you plan on a career in economics, you will study a good deal of math. But the basic ideas of all economic models can be described using words and pictures or diagrams. That is how economic models are described in this text.

A rare exception is a model called the Phillips Economic Hydraulic Computer shown here. Bill Phillips, a New Zealand-born engineer-turned-economist, created this model using plastic tubes and plexiglass tanks at the London School of Economics in 1949. The model still works today in a London museum.

■ Testing

The third step is testing models. A model's predictions might correspond to or conflict with the data. If there is a conflict, the model needs to be modified or rejected. Models that have repeatedly passed the test of corresponding well with real-world data are the basis of economic theories. An **economic theory** is a generalization that summarizes what we understand about the economic choices that people make and the economic performance of industries and nations.

The process of building and testing models creates theories. For example, meteorologists have a theory that if the isobars form a particular pattern at a particular time of the year (a model), then it will snow (reality). They have developed this theory by repeated observation and by carefully recording the weather that follows specific pressure patterns.

Economics is a young science. Although philosophers have written about economic issues since the time of the ancient Greeks, it is generally agreed that as a modern social science, economics was born in 1776 with the publication of Adam Smith's *The Wealth of Nations*. Over the years since then, economists have discovered many useful theories. But in many areas, economists are still looking for answers. The gradual accumulation of economic knowledge gives most economists some faith that their methods will, eventually, provide usable answers.

But progress in economic science comes slowly. A major reason is that it is difficult in economics to unscramble cause and effect.

Economic model
A description of some aspect of the economic world that includes only those features that are needed for the purpose at hand.

Economic theory
A generalization that summarizes what we understand about the economic choices that people make and the economic performance of industries and nations based on models that have repeatedly passed the test of corresponding well with real-world data.

Adam Smith and the Birth of Economics as a Modern Social Science

Many people had written about economics before Adam Smith, but he made economics a social science.

Born in 1723 in Kirkcaldy, a small fishing town near Edinburgh, Scotland, Smith was the only child of the town's customs officer. Lured from his professorship (he was a full professor at 28) by a wealthy Scottish duke who gave him a pension of £300 a year—ten times the average income at that time—he devoted ten years to writing his masterpiece, *An Inquiry into the Nature and Causes of the Wealth of Nations*, published in 1776.

Why, Adam Smith asked in that book, are some nations wealthy while others are poor? He was pondering these questions at the height of the Industrial Revolution. During these years, new technologies were applied to the manufacture of textiles, iron, transportation, and agriculture.

Adam Smith answered his questions by emphasizing the role of the division of labour and free markets. To illustrate his argument, he used the example of a pin factory. He guessed that one person, using the hand tools available in the 1770s, might make 20 pins a day. Yet, he observed, by using those same hand tools but breaking the process into a number of individually small operations in which people specialize—by the division of labour—ten people could make a staggering 48,000 pins a day. One draws out the wire, another straightens it, a third cuts it, a fourth points it, a fifth grinds it. Three specialists make the head, and a fourth attaches it. Finally, the pin is polished and packaged.

But a large market is needed to support the division of labour: one factory employing ten workers would need to sell more than 15 million pins a year to stay in business!

■ Unscrambling Cause and Effect

Are computers getting cheaper because people are buying them in greater quantities? Or are people buying computers in greater quantities because they are getting cheaper? Or is some third factor causing both the price of a computer to fall and the quantity of computers to increase? Economists want to answer questions like these, but doing so is often difficult. The central idea that economists (and all scientists) use to unscramble cause and effect is *ceteris paribus*.

Ceteris Paribus

Ceteris paribus
Other things remaining the same (often abbreviated to *cet. par.*)

Ceteris paribus is a Latin term (often abbreviated as *cet. par.*) that means "other things being equal" or "if all other relevant things remain the same." Ensuring that other things are equal is crucial in many activities, including athletic events, and all successful attempts to make scientific progress use this device. By changing one factor at a time and holding all the other relevant factors constant, we isolate the factor of interest and are able to investigate its effects in the clearest possible way.

Economic models, like the models in all other sciences, enable the influence of one factor at a time to be isolated in the imaginary world of the model. When we use a model, we are able to imagine what would happen if only one factor changed. But *ceteris paribus* can be a problem in economics when we try to test a model.

Laboratory scientists, such as chemists and physicists, perform controlled experiments by actually holding all the relevant factors constant except for the one under investigation. In the non-experimental sciences such as economics (and astronomy), we usually observe the outcomes of the *simultaneous* operation of many factors. Consequently, it is hard to sort out the effects of each individual factor and to compare the effects with what a model predicts. To cope with this problem, economists take three complementary approaches:

- Natural experiments
- Econometric investigations
- Economic experiments

Natural Experiments

A natural experiment is a situation that arises in the ordinary course of economic life in which the one factor of interest is different and other things are equal (or similar). For example, Canada has higher unemployment benefits than the United States, but the people in the two nations are similar. So to study the effects of unemployment benefits on the unemployment rate, economists might compare the United States with Canada.

Econometric Investigations

Econometrics is the use of statistical tools in economics. The most common statistical tool is correlation. **Correlation** is the tendency for the values of two variables to move in a predictable and related way. For example, there is a correlation between the amount of cigarette smoking and the incidence of lung cancer. There is also a correlation between the size of a city's police force and the city's crime rate. Two economic examples are correlation between household income and spending and between the price of a telephone call and the number of calls made. We must be careful to interpret a correlation correctly. Sometimes a correlation shows the strength of a *causal* influence of one variable on the other. For example, smoking causes lung cancer and higher incomes cause higher spending. Sometimes the direction of causation is hard to determine. For example, does a larger police force *detect* more crimes or does a higher crime rate cause a larger police force to be hired? And sometimes a third factor causes *both* of the correlated variables. For example, advances in communication technology have caused both a fall in the price of phone calls and an increase in the quantity of calls. So the correlation between the price and quantity of phone calls arises because both variables are caused by a third factor.

Sometimes, the direction of cause and effect can be determined by looking at the timing of events. But this method must be handled with care because of a problem known as the *post hoc* fallacy.

***Post Hoc* Fallacy** Another Latin phrase—*post hoc ergo propter hoc*—means "after this, therefore because of this." The ***post hoc* fallacy** is the error of reasoning that a first event causes a second event because the first occurred before the second. Suppose you are a visitor from a far off world who observes people shopping in early December and then opening gifts and celebrating on Christmas Day. Does the shopping cause Christmas, you wonder? After a deeper study, you discover that Christmas causes the shopping. A later event causes an earlier event.

Just looking at the timing of events often doesn't help to unravel cause and effect in economics. For example, the stock market booms, and some months later

Econometrics
The use of statistical tools in economics.

Correlation
The tendency for the values of two variables to move in a predictable and related way.

***Post hoc* fallacy**
The error of reasoning that a first event *causes* a second event because the first occurred *before* the second.

the economy expands—jobs and incomes grow. Did the stock market boom cause the economy to expand? Possibly, but perhaps businesses started to plan the expansion of production because a new technology that lowered costs had become available. As knowledge of the plans spread, stock prices rose *in anticipation of* the economic expansion.

To disentangle cause and effect, economists use economic models to interpret correlations in the data and when they can, they perform experiments.

Economic Experiments

Economic experiments are a relatively new approach. These experiments put real subjects in a decision-making situation and vary the influence of interest to discover how the subjects respond to one factor at a time. Most economic experiments are done using students as the subjects. But a few are done using the actual people whose behaviour economists want to understand and predict. An example of an economic experiment on actual subjects is one that was designed to discover the effects of changing the way welfare benefits are paid in Manitoba. Another experiment was conducted to discover how telecommunications companies would bid in different types of auctions for the airwave frequencies they use to transmit cellular telephone messages. Governments have made billions of dollars using the results of this experiment.

CHECKPOINT 1.2

Study Guide pp. 5–7

*e*Foundations 1.2

2 **Describe what economists do and some of the problems they encounter.**

Practice Problems 1.2

1. Classify the following statements as positive or normative:
   a. Unemployed workers have to wait too long before being rehired.
   b. Hockey players earn, on the average, more than doctors.

2. Provide two examples of the *post hoc* fallacy.

Exercise 1.2

1. Classify each statement as positive or normative and suggest how economists might test each positive statement:
   a. The government budget surplus should be spent on health care and education.
   b. Free trade will harm developing countries.
   c. Cuts to public education in Canada have been too great.

Solutions to Practice Problems 1.2

1a. This statement is a normative one because it cannot be tested.
1b. This statement is a positive one because it can be checked against the data.

2. Examples are: New Year celebrations cause January sales. A booming stock market causes a Liberal government to be elected.

1.3 MACROECONOMIC IDEAS

You've seen that to understand what brings changes in the standard of living and the cost of living and what generates economic fluctuations, economists build and test economic models. Four core ideas summarize the way economists think about macroeconomic issues and form the basis of all macroeconomic models. The ideas are:

- Macroeconomic performance results from rational choices.
- The standard of living improves when production per person increases.
- The cost of living rises when the quantity of money increases faster than production.
- The economy fluctuates when expenditure and productivity fluctuate.

■ Rational Choice

The most basic idea of economics is that in making choices, people act rationally. A **rational choice** is one that uses the available resources most effectively to satisfy the wants of the person making the choice.

But how do people choose rationally? How does a person decide how much to save and how much to spend? How does Bell Sympatico decide how many servers and high-speed Internet connections to install? How did governments decide to build highways instead of a high-speed railroad system?

We make rational choices by comparing *costs* and *benefits*. Economists think about costs and benefits in a special and revealing way.

Rational choice
A choice that uses the available resources most effectively to satisfy the wants of the person making the choice.

Cost: What You Must Give Up

Whatever you choose to do, you could have done something else instead. One of these other things is the *best* alternative given up. The best thing that you *must give up* to get something is the **opportunity cost** of the thing that you get. The thing that you could have chosen—the highest-valued alternative forgone—is the cost of the thing that you did choose.

"There's no such thing as a free lunch" is not just a clever but empty saying. It expresses the central idea of economics—that every choice involves a cost.

We use the term *opportunity cost* to emphasize that when we make a choice in the face of scarcity, we give up an opportunity to do something else. You can quit school right now or you can remain in school. Suppose that if you quit school, the best job you can get is at McDonald's, where you can earn $10,000 during the year. The opportunity cost of remaining in school includes the things that you could have bought with this $10,000. The opportunity cost also includes the value of the leisure time that you must forgo to study.

Opportunity cost
The opportunity cost of something is what you must give up to get it.

Benefit: Gain Measured By What You Are Willing To Give Up

The **benefit** of something is the gain or pleasure that it brings. Benefit is how a person *feels* about something. You might be very anxious to get the latest version of a video game. It will bring you a large benefit. And you might have almost no interest in tonight's late movie on television. It will bring you a small benefit.

Economists measure the benefit of something by what a person is *willing to give up* to get it. You can buy CDs, pop, or magazines. The pop or magazines that you are *willing to give up* to get a CD measure the benefit you get from a CD.

Benefit
The benefit of something is the gain or pleasure that it brings.

Margin
A choice at the margin is a choice that is made by comparing *all* the relevant alternatives systematically and incrementally.

Marginal cost
The cost that arises from a one-unit increase in an activity. The marginal cost of something is what you *must give up* to get *one more* unit of it.

Marginal benefit
The benefit that arises from a one-unit increase in an activity. The marginal benefit of something is *measured* by what you are *willing to give up* to get *one more* unit of it.

On The Margin

A choice on the **margin** is a choice that is made by comparing *all* the relevant alternatives systematically and incrementally. For example, you must choose how to divide the next hour between studying or e-mailing your friends. To make this choice, you must evaluate the costs and benefits of the alternative possible allocations of your next hour. You choose on the margin by considering whether you will be better off or worse off if you spend an extra few minutes studying or an extra few minutes e-mailing.

The margin might involve a small change, as it does when you're deciding how to divide an hour between studying and e-mailing friends. Or it might involve a large change, as it does when you're deciding whether to remain in school for another year. Attending school for part of the year is no better (and might be worse) than not attending at all—it is not a *relevant* alternative. So you will likely want to commit the entire year to school or to something else. You still choose on the margin but the marginal change is now a change for one year rather than for a few minutes.

The cost of a one-unit increase in an activity is called marginal cost. **Marginal cost** is what you *must give up* to get *one more* unit of something. For example, the marginal cost of another year in school is a year's forgone income and leisure time. The benefit of a one-unit increase in an activity is called marginal benefit. **Marginal benefit** is what you gain when you get *one more* unit of something. Marginal benefit is *measured by* what you are *willing to give up* to get *one more* unit of something. For example, your marginal benefit of another year in school is measured by the income and leisure time that you are *willing* to forgo.

If the marginal cost of another year in school is less than the marginal benefit, your rational choice is to remain in school. If the marginal cost exceeds the marginal benefit, your rational choice is to drop out of school. We make a rational choice and use our resources in the way that makes us as well off as possible when we take those actions for which marginal benefit exceeds or equals marginal cost.

A change in marginal cost or a change in marginal benefit brings a change in the incentives that we face and leads us to change our actions. For example, suppose that job opportunities improve. Instead of being able to earn $10,000 at McDonald's, you can now get a job that pays $40,000 a year. The marginal cost of remaining in school has increased, and it might now be rational to quit school and take this newly available job. In the choice that we've just described, you are responding to a change in incentives. A central idea of economics is that because people make rational choices, by looking for changes in marginal cost and marginal benefit, we can predict the way choices respond to changes in incentives.

■ The Standard of Living and Productivity

The dollar value of a nation's production can increase for any of three reasons: prices and wage rates rise, the number of people employed increases, or production per person increases. Total production per person is called **productivity**. Only an increase in productivity brings a higher standard of living.

Productivity
Total production per person employed.

A rise in prices and wage rates brings higher incomes, but only in terms of dollars, not in terms of the quantity of goods and services that the income can buy. The extra income is just enough to pay the higher prices, not enough to buy more goods and services.

An increase in the number of people employed brings an increase in *total* production but not an increase in total production *per person*. Living standards increase when people, on the average, consume more goods and services. And on the average, people can consume more only if total production per person increases. So only an increase in total production per person—an increase in productivity—brings an increase in the standard of living.

For example, by automating a car production line, each autoworker can produce a greater output. But if each worker can produce more cars, then there will be more cars for more people to enjoy owning.

Often, automation means that jobs are lost. Automation on farms and in coal mines, steel mills, and car factories has led to a large decrease in the number of jobs in these industries. If automation leads to job loss, how can automation at the same time lead to an increase in the standard of living? The standard of living increases because the people who lose their jobs to automation eventually find new ones that pay an even greater wage, on the average, than the old job did. So by increasing output per person, total production increases, we are able to buy more goods and services, and we enjoy a higher standard of living.

■ The Cost of Living and the Quantity of Money

You've seen that the *cost of living* is the number of dollars it takes to buy the goods and services that achieve a given standard of living. So a rising cost of living, called *inflation*, means that more dollars are needed to buy the same fixed quantity of goods and services.

Inflation is caused by an increase in the quantity of money that is not matched by an increase in the quantity of goods and services. The Bank of Canada determines the quantity of money in the economy by methods that you will learn about in Chapter 12. But to see the *effect* of an increase in the quantity of money, suppose that the Canadian government mailed $1,000 in new $20 bills to every person in Canada. Nothing else has changed. People are doing the same jobs as before and producing the same quantities of goods and services as before.

What do you think happens when people open their mail and find their $1,000? Most people will go out and spend it. But there are no more goods and services to buy. There is "too much money chasing too few goods." As people bring more money to market, sellers see that they can raise their prices. But when sellers go to buy their supplies, they find that the prices they must pay have also increased. With too much money around, prices rise and money loses value.

In some countries, inflation has been rapid. One such country is Russia. During the 1990s, prices in Russia increased at an average rate of 156 percent a year. In Canada during the 1990s, prices increased at an average rate of slightly more than 2 percent a year.

■ Expenditure and Productivity Fluctuations

The economic fluctuations that we call the business cycle are the least well-understood phenomena of macroeconomics. Despite this lack of understanding, economists know a lot about the anatomy of the business cycle. That is, economists have accumulated a great deal of data that describe the ups and downs of economic activity. Economic fluctuations appear to have two broad sources:

- Expenditure fluctuations
- Productivity fluctuations

Expenditure Fluctuations

Expenditure fluctuations bring fluctuations in production and jobs and are a source of economic fluctuations. For example, high interest rates cut spending by businesses and consumers and led to recession in the early 1990s. Increased spending by consumers and businesses increased production and jobs during the late 1990s. Canada exports much of its output, so fluctuations in spending by foreigners, especially Americans, are another source of economic fluctuations in Canada.

Productivity Fluctuations

Productivity fluctuations also bring economic fluctuations. For example, during the 1970s, a disruption of oil supplies and a series of large oil-price increases decreased productivity and brought recession. During the 1990s, the spread of information-age technologies brought an increase in productivity that created an unusually strong and long expansion.

Smoothing the Business Cycle

It is generally agreed that economic fluctuations are undesirable. Recessions bring unemployment, and deep and long recessions like the Great Depression bring enormous economic hardship and even social unrest. An overly strong expansion is undesirable because it brings an increase in prices that outpace the increases in some people's incomes.

Macroeconomics has made a great deal of progress in smoothing the business cycle but not in eliminating it. We cannot predict when a recession or a recovery will occur, and we cannot prevent recession. But we do know how to limit the damage from recession and keep an expansion from becoming too strong. You will learn about these aspects of macroeconomics in Chapters 14 through 18.

CHECKPOINT 1.3

3 **Explain four core ideas that define the way economists think about macroeconomic questions.**

Study Guide pp. 7–9

*e*Foundations 1.3

Practice Problems 1.3

1. Kate usually plays tennis for two hours a week and her grade on math tests is usually 70 percent. Last week, after playing two hours of tennis, Kate thought long and hard about playing for another hour. She decided to play another hour of tennis and cut her study time by one additional hour. But her grade on last week's math test was 60 percent.
    a. What was Kate's opportunity cost of the third hour of tennis?
    b. Was Kate's decision to play the third hour of tennis rational?
    c. Did Kate make her decision at the margin?

2. Classify each of the following events as an influence on the standard of living or the cost of living, and as an expenditure or productivity source of economic fluctuations:
    a. A new computer chip doubles the speed of a PC.
    b. A new process lowers the cost of producing fibre-optic cable.
    c. Telephone companies increase their spending on cellular networks.
    d. Spending is increasing, prices are rising but production is stagnant.

Exercises 1.3

1. Sue has just won $1 billion. Does Sue experience scarcity? Suppose that Sue signs up for a trip to the international space station. Would her choice be rational? Is her choice made at the margin? What is the cost of Sue's trip? What is her benefit from it?

2. Classify each of the following events as an influence on the standard of living or the cost of living, and as an expenditure or productivity source of economic fluctuations:
    a. DVD technology arrives.
    b. Prices that consumers pay rise and so do wages.
    c. New technology increases the average productivity in the nation.
    d. The nation's output increases faster than the inflation rate.

Solutions to Practice Problems 1.3

1a. Kate's opportunity cost of the third hour of tennis was the ten percentage point drop in her grade. If Kate had not played tennis for the third hour, she would have studied and her grade would not have dropped. The best alternative forgone is her opportunity cost of the third hour of tennis.

1b. Her decision was rational if her marginal benefit exceeded her marginal cost.

1c. Kate's decision was made at the margin because she considered the benefit and cost of *one additional hour* of tennis.

2a. Productivity; standard of living.
2b. Productivity; standard of living.
2c. Expenditure; standard of living.
2d. Expenditure; cost of living.

1.4 WHY ECONOMICS IS WORTH STUDYING

In 1961, Mick Jagger, then the 19-year-old lead singer with a group that would become "The Rolling Stones," enrolled in an economics degree program at the London School of Economics. During the day, he was learning about opportunity cost, and each night, his rock group was earning today's equivalent of $120. Mick soon realized that his opportunity cost of remaining in school was too high and so he dropped out. (A faculty advisor is reputed to have told Mick that he wouldn't make much money in a rock band. But within a few months, the Rolling Stones, along with the Beatles, shot to international stardom and multimillion dollar recording contracts!)

Mick Jagger used one of the big ideas of economics to make his own rational decision. And you can do the same. Let's look at the benefits and costs of studying economics and check that the benefits outweigh the costs.

Two main benefits from studying economics are:

- Understanding
- Expanded career opportunities

■ Understanding

George Bernard Shaw, the great Irish dramatist and thinker, wrote: "Economy is the art of making the most of life." Life is certainly full of economic problems, some global or national in scope and some personal.

Every day, on television, on the Internet, and in newspapers and magazines, we hear and read about global or national economic issues: Should Nike pay higher wages to its workers in Asia? Is there too much economic inequality in the world? How can we improve health care, welfare, and education? Are taxes too high or too low? Will the Bank of Canada increase interest rates next week?

And every day in your own life, you're confronted with personal economic choices: Will you buy pizza or pasta? Will you skip class today? Will you put your summer earnings in the bank or the stock market?

Studying economics equips you with tools and insights that help you to understand the world's problems and to participate in the political debate that might eventually lead to their resolution.

John Maynard Keynes, a famous British economist of the twentieth century, wrote: "The ideas of economists…, both when they are right and when they are wrong, are more powerful than is commonly understood. Indeed the world is ruled by little else. Practical men [and women, he would have written today], who believe themselves to be quite exempt from any intellectual influences, are usually the slaves of some defunct economist."

Keynes was correct. You can't ignore economic ideas. They are all around you. You use them every day in your personal life and in your work. You use them when you vote and when you argue with your friends. But you don't need to be the slave of some defunct economist. By studying economics, you will learn how to develop your own ideas and to test them against the ideas of others. As you progress with your study of economics, you will start to listen to the news and read your newspaper with a deeper understanding of what's going on. You will also find yourself increasingly using the economics that you are learning as you make your own economic choices.

■ Expanded Career Opportunities

Robert Reich, a former U.S. Secretary of Labor, predicts that the three big jobs of the 21st century will be what he calls *problem identifying*, *problem solving*, and *strategic brokering*. The people who are good at these tasks command soaring incomes. And there is no better way to train yourself in these skills than to study economics. You can think of economics as a workout regimen for your brain. Almost everything that you study in economics is practice at thinking abstractly and rigorously about concrete things. You will constantly be asking: "what if?" Although students of economics learn many useful economic concepts, it is the training and practice in abstract thinking that really pays off.

Most students of economics don't go on to major in the subject. And even those who do major in economics don't usually go on to become economists. Rather, they work in fields such as banking, business, management, finance, insurance, real estate, marketing, law, government, journalism, health care, and the arts. A course in economics is a very good choice for a pre-med, pre-law, or pre-MBA student.

Economics graduates are not the highest-paid professionals, as you can see in Figure 1.2. Graduates in health sciences, engineering and computer science, and math and other physical sciences earn more than economics graduates. But economics graduates are close to the top and earn more than most others. Significantly, they earn more than commerce graduates.

■ **FIGURE 1.2**
Average Incomes   *e*/**Foundations 1.4**

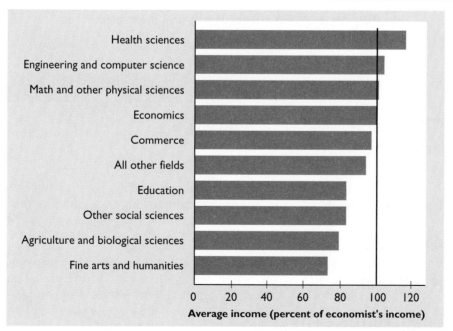

Graduates in disciplines that include economics are at the top of the earnings distribution.

SOURCE: *Earnings of University Graduates in Canada by Discipline*, Ross Finnie, Human Resources Development Canada, paper R-99-13E.b, 2000.

■ The Costs of Studying Economics

Regardless of what you study, you must buy textbooks and supplies and pay tuition. So these expenses are *not* part of the opportunity cost of studying economics.

One cost of studying economics is forgone knowledge of some other subject. If you work hard at studying economics, you must forgo learning some other subject. You can't study everything.

Another cost, and the main cost of studying economics, is forgone leisure time. Economics is a demanding subject and it takes time to master. Most students say that they find it difficult. They often complain that they understand the subject when they read the textbook or listen to their instructor but then, when they take an exam, they just can't figure out the correct answers.

The trick is practice, or "learning-by-doing." Economics is not a subject that you learn by memorizing things. You must memorize definitions and technical terms. But beyond that, memory is not your main mental tool. Working problems and learning how to analyze and solve problems is the key. And this activity is time consuming.

■ Benefits Versus Costs

So which is larger: the benefit or the cost? Economics says that only you can decide. You are the judge of value or benefit to yourself. So you must weigh the benefits and the costs that we've identified (and consider any others that are important to *you*.)

If you're clear that the benefits outweigh the costs, you're well on your way to having a good time in your economics course. If the costs outweigh the benefits, don't waste your time. Life is too short.

If you're on the fence, try to get more information. But if you remain on the fence, complete this one course in economics and then decide.

CHECKPOINT 1.4

Study Guide pp. 10–11

*e*Foundations 1.4

4   **Explain why economics is worth studying.**

Practice Problem 1.4

A student is choosing between an economics course and a popular music course. List two opportunity costs and two benefits from taking the economics course.

Exercise 1.4

Why did Mick Jagger quit his economics course? What are some of the benefits that Mick Jagger might have given up?

Solution to Practice Problem 1.4

Opportunity costs include forgone leisure and forgone appreciation of popular music. Benefits include expanded career opportunities, better understanding of the world, and better problem-solving skills.

CHAPTER CHECKPOINT

Key Points

1 **Define economics, distinguish between microeconomics and macro-economics, and explain the questions of macroeconomics.**

- Economics is the social science that studies the choices that individuals, businesses, governments, and entire societies make as they cope with scarcity.
- Microeconomics is the study of the choices that individuals and businesses make, the way these choices interact, and the influence that governments exert on these choices.
- Macroeconomics studies trends in the standard of living and the cost of living and economic fluctuations—recessions and expansions.

2 **Describe what economists do and some of the problems they encounter.**

- Positive statements are about what *is*, and they can be tested. Normative statements are about what *ought* to be, and they cannot be tested.
- To explain the economic world, economists build and test economic models.
- Economists use the *ceteris paribus* assumption to try to disentangle cause and effect, and they use natural experiments, statistical methods, and economic experiments.

3 **Explain four core ideas that define the way economists think about macroeconomic questions.**

- Macroeconomic performance results from rational choices.
- The standard of living improves when production per person increases.
- The cost of living rises when the quantity of money increases faster than production.
- Economic fluctuations occur when expenditure or productivity fluctuates.

4 **Explain why economics is worth studying.**

- The benefits of studying economics are understanding the economic world and expanded career opportunities.
- The costs of studying economics are forgone knowledge of some other subject and leisure time.

Key Terms

Benefit, 15
Business cycle, 7
Ceteris paribus, 12
Correlation, 13
Cost of living, 7
Econometrics, 13
Economic model, 11
Economic theory, 11

Economics, 5
Goods and services, 6
Great Depression, 8
Inflation, 7
Macroeconomics, 5
Margin, 16
Marginal benefit, 16
Marginal cost, 16

Microeconomics, 5
Opportunity cost, 15
Post hoc fallacy, 13
Productivity, 17
Rational choice, 15
Scarcity, 4
Standard of living, 6
Unemployment, 6

Exercises

1. Devastating rains bring extensive flooding to a nation's agricultural regions. Describe the effects of this event on the nation's standard of living.

2. Here is a choice: You can have $11 and pay the prices of 1800 or you can have $100 and pay the prices of 2000. Which would you prefer? (Use the link to the Inflation Calculator on your Foundations Web site to answer this question.)

3. It is 1931 and close to one in five people is unable to find a job. Describe the effects of such a situation on the standard of living of a family. Compare and contrast this situation with that of 2000.

4. Your school has decided to increase the intake of new students next year. What economic concepts would your school have considered to reach its decision? Did the school make its decision at the margin?

5. Assign each of the following news items to one of the three macroeconomic issues—(i) the standard of living, (ii) the cost of living, and (iii) unemployment—and say whether it is a positive statement or a normative statement.
    a. The government should cut taxes to encourage greater work effort.
    b. An interest rate cut will stimulate job creation.
    c. Gas prices are too high.
    d. Lower gas prices will stimulate production.
    e. Expect a big increase in layoffs.
    f. Mechanization and automation bring rising unemployment.
    g. A government scheme called "workfare" will reduce the number of people unemployed.

6. Which of the following statements are examples of the *post hoc* fallacy? Which statements confuse cause and effect?
    a. After a devastating ice storm, the government allocates millions of dollars to cleaning up the mess. Economic activity increases. An ice storm causes an expansion.
    b. During a strong expansion, production increases, employment increases, and price rises are faster than normal. The cause of the strong expansion is the increase in employment.
    c. Automation eliminates some jobs and brings a recession.
    d. When the stock market plunges, a recession follows.

7. Describe how the standard of living and unemployment vary over the business cycle.

8. Use the link on your Foundations Web site to visit Statistics Canada and the Bank of Canada and obtain information on the current economic condition of Canada. Describe the changes in the standard of living, changes in the cost of living, and the phase of the business cycle through which the economy is passing.

When you have completed your study of this appendix, you will be able to:

1 Interpret a scatter diagram, time-series graph, and cross-section graph.

2 Interpret the graphs used in economic models.

3 Define and calculate slope.

4 Graph relationships among more than two variables.

■ Basic Idea

A graph represents a quantity as a distance and enables us to visualize the relationship between two variables. To make a graph, we set two lines called *axes* perpendicular to each other, like those in Figure A1.1. The vertical line is called the *y*-axis, and the horizontal line is called the *x*-axis. The common zero point is called the *origin*. In Figure A1.1, the *x*-axis measures income in thousands of dollars per year. A movement to the right shows an increase in income and a movement to the left shows a decrease in income. The *y*-axis represents expenditure, measured in thousands of dollars per year. To make a graph, we need a value of the variable *x* and a corresponding value of the variable *y*. For example, if income is $10,000 a year, expenditure is also $10,000 a year at point *A* in the graph. If income is $30,000 a year, expenditure is $25,000 a year at point *B* in the graph. Graphs like that in Figure A1.1 can be used to show any type of quantitative data on two variables and to reveal and describe the relationships between economic variables.

■ **FIGURE A1.1**

Making a Graph

℮ **Foundations A1.1**

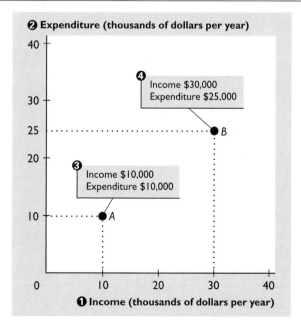

All graphs have axes that measure quantities as distances.

1 The horizontal axis (*x*-axis) measures income. A movement to the right shows an increase in income.

2 The vertical axis (*y*-axis) measures expenditure. A movement upward shows an increase in expenditure.

3 Point *A* shows that when income is $10,000 a year, expenditure is $10,000 a year.

4 Point *B* shows that when income is $30,000 a year, expenditure is $25,000 a year.

■ Interpreting Data Graphs

Scatter diagram
A graph of the value of one variable against the value of another variable.

A **scatter diagram** is a graph of the value of one variable against the value of another variable. It is used to reveal whether a relationship exists between two variables and to describe the relationship. Figure A1.2 shows two examples.

Figure A1.2(a) shows the relationship between expenditure and income. Each point shows expenditure per person and income per person in Canada in a given year from 1990 to 2000. The points are "scattered" within the graph. The label on each point shows its year. The point marked 97 shows that in 1997, income per person was $18,200 and expenditure per person was $17,100. This scatter diagram reveals that as income increases, expenditure also increases.

Figure A1.2(b) shows the relationship between the number of minutes of international phone calls made and the average price per minute. This scatter diagram reveals that as the price per minute falls, the number of minutes called increases.

Time-series graph
A graph that measures time on the x-axis and the variable or variables in which we are interested on the y-axis.

A **time-series graph** measures time (for example, months or years) on the x-axis and the variable or variables in which we are interested on the y-axis. Figure A1.2(c) shows an example. In this graph, time (on the x-axis) is measured in years, which run from 1970 to 2000. The variable that we are interested in is the Canadian unemployment rate, which is measured on the y-axis.

A time-series graph conveys an enormous amount of information quickly and easily, as this example illustrates. It shows when the value is:

1. High or low. When the line is a long way from the x-axis, unemployment is high. When the line is close to the x-axis, unemployment is low.

2. Rising or falling. When the line slopes upward, as in 1981, unemployment is rising. When the line slopes downward, as in 1985, unemployment is falling.

3. Rising or falling quickly or slowly. If the line is steep, then unemployment is rising or falling quickly. If the line is not steep, unemployment is rising or falling slowly. Unemployment rose slowly in 1978 and quickly in 1982. Unemployment fell quickly in 1994 and slowly in 1987.

Trend
A general tendency for the value of a variable to rise or fall.

A time-series graph also reveals if the variable has a trend. A **trend** is a general tendency for the value of a variable to rise or fall. You can see that the unemployment rate had a general tendency to rise through the 1970s and 1980s. That is, although the unemployment rate fluctuated, it rose more than it fell.

With a time-series graph, we can compare different periods quickly. Figure A1.2(c) shows that the 1980s and 1990s were different from the 1970s. Unemployment fluctuated more during the 1980s and 1990s than during the 1970s. This graph conveys a wealth of information, and it does so in much less space than we have used to describe only some of its features.

Cross-section graph
A graph that shows the values of an economic variable for different groups in a population at a point in time.

A **cross-section graph** shows the values of an economic variable for different groups in a population at a point in time. Figure A1.2(d) is an example of a cross-section graph. It shows the unemployment rates in seven major countries in 2000. This graph uses bars rather than dots and lines, and the length of each bar indicates a nation's unemployment rate. Figure A1.2(d) enables you to compare the unemployment rates in these seven countries. And you can do so much more quickly and clearly than by looking at a list of numbers.

■ FIGURE A1.2
Data Graphs

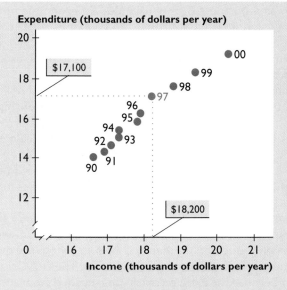

(a) Scatter Diagram: Expenditure and income

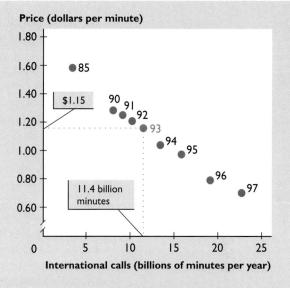

(b) Scatter Diagram: Price and quantity of calls

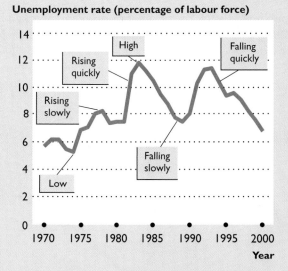

(c) Time Series: The Canadian unemployment rate

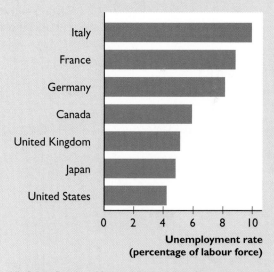

(d) Cross Section: Unemployment rate in seven countries

A scatter diagram reveals the relationship between two variables. In part (a), as income increases, expenditure increases. In part (b), as the price per minute falls, the number of minutes called increases.

A time-series graph plots the value of a variable on the y-axis against time on the x-axis. Part (c) plots the Canadian unemploy-ment rate each year from 1970 to 2000. The graph shows when unemployment was high and low, when it increased and decreased, and when it changed quickly and slowly.

A cross-section graph shows the value of a variable across the members of a population. Part (d) shows the unemployment rate in each of the seven major countries in 2000.

■ Interpreting Graphs Used in Economic Models

We use graphs to show the relationships among the variables in an economic model. An *economic model* is a simplified description of the economy or of a component of the economy such as a business or a household. An economic model consists of statements about economic behaviour that can be expressed as equations or as curves in a graph. Economists use models to explore the effects of different policies or other influences on the economy in ways similar to those used to test model airplanes in wind tunnels and models of the climate.

Figure A1.3 shows graphs of the relationships between two variables that move in the same direction. Such a relationship is called a **positive relationship** or a **direct relationship**.

Part (a) shows a straight-line relationship, which is called a **linear relationship**. The distance travelled in 5 hours increases as the speed increases. For example, point *A* shows that 200 kilometres are travelled in 5 hours at a speed of 40 kilometres per hour. And point *B* shows that the distance travelled increases to 300 kilometres if the speed increases to 60 kilometres per hour.

Part (b) shows the relationship between distance sprinted and recovery time (the time it takes the heart rate to return to its normal resting rate). An upward-sloping curved line that starts out quite flat but then becomes steeper as we move along the curve away from the origin describes this relationship. The curve slopes upward and becomes steeper because the extra recovery time needed from sprinting another 100 metres increases. It takes less than five minutes to recover from sprinting 100 metres but more than 10 minutes to recover from sprinting 200 metres.

Part (c) shows the relationship between the number of problems worked by a student and the amount of study time. An upward-sloping curved line that starts

Positive relationship or direct relationship
A relationship between two variables that move in the same direction.

Linear relationship
A relationship that graphs as a straight line.

■ **FIGURE A1.3**
Positive (Direct) Relationships

*e*Foundations **A1.1**

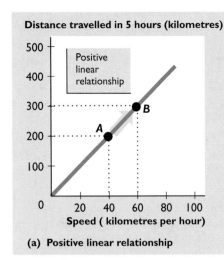

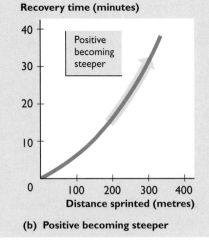

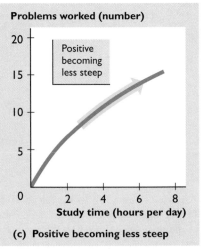

(a) Positive linear relationship

(b) Positive becoming steeper

(c) Positive becoming less steep

Part (a) shows that as speed increases, the distance travelled increases along a straight line.

Part (b) shows that as the distance sprinted increases, recovery time increases along a curve that becomes steeper.

Part (c) shows that as study time increases, the number of problems worked increases along a curve that becomes less steep.

out quite steep and becomes flatter as we move away from the origin shows this relationship. Study time becomes less productive as you increase the hours worked and become more tired.

Figure A1.4 shows relationships between two variables that move in opposite directions. Such a relationship is called a **negative relationship** or an **inverse relationship**.

Part (a) shows the relationship between the number of hours available for playing squash and the number of hours for playing tennis. One extra hour spent playing tennis means one hour less playing squash and vice versa. This relationship is negative and linear.

Part (b) shows the relationship between the cost per kilometre travelled and the length of a journey. The longer the journey, the lower is the cost per kilometre. But as the journey length increases, the cost per kilometre decreases, and the fall in the cost is smaller, the longer the journey. This feature of the relationship is shown by the fact that the curve slopes downward, starting out steep at a short journey length and then becoming flatter as the journey length increases. This relationship arises because some of the costs are fixed, such as auto insurance, and the fixed costs are spread over a longer journey.

Part (c) shows the relationship between the amount of leisure time and the number of problems worked by a student. Increasing leisure time produces an increasingly large reduction in the number of problems worked. This relationship is a negative one that starts out with a gentle slope at a small number of leisure hours and becomes steeper as the number of leisure hours increases. This relationship is a different view of the idea shown in Figure A1.3(c).

Many relationships in economic models have a maximum or a minimum. For example, firms try to make the maximum possible profit and to produce at the lowest possible cost. Figure A1.5 shows relationships that have a maximum or a minimum.

Negative relationship or inverse relationship
A relationship between two variables that move in the opposite direction.

FIGURE A1.4

Negative (Inverse) Relationships

e/**Foundations A1.1**

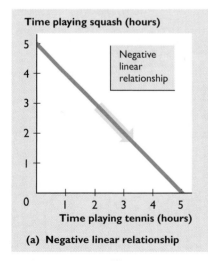

(a) Negative linear relationship

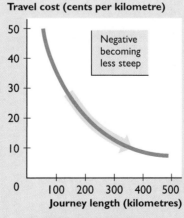

(b) Negative becoming less steep

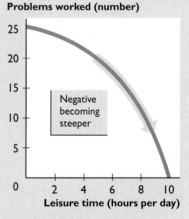

(c) Negative becoming steeper

Part (a) shows that as the time playing tennis increases, the time playing squash decreases along a straight line.

Part (b) shows that as the journey length increases, the travel cost falls along a curve that becomes less steep.

Part (c) shows that as leisure time increases, the number of problems worked decreases along a curve that becomes steeper.

FIGURE A1.5
Maximum and Minimum Points

*e*Foundations **A1.1**

In part (a) as the rainfall increases, the curve ❶ slopes upward as the yield per hectare rises, ❷ is flat at point *A*, the maximum yield, and then ❸ slopes downward as the yield per hectare falls.

In part (b) as the speed increases, the curve ❶ slopes downward as the cost per kilometre falls, ❷ is flat at the minimum point *B*, and then ❸ slopes upward as the cost per kilometre rises.

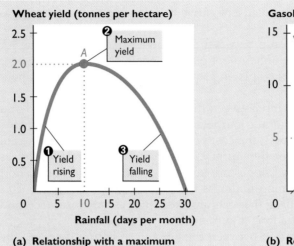

(a) Relationship with a maximum

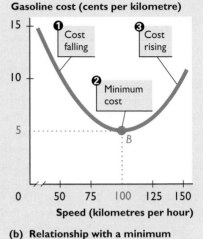

(b) Relationship with a minimum

Part (a) shows the relationship that starts out sloping upward, reaches a maximum, and then slopes downward. And part (b) shows the reverse case: a relationship that begins sloping downward, falls to a minimum, and then slopes upward.

Finally, there are many situations in which no matter what happens to the value of one variable, the other variable remains constant. Sometimes we want to show the independence between two variables in a graph. Figure A1.6 shows two graphs in which the variables are independent.

FIGURE A1.6
Variables That Are Unrelated

*e*Foundations **A1.1**

In part (a), as the price of bananas increases, the student's grade in economics remains at 75 percent. These variables are unrelated and the curve is horizontal.

In part (b), the vineyards of France produce 3 billion litres of wine a year no matter what the rainfall in Alberta is. These variables are unrelated and the curve is vertical.

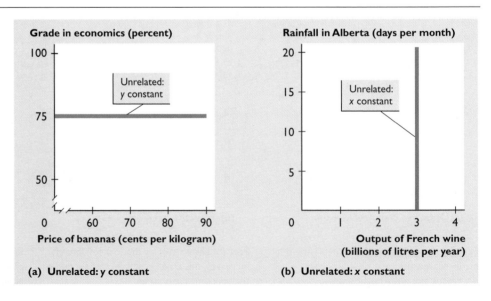

(a) Unrelated: *y* constant

(b) Unrelated: *x* constant

■ The Slope of a Relationship

We can measure the influence of one variable on another by the slope of the relationship. The **slope** of a relationship is the change in the value of the variable measured on the y-axis divided by the change in the value of the variable measured on the x-axis. We use the Greek letter Δ (delta) to represent "change in." So Δy means the change in the value of y, and Δx means the change in the value of x, and the slope of the relationship is

$$\Delta y \div \Delta x.$$

If a large change in y is associated with a small change in x, the slope is large and the curve is steep. If a small change in y is associated with a large change in x, the slope is small and the curve is flat.

Figure A1.7 shows you how to calculate slope. The slope of a straight line is the same regardless of where on the line you calculate it—the slope is constant. In part (a), when x increases from 2 to 6, y increases from 3 to 6. The change in x is +4—that is, Δx is 4. The change in y is +3—that is, Δy is 3. The slope of that line is 3/4. In part (b), when x increases from 2 to 6, y *decreases* from 6 to 3. The change in y is *minus* 3—that is, Δy is −3. The change in x is plus 4—that is, Δx is 4. The slope of the curve is −3/4. In part (c), we calculate the slope at a point on a curve. To do so, place a ruler on the graph so that it touches point A and no other point on the curve, then draw a straight line along the edge of the ruler. The slope of this straight line is the slope of the curve at point A. This slope is 3/4.

Slope
The change in the value of the variable measured on the y-axis divided by the change in the value of the variable measured on the x-axis.

■ FIGURE A1.7

Calculating Slope

*e*Foundations **A1.1**

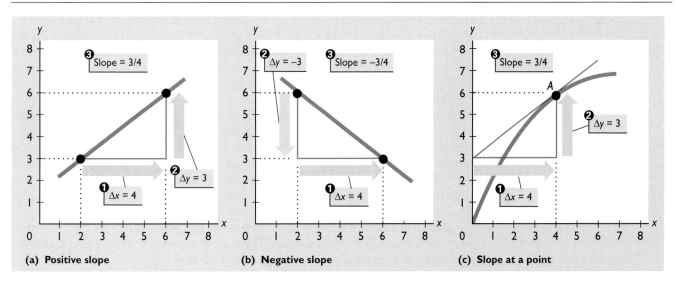

(a) **Positive slope**   (b) **Negative slope**   (c) **Slope at a point**

In part (a), ❶ when Δx is 4, ❷ Δy is 3, so ❸ the slope ($\Delta y/\Delta x$) is 3/4.

In part (b), ❶ when Δx is 4, ❷ Δy is −3, so ❸ the slope ($\Delta y/\Delta x$) is −3/4.

In part (c), the slope of the curve at point A equals the slope of the red line. ❶ When Δx is 4, ❷ Δy is 3, so ❸ the slope ($\Delta y/\Delta x$) is 3/4.

■ Relationships Among More Than Two Variables

We have seen that we can graph the relationship between two variables as a point formed by the x and y values. But most of the relationships in economics involve relationships among many variables, not just two. For example, the amount of ice cream consumed depends on the price of ice cream and the temperature. If ice cream is expensive and the temperature is low, people eat much less ice cream than when ice cream is inexpensive and the temperature is high. For any given price of ice cream, the quantity consumed varies with the temperature; and for any given temperature, the quantity of ice cream consumed varies with its price.

Figure A1.8 shows a relationship among three variables. The table shows the number of litres of ice cream consumed each day at various temperatures and ice cream prices. How can we graph these numbers?

To graph a relationship that involves more than two variables, we use the *ceteris paribus* assumption.

Ceteris Paribus

The Latin phrase, *ceteris paribus*, means "other things remaining the same." Every laboratory experiment is an attempt to create *ceteris paribus* and isolate the relationship of interest. We use the same method to make a graph.

Figure A1.8(a) shows an example. This graph shows what happens to the quantity of ice cream consumed when the price of ice cream varies while the temperature remains the same. The line labelled 20°C shows the relationship between ice cream consumption and the price of ice cream if the temperature is 20°C. The numbers used to plot that line are those in the third column of the table in Figure A1.8. For example, if the temperature is 20°C, 10 litres are consumed when the price is 60¢ a scoop and 18 litres are consumed when the price is 30¢ a scoop. The curve labelled 30°C shows consumption as the price varies if the temperature is 30°C.

We can also show the relationship between ice cream consumption and temperature while the price of ice cream remains constant, as shown in Figure A1.8(b). The curve labelled 60¢ shows how the consumption of ice cream varies with the temperature when ice cream costs 60¢ a scoop, and a second curve shows the relationship when ice cream costs 15¢ a scoop. For example, at 60¢ a scoop, 10 litres are consumed when the temperature is 20°C and 20 litres when the temperature is 30°C.

Figure A1.8(c) shows the combinations of temperature and price that result in a constant consumption of ice cream. One curve shows the combination that results in 10 litres a day being consumed, and the other shows the combination that results in 7 litres a day being consumed. A high price and a high temperature lead to the same consumption as a lower price and a lower temperature. For example, 10 litres of ice cream are consumed at 30°C and 90¢ a scoop, at 20°C and 60¢ a scoop, and at 10°C and 45¢ a scoop.

With what you've learned about graphs in this Appendix, you can move forward with your study of economics. There are no graphs in this textbook that are more complicated than the ones you've studied here.

FIGURE A1.8

Graphing a Relationship Among Three Variables

Price (cents per scoop)	Ice cream consumption (litres per day)			
	0°C	10°C	20°C	30°C
15	12	18	25	50
30	10	12	18	37
45	7	10	13	27
60	5	7	10	20
75	3	5	7	14
90	2	3	5	10
105	1	2	3	6

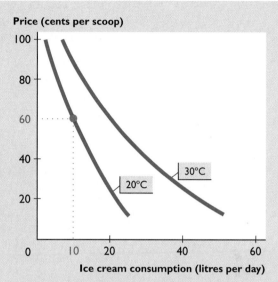

(a) Price and consumption at a given temperature

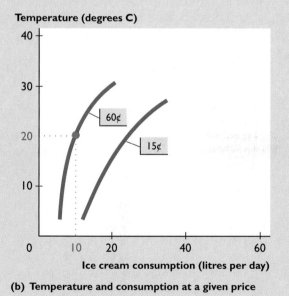

(b) Temperature and consumption at a given price

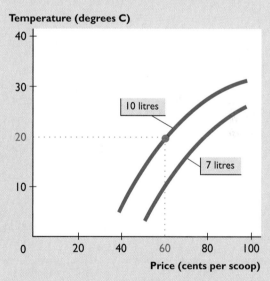

(c) Temperature and price at a given consumption

The table tells us how many litres of ice cream are consumed each day at different prices and different temperatures. For example, if the price is 60¢ a scoop and the temperature is 20°C, 10 litres of ice cream are consumed. This set of values is highlighted in the table and each part of the figure.

Part (a) shows the relationship between price and consumption when temperature is held constant. One curve holds temperature at 30°C and the other at 20°C.

Part (b) shows the relationship between temperature and consumption when price is held constant. One curve holds the price at 60¢ a scoop and the other at 15¢ a scoop.

Part (c) shows the relationship between temperature and price when consumption is held constant. One curve holds consumption at 10 litres and the other at 7 litres.

Study Guide pp. 15–20

e Foundations A1.1

	A	B	C	D
1	1992	43	4	23
2	1993	47	5	24
3	1994	56	6	25
4	1995	57	11	25
5	1996	57	17	27
6	1997	55	26	29
7	1998	56	32	30
8	1999	58	37	31
9	2000	62	43	32
10	2001	66	48	33
11	2002	69	53	34

Exercises

The spreadsheet provides data on consumer spending. Column A is the year, the other columns are actual and projected expenditures per person on recorded music (column B), Internet services (column C), and movies in theatres (column D). Use this spreadsheet to answer Exercises 1, 2, 3, 4, and 5.

1. Draw a scatter diagram to show the relationship between expenditure on recorded music and expenditure on Internet services. Describe the relationship.

2. Draw a scatter diagram to show the relationship between expenditure on Internet services and on movies in theatres. Describe the relationship.

3. Draw a scatter diagram to show the relationship between expenditure on recorded music and expenditure on movies in theatres. Describe the relationship.

4. Draw a time-series graph of expenditure on Internet services. Say in which year(s) (a) expenditure was highest, (b) expenditure was lowest, (c) expenditure increased the most, and (d) expenditure increased the least. Also, say whether the data show a trend and describe its direction.

5. Draw a time-series graph of expenditure on recorded music. Say in which year(s) (a) expenditure was highest, (b) expenditure was lowest, (c) expenditure increased the most, and (d) expenditure increased the least. Also, say whether the data show a trend and describe its direction.

6. Draw a graph to show the relationship between the two variables x and y:

x	0	1	2	3	4	5	6	7	8
y	0	1	4	9	16	25	36	49	64

   a. Is the relationship positive or negative?
   b. Calculate the slope of the relationship between x and y when x equals 2 and when x equals 4.
   c. How does the slope of the relationship change as the value of x increases?
   d. Think of some economic relationships that might be similar to this one.

7. Draw a graph to show the relationship between the two variables x and y:

x	0	1	2	3	4	5	6	7	8
y	60	49	39	30	22	15	9	4	0

   a. Is the relationship positive or negative?
   b. Calculate the slope of the relationship between x and y when x equals 2 and when x equals 4.
   c. How does the slope of the relationship change as the value of x increases?
   d. Think of some economic relationships that might be similar to this one.

Price (dollars each)	Umbrellas (number per day)		
	0	2	4
	(cms per day)		
10	14	16	24
20	8	14	16
30	4	8	14
40	2	4	8

8. The table gives the price of an umbrella, rainfall, and the number of umbrellas purchased. Draw graphs to show the relationship between
   a. The price and the number of umbrellas purchased, if rainfall remains constant.
   b. The number of umbrellas purchased and rainfall, if the price remains constant.
   c. Rainfall and the price, if the number of umbrellas purchased remains constant.

The Canadian and Global Economies

CHAPTER CHECKLIST

When you have completed your study of this chapter, you will be able to:

1 Describe what, how, and for whom goods and services are produced in Canada.

2 Use the circular flow model to provide a picture of how households, firms, and governments interact.

3 Describe the macroeconomic performance—standard of living, cost of living, and economic fluctuations—of the Canadian and other economies.

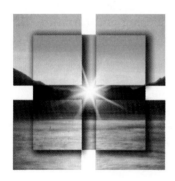

Economic activity arises from scarcity—the available resources are insufficient to meet all our wants. Macroeconomics studies the aggregate (or total) effects on the national economy and the global economy of the choices that individuals, businesses, and governments make. The three big issues that macroeconomics tries to understand are what determines the standard of living, the cost of living, and economic fluctuations—expansions and recessions.

Most of your macroeconomics course is about theories that *explain* and in some cases enable economists to make *predictions* about macroeconomic performance. But in this chapter, we are going to *describe* the main features of the Canadian and global economies. You will learn about the resources available and how they are used, the current levels and changes in the standard of living and the cost of living, and economic fluctuations in Canada and the world as a whole.

2.1   WHAT, HOW, AND FOR WHOM?

Walk around a shopping mall and pay close attention to the range of goods and services that are being offered for sale. Go inside some of the shops and look at the labels to see where various items are manufactured. The next time you travel on a major highway, look at the large trucks and pay attention to the names and products printed on their sides and the places in which the trucks are registered. Open the Yellow Pages and flip through a few sections. Notice the huge range of goods and services that businesses are offering.

You've just done a sampling of *what* goods and services are produced and consumed in Canada today.

■ What Do We Produce?

In macroeconomics, we divide the vast array of goods and services produced into four large groups:

- Consumption goods and services
- Investment goods
- Government goods and services
- Exports of goods and services

Consumption Goods and Services

Consumption goods
and services
Goods and services that are bought by individuals and used to provide personal enjoyment and contribute to a person's standard of living.

Consumption goods and services are items that are bought by individuals and used to provide personal enjoyment and contribute to a person's standard of living. They include items such as housing and furniture, clothing, SUVs, movies and popcorn, vacation trips, coffee and doughnuts, dental care, and dry cleaning services.

Investment Goods

Investment goods
Goods that are bought by businesses to increase their productive resources.

Investment goods are goods bought by businesses to increase their ability to produce goods and services. They include items such as auto assembly lines, machinery and equipment, gas pipelines, banks' computers, and shopping malls.

Government Goods and Services

Government goods
and services
Goods and services that are bought by governments.

Government goods and services are items that are bought by governments. They include items such as health care, education, police protection, law courts, computers, and military equipment.

Exports of Goods and Services

Exports
Goods and services produced in Canada and sold in other countries.

Exports are goods and services produced in Canada and sold in other countries. They include the railway locomotives that General Motors make in London, Ontario that the Irish government buys and the Canada Regional Jets that Bombardier makes in Quebec and that Ansett Airlines of Australia buys.

Figure 2.1 provides a snapshot of the division of total production in Canada in 2000 into these four groups. You can see that the largest component was consumption goods and services, while government goods and services were the smallest. The figure also highlights the large size of exports, which is a key feature of the Canadian economy.

FIGURE 2.1

What We Produce

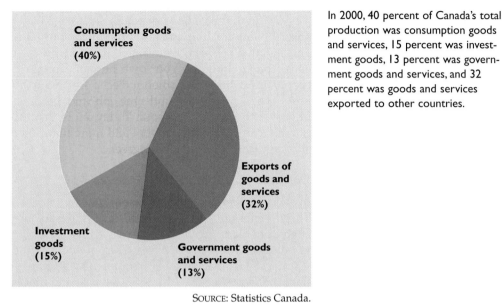

SOURCE: Statistics Canada.

In 2000, 40 percent of Canada's total production was consumption goods and services, 15 percent was investment goods, 13 percent was government goods and services, and 32 percent was goods and services exported to other countries.

How Do We Produce?

Goods and services are produced by using productive resources. Economists call productive resources **factors of production**. Factors of production are grouped into four categories:

- Land
- Labour
- Capital
- Entrepreneurship

Factors of production
The productive resources used to produce goods and services—land, labour, capital, and entrepreneurship.

Land

In economics, **land** includes all the "gifts of nature" that we use to produce goods and services. Land is what, in everyday language, we call *natural resources*. It includes land in the everyday sense, minerals, energy, water, air, wild plants, animals, birds, and fish. Some of these resources are renewable and some are nonrenewable. Natural Resources Canada maintains an inventory of the quantity and quality of Canada's natural resources and monitors changes in that inventory.

Land
The "gifts of nature," or *natural resources*, that we use to produce goods and services.

Labour

Labour is the work time and work effort that people devote to producing goods and services. It includes the physical and mental efforts of all the people who work on farms and construction sites and in factories, shops, and offices. Statistics Canada measures Canada's labour force every month. In Canada today, 16 million people have jobs or are available for work and they provide 27 billion hours of labour a year.

Labour
The work time and work effort that people devote to producing goods and services.

The quantity of labour increases as the adult population increases. The quantity of labour also increases if a larger percentage of the population takes jobs. During the past 50 years, a larger proportion of women have taken paid work and this trend has increased the quantity of labour available.

The quality of labour depends on how skilled people are. Economists use a special name for human skill: human capital. **Human capital** is the knowledge and skill that people obtain from education, on-the-job training, and work experience. You are building your own human capital right now as you work on your economics course and other subjects. And your human capital will continue to grow when you get a full-time job and become better at it. Human capital improves the *quality* of labour. Today, more than 71 percent of Canada's population has completed high school and more than 40 percent has a college or university certificate, diploma, or degree.

Human capital
The knowledge and skill that people obtain from education, on-the-job training, and work experience.

Capital

In everyday language, we talk about money, stocks, and bonds as being "capital." These items are *financial capital,* and they are not productive resources. They enable people to provide businesses with financial resources, but they are *not* used to produce goods and services. They are not capital.

Capital consists of tools, instruments, machines, buildings, and other constructions that have been produced in the past and that businesses now use to produce goods and services. Capital includes auto assembly lines, highways, power plants, airports and airplanes, hammers and screwdrivers, industrial robots, warehouses, retail stores, office towers, computers and electronic communications systems. Statistics Canada keeps track of the total value of capital, which grows over time as new capital goods are produced. In Canada today, it is about $2 trillion.

Capital
Tools, instruments, machines, buildings, and other constructions that have been produced in the past and that businesses now use to produce goods and services.

Eye On The
PAST

Changes in Human Capital

Human capital in Canada has persistently expanded. The number of people in college and university (left figure) is one measure of the growth of human capital. The percentage of the population that has a university degree (right figure) is another measure. You can see that both the growth rate and the level of human capital have increased over the years.

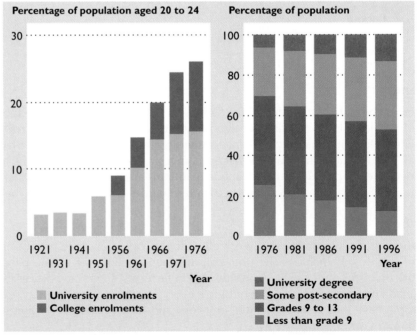

SOURCE: Statistics Canada.

Entrepreneurship

Entrepreneurship is the human resource that organizes labour, land, and capital. Entrepreneurs come up with new ideas about what and how to produce, make business decisions, and bear the risks that arise from these decisions.

The quantity of entrepreneurship is hard to describe or measure. At some periods, there appears to be a great deal of imaginative entrepreneurship around. People such as John Sleeman, who runs one of the fastest growing breweries in North America, Heather Reisman, who created Indigo Books, and Bill Gates, who built Microsoft, are examples of extraordinary entrepreneurial talent. But these highly visible entrepreneurs are just the tip of an iceberg that consists of hundreds of thousands of people who run businesses, large and small.

> **Entrepreneurship**
> The human resource that organizes labour, land, and capital.

■ For Whom Do We Produce?

Who gets the goods and services that are produced depends on the incomes that people earn and the goods and services that they choose to buy. A large income enables a person to buy large quantities of goods and services. A small income leaves a person with few options and small quantities of goods and services.

People earn their incomes by selling the services of the factors of production they own. **Rent** is paid for the use of land, **wages** are paid for the services of labour, **interest** is paid for the use of capital, and entrepreneurs receive a **profit** (or incur a **loss**) from running their businesses.

Which factor of production in Canada earns more income: labour or capital? Figure 2.2 provides the answer. The figure shows the **functional distribution of income**, which is the percentage distribution of income among the factors of production. Labour earns most of the income—69 percent of total income in 2000. Capital income—corporate income plus interest income—was 23 percent in 2000. The proprietors of businesses, whose earnings are a mixture of labour and capital income, earned about 8 percent of total income in 2000. These percentages remain remarkably constant over time.

> **Rent**
> Income paid for the use of land.
>
> **Wages**
> Income paid for the services of labour.
>
> **Interest**
> Income paid for the use of capital.
>
> **Profit (or loss)**
> Income earned by an entrepreneur for running a business.
>
> **Functional distribution of income**
> The percentage distribution of income among the factors of production.

■ FIGURE 2.2

The Functional Distribution of Income in Canada   *e*Foundations **2.1**

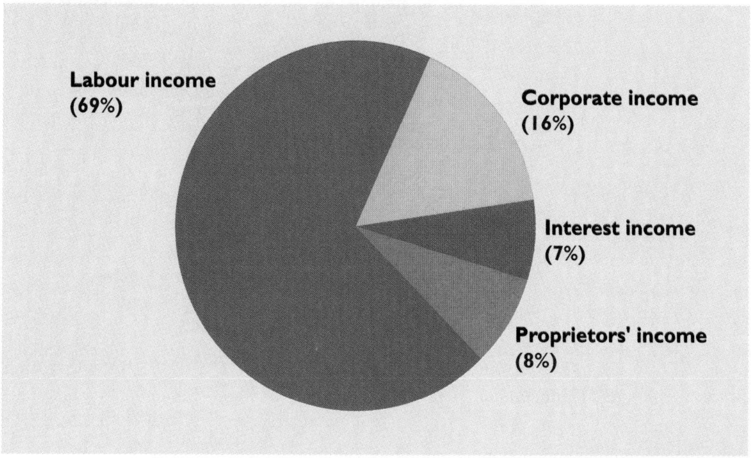

Labour income (69%)

Corporate income (16%)

Interest income (7%)

Proprietors' income (8%)

Incomes determine who consumes the goods and services produced. In 2000, labour income was 69 percent of total income, capital income (corporate income and interest income) was 23 percent, and proprietors' income, which is income to both labour and capital, was 8 percent.

SOURCE: Statistics Canada.

Personal distribution of income

The percentage distribution of income among households.

Figure 2.3 shows the **personal distribution of income**, which is the distribution of income among households. Incomes are shown for five groups, each of which represents 20 percent of households. If incomes were equal, each 20 percent group would earn 20 percent of total income. You know that incomes are unequal, and the figure provides a measure of just how unequal they are.

The poorest 20 percent of households receive only about 4 percent of total income. Servers at McDonald's, who earn less than $7 an hour, checkout clerks and gas station attendants, who earn less than $10 an hour, are in this group. The average income of this group in 1998 was $10,572.

The second poorest 20 percent receive about 10 percent of total income. The average income of this group in 1998 was $24,354.

The middle 20 percent receive about 16 percent of total income, and the average income of this group in 1998 was $39,660. All three of these groups—the lowest 60 percent of households—earn only 30 percent of total income.

The second richest 20 percent receives about 24 percent of total income and had an average household income of $60,480 in 1998. The richest 20 percent of households receive about 46 percent of total income. The average income of this group was $113,933 in 1998. Many famous people are examples of the high earners in this group. Mats Sundin earns almost $11.5 million a year—almost as much as 850 fast-food servers. NHL players' average income is about $3 million a year.

So the 20 percent of households with the highest incomes get 41 percent of the goods and services produced. The other 80 percent of households share the rest.

■ **FIGURE 2.3**

The Personal Distribution of Income in Canada

e/Foundations **2.1**

In 1998, the richest 20 percent of households received 46 percent of total income. The poorest 20 percent received only 4 percent of total income.

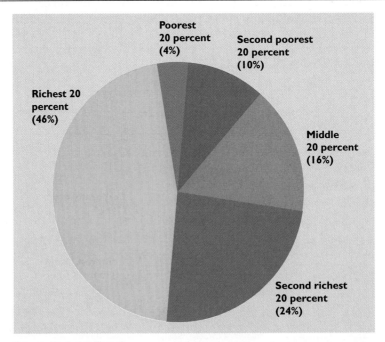

SOURCE: Statistics Canada.

CHECKPOINT 2.1

| | Describe what, how, and for whom goods and services are produced in Canada.

Study Guide **pp. 26–29**

e Foundations **2.1**

Practice Problems 2.1

1. Name the four broad categories of goods and services that we use in macro-economics, provide an example of each (different from those in the chapter), and rank them from largest to smallest in 2000.

2. Name the four factors of production and the incomes they earn.

3. Distinguish between the functional distribution of income and the personal distribution of income.

4. In Canada, which factor of production earns the largest share of income and what percentage of total income does it earn?

Exercises 2.1

1. What is the key distinction between consumption goods and services and investment goods? Which one of them contributes directly to the standard of living?

2. Describe the changes that have occurred in the labour force and human capital of Canada during the last few decades.

3. If everyone were to consume an equal quantity of goods and services, what percentage of total income would the richest 20 percent of individuals have to transfer to lower income groups? What percentage would the second richest 20 percent have to transfer?

4. Compare the percentage of total income that corporations and proprietors earn with the percentage that labour earns in Canada.

Solutions to Practice Problems 2.1

1. The four categories are consumption goods and services, investment goods, government goods and services, and exports of goods and services. An example of a consumption service is a haircut, of an investment good is an oil rig, of a government service is health care, and of an export good is lumber sold to the United States. In 2000, consumption goods and services were the largest component, exports the second largest, investment goods the third largest, and government goods and services the smallest.

2. The factors of production are land, labour, capital, and entrepreneurship. Land earns rent; labour earns wages; capital earns interest; and entrepreneurship earns profit.

3. The functional distribution of income shows the percentage of total income received by each factor of production. The personal distribution of income shows the percentage of total income received by families grouped according to the level of their incomes.

4. Labour is the factor of production that earns the largest share of income in Canada. In 2000, labour earned 69 percent of total income.

2.2 CIRCULAR FLOWS

We can organize the data you've just studied using the **circular flow model**—a model of the economy that shows the circular flow of expenditures and incomes that result from decision makers' choices and the way those choices interact to determine what, how, and for whom goods and services are produced. Figure 2.4 shows the circular flow model.

■ Households and Firms

Circular flow model
A model of the economy that shows the circular flow of expenditure and incomes that result from decision makers' choices, and the way those choices interact to determine what, how, and for whom goods and services are produced.

Households are individuals or groups of people living together as decision-making units. Households own the factors of production—land, labour, capital, and entrepreneurship—and choose the quantities of these resources to provide to firms. Households also choose the quantities of goods and services to buy.

Households
Individuals or groups of people living together as decision-making units.

Firms are the institutions that organize the production of goods and services. Firms choose the quantities of the factors of production to hire and the quantities of goods and services to produce.

Firms
The institutions that organize the production of goods and services.

■ Markets

Households choose the quantities of the factors of production to provide to firms, and firms choose the quantities of the services of the factors of production to hire. Households choose the quantities of goods and services to buy, and firms choose the quantities of goods and services to produce. How are these choices coordinated and made compatible? The answer is: by markets.

A **market** is any arrangement that brings buyers and sellers together and enables them to get information and do business with each other. An example is the market in which oil is bought and sold—the world oil market. The world oil market is not a place. It is the network of oil producers, oil users, wholesalers, and brokers who buy and sell oil. In the world oil market, decision makers do not meet physically. They make deals by telephone, fax, and the Internet.

Market
Any arrangement that brings buyers and sellers together and enables them to get information and do business with each other.

Figure 2.4 identifies two types of markets: goods markets and factor markets. **Goods markets** are markets in which goods and services are bought and sold. **Factor markets** are markets in which factors of production are bought and sold.

Goods markets
Markets in which goods and services are bought and sold.

Factor markets
Markets in which factors of production are bought and sold.

■ Real Flows and Money Flows

When households choose the quantities of land, labour, capital, and entrepreneurship to offer in factor markets, they respond to the incomes they receive—rent for land, wages for labour, interest for capital, and profit for entrepreneurship. When firms choose the quantities of factors to hire, they respond to the rent, wages, interest, and profits they must pay to households.

Similarly, when firms choose the quantities of goods and services to produce and offer for sale in goods markets, they respond to the amounts that they receive from the expenditures that households make. And when households choose the quantities of goods and services to buy, they respond to the amounts they must pay to firms.

Figure 2.4 shows the flows that result from these decisions made by households and firms. The real flows are shown in orange. These are the flows of the factors of production that go from households through factor markets to firms and the goods and services that go from firms through goods markets to households. The money flows go in the opposite direction. These flows are the payments made in exchange for factors of production (blue flow) and expenditures on goods and services (red flow).

Lying behind these real flows and money flows are millions of individual decisions about what to consume, what to produce, and how to produce. These decisions result in buying plans by households and selling plans by firms in goods markets. And the decisions result in selling plans by households and buying plans by firms in factor markets. When these buying plans and selling plans are carried out, they determine the prices that people pay and the incomes they earn and so determine for whom goods and services are produced. You'll learn in Chapter 4 how markets coordinate the buying plans and selling plans of households and firms and make them compatible.

Firms produce most of the goods and services that we consume. But governments provide some of the services that we enjoy. And governments play a big role in modifying for whom goods and services are produced by changing the distribution of income. So we're now going to look at the government sector of the Canadian economy. We'll also add government to the circular flow model.

■ FIGURE 2.4
The Circular Flow Model

 *e*Foundations **2.2**

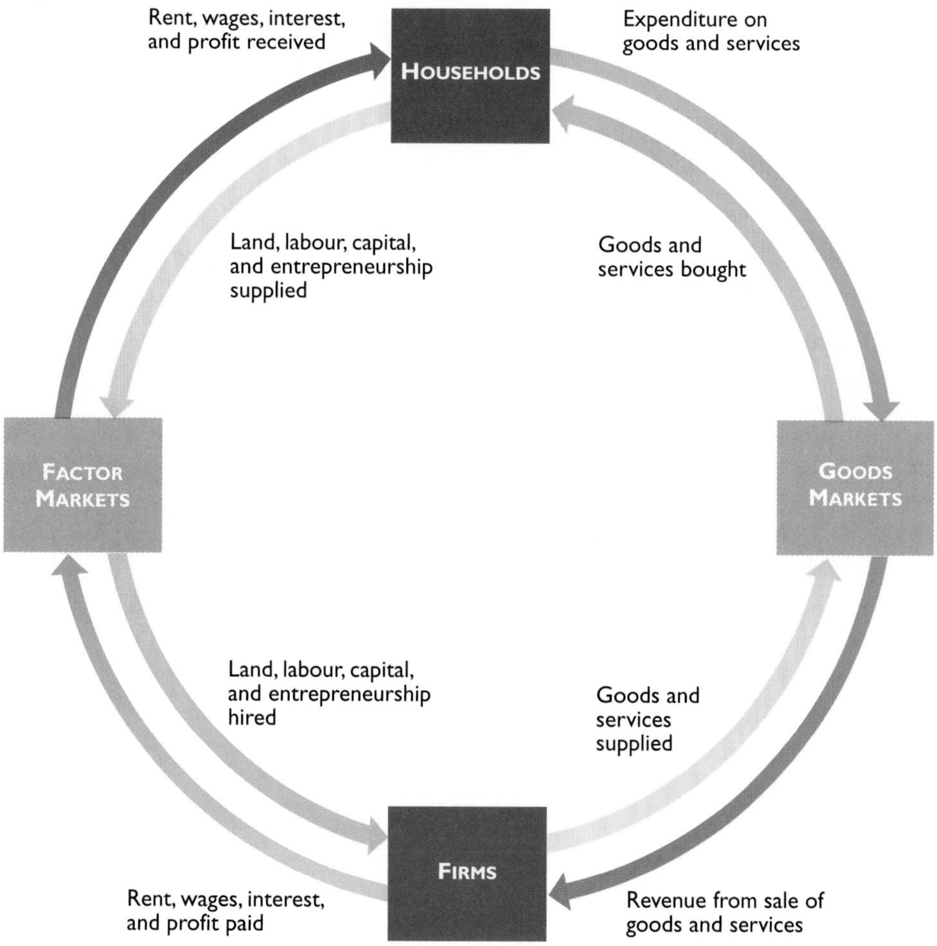

Rent, wages, interest, and profit received

Expenditure on goods and services

HOUSEHOLDS

Land, labour, capital, and entrepreneurship supplied

Goods and services bought

FACTOR MARKETS

GOODS MARKETS

Land, labour, capital, and entrepreneurship hired

Goods and services supplied

FIRMS

Rent, wages, interest, and profit paid

Revenue from sale of goods and services

The orange flows are the factors of production that go from households through factor markets to firms and the goods and services that go from firms through goods markets to households.

The blue flow is the incomes earned by the factors of production and the red flow is the expenditures on goods and services.

The choices that generate these flows determine what, how, and for whom goods and services are produced.

■ The Government Sector

The government sector of the Canadian economy consists of thousands of diverse organizations, some tiny like the Brandon, Manitoba, school board and some enormous like the Government of Canada. We divide the government sector into two parts:

- Federal government
- Provincial and local government

Federal Government

The federal government's major payments are:

1. Expenditures on goods and services
2. Transfers to persons
3. Transfers to provincial and local government

The goods and services provided by the federal government include the legal system, which defines property rights and enforces contracts, national defence, and services such as Environment Canada's weather forecasts. Transfers to persons include benefits to the unemployed and pensions to retired people. Transfers to provincial and local government include payments for health care and post-secondary education.

The federal government finances its payments by collecting taxes. The main taxes paid to the federal government are:

1. Personal income taxes
2. Corporate (business) income taxes
3. GST and excise taxes

In 2000, the federal government's receipts were about $190 billion—nearly 20 percent of the total value of all the goods and services produced in Canada in that year.

Provincial and Local Government

The provincial and local governments' major payments are:

1. Expenditures on goods and services
2. Welfare benefit payments

The major services provided by provincial and local governments are health care and education. Other services include law enforcement, roads, garbage collection and disposal, water supplies, and sewage management.

Provincial and local governments finance these payments by collecting taxes and receiving transfers from the federal government. The main taxes paid to provincial and local governments are:

1. Sales taxes
2. Personal and corporate income taxes
3. Property taxes

In 2000, provincial and local governments spent about $257 billion—75 percent more than was spent by the federal government. About half of provincial and local government spending was on education and health care.

■ Government in the Circular Flow

Figure 2.5 adds the government sector to the circular flow model. As you study this figure, first notice that the outer circle is the same as Figure 2.4. In addition to these private sector flows, the government sector purchases goods and services from firms. The red arrows that run from the government through the goods markets to firms show this flow.

Households and firms pay taxes to the government. The green arrows running directly from households and firms to government show these flows. Also, the government makes cash payments to households and firms—transfers. The green arrows running directly from government to households and firms show these flows. Taxes and transfers are direct transactions with government and do not go through the goods markets and factor markets.

In addition to the roles of government shown by the circular flow model, governments provide the legal framework within which all transactions occur. For example, they operate the courts and legal system that enable the contracts that are the basis for most economic activity to be written and enforced.

■ **FIGURE 2.5**

Government in the Circular Flow   *e*/**Foundations 2.2**

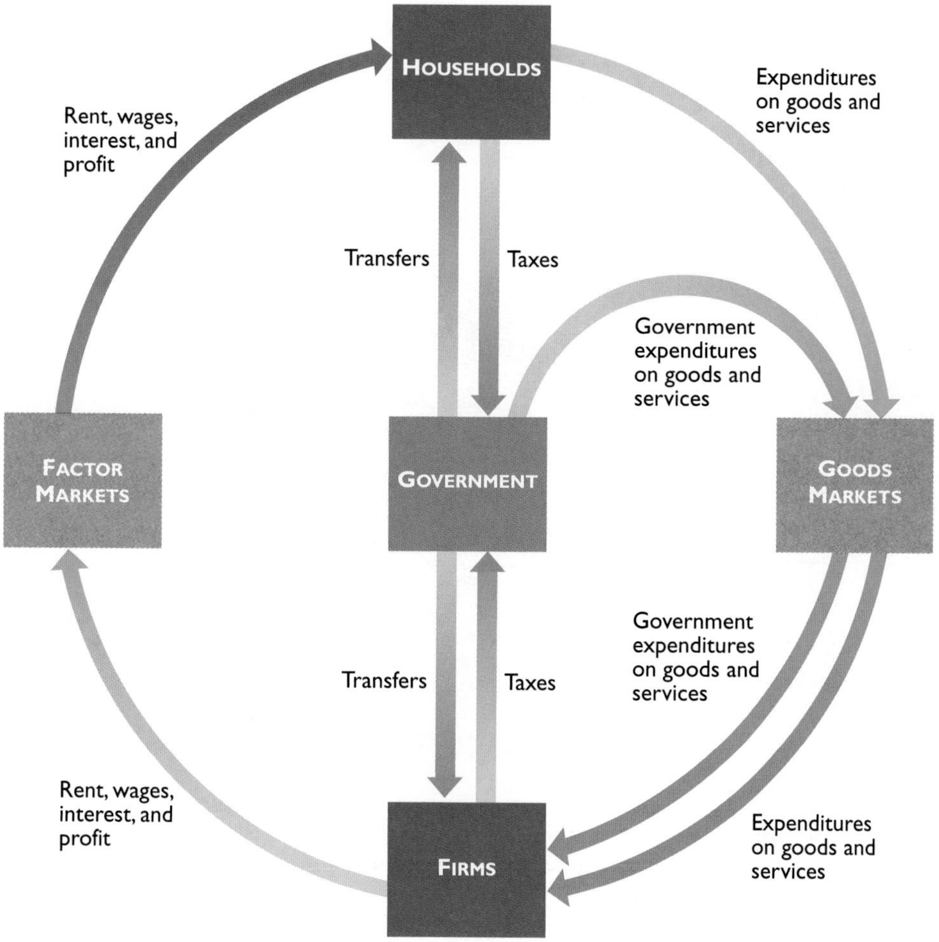

Households and firms pay taxes to and receive transfers from governments (the green arrows). The government purchases goods and services from firms in goods markets.

Rent, wages, interest, and profit

Expenditures on goods and services

Transfers   Taxes

Government expenditures on goods and services

HOUSEHOLDS

FACTOR MARKETS

GOVERNMENT

GOODS MARKETS

Government expenditures on goods and services

Transfers   Taxes

Rent, wages, interest, and profit

FIRMS

Expenditures on goods and services

■ Federal Government Payments and Receipts

Figure 2.6 shows the magnitudes of the federal government's payments and receipts.

National debt
The total amount that the federal government has borrowed in the past to finance its budget deficits (government payments in excess of receipts).

The largest payment that the federal government makes is interest on the national debt. The **national debt** is the total amount that the federal government has borrowed in the past to finance its budget deficits, which are payments that exceed its receipts. The national debt is a bit like a large credit card balance. And paying the interest on the national debt is like paying the minimum required monthly payment. The total interest payment in 2000 was $42 billion or 27 percent of all government payments. Old age security payments and transfers to the provinces (to pay for health services and education) are other large items, each of which accounts for 15 percent of the federal government's total payments. Expenditures on the department of national defence and all other government departments and agencies account for only 22 percent of total government payments.

Personal income taxes are the largest source of federal receipts. The GST and excise taxes (on gasoline, alcohol, and tobacco) are the second-largest source. Only 14 percent of federal tax receipts come from corporate income taxes, and customs duties bring the government almost no revenue.

■ **FIGURE 2.6**
Federal Government Payments and Receipts

*e*Foundations **2.2**

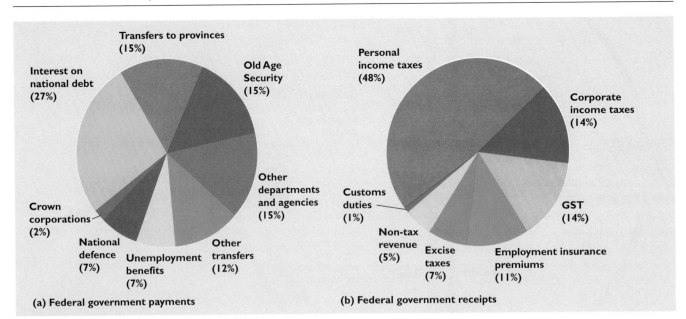

SOURCE: Statistics Canada.

Interest on the national debt is the largest slice of federal government payments. Transfers to provinces, Old Age Security, and payments to other departments and agencies are also large.

Most of the federal government's receipts come from personal and corporate income taxes and the GST.

■ Provincial and Local Government Payments and Receipts

Figure 2.7 shows the magnitudes of the provincial and local governments' payments and receipts.

Under Canada's constitution, provincial and local governments provide health care, education, and welfare and a large part of what these levels of government spend pays for hospitals and other health care facilities, public schools, colleges and universities. In 2000, these items cost $114 billion, or 45 percent of the total amount spent by provincial and local governments. Provincial governments also provide welfare benefits, and provincial and local governments provide a variety of public services such as highways, police services, garbage collection and disposal, sewage management, and water supplies. These other goods and services cost $70 billion in 2000.

Provincial governments get most of their funds from sales taxes ($70 billion or 26 percent of the total in 2000) and personal income taxes ($54 billion or 20 percent of the total in 2000). The provinces also receive transfers of funds from the federal government to help achieve more uniform health care and education services across Canada. In 2000, these transfers were $32 billion, or 12 percent of provincial receipts. Property taxes provide funds for local governments and in 2000, they totalled $33 billion.

■ **FIGURE 2.7**

Provincial and Local Government Payments and Receipts

*e*Foundations 2.2

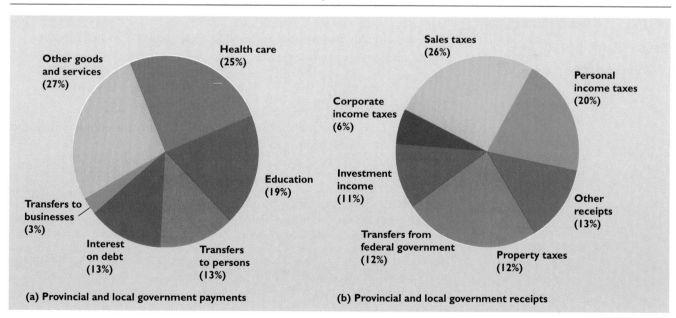

(a) **Provincial and local government payments**

(b) **Provincial and local government receipts**

SOURCE: Statistics Canada.

Health care, education, and other goods and services are the largest components of provincial and local government expenditures.

Most provincial and local government receipts come from sales taxes, income taxes, property taxes, and transfers from the federal government.

Eye On The PAST

The Changing Size of the Government in Canada

The federal government spent 47 percent of total income during World War II. Fluctuations in the state of war and peace drive fluctuations in defence spending. Non-defence spending increased through the 1960s and 1970s with the spread of social programs but was cut back during the 1990s.

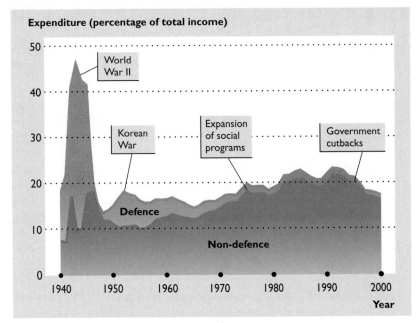

Expenditure (percentage of total income)

World War II

Korean War

Expansion of social programs

Government cutbacks

Defence

Non-defence

1940   1950   1960   1970   1980   1990   2000

Year

SOURCE: Statistics Canada.

CHECKPOINT 2.2

Study Guide pp. 29–31

𝑒Foundations 2.2

2 **Use the circular flow model to provide a picture of how households, firms, and government interact.**

Practice Problem 2.2

What are the real flows and money flows that run between households, firms, and government in the circular flow model?

Exercises 2.2

1. What are the choices made by households and firms that determine what, how, and for whom goods and services are produced? Where, in the circular flow model, do those choices appear?

2. How do the actions of governments modify what, how, and for whom goods and services are produced? Where, in the circular flow model, do those choices appear?

Solution to Practice Problem 2.2

The real flows are the services of factors of production from households to firms and the goods and services from firms to households and government. The money flows are incomes earned by factors of production, household and government expenditures on goods and services, taxes, and transfers.

2.3 MACROECONOMIC PERFORMANCE

Macroeconomic performance has three dimensions:

- Standard of living
- Cost of living
- Economic fluctuations

■ Standard of Living

The standard of living depends of the quantities of goods and services produced and the number of people among whom those goods and services are shared. The greater the value of production per person, the higher is the standard of living, other things remaining the same. For the world as a whole, the average value of goods and services produced is about $30 per person per day. But there is an enormous range around that average. Let's begin our exploration of global living standards by looking at the size and distribution of the population.

World Population

Canada's population in mid-2000 was 30,750,100. During 2000–2001, Canada's population grew by about 1 person every 2 minutes. Visit the Web site of the U.S. Census Bureau and find the population clocks. On December 2, 2000, the world clock recorded a global population of 6,112,917,660 that was growing at a rate of 291 people in the 2 minutes in which Canada's population grew by one person.

Classification of Countries

The world's 6.1 billion and rising population lives in 184 economies classified by the International Monetary Fund into three broad groups:

- Advanced economies
- Developing economies
- Transition economies

Advanced Economies Advanced economies are the 28 countries (or areas) that have the highest living standards. The United States, Japan, Germany, France, Italy, the United Kingdom, and Canada belong to this group. So do four new industrial Asian economies: Hong Kong, South Korea, Singapore, and Taiwan. The other advanced economies include Australia, New Zealand, and most of the rest of Western Europe. Almost 1 billion people live in the advanced economies.

Developing Economies Developing economies are the 128 countries in Africa, Asia, the Middle East, Europe, and Central and South America that have not yet achieved a high standard of living for their people. The standard of living in these economies varies a great deal, but in all cases, it is much lower than that in the advanced economies, and in some cases, it is extremely low. Almost 5 billion people live in the developing economies.

Transition Economies Transition economies are the 28 countries in Europe and Asia that were, until the early 1990s, part of the Soviet Union or its satellites. These countries include Russia, Hungary, Poland, and Mongolia.

The economies in this group are small—only 200 million people in total—but are important because they are in transition (hence the name) from an economic system of state-owned production, central economic planning, and heavily regulated markets to a system of free enterprise and unregulated markets.

Living Standards Around the World

Figure 2.8 shows the distribution of living standards around the world in 2000, measured in Canadian dollars per day. You can see that in Canada, the average income was about $120 per day. This number tells you that an average person in Canada could buy goods and services worth $120, which is about four times the world average. The United States has the highest living standard in the world at about $140 per day, followed by a group that includes Canada, Japan, Germany, France, Italy, the United Kingdom, and the other advanced economies with average incomes roughly two-thirds that of the United States. Living standards fall off quickly as we move farther down the table, with India and the African continent achieving average incomes of $7 per day.

Most people live in countries that have incomes below the world average. You can see this fact by looking at the population numbers shown in the figure. The poorest five countries or regions—China, Central Asia, Other Asia, India, and Africa—have a total population of 4 billion.

FIGURE 2.8
The Standard of Living Around the World

*e*Foundations **2.3**

In 2000, average income per person ranged from $140 per day in the United States to $7 a day in Africa. The world average was $30 per day, and Russia and Central and South America were close to the world average.

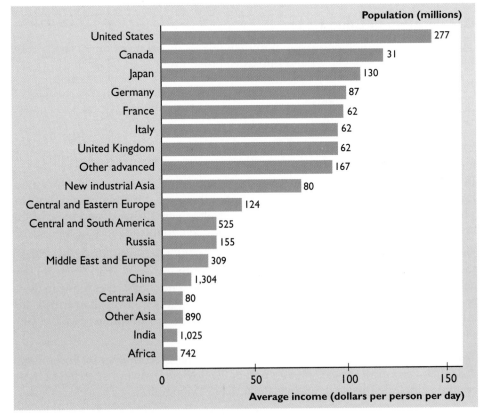

SOURCE: International Monetary Fund, *World Economic Outlook*, October 2000, Washington, D.C.

Unemployment and Living Standards

Unemployment is another factor that influences the standard of living. If jobs are easy to find, then when people lose their jobs they will find new ones after only a short period of unemployment. But if jobs are hard to find, then when people lose their jobs they will find new ones after only a long period of unemployment.

Unemployment rates vary enormously around the world. In Canada, the average unemployment rate during the past 20 years has been slightly more than 9 percent. That is, for every 100 people in the labour force, 91 had jobs and 9 were looking for jobs but couldn't find them.

Figure 2.9 shows the distribution of unemployment rates among developed countries, on the average for the 1980s and 1990s. (Note that the European Union average includes some of the other countries shown separately.)

Canada's unemployment rate has ranked in the middle of the developed nations, along with the European Union. The United States, Japan and the new industrial economies of Asia (Hong Kong, Korea, Singapore, and Taiwan) have lower rates than Canada. And two members of the European Union—Spain and Ireland—have extremely high unemployment rates, with Spain's rate near that experienced in North America during the Great Depression of the 1930s.

Figure 2.9 does *not* show the unemployment rates of the developing and transition economies. Why not? No one knows what they are. Data on unemployment is expensive to collect, and only the rich advanced economies devote resources to its measurement. Even though developing and transition economies do not measure unemployment rates, they are likely to be substantially higher than those in the advanced economies and might even exceed the high rate of Spain.

Why unemployment rates differ across economies is a difficult question to answer and is one of the challenges of macroeconomics.

▓ FIGURE 2.9
Unemployment Rates   *e*/**Foundations 2.3**

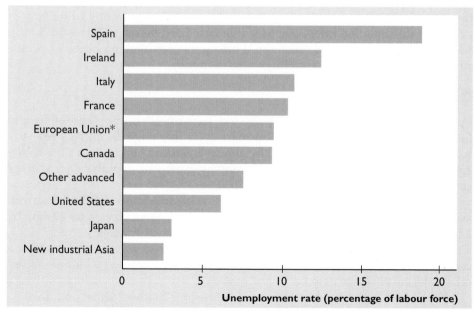

Unemployment rate (percentage of labour force)

During the 1980s and 1990s, the unemployment rate in Canada was in the middle range for developed economies—lower than France, Italy, and Spain but higher than the United States, Japan, and the other advanced Asian economies.

---

* The European Union average is the average for all 15 member countries, including Spain, Ireland, Italy, and

SOURCE: International Monetary Fund, *World Economic Outlook*, October 2000, Washington, D.C.   France.

■ Cost of Living

The cost of living is the amount of money it takes to buy the goods and services that a typical family consumes. In Canada, we measure money in dollars. So the cost of living in Canada is the number of dollars it takes to buy the goods and services that a typical family buys. In the United Kingdom, it is the number of pounds; in Japan, the number of yen; and in Russia, the number of rubles.

Prices in Different Currencies

To make this idea concrete, think about what a Big Mac costs. Table 2.1 shows the prices in eleven countries in 2001. The average price of a Big Mac in Canada was $3.33. This price is expressed in Canadian dollars. In the United Kingdom, a Big Mac cost £1.99 (fewer money units than in Canada), and in Japan, it cost ¥294 (more money units than in Canada). But the cost of a Big Mac was not that different in the three countries. In 2001, the pound was worth a bit more than $2, so a price of £1.90 is higher than the $3.33 that Canadians pay. And a Japanese yen was worth about a cent, so a price of ¥294 is similar to the Canadian price.

Inflation

The number of money units that something costs is not very important, but the rate at which it is changing is. A rising cost of living is called inflation (see page 7), which is measured by the percentage change in the cost of living. Most countries experience inflation, but its rate varies enormously. In Canada, the average inflation rate during the 1980s was 6.5 percent a year and during the 1990s it was only 2.2 percent per year. To put these numbers in perspective, a Big Mac that cost $3.33 in 2001 would have cost $1.77 in 1991 and $1.43 in 1981. A low inflation rate is not generally regarded as a major problem, but we do need to understand its cause.

Most advanced economies have low inflation rates, as you can see in Figure 2.10. But the developing economies have higher inflation rates, some of them spectacularly so. In Central and South America, the average inflation rate during the 1980s and 1990s was 107 percent. A 100 percent change means a doubling of prices. At this inflation rate, a Big Mac that cost 1,260 pesos in 2001 would have cost less than 1 peso in 1991. Such rapid inflation poses huge problems as people struggle to cope with an ever-falling value of money.

■ Economic Fluctuations

Economies expand at an uneven pace and sometimes shrink. These ebbs and flows of economic activity are the business cycle (see page 7). In the 1990–1991 recession in Canada, production fell by almost 2 percent. Following a slow recovery from that recession, the Canadian economy grew very rapidly, at an average annual pace of 4.2 percent from 1996 to 2000.

In 1998, Asia suffered a severe recession that became known as the "Asian crisis." The economies of Japan and the new industrial Asian economies shrank by 2.5 percent amidst a crisis of confidence in their financial systems.

The deepest and longest recession of the 1990s was in the transition economies. Production in Russia and its neighbours decreased by almost 30 percent between 1990 and 1994.

Figure 2.11 shows the recessions and expansions that we've just described.

TABLE 2.1 THE COST OF A BIG MAC IN ELEVEN COUNTRIES

Country	Name of currency	Price of a Big Mac
United Kingdom	Pound	1.99
United States	U.S. dollar	2.50
Canada	Canadian dollar	3.33
Brazil	Real	3.60
South Africa	Rand	9.70
China	Yuan	9.90
France	Franc	18.50
Russia	Ruble	35.00
Japan	Yen	294
Chile	Peso	1,260
Italy	Lire	4,300

FIGURE 2.10

Inflation Rates Around the World: 1982–2000

𝒆Foundations **2.3**

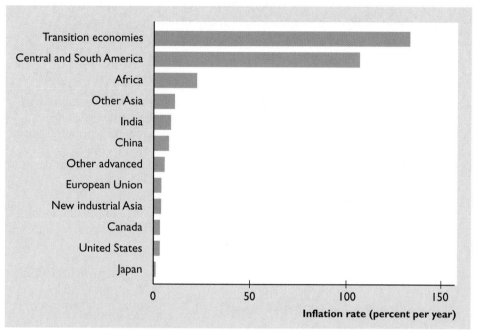

The most severe inflation has occurred in the transition economies (Russia and its neighbours) and in Central and South America. In Canada and the other advanced economies, inflation rates were very low.

SOURCE: International Monetary Fund, *World Economic Outlook*, October 2000, Washington, D.C.

FIGURE 2.11

Business Cycles in the Global Economy

𝒆Foundations **2.3**

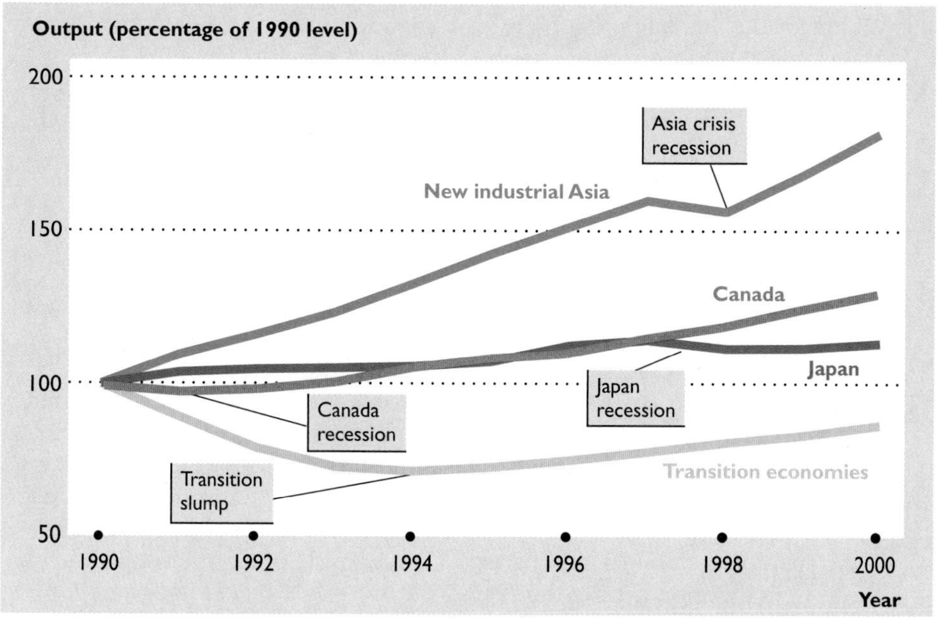

Canada had a recession in 1990–1991. Japan and the new industrial countries of Asia had a sharp recession in 1998. The transition economies had a long and deep recession for most of the 1990s.

Output (percentage of 1990 level)

- 200
- Asia crisis recession
- New industrial Asia
- 150
- Canada
- Japan
- 100
- Japan recession
- Canada recession
- Transition economies
- Transition slump
- 50

1990   1992   1994   1996   1998   2000

Year

SOURCE: International Monetary Fund, *World Economic Outlook*, October 2000, Washington, D.C.

3 Describe the macroeconomic performance—standard of living, cost of living, and economic fluctuations—of the Canadian and other economies.

Practice Problems 2.3

1. What percentage of the world's population lives in developing economies and what was the range of incomes that these people earned in 2000?
2. What percentage of the world's population live in advanced economies and what was the range of incomes that these people earned in 2000?
3. What percentage of the world's population live in Canada and what was the average income that Canadians earned in 2000?
4. Which countries or regions experienced high inflation during the 1990s?
5. Which countries or regions experienced recession during the 1990s?

Exercises 2.3

1. What is the current world population and how rapidly is it growing? What is the current Canadian population and how rapidly is it growing? Is Canada's population becoming larger or smaller relative to the world population?
2. Classify the following countries as (a) advanced, (b) developing, or (c) transition: Australia, Canada, Chile, China, France, India, Indonesia, Hong Kong, Japan, Korea, Mexico, Nigeria, Peru, Russia, Ukraine, United States.
3. What was the average income in the world as a whole in 2000? Which regions or nations were closest to that world average, which were the farthest above it, and which were the farthest below it?
4. What was the average inflation rate in Canada during the 1990s? Is inflation at this rate considered to be a serious problem? Why or why not?
5. Compare and contrast the Canadian recession of 1990–1991 with the recessions in Asia and the transition economies during the 1990s. Which was the deepest? Which lasted the longest?

Solutions to Practice Problems 2.3

1. Approximately 80 percent of the world's population lives in developing economies. In 2000, their average daily incomes ranged from $7 in Africa to $28 in Central and South America.
2. Approximately 16 percent of the world's population lives in advanced economies. In 2000, their average daily incomes ranged from $72 in the new industrial economies of Asia to $140 in the United States.
3. In 2000, the population of Canada was almost 31 million—one-half of one percent of the world's 6 billion population. The average income in Canada was $120 per day.
4. The transition economies and parts of Central and South America experienced high inflation during the 1990s.
5. The transition economies experienced recession during the 1990s. Japan and the new industrial economies of Asia experienced recession during the late 1990s. Canada was in recession in 1990–1991, but for the rest of the 1990s it experienced expansion.

CHAPTER CHECKPOINT

Key Points

1 **Describe what, how, and for whom goods and services are produced in the Canadian economy.**

- Consumption goods and services are 40 percent of total production; investment goods are 15 percent.
- Goods and services are produced by using the four factors of production: land, labour, capital, and entrepreneurship.
- The incomes people earn—rent for land, wages for labour, interest for capital, and profit for entrepreneurship—determine who gets what is produced.

2 **Use the circular flow model to provide a picture of how households, firms, and governments interact.**

- The circular flow model shows the real flows of factors of production and goods and services and the corresponding money flows of incomes and expenditures.
- Government in the circular flow receives taxes, makes transfers, and buys goods and services.
- Transfers to persons and to other levels of government and interest on the national debt make up most of the federal government's payments, and personal income taxes are the largest source of federal receipts.
- Health care and education account for most of the payments of the provincial and local governments, and sales taxes, income taxes, transfers from the federal government, and property taxes pay for these expenditures.

3 **Describe the macroeconomic performance—standard of living, cost of living, and economic fluctuations—of the Canadian and other economies.**

- The standard of living, measured by income per person per day, ranges from an average of $7 in Africa to $140 in the United States.
- Inflation is low in most of the world but has been rapid in the transition economies (Russia and others) and in Central and South America.
- Canada had a recession in 1990–1991. Japan, the new industrial economies of Asia, and the transition economies had recessions during the 1990s.

Key Terms

Capital, 38
Circular flow model, 42
Consumption goods and services, 36
Entrepreneurship, 39
Exports, 36
Factor markets, 42
Factors of production, 37

Firms, 42
Functional distribution of income, 39
Goods markets, 42
Government goods and services, 36
Households, 42
Human capital, 38
Interest, 39
Investment goods, 36

Labour, 37
Land, 37
Market, 42
National debt, 46
Personal distribution of income, 40
Profit (or loss), 39
Rent, 39
Wages, 39

Exercises

1. Use the link on your Foundations Web site to visit Statistics Canada and:
   a. Find the data for the most recent quarter on expenditure on consumption goods and services, investment goods, government goods and services, and exports.
   b. Calculate the percentage of total expenditure that each accounts for.
   c. Compare the numbers that you have calculated with those in Figure 2.1 on page 37. Which items, if any, have increased and which have decreased? Can you think of any reasons that might make these percentages change?

2. Use the link on your Foundations Web site to visit Statistics Canada and:
   a. Find the data for the most recent quarter on the incomes of the factors of production.
   b. Calculate the percentage of total income that each factor of production receives.
   c. Compare the numbers that you have calculated with those in Figure 2.2 on page 39. Which items, if any, have increased and which have decreased?
   d. Can you think of any reasons that might make these percentages change?
   e. What influences might keep these percentages roughly constant?

3. Draw a diagram to show the circular flow model. Use the data from Exercises 1(a) and 2(a), and against each arrow, place the values that represent the Canadian economy in the most recent quarter.

4. Use the link on your Foundations Web site to visit Statistics Canada and:
   a. Find data for the most recent quarter on government payments and receipts.
   b. Calculate the percentage of the total that each item accounts for.
   c. Compare the numbers that you have calculated with those in Figures 2.6 on page 46 and 2.7 on page 47. Which items, if any, have increased and which have decreased?
   d. Can you think of any reasons that might make these percentages change?

5. Draw a diagram to show the circular flow model with a government sector. Use the data from Exercises 1(a), 2(a), and 4(a), and against each arrow, place the values that represent the Canadian economy in the most recent quarter.

6. In 2000, Canada's population was 0.5 percent of the world's population. Use the link on your Foundations Web site to visit Statistics Canada and the U.S. Census Bureau and determine the most recent population of Canada and the world. Has Canada's population increased more rapidly or less rapidly than the world's population?

7. Use the link on your Foundations Web site to visit the International Monetary Fund World Economic Outlook.
   a. Find some data on production and incomes, and compare the growth in living standards in Canada with those in other countries and regions and with the world average.
   b. Find some data on inflation, and compare Canada's inflation with that of other countries and regions and with the world average.

The Economic Problem

When you have completed your study of this chapter, you will be able to:

1 Use the production possibilities frontier to illustrate the economic problem.

2 Calculate opportunity cost.

3 Explain how specialization and trade expand production possibilities.

4 Explain how technological change and increases in capital and human capital expand production possibilities.

You learned in Chapter 1 that all economic problems arise from scarcity, that scarcity forces us to make choices, and that in making choices, we try to get the most value out of our scarce resources by comparing marginal costs and marginal benefits. You learned in Chapter 2 what, how, and for whom goods and services are produced in the Canadian and global economies. And you used your first economic model, the circular flow model, to illustrate the choices and interactions that determine what, how, and for whom goods and services are produced.

In this chapter, you will study another economic model, one that illustrates scarcity, choice, and cost and that helps us to understand the choices that people and societies actually make. You will also discover how we can expand production by specializing and trading with each other and how economic growth expands our production possibilities.

3.1 PRODUCTION POSSIBILITIES

Every working day in the mines, factories, shops, and offices and on the farms and construction sites across Canada, we produce a vast array of goods and services. In Canada in 2000, 27 billion hours of labour equipped with about $2 trillion worth of capital produced more than $1 trillion worth of goods and services. Globally, 6 trillion hours of labour and $100 trillion of capital produced $45 trillion worth of goods and services.

Although our production capability is enormous, it is limited by our available resources and by technology. At any given time, we have fixed quantities of the factors of production, and these factors embody a fixed state of technology. Because our wants exceed our resources, we must make choices. We must rank our wants and decide which wants to satisfy and which to leave unsatisfied.

To illustrate the limits to production, we will focus on two goods only and hold the quantities produced of all the other goods and services constant. That is, we use the *ceteris paribus* assumption. We look at a *model* of the economy in which everything remains the same except for the production of the two goods we are currently considering.

■ Production Possibilities Frontier

Production possibilities frontier

The boundary between combinations of goods and services that can be produced and combinations that cannot be produced, given the available factors of production and the state of technology.

The **production possibilities frontier** is the boundary between the combinations of goods and services that can be produced and the combinations that cannot be produced with a fixed quantity of available factors of production—land, labour, capital, and entrepreneurship—that embody a given state of technology. Let's look at the production possibilities frontier for bottled water and CDs.

Land can be used for either water-bottling plants or CD factories. Labour can be trained to work as water bottlers or as CD makers. Capital can be devoted to tapping springs and making water filtration plants or to the computers and lasers that make CDs. And entrepreneurs can devote their creative talents to managing water resources and bottling factories or to running electronics businesses that make CDs. In every case, the more resources that get used to produce bottled water, the fewer are left for producing CDs.

We can illustrate the production possibilities frontier by using either a table or a graph. The table in Figure 3.1 describes six production possibilities for bottled water and CDs—alternative combinations of quantities of these two goods that we can produce.

One possibility, in column *A*, is to devote no factors of production to making bottled water, so bottled-water production is zero. In this case, we can devote all the factors of production to making CDs and produce 15 million a year. Another possibility, in column *B*, is to devote resources to bottled-water production that are sufficient to produce 1 million bottles a year. But the resources that are being used in water-bottling plants must be taken from CD factories. So we can now produce only 14 million CDs a year. Columns *C*, *D*, *E*, and *F* show other possible combinations of the quantities of these two goods that we can produce. In column *F*, we use all our resources to produce 5 million bottles of water a year and have no resources for producing CDs.

The graph in Figure 3.1 illustrates the production possibilities frontier, *PPF*, for bottled water and CDs. It is a graph of the production possibilities in the table. The *x*-axis shows the production of bottled water, and the *y*-axis shows the production of CDs. Each point on the graph labelled *A* through *F* represents the corresponding column in the table. For example, point *B* represents the production of 1 million bottles of water and 14 million CDs. These quantities also appear in column *B* of the table.

The *PPF* is a valuable tool for illustrating the effects of scarcity and its consequences. It puts three features of production possibilities in sharp focus. They are the distinctions between:

- Attainable and unattainable combinations
- Full employment and unemployment
- Tradeoffs and free lunches

FIGURE 3.1

The Production Possibilities Frontier

The table and the figure show the production possibilities frontier for bottled water and CDs. Point *A* tells us that if we produce no bottled water, the maximum quantity of CDs we can produce is 15 million a year. Points *A*, *B*, *C*, *D*, *E*, and *F* in the figure represent the columns of the table. The line passing through these points is the production possibilities frontier.

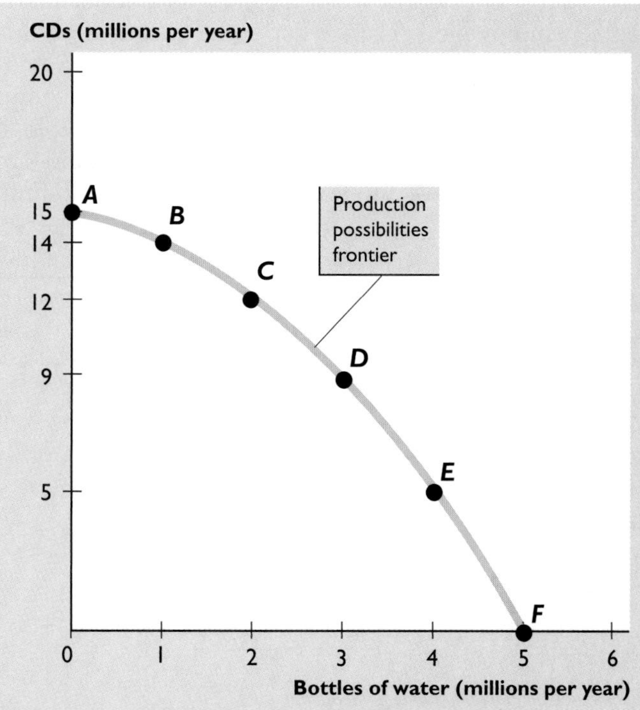

CDs (millions per year)

A   *B*   *C*   *D*   *E*   *F*

Production possibilities frontier

Bottles of water (millions per year)

Bottles of water (millions)	0	1	2	3	4	5
CDs (millions)	15	14	12	9	5	0
Possibility	*A*	*B*	*C*	*D*	*E*	*F*

Attainable and Unattainable Combinations

Because the *PPF* shows the *limits* to production, it separates attainable combinations from unattainable ones. We can produce combinations of bottled water and CDs that are smaller than those on the *PPF*, and we can produce any of the combinations *on* the *PPF*. These combinations of bottled water and CDs are attainable. But we cannot produce combinations that are larger than those on the *PPF*. These combinations are unattainable.

Figure 3.2 emphasizes the attainable and unattainable combinations. Only the points on the *PPF* and inside it (in the orange area) are attainable. The combinations of bottled water and CDs beyond the *PPF* (in the white area), such as the combination at point *G*, are unattainable. These points illustrate combinations that cannot be produced with our current resources and technology. The *PPF* tells us that we can produce 4 million bottles of water and 5 million CDs at point *E* or 2 million bottles of water and 12 million CDs at point *C*. But we cannot produce 4 million bottles of water and 12 million CDs at point *G*.

Full Employment and Unemployment

Full employment occurs when all the available factors of production are being used. Unemployment occurs when some factors of production are not used.

Any factor of production might be unemployed. Some labour is always unemployed, and in a recession, the amount of labour unemployed can be large and socially costly. But land and capital can also be unemployed. Land is often unemployed while its owner is trying to work out the land's most valuable use. Look around where you live and you'll probably be able to find at least one or two city

---

FIGURE 3.2

Attainable and Unattainable Combinations

*e*Foundations **3.1**

The production possibilities frontier, *PPF*, separates attainable combinations from unattainable ones. We can produce at any point inside the *PPF* (the orange area) or *on* the frontier. Points outside the production possibilities frontier such as point *G* are unattainable.

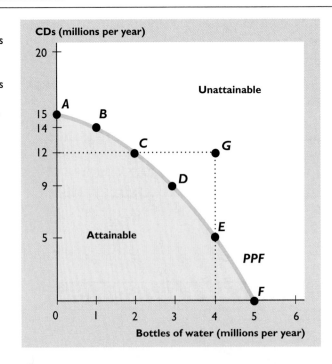

blocks that are currently unemployed. Capital often lies idle. For example, thousands of automobiles are unemployed in parking lots; and restaurant tables and kitchens are often unemployed.

Figure 3.3 illustrates the effects of unemployment. With unemployed resources, the economy might produce at point *H* inside the *PPF*. Here, with some resources *employed*, it is possible to produce 3 million bottles of water and 5 million CDs. But with full employment, it is possible to move to points such as *D* or *E* on the *PPF*. At point *D*, there are more CDs and the same quantity of bottled water as at point *H*. And at point *E*, there are more bottles of water and the same quantity of CDs as at point *H*.

Tradeoffs and Free Lunches

A **tradeoff** is a constraint or limit to what is possible that forces an exchange or a substitution of one thing for something else.

If the federal government allocates more resources to national defence and cuts its transfers to the provincial governments for health care, we face a tradeoff between security and good health. If a provincial government allocates more resources to roads and fewer resources to colleges and universities, we face a tradeoff between transportation services and education. If a city government devotes more resources to art galleries and fewer resources to garbage collection, we face a tradeoff between culture and sanitation.

If lumber producers cut down fewer trees to conserve spotted owls, we face a tradeoff between paper products and wildlife. If Ford Motor Company decreases the production of trucks to produce more SUVs, we face a tradeoff between two

Tradeoff
A constraint or limit to what is possible that forces an exchange or a substitution of one thing for something else.

▨ **FIGURE 3.3**
Full Employment and Unemployment

*e*Foundations **3.1**

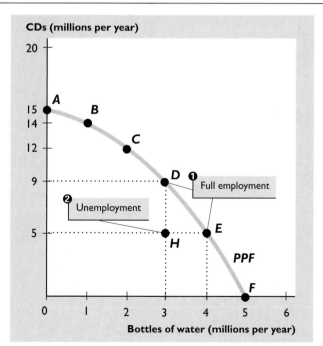

❶ When resources are fully employed, production occurs at points on the *PPF* such as *D* and *E*.

❷ When resources are unemployed, production occurs at a point inside the frontier such as point *H*.

types of vehicle. If a student decides to take an extra course and cut back on her weekend job, she faces a tradeoff between course credits and income.

The *PPF* in Figure 3.4 illustrates the idea of a tradeoff. If we produce at point *E* and would like to produce more CDs, we must forgo some bottled water. For example, we might move from point *E* to point *D*. We exchange some bottles of water for some CDs.

Economists often express the central idea of economics—that every choice involves an opportunity cost—with the saying "There is no such thing as a free lunch" (see Chapter 1, p. 15). But suppose some resources are not being used or are not being used in their most productive way. Isn't it then possible to avoid opportunity cost and get a free lunch?

The answer is yes. You can see this answer in Figure 3.4. If production is taking place *inside* the *PPF* at point *H*, then it is possible to move to point *D* and increase the production of CDs by using currently unused resources or by using resources in their most productive way. There is a free lunch.

So when production takes place at a point on the *PPF*, we face a tradeoff. But we don't face a tradeoff if we produce inside the *PPF*. More of some goods and services can be produced without producing less of some others.

Because of scarcity and the attempt to get the most out of our scarce resources, we do not leave factors of production idle or use them unproductively if we can avoid it. And if such a situation arises, people seek ways of putting their resources to productive employment. It is for these reasons that economists emphasize the tradeoff idea and deny the existence of free lunches. We might *occasionally* get a free lunch, but we *persistently* face tradeoffs.

FIGURE 3.4
Tradeoffs and Free Lunches

*e*Foundations 3.1

❶ When resources are fully employed, we face a tradeoff. If we are producing 5 million CDs a year at point *E*, to produce 9 million CDs at point *D*, we must trade some bottled water for CDs and move along the *PPF*.

❷ When resources are unemployed, there is a free lunch. If we are producing 5 million CDs a year at point *H*, to produce 9 million CDs at point *D*, we move to the *PPF* and get a free lunch.

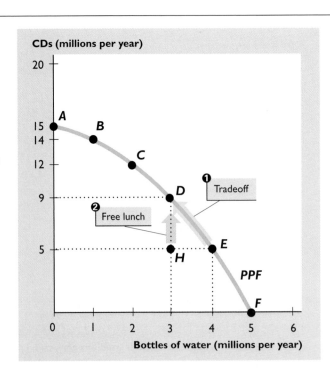

CHECKPOINT 3.1

1 **Use the production possibilities frontier to illustrate the economic problem.**

Study Guide pp. 40–43

*e*Foundations 3.1

Practice Problems 3.1

1. Robinson Crusoe, the pioneer of the television program *Survivor*, lived alone on a deserted island. He spent his day fishing and picking fruit. He varied the time spent on these two activities and kept a record of his production. Table 1 shows the numbers that Crusoe wrote in the sand. Use these numbers to make Crusoe's *PPF* if he can work only 8 hours a day.

2. Which combinations (in kilograms) are attainable and which are unattainable: (i) 10 fish and 30 fruit, (ii) 13 fish and 26 fruit, (iii) 20 fish and 21 fruit?

3. Which combinations (in kilograms) use all of Crusoe's available 8 hours a day: (i) 15 fish and 21 fruit, (ii) 7 fish and 30 fruit, (iii) 18 fish and 0 fruit?

4. Which combinations (in kilograms) provide Crusoe with a free lunch and which confront him with a tradeoff when he increases fruit by 1 kilogram: (i) 18 fish and 0 fruit, (ii) 15 fish and 15 fruit, (iii) 13 fish and 26 fruit?

TABLE 1

Hours	Fish (kilograms)		Fruit (kilograms)
0	0		0
1	4.0	or	8
2	7.5	or	15
3	10.5	or	21
4	13.0	or	26
5	15.0	or	30
6	16.5	or	33
7	17.5	or	35
8	18.0	or	36

Exercises 3.1

1. In the winter, both fish and fruit are harder to find and Robinson Crusoe can work only 5 hours a day. Table 2 shows the quantities that Crusoe can produce in winter. Use these numbers to make Crusoe's *PPF* in winter.

2. Which combinations (in kilograms) are attainable and which are unattainable: (i) 9 fish and 13 fruit, (ii) 10 fish and 13 fruit, (iii) 7 fish and 18 fruit?

3. Which combinations (in kilograms) use all of Crusoe's available 5 hours a day, which provide Crusoe with a free lunch, and which confront him with a tradeoff: (i) 10 fish and 7 fruit, (ii) 4 fish and 20 fruit?

TABLE 2

Hours	Fish (kilograms)		Fruit (kilograms)
0	0		0
1	4	or	7
2	7	or	13
3	9	or	19
4	10	or	24
5	11	or	28

Solutions to Practice Problems 3.1

1. Table 3 sets out Crusoe's *PPF*. He has 8 hours a day for fishing and fruit picking. He can produce the combinations of fish and fruit that lie on his *PPF* if he uses a total of 8 hours a day. If he picks fruit for 8 hours, he picks 36 kilograms and catches no fish—row *A*. If he picks fruit for 7 hours, he picks 35 kilograms and has 1 hour for fishing in which he catches 4 kilograms—row *B*. Check that you can construct the other rows of Table 3.

2. (i) 10 fish and 30 fruit is attainable because on row *D*, Crusoe can produce 10.5 fish and 30 fruit. (ii) 13 fish and 26 fruit is attainable—row *E*. (iii) 20 fish and 21 fruit is unattainable because when Crusoe picks 21 kilograms of fruit, he can catch only 15 kilograms of fish (row *F*).

3. (i) 15 fish and 21 fruit uses all 8 hours—it is on his *PPF* (row *F*). (ii) 7 fish and 30 fruit does not use all 8 hours—it is inside his *PPF* (row *C*). (iii) 18 fish and 0 fruit uses all 8 hours—it is on his *PPF* (row *I*).

4. (i) 18 fish and 0 fruit involves a tradeoff—it is on his *PPF*. (ii) 15 fish and 15 fruit provides a free lunch—it is inside his *PPF*. (iii) 13 fish and 26 fruit involves a tradeoff—it is on his *PPF*.

TABLE 3

Possibility	Fish (kilograms)		Fruit (kilograms)
A	0	and	36
B	4.0	and	35
C	7.5	and	33
D	10.5	and	30
E	13.0	and	26
F	15.0	and	21
G	16.5	and	15
H	17.5	and	8
I	18.0	and	0

3.2 OPPORTUNITY COST

You've just seen that along the *PPF*, all choices involve a tradeoff. But what are the terms of the tradeoff? How much of one item must be forgone to obtain an additional unit of another item—a large amount or a small amount? The answer is given by opportunity cost—What you must give up to get it (see p. 15). The production possibilities frontier enables us to calculate opportunity cost.

■ The Opportunity Cost of a Bottle of Water

The opportunity cost of a bottle of water is the decrease in the quantity of CDs divided by the increase in the number of bottles of water as we move down along the *PPF* in Figure 3.5.

At point *A*, we produce no bottles of water and 15 million CDs. At point *B*, we produce 1 million bottles of water and 14 million CDs. If we move from point *A* to point *B*, the quantity of water increases by 1 million bottles and the quantity of CDs decreases by 1 million. So the opportunity cost of 1 bottle of water is 1 CD.

At point *C*, we produce 2 million bottles of water and 12 million CDs. If we move from point *B* to point *C*, the quantity of water increases by 1 million bottles and the quantity of CDs decreases by 2 million. So the opportunity cost of 1 bottle of water is now 2 CDs.

Repeat these calculations, moving from *C* to *D*, from *D* to *E*, and from *E* to *F*, and check that you can obtain the opportunity costs shown in the table and graph.

■ **FIGURE 3.5**
Calculating the Opportunity Cost of a Bottle of Water

*e*Foundations **3.2**

Movement along *PPF*	Decrease in quantity of CDs	Increase in quantity of bottled water	Decrease in CDs divided by increase in bottled water
A to B	1 million	1 million	1 CD per bottle
B to C	2 million	1 million	2 CDs per bottle
C to D	3 million	1 million	3 CDs per bottle
D to E	4 million	1 million	4 CDs per bottle
E to F	5 million	1 million	5 CDs per bottle

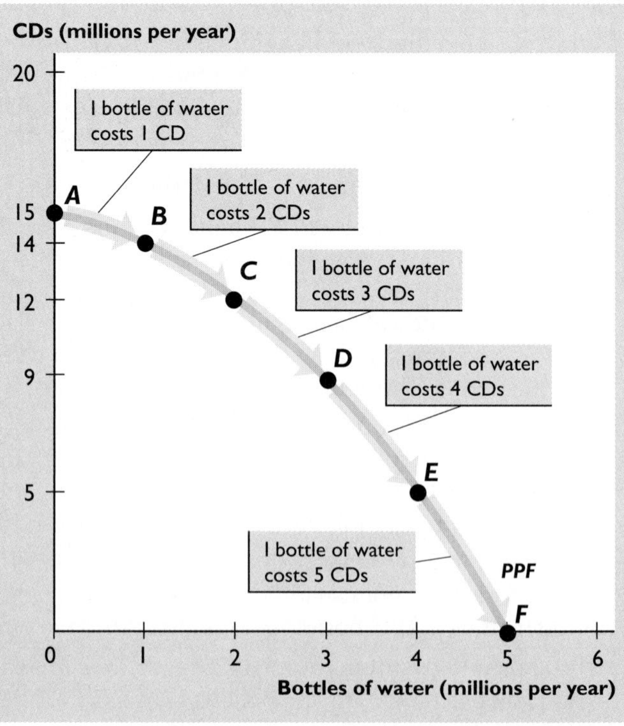

Moving down the *PPF* from *A* to *F*, the opportunity cost of bottled water increases as the quantity of bottled water produced increases.

CDs (millions per year)

I bottle of water costs I CD

I bottle of water costs 2 CDs

I bottle of water costs 3 CDs

I bottle of water costs 4 CDs

I bottle of water costs 5 CDs

PPF

Bottles of water (millions per year)

■ The Opportunity Cost of a CD

The opportunity cost of a CD is the decrease in the quantity of water divided by the increase in the quantity of CDs as we move up along the *PPF* in Figure 3.6.

At point *F*, we produce no CDs and 5 million bottles of water. At point *E*, we produce 5 million CDs and 4 million bottles of water. If we move from point *F* to point *E*, the quantity of CDs increases by 5 million and the quantity of water decreases by 1 million bottles. So the opportunity cost of 1 CD is 1/5 of a bottle of water.

At point *D*, we can produce 9 million CDs and 3 million bottles of water. If we move from point *E* to point *D*, the quantity of CDs increases by 4 million and the quantity of water decreases by 1 million bottles. So the opportunity cost of a CD is now 1/4 of a bottle of water.

At point *C*, we can produce 12 million CDs and 2 million bottles of water. If we move from point *D* to point *C*, the quantity of CDs increases by 3 million and the quantity of water decreases by 1 million bottles. So the opportunity cost of a CD is now 1/3 of a bottle of water.

Again, repeat these calculations moving from *C* to *B* and from *B* to *A* and check that you can obtain the opportunity costs shown in the figure.

■ Opportunity Cost Is a Ratio

You've seen that to calculate the opportunity cost of a bottle of water, we divide the quantity of CDs forgone by the increase in the quantity of water. And to

---

■ **FIGURE 3.6**
Calculating the Opportunity Cost of a CD

e/**Foundations 3.2**

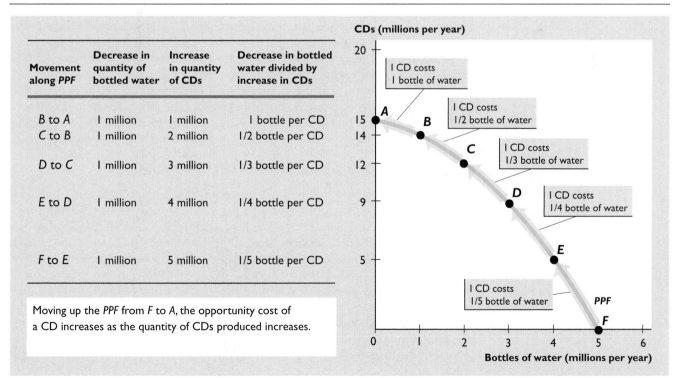

Movement along *PPF*	Decrease in quantity of bottled water	Increase in quantity of CDs	Decrease in bottled water divided by increase in CDs
B to A	I million	I million	I bottle per CD
C to B	I million	2 million	1/2 bottle per CD
D to C	I million	3 million	1/3 bottle per CD
E to D	I million	4 million	1/4 bottle per CD
F to E	I million	5 million	1/5 bottle per CD

Moving up the *PPF* from F to A, the opportunity cost of a CD increases as the quantity of CDs produced increases.

calculate the opportunity cost of a CD, we divide the quantity of bottled water for-gone by the increase in the quantity of CDs. So opportunity cost is a ratio—the change in the quantity of one good divided by the change in the quantity of the other good. The opportunity cost of producing water is equal to the inverse of the opportunity cost of producing CDs. Check this proposition by returning to the cal-culations we've just worked through. When we move along the *PPF* from point *C* to point *D*, the opportunity cost of a bottle of water is 3 CDs. The inverse of 3 is 1/3, so if we increase the production of CDs and decrease the production of water by moving from point *D* to point *C*, the opportunity cost of a CD must be 1/3 of a bottle of water. This number is correct—it is the number we've just calculated.

■ Increasing Opportunity Cost

The opportunity cost of a bottle of water increases as the quantity of bottled water produced increases. And the opportunity cost of a CD increases as the quantity of CDs produced increases. The phenomenon of increasing opportunity cost is reflected in the shape of the *PPF*. It is bowed outward. When a large quantity of CDs and a small quantity of water are produced—between points *A* and *B* in Figure 3.5—the frontier has a gentle slope. A given increase in the quantity of bot-tled water costs a small decrease in the quantity of CDs, so the opportunity cost of a bottle of water is a small quantity of CDs.

When a large quantity of bottled water and a small quantity of CDs are pro-duced—between points *E* and *F* in Figure 3.5—the frontier is steep. A given increase in the quantity of bottled water costs a large decrease in the quantity of CDs, so the opportunity cost of a bottle of water is a large quantity of CDs.

The production possibilities frontier is bowed outward because resources are not equally productive in all activities. Production workers with many years of experience who work for Aqua Springs are very good at bottling water but not very good at making CDs. So if we move some of these people from Aqua Springs to Sony, we get a small increase in the quantity of CDs but a large decrease in the quantity of bottled water.

Similarly, engineers and production workers who work at Sony are good at making CDs but not very good at bottling water. So if we move some of these peo-ple from Sony to Aqua Springs, we get a small increase in the quantity of bottled water but a large decrease in the quantity of CDs. The more we try to produce of either good, the less productive are the additional resources we use to produce that good and the larger is the opportunity cost of a unit of that good.

■ Increasing Opportunity Costs Are Everywhere

Just about every activity that you can think of is one with an increasing opportu-nity cost. We allocate the most skillful farmers and the most fertile land to the pro-duction of food. And we allocate the best doctors and least fertile land to the production of health-care services. If we shift fertile land and tractors away from farming to hospitals and ambulances and ask farmers to become hospital porters, the production of food drops drastically and the increase in the production of health-care services is small. The opportunity cost of a unit of health-care services rises. Similarly, if we shift our resources away from health care towards farming, we must use more doctors and nurses as farmers and more hospitals as hydro-ponic tomato factories. The decrease in the production of health-care services is large, but the increase in food production is small. The opportunity cost of a unit of food rises.

CHECKPOINT 3.2

2 **Calculate opportunity cost.**

Study Guide pp. 43–46

*e*Foundations 3.2

Practice Problems 3.2

1. Use Robinson Crusoe's production possibilities shown in Table 1 to calculate his opportunity cost of a kilogram of fish. Make a table that shows Crusoe's opportunity cost of a kilogram of fish as he increases the time he spends fishing and decreases the time that he spends picking fruit.
2. If Crusoe increases his production of fruit from 21 kilograms to 26 kilograms and decreases his production of fish from 15 kilograms to 13 kilograms, what is his opportunity cost of a kilogram of fruit? Explain your answer.
3. If Crusoe is producing 10 kilograms of fish and 20 kilograms of fruit, what are his opportunity costs of a kilogram of fruit and a kilogram of fish? Explain your answer.

Exercises 3.2

1. Use Robinson Crusoe's production possibilities in winter shown in Table 2 to calculate his opportunity cost of a kilogram of fruit. Make a table that shows Crusoe's opportunity cost of a kilogram of fruit as he increases the time he spends picking fruit and decreases the time he spends fishing.
2. If Crusoe currently catches 7 kilograms of fish and picks 13 kilograms of fruit a day, calculate his opportunity costs of a kilogram of fruit and a kilogram of fish. Explain your answer.
3. If Crusoe increases the fish caught from 7 to 9 kilograms and decreases the fruit picked from 19 to 13 kilograms, what is his opportunity cost of a kilogram of fish? Explain your answer.
4. Does Crusoe's opportunity cost of a kilogram of fruit increase as he spends more time picking fruit? Explain why or why not.

Solutions to Practice Problems 3.2

1. Crusoe's opportunity cost of a kilogram of fish is the decrease in fruit divided by the increase in fish as he moves along his *PPF*, increasing the time he spends fishing and decreasing the time he spends picking fruit. For example, when Crusoe spends no time fishing, he produces the quantities in row *A* in Table 1. When he spends more time fishing and moves to row *B* in Table 1, the increase in fish is 4 kilograms and the decrease in fruit picked is 1 kilogram. So the opportunity cost of a kilogram of fish is 1/4 kilogram of fruit. Check that you can derive the other rows of Table 3.
2. The opportunity cost of a kilogram of fruit is 2/5 kilogram of fish. When fruit increases by 5 kilograms, fish decreases by 2 kilograms. The opportunity cost of a kilogram of fruit is 2 kilograms of fish divided by 5 kilograms of fruit. This opportunity cost is the inverse of the opportunity cost of fish (move from *E* to *F* in Table 3).
3. If Crusoe is producing 10 kilograms of fish and 20 kilograms of fruit, his opportunity costs of fruit and of fish are zero because he can increase the production of both without decreasing the production of either. He is producing a combination inside his *PPF*.

TABLE 1

Possibility	Fish (kilograms)	Fruit (kilograms)
A	0	36
B	4.0	35
C	7.5	33
D	10.5	30
E	13.0	26
F	15.0	21
G	16.5	15
H	17.5	8
I	18.0	0

TABLE 2

Possibility	Fish (kilograms)	Fruit (kilograms)
A	0	28
B	4	24
C	7	19
D	9	13
E	10	7
F	11	0

TABLE 3

Move from	Increase in fish (kilograms)	Decrease in fruit (kilograms)	Opportunity cost of fish (kilograms of fruit)
A to B	4.0	1	0.25
B to C	3.5	2	0.57
C to D	3.0	3	1.00
D to E	2.5	4	1.60
E to F	2.0	5	2.50
F to G	1.5	6	4.00
G to H	1.0	7	7.00
H to I	0.5	8	16.00

3.3 SPECIALIZATION AND EXCHANGE

People can produce several goods, or they can concentrate on producing one good and then exchange some of their own good for those produced by others. Concentrating on the production of only one good is called *specialization*. We are going to discover how people gain by specializing in the production of the good in which they have a *comparative advantage*.

■ Comparative Advantage

Comparative advantage
The ability of a person to perform an activity or produce a good or service at a lower opportunity cost than someone else.

A person has a **comparative advantage** in an activity if that person can perform the activity at a lower opportunity cost than someone else. Let's explore the idea of comparative advantage by looking at two water-bottling plants, one operated by Tom and the other operated by Nancy.

Tom produces both water and bottles, and Figure 3.7 shows his production possibilities frontier. It tells us that if Tom uses all his resources to produce water, he can produce 1,333 litres an hour. The *PPF* in Figure 3.7 also tells us that if Tom uses all his resources to make bottles, he can produce 4,000 bottles an hour. To produce more water, Tom must decrease his production of bottles. For each additional 1,000 litres of water produced, Tom must decrease his production of bottles by 3,000.

Tom's opportunity cost of producing 1 litre of water is 3 bottles.

Similarly, if Tom wants to increase his production of bottles, he must decrease his production of water. For each 1,000 bottles produced, he must decrease his production of water by 333 litres. So

Tom's opportunity cost of producing 1 bottle is 0.333 litres of water.

■ **FIGURE 3.7**
Production Possibilities at Tom's Water-Bottling Plant

*e*Foundations **3.3**

Tom can produce bottles and water along the production possibility frontier *PPF*. For Tom, the opportunity cost of 1 litre of water is 3 bottles and the opportunity cost of 1 bottle is 1/3 of a litre of water. If Tom produces at point *A*, he can produce 1,000 litres of water and 1,000 bottles an hour.

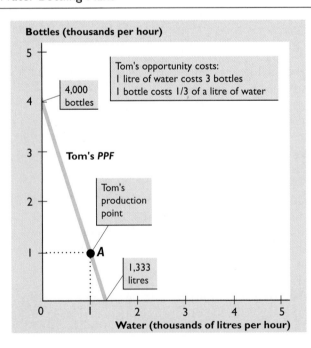

Tom's *PPF* is linear because his workers have similar skills so if he reallocates them from one activity to another, he faces a constant opportunity cost.

Nancy also produces water and bottles. But Nancy owns a much better spring than Tom. At the same time, her bottle-making equipment is less productive than is Tom's. These differences between the two plants mean that Nancy's production possibilities frontier—shown along with Tom's *PPF* in Figure 3.8—is different from Tom's. If Nancy uses all her resources to produce water, she can produce 4,000 litres an hour. If she uses all her resources to make bottles, she can produce 1,333 an hour. Nancy's *PPF* is linear, like Tom's, so she faces a constant opportunity cost. For each 1,000 additional bottles produced, she must decrease her production of water by 3,000 litres.

Nancy's opportunity cost of producing 1 bottle is 3 litres of water.

Similarly, if Nancy wants to increase her production of water, she must decrease her production of bottles. For each additional 1,000 litres of water produced, she must decrease her production of bottles by 333. So

Nancy's opportunity cost of producing 1 litre of water is 0.333 bottles.

Suppose that Tom and Nancy produce both bottles and water and that each produces 1,000 bottles and 1,000 litres of water—1,000 litres of bottled water—per hour. That is, each produces at point *A* on their production possibilities frontiers. Total production is 2,000 litres of bottled water an hour.

In which of the two activities does Nancy have a comparative advantage? Nancy has a comparative advantage in producing a good if her opportunity cost is lower than Tom's opportunity cost of producing that same good. Nancy has a

---

FIGURE 3.8
The Gains from Specialization

*e*Foundations **3.3**

❶ Tom and Nancy each produce at point *A* on their respective *PPFs*. Tom has a comparative advantage in bottles, and Nancy has a comparative advantage in water.

❷ If Tom specializes in bottles, he produces at point *B* on his *PPF*.

❸ If Nancy specializes in water, she produces at point *B'* on her *PPF*.

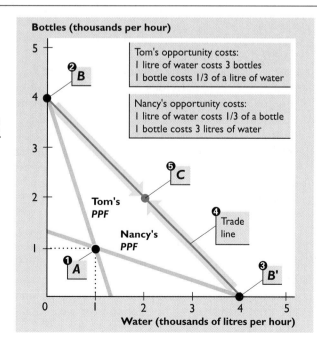

❹ They exchange water for bottles along the red "Trade line." Nancy buys bottles from Tom for less than her opportunity cost of producing them, and Tom buys water from Nancy for less than his opportunity cost of producing it.

❺ Each goes to point *C*—a point outside his or her individual *PPF*—where each has 2,000 bottles of water an hour. Tom and Nancy increase production with no change in resources.

comparative advantage in producing water. Nancy's opportunity cost of a litre of water is 0.333 bottles; Tom's opportunity cost of a litre of water is 3 bottles.

Tom's comparative advantage is in producing bottles. Tom's opportunity cost of a bottle is 0.333 litres of water, which is less than Nancy's opportunity cost of 3 litres of water. So Tom has a comparative advantage in producing bottles.

Because Nancy has a comparative advantage in water and Tom has a comparative advantage in bottles, they can both gain from specialization and exchange.

■ Achieving the Gains from Trade

If Tom specializes in bottles, he can produce 4,000 bottles an hour—point *B* on his *PPF*. If Nancy specializes in water, she can produce 4,000 litres an hour—point *B'* on her *PPF*. By specializing, Tom and Nancy together can produce 4,000 litres of water and 4,000 bottles an hour, which is double their total production without specialization. By specialization and exchange, Tom and Nancy can move to points *outside* their individual production possibilities frontiers.

To achieve the gains from specialization, Tom and Nancy must trade with each other. Suppose that each hour, Nancy produces 4,000 litres of water, Tom produces 4,000 bottles, and Nancy supplies Tom with 2,000 litres of water in exchange for 2,000 bottles. Tom and Nancy move along the red "Trade line" to point *C*. At this point, each produces 2,000 litres of bottled water an hour.

By specializing and trading with each other, both Tom and Nancy can double their production from 1,000 to 2,000 bottles of water an hour. The increases in production that each achieves are the gains from specialization and exchange.

Both Nancy and Tom share in the gains. Nancy gets bottles for 1 litre of water per bottle instead of 3 litres per bottle. Tom gets water for 1 bottle per litre instead of 3 bottles per litre. Nancy gets her bottles more cheaply and Tom gets his water more cheaply than when they produced both water and bottles.

■ Absolute Advantage

Absolute advantage
When one person is more productive than another person in several or even all activities.

Suppose that Nancy invents a production process that makes her four times as productive as she was before in the production of both water and bottles. With her new technology, Nancy now has an **absolute advantage**—she is more productive than Tom in both activities.

But Nancy does not have a *comparative* advantage in both goods. She can produce four times as much of *both* goods as before, but her *opportunity cost* of 1 bottle is still 3 litres of water. Her opportunity cost is higher than Tom's. So Nancy can still get bottles at a lower cost by trading water for bottles with Tom.

The key point to recognize is that it is *not* possible for *anyone* to have a comparative advantage in everything, even though they might have an absolute advantage in everything. So gains from specialization and trade are always available when opportunity costs diverge.

The principle of comparative advantage and the gains from specialization and exchange explain why each individual specializes in a small range of economic activities. It is also the driving force behind international trade. Canada and Mexico, like Tom and Nancy, can *both* gain by specializing in the activities in which they have a comparative advantage and trading with each other. The absolute advantage of Canada is no obstacle to reaping mutual gains from trade.

CHECKPOINT 3.3

3 **Explain how specialization and trade expand production possibilities.**

Study Guide pp. 46–48

*e*Foundations **3.3**

Practice Problem 3.3

Tony and Patty produce scooters and snowboards. Figure 1 shows their production possibilities per day.

a. Calculate Tony's opportunity cost of a snowboard.
b. Calculate Patty's opportunity cost of a snowboard.
c. Who has a comparative advantage in producing snowboards?
d. Who has a comparative advantage in producing scooters?
e. If they specialize and trade, how many snowboards and scooters will they produce?

FIGURE 1

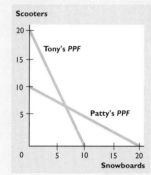

Exercises 3.3

1. Sara and Sid produce boards and sails for windsurfing. Figure 2 shows their production possibilities per day.
  a. Calculate Sara's opportunity cost of a board.
  b. Calculate Sid's opportunity cost of a board.
  c. Who has a comparative advantage in producing boards?
  d. Who has a comparative advantage in producing sails?
  e. If they specialize and trade, how many boards and sails will they produce?

2. If Sid in Exercise 1 installs a new machine that doubles his production possibilities:
  a. Who now has a comparative advantage in producing boards?
  b. Are there any gains for Sara and Sid if they specialize and trade? Explain why or why not.

FIGURE 2

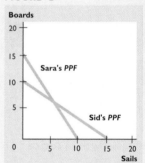

Solution to Practice Problem 3.3

a. Tony's opportunity cost of a snowboard is 2 scooters. If Tony uses all his resources to make scooters, he can make 20 a day. If he uses all his resources to make snowboards, he can make 10 a day. For each snowboard Tony makes, he forgoes making 2 scooters.
b. Patty's opportunity cost of a snowboard is 1/2 of a scooter. If Patty uses all her resources to make scooters, she can make 10 a day. If she uses all her resources to make snowboards, she can make 20 a day. For each snowboard Patty makes, she forgoes making 1/2 of a scooter.
c. Patty has a comparative advantage in producing snowboards because her opportunity cost of a snowboard is less than Tony's.
d. Tony has a comparative advantage in producing scooters. For each scooter made, Tony forgoes making 1/2 of a snowboard. His opportunity cost of a scooter is 1/2 snowboard. For each scooter made, Patty forgoes making 2 snowboards. Her opportunity cost of a scooter is 2 snowboards. Tony's opportunity cost is lower than Patty's.
e. Patty specializes in snowboards, and Tony specializes in scooters. Together, they produce 20 snowboards and 20 scooters.

3.4 EXPANDING PRODUCTION POSSIBILITIES

During the past 30 years, production possibilities per person in Canada have doubled. Such a sustained expansion of production possibilities is called economic growth. Can economic growth enable us to overcome scarcity and avoid opportunity cost? It cannot. The faster we make production possibilities grow, the greater is the opportunity cost of economic growth.

Three key factors influence economic growth: technological change, the expansion of human capital, and capital accumulation. Technological change is the development of new goods and services and of better ways of producing existing goods and services. The expansion of human capital is the improvement in the quality of labour that comes from education, on-the-job training, and work experience. Capital accumulation is the growth of capital resources.

As a consequence of technological change, the expansion of human capital, and capital accumulation, we have cars that enable us to produce more transportation than when we had only horses and carriages; we have satellites that make communications possible on a global scale, far beyond what we could produce using the earlier cable technology. We have water-bottling plants that enable us to produce millions of litres of bottled water each year.

But when we use resources to develop new technologies, educate and train people, and produce new capital equipment, we must decrease our current production of consumption goods and services. This decrease in the current production of consumption goods and services is the opportunity cost of economic growth. Let's look at this opportunity cost.

■ Economic Growth in an Industry

Instead of studying the *PPF* of bottled water and CDs, we'll hold the quantity of CDs produced constant and study the *PPF* for bottled water and water-bottling plants. Figure 3.9 shows this *PPF* as the curve *JKL*. Along this *PPF*, if we use all our resources to produce water-bottling plants, we can produce 3 plants a year at point *J*. In this case, we produce no bottled water. We can produce 2 water-bottling plants and 3 million bottles of water a year at point *K*, or we can produce no water-bottling plants and 5 million bottles of water at point *L*.

The amount by which our production possibilities expands depends on the resources we devote to building new bottling plants and training people to operate them. If we devote no resources to this activity (point *L*), the *PPF* remains at *JKL*—the light orange curve in Figure 3.9. If we decrease the current production of bottled water and build 2 new bottling plants (point *K*), then in the future, we'll have more bottled-water production possibilities and our *PPF* rotates outward to the position shown by the orange curve. Next period if we produce 2 new bottling plants, we produce at point *K'*. The more resources we devote to producing bottling plants now, the greater is the expansion of our production possibilities in the future.

Economic growth brings a benefit—expanded production possibilities in the future. But economic growth is not free. To make it happen, we must decrease the production of goods for consumption now. In Figure 3.9, we move from *L* to *K* and forgo 2 million bottles of water for consumption now. The opportunity cost of more bottling plants in the future is fewer bottles of water today. Also, economic growth is no magic formula for abolishing scarcity. Economic growth rotates the *PPF* outward, but on the new *PPF*, we continue to face opportunity costs. The ideas about economic growth that we have explored in the setting of the water-bottling industry also apply to nations, as you can see in Eye on the Global Economy (on p. 74).

▇ FIGURE 3.9
Expanding Production Possibilities

 *e*Foundations **3.4**

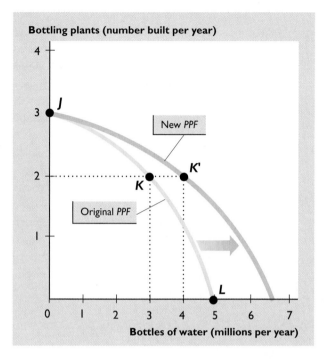

Bottling plants (number built per year)

Bottles of water (millions per year)

The original *PPF* shows the limits to the production of bottled water and water-bottling plants, with the production of all other goods and services remaining the same.

If we devote no resources to producing water-bottling plants and produce 5 million bottles of water a month, we remain stuck at point *L*. But if we decrease water production to 3 million bottles a year and produce 2 water-bottling plants, at point *K*, our production possibilities will expand. After a year, the production possibility frontier shifts outward to the new *PPF* and we can produce at point *K'*, a point outside the original *PPF*. We can shift the *PPF* outward, but we cannot avoid opportunity cost. The opportunity cost of producing more bottled water in the future is less bottled water in the present.

CHECKPOINT 3.4

4 **Explain how technological change and increases in capital and human capital expand production possibilities.**

Study Guide pp. 48–50

*e*Foundations **3.4**

Practice Problem 3.4

Table 1 shows a nation that produces education services and consumption goods. If the nation increases the graduates from 0 to 500 a year, what is the opportunity cost of these 500 graduates?

Exercise 3.4

If the nation in Table 1 uses all its resources to produce consumption goods, at what rate will the economy grow? If the nation increases the graduates from 0 to 750 a year, will the nation experience economic growth? Explain your answer.

Solution to Practice Problem 3.4

The opportunity cost of 500 graduates is 1,000 units (3,000 minus 2,000) of consumption goods forgone.

Possibility	Education services (graduates)	Consumption goods (units)
A	1,000	0
B	750	1,000
C	500	2,000
D	0	3,000

Eye On The GLOBAL ECONOMY

Economic Growth in Canada and Hong Kong

Canada and Hong Kong provide a striking example of how the choices that countries make affect the expansion of their production possibilities. In 1960, the production possibilities per person in Canada were three times those in Hong Kong (see the figure). Canada devoted one-fifth of its resources to accumulating capital and the other four-fifths to consumption. In 1960, Canada chose point A on its PPF. Hong Kong devoted two-fifths of its resources to accumulating capital and three-fifths to consumption. In 1960, Hong Kong chose point A on its PPF.

Since 1960, both countries have experienced economic growth, but growth in Hong Kong has been more rapid than in Canada. Because Hong Kong devoted a bigger fraction of its resources to accumulating capital, its production possibilities have expanded more quickly than those in Canada.

By 2000, the production possibilities per person in Hong Kong and Canada were similar. If Hong Kong (at point B on the 2000 PPF) continues to devote more resources to accumulating capital than does Canada, Hong Kong will continue to grow more rapidly than Canada and its PPF will move out beyond our own. But if Hong Kong increases consumption and decreases capital accumulation (for example, moving to point D on its 2000 PPF), its rate of economic growth will slow.

Canada is typical of the rich industrial countries, which include the United States, Western Europe and Japan. Hong Kong is typical of the fast-growing Asian economies, which include Taiwan, Thailand, South Korea, and China. Growth in these Asian countries slowed during the Asia crisis of 1998, but quickly rebounded. Production in these countries expands by between 5 percent and almost 10 percent a year. If these high growth rates are maintained, these countries will eventually close the gap on Canada.

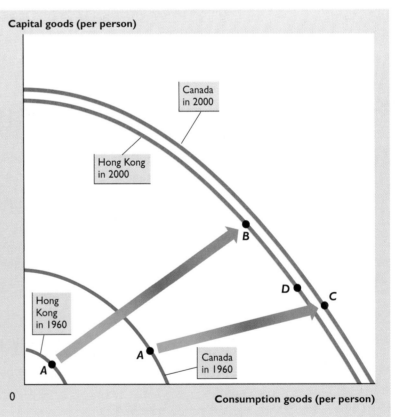

CHAPTER CHECKPOINT

Key Points

1 **Use the production possibilities frontier to illustrate the economic problem.**

- The production possibilities frontier, *PPF,* describes the limits to what we can produce by fully and efficiently using all our available resources.

- Points inside and on the *PPF* are attainable. Points outside the *PPF* are unattainable.

2 **Calculate opportunity cost.**

- Along the *PPF*, the opportunity cost of X (the item on the x-axis) is the decrease in Y (the item on the y-axis) divided by the increase in X.

- The opportunity cost of Y is the inverse of the opportunity cost of X.

- The opportunity cost of producing a good increases as the quantity produced increases.

- The opportunity cost increases because resources are not equally productive in all activities.

3 **Explain how specialization and trade expand production possibilities.**

- People differ in their production abilities.

- A person has a comparative advantage in an activity if he or she can perform that activity at a lower opportunity cost than someone else.

- We gain by specializing in the activity in which we have a comparative advantage and trading.

4 **Explain how technological change and increases in capital and human capital expand production possibilities.**

- Technological change and increases in capital and human capital expand production possibilities.

- The greater the quantity of resources that are devoted to advancing technology, accumulating capital, and increasing human capital, the greater is the expansion of our production possibilities.

- The opportunity cost of economic growth is the decrease in current consumption.

Key Terms

Absolute advantage, 70
Comparative advantage, 68
Production possibilities frontier, 58
Tradeoff, 61

Exercises

1. People can now obtain music from Web sites such as Napster and MP3.
   a. How has the *PPF* for recorded music and other goods and services changed?
   b. Is there still a tradeoff between recorded music and other goods and services, or is the opportunity cost of recorded music now zero?

2. AIDS has become an acute problem in Africa.
   a. How has the spread of AIDS influenced the *PPF* of the economies of Africa?
   b. Has the spread of AIDS increased the opportunity cost of some goods and services? Has it decreased the opportunity cost of anything?

3. On Survivor Island, the only resources are 5 units of capital and 10 hours of labour a day. Table 1 shows the maximum quantities of entertainment and good food that Survivor Island can produce.
   a. Draw Survivor Island's production possibilities frontier.
   b. If Survivor Island produces 50 units of entertainment and 50 units of good food, is its production attainable? Are all its resources fully employed? What is the opportunity cost of a unit of entertainment?
   c. If Survivor Island produces 40 units of entertainment and 60 units of good food, is its production attainable? Is there a tradeoff? What is the opportunity cost of an additional unit of entertainment?
   d. What can you say about the opportunity cost of a unit of good food as Survivor Island allocates more resources to producing good food?

4. In 8 hours, Willy can produce either 50 sundaes or 20 pizzas. In 8 hours, Wendy can produce either 20 sundaes or 50 pizzas.
   a. Calculate Willy's opportunity cost of a sundae.
   b. Calculate Wendy's opportunity cost of a sundae.
   c. Who has a comparative advantage in producing pizzas?
   d. If Willy and Wendy specialize, how many sundaes and how many pizzas will they produce?

5. Tom can produce either 5 kites and 3 jigsaw puzzles an hour or 3 kites and 4 jigsaw puzzles an hour. Tessa can produce either 6 kites and 2 jigsaw puzzles an hour or 2 kites and 5 jigsaw puzzles an hour.
   a. Calculate Tom's opportunity cost of a kite.
   b. Calculate Tessa's opportunity cost of a kite.
   c. Who has a comparative advantage in producing kites?
   d. Who has a comparative advantage in producing jigsaw puzzles?

6. Tom and Tessa in Exercise 5 specialize in producing the good in which they have a comparative advantage.
   a. What are the quantities of jigsaw puzzles and kites produced?
   b. Would Tom and Tessa get any gains from specializing production and trading with each other?

7. Table 2 shows the quantities of robots and other goods and services that the country Alpha can produce along its production possibilities frontier.
   a. If, in a year, Alpha produces 2,000 units of other goods and services, will Alpha experience economic growth? Explain.
   b. If, in a year, Alpha produces 1,100 units of other goods and services, will Alpha experience economic growth? Explain.
   c. If Alpha currently produces no robots and now decides to produce 1 robot, what is the cost of its economic growth?

TABLE 1

Entertainment (units)		Good food (units)
100	and	0
80	and	30
60	and	50
40	and	60
20	and	65
0	and	67

TABLE 2

Robots (units)		Other goods and services (units)
0	and	2,000
1	and	1,900
2	and	1,700
3	and	1,400
4	and	1,000
5	and	500

Demand and Supply

CHAPTER CHECKLIST

When you have completed your study of this chapter,
you will be able to:

1 Distinguish between quantity demanded and demand and explain what determines demand.

2 Distinguish between quantity supplied and supply and explain what determines supply.

3 Explain how demand and supply determine price and quantity in a market and explain the effects of changes in demand and supply.

4 Explain how price ceilings, price floors, and sticky prices cause shortages, surpluses, and unemployment.

Faced with scarcity, we specialize in the activity at which we have a comparative advantage. We sell the services of our factors of production in factor markets and we buy the goods and services that we consume in goods markets.

In this chapter, you study the tools of demand and supply that explain how markets work. You will learn how the choices people make about what to buy and sell determine the quantities and prices of the goods and services produced and consumed and the quantities of the factors of production employed.

Through the rest of your course in macroeconomics, you will use these demand and supply tools to understand the forces that influence the standard of living and the overall level of economic activity. Soon, you will find yourself using the tools of demand and supply every time you think about a price or a quantity in your everyday life.

MARKETS

When you need a new pair of running shoes, want coffee and a doughnut, plan to upgrade your stereo system, or want to fly to Florida for a vacation, you must find a place where people sell those items or offer those services. The place in which you find them is a *market*. You learned in Chapter 2 that a market is any arrangement that brings buyers and sellers together. A market has two sides: buyers (demanders) and sellers (suppliers). There are markets for *goods* such as apples and hiking boots, for *services* such as haircuts and tennis lessons, for *resources* such as computer programmers and earthmovers, and for other manufactured *inputs* such as memory chips and auto parts. There are also markets for money such as Japanese yen and for financial securities such as Nortel stock. Only imagination limits what can be traded in markets.

Some markets are physical places where the buyers and sellers meet and where an auctioneer or a broker helps to determine the prices. Examples of this type of market are the New York Stock Exchange, and wholesale fish, meat, and produce markets.

Some markets are groups of people spread around the world who never meet and know little about each other but are connected via the Internet or phone. Examples of this type of market are the Toronto Stock Exchange and currency markets.

But most markets are unorganized collections of buyers and sellers. You do most of your trading in this type of market. An example is the market for running shoes. The buyers in this vast international market are the millions of joggers (or those who want comfort or to make a fashion statement) who are looking for a new pair of shoes. The sellers are the tens of thousands of retail sports equipment and footwear stores. Each buyer can visit several different stores, and each seller knows that the buyer has a choice of stores.

For most of this chapter, we'll study a market that has so many buyers and sellers that no one can influence the price. In the final section we'll study markets in which the government tries to influence the price or a seller sets the price, or in which buyers and sellers together agree on a price.

4.1 DEMAND

First, we'll study the behaviour of buyers in a market. The **quantity demanded** of any good, service, or resource is the amount that people are willing and able to buy during a specified period and at a specified price. For example, when spring water costs $1 a bottle, you decide to buy 2 bottles a day, so this is your quantity demanded of spring water.

The quantity demanded is measured as an amount *per unit of time*. For example, your quantity demanded of water is 2 bottles *per day*. We could express this quantity as 14 bottles per week or some other number per month or per year. But without a time dimension, a particular number of bottles has no meaning.

Many things influence buying plans, and one of them is price. We look first at the relationship between quantity demanded and price. To study this relationship, we keep all other influences on buying plans the same and we ask: How, other things remaining the same, does the quantity demanded of a good change as its price varies? The law of demand provides the answer.

> **Quantity demanded**
> The amount of any good, service, or resource that people are willing and able to buy during a specified period at a specified price.

■ The Law of Demand

The **law of demand** states:

> **Other things remaining the same, if the price of a good rises, the quantity demanded of that good decreases; if the price of a good falls, the quantity demanded of that good increases.**

So the law of demand states that when all else remains the same, if the price of a laptop computer falls, people will buy more laptops; or if the price of a hockey ticket rises, people will buy fewer tickets.

Why does the quantity demanded increase if the price falls, all other things remaining the same?

The answer is that faced with a limited budget, people always have an incentive to find the best deals they can. If the price of one item falls and the prices of all other items remain the same, the item with the lower price is a better deal than it was before. So people buy more of this item. Suppose, for example, that the price of bottled water fell from $1 a bottle to 25 cents a bottle while the price of Gatorade remained at $1 a bottle. Wouldn't some people switch from Gatorade to water? By doing so, they save 75 cents a bottle, which they can spend on other things that they previously couldn't afford.

Think about the things that you buy and ask yourself: Which of these items does *not* obey the law of demand? If the price of a new textbook were lower, other things remaining the same (including the price of a used textbook), would you buy more new textbooks? Then think about all the things that you do not now buy but would if you could afford them. How cheap would a laptop have to be for you to buy *both* a desktop and a laptop? There is a price that is low enough to entice you!

■ Demand Schedule and Demand Curve

Demand is the relationship between the *quantity demanded* and the *price* of a good when all other influences on buying plans remain the same. The quantity demanded is *one* quantity at *one* price. *Demand* is a *list of quantities at different prices* illustrated by a demand schedule and a demand curve.

> **Demand**
> The relationship between the quantity demanded and the price of a good when all other influences on buying plans remain the same.

Demand schedule

A list of the quantities demanded at each different price when all other influences on buying plans remain the same.

Demand curve

A graph of the relationship between the quantity demanded of a good and its price when all other influences on buying plans remain the same.

A **demand schedule** is a list of the quantities demanded at each different price when *all the other influences on buying plans remain the same*. The table in Figure 4.1 is a demand schedule for bottled water. It tells us that if the price of water is $2.00 a bottle, the quantity demanded is 8.5 million bottles a day. If the price of water is $1.50 a bottle, the quantity demanded is 9 million bottles a day. The quantity demanded increases to 10 million bottles a day at a price of $1.00 a bottle and to 12 million bottles a day at a price of 50 cents a bottle.

A **demand curve** is a graph of the relationship between the quantity demanded of a good and its price when all the other influences on buying plans remain the same. The points on the demand curve labelled *A* through *D* represent the rows *A* through *D* of the demand schedule. For example, point *B* on the graph represents row *B* of the demand schedule and shows that the quantity demanded is 9 million bottles a day when the price is $1.50 a bottle. Point *C* on the demand curve represents row *C* of the demand schedule and shows that the quantity demanded is 10 million bottles a day when the price is $1.00 a bottle.

The downward slope of the demand curve illustrates the law of demand. Along the demand curve, when the price of the good *falls*, the quantity demanded *increases*. When the price of a bottle of water falls from $1.00 to $0.50, the quantity demanded increases from 10 million bottles a day to 12 million bottles a day. And when the price *rises*, the quantity demanded *decreases*. When the price rises from $1.00 to $1.50 a bottle, the quantity demanded decreases from 10 million bottles a day to 9 million bottles a day.

▧ FIGURE 4.1

Demand Schedule and Demand Curve

e/**Foundations 4.1**

The table shows a demand schedule, which lists the quantity of water demanded at each price if all other influences on buying plans remain the same. At a price of $1.50 a bottle, the quantity demanded is 9 million bottles a day.

The demand curve shows the relationship between the quantity demanded and price, everything else remaining the same. The downward-sloping demand curve illustrates the law of demand. When the price falls, the quantity demanded increases; and when the price rises, the quantity demanded decreases.

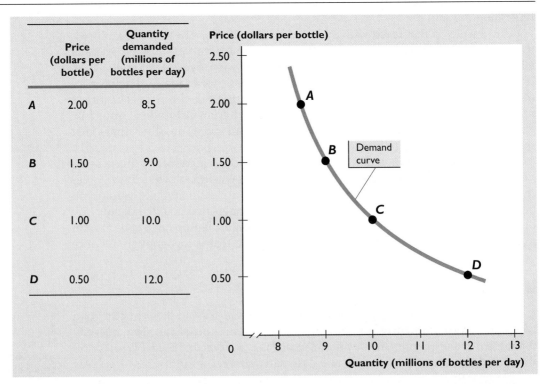

	Price (dollars per bottle)	Quantity demanded (millions of bottles per day)
A	2.00	8.5
B	1.50	9.0
C	1.00	10.0
D	0.50	12.0

■ Changes in Demand

The demand curve shows how the quantity demanded changes when the price changes but *all other influences on buying plans remain the same.* When the price changes, we call the resulting change in buying plans a **change in the quantity demanded.** When any influence on buying plans other than the price of the good changes, there is a **change in demand**.

The main influences on buying plans that change demand are:

- Prices of related goods
- Income
- Expectations
- Number of buyers
- Preferences

Change in the quantity demanded
A change in the quantity of a good that people plan to buy that results from a change in the price of the good.

Change in demand
A change in the quantity that people plan to buy when any influence on buying plans other than the price of the good changes.

Prices of Related Goods

A change in the price of one good can bring a change in the demand for a related good. Related goods are either substitutes or complements. A **substitute** for a good is another good that can be consumed in its place. Chocolate cake is a substitute for cheesecake, a taxi ride is a substitute for a subway ride, and bottled water is a substitute for Gatorade.

The demand for a good *increases* if the price of one of its substitutes *rises*; the demand for a good *decreases* if the price of one of its substitutes *falls*. That is, the demand for a good and the price of one of its substitutes move in the *same direction*. For example, the demand for cheesecake increases when the price of chocolate cake rises.

A **complement** of a good is another good that is consumed with it. Salsa is a complement of tortilla chips, wrist guards are a complement of in-line skates, and bottled water is a complement of fitness centre services.

The demand for a good *decreases* if the price of one of its complements *rises*; and the demand for a good *increases* if the price of one of its complements *falls*. That is, the demand for a good and the price of one of its complements move in *opposite directions*. For example, the demand for salsa decreases when the price of tortilla chips rises.

Substitute
A good that can be consumed in place of another good.

Complement
A good that is consumed with another good.

Income

A good is a **normal good** if a rise in income brings an *increase* in demand and a fall in income brings a *decrease* in demand. For example, if you buy more bottled water when your income increases, then bottled water is a normal good. Most goods are normal goods (hence the name).

A good is an **inferior good** if a rise in income brings a *decrease* in demand and a fall in income brings an *increase* in demand. For example, if you buy fewer macaroni and cheese dinners and more fast-food restaurant dinners when your income increases, then a macaroni and cheese dinner is an inferior good.

Normal good
A good for which the demand increases when income increases.

Inferior good
A good for which the demand decreases when income increases.

Expectations

Expected future income and prices influence demand. For example, you're offered a well-paid job that starts next summer, so you go to Cancun during spring break. Your demand for vacation travel has increased. Or if you expect the price of a macaroni and cheese dinner to rise next week, you buy enough of them to get you through the term. Your demand for macaroni and cheese dinners has increased.

Number of Buyers

The greater the number of buyers in a market, the larger is demand. For example, the demand for parking spaces, movies, bottled water, or just about anything is greater in Vancouver than it is in Charlottetown, P.E.I.

Preferences

When *preferences* change, the demand for one item decreases and the demand for another item (or items) increases. Better information about the health hazards of tobacco has changed preferences. This change in preferences has decreased the demand for cigarettes and increased the demand for nicotine patches.

Preferences also change when new goods become available. For example, the development of MP3 has decreased the demand for CDs and increased the demand for Internet services and personal computers.

Illustrating a Change in Demand

Figure 4.2 illustrates a change in demand and distinguishes it from a change in the quantity demanded. When the price of the good changes, there is *change in the quantity demanded*, shown by a *movement along the demand curve*. When demand changes, *the demand curve shifts*. Figure 4.2 illustrates two changes in demand. Initially, the demand curve is D_0. When the demand for bottled water decreases, the demand curve shifts leftward to D_1. On demand curve D_1, the quantity demanded is smaller at each price. And when the demand for bottled water increases, the demand curve shifts rightward to D_2. On demand curve D_2, the quantity demanded is greater at each price.

■ **FIGURE 4.2**

Change in Quantity Demanded Versus Change in Demand

*e/*Foundations **4.1**

❶ **A decrease in the quantity demanded**

If the price of a good rises, *cet. par.*, the quantity demanded decreases. There is a movement up along the demand curve D_0.

❷ **A decrease in demand**

Demand decreases and the demand curve shifts leftward (from D_0 to D_1) if:

■ The price of a substitute falls.
■ The price of a complement rises.
■ The price of the good is expected to fall or income is expected to fall in the future.
■ Income decreases.*
■ The number of buyers decreases.

  * Bottled water is a normal good

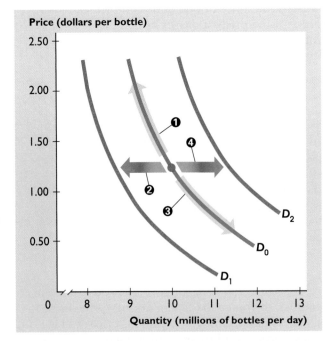

❸ **An increase in the quantity demanded**

If the price of a good falls, *cet. par.*, the quantity demanded increases. There is a movement down along the demand curve D_0.

❹ **An increase in demand**

Demand increases and the demand curve shifts rightward (from D_0 to D_2) if:

■ The price of a substitute rises.
■ The price of a complement falls.
■ The price of the good is expected to rise or income is expected to rise in the future.
■ Income increases.*
■ The number of buyers increases.

CHECKPOINT 4.1

1 **Distinguish between quantity demanded and demand and explain what determines demand.**

Study Guide pp. 57–59

*e*Foundations 4.1

Practice Problem 4.1

In the market for scooters, the following events occur, one at a time. Explain the influence of each event on the quantity demanded of scooters and on the demand for scooters. Illustrate the effects of each event by either a movement along the demand curve or a shift in the demand curve for scooters and say which event (or events) illustrates the law of demand in action. These events are:
a. The price of a scooter falls.
b. The price of a bicycle falls.
c. Citing rising injury rates, cities and towns ban scooters from sidewalks.
d. Average income increases.
e. Rumour has it that the price of a scooter will rise next month.
f. The number of buyers increases.

Exercise 4.1

The Internet was born in 1969. For the next 20 years, mainly scientists in universities and research laboratories used it. But in the 1990s, the use of Internet service increased dramatically and the price per hour of Internet service fell.
a. Are there any substitutes for Internet service? If so, provide an example.
b. Are there any complements of Internet service? If so, provide an example.
c. What are the main developments that brought about the dramatic increase in the quantity of Internet service during the 1990s?
d. Which developments that you identified in (c) increased the demand for Internet service? Illustrate these effects by using the demand curve for Internet service.
e. Which developments that you identified in (c) increased the quantity demanded of Internet service? Illustrate these effects by using the demand curve for Internet service.

Solution to Practice Problem 4.1

a. A fall in the price of a scooter increases the quantity demanded of scooters, shown by a movement down along the demand curve for scooters (Figure 1). It is an example of the law of demand in action.
b. A bicycle is a substitute for a scooter. So when the price of a bicycle falls, the demand for scooters decreases.
c. The ban on scooters changes preferences and decreases the demand for scooters.
   In (b) and (c), the demand curve shifts leftward (Figure 2).
d. A scooter is (likely) a normal good. So when the average income increases, the demand for scooters increases.
e. A rise in the expected price of a scooter next month increases the demand for scooters now.
f. An increase in the number of buyers increases the demand for scooters.
   In (d), (e), and (f), the demand curve for scooters shifts rightward (Figure 2).

FIGURE 1

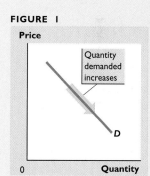

FIGURE 2

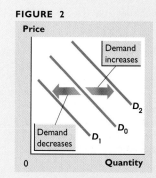

4.2 SUPPLY

A market has two sides. On one side are the buyers, or demanders, that we've just studied. On the other side of the market are the sellers, or suppliers. We now study the forces that determine suppliers' plans.

The **quantity supplied** of a good, service, or resource is the amount that people are willing and able to sell during a specified period and at a specified price. For example, when the price of spring water is $1.50 a bottle, a spring owner decides to sell 2,000 bottles a day, so this is the quantity supplied of spring water by this individual producer. (As in the case of demand, the quantity supplied is measured as an amount *per unit of time*.)

Many things influence selling plans, and one of them is the price. We look first at the relationship between quantity supplied of a good and its price. To study this relationship, we keep all other influences on selling plans the same. And we ask: How, other things remaining the same, does the quantity supplied of a good change as its price varies? The law of supply provides the answer.

Quantity supplied
The amount of any good, service, or resource that people are willing and able to sell during a specified period at a specified price.

■ The Law of Supply

The **law of supply** states:

> **Other things remaining the same, if the price of a good rises, the quantity supplied of that good increases; and if the price of a good falls, the quantity supplied of that good decreases.**

So the law of supply states that when all else remains the same, if the price of bottled water rises, spring owners will offer more water for sale; if the price of a CD falls, Sony Corp. will offer fewer CDs for sale.

Why, other things remaining the same, does the quantity supplied increase if the price rises? The basic answer is that when the production of a good or service increases, the opportunity cost of producing it increases (Chapter 3, p. 66). But if the price exceeds the opportunity cost of production, then it is profitable to increase the quantity supplied. So a higher price makes it profitable to produce a larger quantity and incur a higher opportunity cost.

For example, to increase the quantity of bottled water produced per day, spring owners must hire more labour and run the bottling plant at a faster rate. The opportunity cost per bottle produced increases. If the price of a bottle of water rises from $1 a bottle to $2 a bottle while the prices of everything else, including wage rates and the prices of other inputs, remain the same, spring owners will increase production and incur the higher opportunity cost. By doing so, the spring owner will earn a larger profit.

The law of supply applies to the things that you own and can offer for sale. If, for example, the used book dealer offered a higher price for last year's textbooks, wouldn't you think about selling that handy math text?

■ Supply Schedule and Supply Curve

Supply
The relationship between the quantity supplied and the price of a good when all other influences on selling plans remain the same.

Supply is the relationship between the quantity supplied and the price of a good when all other influences on selling plans remain the same. The quantity supplied is *one* quantity at *one* price. *Supply* is a *list of quantities at different prices* illustrated by a supply schedule and a supply curve.

A **supply schedule** lists the quantities supplied at each different price when all the other influences on selling plans remain the same. The table in Figure 4.3 is a supply schedule for bottled water. It tells us that if the price of water is 50 cents a bottle, the quantity supplied is 8 million bottles a day. If the price of water is $1.00, the quantity supplied is 10 million bottles a day. The quantity supplied increases to 11 million bottles a day at a price of $1.50 a bottle and to 11.5 million bottles a day at a price of $2.00 a bottle.

A **supply curve** is a graph of the relationship between the quantity supplied of a good and its price when all the other influences on selling plans remain the same. The points on the supply curve labelled *A* through *D* represent the rows *A* through *D* of the supply schedule. For example, point *C* on the graph represents row *C* of the supply schedule and shows that the quantity supplied is 10 million bottles a day when the price is $1.00 a bottle. Point *B* on the supply curve represents row *B* of the supply schedule and shows that the quantity supplied is 11 million bottles a day when the price is $1.50 a bottle.

The upward slope of the supply curve illustrates the law of supply. Along the supply curve, when the price of the good *rises*, the quantity supplied *increases*. When the price of a bottle of water rises from $1.50 to $2.00, the quantity supplied increases from 11 million bottles a day to 11.5 million bottles a day. And when the price *falls*, the quantity supplied *decreases*. When the price falls from $1.50 to $1.00 a bottle, the quantity supplied decreases from 11 million bottles a day to 10 million bottles a day.

Supply schedule
A list of the quantities supplied at each different price when all other influences on selling plans remain the same.

Supply curve
A graph of the relationship between the quantity supplied of a good and its price when all other influences on selling plans remain the same.

FIGURE 4.3
Supply Schedule and Supply Curve

*e*Foundations **4.2**

	Price (dollars per bottle)	Quantity supplied (millions of bottles per day)
A	2.00	11.5
B	1.50	11.0
C	1.00	10.0
D	0.50	8.0

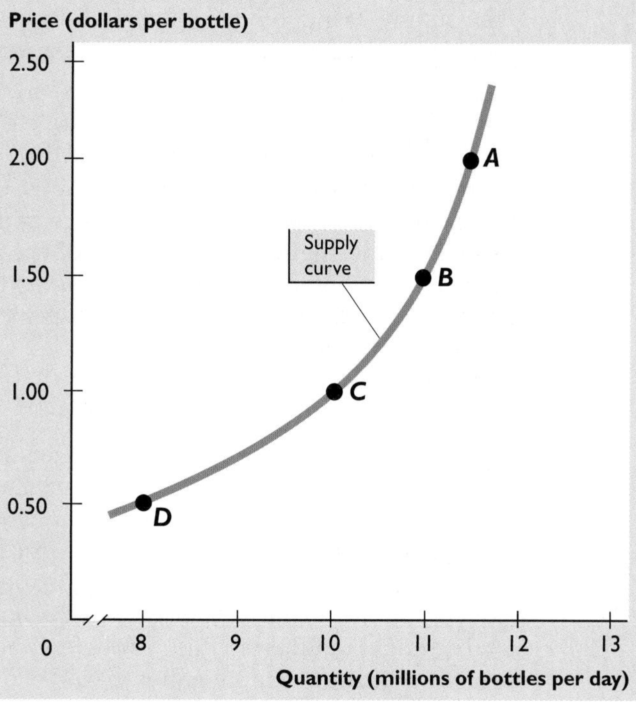

The table shows a supply schedule, which lists the quantity of water supplied at each price if all other influences on selling plans remain the same. At a price of $1.50 a bottle, the quantity supplied is 11 million bottles a day.

The supply curve shows the relationship between the quantity supplied and price, everything else remaining the same. The upward-sloping supply curve illustrates the law of supply. When the price rises, the quantity supplied increases; and when the price falls, the quantity supplied decreases.

■ Changes in Supply

The supply curve shows how the quantity supplied changes when the price changes and *when all other influences on selling plans remain the same.* When the price changes, we call the resulting influence on selling plans the **change in the quantity supplied**. When any influence on selling plans other than the price of the good changes, there is a **change in supply**.

The main influences on selling plans that change supply are:

- Prices of related goods
- Prices of resources and other inputs
- Expectations
- Number of sellers
- Productivity

Prices of Related Goods

A change in the price of one good can bring a change in the supply of a related good. Related goods are substitutes in production or complements in production. A **substitute in production** for a good is another good that can be produced in its place. Button-fly jeans are substitutes in production for cargo pants in a clothing factory. The supply of a good *decreases* if the price of one of its substitutes in production *rises*; and the supply of a good *increases* if the price of one of its substitutes in production *falls*. That is, the supply of a good and the price of one of its substitutes in production move in *opposite directions*. For example, the supply of cargo pants decreases when the price of button-fly jeans rises.

A **complement in production** of a good is another good that is produced along with it. Leather is a complement in production of beef. The supply of a good *increases* if the price of one of its complements in production *rises*; and the supply of a good *decreases* if the price of one of its complements in production *falls*. That is, the supply of a good and the price of one of its complements in production move in the *same direction*. For example, the supply of cowhide increases when the price of beef rises.

Prices of Resources and Other Inputs

Supply changes when the price of a resource or other input used to produce the good changes. The reason is that resource and input prices influence the cost of production. And the more it costs to produce a good, the smaller is the quantity supplied of that good (other things remaining the same). For example, if the wage rate of bottling-plant workers rises, it costs more to produce a bottle of water. So the supply of bottled water decreases.

Expectations

Expectations about future prices influence supply. For example, a real estate developer in Yellowknife expects the price of houses to rise as the Diavik diamond mine steps up production and hires more workers. So instead of selling houses now, she plans to sell them later when the price is higher. This action decreases the current supply of houses in Yellowknife. Expectations of future input prices also influence supply. If the developer expects builders' wages to rise sharply next year, she might build more this year before the wage increase occurs. This action increases the current supply of houses in Yellowknife.

Change in the quantity supplied
A change in the quantity of a good that suppliers plan to sell that results from a change in the price of the good.

Change in supply
A change in the quantity that suppliers plan to sell when any influence on selling plans other than the price of the good changes.

Substitute in production
A good that can be produced in place of another good.

Complement in production
A good that is produced along with another good.

Number of Sellers

The greater the number of sellers in a market, the larger is supply. For example, many new sellers have developed springs and water-bottling plants in Canada and the supply of bottled water has increased.

Productivity

Productivity is output per unit of input. An increase in productivity lowers costs and increases supply. A decrease in productivity has the opposite effect and decreases supply. Technological change is the main influence on productivity. For example, advances in electronic technology have lowered the cost of computers and increased their supply. Natural events such as weather patterns change farm productivity and change the supply of agricultural products.

Illustrating a Change in Supply

Figure 4.4 illustrates a change in supply and distinguishes it from a change in the quantity supplied. When the price of the good changes, there is *change in the quantity supplied*, shown by a *movement along the supply curve*. When supply changes, *the supply curve shifts*. Figure 4.4 illustrates two changes in supply. Initially, the supply curve is S_0. When the supply of bottled water decreases, the supply curve shifts leftward to S_1. On supply curve S_1, the quantity supplied is smaller at each price. And when the supply of bottled water increases, the supply curve shifts rightward to S_2. On supply curve S_2, the quantity supplied is greater at each price.

■ **FIGURE 4.4**

Change in Quantity Supplied Versus Change in Supply　　　　　*e*Foundations **4.2**

❶ A decrease in the quantity supplied

If the price of a good falls, *cet. par.*, the quantity supplied decreases. There is a movement down along the demand curve S_0.

❷ A decrease in supply

Supply decreases and the supply curve shifts leftward (from S_0 to S_1) if:

- The price of a substitute in production rises.
- The price of a complement in production falls.
- A resource price or other input price rises.
- The price of the good is expected to rise.
- The number of sellers decreases.
- Productivity decreases.

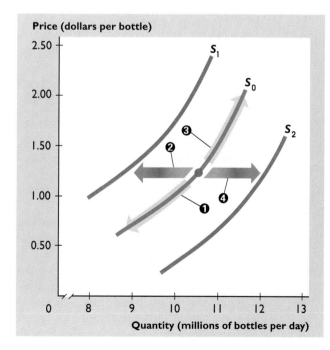

❸ An increase in the quantity supplied

If the price of a good rises, *cet. par.*, the quantity supplied increases. There is a movement up along the supply curve S_0.

❹ An increase in supply

Supply increases and the supply curve shifts rightward (from S_0 to S_2) if:

- The price of a substitute in production falls.
- The price of a complement in production rises.
- A resource price or other input price falls.
- The price of the good is expected to fall.
- The number of sellers increases.
- Productivity increases.

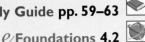
2 **Distinguish between quantity supplied and supply and explain what determines supply.**

Practice Problem 4.2

In the market for timber beams, several events occur one at a time. Explain the influence of each event on the quantity supplied of timber beams and the supply of timber beams. Illustrate the effects of each event by either a movement along the supply curve or a shift in the supply curve of timber beams and say which event (or events) illustrates the law of supply in action. The events are:

a. The wage rate of sawmill workers rises.
b. The price of sawdust rises.
c. The price of a timber beam rises.
d. The price of a timber beam is expected to rise next year.
e. Environmentalists convince Parliament to pass a new law that reduces the amount of forest that can be cut for timber products.
f. A new technology lowers the cost of producing timber beams.

Exercise 4.2

In the market for SUVs, several events occur one at a time. Explain the influence of each event on the quantity supplied of SUVs and the supply of SUVs. Illustrate the effects of each event by either a movement along the supply curve or a shift in the supply curve of SUVs and say which event (or events) illustrates the law of supply in action. The events are:

a. The price of a truck rises.
b. The price of an SUV falls.
c. The price of an SUV is expected to fall next year.
d. An SUV engine defect requires a huge and costly manufacturer's recall to replace the defective engines.
e. A new robot technology lowers the cost of producing SUVs.

Solution to Practice Problem 4.2

a. A rise in the wage rate of sawmill workers decreases the supply of timber beams. The supply curve of timber beams shifts leftward (Figure 1).
b. Sawdust and timber beams are complements in production. A rise in the price of sawdust increases the supply of timber beams. The supply curve of timber beams shifts rightward (Figure 1).
c. A rise in the price of a timber beam increases the quantity supplied of timber beams, which is shown as a movement up along the supply curve of timber beams (Figure 2). It is an example of the law of supply in action.
d. The expected rise in the price of a timber beam decreases the supply of timber beams. The supply curve of timber beams shifts leftward (Figure 1).
e. The new law decreases the supply of timber beams. The supply curve of timber beams shifts leftward (Figure 1).
f. The new technology increases the supply of timber beams and shifts the supply curve rightward (Figure 1).

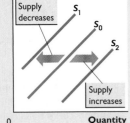

FIGURE 1

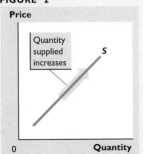

FIGURE 2

4.3 MARKET EQUILIBRIUM

In everyday language, "equilibrium" means "opposing forces are in balance." In a market, the opposing forces are those of demand and supply. Buyers want the lowest possible price, and the lower the price, the greater is the quantity that they plan to buy. Sellers want the highest possible price, and the higher the price, the greater is the quantity that they plan to sell.

Market equilibrium occurs when the quantity demanded equals the quantity supplied—when buyers' and sellers' plans are consistent. The **equilibrium price** is the price at which the quantity demanded equals the quantity supplied. The **equilibrium quantity** is the quantity that is bought and sold at the equilibrium price.

Figure 4.5 shows the market for bottled water. The market equilibrium occurs where the demand curve and the supply curve intersect. The equilibrium price is $1 a bottle, and the equilibrium quantity is 10 million bottles a day.

At the equilibrium price, buying plans and selling plans are balanced. People would buy more water at a lower price, and bottlers would sell more water at a higher price. But at a price of $1 a bottle, the quantity that people plan to buy equals the quantity that bottlers plan to sell. The opposing forces of buying plans and selling plans are exactly balanced at a price of $1 a bottle.

An equilibrium might be stable or unstable. Balance an egg on its pointed end (if you can!) and then give it a nudge. The egg rolls over onto its side. The equilibrium was unstable. Now balance an egg on its side and give it a nudge. The egg rocks for a moment but soon settles down in its equilibrium again. Market equilibrium is like an egg balanced on its side. The market is constantly pulled towards a stable equilibrium in which neither buyers nor sellers can improve their positions by changing either the price or the quantity.

Market equilibrium
When the quantity demanded equals the quantity supplied—when buyers' and sellers' plans are consistent.

Equilibrium price
The price at which the quantity demanded equals the quantity supplied.

Equilibrium quantity
The quantity that is bought and sold at the equilibrium price.

FIGURE 4.5
Equilibrium Price and Quantity

*e*Foundations **4.3**

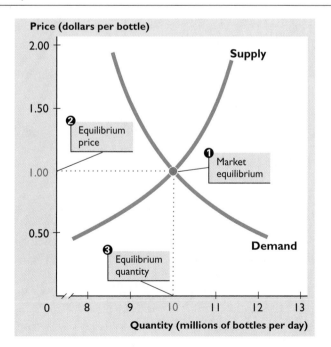

❶ Market equilibrium occurs at the intersection of the demand curve and the supply curve.

❷ The equilibrium price is $1.00 a bottle.

❸ At the equilibrium price, the quantity demanded and the quantity supplied are 10 million bottles a day, which is the equilibrium quantity.

■ Price: A Market's Automatic Regulator

When equilibrium is disturbed, the market forces restore it. The **law of market forces** states:

> **When there is a shortage, the price rises; and when there is a surplus, the price falls.**

Price is the regulator that pulls the market towards its equilibrium. If the price is above the equilibrium price, there is a **surplus** or **excess supply**—the quantity supplied exceeds the quantity demanded—and the price falls. If the price is below the equilibrium price, there is a **shortage** or **excess demand**—the quantity demanded exceeds the quantity supplied—and the price rises.

In Figure 4.6(a), when the price is $1.50 a bottle, suppliers would like to sell 11 million bottles but demanders buy only 9 million bottles. There is a surplus of 2 million bottles. To sell the surplus, suppliers cut the price. As the price falls, the quantity demanded increases, the quantity supplied decreases, and the surplus decreases. The price falls until there is no surplus and comes to rest at $1 a bottle.

In Figure 4.6(b), at 75 cents a bottle, demanders would like to buy 11 million bottles but suppliers sell only 9 million bottles. There is a shortage of 2 million bottles. Suppliers raise the price. As the price rises, the quantity supplied increases, the quantity demanded decreases, and the shortage decreases. The price rises until there is no shortage and comes to rest at $1 a bottle.

Surplus or excess supply
A situation in which the quantity supplied exceeds the quantity demanded.

Shortage or excess demand
A situation in which the quantity demanded exceeds the quantity supplied.

■ **FIGURE 4.6**
The Forces That Achieve Equilibrium

*e*Foundations **4.3**

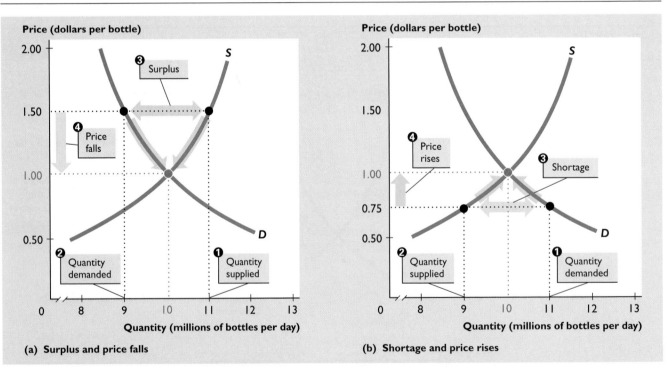

(a) Surplus and price falls

(b) Shortage and price rises

At $1.50 a bottle, ❶ the quantity supplied is 11 million bottles, ❷ the quantity demanded is 9 million bottles, ❸ the surplus is 2 million bottles, and ❹ the price falls.

At 75 cents a bottle, ❶ the quantity demanded is 11 million bottles, ❷ the quantity supplied is 9 million bottles, ❸ the shortage is 2 million bottles, and ❹ the price rises.

■ Effects of Changes in Demand

Markets are constantly hit by events that change demand and supply and bring changes in price and quantity. Some events change only demand, some change only supply, and some change *both* demand and supply. We'll look at all the possible cases. But we'll look first at the effects of changes in demand.

In Figure 4.7, the supply curve is S and initially, the demand curve is D_0. The equilibrium price is $1 a bottle, and the equilibrium quantity is 10 million bottles.

Suppose that a new study is published that raises concerns about the safety of the public water supply. The demand for bottled water increases. In Figure 4.7(a), the demand curve *shifts rightward* to D_1. At $1 a bottle, there is now a shortage, so the price rises and the quantity supplied increases. The price rises to $1.50 a bottle, and the quantity increases to 11 million bottles a day.

When demand changes, there is *no change in supply*. But there is a *change in the quantity supplied*—a movement along the supply curve.

Next, suppose that a new zero-calorie sports drink is invented and the demand for bottled water decreases. In Figure 4.7(b), the demand curve *shifts leftward* to D_2. At the initial price of $1.00 a bottle, there is now a surplus, so the price falls and the quantity supplied decreases. The price falls to 75 cents a bottle, and the quantity decreases to 9 million bottles a day.

■ **FIGURE 4.7**

The Effects of a Change in Demand   *e*Foundations **4.3**

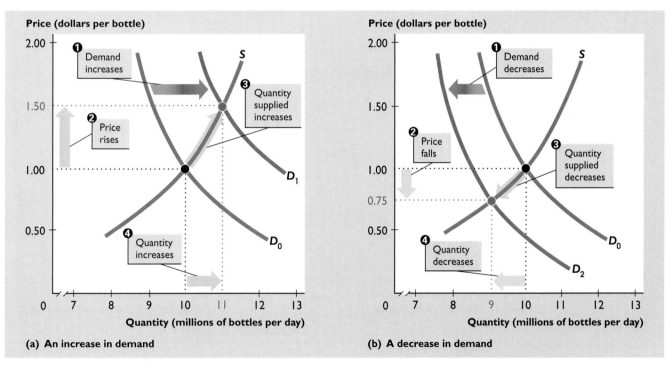

(a) An increase in demand

(b) A decrease in demand

An increase in demand ❶ shifts the demand curve rightward to D_1, ❷ raises the price, ❸ increases the quantity supplied, and ❹ increases the equilibrium quantity.

A decrease in demand ❶ shifts the demand curve leftward to D_2, ❷ lowers the price, ❸ decreases the quantity supplied, and ❹ decreases the equilibrium quantity.

■ Effects of Changes in Supply

Let's now work out what happens when supply changes.

In Figure 4.8, the demand curve is D and initially, the supply curve is S_0. The equilibrium price is $1 a bottle, and the equilibrium quantity is 10 million bottles.

Suppose that European water bottlers buy springs and open up bottling plants in Canada. The supply of bottled water increases. In Figure 4.8(a), the supply curve shifts rightward to S_1. At the initial price of $1.00 a bottle, there is now a surplus, so the price falls and the quantity demanded increases. The price falls to 75 cents a bottle, and the quantity increases to 11 million bottles a day.

When supply changes, there is *no change in demand*. But there is a *change in the quantity demanded*—a movement along the demand curve.

Next, suppose that a drought dries up some springs and the supply of bottled water decreases. In Figure 4.8(b), the supply curve shifts leftward to S_2. At the initial price of $1 a bottle, there is now a shortage, so the price rises and the quantity demanded decreases. The price rises to $1.50 a bottle, and the quantity decreases to 9 million bottles a day.

The new equilibrium price is $1.50 a bottle. Again, there is *no change in demand*. There is a *decrease in the quantity demanded* (movement along the demand curve). The equilibrium quantity decreases to 9 million bottles a day.

FIGURE 4.8

The Effects of a Change in Supply

*e*Foundations **4.3**

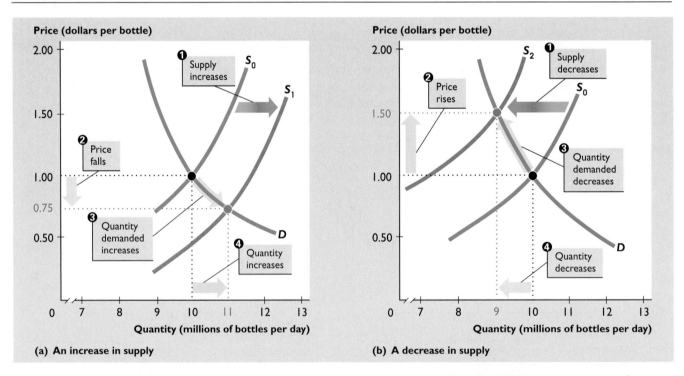

(a) An increase in supply

(b) A decrease in supply

An increase in supply ❶ shifts the supply curve rightward to S_1, ❷ lowers the price, ❸ increases the quantity demanded, and ❹ increases the equilibrium quantity.

A decrease in supply ❶ shifts the supply curve leftward to S_2, ❷ raises the price, ❸ decreases the quantity demanded, and ❹ decreases the equilibrium quantity.

Eye On The GLOBAL ECONOMY

A Change in the Demand for Roses

Colombia and Ecuador grow most of the world's roses. On the average, the quantity of roses sold worldwide is around 6 million bunches a month. And the average price that consumers pay is around $40 a bunch.

But one month, February, is not a normal month. Each year in February, the quantity of roses bought increases to four times that of any other month. The reason: Valentine's Day. And on Valentine's Day, the price of a bunch of roses doubles.

The demand-supply model explains these facts. The figure shows the supply curve of roses and two demand curves. The blue demand curve is the demand for roses in a normal month. This demand curve intersects the supply curve at an equilibrium price of $40 a bunch and an equilibrium quantity of 6 million bunches.

In February, the demand curve shifts rightward to the red curve. The February demand curve for roses intersects the supply curve at an equilibrium price of $80 a bunch and an equilibrium quantity of 24 million bunches.

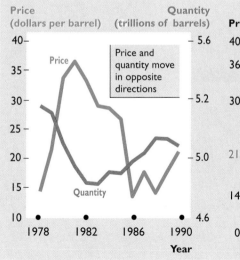

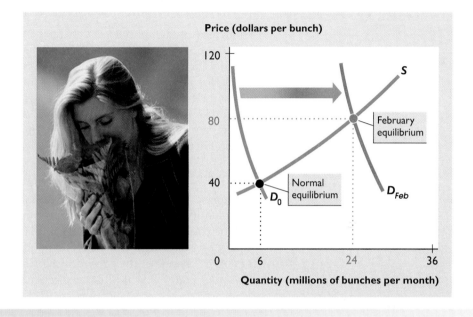

Eye On The PAST

Changes in the Supply of Oil

Between 1978 and 1981, the price of oil rocketed from $14 a barrel to $36 a barrel. Then, through the 1980s, the price fell. In 1990, the price stood at $21 a barrel. The quantity of oil consumed fluctuated in the direction opposite to these price changes.

Over this period, rising income increased demand. But more fuel-efficient cars, airplanes, and furnaces offset this increase, and the demand for oil remained constant. Supply decreased from 1978 through 1981, and this decrease raised the equilibrium price and decreased the quantity. Supply increased through the 1980s, which lowered the equilibrium price and increased the quantity.

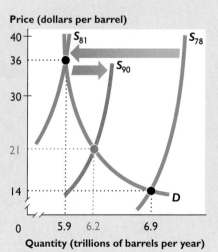

SOURCE: Energy Information Administration.

■ Changes in Both Demand and Supply

Often, in real markets, events occur that change *both* demand and supply. To study the effects of such changes on price and quantity, we combine the effects of a change in demand and a change in supply.

Increase in Demand and Increase in Supply

An increase in demand increases the quantity, and an increase in supply increases the quantity. So when demand and supply increase together, the equilibrium quantity increases. But an increase in demand raises the price, and an increase in supply lowers the price. So when demand and supply increase together, the direction of the change in the equilibrium price is ambiguous. It might rise, fall, or stay the same. Figure 4.9(a) illustrates an increase in both demand and supply in the market for personal computers. In this example, the price falls because the increase in supply is greater than the increase in demand.

Decrease in Demand and Decrease in Supply

A decrease in demand decreases the quantity, and a decrease in supply decreases the quantity. So when demand and supply decrease together, the equilibrium quantity decreases. But a decrease in demand lowers the price, and a decrease in supply raises the price. So when demand and supply decrease together, the direction of the change in the equilibrium price is ambiguous. It might rise, fall, or stay the same. Figure 4.9(b) illustrates a decrease in both demand and supply in the

---

■ FIGURE 4.9
Demand and Supply Change in the Same Direction

*e*Foundations **4.3**

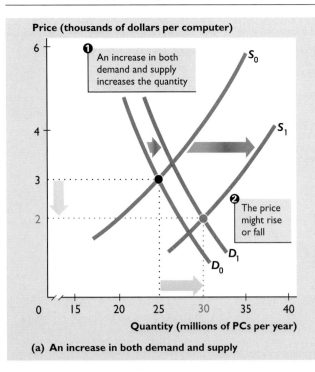

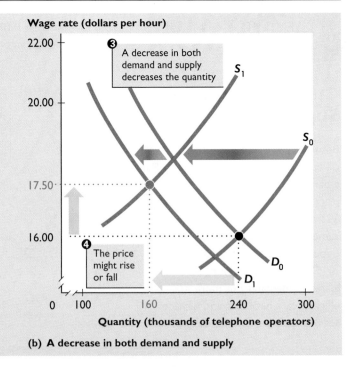

(a) An increase in both demand and supply

(b) A decrease in both demand and supply

market for telephone operators in Canada over the past 20 years. In this example, the price (the telephone operator's wage rate) rises because the decrease in supply exceeds the decrease in demand.

Increase in Demand and Decrease in Supply

When demand increases, the price rises. When supply decreases, the price rises. So when demand increases at the same time as supply decreases, the equilibrium price rises. But an increase in demand increases the quantity, and a decrease in supply decreases the quantity. So when demand increases at the same time as supply decreases, the equilibrium quantity can increase, decrease, or remain the same. Figure 4.10(a) illustrates this case in the market for Yahoo! stock. In this example, the quantity remains the same because the increase in demand equals the decrease in supply.

Decrease in Demand and Increase in Supply

When demand decreases, the price falls. When supply increases, the price falls. So when demand decreases at the same time as supply increases, the equilibrium price falls. But a decrease in demand decreases the quantity, and an increase in supply increases the quantity. So when demand decreases at the same time as supply increases, the equilibrium quantity can increase, decrease, or remain the same. Figure 4.10(b) illustrates this case in the market for the currency of Thailand, called the baht, in 1997. In this example, the quantity remains the same because the decrease in demand equals the increase in supply.

ECONOMICS *in the* **NEWS**

July 7, 2001

Price of Coffee Seems to be Bottomless

World coffee prices…dipped again to just under 56 U.S. cents a pound…

…global coffee production is expected to reach record levels this year, thanks largely to Vietnam, which has vaulted past Colombia and become the second-biggest coffee producing nation.

NATIONAL POST

Draw graphs showing the world coffee market before and after Vietnam's entry into the market.

*e*Foundations **4.3**

FIGURE 4.10
Demand and Supply Change in Opposite Directions

*e*Foundations **4.3**

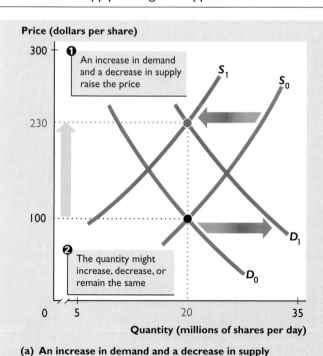

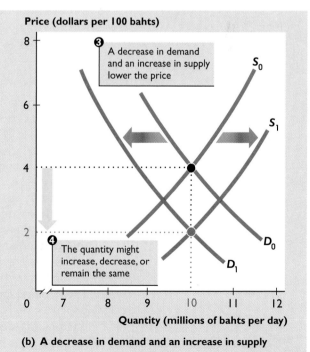

(a) An increase in demand and a decrease in supply

(b) A decrease in demand and an increase in supply

Study Guide pp. 63–66

e/Foundations 4.3

3 Explain how demand and supply determine price and quantity in a market and explain the effects of changes in demand and supply.

Practice Problem 4.3

The table shows the demand and supply schedules for milk:

Price (dollars per carton)	Quantity demanded	Quantity supplied
	(cartons per day)	
1.00	200	110
1.25	175	130
1.50	150	150
1.75	125	170
2.00	100	190

a. What is the market equilibrium in the milk market?
b. Describe the situation in the milk market if the price is $1.75 a carton.
c. If the price is $1.75 a carton, explain how the market reaches equilibrium.
d. A drought decreases the quantity supplied by 45 cartons a day at each price. What is the new equilibrium and how does the market adjust to it?
e. Milk becomes more popular, and the quantity demanded increases by 5 cartons a day at each price. Improved feeds for dairy cows increase the quantity of milk supplied by 50 cartons a day at each price. If there is no drought, what is the new equilibrium and how does the market adjust to it?

Exercise 4.3

The table shows the demand and supply schedules for CDs:

Price (dollars per CD)	Quantity demanded	Quantity supplied
	(CDs per day)	
5.00	300	100
6.00	250	150
7.00	200	200
8.00	150	250
9.00	100	300

a. What is the market equilibrium?
b. If the price of a CD is $6.00, describe the situation in the CD market. Explain how market equilibrium is restored.
c. A rise in incomes increases the quantity of CDs demanded by 100 a day at each price. What is the new equilibrium and how does the market adjust?
d. A rise in the number of recording studios increases the quantity of CDs supplied by 75 a day at each price. People download more music from the Internet and the quantity demanded of CDs decreases by 25 a day at each price. With no change in incomes, what is the new equilibrium and how does the market adjust?

FIGURE 1

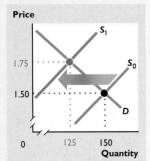

Solution to Practice Problem 4.3

a. Figure 1 shows the market equilibrium at $1.50 a carton and 150 cartons a day.
b. At $1.75 a carton, the quantity demanded (125 cartons) is less than the quantity supplied (170 cartons), so there is a surplus of 45 cartons a day.
c. At $1.75 a carton, there is a surplus of milk. As suppliers lower the price, the quantity demanded increases, the quantity supplied decreases, and the surplus decreases. The price falls until the surplus disappears at $1.50 a carton.
d. The supply curve *shifts leftward* by 45 cartons a day at each price. At $1.50, the quantity demanded (150 cartons) exceeds the quantity supplied (105 cartons) and there is a shortage of milk. As suppliers raise the price, the quantity demanded decreases, the quantity supplied increases, and the shortage decreases. The price rises to $1.75 a carton, and the quantity decreases to 125 cartons a day (Figure 1).
e. The demand curve *shifts rightward* by 5 cartons a day at each price. The supply curve *shifts rightward* by 50 cartons a day at each price. At $1.50 a carton, the quantity demanded (155 cartons) is less than the quantity supplied (200 cartons). Suppliers lower the price. The price falls to $1.25 a carton, and the quantity increases to 180 cartons a day (Figure 2).

FIGURE 2

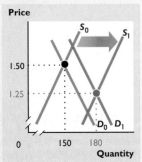

4.4 PRICE RIGIDITIES

You've seen that price adjustments bring market equilibrium. But suppose that for some reason, the price in a market does not adjust. What happens then? The answer depends on why the price doesn't adjust. There are three broad reasons:

- Price ceiling
- Price floor
- Sticky price

■ Price Ceiling

A **price ceiling** is the highest price at which it is legal to trade a particular good, service, or factor of production. An example of a price ceiling is a **rent ceiling** on houses and apartments—a law that makes it illegal for landlords to charge a rent that exceeds a set limit. How does a rent ceiling affect the rental market for apartments?

Landlords decide the quantity of apartments to supply, and the higher the rent, the greater is the quantity of apartments supplied. Families decide the quantity of apartments to demand, and the lower the rent, the greater is the quantity of apartments demanded. The rent adjusts to make the quantity of apartments demanded equal to the quantity supplied.

Figure 4.11 illustrates a rental apartment market. In this market, the demand for apartments curve is D and the supply of apartments curve is S. Market equilibrium occurs at a rent of $550 a month with 4,000 apartments rented.

Suppose a government thinks that no one should have to pay a rent as high as $550 a month and decides it wants to lower the rent. Can the government help families by passing a rent ceiling law?

Price ceiling
The highest price at which it is legal to trade a particular good, service, or factor of production.

Rent ceiling
A law that makes it illegal for landlords to charge a rent that exceeds a set limit—an example of a price ceiling.

■ **FIGURE 4.11**
A Rental Apartment Market

e/**Foundations 4.4**

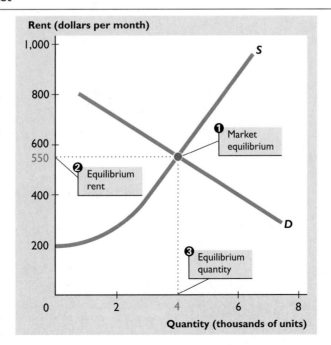

❶ Market equilibrium is determined by the demand for apartments and the supply of apartments for rent.

❷ The equilibrium rent is $550 a month.

❸ At the equilibrium rent, the equilibrium quantity of apartments rented is 4,000.

The effect of a rent ceiling depends on whether it is imposed at a level above or below the equilibrium rent. In Figure 4.11, the equilibrium rent is $550 a month. With a rent ceiling above $550 a month, nothing would change. The reason is that people are already paying $550 a month, and because this rent is below the rent ceiling, the rent paid doesn't change.

But a rent ceiling set *below* the equilibrium rent has powerful effects on the market. The reason is that it attempts to prevent the rent rising high enough to regulate the quantities demanded and supplied. The law and the market are in conflict, and one (or both) of them must yield.

Figure 4.12 shows one effect of a rent ceiling that is set below the equilibrium rent. The rent ceiling is $400 a month. We've shaded the area above the rent ceiling because a rent in this region is illegal. At a rent of $400 a month, the quantity of apartments supplied is 3,000 and the quantity demanded is 6,000. So there is a shortage of 3,000 apartments.

The first effect, then, of a rent ceiling is a housing shortage. People are seeking a larger amount of housing than builders and owners of existing buildings have an incentive to make available.

But the story does not end here. Somehow the 3,000 apartments that owners are willing to make available must be allocated among people who are seeking 6,000 units. Blocking rent adjustments that bring the quantity of apartments demanded into equality with the quantity supplied doesn't end scarcity. So when the law prevents the rent from adjusting and blocks the price mechanism from allocating scarce housing, some other allocation mechanism must be used. But the mechanisms that get used do not usually achieve an outcome that improves on a higher rent. First-come-first-served is one allocation mechanism; discrimination can be another.

FIGURE 4.12
A Rent Ceiling Creates a Shortage of Apartments

e/**Foundations 4.4**

A rent ceiling is imposed below the equilibrium rent. In this example, the rent ceiling is $400 a month.

❶ The quantity of apartments supplied decreases to 3,000.

❷ The quantity of apartments demanded increases to 6,000.

❸ A housing shortage of 3,000 apartments arises.

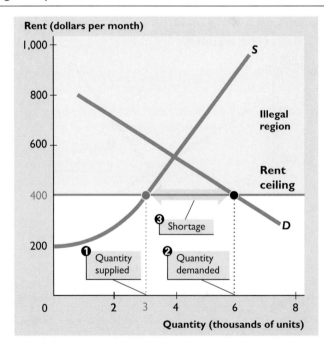

■ Price Floor

A **price floor** is the lowest price at which it is legal to trade a particular good, service, or factor of production. An example of a price floor is the **minimum wage law**, which is a government regulation that makes hiring labour for less than a specified wage illegal. Firms are free to pay a wage rate that exceeds the minimum wage but may not pay less than the minimum. How does the minimum wage affect the labour market?

Firms hire labour, so they decide how much labour to demand. The lower the wage rate, the greater is the quantity of labour that firms demand. Households decide how much labour to supply. The higher the wage rate, the greater is the quantity of labour households are willing to supply. The wage rate adjusts to make the quantity of labour demanded equal to the quantity supplied.

Figure 4.13 shows the market for fast-food servers in Vancouver. In this market, the demand for labour curve is D and the supply of labour curve is S. Equilibrium occurs at a wage rate of $5 an hour with 5,000 people employed as servers.

Suppose that the government thinks that no one should have to work for a wage rate as low as $5 an hour and decides that it wants to increase the wage rate. Can the government improve conditions for these workers by passing a minimum wage law?

The effect of a price floor depends on whether it is set below or above the equilibrium price. In Figure 4.13, the equilibrium wage rate is $5 an hour, and at this wage rate, firms hire 5,000 workers. If the government introduced a minimum wage below $5 an hour, nothing would change. The reason is that firms are already paying $5 an hour, and because this wage exceeds the minimum wage, the wage rate paid doesn't change. And firms continue to hire 5,000 workers.

Price floor
The lowest price at which it is legal to trade a particular good, service, or factor of production.

Minimum wage law
A government regulation that makes hiring labour for less than a specified wage illegal—an example of a price floor.

■ FIGURE 4.13
A Market for Fast-Food Servers

*e/*Foundations **4.4**

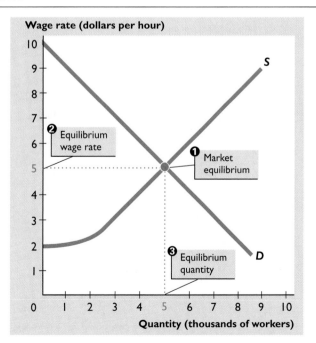

❶ Market equilibrium is determined by the demand for and the supply of fast-food servers.

❷ The equilibrium wage rate is $5 an hour.

❸ At the equilibrium wage rate, the equilibrium quantity of fast-food servers is 5,000.

But the aim of a minimum wage is to boost the incomes of low-wage earners. So the minimum wage will exceed the equilibrium wage of the lowest-paid labour.

Suppose that the government introduces a minimum wage of $7 an hour. Figure 4.14 shows the effects of this law. Wage rates below $7 an hour are illegal, so we've shaded the illegal region below the minimum wage. Firms and workers are no longer permitted to operate at the equilibrium point in this market because it is in the illegal region. Market forces and political forces are in conflict.

The government can set a minimum wage. But it can't tell employers how many workers to hire. If firms must pay $7 an hour for labour, they will hire only 3,000 workers. At the equilibrium wage rate of $5 an hour, they hired 5,000 workers. So when the minimum wage is introduced, firms fire 2,000 workers.

But at a wage rate of $7 an hour, another 2,000 people who didn't want to work for $5 an hour now try to find work as servers, so at $7 an hour, the quantity supplied is 7,000 workers. With 2,000 workers fired and another 2,000 looking for work at the higher wage rate, 4,000 people who would like to work as servers are unemployed.

Somehow, the 3,000 jobs available must be allocated among the 7,000 people who are available for and willing to work. How is this allocation achieved? The answer is the same as in the housing market: first-come-first-served and discrimination replace price as the means of allocating resources. Also, workers might illegally accept wages below the minimum wage.

■ Sticky Price

In most markets, a law does not restrict the price. But in some markets, the buyer and seller agree on a price for a fixed period, and in others, the seller sets a price

---

■ FIGURE 4.14

A Minimum Wage Creates Unemployment

e/**Foundations 4.4**

A minimum wage is introduced above the equilibrium wage rate. In this example, the minimum wage rate is $7 an hour.

❶ The quantity of labour demanded decreases to 3,000.

❷ The quantity of labour supplied increases to 7,000.

❸ 4,000 people are unemployed.

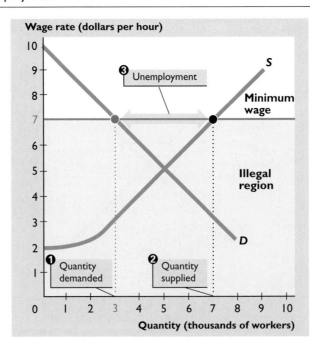

that changes infrequently. For example, in some labour markets, firms enter into long-term contracts with labour unions that fix wage rates for at least one year and often for as many as three years. Borrowers and lenders often agree on an interest rate that is fixed for the term of a loan, which could be for as long as 20 years. And many commodities such as sugar, oil, and coal are traded on long-term contracts.

In these markets, the price adjustment process that is described in Figure 4.6 on p. 90 is slowed down. Prices do adjust, but not quickly enough to avoid shortages or surpluses.

If demand increases or if supply decreases after a price (or wage) contract is struck, there is a shortage. The quantity supplied is less than the quantity demanded. So the quantity supplied determines the quantity that is actually traded, and buyers' plans are frustrated. The price gradually rises as contracts come up for renewal, but in the intervening period, a shortage persists.

Similarly, if demand decreases or if supply increases after a price (or wage) contract is struck, there is a surplus. The quantity demanded is less than the quantity supplied. So the quantity demanded determines the quantity that is actually traded, and sellers' plans are frustrated. In the labour market, the sellers are workers, and some of them become unemployed. The price (or wage rate) gradually falls as contracts come up for renewal, but in the intervening period, a surplus and above-normal unemployment persist.

Eye On The CANADIAN ECONOMY

The Effects of a Minimum Wage Law

A law that raises the minimum wage above the market equilibrium wage has been described as creating a lottery. The winners are workers whose wages rise and the losers are unemployed workers who can't find jobs at the higher wage.

Advocates of the minimum wage assert that it benefits low-wage workers by ending their exploitation by employers.

The employers of low-paid workers (such as fast-food producers) say that a minimum wage backfires because it limits employment opportunities for low-paid workers.

Who is correct in this debate? How much unemployment does a minimum wage law create?

Economists have estimated that a 10 percent rise in the minimum wage rate decreases teenager employment by between 1 percent and 3 percent.

Many economists believe that the effects of the minimum wage on employment are more subtle than simply layoffs of employees shortly after the minimum wage rate is increased. They believe that few employers quickly lay off employees because the minimum wage rate has increased; but as their profits are

squeezed by higher labour costs, employers do not replace all of their employees who leave. So unemployment increases not because of layoffs but because of this "non-hiring effect."

This effect on hiring explains why the minimum wage rate particularly affects the employment of teenagers, many of whom are seeking work for the first time. The other group that is most affected is females with less education, largely because so many are employed in the food service industry.

Finally, looking only at employment misses the effect of the minimum wage on the supply of labour. A higher minimum wage rate also increases the number of people who drop out of high school to look for work.

Study Guide pp. 66–69

*e*Foundations 4.4

4 Explain how price ceilings, price floors, and sticky prices cause shortages, surpluses, and unemployment.

Practice Problems 4.4

FIGURE 1

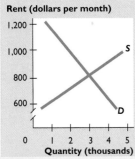

1. Figure 1 shows the rental market for apartments in a Winnipeg suburb:
   a. What is the rent in this suburb and how many apartments are rented?
   b. If the city of Winnipeg imposes a rent ceiling of $900 a month, what is the rent in this suburb and how many apartments are rented?
   c. If the city of Winnipeg imposes a rent ceiling of $600 a month, what is the rent in this suburb and how many apartments are rented?

2. Figure 2 shows the market for tomato pickers in southern Ontario.
   a. What is the equilibrium wage rate of tomato pickers and what is the equilibrium quantity of tomato pickers employed?
   b. If Ontario introduces a minimum wage for tomato pickers of $4 an hour, how many tomato pickers are employed and how many are unemployed?
   c. If Ontario introduces a minimum wage for tomato pickers of $8 an hour, how many tomato pickers are employed and how many are unemployed?

FIGURE 2

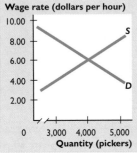

Exercises 4.4

Figure 3 shows a market for private math tutors organized by the Students' Union at a community college.
   a. What is the wage rate that math tutors earn and how many are employed?
   b. If the Students' Union sets the minimum wage for private math tutors at $8 an hour, how many tutors are employed and what wage rate do they earn?
   c. If the Students' Union sets the minimum wage for private tutors at $15 an hour, how many tutors are employed and what wage rate do they earn?
   d. At which minimum wage ($8 an hour or $15 an hour) will some math tutors be unemployed? How many will be unemployed?

FIGURE 3

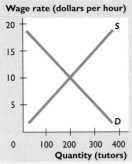

Solutions to Practice Problems 4.4

1a. Equilibrium rent is $800 a month, and 3,000 apartments are rented (Figure 4).
1b. A rent ceiling of $900 a month is above the equilibrium rent, so the outcome is the market equilibrium rent of $800 a month with 3,000 apartments rented.
1c. With a rent ceiling of $600 a month, 1,000 apartments are rented (on the supply curve) and the rent is $600 a month (the rent ceiling) (Figure 4).
2a. Equilibrium wage is $6 an hour, and 4,000 pickers are employed (Figure 5).
2b. The minimum wage of $4 an hour is below the equilibrium wage rate, so 4,000 tomato pickers are employed and none are unemployed.
2c. The minimum wage of $8 an hour is above the equilibrium wage rate, so 3,000 tomato pickers are employed (on the demand curve), and 5,000 people would like to work as tomato pickers for $8 an hour (on the supply curve), so 2,000 are unemployed (Figure 5).

FIGURE 4

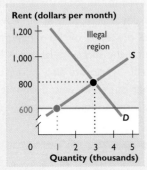

FIGURE 5

CHAPTER CHECKPOINT

Key Points

1 **Distinguish between quantity demanded and demand and explain what determines demand.**

- Other things remaining the same, the quantity demanded increases as the price falls and decreases as the price rises—the law of demand.
- Changes in the price of a related good, income, expectation about future prices and income, the number of buyers, and preferences change demand.

2 **Distinguish between quantity supplied and supply and explain what determines supply.**

- Other things remaining the same, the quantity supplied increases as the price rises and decreases as the price falls—the law of supply.
- Changes in the price of a related good, prices of resources and other inputs, expectation about future prices and profits, number of sellers, and productivity change supply.

3 **Explain how demand and supply determine price and quantity in a market and explain the effects of changes in demand and supply.**

- The price adjusts to maintain market equilibrium—to keep the quantity demanded equal to the quantity supplied. A surplus brings a fall in the price; a shortage brings a rise in the price.
- An increase in demand increases both the price and the quantity; a decrease in demand decreases both the price and the quantity. An increase in supply increases the quantity but decreases the price; a decrease in supply decreases the quantity but increases the price.

4 **Explain how price ceilings, price floors, and sticky prices cause shortages, surpluses, and unemployment.**

- A price ceiling below the equilibrium price creates a shortage.
- A price floor above the equilibrium price creates a surplus (unemployment in the labour market).
- Sticky prices create temporary shortages and surpluses (unemployment in the labour market).

Key Terms

Exercises

1. Use the link on your Foundations Web site to obtain information about the market for bottled water.
   a. How many producers are there? Do you think a single producer could influence the average price?
   b. Use the law of market forces and demand-supply diagrams to explain the changes in the price and quantity of bottled water in the past few years.
   c. Explain the effects of the bottled-water market on the market for soft drinks.
   d. Explain the effects of the spread of fitness centres on the market for bottled water.

2. What is the effect on the price and quantity of orange juice if:
   a. The price of apple juice decreases?
   b. The price of apple juice decreases and the wage rate paid to orange grove workers increases?
   c. Orange juice becomes more popular and a cheaper machine for picking oranges is used?
   d. Joggers switch from bottled water to orange juice?

3. Gasoline producers invent a new fuel that is cheaper and cleaner than gasoline. All new cars use the new fuel. Use a demand-supply diagram to explain the effect of this new fuel on:
   a. The price of gasoline and the quantity of gasoline bought.
   b. The price of a used car.

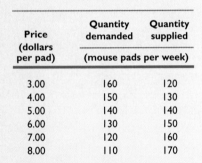

Price (dollars per pad)	Quantity demanded	Quantity supplied
	(mouse pads per week)	
3.00	160	120
4.00	150	130
5.00	140	140
6.00	130	150
7.00	120	160
8.00	110	170

4. The table shows the demand and supply schedules for mouse pads.
   a. What is the market equilibrium?
   b. If the price of a mouse pad is $7.00, describe the situation in the market. Explain how the market equilibrium is restored.
   c. Explain what happens to the market equilibrium and how the market adjusts to its new equilibrium if a fall in the price of a computer changes the quantity demanded of mouse pads by 20 a week at each price.
   d. Explain what happens to the initial market equilibrium and how the market adjusts if new voice-recognition software changes the quantity demanded by 10 mouse pads a week at each price and at the same time the cost of producing a mouse pad falls and changes the quantity supplied by 30 a week at each price.

5. "As more people buy computers, the demand for Internet service will increase and the price of Internet service will decrease. The decrease in the price of Internet service will decrease the supply of Internet service." Is this statement true or false? Explain your answer.

6. Concerned about the political fallout from rising gas prices, the government decides to impose a ceiling on the price of gasoline of $0.50 a litre. Explain how the market for gasoline would react to this price ceiling if:
   a. The oil-producing nations increased production and drove the equilibrium price of gasoline to $0.45 a litre.
   b. A global shortage of oil sent the equilibrium price of gasoline to $0.90 a litre.

7. Bakers earn $10 an hour, gas pump attendants earn $4 an hour, and copy shop workers earn $5 an hour. If the government introduces a minimum wage of $5 an hour, explain how the markets for bakers, gas pump attendants, and copy shop workers will respond initially to the minimum wage.

Monitoring the Macroeconomy

Part 2

Chapter
5

GDP and the Standard of Living

CHAPTER CHECKLIST

When you have completed your study of this chapter, you will be able to:

1 Define **GDP** and explain why the value of production, income, and expenditure are the same for an economy.

2 Describe how economic statisticians measure **GDP** in Canada.

3 Distinguish between nominal **GDP** and real **GDP** and define the **GDP** deflator.

4 Explain and describe the limitations of real **GDP** as a measure of the standard of living.

You've seen that equilibrium quantities and prices in the markets for goods, services, and factors of production determine *what, how,* and *for whom* goods and services are produced. What and for whom goods and services are produced influence the standard of living, a central concern of macroeconomics.

A focus on the standard of living directs our attention to the value of *total* production rather than the production of each individual good or service. You will discover that several different factors contribute to the standard of living, but one indicator dominates the others. It is called gross domestic product, or GDP. In this chapter, you will find out how economic statisticians measure GDP. You will also learn about other indicators of the standard of living as well as the scope and limitations of GDP as a measure of the standard of living.

5.1 GDP, INCOME, AND EXPENDITURE

How does your standard of living compare with that of your parents when they were your age? Who is better off: you or a college student in Beijing, China?

We defined the *standard of living* in Chapter 1 (p. 6) as the level of consumption of goods and services that people enjoy, *on the average*, measured by average income per person. So to answer the questions we've just posed, you might try to discover who has the higher income: you today or your parents in the 1970s, and you or a college student in China.

But it is the quantities of goods and services consumed that determine how well off people are. To consume goods and services, they must be produced. So another way to answer the questions posed is to discover who produces the greater total value of goods and services. Do we produce more per person today than our parents' generation did in the 1970s, and do we produce more per person than the people of China produce? To answer these questions, we need to measure total production.

■ GDP Defined

Gross domestic product (GDP)
The market value of all the final goods and services produced within a country in a given time period.

We measure total production as **gross domestic product,** or **GDP,** which is the market value of all the final goods and services produced within a country in a given time period. This definition has four parts that we'll examine in turn.

Value Produced

To measure total production, we must add together the production of apples and oranges, computers and popcorn. Just counting the items doesn't get us very far. Which is the greater total production: 100 apples and 50 oranges or 50 apples and 100 oranges?

GDP answers this question by valuing items at their *market value*—at the prices at which each item is traded in markets. If the price of an apple is 10 cents and the price of an orange is 20 cents, the market value of 100 apples plus 50 oranges is $20 and the market value of 50 apples and 100 oranges is $25. So by using market prices to value production, we can add apples and oranges.

What Produced

Final good or service
A good or service that is produced for its final user and not as a component of another good or service.

Intermediate good or service
A good or service that is produced by one firm, bought by another firm, and used as a component of a final good or service.

To calculate GDP, we value *all the final goods and services.* A **final good or service** is a good or service that is produced for its final user and not as a component of another good or service. It contrasts with an **intermediate good or service,** which is a good or service that is produced by one firm, bought by another firm, and used as a component of a final good or service. For example, a Ford SUV is a final good, but the Goodyear tires on the SUV are intermediate goods.

GDP aims to be a full count of the value of everything that is produced. In practice, with one exception, GDP includes only items that are bought and sold in markets. It does not include the market value of goods and services that people produce for their own use. For example, if you wash your own car, the value of the car wash is not counted as part of GDP but if you buy a car wash, your expenditure is counted as part of GDP. The exception is the market value of homes that people own. GDP puts a rental value on such homes and pretends that their owners rent them to themselves.

Where Produced

Only goods and services that are produced *within a country* count as part of that country's GDP. Bata Shoes, a Canadian firm, produces outdoor shoes in India, and the market value of those shoes is part of India's GDP, not part of Canada's GDP. Honda, a Japanese firm, produces cars in Alliston, Ontario, and the market value of this production is part of Canada's GDP, not part of Japan's GDP.

When Produced

GDP measures the value of production *during a given time period*. This time period is either a quarter of a year—called the quarterly GDP data—or a year—called the annual GDP data. The Bank of Canada and others use the quarterly GDP data to keep track of the short-term evolution of the economy, and economists use the annual GDP data to examine long-term trends.

GDP measures not only the value of total production but also total income and total expenditure. The circular flow model that you studied in Chapter 2 explains why.

■ Circular Flows in the Canadian Economy

Four groups buy the final goods and services produced: households, firms, governments, and the rest of the world. Four types of expenditure correspond to these groups:

- Consumption expenditure
- Investment
- Government expenditure on goods and services
- Net exports of goods and services

Consumption Expenditure

Consumption expenditure is the expenditure by households on consumption goods and services. It includes expenditures on food and clothing, popcorn and movies, and dental and dry cleaning services. Consumption expenditure also includes house and apartment rents, including the rental value of owner-occupied housing.

Consumption expenditure
The expenditure by households on consumption goods and services.

Investment

Investment is the purchase of new *capital goods* (tools, instruments, machines, buildings and other constructions) and additions to inventories. Some firms produce capital goods, and other firms buy them. For example, Nortel produces telecommunications equipment and banks buy some of it. Bombardier produces airplanes and Air Canada buys some of them.

Some of a firm's output might remain unsold at the end of a year. For example, if GM produces 400,000 cars and sells 390,000 of them, the other 10,000 cars remain unsold. In this case, GM's inventory of cars increases by 10,000. When a firm adds unsold output to inventory, we count those items as part of investment.

It is important to note that investment does *not* include the purchase of stocks and bonds. In macroeconomics, we reserve the term "investment" for the purchase of new capital goods and the additions to inventories.

Investment
The purchase of new *capital goods* (tools, instruments, machines, buildings, and other constructions) and additions to inventories.

Government Expenditure on Goods and Services

Government expenditure on goods and services
The expenditure by all levels of governments on goods and services.

Government expenditure on goods and services is the expenditure by all levels of governments on goods and services. You saw in Chapter 2 (pp. 44–47) that governments buy a wide range of goods and services. For example, the federal government buys helicopters and submarines, computers, and Internet service; provincial governments buy education and health care; municipal governments buy buses, fire engines, and garbage collection services.

Net Exports of Goods and Services

Net exports of goods and services
The value of exports of goods and services minus the value of imports of goods and services.

Exports of goods and services
Items that firms in Canada sell to the rest of the world.

Imports of goods and services
Items that households, firms, and governments in Canada buy from the rest of the world.

Net exports of goods and services are the value of exports of goods and services minus the value of imports of goods and services. **Exports of goods and services** are items that firms in Canada produce and sell to the rest of the world. **Imports of goods and services** are items that households, firms, and governments in Canada buy from the rest of the world. Imports are produced in other countries, so expenditure on imports is not an expenditure on Canadian-produced goods and services. Net exports might be positive (exports exceed imports) or negative (imports exceed exports).

Total Expenditure

Total expenditure on goods and services produced in Canada is the sum of the four items that you've just examined. We call consumption expenditure C, investment I, government expenditure on goods and services G, and net exports of goods and services NX. Using these symbols, total expenditure is:

$$\text{Total expenditure} = C + I + G + NX.$$

Total expenditure is the total amount received by producers of final goods and services.

Income

Labour earns wages, capital earns interest, land earns rent, and entrepreneurship earns profits. Households receive these incomes. A part of total income, called *undistributed profit*, is a combination of interest and profit that firms do not pay to the households that own them. But from an economic viewpoint, undistributed profit is income paid to households and then loaned to firms.

■ Expenditure Equals Income

Figure 5.1 shows the circular flows of expenditure and income that we've just described. The figure is based on Figures 2.4 and 2.5 (on p. 43 and p. 45), but it includes some more details and additional flows.

We call total income Y and show it by the blue flow from firms to households.

When households receive their incomes, they pay some in taxes and save some. Some households receive benefits from government. *Net taxes* equal taxes paid minus benefits received and are the green flow from households to government labelled NT. Saving flows from households to financial markets and is the green flow labelled S. These two green flows are not expenditures on goods and services. They are just flows of money.

The red flows show the four expenditure flows described above: consumption expenditure from households to firms, government expenditure from government to firms, and net exports from the rest of world to firms. Investment flows from financial markets, where firms borrow, to the firms that produce capital goods.

Because firms pay out everything they receive as incomes to the factors of production, total expenditure equals total income. That is:

$$Y = C + I + G + NX.$$

From the viewpoint of firms, the value of production is the cost of production, which equals income. From the viewpoint of purchasers of goods and services, the value of production is the cost of buying it, which equals expenditure. So:

The value of production equals income equals expenditure.

The circular flow and the equality of income and expenditure provide two approaches to measuring GDP that we'll study in the next section.

FIGURE 5.1

The Circular Flow of Income and Expenditure   *e*Foundations **5.1**

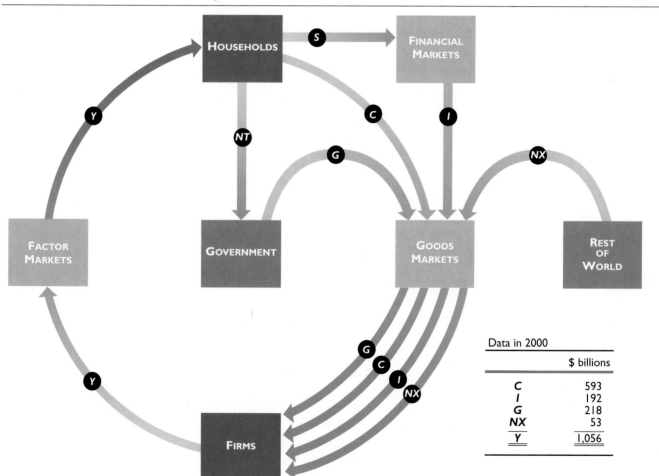

Data in 2000	
	$ billions
C	593
I	192
G	218
NX	53
Y	1,056

In the circular flow, the blue flow (Y) is income and the red flows (C, I, G, and NX) are expenditures on goods and services. The green flows are flows of money: Households pay net taxes (NT) to the government and save some of their income (S). Firms borrow in financial markets to buy goods (I) from other firms. Expenditure equals income and equals the value of production.

CHECKPOINT 5.1

Study Guide pp. 75–77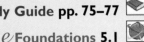

𝑒 Foundations 5.1

1 **Define GDP and explain why the value of production, income, and expenditure are the same for an economy.**

Practice Problems 5.1

1. Classify each of the following items as a final good or service or an intermediate good or service:
   a. Banking services bought by a student.
   b. New cars bought by Hertz, the car rental firm.
   c. Newsprint bought by *The Globe and Mail* from Abitibi Paper.
   d. Ice cream bought by a diner and used to produce sundaes.

2. During 2001 on Lotus Island, net taxes were $10 billion; consumption expenditure was $30 billion; government expenditure was $12 billion; investment was $15 billion; and net exports were $3 billion. Calculate:
   a. Total expenditure.
   b. Total income.
   c. GDP.

Exercises 5.1

1. Classify each of the following items as a final good or service, an intermediate good or service, or neither:
   a. The fertilizer bought by a Saskatchewan wheat farmer.
   b. The *Maclean's* magazine you bought today.
   c. The PlayStation 2 that you bought on eBay.
   d. The aircraft fuel bought by Air Canada.

2. During 2002 on Lotus Island, households spent $60 million of their income on goods and services, saved $20 million, and paid the rest of their income in net taxes; government expenditure was $15 million; investment was $25 million; and net exports were zero. Calculate:
   a. Total expenditure.
   b. Net taxes.
   c. Total income.
   d. GDP.

Solutions to Practice Problems 5.1

1a. A final service—The student is the final user.
1b. Final goods—The new cars that Hertz buys are additions to its capital and as such they are investment.
1c. An intermediate good—Newsprint is a component of the newspaper.
1d. An intermediate good—Ice cream is a component of sundaes.

2a. Total expenditure is $60 billion. Total expenditure $= C + I + G + NX$. Inserting the values into the equation, we have:
Total expenditure $= \$(30 + 15 + 12 + 3)$ billion $= \$60$ billion.
2b. Total income = total expenditure = $60 billion.
2c. GDP = total expenditure = $60 billion.

5.2 MEASURING CANADA'S GDP

Canada's GDP is the market value of all the final goods and services produced within Canada during a year. In 2000, Canada's GDP exceeded the $1 trillion mark for the first time ever. Statistics Canada measures GDP, using two different approaches:

- Expenditure approach
- Income approach

■ Expenditure Approach

Table 5.1 shows the expenditure approach. It measures GDP by using data on consumption expenditure, investment, government expenditure, and net exports. This approach is like attaching a meter to the circular flow diagram on all the flows running through the markets for goods and services to firms and measuring the magnitudes of those flows.

Using the expenditure approach, GDP is the sum of consumption expenditure (C), investment (I), government expenditure on goods and services, (G), and net exports of goods and services (NX).

The table shows the amount of each type of expenditure in 2000. GDP measured by the expenditure approach was $1,056 billion in 2000.

Net exports were positive in 2000 because exports exceeded imports. Exports were $479 billion and imports were $426 billion, so net exports—exports minus imports—were +$53 billion, as shown in the table.

Table 5.1 also shows the relative magnitudes of the expenditures. Consumption expenditure makes up more than half of total expenditure; investment and government expenditure are about the same percentage of total expenditure; and net exports is the smallest.

In 2000, consumption expenditure was 56 percent, investment was 18 percent, government expenditure was 21 percent, and net exports were 5 percent.

■ **TABLE 5.1**
GDP: The Expenditure Approach

*e*Foundations **5.2**

Item	Symbol	Amount in 2000 (billions of dollars)	Percentage of GDP
Consumption expenditure	C	593	56
Investment	I	192	18
Government expenditure	G	218	21
Net exports	NX	53	5
GDP	Y	1,056	100

The expenditure approach measures GDP by adding together consumption expenditures (C), investment (I), government expenditure (G), and net exports (NX). In 2000, GDP measured by the expenditure approach was $1,056 billion.

SOURCE: Statistics Canada.

Expenditures Not in GDP

Total expenditure (and GDP) does not include all the things that people and businesses buy. GDP is the value of *final goods and services*, so spending that is *not* on final goods and services is not part of GDP. Spending on intermediate goods and services is not part of GDP, although it is not always obvious whether an item is an intermediate good or a final good; see Eye on the Canadian Economy. Also, we do not count as part of GDP spending on:

- Used goods
- Financial assets

Used Goods   Expenditure on used goods is not part of GDP because these goods were part of GDP in the period in which they were produced and during which time they were new goods. For example, a 1999 automobile was part of GDP in 1999. If the car is traded on the used car market in 2001, the amount paid for the car is not part of GDP in 2001 because the car was not produced in 2001.

Financial Assets   When households buy financial assets such as bonds and stocks, they are making loans, not buying goods and services. The expenditure on newly produced capital goods is part of GDP, but the purchase of financial assets is not.

Is a Computer Program an Intermediate Good or a Final Good?

When Air Canada buys a new reservations software package, is that like General Motors buying tires? If it is, then software is an *intermediate good* and it is not counted as part of GDP. Airline ticket sales, like GM cars, are part of GDP, but the intermediate goods that are used to produce air transportation or cars are not part of GDP.

Or when Air Canada buys new software, is that like General Motors buying a new assembly-line robot? If it is, then the software is a capital good and its purchase is the purchase of a final good. In this case, the software purchase is an *investment* and it *is* counted as part of GDP.

Until 2001, Statistics Canada treated business expenditure on developing and purchasing software as expenditure on *intermediate goods* and did not count it as part of GDP. But since 2001, Statistics Canada has classified such expenditure as part of *investment*.

As a result of this change, measured GDP will rise more rapidly. Initial projections suggested that GDP might be 0.1 to 0.2 percent higher each year. While this is a small amount in percentage terms, it amounts to $1 billion to $2 billion a year and the effect will accumulate over time. In addition, the change makes

Canada's GDP statistics more comparable to those of other major countries, notably the United States.

This change is a nice example of the ongoing effort by Statistics Canada to keep the GDP measure as accurate as possible.

■ Income Approach

Statistics Canada measures GDP using the income approach by collecting data (from Canada Customs and Revenue Agency and other sources) on the incomes that firms pay households for the services of factors of production they hire—wages for labour, interest for the use of capital, rent for the use of land, and profits for entrepreneurship—and summing those incomes. This approach is like attaching a meter to the circular flow diagram on all the flows of factor incomes from firms to households and measuring the magnitudes of those flows. Let's see how the income approach works.

The national accounts do not separately identify each of the four factor incomes—wages, interest, rent, and profit. Instead, they group the incomes into the following four categories:

- Wages, salaries, and supplementary labour income
- Interest and investment income
- Profits of corporations and government enterprises
- Income from farms and unincorporated businesses

Wages, Salaries, and Supplementary Labour Income

Wages, salaries, and supplementary labour income are the payments for labour services. This category includes all wages and salaries plus fringe benefits paid by employers such as extended health insurance and pension fund contributions.

Interest and Investment Income

Interest income is the total interest earned by households from assets (such as bonds) and loans they have made minus the interest payments they make on their debts (such as credit card debt). Investment income includes rent received by households for the use of their property and other assets, as well as "imputed rent" for owner-occupied housing. (Imputed rent is an estimate of what homeowners would pay to rent the housing they own and use themselves. By including this item in the national income accounts, we measure the total value of housing services, whether they are owned or rented.)

Profits of Corporations and Government Enterprises

The profits of corporations and government enterprises are a combination of interest on capital and profit for entrepreneurship. The profits of corporations include the profits paid out as dividends as well as profits retained by firms—called undistributed profits. Undistributed profits are counted as income because they are like an addition to the income of shareholders. These undistributed profits are equivalent to profits paid out as dividends and then lent back to the corporations that earned them.

Income from Farms and Unincorporated Businesses

The income from farms and unincorporated business is a mixture of wages, interest, rent, and profit. Farmers and the owners of unincorporated businesses earn a wage for their labour, interest for the use of their capital, rent for the use of their land, and profit for their entrepreneurial ability. The national income accounts lump all these incomes into a single category.

■ TABLE 5.2
GDP: The Income Approach

*e/*Foundations **5.2**

The sum of all incomes equals net domestic product at factor cost. GDP equals net domestic product at factor cost plus indirect taxes less subsidies plus capital consumption (depreciation). In 2000, GDP measured by the income approach was $1,056 billion. Wages, salaries, and supplementary labour income was by far the largest part of aggregate income.

Item	Amount in 2000 (billions of dollars)	Percentage of GDP
Wages, salaries, and supplementary labour income	537	50.9
Interest and investment income	54	5.1
Profits of corporations and government enterprises	140	13.2
Income from farms and unincorporated businesses	65	7.9
Net domestic product at factor cost	796	75.4
Indirect taxes *less* subsidies*	126	11.9
Capital consumption	134	12.7
GDP	1,056	100.0

*Includes adjustments and statistical discrepancy.

SOURCE: Statistics Canada.

Net domestic product at factor cost
The sum of the four factor incomes—wages, interest, rent, and profit.

Table 5.2 shows these four components of incomes and their relative magnitudes. These four components of incomes sum to **net domestic product at factor cost**. Net domestic product at factor cost is not GDP. We must make two further adjustments to get to GDP: one from factor cost to market prices and another from net product to gross product.

From Factor Cost to Market Price

The expenditure approach values goods and services at market prices, and the income approach values them at factor cost—the cost of the factors of production used to produce them. Indirect taxes (such as sales taxes) and subsidies (payments by government to firms) make these two values differ. Sales taxes make market prices greater than factor cost, and subsidies make market prices less than factor cost. So to get GDP at market prices, we must add indirect taxes less subsidies to GDP at factor cost.

From Net to Gross

Depreciation
The decrease in the value of capital that results from its use and from obsolescence—also called capital consumption.

The expenditure approach measures gross product and the income approach measures net product. The difference is **depreciation**, the decrease in the value of capital that results from its use and from obsolescence—also called capital consumption. A firm's profit before subtracting the depreciation of capital is its gross profit. And its profit after subtracting the depreciation of capital is its net profit. Income includes net profit, so the income approach gives a *net* measure. Expenditure includes investment, which is the purchase of new capital. Because some new capital is purchased to replace depreciated capital, the expenditure approach gives a *gross* measure. So to get *gross* domestic product from the income approach, we must add depreciation to total income.

Table 5.2 summarizes these adjustments and shows that the income approach gives the same estimate of GDP as the expenditure approach.

■ Valuing the Output of Industries

The methods that are used to measure GDP can be used to measure the contribution that each industry makes to GDP. To measure the value of production of an industry, we count only the value added by that industry. **Value added** is the value of a firm's production minus the value of the intermediate goods it buys from other firms. Equivalently, a firm's value added equals the sum of the incomes (including profits) that the firm paid for the factors of production it used.

Figure 5.2 illustrates value added by looking at the brief life of a loaf of bread. It starts with the farmer, who hires factors of production and grows wheat. We'll assume that the farmer uses no intermediate goods. The miller buys the wheat (for one loaf) from the farmer for 20¢. The value of the farmer's production is 20¢, and the farmer's value added is 20¢. The farmer's value added equals the incomes that the farmer paid for the factors of production plus the farmer's profit.

The miller hires factors of production to turn the wheat into flour. The baker buys the flour from the miller for 70¢. The miller's value added is 50¢—the value of the flour (70¢) minus the cost of the intermediate good (20¢ for wheat). The miller's value added equals the incomes that the miller paid for the factors of production plus the miller's profit.

The baker adds a further 80¢ of value by turning the flour into bread. The consumer buys the bread for its market price, $1.50. The market price equals the value added by the farmer (20¢), the miller (50¢), and the baker (80¢).

To value output, we count *only* value added because the total of the values added at all stages of production equals expenditure on the final good. By totalling values added, we avoid double counting. In Figure 5.2, the only final good is a loaf of bread. The red bar shows the value of the final good. The blue bars show the value added at each stage, and the sum of the blue bars equals the red bar. The transactions involving intermediate goods, shown by the green bars, are not part of value added and are *not* counted as part of the value of output or of GDP.

Value added
The value of a firm's production minus the value of the intermediate goods it buys from other firms.

■ **FIGURE 5.2**
Value Added and Final Expenditure

*e*Foundations **5.2**

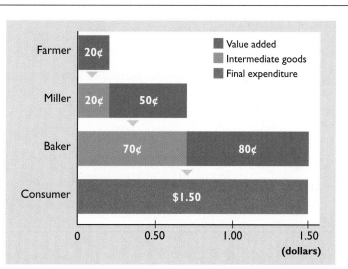

Value added is the value of a firm's production minus the value of the intermediate goods it buys from other firms. The baker's value added is the consumer's expenditure on bread minus the baker's intermediate expenditure on flour. The baker's value added equals the incomes paid, including profit, for the factors of production hired by the baker. The value of the bread (the final good) is equal to the sum of all values added.

Study Guide pp. 77–80

*e*Foundations 5.2

2 **Describe how economic statisticians measure GDP in Canada.**

Practice Problem 5.2

Table 1 gives some of the items in Canada's national accounts in 1998.
a. Calculate Canada's GDP in 1998.
b. Did you use the expenditure approach or the income approach to make this calculation?
c. How much did Canadian governments spend on goods and services in 1998?
d. By how much did capital in the Canadian economy depreciate in 1998?

Exercises 5.2

1. Table 2 gives some of the items in Canada's national accounts in 1999.
   a. Use the expenditure approach to calculate Canada's GDP in 1999.
   b. Use the income approach to calculate Canada's net domestic product at factor cost in 1999.
   c. Calculate GDP minus net domestic product at factor cost in 1999.
   d. Calculate indirect taxes less subsidies in 1999.

2. At the Skweeze Juice Bar, the price of a mango smoothie is $3.00. The juice bar buys the mango for 50¢, skim milk for 20¢, and flavouring for 1¢ from other firms and pays 25¢ for the labour and capital. Calculate the value added by the Skweeze Juice Bar when it produces a mango smoothie.

Solution to Practice Problem 5.2

a. GDP = $C + I + G + NX$ (the expenditure approach) and GDP = Wages, salaries, and supplementary labour income + Profit of corporations and government enterprises + Interest and investment income + Income of farmers and unincorporated businesses + Indirect taxes less subsidies + Capital consumption (the income approach). Inspect the data and notice that Government expenditure (G) is missing. So you can't use the expenditure approach. But you can use the income approach. Insert the items in the equation and get:

   GDP in billions = $475 + $93 + $48 + $60 + $120 + $122 = $918 billion.

b. You totalled the incomes for factors of production, so you used the income approach.
c. Use the expenditure approach to calculate G:

$$GDP = C + I + G + NX.$$

Insert the numbers that you know into this equation:

$$GDP \text{ in billions} = \$918 = \$534 + \$167 + G + \$17.$$

$$G = \$918 \text{ billion} - \$718 \text{ billion} = \$ 200 \text{ billion}.$$

d. Depreciation equals capital consumption, which in 1998 was $122 billion.

TABLE 1

Item	Amount (billions of dollars)
Wages, salaries, and supplementary labour income	475
Consumption expenditure	534
Indirect taxes *less* subsidies	120
Interest and investment income	48
Profits of corporations and government enterprises	93
Capital consumption	122
Investment	167
Net exports	17
Income from farms and unincorporated businesses	60

TABLE 2

Item	Amount (billions of dollars)
Consumption expenditure	559
Government expenditure	200
Interest and investment income	48
Profit from corporations and government enterprises	113
Income from farms and unincorporated businesses	62
Investment	170
Net exports	28
Wages, salaries, and supplementary labour income	499
Capital consumption	120

5.3 NOMINAL GDP VERSUS REAL GDP

You've seen that GDP measures total expenditure on final goods and services in a given period. In 1999, GDP was $975 billion. In 2000, GDP was $1,056 billion. Because GDP in 2000 was greater than in 1999, we know that one or two things must have happened during that period:

- We produced more goods and services.
- We paid higher prices for our goods and services.

Producing more goods and services contributes to an improvement in our standard of living. Paying higher prices means that our cost of living has increased but our standard of living has not. So it matters a great deal why GDP has increased.

You're going to learn how economists at Statistics Canada split the increase in GDP into two parts: one part that tells us the change in production and the other that tells us the change in prices. The method Statistics Canada uses has changed recently, and we will describe the new method.

We measure the increase in production by a number called real GDP. **Real GDP** is the value of the final goods and services produced in a given year when valued at constant prices. By comparing real GDP in two years, we can measure the increase in production.

Real GDP
The value of the final goods and services produced in a given year when valued at constant prices.

■ Calculating Real GDP

Table 5.3 shows the quantities produced and prices in 2001 for an economy that produces only apples and oranges. The first step towards calculating real GDP is to calculate **nominal GDP,** which is the value of the final goods and services produced in a given year valued at the prices that prevailed in that same year. Nominal GDP is just a more precise name for GDP that we use when we want to make it clear that we are not talking about real GDP.

Nominal GDP
The value of the final goods and services produced in a given year valued at the prices that prevailed in that same year.

Nominal GDP Calculation

To calculate nominal GDP in 2001, sum the expenditures on apples and oranges in 2001 as follows:

Expenditure on apples	= 100 apples × $1	= $100.
Expenditure on oranges	= 200 oranges × $0.50	= $100.
Nominal GDP in 2001	= $100 + $100	= $200.

TABLE 5.3   GDP DATA FOR 2001

Item	Quantity	Price
Apples	100	$1.00
Oranges	200	$0.50

Table 5.4 shows the quantities produced and prices in 2002. The quantity of apples produced increased to 160 and the quantity of oranges produced increased to 220. The price of an apple fell to 50¢, and the price of an orange increased to $2.25. To calculate nominal GDP in 2002, sum the expenditures on apples and oranges in 2002 as follows:

Expenditure on apples	= 160 apples × $0.50	= $80.
Expenditure on oranges	= 220 oranges × $2.25	= $495.
Nominal GDP in 2002	= $80 + $495	= $575.

TABLE 5.4   GDP DATA FOR 2002

Item	Quantity	Price
Apples	160	$0.50
Oranges	220	$2.25

To calculate real GDP, we choose one year, called the *base year*, against which to compare the other years. The choice of the base year is not important. It is just a common reference point. We'll use 2001 as the base year. By definition, real GDP equals nominal GDP in the base year. So real GDP in 2001 is $200.

Traditional Real GDP Calculation

The traditional method of calculating real GDP valued the quantities produced in each year at the prices of the base year. Table 5.5 summarizes these prices and quantities for 2001 and 2002. The value of the 2002 quantities at the 2001 prices is calculated as follows:

TABLE 5.5 2002 QUANTITIES AND 2001 PRICES

Item	Quantity	Price
Apples	160	$1.00
Oranges	220	$0.50

Expenditure on apples = 160 apples × $1.00 = $160.
Expenditure on oranges = 220 oranges × $0.50 = $110.
Value of the 2002 quantities at 2001 prices = $270.

Using the traditional method, $270 would be recorded as real GDP in 2002.

New Method of Calculating Real GDP

The new method of calculating real GDP builds on the old method but takes a further step. The new method compares the quantities produced in 2001 and 2002 by using not only 2001 prices but also the 2002 prices. It then averages the two sets of numbers in a special way that we'll now describe.

To compare the quantities produced in 2001 and 2002 at 2002 prices, we need to calculate the value of 2001 quantities at 2002 prices. Table 5.6 summarizes these quantities and prices. The value of the 2001 quantities at the 2002 prices is calculated as follows:

TABLE 5.6 2001 QUANTITIES AND 2002 PRICES

Item	Quantity	Price
Apples	100	$0.50
Oranges	200	$2.25

Expenditure on apples = 100 apples × $0.50 = $50.
Expenditure on oranges = 200 oranges × $2.25 = $450.
Value of the 2001 quantities at 2002 prices = $500.

We now have two comparisons between 2001 and 2002. At the 2001 prices, the value of production increased from $200 in 2001 to $270 in 2002. The increase in value is $70, and the percentage increase is ($70 ÷ $200) × 100, which is 35 percent.

At the 2002 prices, the value of production increased from $500 in 2001 to $575 in 2002. The increase in value is $75, and the percentage increase is ($75 ÷ $500) × 100, which is 15 percent.

When we value production in 2001 prices, it increased by 35 percent in 2002. When we value production in 2002 prices, it increased by 15 percent in 2002. The new method of calculating real GDP uses the average of these two percentage increases. The average of 35 percent and 15 percent is (35 + 15) ÷ 2, which equals 25 percent. Real GDP is 25 percent greater in 2002 than in 2001. Real GDP in 2001 is $200, so real GDP in 2002 is $250.

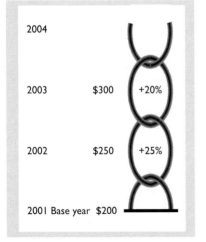

Chain Linking

The calculation that we've just described is repeated each year. Each year is compared with its preceding year. So, in 2003, the calculations are repeated but using the prices and quantities of 2002 and 2003. Real GDP in 2003 equals real GDP in 2002 increased by the calculated percentage change in real GDP for 2003. For example, suppose that real GDP for 2003 is calculated to be 20 percent greater than in 2002. You know that real GDP in 2002 is $250. So real GDP in 2003 is 20 percent greater than this value and is $300. In every year, real GDP is valued in base-year (2001) dollars.

By applying the calculated percentage change to the real GDP of the preceding real GDP, each year is linked back to the dollars of the base year like the links in a chain.

Deflating the GDP Balloon

Nominal GDP has increased every year during the 1990s. Part of the increase reflects increased production, and part of it reflects rising prices.

You can think of GDP as a balloon that is blown up by growing production and rising prices. In the figure, the GDP deflator lets the inflation air—the contribution of rising prices—out of the nominal GDP balloon so that we can see what has happened to real GDP. The red balloon for 1990 shows real GDP in that year. The green balloon shows nominal GDP in 2000. The red balloon for 2000 shows real GDP for that year. To see real GDP in 2000, we use the GDP deflator to deflate nominal GDP.

With the inflation air removed, real GDP shows how the total value of production has changed. Over the long term, real GDP has grown by less than 3 percent a year. The 1990s began with a recession in which real GDP shrank by 1.9 percent. Recovery from the recession was slow, but in the four years after 1996, real GDP grew by 4.2 percent per year. By the end of the decade (2000), real GDP was 25 percent higher than in 1990.

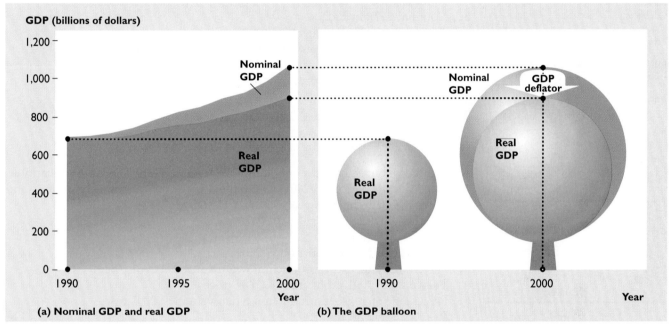

(a) Nominal GDP and real GDP

(b) The GDP balloon

SOURCE: Statistics Canada.

■ Calculating the GDP Deflator

The **GDP deflator** is an average of current prices expressed as a percentage of base-year prices. The GDP deflator measures the price level. We calculate the GDP deflator by using nominal GDP and real GDP in the following formula:

$$\text{GDP deflator} = (\text{Nominal GDP} \div \text{Real GDP}) \times 100.$$

You can see why the GDP deflator is a measure of the price level. If nominal GDP rises but real GDP remains unchanged, it must be that prices have risen. The formula would deliver that result in the form of a higher GDP deflator. The larger the nominal GDP for a given real GDP, the higher are prices and the larger is the GDP deflator.

Table 5.7 shows how the GDP deflator is calculated. In 2001, the deflator is 100. In 2002, it is 230, which equals nominal GDP of $575 divided by real GDP of $250 and then multiplied by 100.

GDP deflator
An average of current prices expressed as a percentage of base-year prices.

TABLE 5.7 CALCULATING THE GDP DEFLATOR

Year	Nominal GDP	Real GDP	GDP Deflator
2001	$200	$200	100
2002	$575	$250	230

Study Guide pp. 80–82

*e*Foundations 5.3

3 **Distinguish between nominal GDP and real GDP and define the GDP deflator.**

Practice Problem 5.3

An island economy produces only bananas and coconuts. Table 1 gives the quantities produced and prices in 2001, and Table 2 gives the quantities produced and prices in 2002. The base year is 2001. Calculate:

a. Nominal GDP in 2001.
b. Nominal GDP in 2002.
c. The value of 2002 production in 2001 prices.
d. Percentage increase in production when valued at 2001 prices.
e. The value of 2001 production in 2002 prices.
f. Percentage increase in production when valued at 2002 prices.
g. Real GDP in 2001 and 2002.
h. The GDP deflator in 2002.

Exercise 5.3

An island economy produces only lobsters and crabs. Table 3 gives the quantities produced and the prices in 2001, and Table 4 gives the quantities produced and the prices in 2002. The base year is 2001. Calculate:

a. Nominal GDP in 2001.
b. Nominal GDP in 2002.
c. The value of 2002 production in 2001 prices.
d. Percentage increase in production when valued at 2001 prices.
e. The value of 2001 production in 2002 prices.
f. Percentage increase in production when valued at 2002 prices.
g. Real GDP in 2001 and 2002.
h. The GDP deflator in 2002.

Solution to Practice Problem 5.3

a. Nominal GDP in 2001 is $1,600—expenditure is $1,000 on bananas and $600 on coconuts (Table 1).
b. Nominal GDP in 2002 is $2,250—expenditure is $1,650 on bananas and $600 on coconuts (Table 2).
c. The value of 2002 production in 2001 prices is $1,820 (Table 5).
d. In 2001 prices, the value of production increased from $1,600 to $1,820, an increase of $220. The percentage increase is (220 ÷ 1,600) × 100, or 13.75 percent.
e. The value of 2001 production in 2002 prices is $2,000 (Table 6).
f. In 2002 prices, the value of production increased from $2,000 to $2,250, an increase of $250. The percentage increase is (250 ÷ 2,000) × 100, or 12.5 percent.
g. Real GDP in 2001 is $1,600. The average percentage increase in production is (13.75 + 12.5) ÷ 2, which is 13.125 percent. Real GDP in 2002 is 13.125 percent greater than $1,600, which is $1,810.
h. The GDP deflator in 2002 is (nominal GDP ÷ real GDP) × 100, which is 124.3.

TABLE 1

In 2001:

Item	Quantity	Price
Bananas	100	$10 a bunch
Coconuts	50	$12 a bag

TABLE 2

In 2002:

Item	Quantity	Price
Bananas	110	$15 a bunch
Coconuts	60	$10 a bag

TABLE 3

In 2001:

Item	Quantity	Price
Lobsters	100	$20 each
Crabs	25	$25 each

TABLE 4

In 2002:

Item	Quantity	Price
Lobsters	110	$25 each
Crabs	30	$30 each

TABLE 5

2002 quantities and 2001 prices

Item	Quantity	Price	Expenditure
Bananas	110	$10	$1,100
Coconuts	60	$12	$720
Value in 2001 prices			$1,820

TABLE 6

2001 quantities and 2002 prices

Item	Quantity	Price	Expenditure
Bananas	100	$15	$1,500
Coconuts	50	$10	$500
Value in 2002 prices			$2,000

5.4 REAL GDP AND THE STANDARD OF LIVING

We use estimates of real GDP to compare the standard of living across countries and over time. In 2000, real GDP per person in Canada was almost $30,000, which (at 2000 prices) was more than twice what it was in 1965. But are we twice as well off? Does this expansion of real GDP provide a full and accurate measure of the change in our standard of living?

It does not, for two reasons. First, the standard of living depends on *all* goods and services, not only on those included in GDP. Second, the standard of living depends on factors other than the goods and services produced.

■ Goods and Services Omitted from GDP

GDP measures the value of goods and services that are bought in markets. But it excludes:

- Household production
- Underground production
- Leisure time
- Environment quality

Household Production

An enormous amount of production takes place every day in our homes. Preparing meals, cleaning the kitchen, changing a light bulb, cutting the grass, washing the car, and helping a student with homework are all examples of productive activities that do not involve market transactions and are not counted as part of GDP.

Because real GDP omits household production, it underestimates the value of the production of many people, most of them women. But market production is increasingly replacing household production. Two trends point in this direction. One is the number of people who have jobs outside the home, which has increased from 54 percent in 1965 to 66 percent in 2000. The other is the purchase of more goods and services that traditionally were produced in the home. For example, more and more families now eat in fast-food restaurants—one of the fastest-growing industries in Canada—and use day-care services. These trends mean that an increasing proportion of food preparation and childcare that were once part of household production are now measured as part of GDP. So real GDP grows more rapidly than does real GDP plus home production.

Underground Production

The underground economy is the part of the economy that is hidden from the view of the government either because people want to avoid taxes and regulations or because the goods and services being produced are illegal. Because underground economic activity is unreported, it is omitted from GDP.

The underground economy is easy to describe, even if it is hard to measure. It includes the production and distribution of illegal drugs, production that uses illegal workers who are paid less than the minimum wage, and jobs done for cash to avoid paying income and sales taxes. This last category might be quite large and includes tips earned by hotel and restaurant workers, cab drivers, hairdressers, and a large range of other legal cash transactions that are illegally unreported.

ECONOMICS *in the* NEWS

October 31, 2001

GDP Relatively Flat Since May

Gross Domestic Product (GDP) remained largely flat for the fourth straight month. The economy increased a marginal 0.1% in August, only the fifth time in the past 12 months that the economy as a whole showed any improvement.

STATISTICS CANADA, *THE DAILY*

Questions
1. What does this information tell you about the state of the economy in mid-2001?
2. What do you think has happened to the standard of living in Canada over this 12-month period?

 *e*Foundations **5.4**

The Department of Finance estimates the size of Canada's underground economy to be about 5 percent of GDP. Other estimates range from as small as 3 percent to as large as 10–15 percent of GDP. The underground economy is much larger in some Eastern European countries, which are making a transition from communist economic planning to a market economy.

Leisure Time

Leisure time is an economic good. Other things remaining the same, the more leisure we have, the better off we are. Our working time is valued as part of GDP, but our leisure time is not. Yet an hour of our leisure time must be at least as valuable to us as the wage rate we earn by working. If it were not, we would work instead. Over the years, leisure time has steadily increased. The workweek has become shorter, the number of vacation days has increased, and more people retire early. Real GDP does not measure these improvements in our standard of living.

Environment Quality

An industrial society produces more atmospheric pollution than an agricultural society does. For example, an industrial society burns more coal, oil, and gas. And it depletes resources, clears forests, and pollutes lakes and rivers.

But industrial activity increases wealth, and wealthy people value a clean environment and are better able to devote resources to protecting it. So pollution does not necessarily increase when production increases. Pollution in Germany provides an example. When East Germany, a relatively poor part of the country, opened its borders with West Germany in the late 1980s, it was discovered that East German rivers, lakes, and air were much more severely polluted than those of its richer West German neighbour.

Resources that are used to protect the environment are valued as part of GDP. For example, the production of catalytic converters that help to protect the atmosphere from automobile emissions is part of GDP. But pollution is not subtracted from GDP. If we didn't produce catalytic converters but instead polluted the atmosphere, we would not count the deteriorating atmosphere as a negative part of GDP. So if our standard of living is adversely affected by pollution, our GDP measure does not show this fact.

■ Other Influences on the Standard of Living

The quantity of goods and services consumed is a major influence on the standard of living. But other influences are:

- Health and life expectancy
- Political freedom and social justice

Health and Life Expectancy

Good health and a long life—the hopes of everyone—do not show up directly in real GDP. A higher real GDP enables us to spend more on medical research, health care, a good diet, and exercise equipment. And as real GDP has increased, our life expectancy has lengthened—from 70 years at the end of World War II to nearly 80 years today. Infant deaths and death in childbirth, two scourges of the nineteenth century, have almost been eliminated.

But we face new health and life expectancy problems every year. Diseases such as AIDS and drug abuse are taking young lives at a rate that causes serious concern. When we take these negative influences into account, real GDP growth overstates the improvements in the standard of living.

Political Freedom and Social Justice

A country might have a very large real GDP per person but have limited political freedom and social justice. For example, a small elite might enjoy political liberty and extreme wealth while the majority of people have limited freedom and live in poverty. Such an economy would generally be regarded as having a lower standard of living than one that had the same amount of real GDP but in which everyone enjoyed political freedom. Today, China has rapid real GDP growth but limited political freedom, while Russia has slower real GDP growth and an emerging democratic political system.

Because of the limitations of real GDP, other measures such as the Human Development Index have been proposed (see Eye on the Global Economy).

Eye On The GLOBAL ECONOMY

The Human Development Index

The limitations of real GDP that we've reviewed in this chapter affect the standard of living of every country. So to make international comparisons of the standard of living, we must look at real GDP and other indicators. Nonetheless, real GDP per person is a major component of international comparisons.

The United Nations has constructed a broader measure called the Human Development Index, or HDI, which combines real GDP, life expectancy and health, and education levels.

The figure shows the relationship between GDP and the HDI. Each dot represents a country. The United States, labelled in the figure, has the

highest real GDP per person but the fourth highest HDI. The small African nation of Sierra Leone, also labelled, has the lowest HDI (but not the lowest real GDP per person).

Why is Canada ranked higher than the United States on the HDI? There

are two reasons: Life expectancy in Canada is a bit longer than in the United States, and the quality of Canadian schools is ranked more highly than the quality of schools in the United States.

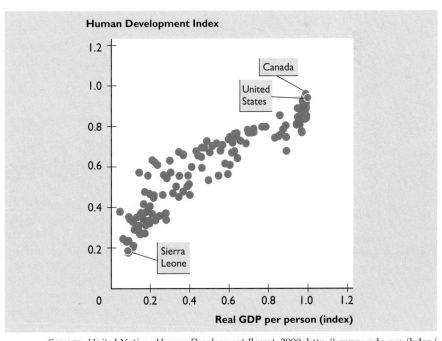

SOURCE: *United Nations Human Development Report*, 2000, http://www.undp.org/hdro/

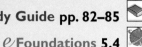
4 **Explain and describe the limitations of real GDP as a measure of the standard of living.**

Practice Problem 5.4

The International Monetary Fund reports the following data for real GDP per person in 1999: China, $3,762; Russia, $6,803; Canada, $28,346; United States, $34,530. Other information suggests that household production is similar in Canada and the United States and smaller in these two countries than in the other two. The underground economy is largest in Russia and China and a similar proportion of the economy in these two cases. Canadians and Americans enjoy more leisure hours than do the Chinese and Russians. Canada and the United States spend significantly more to protect the environment, so air, water, and land pollution is less in those countries than in China and Russia. Given this information and ignoring any other influences on the standard of living:

a. In which pair (or pairs) of these four countries is it easier to compare the standard of living? Why?

b. In which pair (or pairs) of these four countries is it more difficult to compare the standard of living? Why?

c. What more detailed information would we need to be able to make an accurate assessment of the relative standard of living in these four countries?

d. Do you think that the differences in real GDP per person correctly rank the standard of living in these four countries?

Exercise 5.4

Life expectancy at birth is 79.1 in Canada, 76.4 in the United States, 69.2 in China, and 65.5 in Russia. Freedom House rates political freedom each year, and its ratings are as follows: Canada and the United States, 1.1 (1.0 is the most free); Russia, 4.5; and China, 7.6 (ratings in the 7+ range are the least free). How do these facts change the relative rankings of living standards indicated by differences in real GDP per person?

Solution to Practice Problem 5.4

a. Two pairs—Canada and the United States, and China and Russia—are easy to compare because household production, the underground economy, leisure hours, and the environment are similar in the two countries in each pair.

b. Canada and the United States are the more difficult to compare with China and Russia because household production and the underground economy narrow the differences and leisure hours and the environment widen them.

c. We would need more detailed information on the value of household production, the underground economy, the value of leisure, and the value of environmental differences.

d. Differences in real GDP per person probably correctly rank the standard of living in these four countries because where the gap is small (Canada and the United States), other factors are similar, and where other factors differ, the gaps are huge.

CHAPTER CHECKPOINT

Key Points

1 **Define GDP and explain why the value of production, income, and expenditure are the same for an economy.**

- GDP is the value of production of final goods and services in a given time period.
- We can value goods and services either by what it costs to produce (incomes) or by what people are willing to pay (expenditures).
- The value of production equals income equals expenditure.

2 **Describe how economic statisticians measure GDP in Canada.**

- We measure GDP by summing either expenditures on final goods and services (the expenditure approach) or incomes of all the factors of production (the income approach).
- GDP measures expenditure on final goods and services but excludes expenditure on intermediate goods, used goods, and financial assets.
- To value the output of a sector, we measure only the sector's value added.

3 **Distinguish between nominal GDP and real GDP and define the GDP deflator.**

- Nominal GDP is the value of production using the prices of the current year and quantities produced of the current year.
- Real GDP is the value of production using the prices of a base year and the quantities of a current year.
- Changes in real GDP measure changes in production. Changes in nominal GDP combine changes in both production and prices.
- The GDP deflator is the ratio of nominal GDP to real GDP (multiplied by 100).

4 **Explain and describe the limitations of real GDP as a measure of the standard of living.**

- Real GDP per person is a major indicator of the standard of living.
- Real GDP omits household production, underground production, leisure time, environment quality, health and life expectancy, and political freedom and social justice.
- Broader indexes of the standard of living, such as the Human Development Index, take some of these omitted factors into account.

Key Terms

Consumption expenditure, 109
Depreciation, 116
Exports of goods and services, 110
Final good or service, 108
GDP deflator, 121

Government expenditure on goods and services, 110
Gross domestic product (GDP), 108
Imports of goods and services, 110
Intermediate good or service, 108
Investment, 109

Net domestic product at factor cost, 116
Net exports of goods and services, 110
Nominal GDP, 119
Real GDP, 119
Value added, 117

Exercises

FIGURE 1

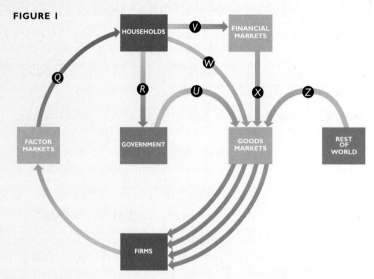

1. Refer to Figure 1. In the Canadian economy in 1998, W was $533 billion, X was $162 billion, Z was $13 billion, and U was $194 billion. Calculate:
    a. Q.
    b. $R + V$.
    c. GDP.

2. The national accounts of Parchment Paradise are kept on (you guessed it) parchment. A fire destroyed the national statistical office and the national accounts are now incomplete. But they contain the following information for 2001: Net domestic product at factor cost is $2,900; consumption expenditure is $2,000; indirect taxes less subsidies are $80; interest and investment income is $200; farmers' income is $100; investment is $800; government expenditure on goods and services is $800; income of unincorporated businesses is $200; wages, salaries and supplementary labour income is $2,000; net exports are –$200. You've been hired as an economist to reconstruct the missing numbers by calculating for 2001:
    a. GDP.
    b. Corporate profits.
    c. Capital consumption.

3.   Use the link on your Foundation's Web site to visit Statistics Canada and use the national accounts for 1999.
    a. What are the values of consumption expenditure, investment, government expenditure, and net exports? Check that the expenditure approach delivers GDP.
    b. The GDP deflator in 1999 was 108.8 when the base year was 1992. Calculate real GDP in 1999.
    c. Was the cost of living higher in 1999 than in 1992? Explain your answer.

4. In 1999, a devastating oil spill occurred in the Bay of Biscay that washed ashore on the beaches of France. Millions of dollars were spent cleaning up the mess, and much wildlife was killed. Describe how the effects of this oil spill appear in the national accounts of France. Does the national accounts treatment of this event properly record the effects of the spill on the standard of living of the people affected? Explain why or why not.

Jobs and Unemployment

Chapter
6

CHAPTER CHECKLIST

When you have completed your study of this chapter,
you will be able to:

1 Define the unemployment rate and other labour market indicators.

2 Describe the trends and fluctuations in the indicators of labour market performance in Canada.

3 Describe the sources and types of unemployment, define full employment, and explain the link between unemployment and real GDP.

Macroeconomics studies three big issues: the standard of living, unemployment, and the cost of living. You've just learned how we measure a main indicator of the standard of living: real GDP. Most of us earn the incomes that make up GDP by working. We become concerned when jobs are hard to find and more relaxed when jobs are plentiful. We also care about the kinds of jobs that are available. We want well-paid and interesting jobs, so we spend time searching for the right job.

In this chapter, we study the way that economists track the health of the labour market. First, we'll describe a monthly survey that discovers the labour market status of the population and provides the raw material for job market statistics. Second, we'll describe the trends and fluctuations in the indicators of labour market performance. Third, we'll look at the sources and types of unemployment and learn what we mean by "full employment."

6.1 | LABOUR MARKET INDICATORS

Every month, 720 Statistics Canada interviewers contact 54,000 Canadian households and ask questions about the age and employment status of the members of each household. This survey is called the Labour Force Survey. Statistics Canada uses the results of this survey to keep track of the state of Canada's labour market. Let's look at some of the data collected by this survey.

■ Labour Force Survey

Working-age population
The total number of people aged 15 years and over.

Figure 6.1 shows the categories into which Statistics Canada divides the population. It also shows the relationships among the categories. The first category divides the population into two groups: the working-age population and others who are too young to work. The **working-age population** is the total number of people aged 15 years and over. In May 2001, the estimated population of Canada was 31 million. The working-age population was 24.58 million, and 6.42 million were under 15 years of age.

Labour force
The number of people employed plus the number unemployed.

The second category divides the working-age population into two groups: those in the labour force and those not in the labour force. The **labour force** is the number of people employed plus the number unemployed. In May 2001, the Canadian labour force was 16.39 million and 8.21 million people of working age were not in the labour force. Most of those not in the labour force were in full-time school or had retired from work.

The third category divides the labour force into two groups: the employed and the unemployed. In May 2001, the Canadian labour force was made up of 15.23 million people employed and 1.16 million unemployed.

■ Labour Force Survey Criteria

The survey counts as employed all persons who, during the week before the survey:

1. Did any work at all for pay or profit (including unpaid work for a business operated by a member of the household).
2. Had a job but were not at work due to factors such as their own illness or disability, personal or family responsibilities, bad weather, labour dispute, or vacation.

The survey counts as unemployed all persons who, during the week before the survey:

1. Had no employment.
2. Were available for work.

and either:

1. Were on temporary layoff with an expectation of recall, or
2. Had actively looked for work during the past four weeks, or
3. Had a new job to start within four weeks.

People in the working-age population who by the above criteria are neither employed nor unemployed are classified as not in the labour force.

■ **FIGURE 6.1**
Population Labour Force Categories

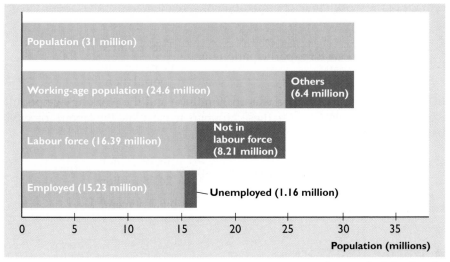

The Canadian population is divided into the working-age population and others who are too young to work. The working-age population is divided into the labour force and those not in the labour force. The labour force is divided into the employed and the unemployed. The figure shows the data for May 2001.

SOURCE: Statistics Canada.

■ Two Main Labour Market Indicators

Using the numbers from the Labour Force Survey, Statistics Canada calculates several indicators of the state of the labour market. The two main labour market indicators are:

- The unemployment rate
- The labour force participation rate

The Unemployment Rate

The amount of unemployment is an indicator of the extent to which people who want jobs can't find them. It tells us the amount of slack in the labour market. The **unemployment rate** is the percentage of the people in the labour force who are unemployed. That is,

Unemployment rate
The percentage of the people in the labour force who are unemployed.

$$\text{Unemployment rate} = \frac{\text{Number of people unemployed}}{\text{Labour force}} \times 100.$$

In May 2001, the number of people unemployed was 1.16 million and the labour force was 16.39 million. We can use these numbers to calculate the unemployment rate in May 2001, which was

$$\text{Unemployment rate} = \frac{1.16 \text{ million}}{16.39 \text{ million}} \times 100$$

$$= 7.1 \text{ percent.}$$

Labour force participation rate
The percentage of the working-age population who are members of the labour force.

The Labour Force Participation Rate

The number of people in the labour force is an indicator of the willingness of people of working age to take jobs. The **labour force participation rate** is the percentage of the working-age population who are members of the labour force. That is:

$$\text{Labour force participation rate} = \frac{\text{Labour force}}{\text{Working-age population}} \times 100.$$

In May 2001, the labour force was 16.39 million and the working-age population was 24.58 million. We can use these numbers to calculate the labour force participation rate in May 2001, which was:

$$\text{Labour force participation rate} = \frac{16.39 \text{ million}}{24.58 \text{ million}} \times 100$$

$$= 66.7 \text{ percent.}$$

■ Discouraged Workers

Discouraged worker
A person who does not have a job, is available and willing to work but has not made specific efforts to find a job within the previous four weeks.

Neither the unemployment rate nor the labour force participation rate includes an important group of unemployed people called discouraged workers. A **discouraged worker** is a person who does not have a job, is available and willing to work, but has not made specific efforts to find a job within the previous four weeks. The presence of discouraged workers means that the measured unemployment rate underestimates the true amount of unemployment.

■ Part-Time Workers

Full-time workers
People who usually work 30 hours or more a week.

Part-time workers
People who usually work less than 30 hours per week.

Involuntary part-time workers
People who work part time but want a full-time job.

The Labour Force Survey measures the number of full-time workers and part-time workers. **Full-time workers** are those who usually work 30 hours or more a week. **Part-time workers** are those who usually work less than 30 hours a week. In May 2001, the number of people employed was 15.23 million. Of these, 12.48 million were full-time workers and 2.75 million were part-time workers.

Part-time workers are divided into two groups: voluntary part-time workers (those who chose to work part time) and **involuntary part-time workers** (those who work part time but want a full-time job). In May 2001, the number of voluntary part-time workers was 2.05 million and the number of involuntary part-time workers was 0.7 million.

Part-time workers who want full-time jobs are underemployed. To measure the extent of this type of underemployment, Statistics Canada calculates the involuntary part-time rate, which is the number of involuntary part-time workers as a percentage of the labour force. That is:

$$\text{Involuntary part-time rate} = \frac{\text{Number of involuntary part-time workers}}{\text{Labour force}} \times 100.$$

In May 2001, the number of involuntary part-time workers was 0.7 million, the labour force was 16.39 million, and the involuntary part-time rate was 4.27 percent.

The Labour Force Survey

Statistics Canada goes to great lengths to collect accurate labour force data. They constantly train and retrain 720 interviewers. Each month, each interviewer contacts 75 households and asks basic demographic questions about all persons living at the address and detailed labour force questions about persons aged 15 or over.

Once a household has been selected for the survey, it is questioned for six consecutive months. Each month, one-sixth of the households in the sample are removed and replaced by new households in the same or a similar area. The result of this approach is a combined rotation and overlap of households in the sample that provides very reliable information about month-to-month and year-to-year changes in the labour market.

The first time that a household is in the panel, it is visited by an interviewer armed with a laptop computer with a computerized questionnaire. If the household has a telephone, most of the subsequent interviews are conducted by phone, and approximately 85 percent of interviews are by telephone.

■ Aggregate Hours

The labour market indicators that we've just examined are useful signs of the health of the economy and directly measure what matters to most people: jobs and whether those jobs are full time or part time. But they don't tell us the *quantity of labour* that was employed.

The reason the number of people employed does not measure the quantity of labour employed is that jobs are not all the same. You've seen that people in part-time jobs work between 1 and 29 hours a week and people in full-time jobs work 30 or more hours a week. A Second Cup coffee shop might hire six students who work for three hours a day each. Another Second Cup might hire two full-time workers who work nine hours a day each. The total number of people employed is eight, but the total hours worked by six part-time workers is the same as the total hours worked by the two full-time workers.

To determine the total amount of labour employed, we measure labour in hours rather than in jobs. **Aggregate hours** are the total number of hours worked by all the people employed, both full time and part time, during a year and equal the number of people employed multiplied by the average work hours per person.

In May 2001, 15.23 million people worked an average of 34.5 hours per week. With 50 workweeks a year, aggregate hours for the year were:

Aggregate hours = 15.23 million × 34.5 × 50 = 26.27 billion.

The measurement of aggregate hours is not very precise. But the estimation of the percentage change in aggregate hours from one month to another is more precise, making both aggregate hours worked and average weekly hours worked useful statistics.

Aggregate hours
The total number of hours worked by all the people employed, both full time and part time, during a year.

Study Guide pp. 91–93

e Foundations 6.1

1 **Define the unemployment rate and other labour market indicators.**

Practice Problem 6.1

Statistics Canada reported that in January 2001, the labour force was 15.9 million; employment was 14.7 million; and the working-age population was 24.5 million. Average weekly hours were 34.5. Calculate for that month the:

   a. Unemployment rate.
   b. Labour force participation rate.
   c. Aggregate hours worked in a week.

Exercises 6.1

1. Statistics Canada reported that in March 2001, the labour force was 15.97 million; employment was 14.76 million; and the working-age population was 24.52 million. Calculate for that month the Canadian:
   a. Unemployment rate.
   b. Labour force participation rate.

2. The U.S. Census Bureau reported that in March 2001, the U.S. labour force was 141.9 million; employment was 135.8 million; and the working-age population was 211.2 million. Calculate for that month the U.S.:
   a. Unemployment rate.
   b. Labour force participation rate.

3. Given the data in Exercises 1 and 2, do you think that in March 2001 jobs were harder to find in Canada or the United States? Why?

4. Use the link on your Foundations Web site to obtain data on the labour force, employment, unemployment, and the working-age population for your own province in the most recent month for which data are available. For that month:
   a. Calculate your province's unemployment rate.
   b. Calculate your province's labour force participation rate.
   c. Compare the labour market indicators in your province with those for Canada.

Solution to Practice Problem 6.1

1a. Unemployment rate: The labour force is the sum of the number employed plus the number unemployed. So the number unemployed equals the labour force minus the number employed, which equals 15.9 million − 14.7 million = 1.2 million. The unemployment rate is the number unemployed as a percentage of the labour force, which is (1.2 million ÷ 15.9 million) × 100 = 7.5 percent.

1b. Labour force participation rate: The labour force participation rate is the labour force as a percentage of the working-age population, which equals (15.9 million ÷ 24.5 million) × 100 = 64.9 percent.

1c. In January 2001, average weekly hours were 34.5 and employment was 14.7 million. So the aggregate hours worked in a week were 34.5 × 14.7 million = 507.15 million.

6.2 LABOUR MARKET TRENDS AND FLUCTUATIONS

What do we learn about the Canadian labour market from changes in the unemployment rate, the labour force participation rate, part-time employment, and work hours? Let's explore the trends and fluctuations in these indicators.

■ Unemployment

You've seen that in May 2001, Canada's unemployment rate was 7.1 percent. This unemployment rate might seem high, but it was the lowest unemployment rate in 26 years. Figure 6.2 shows the record on the unemployment rate from 1960 to 2000. It also shows the average unemployment rate over this period.

During the 40 years from 1960 to 2000, the average unemployment rate in Canada was 7.6 percent. Unemployment rates in the 1960s were low, and dipped to 3.3 percent in 1966. From the late 1960s to the mid-1990s, the unemployment rate drifted upward. During the 1970s, the unemployment rate rose persistently, mainly because a large number of baby boomers entered the labour force. The 1982 recession pushed the unemployment rate up to 11.9 percent in 1983, the highest since the 1930s. During the rest of the 1980s, a period of expansion brought the unemployment rate down to the long-term average by 1989. But another recession followed in the early 1990s. In this recession, the unemployment rate peaked at 11.3 percent in 1992, and remained high in a slow recovery.

After 1996, the recovery gained momentum, led by rising exports to the booming U.S. economy. During this strong expansion, the unemployment rate fell rapidly to dip below its long-term average.

■ **FIGURE 6.2**

The Canadian Unemployment Rate: 1960–2000

*e*Foundations **6.2**

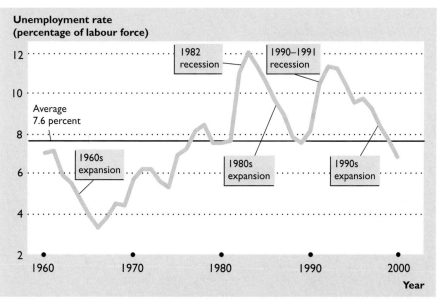

The average unemployment rate between 1960 and 2000 was 7.6 percent. The unemployment rate increases in recessions and decreases in expansions. Unemployment fell rapidly to below its long-term average during the expansion of the late 1990s.

SOURCE: Statistics Canada.

The Labour Market in the Great Depression

The Great Depression of the 1930s was a period of prolonged and extreme economic hardship. Not until 1939 did real GDP recover to the peak it had reached in 1929.

By 1933, the worst of the Depression years, real GDP had fallen by a huge 30 percent. And, as the figure shows, one in five of the people who wanted jobs couldn't find one.

The horrors of the Great Depression shaped political attitudes that still influence economic policy today.

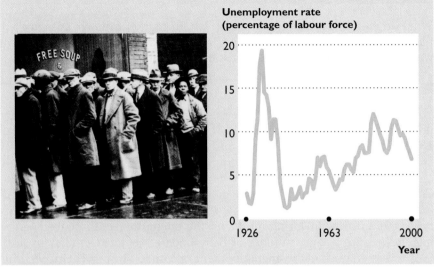

SOURCE: Statistics Canada.

■ The Participation Rate

Figure 6.3 shows the labour force participation rate, which you can see has followed an upward trend. It increased from 54 percent during the 1950s to 66 percent during the 1990s. The cyclical fluctuations in the participation rate are mild and result from unsuccessful job seekers becoming *discouraged workers*—people who leave the labour force in a recession and re-enter in an expansion.

| FIGURE 6.3 | |
The Changing Face of the Labour Market: 1950–2000

*e*Foundations **6.2**

During the past 50 years, the labour force participation rate of men has decreased and that of women has increased. The total participation rate also increased.

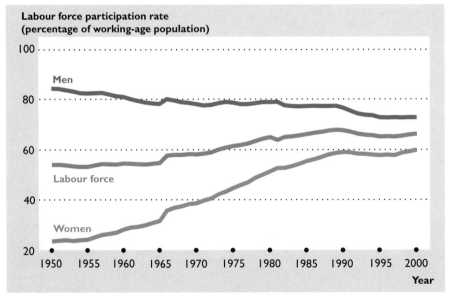

SOURCE: Statistics Canada.

Eye On The GLOBAL ECONOMY

Unemployment Around the World

Unemployment in Canada fell from 1992 through 2000. But only two other countries shown in the figure shared the Canadian experience: the United States and the United Kingdom. Although Canadian unemployment fell, its rate remained about 2 percentage points higher than U.S. unemployment in 2000.

Unemployment in the three main countries of Europe—France, Germany, and Italy—has climbed steadily to three times the U.S. rate. Unemployment in Japan has also increased from 2 percent in 1990 to more than the U.S. level in 2000.

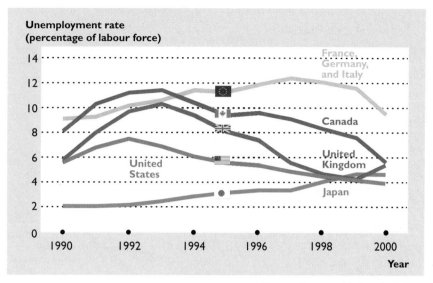

SOURCE: Bureau of Labor Statistics.

Why has the labour force participation rate increased? The main reason is an increase in the number of women in the labour force. Figure 6.3 shows this increase. Between 1950 and 2000, the participation rate of women increased from 23 percent to 60 percent. This increase is spread across women of all age groups and occurred for four main reasons. First, more women pursued a college education and so increased their earning power. Second, technological change in the workplace created a large number of white-collar jobs with flexible work hours that a large number of women found attractive. Third, technological change in the home increased the time available for paid employment. And fourth, families looked increasingly to a second income to balance tight budgets.

Figure 6.3 also shows another remarkable trend in Canada's labour force: The participation rate of men *decreased* from 84 percent in 1950 to 73 percent in 2000. Decreased labour force participation by men occurred mostly among men aged 55–64. The participation rate of this group fell from 76 percent in 1976 to 61 percent in 2000. Most of this decrease occurred because more men retired at an earlier age. Some of this earlier retirement was by choice and was made possible by an increase in wealth. But some arose from forced "early retirements" at an age at which finding a new job was difficult. For younger men, decreased labour force participation occurred because more remained in full-time education.

■ Part-Time Workers

A part-time job is attractive to many workers because it enables them to balance family and other commitments with work. Part-time jobs are attractive to employers because they don't have to pay benefits to part-time workers and are less constrained by government regulations. Figure 6.4 shows some interesting facts about part-time workers. First, the percentage of workers who are part time has

■ FIGURE 6.4

Part-Time Workers: 1976–2000

*e*Foundations **6.2**

Part-time workers are an increasing proportion of the labour force, up from 13 percent in 1976 to 18 percent in 2000. The percentage of workers who are part time and the percentage of part-time workers who would like full-time work increase in a recession and decrease in an expansion.

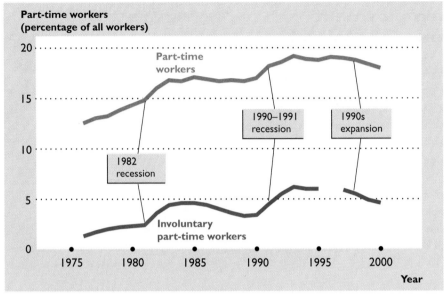

SOURCE: Statistics Canada.

increased gradually from 13 percent in 1976 to 18 percent in 2000. Second, the percentage of part-time workers fluctuates with the business cycle. During recessions in the early 1980s and early 1990s, the part-time employment rate increased. Following each recession, the part-time employment rate first stabilized and then decreased.

The percentage of all workers who are involuntary part-time workers increased from 1.3 percent in 1976 to 5.3 percent in 2000. But more striking are the large swings in the percentage of workers who are involuntary part-time workers. After the 1982 recession, the percentage climbed to 4.4 percent in 1985. And after the 1990–1991 recession, the percentage climbed to 5.9 percent in 1995. In the 1990s expansion, the percentage decreased rapidly.

■ Aggregate and Average Hours

Figure 6.5(a) shows aggregate hours in the Canadian economy from 1960 to 2000. Aggregate hours have an upward trend, but they have not grown as quickly as have the number of people employed. Between 1960 and 2000, the number of people employed in Canada increased by 150 percent. During that same period, aggregate hours increased by 107 percent. Why the difference? Because average hours per worker decreased.

Figure 6.5(b) shows average hours per worker. Average hours per worker decreased from 40 hours a week during the early 1960s to 34.5 hours a week during the 1990s. This shortening of the average workweek by about 14 percent occurred partly because the average hours worked by full-time workers decreased and partly because the number of part-time jobs increased faster than the number of full-time jobs.

Fluctuations in aggregate hours and average hours per worker line up with the business cycle. Figure 6.5 identifies the past two recessions, during which aggregate hours decreased and average hours per worker decreased more quickly than their long-term trend.

■ **FIGURE 6.5**

Work Hours: 1960–2000   *e*Foundations **6.2**

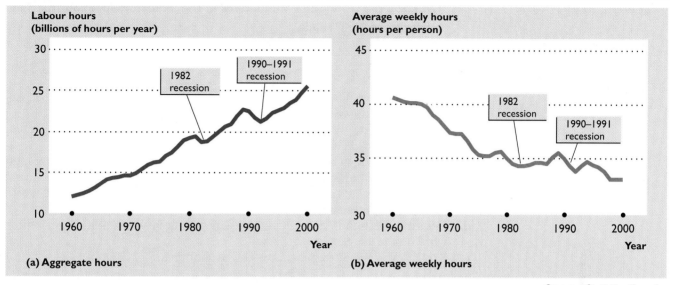

**Labour hours
(billions of hours per year)**

1982 recession

1990–1991 recession

(a) Aggregate hours

**Average weekly hours
(hours per person)**

1982 recession

1990–1991 recession

(b) Average weekly hours

SOURCE: Statistics Canada.

Between 1960 and 2000, aggregate hours increased by an average of 1.9 percent a year. Fluctuations in aggregate hours coincide with business cycle fluctuations.

Average weekly hours have decreased because the full-time workweek has shortened and the number of part-time workers has increased.

Eye On The
GLOBAL
ECONOMY

Women in the Labour Force

The participation rate of women in the Canadian labour force has increased from 23 percent in 1950 to nearly 60 percent in 2000. This upward trend is found in most of the world's rich advanced nations.

But the *level* of women's participation in the labour force varies a great deal around the world. Here, we compare seven other countries— Australia, France, Japan, Spain, Sweden, the United Kingdom and the United States—with Canada.

Among these countries, Sweden's labour force has the largest participation rate of women and the United States comes second. Spain and Japan have the lowest rates.

Cultural factors play a role in determining national differences in women's work choices. But economic factors such as the percentage of women with a college degree will ultimately dominate cultural influences and bring a convergence of outcomes.

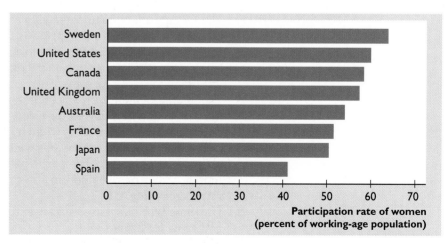

**Participation rate of women
(percent of working-age population)**

SOURCE: OECD.

CHECKPOINT 6.2

Study Guide pp. 94–96

e Foundations 6.2

2 **Describe the trends and fluctuations in the indicators of labour market performance in Canada.**

Practice Problem 6.2

Use the link on your Foundations Web site and view the data for Figures 6.2, 6.3, 6.4, and 6.5. Then answer the following questions:

a. In which decade—the 1960s, 1970s, 1980s, or 1990s—was the unemployment rate the lowest? What brought low unemployment in that decade?

b. In which decade was the unemployment rate the highest? What brought high unemployment in that decade?

c. Describe the trends in the participation rates of men and women and all workers. Why did these trends occur?

d. Describe the trends and fluctuations in part-time work. Why is part-time work on the increase?

e. Explain why the average workweek has shortened.

Exercise 6.2

Use the link on your Foundations Web site and view the data for Figures 6.2, 6.3, 6.4 and 6.5. Then answer the following questions:

a. During which decade—the 1960s, 1970s, 1980s, or 1990s—did the labour force participation rate of women increase most? Suggest some reasons why this rapid increase occurred during this particular decade.

b. In which decade did the labour force participation rate of men decrease most? Suggest some reasons why this rapid decrease occurred during this particular decade.

c. Describe the trends in the unemployment rate, the labour force participation rates of men and women, part-time workers, involuntary part-time workers, and aggregate hours since 1994. Why did these trends occur?

Solution to Practice Problem 6.2

a. The average unemployment rates in each decade were: 1960s, 5.0 percent; 1970s, 6.7 percent; 1980s, 9.4 percent; 1990s, 9.6 percent. The unemployment rate was the lowest during the 1960s, due to a strong economic expansion generated by large increases in government spending on social programs and rapidly-rising exports to the U.S. economy.

b. The unemployment rate was highest during the 1990s, when a deep recession in 1991–1992 was followed by a slow recovery.

c. The participation rate of women increased because (1) better-educated women earn more, (2) more jobs were created, and (3) people have more time for paid employment. The participation rate of men decreased because men retired earlier or remained in full-time education. The overall participation rate increased.

d. Part-time work increased because it provides flexible hours for workers and cuts costs for firms.

e. Average workweek shortened because average hours of full-time workers decreased and the percentage of workers who were part time increased.

6.3 THE SOURCES AND TYPES OF UNEMPLOYMENT

How do people become unemployed, how long do they remain unemployed, and who is at greatest risk to become unemployed? Let's begin to answer these questions by looking at the events that move people into and out of the labour market and into and out of jobs.

■ Sources of Unemployment

The labour market is constantly churning. New jobs are created and old ones destroyed. Some people move into the labour force, and some move out of it. Job creation and job destruction and the movement into and out of the labour force create unemployment.

People who become unemployed are:

1. Job losers
2. Job leavers
3. Entrants or re-entrants

Job Losers

People who are laid off, either permanently or temporarily, from their jobs are called *job losers*. People lose their jobs for a variety of reasons. Some are just not a good match for the job they're doing, and they get fired. Firms fail, so their workers get laid off. And new technology destroys some jobs.

A job loser has two choices: either look for another job or withdraw from the labour force. A job loser who decides to look for a new job remains in the labour force and becomes unemployed. A job loser who decides to withdraw from the labour force does not get counted as being unemployed. Such a person is classified as "not in the labour force." Most job losers decide to look for a new job and some of them take a long time to find one.

Job Leavers

People who voluntarily quit their jobs are called *job leavers*. Most people who leave their jobs do so for one of two reasons: either they've got a better job, or they've decided to withdraw from the labour force. Neither of these job leavers becomes unemployed. But a few people quit their jobs because they want to spend time looking for a better one. These job leavers become unemployed.

Entrants and Re-Entrants

People who have just left school and entered the job market are called *entrants*. Some entrants have a job lined up before leaving school and are never unemployed. But many entrants spend time searching for their first job, and during this period, they are unemployed.

People who previously had jobs but quit and left the labour force and who have now decided to look for jobs are called *re-entrants*. Some re-entrants are people who have been out of the labour force rearing children, but most are discouraged workers—people who gave up searching for jobs because they were not able to find suitable ones and who have now decided to look again.

Figure 6.6 shows the magnitudes of the three sources of unemployment. Most of the unemployed are job losers. Also, their number fluctuates most. Entrants and

Everyone who is unemployed is a job loser, a job leaver, or an entrant or re-entrant into the labour force. Job losers are the biggest group and their number fluctuates most. Entrants and re-entrants are the second biggest group. Their number also fluctuates. Job leavers are the smallest group.

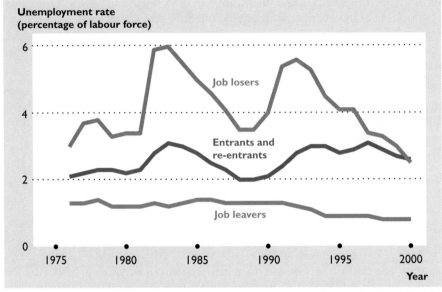

SOURCE: Statistics Canada.

re-entrants are also a large component and their number also fluctuates. Job leavers are the smallest and most stable source of unemployment.

■ How Unemployment Ends

People who end a period of unemployment are either:

1. Hires or recalls
2. Withdrawals

Hires and Recalls

People who have been unemployed but have been hired to start a new job are called *hires*. And people who have been temporarily laid off (which is classified as unemployment) and who start work again are called *recalls*. Firms are constantly hiring and recalling workers, so there are always people moving from unemployment to employment.

Withdrawals

People who have been unemployed and who decide to stop looking for jobs are called *withdrawals* from the labour force. Most of these people are *discouraged workers*. They will most likely re-enter the labour force later when they think that job prospects have improved.

■ Labour Market Flows: A Summary

Figure 6.7 provides a summary of the labour market flows that begin and end a period of unemployment.

FIGURE 6.7
Labour Market Flows

*e*Foundations **6.3**

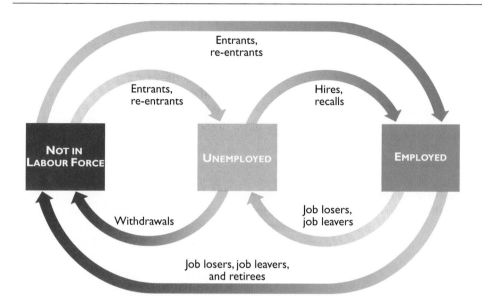

Unemployment results from employed people losing or leaving their jobs (job losers and job leavers) and from people entering the labour force (entrants and re-entrants). Unemployment ends because people get hired or recalled or because they withdraw from the labour force.

■ Types of Unemployment

Unemployment is classified into four types:

- Frictional
- Structural
- Seasonal
- Cyclical

Frictional Unemployment

Frictional unemployment is the unemployment that arises from normal labour turnover—from people entering and leaving the labour force and from the ongoing creation and destruction of jobs. Frictional unemployment is a permanent and healthy phenomenon in a dynamic, growing economy.

The unending flow of people into and out of the labour force and the processes of job creation and job destruction create the need for people to search for jobs and for businesses to search for workers. There are always businesses with unfilled jobs and people seeking jobs.

Look in your local newspaper, and you will see that there are always jobs being advertised. Businesses don't usually hire the first person who applies for a job, and unemployed people don't usually take the first job that comes their way. Instead, both firms and workers spend time searching out what they believe will be the best attainable match. By this search process, people can match their own skills and interests with the available jobs and find a satisfying job and income. While these unemployed people are searching, they are frictionally unemployed.

The amount of frictional unemployment depends on the rate at which people enter and re-enter the labour force and on the rate at which jobs are created and

Frictional unemployment
The unemployment that arises from normal labour turnover—from people entering and leaving the labour force and from the ongoing creation and destruction of jobs.

destroyed. During the 1970s, the amount of frictional unemployment increased because of the postwar baby boom that began during the 1940s. By the 1970s, the baby boom was creating a bulge in the number of people leaving school. As these people entered the labour force, the amount of frictional unemployment increased.

The amount of frictional unemployment is also influenced by unemployment compensation. The greater the number of unemployed people eligible for benefits and the more generous those benefits, the longer is the average time taken in job search and the greater is the amount of frictional unemployment. Unemployment benefits in Canada and Western Europe exceed those in the United States, which is one reason why these economies have higher unemployment rates than the United States.

Structural Unemployment

Structural unemployment
The unemployment that arises when changes in technology or international competition change the skills needed to perform jobs or change the locations of jobs.

Seasonal unemployment
The unemployment that arises because of seasonal weather patterns.

Cyclical unemployment
The fluctuating unemployment over the business cycle that increases during a recession and decreases during an expansion.

Structural unemployment is the unemployment that arises when changes in technology or international competition change the skills needed to perform jobs or change the locations of jobs. Structural unemployment usually lasts longer than frictional unemployment because workers must usually retrain and possibly relocate to find a job. For example, when a telephone exchange in Halifax is automated, some jobs in that city are destroyed. Meanwhile, new jobs for life-insurance salespeople and retail clerks are created in cities in Ontario, Alberta, and British Columbia. The former telephone operators remain unemployed for several months until they move, retrain, and get one of these jobs. Structural unemployment is painful, especially for older workers for whom the best available option might be to retire early but with a lower income than they had expected.

Sometimes, the amount of structural unemployment is modest. At other times, it is large, and at such times, structural unemployment can become a serious long-term problem. It was especially large during much of the 1980s when foreign competition destroyed jobs in traditional Canadian industries, such as steel making, and created jobs in new industries, such as information processing and electronics. In the early 1990s, structural unemployment increased again as many businesses and governments downsized.

Seasonal Unemployment

Seasonal unemployment is the unemployment that arises because of seasonal weather patterns. Seasonal unemployment increases during the winter months and decreases during the spring and summer. A fruit picker who is laid off after the fall harvest and who gets rehired the following summer experiences seasonal unemployment. Seasonal factors increase unemployment by about 200,000 during the Canadian winter.

Cyclical Unemployment

Cyclical unemployment is the fluctuating unemployment over the business cycle. Cyclical unemployment increases during a recession and decreases during an expansion. An autoworker who is laid off because the economy is in a recession and who gets recalled some months later when the expansion begins has experienced cyclical unemployment.

■ Duration and Demographics of Unemployment

Some people are unemployed for a week or two, and others for a year or more. The longer the period of unemployment, the greater the personal cost to the unemployed. The average duration of unemployment varies over the business cycle. In a recession, the average duration increases, and during an expansion, the average duration decreases.

Figure 6.8(a) compares the duration of unemployment in 1992, the last business cycle trough, with that in 1989, the last business cycle peak. In the peak of 1989, almost 32 percent of the unemployed were in that state for 4 weeks or less and 40 percent of the unemployed were jobless for longer than 13 weeks. In the trough of 1992, only 25 percent of the unemployed found a new job in 4 weeks or less and 50 percent were unemployed for more than 13 weeks.

Unemployment does not affect all demographic groups and regions in the same way. And the differences between the groups and regions most and least affected by unemployment are large. Figure 6.8(b) shows the differences in 2000. The unemployment rate for young people (age 15–24) was more than twice as high as for people over 25. It also shows that the unemployment rate in Atlantic Canada was more than twice that in the Prairies.

Why do these large differences arise? Young people try different lines of work and leave their jobs more frequently than do older workers. Also, firms hire teenagers on a trial basis and lay off younger workers first. Fewer firms locate in Atlantic Canada so the rate of job creation there is low.

■ FIGURE 6.8
Unemployment Rates by Duration, Age, and Region   *e*Foundations **6.3**

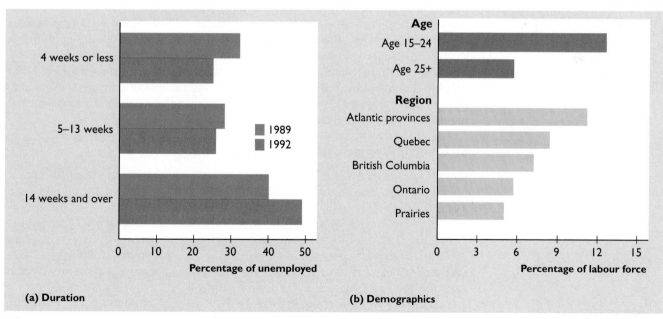

(a) Duration

(b) Demographics

SOURCE: Statistics Canada.

In a business cycle peak year (1989 was the most recent), unemployed people find jobs faster than in a business cycle trough year (1992 was the most recent).

The unemployment rate of people aged 15–24 is more than twice that of people aged 25 and over. The unemployment rate in Atlantic Canada is more than twice that in the Prairies.

You've seen that there is always *some* unemployment—someone looking for a job or laid off and waiting to be recalled. Yet one of the goals of economic policy is to achieve full employment. What do we mean by *full employment*?

■ Full Employment

There can be a lot of unemployment at full employment, and the term "full employment" is an example of a technical economic term that does not correspond with everyday language. **Full employment** occurs when there is no cyclical unemployment or, equivalently, when all the unemployment is frictional, structural, and seasonal. The divergence of the unemployment rate from full employment is cyclical unemployment.

The unemployment rate at full employment is called the **natural unemployment rate.** The term "natural unemployment rate" is another example of a technical economic term that does not correspond with everyday language. For most people—especially for unemployed workers—there is nothing *natural* about unemployment.

So, why do economists call a situation with a lot of unemployment one of full employment? And why is the unemployment rate at full employment called the "natural" unemployment rate? The reason is that the Canadian economy is a complex mechanism that undergoes constant change in its players, structure, and direction. For example in 2000, around 300,000 people retired and more than 300,000 new workers entered the labour force. Thousands of businesses, including new start-ups, expanded and created jobs while thousands of others downsized or failed and destroyed jobs. This process of change creates frictions and dislocations that are unavoidable—that are natural. And they create unemployment.

There is not much controversy about the existence of a natural unemployment rate. But economists don't agree about its size or the extent to which it fluctuates. Most would agree that the natural unemployment rate has been in the 8–9 percent range in recent years and that during the late 1990s it decreased below 8 percent.

An increasing number of economists say that the natural unemployment rate is not constant but rather fluctuates as the amount of frictional and structural unemployment fluctuates. These economists believe that at times of rapid demographic change and rapid structural change, the natural unemployment rate can be high. (You will learn more about the uncertain value of the natural unemployment rate in Chapters 8 and 17.)

■ Unemployment and Real GDP

Cyclical unemployment is the fluctuating unemployment over the business cycle—unemployment that increases during a recession and decreases during an expansion. At full employment, there is no cyclical unemployment. At a business cycle trough, cyclical unemployment is positive and at a business cycle peak, it is *negative*.

Figure 6.9(a) shows the unemployment rate in Canada between 1980 and 2000. It also shows our estimate of the natural unemployment rate (the black line) and cyclical unemployment (the areas shaded red, when cyclical unemployment was positive, and blue, when cyclical unemployment was negative).

Figure 6.9(b) shows Canada's real GDP between 1980 and 2000. The figure also shows **potential GDP**, which is the level of real GDP that the economy would produce if it were at full employment. Because the unemployment rate fluctuates around the natural unemployment rate, real GDP fluctuates around potential

---

Full employment
When there is no cyclical unemployment or, equivalently, when all the unemployment is frictional, structural, and seasonal.

Natural unemployment rate
The unemployment rate at full employment.

ECONOMICS
in the
NEWS

September 20, 2001

Employment Insurance

The estimated number of Canadians who received regular Employment Insurance (EI) benefits in July rose 7.4 percent from June to 542,520. This marks the largest of three consecutive monthly increases.

STATISTICS CANADA, *THE DAILY*

Questions
1. Which type of unemployment—frictional, structural, seasonal, or cyclical—do you think increased when the number of people receiving EI benefits increased in the summer of 2001?
2. What does this information suggest about the state of the economy in the summer of 2001?

 *e*Foundations **6.3**

Potential GDP
The level of real GDP that the economy would produce if it were at full employment.

■ **FIGURE 6.9**

The Relationship Between Unemployment and Real GDP

e/**Foundations 6.3**

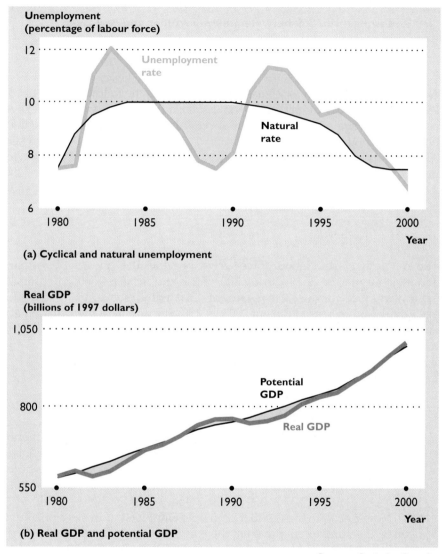

As the unemployment rate fluctuates around the natural unemployment rate (part a), real GDP fluctuates around potential GDP (part b).

SOURCE: Statistics Canada.

GDP. When the unemployment rate is above the natural unemployment rate (in part a), real GDP is below potential GDP (in part b); when the unemployment rate is below the natural unemployment rate, real GDP is above potential GDP; and when the unemployment rate equals the natural unemployment rate, real GDP equals potential GDP.

You will learn what determines full employment and potential GDP in Chapter 8. And you'll learn what determines the fluctuations around full employment and potential GDP in Chapters 14 and 15.

3 **Describe the sources and types of unemployment, define full employment, and explain the link between unemployment and real GDP.**

Practice Problem 6.3

A labour force survey in a Polynesian island records the following data for December 31, 2001: number employed, 13,500; number unemployed, 1,500; number not in the labour force, 7,500. The survey also provides the following information about labour market flows during 2002: hires and recalls, 1,000; job losers, 750; job leavers, 300; entrants, 150; re-entrants, 450; withdrawals, 500. The working-age population increased during 2002 by 100. Calculate for the end of 2002:

a. The unemployment rate.
b. The labour force participation rate.

Exercise 6.3

The Polynesian island labour force survey provides the following information about labour market flows during 2003: hires and recalls, 1,500; job losers, 550; job leavers, 300; entrants, 200; re-entrants, 500; withdrawals, 450. The working-age population increased during 2003 by 150. Starting with the situation at the end of 2002 in the practice problem, calculate for the end of 2003:

a. The unemployment rate.
b. The labour force participation rate.
c. What do you predict happened to real GDP in 2003? Why?

Solution to Practice Problem 6.3

a. The number of people unemployed at the end of 2002 equals the number unemployed at the end of 2001, which is 1,500 plus the number of job losers, 750; job leavers, 300; entrants, 150; and re-entrants, 450; minus the number of hires and recalls, 1,000; and withdrawals, 500. That is,

$$1,500 + 750 + 300 + 150 + 450 - 1,000 - 500 = 1,650.$$

Now calculate the number of people employed at the end of 2002. It equals the number employed at the end of 2001, which is 13,500 plus the number of hires and recalls, 1,000; minus the number of job losers, 750; and the number of job leavers, 300. That is,

$$13,500 + 1,000 - 750 - 300 = 13,450.$$

Next calculate the labour force, which is the sum of the number unemployed and the number employed, which equals 1,650 + 13,450 = 15,100.

The unemployment rate is the number unemployed as a percentage of the labour force, which is (1,650 ÷ 15,100) × 100 = 10.9 percent.

b. The labour force participation rate is the labour force as a percentage of the working-age population. The working-age population at the end of 2001 is the sum of number employed (13,500), number unemployed (1,500), and the number not in the labour force (7,500). That is,

$$13,500 + 1,500 + 7,500 = 22,500.$$

The working-age population increased during 2002 by 100, so at the end of 2002 it is 22,600.

The labour force participation rate is (15,100 ÷ 22,600) × 100 = 66.8 percent.

CHAPTER CHECKPOINT

Key Points

1 **Define the unemployment rate and other labour market indicators.**

- The unemployment rate is the number unemployed as a percentage of the labour force and the labour force is the sum of the number employed and the number unemployed.
- The labour force participation rate is the labour force as a percentage of the working-age population.

2 **Describe the trends and fluctuations in the indicators of labour market performance in Canada.**

- The unemployment rate fluctuates with the business cycle.
- The female labour force participation rate has increased, and the male rate has decreased.
- Aggregate hours trend upward more slowly than employment because average hours decrease. Aggregate hours and average hours fluctuate with the business cycle.

3 **Describe the sources and types of unemployment, define full employment, and explain the link between unemployment and real GDP.**

- Unemployment arises from a process of job creation and job destruction and from the movement of people into and out of the labour force.
- Unemployment can be frictional, structural, seasonal, or cyclical.
- The duration of unemployment fluctuates over the business cycle.
- The unemployment rate is highest among young people.
- The unemployment rate is highest in Atlantic Canada.
- Full employment occurs when there is no cyclical unemployment; the unemployment rate equals the natural unemployment rate.
- As the unemployment rate fluctuates around the natural unemployment rate, real GDP fluctuates around potential GDP.

Key Terms

Aggregate hours, 133
Cyclical unemployment, 144
Discouraged worker, 132
Frictional unemployment, 143
Full employment, 146
Full-time workers, 130
Involuntary part-time workers, 132
Labour force, 130

Labour force participation rate, 132
Natural unemployment rate, 146
Part-time workers, 130
Potential GDP, 146
Seasonal unemployment, 144
Structural unemployment, 144
Unemployment rate, 131
Working-age population, 130

Exercises

 1. Use the link on your Foundations Web site to visit Statistics Canada and find the following labour market data for Canada in the most recent month and for the same month one year ago: the labour force, the number employed, the number unemployed, and the working-age population.
  a. Calculate for the two months the
     i. Unemployment rate.
     ii. Labour force participation rate.
  b. Describe the change in the labour market over the past year.

 2. Use the link on your Foundations Web site to visit Statistics Canada and find the data on real GDP for the past year through the most recent quarter.
  a. Describe the change in real GDP over the past year.
  b. Explain how the change in real GDP relates to the changes in the labour market that you described in Exercise 1b.

 3. Use the link on your Foundations Web site to visit Statistics Canada and find labour market data for your own province.
  a. What have been the trends in employment, unemployment, and labour force participation in your own province during the past two years?
  b. Based on what you know about your own region, how would you set about explaining these trends?
  c. Try to identify those industries that have expanded most and those that have shrunk.
  d. What are the problems with your own regional labour market that you think need government action to resolve?
  e. What actions do you think your provincial government must take to resolve them? Answer this question by using the demand and supply model of the labour market and predict the effects of the actions you prescribe.
  f. Compare the labour market performance of your own province with that of the nation as a whole.
  g. If your province is performing better than the national average, to what do you attribute the success? If your region is performing worse than the national average, to what do you attribute its problems?

 4. Use the link on your Foundations Web site to obtain labour market data for the United States.
  a. What have been the trends in employment, unemployment, and labour force participation in the United States during the past two years?
  b. Compare and contrast Canadian and U.S. labour market trends during these years.
  c. Based on what you've learned in this chapter about the types of unemployment, which types of unemployment do you think Canada has more of than the United States? Why?
  d. Is the natural unemployment rate in Canada higher or lower than in the United States?
  e. To what do you attribute the difference in the natural unemployment rate in the two countries?

The CPI and the Cost of Living

CHAPTER CHECKLIST

When you have completed your study of this chapter,
you will be able to:

1 Explain what the Consumer Price Index (CPI) is and how it is calculated.

2 Explain the limitations of the CPI as a measure of the cost of living.

3 Adjust money values for inflation and calculate real wage rates and real interest rates.

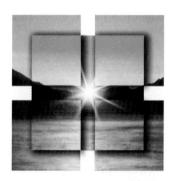

You learned in Chapters 5 and 6 how economists at Statistics Canada measure GDP and how they keep track of the developments in the labour market. These economic indicators provide information on the standard of living. In this chapter, we focus on measuring the cost of living.

The main measure of the cost of living is called the Consumer Price Index, or CPI. Statistics Canada publishes new figures each month, and analysts in newspapers and on TV quickly leap to conclusions about the causes of recent changes in prices and the implications of the latest numbers for the economy and interest rate actions by the Bank of Canada.

How does the government determine the CPI? How well does it measure the cost of living and the inflation rate?

In this chapter, you will find out how economic statisticians measure the price level and the inflation rate and you will discover the limitations of these measures. You will also learn how we use price index numbers to strip away the veil of money and dollar values to see the real values that they represent.

7.1 THE CONSUMER PRICE INDEX

Consumer Price Index (CPI)
A measure of the average of the prices paid by households for a fixed market basket of consumer goods and services.

The **Consumer Price Index (CPI)** is a measure of the average of the prices paid by households for a fixed market basket of consumer goods and services. Statistics Canada calculates the CPI every month, and by using these numbers, we can compare what the fixed market basket costs this month with what it cost in some previous month or year.

■ Reading the CPI Numbers

Base period
A period for which the CPI is defined to equal 100. Currently, the base period is 1992.

Statistics Canada defines the value of the CPI to be 100 in a period called the **base period.** Currently, the base period is 1992. That is, the Consumer Price Index in 1992 is defined to be 100.

In September 2001, the CPI was 117.4. This number tells us that the average of the prices paid by households for a fixed market basket of consumer goods and services was 17.4 percent higher in September 2001 than it was on the average in 1992.

In August 2001, the CPI was 117.1. Comparing the September CPI with the August CPI tells us that the average of the prices paid by households for a fixed market basket of consumer goods and services increased by 0.3 percent in September 2001.

■ Constructing the CPI

Constructing the CPI is a huge operation that costs millions of dollars and involves three stages:

- Selecting the CPI basket
- Conducting the monthly price survey
- Calculating the CPI

■ The CPI Basket

The first stage in constructing the CPI is to select what is called the *CPI basket*. This "basket" contains the goods and services represented in the index and the relative importance attached to each of them. The idea is to make the relative importance of the items in the CPI basket the same as in the budget of an average household. For example, because people spend more on housing than on bus rides, the CPI places more weight on the price of housing than on the price of a bus ride.

To determine the spending patterns of households and to select the CPI basket, Statistics Canada uses information gathered in the Family Expenditure Survey and Survey of Household Spending. Today's CPI is based on data gathered in a survey conducted in 1996. It is important that the CPI basket be updated regularly, because for reasons that we will soon see, changes in consumer spending patterns can affect the accuracy of the CPI statistics.

Statistics Canada uses two baskets and calculates two CPIs. One, called "CPI All-items," measures the average of the prices paid by all households and covers all goods and services. The other is called "CPI All-items excluding the 8 most volatile components." These volatile items include the prices of fruit and vegetables; natural gas and oil; gasoline; inter-city transportation; tobacco products and smokers' supplies; and mortgage interest cost. Here, we'll focus on the CPI All-items, the broader measure.

Figure 7.1 shows the CPI basket at the end of 2000. The basket contains around 600 goods and services arranged in the eight large groups shown in the figure. The largest item in a household's budget is shelter, which accounts for 27 percent of the average household's expenditure; when household operations and furnishings are added, the total of these two housing-related items is 38 percent. Transportation is 19 percent. Third in relative importance is food at 18 percent. These four major groups account for almost three-quarters of the average household's budget. Recreation, education, and reading are quite large at 11 percent, followed by clothing and footwear, health and personal care and alcoholic beverages and tobacco products.

Statistics Canada breaks each of these categories into smaller ones. For example, transportation includes automobiles; gasoline; car insurance and repairs; airline, bus, and train tickets; taxi fares; and other items involving transportation.

As you look at these relatively important numbers, remember that they apply to the average household. Individual households are spread around the average. Think about your own expenditure and compare it with the average.

■ The Monthly Price Survey

Each month, employees of Statistics Canada record the prices of the 600 goods and services in the CPI basket in retail outlets across Canada. Because the CPI aims to measure price changes, it is important that the prices recorded each month refer to exactly the same item. For example, suppose the price of a can of peanuts has increased but a can now contains more peanuts. Has the price of peanuts increased? The economic assistant must record the details of changes in quality, size, weight, or packaging so that price changes can be isolated from other changes.

Once the raw price data are in hand, the next task is to calculate the CPI.

▓ FIGURE 7.1
The CPI Basket   *e*Foundations **7.1**

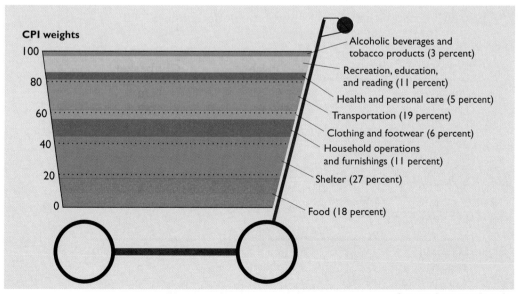

This shopping cart is filled with the items that an average Canadian household buys. Food (18 percent), shelter (27 percent), household operations and furnishings (11 percent), clothing and footwear (6 percent), and transportation (19 percent) take more than 80 percent of household income.

SOURCE: Statistics Canada.

■ Calculating the CPI

The CPI calculation has three steps:

- Find the cost of the CPI basket at base period prices.
- Find the cost of the CPI basket at current period prices.
- Calculate the CPI for the base period and the current period.

We'll work through these three steps for a simple example. Suppose the CPI basket contains only two goods and services: oranges and haircuts. We'll construct an annual CPI rather than a monthly CPI with the base period 2000 and the current period 2001.

Table 7.1 shows the quantities in the CPI basket and the prices in the base period and the current period. Part (a) contains the data for the base period. In that period, consumers bought 10 oranges at $1 each and 5 haircuts at $8 each. To find the cost of the CPI basket in the base period prices, multiply the quantities in the CPI basket by the base period prices. The cost of oranges is $10 (10 at $1 each), and the cost of haircuts is $40 (5 at $8 each). So total expenditure in the base period on the CPI basket is $50 ($10 + $40).

Part (b) contains the price data for the current period. The price of an orange increased from $1 to $2, which is a 100 percent increase ($1 ÷ $1 × 100 = 100). The price of a haircut increased from $8 to $10, which is a 25 percent increase ($2 ÷ $8 × 100 = 25).

The CPI provides a way of averaging these price increases by comparing the cost of the basket rather than the price of each item. To find the cost of the CPI basket in the current period, 2001, multiply the quantities in the basket by their 2001 prices. The cost of oranges is $20 (10 at $2 each), and the cost of haircuts is $50 (5 at $10 each) So total expenditure on the fixed CPI basket at current period prices is $70 ($20 + $50).

■ **TABLE 7.1**

The Consumer Price Index: A Simplified CPI Calculation

e/**Foundations 7.1**

(a) The cost of the CPI basket at base period prices: 2000

Item	CPI basket Quantity	Price	Cost of CPI basket
Oranges	10	$1 each	$10
Haircuts	5	$8 each	$40
		Cost of CPI basket at base period prices	$50

(b) The cost of the CPI basket at current period prices: 2001

Item	CPI basket Quantity	Price	Cost of CPI basket
Oranges	10	$2 each	$20
Haircuts	5	$10 each	$50
		Cost of CPI basket at current period prices	$70

You've now taken the first two steps towards calculating the CPI. The third step uses the numbers you've just calculated to find the CPI for 2000 and 2001. The formula for the CPI is:

$$\text{CPI} = \frac{\text{Cost of CPI basket at current period prices}}{\text{Cost of CPI basket at base period prices}} \times 100.$$

In Table 7.1, you established that in 2000, the cost of the CPI basket was $50 and in 2001, it was $70. If we use these numbers in the CPI formula, we can find the CPI for 2000 and 2001. For 2000, the CPI is:

$$\text{CPI in 2000} = \frac{\$50}{\$50} \times 100 = 100.$$

For 2001, the CPI is:

$$\text{CPI in 2001} = \frac{\$70}{\$50} \times 100 = 140.$$

The principles that you've applied in this simplified CPI calculation apply to the more complex calculations performed every month by Statistics Canada.

■ Measuring Inflation

A major purpose of the CPI is to measure *changes* in the cost of living and in the value of money. To measure these changes, we calculate the **inflation rate,** which is the percentage change in the price level from one year to the next. To calculate the inflation rate, we use the formula:

$$\text{Inflation rate} = \frac{(\text{CPI in current year} - \text{CPI in previous year})}{\text{CPI in previous year}} \times 100.$$

Inflation rate
The percentage change in the price level from one year to the next.

We can use this formula to calculate the inflation rate in 2001 using the CPI numbers that you've just calculated. The CPI in the current year (2001) is 140, and that in the previous year (2000) is 100. So the inflation rate in 2001 was:

$$\text{Inflation rate} = \frac{(140 - 100)}{100} \times 100 = 40 \text{ percent.}$$

This inflation rate is very high—much higher than anything that we experience in Canada. You can check the latest inflation rate by visiting the Statistics Canada Web site. Let's calculate a recent Canadian inflation rate. In September 2001, the CPI was 117.4, and in September 2000, it was 114.4. So the inflation rate during the year to September 2001 was:

$$\text{Inflation rate} = \frac{(117.4 - 114.4)}{114.4} \times 100 = 2.6 \text{ percent.}$$

Figure 7.2(a) shows the CPI in Canada during the 30 years between 1970 and 2000. The CPI increased every year during this period. During the late 1970s and 1980, it was increasing rapidly, but the rate of increase slowed during the 1980s and 1990s. Figure 7.2(b) shows the inflation rate between 1970 and 2000. The two parts of Figure 7.2 are related. When the *price level* in part (a) rises rapidly, the *inflation rate* in part (b) is high, and when the price level in part (a) rises slowly, the inflation rate in part (b) is low.

■ FIGURE 7.2
The CPI and the Inflation Rate: 1970–2000

 *e*Foundations 7.1

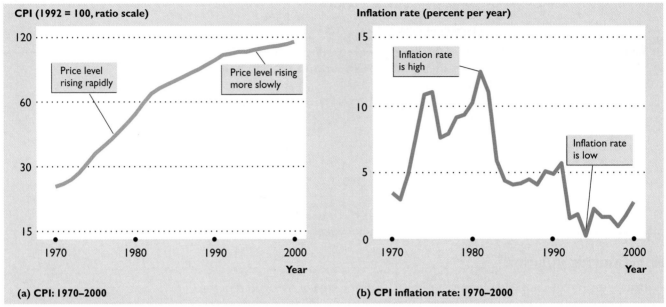

(a) CPI: 1970–2000   (b) CPI inflation rate: 1970–2000

SOURCE: Statistics Canada.

Part (a) shows that the CPI (the price level) has increased every year. Part (b) shows that the inflation rate (the percentage change in the price level) has ranged between 12 percent a year and almost zero. When the price level increases rapidly, the inflation rate is high. When the price level increases slowly, the inflation rate is low.

 **Eye On The PAST**

700 Years of Inflation and Deflation

These extraordinary data show century averages of inflation in England since the 1300s. There was a burst of inflation during the sixteenth century after Europeans discovered America. But this inflation was less than 2 percent a year—less than we have today—and eventually subsided. During the Industrial Revolution, inflation was less than 1 percent a year. Only in the twentieth century did inflation become a serious problem.

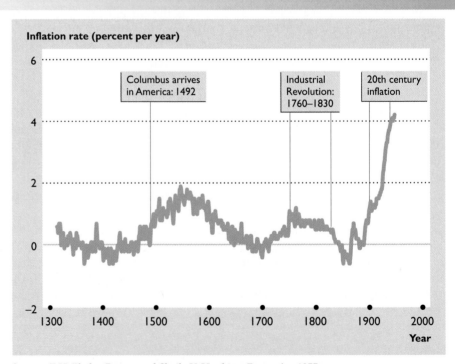

SOURCE: E.H. Phelps Brown and Sheila V. Hopkins, *Economica*, 1955.

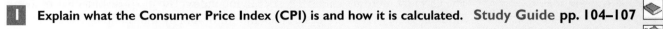

CHECKPOINT 7.1

1 **Explain what the Consumer Price Index (CPI) is and how it is calculated.** Study Guide pp. 104–107

*e*Foundations **7.1**

Practice Problems 7.1

1. A Survey of Household Spending in Sparta shows that people consume only juice and cloth. In 2001, the year of the survey and also the base period, the average household spent $40 on juice and $25 on cloth. The price of juice in 2001 was $4 a bottle, and the price of cloth was $5 a metre. In the current year, 2002, the price of juice is $4 a bottle and the price of cloth is $6 a metre. Calculate:
   a. The CPI basket.
   b. The percentage of the average household budget spent on juice in the base period.
   c. The CPI in 2002.

2. Table 1 shows the CPI in Russia. Calculate Russia's inflation rate in 2000 and 2001. Did the price level rise or fall in 2001? Did the inflation rate increase or decrease in 2001?

TABLE 1

Year	CPI
1999	186
2000	221
2001	251

Exercise 7.1

1. A Survey of Household Spending in the city of Firestorm shows that people consume only firecrackers and bandages. In 2000, the year of the survey and also the base period, the average household spent $100 on firecrackers and $10 on bandages. The price of a firecracker in 2000 was $2, and the price of bandages was $1 a pack. In the current year, 2001, the price of a firecracker is $3 and the price of bandages is $1.25 a pack. Calculate:
   a. The CPI basket.
   b. The percentage of the average household's budget spent on firecrackers in the base period.
   c. The CPI in 2001.
   d. The inflation rate in 2001.

Solutions to Practice Problems 7.1

1a. The CPI basket is the quantities bought during the Survey year, 2001. The average household spent $40 on juice at $4 a bottle so the quantity of juice bought was 10 bottles. The average household spent $25 on cloth at $5 a metre, so the quantity of cloth bought was 5 metres. The CPI basket is 10 bottles of juice and 5 metres of cloth.

1b. In the base period, expenditure on juice was $40 and expenditure on cloth was $25, so the household budget was $65. Expenditure on juice was 61.5 percent of the household budget: ($40 ÷ $65) × 100 = 61.5 percent.

1c. To calculate the CPI in 2002, find the cost of the CPI basket in 2001 and 2002. In 2001, the CPI basket costs $65 ($40 for juice and $25 for cloth). In 2002, the CPI basket costs $40 for juice (10 bottles at $4 a bottle) plus $30 for cloth (5 metres at $6 a metre), which sums to $70. The CPI in 2002 equals ($70÷$65) × 100 = 107.7.

2. The inflation rate in 2000 is [(221 − 186) ÷ 186] × 100 = 18.8 percent. The inflation rate in 2001 is [(251 − 221) ÷ 221] × 100 = 13.6 percent. The price level rose and the inflation rate decreased in 2001.

7.2 THE CPI AND THE COST OF LIVING

Cost of living index
A measure of changes in the amount of money that people would need to spend to achieve a given standard of living.

The CPI is sometimes called a cost of living index. The purpose of a **cost of living index** is to measure changes in the amount of money that people would need to spend to achieve a given standard of living. The CPI does not measure the cost of living for two broad reasons.

First, the CPI does not try to measure all the components of the cost of living. For example, a severe winter might cause people to buy more natural gas and electricity to heat their homes. An increase in the prices of these items would increase the CPI, but the increased quantities bought would not change the CPI because the CPI basket is fixed. So part of this increase in spending, which is an increase in the cost of maintaining a given standard of living, would not show up as an increase in the CPI.

Second, even those components of the cost of living that are included in the CPI are not always measured accurately. The result is that the CPI is possibly a biased measure of changes in the cost of living. Let's look at some of the problems faced by Statistics Canada that might lead to bias in the CPI.

■ The Biased CPI

The main sources of bias in the CPI are:

- New goods bias
- Quality change bias
- Commodity substitution bias
- Outlet substitution bias

New Goods Bias

New goods keep replacing old ones. For example, the PC has replaced the typewriter. The DVD is gradually replacing the videocassette player. The digital camera is replacing the film camera. These are just a few examples of a very long list of new goods to which you can easily add.

If you want to compare the price level in 2001 with that in 1991, you must somehow compare the price of a DVD today with that of a videocassette player in 1991. Because DVDs do a better job than videocassette players, you are better off with the new technology if the prices are the same. But DVDs are more expensive than videocassette players. How much of the higher price is a sign of the higher quality?

Statistics Canada does its best to answer this type of question and employs many experts to help get the correct answer. But there is no sure way of making the necessary adjustment, and most likely, the arrival of new goods puts an upward bias into the CPI and its measure of the inflation rate.

Quality Change Bias

Cars, CD players, and many other items get better every year. For example, central locking, airbags, and antilock braking systems all add to the quality of a car. But they also add to the cost. Is the improvement in quality greater than the increase in cost? Or do car prices rise by more than can be accounted for by quality improvements? To the extent that a price rise is a payment for improved quality, it is not inflation. Again, Statistics Canada does the best job it can to estimate the effects of quality improvements on price changes. But the CPI probably counts too much of any price rise as inflation and so overstates inflation.

Commodity Substitution Bias

Changes in relative prices lead consumers to change the items they buy. People cut back on items that become relatively more costly and increase their consumption of items that become relatively less costly. For example, suppose the price of beef rises while the price of chicken remains constant. Now that beef is more costly relative to chicken, you might decide to buy more chicken and less beef. Suppose that you switch from beef to chicken, spend the same amount on meat as before, and get the same enjoyment as before. Your cost of meat has not changed. But the CPI says that the price of meat has increased because it ignores your substitution between goods in the CPI basket.

Outlet Substitution Bias

When confronted with higher prices, people use discount stores more frequently and convenience stores less frequently. This phenomenon is called *outlet substitution*. Suppose, for example, that gas prices rise by 10 cents a litre. Instead of buying from your nearby gas station for $0.75 a litre, you now drive farther to a gas station that charges $0.65 a litre. Your cost of gas has increased because you must factor in the cost of your time and the gas that you use driving several blocks down the road. But your cost has not increased by as much as the 10 cents a litre increase in the pump price. However, the CPI says that the price of gas has increased by 10 cents a litre because it does not measure outlet substitutions.

The growth of online shopping in recent years has provided an alternative to discount stores, which makes outlet substitution even easier and potentially makes this source of bias more serious.

■ The Magnitude of the Bias

You've reviewed the sources of bias in the CPI. But how big is the bias? The answer varies from country to country. In the United States, a study conducted in 1996 estimated that the U.S. CPI overstates inflation by 1.1 percentage points a year. That is, if the CPI reports that inflation is 3.1 percent a year, most likely inflation is actually 2 percent a year.

It is believed that the bias in Canada's CPI is smaller than 1.1 percentage points a year, largely because Statistics Canada updates the basket of goods and services that it uses for calculating the CPI about every 5 years. In addition, Statistics Canada tries to estimate the quantitative effects of the various sources of bias in the CPI and eliminate them by making statistical adjustments. These adjustments make Canada's CPI a more reliable measure of the price level than the U.S. CPI is of the U.S. price level.

■ Two Consequences of the CPI Bias

The bias in the CPI has two main consequences. It

- Distorts private contracts.
- Increases government outlays.

October 18, 2001

Consumer Price Index

Consumers paid 2.6% more for the goods and services in the Consumer Price Index (CPI) basket than they did in September 2000. After remaining unchanged from July to August, the CPI rose 0.3% from August to September.

STATISTICS CANADA, *THE DAILY*

Questions

1. What does the percentage increase in the CPI measure?

2. Did the inflation rate increase, decrease, or remain constant in September 2001?

3. If inflation persists at its September 2001 rate for a year, by how much would the CPI have increased by September 2002?

4. Do you think the September 2001 rate of price increase was a cause for concern? Why or why not?

 *e*Foundations **7.2**

Distortion of Private Agreements

Many private agreements, such as wage contracts, are linked to the CPI. For example, suppose that the Canadian Auto Workers Union and Ford sign a three-year wage agreement. The deal sets the wage rate for the first year at $28 an hour and further specifies that it will increase by 2.5 percent a year plus the percentage increase in the CPI during each of the three years. Suppose that the CPI increases by 3 percent each year but the true price increase is 2 percent a year (a 1 percent point bias in the CPI). Table 7.2 shows the wage rates each year and the effects of the bias. At the end of the first year, the wage rate rises by 5.5 percent to $29.54 an hour. Already, there is a 28¢ an hour upward bias compared with what the wage rate would have been with a correctly measured CPI. After the second year, the wage rate rises by a further 5.5 percent to $31.16 an hour. The bias is now 54¢ an hour. After three years, the workers are receiving 93¢ an hour more than they would have received if the CPI measured the true increase in prices.

Increases in Government Outlays

Because rising prices decrease the buying power of the dollar, the CPI is used to adjust the incomes of Canadians who receive income assistance such as welfare benefits and pensions. For many such people, a 2.5 percent increase in the CPI would mean that the income assistance and pensions that they receive from the government would also increase by 2.5 percent, so that their purchasing power and standard of living would not be constantly eroded by inflation.

Close to a third of federal government outlays are linked directly to the CPI. If the CPI overstates the inflation rate, all of these expenditures increase by more than that required to compensate for the fall in the buying power of the dollar. And although the effect in each year might be small, over longer periods of time it can accumulate into a substantial effect on government outlays and finances.

■ The GDP Deflator: A Better Measure?

In Chapter 5, you learned about another measure of average prices: the *GDP deflator*. When we calculate the GDP deflator, we compare the current year's prices with the previous year's prices by using the current year's and a previous year's baskets of goods and services. Because the GDP deflator uses current year quantities, real GDP includes new goods and quality improvements and even allows for substitution effects of both commodities and retail outlets. So in principle, the GDP deflator is not subject to the biases of the CPI.

But in practice, the GDP deflator suffers from some of the CPI's problems. To arrive at its estimate of real GDP, Statistics Canada does not directly measure the

---

■ **TABLE 7.2**
A Three-Year Wage Agreement
*e*Foundations **7.2**

	Fixed increase (percent)	CPI increase (percent)	True price increase (percent)	Wage rate (dollars per hour)	Wage bias (dollars per hour)
Initially				28.00	—
After 1 year	2.5	3	2	29.54	0.28
After 2 years	2.5	3	2	31.16	0.54
After 3 years	2.5	3	2	32.88	0.93

physical quantities that are produced. Instead, it estimates quantities by dividing expenditures by price indexes. And one of these price indexes is the CPI. So the biased CPI injects its bias into the GDP deflator.

Also, the GDP deflator is broader than the CPI. GDP is the sum of expenditures on all final goods and services, not just consumption expenditures. So the GDP deflator reflects the prices of such items as industrial robots bought by Daimler-Chrysler to make cars, Bombardier jets bought by foreign airlines, and helicopters bought by the Department of National Defence. So the GDP deflator is not an alternative to the CPI as a measure of the cost of living.

Figure 7.3(a) shows the two measures of inflation based on the CPI and the GDP deflator. The two inflation rates fluctuate in similar ways, and over the thirty years shown here are almost the same. Figure 7.3(b) shows the price levels. Again, both measures follow a similar path.

FIGURE 7.3

Two Measures of Inflation and the Price Level

(a) Two measures of inflation

(b) Two measures of price level

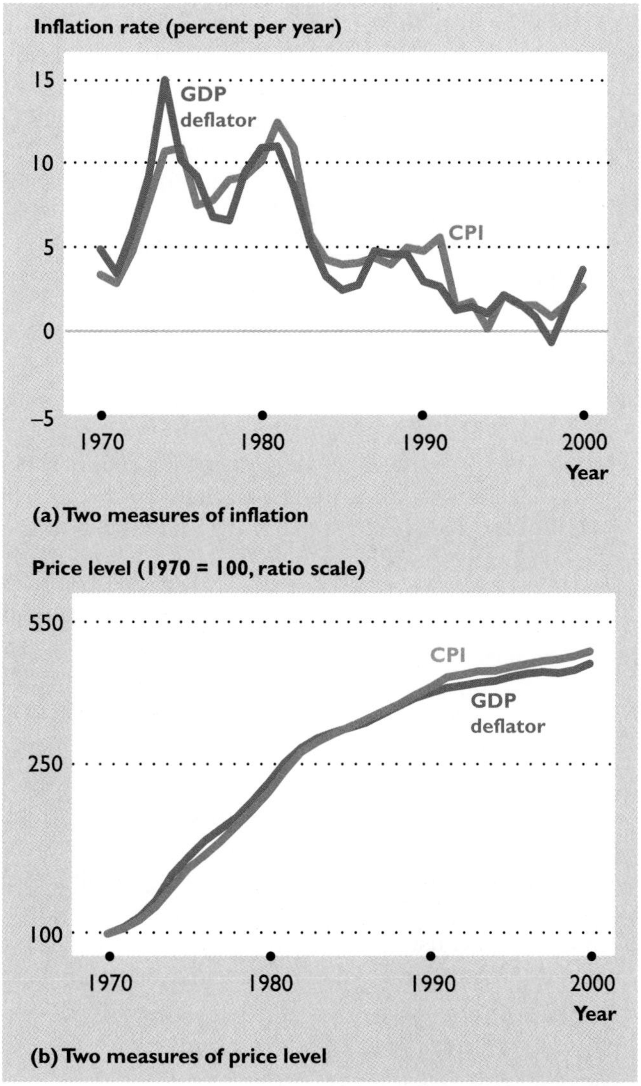

SOURCE: Statistics Canada.

The two measures of the inflation rate in part (a) fluctuate together and over the thirty years shown are almost the same. The two measures of the price level in part (b) also follow similar paths. Both measures probably overstate the inflation rate.

Study Guide pp. 107–109

*e*Foundations 7.2

2 **Explain the limitations of the CPI as a measure of the cost of living.**

Practice Problem 7.2

Economists in the Statistics Bureau decide to check the substitution bias in the CPI. To do so, they conduct an expenditure survey in both 2001 and 2002. Table 1 shows the results of the survey. It shows the items consumers buy and their prices. The Statistics Bureau fixes the base period as 2001 and asks you to:

a. Calculate the CPI in 2002 using the 2001 CPI basket.
b. Calculate the CPI in 2002 using the 2002 CPI basket.
c. Explain whether there is any substitution bias in the CPI that uses the 2001 basket.

TABLE 1

	2001		2002	
Item	Quantity	Price	Quantity	Price
Broccoli	10	$3.00	15	$3.00
Carrots	15	$2.00	10	$4.00

Exercise 7.2

In Virtual Reality, time travel became possible only in 3002. Economists in the Statistics Bureau decided to conduct an expenditure survey in both 3001 and 3002 to check the substitution bias of the CPI. Table 2 shows the results of the survey. It shows the items that consumers buy and their prices. The Statistics Bureau fixes the base period as 3001 and asks you to:

a. Calculate the CPI in 3002 using the 3001 CPI basket.
b. Calculate the CPI in 3002 using the 3002 CPI basket.
c. Explain whether there is any substitution bias in the CPI that uses the 3001 basket.

TABLE 2

	3001		3002	
Item	Quantity	Price	Quantity	Price
Games	10	$30	5	$35
Time travel	0	–	10	$4,000

Solution to Practice Problem 7.2

a. Table 3 shows the calculation of the CPI in 2001 using the 2001 basket. The cost of the 2001 basket at 2001 prices is $60, and the cost of the 2001 basket in 2002 prices is $90. So the CPI in 2002 using the 2001 basket is ($90 ÷ $60) × 100 = 150.

b. Table 4 shows the calculation of the CPI in 2002 using the 2002 basket. The cost of the 2002 basket at 2001 prices is $65, and the cost of the 2002 basket in 2002 prices is $85. So the CPI in 2002 using the 2002 basket is ($85 ÷ $65) × 100 = 134.

c. There is some substitution bias in the CPI that uses the 2001 basket. The price of broccoli remains constant, but the price of carrots rises by 100 percent. So consumers cut the quantity of carrots consumed and increase the quantity of broccoli consumed. They end up spending $85 on vegetables. But they would have spent $90 if they had not substituted the now relatively less costly broccoli. The cost of vegetables does not rise by 50 percent as shown by the CPI. Instead, because of substitution, the cost of vegetables increases by only 42 percent ($85 is 42 percent greater than $60). When we calculate the increase in the price of vegetables using the 2002 CPI basket, the increase is only 31 percent ($85 compared with $65). So the CPI is biased upward because it ignores the substitutions that people make in response to changes in the price of one item relative to the price of another.

TABLE 3

Item	2001 basket at 2001 prices	2001 basket at 2002 prices
Broccoli	$30	$30
Carrot	$30	$60
Totals	$60	$90

TABLE 4

Item	2002 basket at 2001 prices	2002 basket at 2002 prices
Broccoli	$45	$45
Carrot	$20	$40
Totals	$65	$85

7.3 NOMINAL AND REAL VALUES

In 2000, it cost 47 cents to mail a first-class letter. One hundred years earlier, in 1900, that same letter would have cost 2 cents to mail. Does it *really* cost you 23.5 times the amount that it cost your great-great-grandmother to mail a letter?

You know that it does not. You know that a dollar today buys less than what a dollar bought in 1900, so the cost of a stamp has not really increased to 23.5 times its 1900 level. But has it increased at all? Did it really cost you any more to mail a letter in 2000 than it cost your great-great-grandmother in 1900?

The CPI can be used to answer questions like these. In fact, that is one of the main reasons for constructing a price index. Let's see how we can compare the price of a stamp in 1900 and the price of a stamp in 2000.

■ Dollars and Cents at Different Dates

To compare dollar amounts at different dates, we need to know the CPI at those dates. Currently, the CPI has a base of 100 for 1992.

In 2000, the CPI was 113.5, and in 1900, it was 5.3. By using these two numbers, we can calculate the relative value of the dollar in 1900 and 2000. To do so, we divide the 2000 CPI by the 1900 CPI. That ratio is 113.5 ÷ 5.3 = 21.4. That is, prices on the average were a bit more than 21 times higher in 2000 than in 1900.

We can use this ratio to convert the price of a 2-cent stamp in 1900 into its 2000 equivalent. The formula for this calculation is:

$$\text{Price of stamp in 2000 dollars} = \text{Price of stamp in 1900 dollars} \times \frac{\text{CPI in 2000}}{\text{CPI in 1900}}.$$

$$= 2 \text{ cents} \times \frac{113.5}{5.3} = 42.8 \text{ cents}.$$

So it *really* cost great-great-grandmother almost as much to mail that first-class letter as it cost you in 2000. She paid the equivalent of 42.8 cents, and you paid 47 cents.

The calculation that we've just done is an example of converting a *nominal* value into a *real* value. A nominal value is one that is expressed in current dollars. A real value is one that is expressed in the dollars of a given year.

■ Nominal and Real Values in Macroeconomics

Macroeconomics makes a big issue of the distinction between nominal and real values. You saw that distinction in Chapter 5, where you learned the difference between nominal GDP and real GDP.

To calculate real GDP, we use the same idea that you've just used to calculate the real price of a stamp. But usually, in macroeconomics, we use the GDP deflator rather than the CPI as our measure of the price level. The reason is that we are dealing with economy totals, of which consumer spending is just one part. So real GDP is equal to nominal GDP divided by the GDP deflator and *not* nominal GDP divided by the CPI.

The Nominal and Real Price of Mailing a Letter

The figure shows the cost of mailing a letter since 1900. The green line is the nominal price—the actual price of a postage stamp in the dollars (cents) of the year in question. The red line is the real price—the price in terms of the 2000 dollar. You can see that the nominal price has increased but that the real price has fluctuated, sometimes rising and sometimes falling. The highest real price, 53 cents, occurred in 1983 and the lowest price, 17 cents, occurred in 1920.

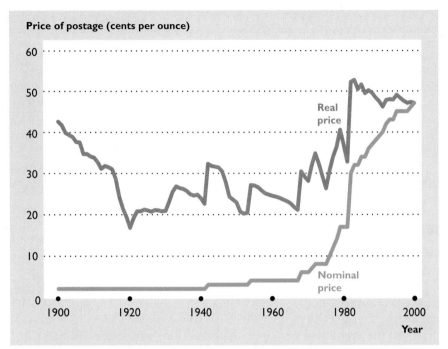

SOURCE: Canada Post and Statistics Canada.

Two other nominal–real distinctions play a big role in macroeconomics—and in your life. They are the distinctions between:

- The nominal wage rate and the real wage rate
- The nominal interest rate and the real interest rate

Let's study these vital distinctions.

■ Nominal and Real Wage Rates

The price of labour is the wage rate—the income that an hour of labour earns. In macroeconomics, we are interested in economy-wide performance, so we focus on the *average* hourly wage rate. The **nominal wage rate** is the average hourly wage rate measured in *current* dollars. The **real wage rate** is the average hourly wage rate measured in the dollars of a given base year.

To calculate the real wage rate, we divide the nominal wage rate by the CPI and multiply by 100. That is:

$$\text{Real wage rate in 2000} = \frac{\text{Nominal wage rate in 2000}}{\text{CPI in 2000}} \times 100.$$

In 2000, the nominal wage rate (average hourly wage rate) was \$20.01 and the CPI was 113.5 (1992 = 100), so the real wage rate in 2000 was:

$$\text{Real wage rate in 2000} = \frac{\$20.01}{113.5} \times 100 = \$17.63 \ (1992 \text{ dollars}).$$

Nominal wage rate
The average hourly wage rate measured in *current* dollars.

Real wage rate
The average hourly wage rate measured in the dollars of a given base year.

Because we measure the real wage rate in constant base-year dollars, a change in the real wage rate measures the change in the quantity of goods and services that an hour's work can buy. In contrast, a change in the nominal wage rate measures a combination of a change in the quantity of goods and services that an hour's work can buy and a change in the price level. So the real wage rate takes the effects of inflation out of changes in the nominal wage rate.

The real wage rate is a significant economic variable because it measures the real reward for labour, which is a major determinant of the standard of living. The real wage rate is also significant because it measures the real cost of labour, which influences the quantity of labour that firms are willing to hire.

Figure 7.4 shows what has happened to the nominal wage rate and the real wage rate in Canada between 1960 and 2000. The nominal wage rate is the average hourly earning of all workers including wages and salaries and supplementary labour income such as health and insurance benefits. This measure is probably the most appropriate because the true amount paid to workers for labour services includes the value of the noncash benefits.

The nominal wage rate increased from $1.86 an hour in 1960 to $20.01 an hour in 2000. The real wage rate also increased, but more slowly. In 1992 dollars (the CPI base-period dollars), the real wage rate was $10.06 an hour in 1960 and $17.63 an hour in 2000.

The increase in the real wage rate is smaller than the increase in the nominal wage rate because of the effects of inflation. When the effects of inflation are removed from the nominal wage rate, we can see what is happening to the buying power of the average wage rate.

You can also see that the real wage rate has grown at an uneven pace. It grew rapidly during the 1960s and early 1970s and very slowly after 1975.

▊ FIGURE 7.4
Nominal and Real Wage Rates: 1970–2000

 *e*/**Foundations 7.3**

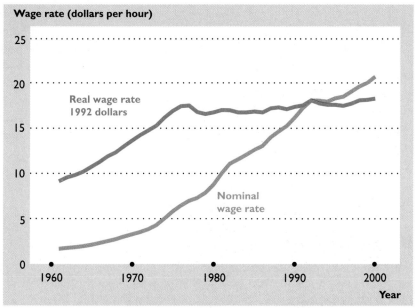

The nominal wage rate has increased in every year since 1960. During the 1960s and early 1970s, the real wage rate grew rapidly but after 1975, it grew very slowly. The real wage rate has decreased at times, most notably in the late 1970s and the first half of the 1990s.

SOURCE: Statistics Canada.

The Nominal and Real Wage Rates of Prime Ministers of Canada

Does an airline pilot in 2001 earn a higher real wage rate than a pilot earned in 1960? Does a nickel miner in 2001 earn more than a nickel miner earned in 1960? We can use the formula that you've learned in this chapter to calculate the real wage rates of pilots and miners in 1960 and 2001 and compare them. But the comparison will be imprecise because new technology has changed these jobs a great deal.

One job that has not changed much over time is that of Prime Minister of Canada. The job description hasn't changed, and the level of stress of the job has probably remained similar over the decades.

It is tempting, therefore, to calculate the real wage rates of Canadian Prime Ministers to see how the salaries they received for their efforts have changed over the years.

The figure provides the data. The nominal wage rate (the green line) was set at $12,000 a year in 1905 and increased only slightly for nearly 50 years.

During the First World War, inflation reduced the Prime Minister's real wage rate (as shown by the red line). Following the war, deflation (falling prices) helped to restore some of these losses.

During the early 1930s, the combined effects of the addition of a car allowance and falling prices made R. B. Bennett the highest-paid Prime Minister of the twentieth century (in real dollars), despite the fact that the Great Depression was underway.

For the next 22 years, inflation eroded the Prime Minister's real income to around half its 1933 peak. In 1954, a 59 percent pay raise restored the Prime Minister's real wage to its 1913 level.

But since 1954, inflation has placed the Prime Minister's purchasing power on a downhill slide, despite more frequent increases in the nominal wage rate. By the late 1990s, Jean Chrétien had become the lowest-paid Prime Minister of the twentieth century.

Not counted in the Prime Minister's salary are the paid expenses and other perks that go with the job. These are considerable and have grown over the years, so when all is said and done, perhaps Jean Chrétien doesn't have such a raw deal after all.

SOURCE: Library of Parliament and Statistics Canada.

■ Nominal and Real Interest Rates

You've just seen that we can calculate real values from nominal values by deflating them using the CPI. And you've seen that to make this calculation, we *divide* the nominal value by a price index. Converting a nominal interest rate to a real interest rate is a bit different. To see why, we'll start with their definitions.

A **nominal interest rate** is the interest payable on a loan expressed as a percentage of the loan. For example, if your bank lends you $100 for which you pay interest of $5 a year, the nominal interest rate is 5 percent. The **real interest rate** is the interest rate payable on the loan expressed in the purchasing power of the interest received. That is, the real interest rate is the nominal interest rate adjusted for the effects of inflation.

Suppose that your bank lends you $100 and that after one year, you repay the loan. You pay the bank the $100 that you borrowed plus the $5 interest that you owe (at 5 percent a year). But suppose that during the year, prices have increased by 3 percent. You pay the bank $105, but the bank needs $103 just to buy what $100 would have bought when you borrowed the money. So how much interest has your bank really earned? It has earned $2, or a real interest rate of 2 percent a year.

To convert a nominal interest rate to a real interest rate, we *subtract* the *inflation rate*. That is:

Real interest rate = Nominal interest rate – Inflation rate.

Plug your numbers into this formula. The nominal interest rate is 5 percent a year, the inflation rate is 3 percent a year, and the real interest rate is 5 percent minus 3 percent, which equals 2 percent a year.

Figure 7.5 shows the nominal interest rate and the real interest rate in Canada between 1970 and 2000. The vertical distance between the nominal interest rate and the real interest rate is the inflation rate. When the inflation rate was high during the 1970s, the real interest rate was negative—a situation in which the lender pays the borrower!

Nominal interest rate
The interest payable on a loan expressed as a percentage of the loan.

Real interest rate
The interest rate payable on the loan expressed in the purchasing power of the interest received—the nominal interest rate adjusted for the effects of inflation.

FIGURE 7.5
Nominal and Real Interest Rates: 1970–2000

*e*Foundations **7.3**

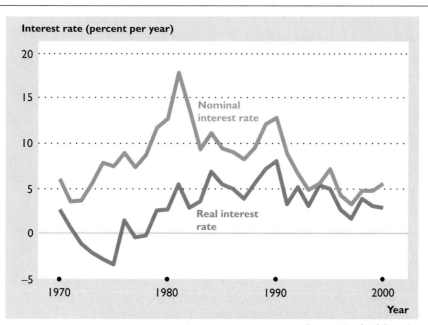

SOURCE: Bank of Canada.

The real interest rate equals the nominal interest rate minus the inflation rate. During the 1970s, the real interest rate became negative. In the late 1980s and early 1990s, the real interest rate reached very high levels before decreasing and becoming more stable.

Study Guide pp. 109–112

e Foundations 7.3

3 **Adjust money values for inflation and calculate real wage rates and real interest rates.**

Practice Problems 7.3

TABLE 1

Year	Price of gasoline (cents per litre)	CPI (1992 = 100)
1970	10	24.2
1985	51	75.0
2001	75	115.6

1. Table 1 shows some gas prices and the CPI for three years:
   a. Calculate the real price of gasoline in each year in 1992 dollars.
   b. In which year was gasoline the most costly in real terms?
   c. By how much did the real price of gasoline change from 1985 to 2001?

2. Canadian Industries Ltd. agreed to pay its workers $22 an hour in 2002, a 10 percent increase over the 2000 wage rate of $20 an hour. The CPI for these years was 114 in 2000 and 122 in 2002.
   a. Calculate the real wage rate in each year.
   b. What was the change in the real wage rate between 2000 and 2002?

3. Sally worked hard all year so that she could go to school full time the following year. She put her savings into a mutual fund that paid a nominal interest rate of 7 percent a year. The CPI was 123 at the beginning of the year and 132 at the end of the year. What was the real interest rate that Sally earned?

Exercise 7.3

TABLE 2

Year	Nominal interest rate	Inflation rate
	(percent per year)	
1992	4.6	1.7
1993	3.0	1.2
1994	2.1	0.7
1995	1.2	–0.1
1996	0.4	0.1
1997	0.4	1.7
1998	0.4	0.6
1999	0.1	–0.3
2000	0.1	–0.6

Table 2 shows the nominal interest rate and inflation rate in Japan for several years.
   a. Calculate the real interest rate for each year.
   b. In which year was the real interest rate the highest?
   c. In which year was the real interest rate the lowest?
   d. Was the real interest rate in Japan negative in any year?

Solutions to Practice Problems 7.3

1a. To calculate the real price of gasoline in each year in 1992 dollars, divide the nominal price by the CPI and multiply by 100. See Table 3.

1b. Gasoline was the most costly in real terms in 1985, when it was 68.0 cents (1992 cents) per litre.

1c. From 1985 to 2001, the real price of gasoline fell from 68.0 to 64.9 cents per litre, a decline of nearly 5 percent.

TABLE 3

Year	Price of gasoline (cents per litre)	CPI (1992 = 100)	Price of gasoline (1992 cents per litre)
1970	10	24.2	41.3
1985	51	75.0	68.0
2001	75	115.6	64.9

2a. The real wage rate in 2000, expressed in 1992 dollars, was ($20 ÷ 114) × 100 = $17.54. The real wage rate in 2002, expressed in 1992 dollars, was ($22 ÷ 122) × 100 = $18.03 an hour.

2b. Their real wage rate increased by 49 cents an hour.

3. The inflation rate during the year that Sally was working was (132 – 123) ÷ 123 × 100 = 7.3 percent. On the savings that Sally had in the mutual fund for the full year, she earned a real interest rate equal to the nominal interest rate minus the inflation rate, which is 7 – 7.3 = –0.3. Sally's real interest rate was negative. (Sally would have been even worse off if she had just kept her saving in cash. Her nominal interest rate would then have been zero, and her real interest rate would have been equal to –7.3 percent.)

CHAPTER CHECKPOINT

Key Points

1 Explain what the Consumer Price Index (CPI) is and how it is calculated.

- The Consumer Price Index (CPI) is a measure of the average prices of the goods and services that an average household buys.
- The CPI is calculated by dividing the cost of the CPI basket in the current period with its cost in the base period and multiplying by 100.

2 Explain the limitations of the CPI as a measure of the cost of living.

- The CPI does not include all the items that contribute to the cost of living.
- The CPI cannot provide an accurate measure of the price changes because of new goods, quality improvements, and substitutions that consumers make when relative prices change.

3 Adjust money values for inflation and calculate real wage rates and real interest rates.

- To adjust a money value (also called a nominal value) for inflation, we express the value in terms of the dollar of a given year.
- To convert a dollar value of year B to the dollars of year A, multiply the value in year B by the price level in year A and divide by the price level in year B.
- The real wage rate equals the nominal wage rate divided by the CPI and multiplied by 100.
- The real interest rate equals the nominal interest rate minus the inflation rate.

Key Terms

Consumer Price Index (CPI), 152
Cost of living index, 158
Inflation rate, 155
Nominal interest rate, 167

Nominal wage rate, 164
Real interest rate, 167
Real wage rate, 164
Base period, 152

Exercises

1. Make a careful record of your own expenditures during two weeks (week *A* and week *B*). In particular, record the items that you bought, their prices, and the quantities. Use these records to calculate:
   a. Your own CPI basket based on your week *A* expenditures.
   b. The percentage of your expenditures on each item.
   c. The cost of your CPI basket in week *A*.
   d. The cost of your CPI basket in week *B*.
   e. Your personal CPI for week *B*.
   f. Your personal inflation rate in week *B*.

2. On the basis of your observations of your own expenditures in weeks *A* and *B* (recorded in your answer to Exercise 1), explain and discuss the way in which your personal CPI is influenced by:
   a. New goods
   b. Quality changes
   c. Commodity substitution
   d. Outlet substitution

3. Use the link on your Foundations Web site to find CPI data for the province in which you live.
   a. Is the CPI in your province higher or lower than the Canadian average?
   b. Explain the deviation of your province's CPI from the Canadian average.

4. Use the link on your Foundations Web site to find data on the CPI All-items and the CPI All-items excluding the 8 most volatile components.
   a. How do these two versions of the CPI differ?
   b. Which version of the CPI showed the higher inflation rate during 2001?
   c. Which of the two CPI measures do you think most closely matches your personal inflation experience? Explain why.

5. Recently, a student brought to one of the authors a 1936 $10.00 bill that his great-grandfather had hidden for safekeeping during the Great Depression and had not been found for 65 years. Use the link on your Foundations Web site to visit the Bank of Canada's Inflation Calculator to estimate in today's dollars the purchasing power of this $10 bill in 1936.

6. Use the link on the Foundations Web site to find data on nominal interest rates and inflation rates for Canada and Italy during the 1990s.
   a. Calculate the real interest rate for each country and each year.
   b. In which country was the real interest rate higher on the average?
   c. Describe the similarities, if any, and the differences between the real and nominal interest rates for the two countries.

The Real Economy

Part 3

AS-AD and Potential GDP

CHAPTER CHECKLIST

When you have completed your study of this chapter, you will be able to:

1 Use the aggregate supply–aggregate demand (*AS-AD*) model to illustrate economic growth, inflation, and the business cycle.

2 Explain the forces that determine potential GDP and the distribution of income between labour and other factors of production.

3 Explain what creates unemployment when the economy is at full employment and describe the influences on the natural unemployment rate.

In the three previous chapters, you've learned how we define and measure the indicators of macroeconomic performance. You are now going to shift gears and turn from defining and measuring these variables to understanding the forces that determine them.

Why does our economy fluctuate in a business cycle? *Why* is real GDP per person in Canada almost 20 times that in Nigeria? *Why* was real GDP per person in Canada in 2000 more than twice what it was in 1965? *Why* is the unemployment rate in Spain more than twice that in Canada? *Why* has the inflation rate in Russia been six times that of Canada? *Why* does our economy fluctuate in a business cycle?

This chapter lays the foundation. It begins with a preview of the workhorse model of macroeconomics, the aggregate supply–aggregate demand model. But its major task is to explain the forces that determine real GDP and the unemployment rate when the economy is at full employment.

UNDERSTANDING MACROECONOMIC PERFORMANCE

Macroeconomists have made progress in understanding how the economy works by dividing the variables that describe macroeconomic performance into two lists:

- Real variables
- Nominal variables

Real variables are items such as real GDP, the real wage rate, real interest rate, and other real items such as the levels of employment and unemployment. These variables describe the real economy and tell us what is *really* happening to production and consumption, saving and investment, work and leisure, all of which contribute to the standard of living.

Nominal variables are items such as the price level (CPI or GDP deflator) and the inflation rate along with nominal GDP, the nominal wage rate, and the nominal interest rate. These variables describe the nominal economy and tell us how *dollar values* and the cost of living are changing.

This separation of macroeconomic performance into a real part and a nominal part is the basis of a huge discovery called the **classical dichotomy**, which states:

> **When the economy is operating at full employment, the forces that determine the real variables are independent of those that determine the nominal variables.**

In practical terms, the classical dichotomy means that if we want to explain why real GDP per person in Canada is almost 20 times that in Nigeria, we can do so by looking only at the real parts of the two economies and ignoring differences in their price levels and inflation rates. Similarly, to explain why real GDP per person in 2000 was around twice that in 1965, we don't need to consider what has happened to the value of the dollar between those two years.

The classical dichotomy describes the economy at full employment. But it does *not* hold over the business cycle as the economy fluctuates around full employment. The forces that shape the real economy and those that shape the nominal economy interact to create the business cycle.

Another practical implication of the classical dichotomy is that it simplifies your task of learning macroeconomics. It allows you to take it in bite-size pieces rather than in one big meal. The subject conveniently divides into the following parts:

- The real economy (Chapters 8–10)
- The money (nominal) economy (Chapters 11–13)
- Economic fluctuations (Chapters 14–18)

In this chapter and the two that follow it, you will learn about the real economy and the process of economic growth. You will then study the nominal economy and the forces that bring inflation. Finally, you will see how real and nominal forces interact to bring about the business cycle. You will also review the ongoing debate about how the government and the Bank of Canada can use policies to improve economic performance. But first, this chapter places the full-employment economy in a broader perspective by previewing the *AS-AD* model.

8.1 THE *AS-AD* MODEL

We are going to begin this chapter with a preview of the aggregate supply-aggregate demand (or *AS-AD*) model, which provides a framework for thinking about all three of the big macroeconomic issues—economic growth, inflation, and the business cycle. What you will learn in this chapter is an outline, the details of which we will fill in as you progress through the rest of your study of macroeconomics. But keeping this outline in view will help you to navigate through the rest of your course.

As its name suggests, the *AS-AD* model applies to the economy as a whole—the aggregate or total economy—the ideas of supply and demand that you studied in Chapter 4. We'll explore the *AS-AD* model by looking at:

- Aggregate supply
- Aggregate demand
- Macroeconomic equilibrium

■ Aggregate Supply

Loblaws, Bell Canada, Canadian Tire, McCain Foods, the Royal Bank, and other businesses in Canada, large and small, have wage agreements with their workers that run for a year or more into the future. They also have loan, rental, and long-term supply agreements. Most of these agreements are specified in nominal—dollar—terms. They commit firms to pay agreed dollar amounts.

When firms make long-term commitments to pay agreed dollar amounts, they make bets about the future prices they will be able to obtain for their products. If their bets are accurate and the prices they obtain turn out to be what they expected, each firm operates at its desired output rate. The economy as a whole operates at full employment, and real GDP equals **potential GDP**. (We study the forces that determine potential GDP on pages 181–187.)

Potential GDP
The level of real GDP that the economy would produce if it were at full employment.

If the prices that firms can obtain for their products fall below the levels they expected, they take defensive actions. For some of the firms, the fall in prices brings layoffs and a decrease in production. For other firms, the fall in prices is more serious: It shuts them down and destroys jobs. Real GDP decreases.

If in a happier time for businesses, the prices that they obtain for their products rise above the levels they expected, they will act to take advantage of the higher prices. Existing firms hire new workers and increase production. New firms set up, hire workers, and start to produce. Real GDP increases.

We've just described the actions of firms that generate **aggregate supply**—the relationship between the quantity of real GDP supplied and the price level when all other influences on production plans remain the same. This relationship can be described as follows:

Aggregate supply
The relationship between the quantity of real GDP supplied and the price level when all other influences on production plans remain the same.

> **Other things remaining the same, the higher the price level, the greater is the quantity of real GDP supplied, and the lower the price level, the smaller is the quantity of real GDP supplied.**

Figure 8.1 illustrates aggregate supply as an aggregate supply schedule and aggregate supply curve. The aggregate supply schedule lists the quantities of real GDP supplied at each price level, and the upward sloping *AS* curve graphs these points. The figure also shows potential GDP—$1,000 billion in the figure.

FIGURE 8.1

Aggregate Supply Schedule and Aggregate Supply Curve

e Foundations **8.1**

The aggregate supply schedule and aggregate supply curve, *AS*, show the relationship between the quantity of real GDP supplied and the price level when all other influences on production plans remain the same. Each point *A* through *E* on the *AS* curve corresponds to the row identified by the same letter in the schedule.

❶ Potential GDP is $1,000 billion and when the price level is 105, real GDP equals potential GDP.

❷ If the price level is above 105, real GDP exceeds potential GDP.

❸ If the price level is below 105, real GDP is less than potential GDP.

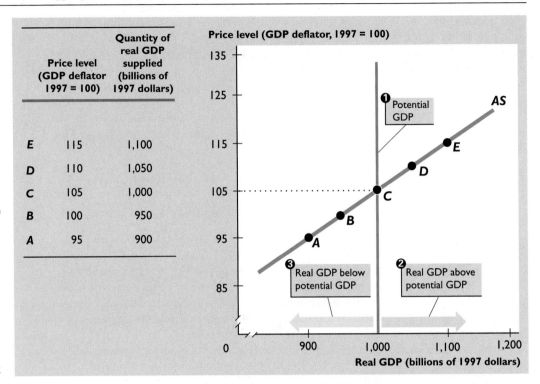

	Price level (GDP deflator 1997 = 100)	Quantity of real GDP supplied (billions of 1997 dollars)
E	115	1,100
D	110	1,050
C	105	1,000
B	100	950
A	95	900

When the price level is 105, the quantity of real GDP supplied is $1,000 billion, which equals potential GDP (at point *C* on the *AS* curve). If the price level is above 105, the quantity of real GDP supplied exceeds potential GDP; if the price level is below 105, the quantity of real GDP supplied is less than potential GDP. These departures from potential GDP, especially on the upside, can occur only temporarily while firms' money costs are fixed.

Changes in Aggregate Supply

Aggregate supply changes when potential GDP changes. If potential GDP increases, aggregate supply increases and the *AS* curve shifts rightward. Aggregate supply also changes when the money wage rate or any other money costs such as the price of oil changes. A rise in the money wage rate or the price of oil raises firms' costs, decreases aggregate supply, and shifts the *AS* curve leftward.

■ Aggregate Demand

You and the other 31 million people in Canada have some money in the bank, some debts, and some available funds on your credit card, all of which influence your spending plans. Firms also have funds available for spending on new capital. All of these funds and lines of credit are set in nominal—dollar—terms.

Suppose that suddenly, the prices that we must all pay for the things that we buy increase. With a fall in the buying power of money, people scale back their consumption expenditure plans and firms scale back their investment plans. Foreigners buy less of our production, so exports decrease.

In a happier time for buyers, the prices that we must pay for the things that we buy decrease. With a rise in the buying power of money, people increase consumption expenditure and businesses increase investment. Foreigners buy more of our production, so exports increase.

We've just described the actions of households, firms, and foreigners that generate **aggregate demand**—the relationship between the quantity of real GDP demanded and the price level when all other influences on expenditure plans remain the same. This relationship can be described as follows:

Aggregate demand
The relationship between the quantity of real GDP demanded and the price level when all other influences on expenditure plans remain the same.

Other things remaining the same, the higher the price level, the smaller is the quantity of real GDP demanded, and the lower the price level, the greater is the quantity of real GDP demanded.

Figure 8.2 illustrates aggregate demand by using an aggregate demand schedule and aggregate demand curve. The aggregate demand schedule lists the quantities of real GDP demanded at each price level, and the downward-sloping *AD* curve graphs these points.

Changes in Aggregate Demand

Many factors change aggregate demand and shift the *AD* curve. Here, we will just list the major ones. A fall in the interest rate, an increase in the quantity of money in the economy, an increase in government expenditure or a tax cut, and an increase in real GDP in the rest of the world all stimulate spending and increase aggregate demand. Changes in these variables in the opposite direction decrease aggregate demand. (Chapters 14 and 15 explain these influences.)

FIGURE 8.2

Aggregate Demand Schedule and Aggregate Demand Curve

*e*Foundations **8.1**

	Price level (GDP deflator 1997 = 100)	Quantity of real GDP demanded (billions of 1997 dollars)
A	125	900
B	115	950
C	105	1,000
D	95	1,050
E	85	1,100

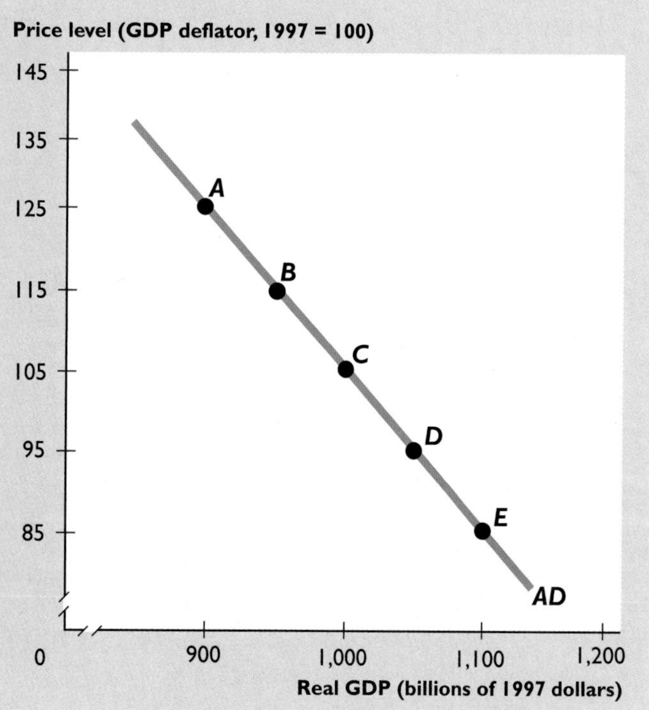

The aggregate demand schedule and aggregate demand curve, *AD*, show the relationship between the quantity of real GDP demanded and the price level when all other influences on expenditure plans remain the same. Each point *A* through *E* on the *AD* curve corresponds to the row identified by the same letter in the schedule.

Macroeconomic equilibrium
When the quantity of real GDP demanded equals the quantity of real GDP supplied at the point of intersection of the *AD* curve and the *AS* curve.

■ Macroeconomic Equilibrium

Aggregate supply and aggregate demand determine real GDP and the price level. **Macroeconomic equilibrium** occurs when the quantity of real GDP demanded equals the quantity of real GDP supplied at the point of intersection of the *AD* curve and the *AS* curve. Figure 8.3(a) shows such an equilibrium at a price level of 105 and real GDP of $1,000 billion.

To see why this position is the equilibrium, think about what happens if the price level is something other than 105. Suppose that the price level is 115 and that real GDP is $1,100 billion (point *E* on the *AS* curve). The quantity of real GDP demanded is less than $1,100 billion, so firms are unable to sell all their output. Unwanted inventories pile up. So firms cut production and prices until they can sell all their output, which occurs only when real GDP is $1,000 billion and the price level is 105.

Now suppose the price level is 95 and real GDP is $900 billion (point *A* on the *AS* curve). The quantity of real GDP demanded exceeds $900 billion, so firms are unable to meet the demand for their output. Inventories decrease, and customers clamour for goods and services. So firms increase production and raise prices until firms can meet demand, which occurs only when real GDP is $1,000 billion and the price level is 105.

■ **FIGURE 8.3**
Macroeconomic Equilibrium

*e*Foundations **8.1**

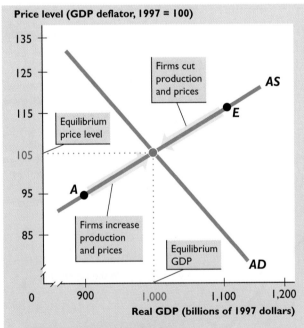

(a) Macroeconomic equilibrium

Macroeconomic equilibrium occurs at the intersection of the *AD* and *AS* curves. Macroeconomic equilibrium might be below full employment, at full employment, or above full employment

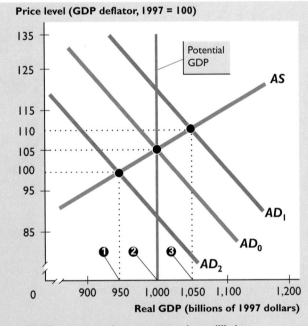

(b) Three types of macroeconomic equilibrium

❶ Below full-employment equilibrium
❷ Full-employment equilibrium
❸ Above full-employment equilibrium

In macroeconomic equilibrium, the economy might be at full employment or above or below full employment, and Figure 8.3(b) shows these three possibilities. **Full-employment equilibrium**—equilibrium real GDP equals potential GDP—occurs where AD_0 intersects the aggregate supply curve AS. Fluctuations in aggregate demand bring fluctuations in real GDP around potential GDP. If aggregate demand increases to AD_1, firms increase production and raise prices until they can meet the higher demand. Real GDP increases to $1,050 billion and exceeds potential GDP in an **above full-employment equilibrium**. If aggregate demand decreases to AD_2, firms decrease production and cut prices until they can sell all their output. Real GDP decreases to $950 billion and is less than potential GDP in a **below full-employment equilibrium**.

Full-employment equilibrium
When equilibrium real GDP equals potential GDP.

Above full-employment equilibrium
When equilibrium real GDP exceeds potential GDP.

Below full-employment equilibrium
When potential GDP exceeds equilibrium real GDP.

Eye On The CANADIAN ECONOMY

Real GDP Growth, Inflation, and the Business Cycle

Each dot in the figure represents a year. In 1970, the economy was at the point of intersection of aggregate demand curve AD_{70} and aggregate supply curve AS_{70}. Real GDP was $381 billion, and the GDP deflator was 24. Real GDP was close to potential GDP.

By 2000, the economy had reached the point marked by the intersection of aggregate demand curve AD_{00} and aggregate supply curve AS_{00}. Real GDP was $1,009 billion, and the GDP deflator was 105. The figure shows potential GDP in 2000 as $1,000 billion. (This value is an assumption.)

Real GDP grows because potential GDP grows. Inflation occurs because aggregate demand increases more rapidly than aggregate supply. Business cycles occur because aggregate demand and aggregate supply grow at fluctuating rates.

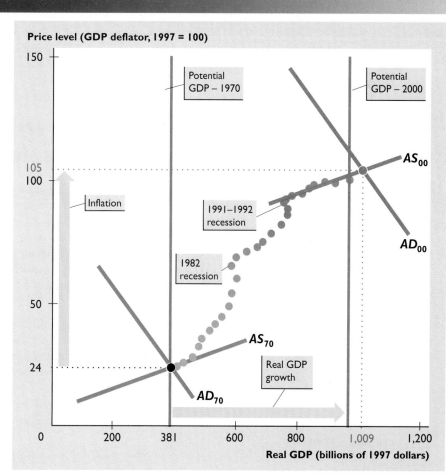

SOURCE: Statistics Canada.

The dominant macroeconomic problem of the 1970s was rapid inflation. By 1980, the Bank of Canada took strong action against inflation and the economy went into the deep 1982 recession. When the inflation rate increased again in the late 1980s, the Bank of Canada again took action and brought on the recession of 1991–1992.

Study Guide pp. 117–120

*e*Foundations 8.1

1 Use the aggregate supply–aggregate demand (*AS-AD*) model to illustrate economic growth, inflation, and the business cycle.

TABLE 1

Price level (GDP deflator)	Real GDP demanded	Real GDP supplied
	(billions of 1995 pounds)	
90	800	650
100	775	700
110	750	750
120	725	800
130	700	850

TABLE 2

Price level (GDP deflator)	Real GDP demanded	Real GDP supplied
	(billions of 1990 dollars)	
90	420	360
100	410	380
110	400	400
120	390	420
130	380	440

FIGURE 1

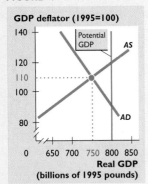

FIGURE 2

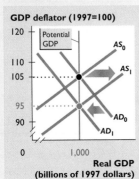

Practice Problems 8.1

1. Table 1 shows aggregate demand and aggregate supply schedules for the United Kingdom.
   a. Plot the aggregate demand curve.
   b. Plot the aggregate supply curve.
   c. What is the macroeconomic equilibrium?
   d. If potential GDP in the United Kingdom is £800 billon, what is the type of macroeconomic equilibrium?

2. The Canadian economy is at full employment when two events occur:
   • A deep recession hits the world economy, and real GDP in the rest of the world decreases.
   • The world oil price tumbles.
   a. Explain the effect of each event separately on aggregate demand and aggregate supply in Canada.
   b. Explain the combined effect of the two events on the Canadian price level and real GDP.

Exercises 8.1

1. Table 2 shows aggregate demand and aggregate supply schedules for Australia.
   a. Plot the aggregate demand curve.
   b. Plot the aggregate supply curve.
   c. What is the macroeconomic equilibrium?
   d. If potential GDP in Australia is $380 billion, what is the type of macroeconomic equilibrium?

2. The U.S. economy is at full employment when two events occur:
   • A strong expansion increases real GDP in the rest of the world.
   • The U.S. government cuts taxes.
   a. Explain the effect of each event separately on U.S. aggregate demand and aggregate supply.
   b. Explain the combined effect of the two events on the U.S. price level and real GDP.

Solutions to Practice Problems 8.1

1. Figure 1 shows the *AD* and *AS* curves and potential GDP. Real GDP is less than potential GDP, so the economy is at a below full-employment equilibrium.

2a. A decrease in real GDP in the rest of the world decreases Canadian aggregate demand. The *AD* curve shifts leftward. A fall in the world oil price lowers firms' costs and increases aggregate supply. The *AS* curve shifts rightward (Figure 2).

2b. Because *AD* decreases and *AS* increases, the price level falls. But real GDP might increase or decrease depending on which of the two changes is larger (Figure 2).

8.2 POTENTIAL GDP

Potential GDP is the level of real GDP that the economy would produce if it were at full employment. It is vital to understand the forces that determine potential GDP for three reasons. First, when the economy is *at* full employment, real GDP equals potential GDP; so actual real GDP is determined by the same factors that determine potential GDP. Second, real GDP can exceed potential GDP only temporarily as it approaches and then recedes from a business cycle peak. So potential GDP is the *sustainable* upper limit of production. Third, real GDP fluctuates around potential GDP, which means that on the average over the business cycle, real GDP equals potential GDP.

We produce the goods and services that make up real GDP by using the *factors of production*: labour and human capital, physical capital, land (and natural resources), and entrepreneurship. At any given time, the quantities of capital, land, and entrepreneurship and the state of technology are fixed. But the quantity of labour is not fixed. It depends on the choices that people make about the allocation of time between work and leisure. So with fixed quantities of capital, land, and entrepreneurship and fixed technology, real GDP depends on the quantity of labour employed. To describe this relationship between real GDP and the quantity of labour employed, we use a relationship that is similar to the production possibilities frontier, which is called the production function.

Eye On The CANADIAN ECONOMY

Potential GDP in the 1960s and 1990s

Back in the 1960s, we had six television channels, black vinyl phonograph records, rotary telephones, roller skates, cars that barely ran 4 kilometres on a litre of gasoline, typewriters, and human telephone operators and bank tellers. By the 1990s, we had hundreds of television channels, MP3 and CDs, cell phones small enough to slip into our shirt pockets and smart enough to remember a hundred numbers, in-line skates, cars that ran 16 kilometres on a litre of gasoline, PCs that we could talk to, and ATMs in every shopping mall and main street.

This chapter explains the forces that determined real GDP and the real wage rate on the average during these two decades.

The figure provides a snapshot of the contrasts and a similarity across these decades using some standard macroeconomic indicators.

Real GDP averaged $835 billion (all values are in 1997 dollars) during the 1990s but only $305 billion during the 1960s. Real wage rates per hour of work averaged $19.22 during the 1990s but only $11.55 during the 1960s. But the share of GDP earned by labour was similar in the 1960s and the 1990s.

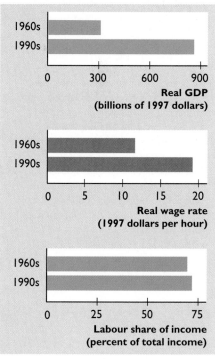

Source: Statistics Canada.

■ The Production Function

Production function
A relationship that shows the maximum quantity of real GDP that can be produced as the quantity of labour employed changes and all other influences on production remain the same.

The **production function** is a relationship that shows the maximum quantity of real GDP that can be produced as the quantity of labour employed changes and all other influences on production remain the same. Figure 8.4 shows a production function, which is the curve labelled *PF*.

In Figure 8.4, when 10 billion labour hours are employed, real GDP is $600 billion (at point *A*). When 20 billion labour hours are employed, real GDP is $1,000 billion (at point *B*). And when 30 billion labour hours are employed, real GDP is $1,200 billion (at point *C*).

The production function shares a feature of the *production possibilities frontier* that you studied in Chapter 3 (p. 58). Like the *PPF*, the production function is a boundary between the attainable and the unattainable. It is possible to produce at any point along the production function and beneath it in the shaded area. But points above the production function are unattainable.

Diminishing returns
The tendency for each additional hour of labour employed to produce a successively smaller additional amount of real GDP.

The production function displays **diminishing returns**—each additional hour of labour employed produces a successively smaller additional amount of real GDP. The first 10 billion hours of labour produces $600 billion of real GDP. The second 10 billion hours increases real GDP to $1,000 billion and so produces only

---

■ **FIGURE 8.4**

The Production Function

e/Foundations **8.2**

The production function shows the maximum level of real GDP that can be produced as the quantity of labour employed changes and all other influences on production remain the same.

The production function separates attainable combinations of labour hours and real GDP from unattainable combinations and displays diminishing returns: Each additional hour of labour produces a successively smaller additional amount of real GDP. In this example, 10 billion hours of labour can produce $600 billion of real GDP at point *A*, 20 billion hours of labour can produce $1,000 billion of real GDP at point *B*, and 30 billion hours of labour can produce $1,200 billion of real GDP at point *C*.

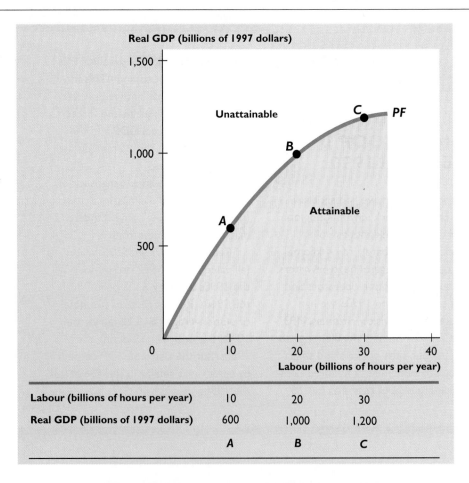

Labour (billions of hours per year)	10	20	30
Real GDP (billions of 1997 dollars)	600	1,000	1,200
	A	*B*	*C*

an additional $400 billion of real GDP. The third 10 billion hours increases real GDP to $1,200 billion and so produces only an additional $200 billion of real GDP.

Diminishing returns arise because the quantity of capital (and other factors of production) is fixed. As more labour is hired, the additional output produced decreases because the extra workers have less capital to work with. For example, a forest service has three chain saws and an axe and hires three workers to clear roads and trails of fallen trees and debris during the spring thaw. Hiring a fourth worker will contribute less to the amount cleared than the third worker added and hiring a fifth worker will add even less.

Because real GDP depends on the quantity of labour employed, potential GDP depends on the point on the production function at which the economy operates. To find that point, we must understand what determines the quantity of labour employed.

■ The Labour Market

You've already studied the tool that we use to determine the quantity of labour employed: demand and supply. In macroeconomics, we apply the concepts of demand, supply, and market equilibrium to economy-wide markets. In the present case, we apply the same concepts to the economy-wide labour market.

The quantity of labour employed depends on firms' decisions about how much labour to hire (the demand for labour). It also depends on households' decisions about how to allocate time between employment and other activities (the supply of labour). And it depends on how the labour market coordinates the decisions of firms and households (labour market equilibrium). So we will study:

- The demand for labour
- The supply of labour
- Labour market equilibrium

The Demand for Labour

The **quantity of labour demanded** is the total labour hours that all the firms in the economy plan to hire during a given time period at a given real wage rate. The **demand for labour** is the relationship between the quantity of labour demanded and the *real wage rate* when all other influences on firms' hiring plans remain the same. The lower the real wage rate, the greater is the quantity of labour demanded.

The real wage rate is the *nominal wage rate* (the dollars per hour that people earn on the average) divided by the price level (see Chapter 7, p. 164). We express the real wage rate in constant dollars—today in 1997 dollars. Think about the real wage rate as the quantity of real GDP that an hour of labour earns.

The lower the real wage rate, the greater is the quantity of labour that firms find it profitable to hire. The real wage rate influences the quantity of labour demanded because what matters to firms is not the number of dollars they pay for an hour of labour (the nominal wage rate) but how much output they must sell to earn those dollars. So firms compare the extra output that an hour of labour can produce with the real wage rate.

Firms are in business to maximize profit. So they hire labour as long as each additional hour hired produces at least as much additional output as the real wage rate. When a small quantity of labour is hired, an extra hour of labour produces more output than the real wage rate. But each additional hour of labour produces less additional output than the previous hour. As a firm hires more labour, eventually the

ECONOMICS *in the* **NEWS**

May 7, 2001

Canada Further Behind U.S.: Study

Labour productivity … rose by an average of 1.2% a year in Canada from 1989 to 2000. In the United States, it was 1.9%.

NATIONAL POST

Questions

1. What is labour productivity?
2. What makes labour productivity increase?
3. How would you use the production function to illustrate an increase in labour productivity?
4. How does an increase in labour productivity influence potential GDP in Canada and the United States?

 e **Foundations 8.2**

Quantity of labour demanded
The total labour hours that all the firms in the economy plan to hire during a given time period at a given real wage rate.

Demand for labour
The relationship between the quantity of labour demanded and real wage rate when all other influences on firms' hiring plans remain the same.

extra output from an extra hour of labour exactly equals the real wage rate. This equality determines the quantity of labour demanded at the real wage rate.

The Demand for Labour in a Soft Drink Factory You can understand the demand for labour better by thinking about a single firm rather than the economy as a whole. Suppose that the money wage rate is $15 an hour. And suppose that the price of a bottle of pop is $1.50. For a pop factory, the real wage rate is a number of bottles of pop. To find the pop factory's real wage rate, divide the money wage rate by the price of its output—$15 per hour ÷ $1.50 per bottle = 10 bottles of pop per hour. It costs the factory 10 bottles of pop to hire an hour of labour. As long as the factory can hire labour that produces more than 10 additional bottles of pop an hour, it is profitable to hire more labour. Only when the extra output produced by an extra hour of labour falls to 10 bottles an hour has the factory reached the profit-maximizing quantity of labour.

Labour Demand Schedule and Labour Demand Curve For the economy as a whole, we can represent the demand for labour as either a demand schedule or a demand curve. The table in Figure 8.5 shows part of a demand for labour schedule. It tells us the quantity of labour demanded at three real wage rates. For example, if the real wage rate is $50 an hour (row *A*), the quantity of labour demanded is 10 billion hours a year. If the real wage rate falls to $30 an hour (row *B*), the quantity of labour demanded increases to 20 billion hours a year. If the real wage rate falls to $10 an hour (row *C*), the quantity of labour demanded increases to 30 billion hours a year.

Figure 8.5 shows the demand for labour curve. Points *A*, *B*, and *C* on the demand curve correspond to rows *A*, *B*, and *C* of the demand schedule.

■ FIGURE 8.5
The Demand for Labour

e/Foundations **8.2**

Firms are willing to hire labour only if it produces more than the real wage rate it costs. So the lower the real wage rate, the greater is the quantity of labour demanded.

At a real wage rate of $50 an hour, the quantity of labour demanded is 10 billion hours at point *A*; at a real wage rate of $30 an hour, the quantity of labour demanded is 20 billion hours at point *B*; and at a real wage rate of $10 an hour, the quantity of labour demanded is 30 billion hours at point *C*.

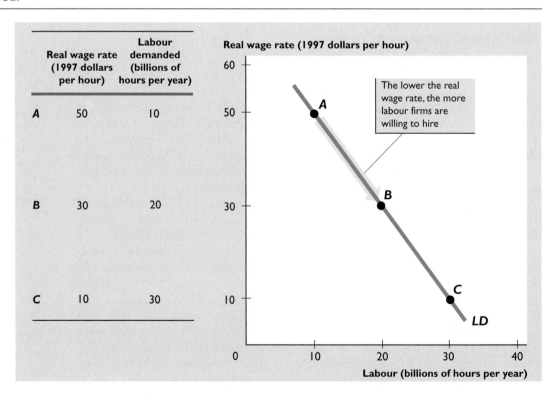

	Real wage rate (1997 dollars per hour)	Labour demanded (billions of hours per year)
A	50	10
B	30	20
C	10	30

The Supply of Labour

The **quantity of labour supplied** is the number of labour hours that all the households in the economy plan to work during a given time period and at a given real wage rate. The **supply of labour** is the relationship between the quantity of labour supplied and the real wage rate when all other influences on work plans remain the same.

We can represent the supply of labour as either a supply schedule or a supply curve. The table in Figure 8.6 shows a supply of labour schedule. It tells us the quantity of labour supplied at three real wage rates. For example, if the real wage rate is $15 an hour (row *A*), the quantity of labour supplied is 10 billion hours a year. If the real wage rate rises to $30 an hour (row *B*), the quantity of labour supplied increases to 20 billion hours a year. And if the real wage rate rises to $50 an hour (row *C*), the quantity of labour supplied increases to 30 billion hours a year.

Figure 8.6 shows the supply of labour curve. It corresponds to the supply schedule, and the points *A*, *B*, and *C* on the curve correspond to the rows *A*, *B*, and *C* of the supply schedule.

The real wage rate influences the quantity of labour supplied because what matters to people is not the number of dollars they earn but what those dollars will buy.

The quantity of labour supplied increases as the real wage rate increases, for two reasons:

- Hours per person increase.
- Labour force participation increases.

Quantity of labour supplied
The number of labour hours that all the households in the economy plan to work during a given time period and at a given real wage rate.

Supply of labour
The relationship between the quantity of labour supplied and the real wage rate when all other influences on work plans remain the same.

■ **FIGURE 8.6**
The Supply of Labour

 *e* Foundations **8.2**

	Real wage rate (1997 dollars per hour)	Labour supplied (billions of hours per year)
C	50	30
B	30	20
A	15	10

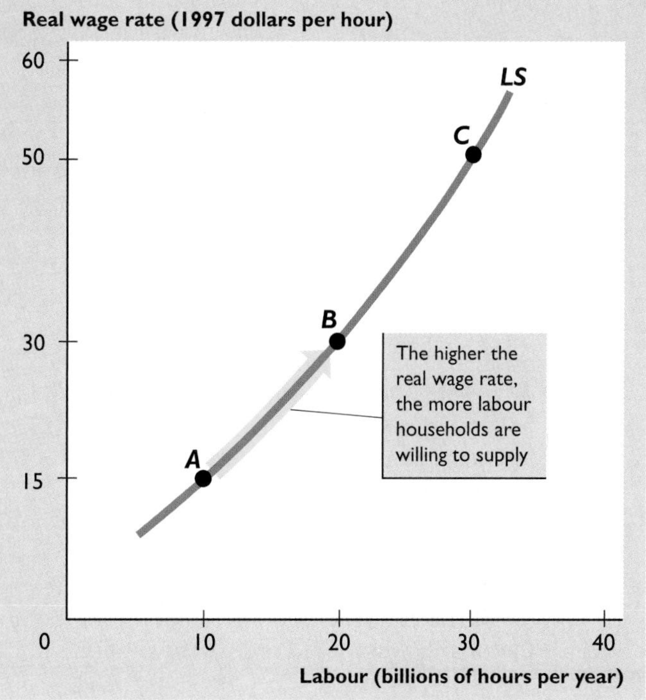

Households are willing to supply labour only if the real wage rate is high enough to attract them from other activities. The higher the real wage rate, the greater is the quantity of labour supplied.

At a real wage rate of $15 an hour, the quantity of labour supplied is 10 billion hours at point *A*; at a real wage rate of $30 an hour, the quantity of labour supplied is 20 billion hours at point *B*; and at a real wage rate of $50 an hour, the quantity of labour supplied is 30 billion hours at point *C*.

[Graph: Real wage rate (1997 dollars per hour) on vertical axis vs Labour (billions of hours per year) on horizontal axis. Upward-sloping curve LS passing through points A (10, 15), B (20, 30), and C (30, 50). Annotation: "The higher the real wage rate, the more labour households are willing to supply"]

Hours per Person In choosing how many hours to work, a household considers the opportunity cost of not working. This opportunity cost is the real wage rate. The higher the real wage rate, the greater is the opportunity cost of taking leisure and not working. And as the opportunity cost of taking leisure rises, other things remaining the same, the more the household chooses to work.

But other things don't remain the same. The higher the real wage rate, the greater is the household's income. And the higher the household's income, the more the household wants to consume. One item that it wants to consume more of is leisure.

So a rise in the real wage rate has two opposing effects. By increasing the opportunity cost of leisure, it makes the household want to consume less leisure and to work more. And by increasing the household's income, it makes the household want to consume more leisure and to work fewer hours—an effect called the backward-bending supply response. For most households, the opportunity cost effect is stronger than the income effect. So the higher the real wage rate, the greater is the amount of work that the household chooses to do. That is, the labour supply curve does not bend backward.

Labour Force Participation Most people have productive opportunities outside the labour force and choose to work only if the real wage rate exceeds the value of other productive activities. For example, a parent might spend time caring for her or his child. The alternative is day care. The parent will choose to work only if he or she can earn enough per hour to pay the cost of day care and have enough left to make the work effort worthwhile. The higher the real wage rate, the more likely it is that a parent will choose to work and so the greater is the labour force participation rate.

Labour Supply Response The quantity of labour supplied increases as the real wage rate rises. But the quantity of labour supplied is not highly responsive to the real wage rate. A large percentage change in the real wage rate brings a small percentage change in the quantity of labour supplied.

Let's now see how the labour market determines employment, the real wage rate, and potential GDP.

Labour Market Equilibrium

Figure 8.7(a) shows the labour market equilibrium. The demand curve and the supply curve are the same as those in Figures 8.5 and 8.6. The forces of supply and demand operate in labour markets just as they do in the markets for goods and services. The price of labour is the real wage rate. A rise in the real wage rate eliminates a shortage of labour by decreasing the quantity demanded and increasing the quantity supplied. A fall in the real wage rate eliminates a surplus of labour by increasing the quantity demanded and decreasing the quantity supplied. If there is neither a shortage nor a surplus, the labour market is in equilibrium.

In Figure 8.7(a), if the real wage rate is less than $30 an hour, the quantity of labour demanded exceeds the quantity supplied and there is a shortage of labour. In this situation, the real wage rate rises.

If the real wage rate exceeds $30 an hour, the quantity of labour supplied exceeds the quantity demanded and there is a surplus of labour. In this situation, the real wage rate falls.

If the real wage rate is $30 an hour, the quantity of labour demanded equals the quantity supplied and there is neither a shortage nor a surplus of labour. In

▨ FIGURE 8.7
Labour Market Equilibrium and Potential GDP

e/**Foundations 8.2**

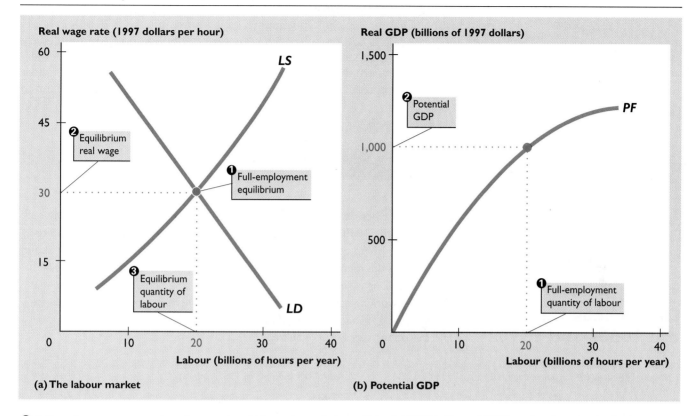

(a) The labour market

(b) Potential GDP

❶ Full employment occurs when the quantity of labour demanded equals the quantity of labour supplied. ❷ The equilibrium real wage rate is $30 an hour, and ❸ equilibrium employment is 20 billion hours a year.

Potential GDP is the real GDP produced on the production function by the full-employment quantity of labour. ❶ The full-employment quantity of labour, 20 billion hours a year, produces a ❷ potential GDP of $1,000 billion.

this situation, the labour market is in equilibrium and the real wage rate remains constant. The equilibrium level of employment is 20 billion hours a year. At the equilibrium level of employment, there is full employment. So full employment is 20 billion hours a year.

Full Employment and Potential GDP

You've seen that the quantity of real GDP depends on the quantity of labour employed. The production function tells us how much real GDP a given amount of employment can produce. Now that we've determined the full-employment quantity of labour, we can find potential GDP.

Figure 8.7(b) shows the relationship between labour market equilibrium and potential GDP. The equilibrium quantity of labour employed in Figure 8.7(a) is 20 billion hours. The production function in Figure 8.7(b) tells us that 20 billion hours of labour produces $1,000 billion of real GDP. This level of real GDP is potential GDP. When the labour market is in equilibrium, the economy is at full employment and real GDP equals potential GDP.

■ The Functional Distribution of Income

We can use the full-employment model to explain the *functional distribution of income*—the percentage distribution of income among labour and the factors of production (Chapter 2, p. 39). The quantity of labour employed is 20 billion hours and the wage rate is $30 an hour, so labour earns 20 billion hours multiplied by $30 an hour, which equals $600 billion. Real GDP is $1,000 billion, so the other factors of production earn the remaining $400 billion. In this economy, labour's share of real GDP is 60 percent and the shares of the other factors of production sum to 40 percent.

Eye On The CANADIAN ECONOMY

Explaining the Differences Between the 1960s and 1990s

Labour was twice as productive in the 1990s as in the 1960s, so the production function shifts upward from PF_{60s} to PF_{90s}, and the demand for labour curve shifted rightward from LD_{60s} to LD_{90s}. The working-age population was larger in the 1990s than in the 1960s, and the labour supply curve shifted rightward from LS_{60s} to LS_{90s}. The real wage rate increased from $11.55 to $19.22 an hour; the quantity of labour employed increased from 13.6 billion hours to 22.8 billion hours. Potential GDP increased from $305 billion to $832 billion.

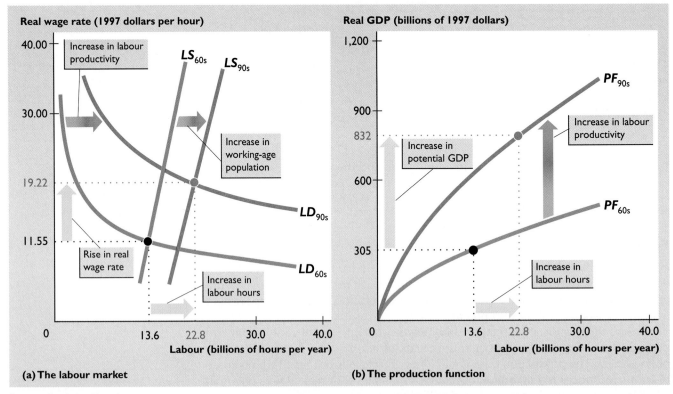

(a) The labour market

(b) The production function

SOURCE: Statistics Canada.

CHECKPOINT 8.2

2 Explain the forces that determine potential GDP and the distribution of income between labour and other factors of production.

Study Guide pp.120–123

𝑒Foundations 8.2

Practice Problem 8.2

Table 1 describes an economy's production function and its demand for labour.

Table 1

Quantity of labour (billions of hours per year)	0	1	2	3	4
Real GDP (billions of 2001 dollars)	0	40	70	90	100
Real wage rate (2001 dollars per hour)		40	30	20	10

Table 2 describes the supply of labour in this economy.

Table 2

Quantity of labour (billions of hours per year)	0	1	2	3	4
Real wage rate (2001 dollars per hour)	10	20	30	40	50

a Make graphs of the production function and the labour market.
b. Find the equilibrium employment, real wage rate, and potential GDP.
c. What percentage of GDP does labour earn?

Exercise 8.2

Table 3 describes an economy's production function and its demand for labour.

Table 3

Quantity of labour (billions of hours per year)	0	1	2	3	4	5
Real GDP (billions of 2001 dollars)	0	5	9	12	14	15
Real wage rate (2001 dollars per hour)		5	4	3	2	1

Table 4 describes the supply of labour in this economy.

Table 4

Quantity of labour (billions of hours per year)	0	1	2	3	4
Real wage rate (2001 dollars per hour)	1.50	2.00	2.50	3.00	3.50

a. Make graphs of the production function and the labour market.
b. Find the equilibrium employment, real wage rate, and potential GDP.
c. What percentage of GDP does labour earn?

Solution to Practice Problem 8.2

a. The production function is a graph of the first two rows of Table 1 (Figure 1). The demand for labour is a graph of the first and last rows of Table 1 and the supply of labour is a graph of the data in Table 2 (Figure 2).
b. Labour market equilibrium occurs when the real wage rate is $30 an hour and 2 billion hours of labour are employed (Figure 2). Potential GDP is the real GDP produced by the equilibrium quantity of labour (2 billion hours in Figure 2). Potential GDP is $70 billion (Figure 1).
c. Labour earns $30 an hour on 2 billion hours, which equals $60 billion. GDP is $70 billion. So labour earns ($60 ÷ $70) × 100 = 85.7 percent of GDP.

FIGURE 1

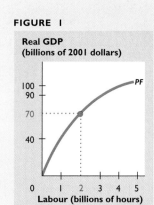

Real GDP (billions of 2001 dollars)

FIGURE 2

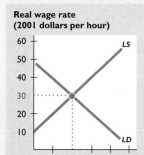

Real wage rate (2001 dollars per hour)

8.3 THE NATURAL UNEMPLOYMENT RATE

So far, we've focused on the forces that determine the real wage rate, the quantity of labour employed, and real GDP at full employment. We're now going to bring unemployment into the picture.

You learned in Chapter 6 (pp. 130–131) how unemployment is measured. And you learned how people become unemployed by losing or leaving their jobs and by entering or re-entering the labour force. You also learned how we classify unemployment as frictional, structural, seasonal, or cyclical. Finally, you learned that the unemployment rate at full employment, which consists of frictional, structural, and seasonal unemployment, is called the *natural unemployment rate*.

Measuring, describing, and classifying unemployment tell us a lot about it. But these activities do not *explain* the amount of unemployment that exists or why its rate changes over time.

Many forces interact to determine the unemployment rate. Understanding these forces is a challenging task. Economists approach this task in two steps. The first step is to understand what determines the natural unemployment rate—the unemployment rate at full employment. The second step is to understand what makes unemployment fluctuate around the natural unemployment rate. In this chapter, we take the first of these steps. We take the second step in Chapters 14–18 when we study economic fluctuations.

Eye On The PAST

Average Unemployment Rates over Five Decades

If we look back at the Canadian economy decade by decade, we can see through the ups and downs of the business cycle and focus on the broad trends. By looking at the average unemployment rates across the decades, we get an estimate of movements in the natural unemployment rate.

The figure shows that during the 1950s and 1960s, the average unemployment rate was below 5 percent. In each successive decade, the unemploy-

ment rate increased and in the 1990s it was twice that of the 1950s and 1960s. But in the late 1990s, the unemployment rate fell sharply and in 2000 it was at its lowest level in 26 years.

You will be a member of the labour force of the 2000s. And the average unemployment rate of the first decade of the 2000s will have a

big effect on your job market success. Will the average unemployment rate of the 2000s continue to rise as in the past? Or will the improvement of the 1998–2000 period continue? No one knows for sure. But what you learn in this section will help you understand the forces that are at work.

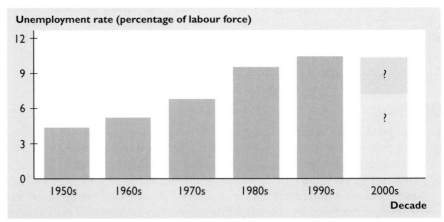

Unemployment rate (percentage of labour force)

SOURCE: Statistics Canada.

To understand the amount of frictional and structural unemployment that exists at the natural unemployment rate, economists focus on two fundamental causes of unemployment that cut across the frictional–structural classification. The two fundamental causes of unemployment are:

- Job search
- Job rationing

■ Job Search

Job search is the activity of looking for an acceptable vacant job. There are always some people who have not yet found suitable jobs and who are actively searching for jobs. The reason is that the labour market is in a constant state of change. The failure of existing businesses destroys jobs. The expansion of existing businesses and the startup of new businesses that use new technologies and develop new markets create jobs. As people pass through different stages of life, some enter or re-enter the labour market. Still others leave their jobs to look for better ones, and others retire. This constant churning in the labour market means that there are always some people looking for jobs, and these people are part of the unemployed.

The amount of job search depends on a number of factors that change over time. The main ones are:

- Demographic change
- Unemployment benefits
- Structural change

Job search
The activity of looking for an acceptable vacant job.

Demographic Change

An increase in the proportion of the population that is of working age brings an increase in the entry rate into the labour force and an increase in the unemployment rate. This factor was important in the Canadian labour market during the 1970s. The bulge in the birth rate that occurred in the late 1940s and early 1950s increased the proportion of new entrants into the labour force during the 1970s and early 1980s and brought an increase in the unemployment rate.

As the birth rate declined, the bulge moved into higher and higher age groups and the proportion of new entrants declined. This factor slowed the increase in the unemployment rate.

Another source of demographic change has been an increase in the number of households with two incomes. When unemployment comes to one of these workers, it is possible, with income still flowing in, to take longer to find a new job. This factor might have increased frictional unemployment.

Unemployment Benefits

The length of time that an unemployed person spends searching for a job depends, in part, on the opportunity cost of job search. An unemployed person who receives no unemployment benefits faces a high opportunity cost of job search. In this situation, the search is likely to be short and the person is likely to accept a less attractive job that is found quickly rather than continue a costly search process. An unemployed person who receives generous unemployment benefits faces a lower opportunity cost of job search. In this situation, the unemployed worker will likely spend a long time searching for the ideal job.

Eye On The CANADIAN ECONOMY

Demographics and the Natural Unemployment Rate

The natural unemployment rate increased during the 1970s and 1980s. One cause of this increase was the arrival of the Baby Boomers—the large group of Canadians born between 1946 and 1956. When the Baby Boomers reached working age, there was an increase in the 15–24 age group as a proportion of the working-age population in the 1970s and early 1980s. As the graph shows,

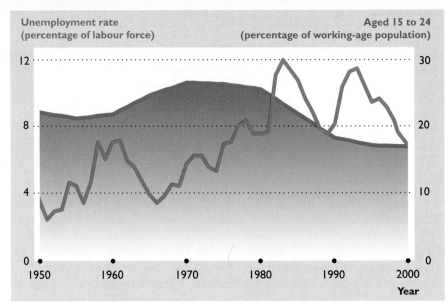

SOURCE: Statistics Canada.

Canada's unemployment rate also increased during this period.

In the decade starting in 2010, large numbers of Baby Boomers will retire and pose new and very different challenges for the Canadian economy.

Structural Change

Labour market flows and unemployment are influenced by the pace and direction of technological change. Sometimes, technological change brings a structural slump, a condition in which some industries die and some regions suffer while other industries are born and other regions flourish. When these events occur, labour turnover is high, job search increases, and the natural unemployment rate is high. At other times, technological change brings a structural boom by creating new jobs that are a good match for the people who are losing their jobs. When these events occur, labour turnover might be high but job search decreases because new jobs are found quickly. The natural unemployment rate is low. The Internet economy of the 1990s is an example of a structural boom. Lots of new jobs have been created in every major population centre that are a good match for the skills available. As these job opportunities grew, the natural unemployment rate decreased.

■ Job Rationing

Job rationing
A situation that arises when the real wage rate is above the equilibrium level.

Job rationing occurs when the real wage rate is above the equilibrium level. You have learned that markets allocate scarce resources by adjusting the market price to bring buying plans and selling plans into balance. You can think of the market as *rationing* scarce resources. In the labour market, the real wage rate rations employment and therefore rations jobs. Changes in the real wage rate keep the number of people seeking work and the number of jobs available in balance. But the real wage rate is not the only possible instrument for rationing jobs. And in some industries, the real wage rate is set above the market equilibrium level, which brings a surplus of labour. So in these labour markets, jobs are rationed by some other means.

The real wage rate might be set above the equilibrium level for three reasons:

- Efficiency wage
- Minimum wage
- Union wage

Efficiency Wage

An **efficiency wage** is a real wage rate that is set above the market equilibrium wage rate to induce a greater work effort. The idea is that if a firm pays only the going market average wage, employees have no incentive to work hard because they know that even if they are fired for shirking, they can find a job with another firm at a similar wage rate. But if a firm pays *more* than the going market average wage, employees have an incentive to work hard because they know that if they are fired, they *cannot* expect to find a job with another firm at a similar wage rate.

Further, by paying an efficiency wage, a firm can attract the most productive workers. Also, its workers are less likely to quit their jobs, so the firm faces a lower rate of labour turnover and lower training costs. Finally, the firm's recruiting costs are lower because it always faces a steady stream of available new workers.

Paying an efficiency wage is costly, so only those firms that can't directly monitor the work effort of their employees use this device. But if enough firms pay an efficiency wage, the average real wage rate will exceed the full-employment equilibrium level.

The Minimum Wage

A *minimum wage law* is a government regulation that makes hiring labour for less than a specified wage illegal. If the minimum wage is set below the equilibrium wage, the minimum wage has no effect. But if a minimum wage is set above the equilibrium wage, the minimum wage is in conflict with market forces and unemployment arises.

Minimum wage laws have the strongest effects on unemployment in the markets for low-skilled labour. And because skill grows with work experience, teenage labour is particularly affected by the minimum wage.

Union Wage

A **union wage** is a wage rate that results from collective bargaining between a labour union and an employer. Because a union increases the bargaining power of a group of workers, it can usually achieve a wage rate that exceeds the level that would prevail in a competitive labour market.

It is estimated that on the average, union wage rates are 30 percent higher than nonunion wage rates. Around that average, the union-nonunion wage difference is close to zero in mining and financial services. In other services, manufacturing, and transportation, the difference lies between 11 and 19 percent. In wholesale and retail trades, the difference is 28 percent, and in construction, it is 65 percent.

But these union-nonunion wage differences probably overstate the effects of unions on wage rates. In some industries, union wages are higher than nonunion wages because union members do jobs that involve greater skill. In these cases,

Efficiency wage
A real wage rate that is set above the full-employment equilibrium wage rate to induce greater work effort.

Union wage
A wage rate that results from collective bargaining between a labour union and an employer.

even without a union, those workers would earn a higher wage. To calculate the effects of unions, we must examine the wages of union and nonunion workers who do nearly identical work. The evidence suggests that for comparable skill, the union-nonunion wage difference lies between 10 percent and 25 percent. For example, airline pilots who are members of the Air Line Pilots Association earn about 25 percent more than nonunion pilots with the same level of skill.

Job Rationing and Unemployment

Whether because of efficiency wages, a minimum wage law, or the actions of labour unions, if the real wage rate is above the full-employment equilibrium level, the natural unemployment rate increases. The above-equilibrium real wage rate decreases the quantity of labour demanded and increases the quantity of labour supplied.

Figure 8.8 illustrates job rationing and the frictional and structural unemployment it creates. The full-employment equilibrium real wage rate is $30 an hour, and the equilibrium quantity of labour is 20 billion hours a year. The existence of efficiency wages, the minimum wage, and union wages raises the economy's average real wage rate to $40 an hour. At this wage rate, the quantity of labour demanded decreases to 15 billion hours and the quantity of labour supplied increases to 25 billion hours. Firms ration jobs and choose the workers to hire on the basis of criteria such as education and previous job experience. The labour market is like a game of musical chairs in which a large number of chairs have been removed. So the quantity of labour supplied persistently exceeds the quantity demanded, and additional unemployment arises from job rationing.

◼ FIGURE 8.8

Job Rationing Increases the Natural Unemployment Rate

e/**Foundations 8.3**

The full-employment equilibrium real wage rate is $30 an hour. Efficiency wages, the minimum wage, and union wages put the average real wage rate above the full-employment equilibrium level—at $40 an hour.

❶ The quantity of labour demanded decreases to 15 billion hours.

❷ The quantity of labour supplied increases to 25 billion hours.

❸ A surplus of labour arises and increases the natural unemployment rate.

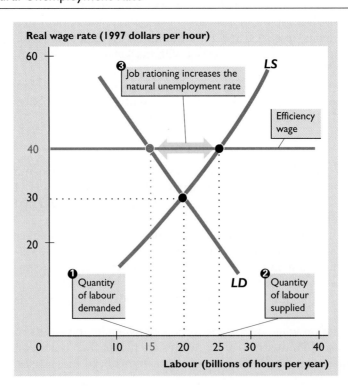

Eye On The CANADIAN ECONOMY

Canada's High Unemployment Rate

The figure highlights three facts about the unemployment rates in Canada and the United States over the fifty years from 1950 to 2000. First, during the 1950s and 1960s, Canada's unemployment rate was almost the same as that in the United States. Second, during the 1970s and 1980s, the unemployment rates in both countries increased. And third, after the mid-1970s, the Canadian unemployment rate moved above and remained stubbornly higher than that of our American neighbour.

Why did the unemployment rate increase in both countries and why did the Canadian rate move above the U.S. rate? These questions have troubled economists and been much studied by them. The most recent study is by Pierre Fortin of the Université du Québec à Montréal, Manfred Keil of Claremont McKenna College, and James Symons of the London School of Economics[*].

High interest rates and recession contributed to cyclical unemployment in both countries, and more so in Canada. And two demographic changes contributed to a higher natural unemployment rate in both countries. First, during the 1970s, the proportion of young workers increased. This group of workers has a higher job turnover rate and higher unemployment rate than older workers. Second, the number of women in the labour force increased. With two or more earners in a household, when other household members lost their jobs, they could be more selective in searching for new jobs.

Three factors that might have contributed to a higher natural unemployment rate in Canada than in the United States are Canada's:

- More generous unemployment benefits
- Higher minimum wage
- Stronger labour unions

Canada's unemployment benefits were so generous during the 1970s and 1980s, especially in high-unemployment regions, that a person could take a job for 8 weeks and then qualify for benefits that lasted for 44 weeks. This arrangement increased the labour force participation rate and the unemployment rate.

Canada's minimum wage increased from 40 percent to almost 50 percent of the average wage during the 1970s and fell back to 35 percent of the average wage during the 1990s.

The percentage of the labour force unionized decreased in the United States but remained high in Canada. Stronger unionization in Canada might have kept wage rates higher here but at the expense of some jobs.

[*] "The sources of unemployment in Canada, 1967-91: evidence from a panel of regions and demographic groups" *Oxford Economic Papers* 53 (2001), pp. 67–93.

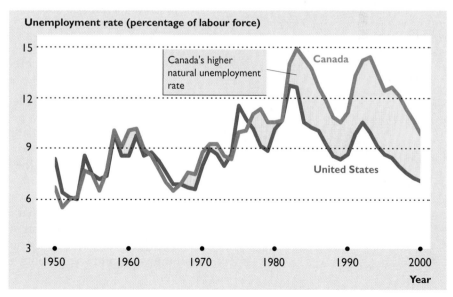

SOURCE: Statistics Canada.

Study Guide pp. 124–126

*e*Foundations 8.3

3 Explain what creates unemployment when the economy is at full employment and describe the influences on the natural unemployment rate.

Practice Problem 8.3

The economy of Singapore has seen huge changes during the past 50 years. It has experienced rapid population growth and has restructured its economy several times to remain at the forefront of the latest technology. Singapore has modest unemployment benefits, no minimum wage, and weak labour unions.

  a. Does the unemployment that Singapore experiences arise primarily from job search or job rationing?
  b. Which factors mentioned above suggest that Singapore has a higher natural unemployment rate than Canada?
  c. Which factors mentioned above suggest that Singapore has a lower natural unemployment rate than Canada?

Exercise 8.3

1. The economy of Sweden has seen changes during the past 50 years, but the change has been steady and population growth has been modest. Sweden has high unemployment benefits, a high minimum wage, and strong labour unions.
   a. Does the unemployment that Sweden experiences arise primarily from job search or job rationing?
   b. Which factors mentioned above suggest that Sweden has a higher natural unemployment rate than Canada?
   c. Which factors mentioned above suggest that Sweden has a lower natural unemployment rate than Canada?

Solution to Practice Problem 8.3

  a. Singapore's unemployment is likely to arise primarily from job search. Of the sources of job rationing (efficiency wages, minimum wages, and union wages) only efficiency wages applies.
  b. The factors mentioned above that point towards a higher natural unemployment rate in Singapore than in Canada are rapid population growth and restructuring to remain at the forefront of new technologies, both of which will create a large amount of job search, other things remaining the same.
  c. The factors mentioned above that point towards a lower natural unemployment rate in Singapore than in Canada are modest unemployment benefits, which will limit the amount of job search, and the absence of a minimum wage and weak labour unions, which will limit the amount of job rationing.

CHAPTER CHECKPOINT

Key Points

1 **Use the aggregate supply–aggregate demand (*AS-AD*) model to illustrate economic growth, inflation, and the business cycle.**

- A rise in the price level brings an increase in the quantity of real GDP supplied and a decrease in the quantity of real GDP demanded, other influences on production and expenditure remaining the same.
- When the quantity of real GDP supplied equals the quantity of real GDP demanded, real GDP might equal, exceed, or be less than potential GDP.

2 **Explain the forces that determine potential GDP and the distribution of income between labour and other factors of production.**

- The production function describes the relationship between real GDP and the quantity of labour employed when all other influences on production remain the same. As the quantity of labour increases, real GDP increases.
- The quantity of labour demanded increases as the real wage rate falls, other things remaining the same.
- The quantity of labour supplied increases as the real wage rate rises, other things remaining the same.
- At full-employment equilibrium, the real wage makes the quantity of labour demanded equal the quantity of labour supplied.
- Potential GDP is the level of real GDP that the full-employment quantity of labour produces.

3 **Explain what creates unemployment when the economy is at full employment and describe the influences on the natural unemployment rate.**

- The unemployment rate at full employment is the natural unemployment rate.
- Unemployment is ever present because of job search and job rationing.
- Job search is influenced by demographic change, unemployment benefits, and structural change.
- Job rationing arises from efficiency wages, the minimum wage, and union wages.

Key Terms

Exercises

1. The people of Nautica can work a maximum of 100 hours every day. The first 10 hours of work produce $10 of real GDP. The second 10 hours a day produce an additional $9 of real GDP. The third 10 hours a day produce an additional $8 of real GDP. Each additional 10 hours of work a day produces additional GDP of $1 a day less than the previous 10 hours. Make a table and a graph of Nautica's production function.

2. Use the information provided in Exercise 1 about the economy of Nautica. Also, use the information that the firms in Nautica are willing to hire 10 hours of labour a day for a real wage rate of $1 an hour and 20 hours of labour a day for a real wage rate of 90¢ an hour. In addition, for each 10¢ cut in the real wage rate, they are willing to hire an additional 10 hours of labour a day. The people of Nautica are willing to work 10 hours a day for a real wage rate of 10¢ an hour. And for each 10¢ an hour increase in the real wage, they are willing to work an additional 10 hours a day.
   a. Make a table that shows Nautica's demand for labour schedule and draw Nautica's demand for labour curve.
   b. Make a table that shows Nautica's supply of labour schedule and draw Nautica's supply of labour curve.
   c. Find the equilibrium real wage rate and quantity of labour in Nautica.
   d. Find Nautica's potential GDP.

3. Two island economies, Cocoa Island and Plantation Island, are identical in every respect except one. A survey tells us that when Cocoa Island is at full employment, people spend 1,000 hours a day in job search, while the people on Plantation Island spend 2,000 hours a day in job search when their island is at full employment. Which economy has:
   a. The greater level of potential GDP?
   b. The higher real wage rate?
   c. The higher natural unemployment rate?

4. On Cocoa Island described in Exercise 3, the government sets a minimum wage that creates an additional 1,000 hours a day of unemployment. On Plantation Island, nothing changes from the situation described in Exercise 3.
   a. Which economy now has the greater level of potential GDP?
   b. Which economy now has the higher real wage rate?
   c. Which economy now has the higher natural unemployment rate?
   d. How much of each economy's unemployment results from job search and how much from job rationing?

5. Visit your Foundations Web site and use the links provided to obtain information about the economy of Russia during the 1990s. Try to figure out what happened to the production function, the demand for labour, and the supply of labour in Russia during the 1990s.

6. Visit your Foundations Web site and use the links provided to obtain information about the economy of Russia during the 1990s. Use the concepts and tools that you have learned about in this chapter to describe the influences on and the course of the Russian economy during the 1990s. Pay special attention to the changes in aggregate supply and aggregate demand and explain the type of macroeconomic equilibrium that Russia has experienced.

Investment and Saving

CHAPTER CHECKLIST

When you have completed your study of this chapter,
you will be able to:

1 Define and explain the relationships among capital, investment, wealth, and saving.

2 Explain how investment and saving decisions are made and how these decisions interact in financial markets to determine the real interest rate.

3 Explain how government influences the real interest rate, investment, and saving.

You learned in Chapter 8 how real GDP at full employment is determined. And you saw the large differences between the full-employment economies of the 1960s and 1990s. In Chapter 3, you took a quick first look at how the economy gets from one level of real GDP (such as that of the 1960s) to a higher level (such as that of the 1990s). Real GDP expands when the *PPF* shifts rightward. And the *PPF* shifts rightward when the quantity of capital increases and technology advances.

The quantity of capital increases because we save and invest. So the amount of saving and the amount of investment determine the pace at which the quantity of capital increases.

In this chapter, you are going to learn about the choices that businesses, households, and governments make that determine investment and saving. And you're going to see how a global financial market coordinates these choices to determine the quantity of capital and the real interest rate.

9.1   CAPITAL, INVESTMENT, WEALTH, AND SAVING

Physical capital
The tools, instruments, machines, buildings, and other constructions that have been produced in the past and that are used to produce goods and services.

Financial capital
The funds that firms use to buy and operate physical capital.

Gross investment
The total amount spent on new capital goods.

Net investment
The change in the quantity of capital—equals gross investment minus depreciation.

Capital, or **physical capital,** is the tools, instruments, machines, buildings, and other constructions that have been produced in the past and that are used to produce goods and services. When economists use the term *capital,* they mean physical capital. **Financial capital** is the funds that firms use to buy and operate physical capital. The quantity of physical capital influences our production possibilities and real GDP. But the quantity of financial capital, which depends on the decisions that people and businesses make about spending, saving, borrowing, and lending, influences the quantity of physical capital. We begin by describing the links between the quantity of physical capital and investment.

■ Capital and Investment

Investment and depreciation change the quantity of capital. *Investment* (Chapter 5, p. 109) is the purchase of new capital goods and additions to inventories. *Depreciation* (Chapter 5, p. 116) is the decrease in the value of capital that results from its use and from obsolescence. Also called *capital consumption,* depreciation is the opportunity cost of owning and using capital. It is the market price of capital at the beginning of a period minus its market price at the end of a period. The total amount spent on new capital goods is called **gross investment.** The change in the quantity of capital is called net investment. **Net investment** equals gross investment minus depreciation.

Figure 9.1 illustrates these concepts. On January 1, 2001, Tom's DVD Burning, Inc. had DVD recording machines worth $30,000—Tom's initial capital. During 2001, the market value of Tom's machines fell by 67 percent—$20,000. After this depreciation, Tom's machines were valued at $10,000. During 2001, Tom spent $30,000 on new machines. This amount is Tom's gross investment. By December 31, 2001, Tom had capital valued at $40,000, so his capital had increased by $10,000. This amount is Tom's net investment. Tom's net investment equals his gross investment of $30,000 minus depreciation of $20,000.

■ **FIGURE 9.1**
Capital and Investment

*e*Foundations **9.1**

On January 1, 2001, Tom's DVD Burning, Inc. had DVD recording machines valued at $30,000. During 2001, the value of Tom's machines fell by $20,000—depreciation—and he spent $30,000 on new machines—gross investment. Tom's net investment was $10,000, so at the end of 2001, Tom had capital valued at $40,000.

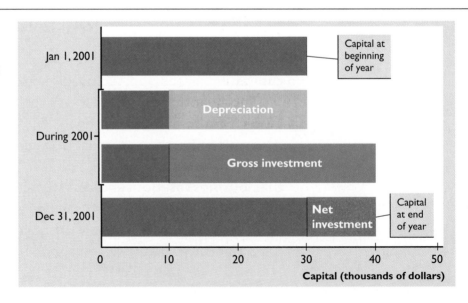

Investment and Capital, 1970–2000

Gross investment, shown in part (a) of the figure, increases in most years and especially during periods of economic expansion; but it decreases during recessions (highlighted in the figure).

Depreciation, also shown in part (a), increases in most years, but it fluctuates less than gross investment.

Gross investment minus depreciation is net investment. You can see net investment in part (a) as the gap between the two curves.

Part (b) of the figure provides a sharper view of net investment. You can see that it fluctuates a great deal and decreases sharply during a recession. Like gross investment, it increased rapidly during the late 1990s.

Although net investment fluctuates, it rarely (and never during the 30 years shown here) becomes negative. Negative net investment would mean that the quantity of capital was shrinking. Because net investment is always positive, the quantity of capital, shown in part (c) of the figure, increases each year.

The quantity of capital grows steadily despite huge swings in net investment. The reason is that net investment is tiny in comparison with the quantity of capital. Between 1970 and 2000, net investment averaged 3 percent of the quantity of capital.

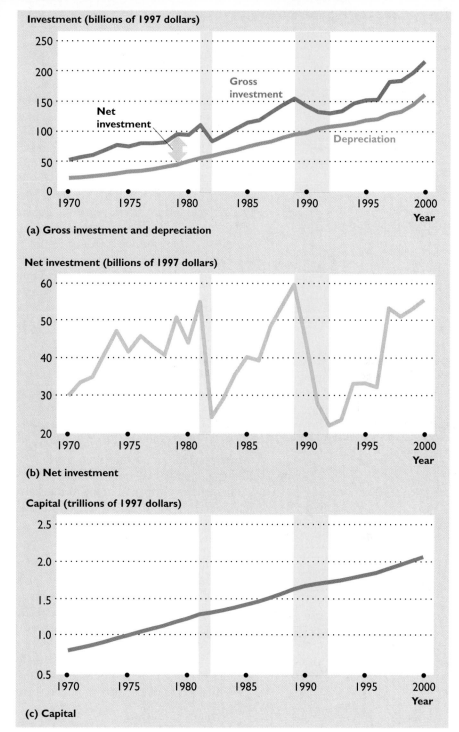

(a) Gross investment and depreciation

(b) Net investment

(c) Capital

SOURCE: Statistics Canada.

Each nation's capital and investment work just like the example of Tom's DVD-recording shop. A nation's capital today equals its capital a year ago plus its net investment during the past year. A nation's net investment during the past year equals its gross investment minus depreciation. The Eye on the Canadian Economy takes a look at Canada's investment and capital growth from 1970 to 2000.

■ Wealth and Saving

Wealth
The value of all the things that a person owns.

Saving
The amount of income that is not paid in taxes or spent on consumption goods and services—adds to wealth.

A person's **wealth** is the value of all the things that the person owns. What people *own* is related to what they *earn*. But it is not the same thing. People *earn* an *income*, which is the amount they receive during a given time period from supplying the services of the resources they own. **Saving** is the amount of income that is not paid in taxes or spent on consumption goods and services, and saving adds to wealth. Wealth also increases when the value of assets rises—called *capital gains*.

Suppose that at the end of the school year, you have $250 in a savings account and some textbooks that are worth $300. That's all you own. Your wealth is $550. During the summer, you earn an income (after tax) of $5,000. You spend only $1,000 through the summer on consumption. At the end of the summer, you have $4,250 in your savings account. Your wealth is now $4,550. Your wealth has increased by $4,000, which equals your saving of $4,000. Your saving of $4,000 equals your income of $5,000 minus your consumption expenditure of $1,000.

National wealth and national saving work just like this personal example. The wealth of a nation at the start of a year equals its wealth at the start of the previous year plus its saving during the year. Its saving equals its income minus its consumption expenditure.

■ Financial Markets

Financial markets
The collection of households, firms, governments, banks, and other financial institutions that lend and borrow.

Financial markets are the collections of households, firms, governments, banks, and other financial institutions that lend and borrow. Financial markets are where firms get the funds that they use to buy capital. Firms are demanders and households are suppliers in financial markets. Governments are demanders if they have a budget deficit and suppliers if they have a budget surplus. Banks and other financial institutions help to match the lending plans of households and the borrowing plans of firms. Financial markets determine the price of financial capital, which is expressed as an interest rate (percent per year).

■ Global Financial Markets

Financial markets span the globe. Lenders want to earn the highest possible real interest rate. If, for equal risk, they can get a higher real interest rate in Europe than in Canada, lenders will move their funds to Europe. Borrowers want to pay the lowest possible real interest rate. If they can borrow at a lower interest rate in Japan than in Canada, they will borrow in Japan.

Because funds are free to roam the globe looking for the highest possible real interest rate and because borrowers are free to seek the lowest possible real interest rate in any country, the financial markets form a single global market.

Financial markets are organized into four groups:

- Stock markets
- Bond markets
- Short-term securities markets
- Loans markets

Stock Markets

Stock
A certificate of ownership and claim to the profits that a firm makes.

When VHQ Entertainment wanted to raise funds to expand its chain of video rental stores in western Canada, it issued stock. A **stock** is a certificate of ownership and claim to the profits that a firm makes. VHQ has issued about 11.5

million shares of its stock. So if you owned 11,500 VHQ shares, you would own one thousandth of VHQ and be entitled to receive one thousandth of the company's profits.

A **stock market** is a financial market in which shares in companies' stocks are traded. The Toronto Stock Exchange and the New York Stock Exchange are the largest stock markets in Canada and the United States respectively. The London Stock Exchange (in England) and the Frankfurt Stock Exchange (in Germany) are the main stock markets in Europe. In Asia, the Tokyo and Hong Kong stock exchanges are the dominant ones. You can visit the Web sites of stock markets and see the prices and the quantities of shares that are being traded minute by minute throughout the business day.

Stock market
A financial market in which shares of companies' stocks are traded.

If you buy some VHQ Entertainment stock today, you pay the current owner of the stock, not VHQ. VHQ received the value of the stock when it first issued it.

Demand and supply in stock markets determine the prices of individual stocks and the returns on them. The return on a stock is the dividend that the firm pays plus the change in the market value of the stock—the capital gain or loss.

Bond Markets

In 1999, Bell Canada wanted to raise $200 million to expand its communications services. Instead of issuing stock, Bell Canada sold bonds. A **bond** is a promise to pay specified sums of money on specified dates and is a debt of the issuer of the bond. The buyer of a $1,000 bond loaned Bell Canada that amount for 20 years. Each year, the bondholder receives $65.50 interest (6.55 percent of the $1,000 loaned), and after 20 years, is repaid the $1,000 that was loaned. Governments—federal, provincial, and local—also issue bonds. The buyer of a bond is entitled only to the payments promised by the bond and unlike a stockholder is not a part owner of the firm. When a person buys a newly issued bond, he or she might hold the bond until the borrower repays the amount borrowed or sell it to someone else. The **bond market** is a financial market in which bonds issued by firms and governments are traded. Demand and supply in the bond market determine the prices of bonds and the interest rates on them.

Bond
A promise to pay specified sums of money on specified dates; it is a debt for the issuer.

Bond market
A financial market in which bonds issued by firms and governments are traded.

Short-Term Securities Markets

When General Motors sells $100 million of railway locomotives to Canadian Pacific, GM wants to be paid as soon as the items are shipped. But Canadian Pacific doesn't want to pay until the locomotives are operating and earning an income. In this situation, GM can issue a short-term security called a commercial bill. Each bill would be a promise by GM to pay $100 on a date three months in the future. A bank would be willing to buy these bills for an amount less than $100, and the difference between the price paid and $100 would be the interest on the bill. The Government of Canada also issues bills of this type, called Treasury bills.

Demand and supply in the short-term securities market determine the price and interest rate on commercial bills and Treasury bills.

Loans Markets

Many businesses finance their short-term capital, such as inventories, with a loan from a bank. Banks and other financial institutions lower the cost of financing firms' capital expenditures by accepting short-term deposits and making longer-term loans. They enable the small savings of millions of individuals to be pooled to finance investment. (You will study banks in some detail in Chapter 11.)

Study Guide pp. 133–135

*e*Foundations 9.1

1 Define and explain the relationships among capital, investment, wealth, and saving.

Practice Problems 9.1

1. Michael is an Internet service provider. On December 31, 2000, he bought an existing business with servers and a building worth $400,000. During his first year of operation, his business grew and he bought new servers for $500,000. The market value of some of his older servers fell by $100,000.
   a. What was Michael's gross investment during 2001?
   b. What was Michael's depreciation during 2001?
   c. What was Michael's net investment during 2001?
   d. What was Michael's capital at the end of 2001?

2. Lori is a student who teaches golf on the weekend and in a year earns $20,000 in fees after paying her taxes. At the beginning of 2000, Lori owned $1,000 worth of books, CDs, and golf clubs and she had $5,000 in a savings account at the bank. During 2000, the interest on her savings account was $300 and she spent a total of $15,300 on consumption goods and services.
   a. How much did Lori save in 2000?
   b. What was Lori's wealth at the end of 2000?

Exercises 9.1

1. Annie runs a fitness centre. On December 31, 2000, she bought an existing business with exercise equipment and a building worth $600,000. During her first year of operation, business was poor. She sold some of her equipment to a competitor for $200,000.
   a. What was Annie's gross investment during 2001?
   b. What was Annie's depreciation during 2001?
   c. What was Annie's net investment during 2001?
   d. What was the value of Annie's capital at the end of 2001?

2. Karrie is a golf pro, and after she paid taxes, her total income from golf and from the stocks and bonds that she owns was $1,000,000 in 2000. At the beginning of 2000, she owned $600,000 worth of stocks and bonds. At the end of 2000, Karrie's stocks and bonds were worth $1,400,000. How much did Karrie save during 2000 and how much did she spend on consumption goods and services?

Solutions to Practice Problems 9.1

1a. Michael's gross investment during 2001 was $500,000.
1b. Michael's depreciation during 2001 was $100,000.
1c. Michael's net investment during 2001 was $400,000.
1d. At the end of 2001, Michael's capital was $800,000.

2a. Lori's saving equals her income (after tax) minus the amount she spent. That is, her saving equalled $20,300 minus $15,300, or $5,000.
2b. Lori's wealth at the end of 2000 was $11,000—the sum of her wealth at the start of 2000 ($6,000) plus her saving during 2000 ($5,000).

9.2 INVESTMENT, SAVING, AND INTEREST

Firms' investment decisions (investment demand) and households' consumption and saving decisions (saving supply) are coordinated in a global financial market to determine the quantity of capital and the real interest rate (financial market equilibrium). You learned how we define and measure the real interest rate in Chapter 7 (p. 167). We're now going to learn how the forces of demand and supply in the global financial market determine the real interest rate. We will study:

- Investment demand
- Saving supply
- Financial market equilibrium

■ Investment Demand

How does Canadian Tire decide whether to invest in a new warehouse? How does McCain Foods decide whether to build a new food-processing plant? Many details influence business investment decisions like these, but we can summarize them in two factors: the real interest rate and the expected rate of profit.

The real interest rate is the opportunity cost of the funds used to finance the purchase of capital, and firms compare the opportunity cost with the rate of profit they expect to earn on their new capital. Firms invest only when they expect to earn a rate of profit that exceeds the real interest rate. The higher the real interest rate, the fewer the projects that are profitable, so the smaller is the amount of investment demanded.

> **Other things remaining the same, the higher the real interest rate, the smaller is the quantity of investment demanded; and the lower the real interest rate, the greater is the quantity of investment demanded.**

Suppose that Canadian Tire expects to earn an additional $5 million (before paying its interest costs) if it builds a new $100 million warehouse. If the real interest rate is 4 percent a year, Canadian Tire's interest bill for this warehouse is $4 million a year, so the investment earns $1 million a year. But if the real interest rate is 6 percent a year (other things remaining the same), Canadian Tire's interest bill is $6 million a year, so the investment incurs a loss of $1 million a year. So Canadian Tire will invest in the warehouse at a real interest rate of 4 percent a year but not at 6 percent a year.

The funds used to finance investment might be borrowed, or they might be the financial resources of the firm's owners (the firm's retained earnings). The opportunity cost of both sources of funds is the real interest rate because they could be loaned and earn the real interest rate.

We summarize the influences on investment decisions in an investment demand curve.

Investment Demand Curve

The relationship between the quantity of investment demanded and the real interest rate, other things remaining the same, is called **investment demand.** If the real interest rate rises, other things remaining the same, the quantity of investment demanded decreases. The table in Figure 9.2 shows an example of this relationship.

Investment demand
The relationship between the quantity of investment demanded and the real interest rate, other things remaining the same.

*e*Foundations **9.2**

The table shows the quantity of investment demanded at five real interest rates. For example, when the real interest rate is 6 percent a year, the quantity of investment demanded is $10 trillion. The figure shows the investment demand curve, *ID*. Points *A* through *E* on the investment demand curve correspond to the rows in the table.

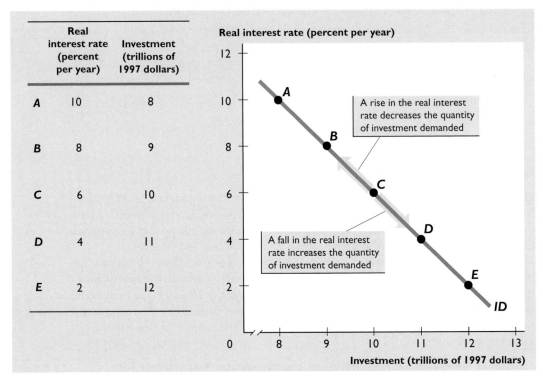

	Real interest rate (percent per year)	Investment (trillions of 1997 dollars)
A	10	8
B	8	9
C	6	10
D	4	11
E	2	12

Figure 9.2 shows an investment demand curve in the global financial market. Each point (*A* through *E*) corresponds to a row in the table. If the real interest rate is 6 percent a year, the quantity of investment demanded is $10 trillion. A change in the real interest rate brings a movement along the investment demand curve. If the real interest rate rises to 8 percent a year, the quantity of investment demanded decreases to $9 trillion; there is a movement up the investment demand curve. If the real interest rate falls to 4 percent a year, the quantity of investment demanded increases to $11 trillion; there is a movement down the investment demand curve.

Changes in Investment Demand

When the expected rate of profit changes, investment demand changes. Other things remaining the same, the greater the expected profit from new capital, the greater is the amount of investment. The many influences on expected profit can be placed in three groups:

- Objective influences such as the phase of the business cycle, technological change, and population growth
- Subjective influences summarized in the phrase "animal spirits"
- Contagion effects summarized in the phrase "irrational exuberance"

Expected profits rise in an expansion and fall in a recession and so bring swings in investment demand over the business cycle. For example, investment soared during the information-based expansion of the late 1990s and sagged during the recession of the early 1990s.

Technological change lowers costs and creates new and profitable products. But to take advantage of new technologies, firms must invest in the equipment that employs them. For example, to produce a new generation of enormously profitable computer chips, Intel Corporation must invest several billion dollars in chip-making equipment that incorporates the latest technology.

Population growth brings a steady increase in the demand for all goods. Greater demand leads to greater profits. But to meet the increased demand and earn the profits available, firms must invest in additional capital.

Because investment decisions are forward looking, they are based on subjective feelings about the future. Sometimes "animal spirits" are optimistic and sometimes pessimistic, and these swings of mood bring swings in investment demand.

Also, mood swings can be contagious. U.S. Federal Reserve Chairman Alan Greenspan called the contagious optimism of the 1990s "irrational exuberance."

Shifts of the Investment Demand Curve

When investment demand changes, the investment demand curve shifts. Figure 9.3 shows how the investment demand curve depends on expected profit. When firms expect average profits, investment demand is ID_0, which is the same investment demand curve as the one in Figure 9.2.

When the expected profit increases, investment demand increases and the investment demand curve shifts rightward to ID_1. When expected profit decreases, investment demand decreases and the investment demand curve shifts leftward to ID_2.

■ **FIGURE 9.3**

Changes in Investment Demand   *e*/**Foundations 9.2**

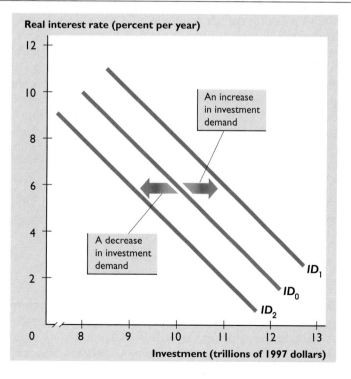

A change in profit expectations shifts the investment demand curve. An increase in the expected profit increases investment demand and shifts the investment demand curve rightward to ID_1. A decrease in the expected profit decreases investment demand and shifts the investment demand curve leftward to ID_2.

June 21, 2001

Canadians Saving More than Americans

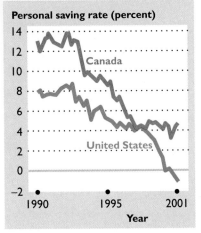

NATIONAL POST

Questions
1. What might explain the sharp decline in the U.S. savings rate?

 *e*Foundations **9.2**

Saving supply
The relationship between the quantity of saving supplied and the real interest rate, other things remaining the same.

Disposable income
Income earned minus net taxes.

■ Saving Supply

You've graduated and landed a great job that pays you $40,000 a year. How do you decide how much of your income to spend on consumption goods and services and how much to save? Your decision would be influenced by many factors that we'll now review. But we'll begin by focusing on one of them: the real interest rate.

> **Other things remaining the same, the higher the real interest rate, the greater is the quantity of saving supplied; and the lower the real interest rate, the smaller is the quantity of saving supplied.**

The real interest rate is the *opportunity cost* of consumption expenditure. A dollar spent is a dollar not saved, so the interest that could have been earned on that saving is forgone. This opportunity cost arises regardless of whether a person is a lender or a borrower. For a lender, saving less this year means receiving less interest next year. For a borrower, saving less this year means paying less off a loan this year and paying more interest next year.

By thinking about student loans, you can see why the real interest rate influences saving. If the real interest rate on student loans jumped to 20 percent a year, graduates would save more (buying cheaper food and finding lower-rent accommodations) to pay off their loans as quickly as possible and avoid, as much as possible, paying the higher interest cost of their loan. If the real interest rate on student loans fell to 1 percent a year, graduates would save less and take longer to pay off their loan because the interest burden was easier to bear.

Saving Supply Curve

The relationship between the quantity of saving supplied and the real interest rate, other things remaining the same, is called **saving supply.**

Figure 9.4 illustrates saving supply in the global financial market. The table shows a saving supply schedule, and the graph shows the saving supply curve. The points *A* through *E* on the saving supply curve *SS* in Figure 9.4 correspond to the rows of the table. For example, point *C* shows that when the real interest rate is 6 percent a year, the quantity of saving supplied is $10 trillion. If the real interest rate rises from 6 percent a year to 8 percent a year, the quantity of saving supplied increases from $10 trillion to $11 trillion and there is a movement along the saving supply curve from *C* to *B*. If the real interest rate falls from 6 percent a year to 4 percent a year, the quantity of saving supplied decreases from $10 trillion to $9 trillion and there is a movement along the saving supply curve from *C* to *D*.

Changes in Saving Supply

When any influence on saving other than the real interest rate changes, saving supply changes. The three main factors that influence saving supply are:

- Disposable income
- The buying power of net assets
- Expected future disposable income

Disposable Income A household's **disposable income** is the income earned minus net taxes. The greater a household's disposable income, other things remaining the same, the greater is its saving. For example, a student works part time and earns a disposable income of $10,000. She spends the entire $10,000 on

FIGURE 9.4

Saving Supply   *e*Foundations **9.2**

Real interest rate (percent per year)	Saving (trillions of 1997 dollars)
A 10	12
B 8	11
C 6	10
D 4	9
E 2	8

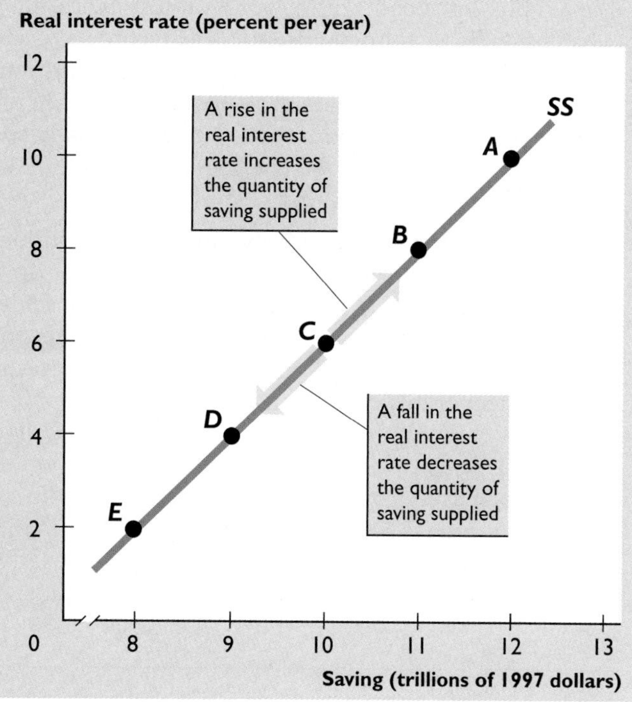

Real interest rate (percent per year)

A rise in the real interest rate increases the quantity of saving supplied

A fall in the real interest rate decreases the quantity of saving supplied

Saving (trillions of 1997 dollars)

The table shows the quantity of saving supplied at five real interest rates. For example, when the real interest rate is 6 percent a year, the quantity of saving supplied is $10 trillion. The figure shows the saving supply curve, SS. Points A through E on the saving supply curve correspond to the rows in the table.

consumption and saves nothing. When she graduates as an economics major, her disposable income increases to $35,000 a year. She now saves $10,000 and spends $25,000 on consumption. The increase in disposable income of $25,000 has increased saving by $10,000.

Buying Power of Net Assets   A household's net assets are what it owns minus the debts that it owes. The buying power of a household's net assets is the quantity of goods and services that its net assets can buy. The greater the buying power of the net assets that a household has accumulated, other things remaining the same, the less will the household save.

Patty is a department store executive who earns $50,000 a year. She has been saving $5,000 a year and now has $15,000 in the bank and no debts. With $15,000 in the bank, Patty decides to spend $5,000 on a vacation and save nothing this year. Tony, another department store executive who also earns $50,000, has saved nothing and has an outstanding balance of $10,000 on his credit card. With nothing in the bank and a big debt, Tony feels financially insecure, so he decides to cut his consumption and start saving.

Expected Future Disposable Income   The higher a household's expected future disposable income, other things remaining the same, the smaller is its saving today. That is, if two households have the same disposable income in the current year, the household with the larger expected future disposable income will spend a larger portion of current disposable income on consumption goods and services and so save less today.

Look at Patty and Tony again. Patty has just been promoted and will receive a $10,000 pay raise next year. Tony has just been told that he will be fired at the end of the year. On receiving this news, Patty buys a new car—increases her consumption expenditure and cuts her saving—and Tony sells his car and takes the bus—decreases his consumption expenditure and increases his saving.

Most young households expect to have a higher future income for some years and then to have a lower income during retirement. Because of this pattern of income over the life cycle, young people save a small amount, middle-aged people save a lot, and retired people gradually spend their accumulated savings.

Shifts of the Saving Supply Curve

Along the saving supply curve, all the influences on saving other than the real interest rate remain the same. A change in any of these influences on saving changes the saving supply and shifts the saving supply curve. An increase in disposable income, a decrease in the buying power of net assets, or a decrease in expected future disposable income increases saving supply. Figure 9.5 shows the effect of this change on the saving supply curve.

Initially, the saving supply curve is SS_0. Then disposable income increases, the buying power of net assets decreases, or expected future disposable income decreases. Saving supply increases, and the saving supply curve shifts rightward from SS_0 to SS_1. Changes in these factors in the opposite direction decrease saving supply and shift the saving supply curve leftward from SS_0 to SS_2.

■ **FIGURE 9.5**

Changes in Saving Supply

*e*Foundations **9.2**

An increase in disposable income, a decrease in the buying power of net assets, or a decrease in expected future disposable income increases saving and shifts the saving supply curve rightward from SS_0 to SS_1.

A decrease in disposable income, an increase in the buying power of net assets, or an increase in expected future disposable income decreases saving and shifts the saving supply curve leftward from SS_0 to SS_2.

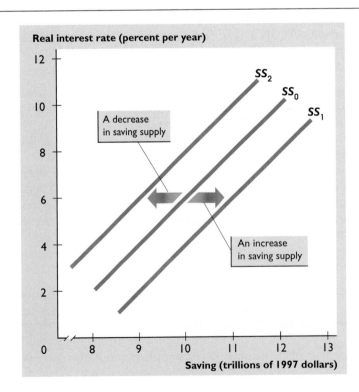

■ Financial Market Equilibrium

Figure 9.6 shows how the real interest rate is determined. The *ID* curve is the global investment demand curve. The *SS* curve is the global saving supply curve. The higher the real interest rate, the greater is the amount of saving and the smaller is the amount of investment.

In Figure 9.6, when the real interest rate exceeds 6 percent a year, the quantity of saving supplied exceeds the quantity of investment demanded. There is a surplus of saving, and borrowers have an easy time finding the loans they want, but lenders are unable to lend all the funds they have available. The real interest rate falls, and as it does so, the quantity of investment demanded increases and the quantity of saving supplied decreases.

Alternatively, when the interest rate is less than 6 percent a year, the quantity of saving supplied is less than the quantity of investment demanded. There is a shortage of saving. Borrowers can't find the loans they want, but lenders are able to lend all the funds they have available. So the real interest rate rises. As the real interest rate rises, the quantity of investment demanded decreases and the quantity of saving supplied increases.

Regardless of whether there is a surplus or a shortage of saving, the real interest rate changes and is pulled towards an equilibrium level. In Figure 9.6, this equilibrium is 6 percent a year. At this interest rate there is neither a surplus nor a shortage of saving. Investors can get the funds they demand, and savers can lend all the funds they have available. The plans of savers and investors are consistent with each other.

■ **FIGURE 9.6**
Financial Market Equilibrium   *e***Foundations 9.2**

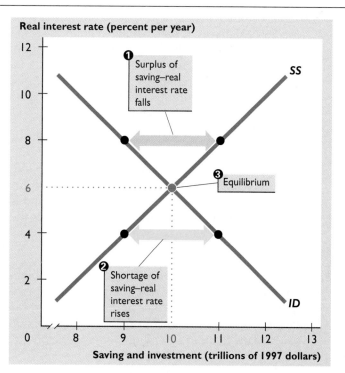

❶ If the real interest rate is 8 percent a year, the quantity of investment demanded is less than the quantity of saving supplied. There is a surplus of saving, and the real interest rate falls.

❷ If the real interest rate is 4 percent a year, the quantity of investment demanded exceeds the quantity of saving supplied. There is a shortage of saving, and the real interest rate rises.

❸ When the real interest rate is 6 percent a year, the quantity of investment demanded equals the quantity of saving supplied. There is neither a shortage nor a surplus of saving, and the real interest rate is at its equilibrium level.

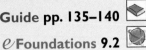
2 Explain how investment and saving decisions are made and how these decisions interact in financial markets to determine the real interest rate.

Practice Problems 9.2

1. First Call, Inc. is a cellular phone company. It plans to build an assembly plant that costs $10 million if the real interest rate is 6 percent a year. If the real interest rate is 5 percent a year, First Call will build a larger plant that costs $12 million. If the real interest rate is 7 percent a year, First Call will build a smaller plant that costs $8 million.
   a. Draw a graph of First Call's investment demand curve.
   b. First Call expects its profit from the sale of cellular phones to double next year. If everything else remains the same, explain how this increase in expected profit influences First Call's investment demand.
   c. In 2005, First Call plans to incorporate a new technology into its cellular phones. If the demand for its phones increases and other things remain the same, explain how the new technology influences First Call's investment demand.

2. In 2000, the King family had a disposable income of $50,000, net assets of $100,000, and an expected future disposable income of $50,000 a year. At a real interest rate of 4 percent a year, the King family would save $10,000 a year; at a real interest rate of 6 percent a year, they would save $12,500 a year; and at a real interest rate of 8 percent a year, they would save $15,000 a year.
   a. Draw a graph of the King family's saving supply curve.
   b. In 2001, the King family expects its future disposable income to increase to $60,000 a year. If other things remain the same, explain how this change influences the King family's saving supply.
   c. In 2002, the stock market booms and the King family's net assets increase in value. If the King family expects its future disposable income to be $50,000 and other things remain the same, explain how this change influences the King family's saving supply.

3. Draw graphs of the global financial market that illustrate how an increase in saving supply and:
   a. A decrease in investment demand can lower the real interest rate and leave the equilibrium quantity of saving and investment unchanged.
   b. An even larger increase in investment demand increases the equilibrium quantity of saving and investment and raises the real interest rate.

Exercises 9.2

1. Clean Energy, Inc. is a natural gas company. It plans to build pipelines to metropolitan areas. If the real interest rate is 4 percent a year, it plans to build $20 million of pipelines. If the real interest rate is 6 percent a year, it plans to build $15 million of pipelines. If the real interest rate is 8 percent a year, it plans to build $10 million of pipelines.

a. Draw a graph of Clean Energy's investment demand curve.
b. Clean Energy expects the households that use gas to increase in the next few years. Explain how this change influences Clean Energy's investment demand.

2. In 2000, the Lee family had a disposable income of $60,000, net assets of $120,000, and an expected future disposable income of $60,000 a year. At a real interest rate of 4 percent a year, the Lee family would save $10,000 a year; at a real interest rate of 6 percent a year, they would save $15,000 a year; and at a real interest rate of 8 percent, they would save $20,000 a year.
a. Draw a graph of the Lee family's saving supply curve.
b. In 2001, the stock market booms and the Lee family's net assets increase. Explain how this change influences the Lee family's saving supply.
c. In 2002, the stock market crashes and the Lee family loses all its assets. Explain how this change influences the Lee family's saving supply.

3. Draw graphs of the global financial market that illustrate how:
a. A decrease in saving supply and a decrease in investment demand can decrease the equilibrium quantity of saving and investment and leave the real interest rate unchanged.
b. An increase in investment demand and an even larger increase in saving supply can lower the real interest rate and increase the equilibrium quantity of saving and investment.

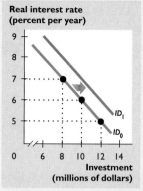

FIGURE 1

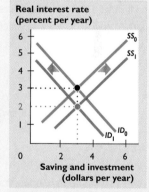

FIGURE 2

Solutions to Practice Problems 9.2

1a. The investment demand curve is the downward-sloping curve ID_0 and passes through the points highlighted in Figure 1.
1b. An increase in the expected profit increases the amount of investment at each real interest rate. First Call's investment demand increases, and the investment demand curve shifts rightward to ID_1 (Figure 1).
1c. To incorporate the new technology, First Call increases the amount of investment at each real interest rate. First Call's investment demand increases, and the investment demand curve shifts rightward to ID_1 (Figure 1).

2a. The saving supply curve is the upward-sloping curve SS_0 and passes through the points highlighted in Figure 2.
2b. An increase in expected future disposable income decreases the amount of saving at each real interest rate. The King family's saving supply decreases, and the saving supply curve shifts leftward to SS_1 (Figure 2).
2c. An increase in the buying power of net assets decreases the amount of saving at each real interest rate. The King family's saving supply decreases, and the saving supply curve shifts leftward to SS_1 (Figure 2).

3a. The increase in saving supply shifts the saving supply curve rightward. The decrease in investment demand shifts the investment demand curve leftward. If the shifts are of the same magnitude, then the real interest rate falls and the equilibrium quantity of saving and investment remains unchanged (Figure 3).
3b. The increase in saving supply shifts the saving supply curve rightward, and the increase in investment demand shifts the investment demand curve rightward, but the investment demand curve shifts farther than the saving supply curve. The real interest rate rises, and the equilibrium quantity of saving and investment increases (Figure 4).

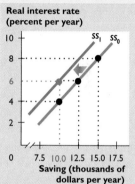

FIGURE 3

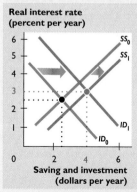

FIGURE 4

Eye On The GLOBAL ECONOMY

The Real Interest Rate Roller Coaster— 1973 to 1999

In 1973, the real interest rate was 2 percent a year. But by 1975, it had fallen to *minus* 1 percent a year. This low real interest rate was caused by an increase in saving supply and a decrease in investment demand. The changes in both saving and investment resulted from a single event: a large increase in the price of oil. The suppliers of oil were awash with funds to lend. And the users of oil suffered a big fall in profits and decreased their investment in new capital. Equilibrium saving and investment didn't change much, as part (a) of the figure shows.

By 1984, the real interest rate had increased to 8 percent a year. This increase resulted from a large increase in investment demand accompanied by a smaller increase in saving supply, as part (b) of the figure shows.

Through the 1990s, the real interest rate was around 6 percent a year, and the equilibrium quantity of saving and investment was around twice its mid-1970s level. An increase in the population and in income brought an increase in saving supply. And extraordinary technological advances, especially in communications and information technologies and biotechnologies, brought a large increase in investment demand.

By 1999, an even larger increase in saving supply than the large increase in investment demand lowered the real interest rate to 4 percent a year, as part (c) of the figure shows.

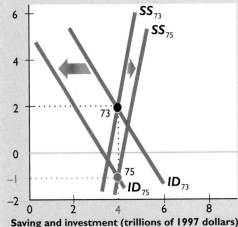

(a) 1973–1975

A large rise in the world price of oil increased saving supply and decreased investment demand

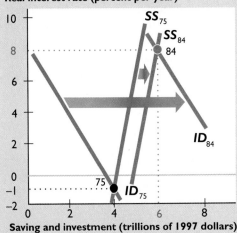

(b) 1975–1984

Slow income growth increased saving supply by less than investment demand and brought a rise in the real interest rate

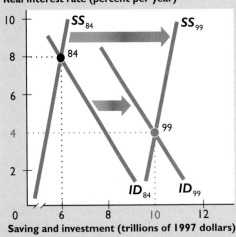

(c) 1984–1999

Rapid income growth increased saving supply by more than investment demand and brought a fall in the real interest rate

9.3 GOVERNMENT IN THE FINANCIAL MARKET

Part of each nation's saving is government saving. Government actions that change the global saving supply influence the real interest rate and the equilibrium quantity of investment. To complete our study of the forces that determine the quantity of capital and the real interest rate, we investigate the role played by government saving.

■ Government Budget and Government Saving

You learned in Chapter 5 (p. 111) that GDP, Y, equals the sum of consumption expenditure, C; investment, I; government expenditure on goods and services, G; and net exports, NX. Table 9.1 shows data on these variables for Canada, the rest of the world, and the global economy in 2000. Because we are studying the global financial market, we focus on the global economy in which net exports are zero. For the global economy:

$$Y = C + I + G.$$

GDP equals total income, which is the sum of consumption expenditure; saving, S; and net taxes, NT. So:

$$Y = C + S + NT.$$

By combining these two ways of looking at GDP, you can see that:

$$C + I + G = C + S + NT.$$

Because consumption expenditure, C, is on both sides of this equation, we can subtract C and simplify the equation to:

$$I + G = S + NT.$$

Now subtract government expenditure, G, from both sides of this equation to obtain:

$$I = S + (NT - G).$$

This equation tells us that investment, I, is financed by private saving, S, and government saving, $NT - G$. Government saving, $NT - G$, is also the government budget surplus. Table 9.2 shows that data for Canada, the rest of the world, and the global economy in 2000.

Total saving equals private saving plus government saving. So when governments have a budget surplus, they contribute towards financing investment. But when governments have a budget deficit, they compete with businesses for private saving and decrease the amount available for investment.

■ Effect of Government Saving

A government budget surplus increases total saving supply. To find total saving supply, we must add the government budget surplus to the private saving supply. An increase in total saving supply brings a lower interest rate, which decreases the quantity of private saving supplied and increases the quantity of investment.

Figure 9.7 shows these effects of government saving. The private saving supply curve, *PS*, shows the relationship between private saving and the real interest rate. The saving supply curve, *SS*, shows the sum of private saving and government saving. Here, government saving is a constant $2 trillion at each real

TABLE 9.1 INCOME AND EXPENDITURE IN THE GLOBAL ECONOMY

	Y = C + I + G + NX (trillions of dollars)				
Canada	1.05	0.60	0.21	0.19	0.05
Rest of world	43.50	26.15	8.74	8.66	–0.05
Global economy	44.55	26.75	8.95	8.85	0

SOURCES: Statistics Canada and International Monetary Fund.

TABLE 9.2 INVESTMENT, SAVING, AND NET TAXES IN THE GLOBAL ECONOMY

	I = S + NT – G – NX (trillions of dollars)				
Canada	0.21	0.24	0.21	0.19	0.05
Rest of world	8.74	9.73	7.62	8.66	–0.05
Global economy	8.95	9.97	7.83	8.85	0

SOURCES: Statistics Canada and International Monetary Fund.

interest rate, so the saving supply curve lies $2 trillion to the right of the private saving supply curve. That is, the horizontal distance between the private saving curve and the saving supply curve is government saving.

The investment demand curve, *ID*, is the same as that in Figure 9.6. In the absence of government saving, the real interest rate would be 6 percent a year and saving and investment would be $10 trillion a year. But with the government saving $2 trillion a year, the equilibrium real interest rate falls to 4 percent a year. Investment increases to $11 trillion. Private saving decreases to $9 trillion. Private saving plus government saving equals investment.

So government saving—a government budget surplus—lowers the real interest rate and increases investment.

■ Government Deficit and Crowding Out

A government budget deficit works in the opposite way to the surplus that we've just examined. It decreases total saving supply. So to find total saving supply, we must subtract the government budget deficit from private saving. But a decrease in total saving supply brings a higher real interest rate, which increases the quantity of private saving supplied and increases the quantity of investment.

In Figure 9.8, the private saving supply curve, *PS*, and the investment demand curve, *ID*, are the same as those in Figure 9.7. The horizontal distance between the private saving curve and the saving supply curve is the government budget deficit. In this example, government saving is a negative $2 trillion. That is, governments have budget deficits totalling $2 trillion.

The effect of government negative saving (also called dissaving) is to decrease total saving and increase the real interest rate. Investment decreases. In Figure 9.8,

---

FIGURE 9.7
Government Saving

e/**Foundations 9.3**

The investment demand curve is *ID*, and the private saving supply curve is *PS*. With balanced government budgets, the real interest rate is 6 percent a year and investment equals saving at $10 trillion a year.

❶ A government budget surplus of $2 trillion is added to private saving to determine the saving supply curve *SS*.

❷ The real interest rate falls to 4 percent a year, ❸ private saving decreases to $9 trillion, and ❹ total saving and investment increase to $11 trillion.

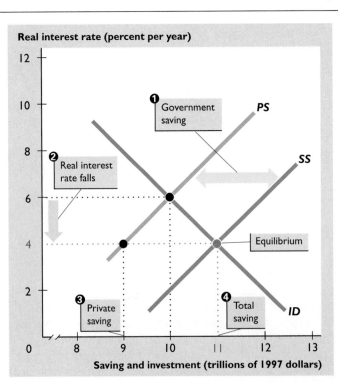

with government budget deficits of $2 trillion, the saving supply curve shifts left-ward and the real interest rate rises from 6 percent a year to 8 percent a year. Total saving and investment decrease from $10 trillion to $9 trillion. By raising the real interest rate, the government budget deficits crowd out investment. The tendency for a government budget deficit to decrease private investment is called the **crowding-out effect.**

Investment does not decrease by the full amount of the government budget deficit because the higher real interest rate induces an increase in private saving. In this example, private saving increases by $1 trillion to $11 trillion. In reality, the increase in private saving might be quite small.

Crowding-out effect
The tendency for a government budget deficit to decrease private investment.

The Ricardo-Barro Effect

First suggested by the English economist David Ricardo in the nineteenth century and refined by Robert J. Barro of Harvard University during the 1980s, the Ricardo-Barro effect holds that the effects we've just shown are wrong and that the government budget deficit has no effect on the real interest rate or investment. The reason is that the private saving supply changes to offset any change in government saving, so the total saving supply is unchanged. It is argued that rational taxpayers can see that a deficit today means that future taxes will be higher and disposable incomes will be smaller. With a smaller expected future disposable income, saving increases. Most economists regard this view as extreme. But there is probably some partial change in private saving supply that goes in the direction suggested by Ricardo and Barro that lessens the effect of the government budget deficit on the real interest rate and investment.

FIGURE 9.8
A Crowding-Out Effect

*e*Foundations **9.3**

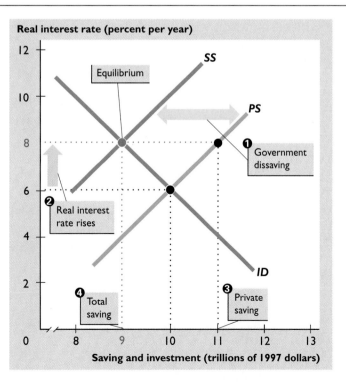

The investment demand curve is *ID*, and the private saving supply curve is *PS*. With balanced government budgets, the real interest rate is 6 percent a year and investment equals saving at $10 trillion a year.

❶ A government budget deficit of $2 trillion is subtracted from private saving to determine the saving supply curve *SS*.

❷ The real interest rate rises to 8 percent a year, ❸ private saving increases to $11 trillion, and ❹ total saving and investment decrease to $9 trillion. Investment is crowded out.

3 **Explain how government influences the real interest rate, investment, and saving.**

Practice Problem 9.3

Table 1 shows the investment demand schedule and the supply schedule of private saving.

a. If the government budget surplus is $1 trillion, what are the real interest rate, the quantity of investment, and the quantity of private saving? Is there any crowding out in this situation?

b. If the government budget deficit is $1 trillion, what are the real interest rate, the quantity of investment, and the quantity of private saving? Is there any crowding out in this situation?

c. If the Ricardo-Barro effect occurs, how do your answers to part (a) and part (b) change?

TABLE 1

Real interest rate (percent per year)	Investment	Private saving
	(trillions of 1997 dollars per year)	
4	8.5	5.5
5	8.0	6.0
6	7.5	6.5
7	7.0	7.0
8	6.5	7.5
9	6.0	8.0
10	5.5	8.5

Exercise 9.3

Starting from the situation in Table 1, investment demand increases by $2 trillion at each level of the real interest rate and the supply of private saving increases by $1 trillion at each interest rate.

a. If the government budget has neither a surplus nor a deficit, what are the real interest rate, the quantity of investment, and the quantity of private saving? Is there any crowding out in this situation?

b. If the government budget deficit is $1 trillion, what are the real interest rate, the quantity of investment, and the quantity of private saving? Is there any crowding out in this situation?

c. If governments want to stimulate the quantity of investment and increase it to $10 trillion, what must they do?

FIGURE 1

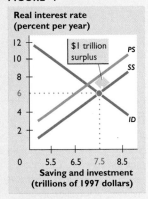

Real interest rate (percent per year)

$1 trillion surplus

Saving and investment (trillions of 1997 dollars)

Solution to Practice Problem 9.3

a. If the government budget surplus is $1 trillion, the equilibrium real interest rate is 6 percent a year, the quantity of investment is $7.5 trillion, and the quantity of private saving is $6.5 trillion. There is no crowding out in this situation (Figure 1).

b. If the government budget deficit is $1 trillion, the equilibrium real interest rate is 8 percent a year, the quantity of investment is $6.5 trillion, and the quantity of private saving is $7.5 trillion. There is crowding out in this situation because the deficit increases the real interest rate, which decreases the quantity of investment demanded (Figure 2).

c. If the Ricardo-Barro effect occurs, private saving changes to offset the budget surplus or deficit, and the equilibrium real interest rate equals 7 percent a year. With a balanced government budget, the equilibrium quantity of investment is $7 trillion and the quantity of private saving is $7 trillion minus government saving. There is no crowding out because the government saving has no effect on the real interest rate.

FIGURE 2

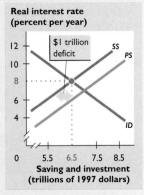

Real interest rate (percent per year)

$1 trillion deficit

Saving and investment (trillions of 1997 dollars)

CHAPTER CHECKPOINT

Key Points

1 **Define and explain the relationships among capital, investment, wealth, and saving.**

- Firms borrow financial capital to buy and operate physical capital.
- Gross investment is the total amount spent on physical capital in a given period. Net investment equals gross investment minus depreciation.
- Wealth is the value of what people own; saving is the amount of income that is not spent, and it adds to wealth.
- A financial market (stock, bond, short-term securities, or loans market) is the collection of households, firms, government, banks, and other financial institutions that lend and borrow to finance the purchase of physical capital.

2 **Explain how investment and saving decisions are made and how these decisions interact in financial markets to determine the real interest rate.**

- Other things remaining the same, the lower the real interest rate or the higher the expected profit rate, the greater is the amount of investment.
- Investment demand is the relationship between investment and the real interest rate, other things remaining the same. Investment demand changes when the expected profit rate changes.
- Other things remaining the same, the higher the real interest rate, the greater is saving.
- Saving supply is the relationship between saving and the real interest rate, other things remaining the same. Saving supply changes when disposable income, the buying power of net assets, or expected future disposable income changes.
- Because capital is free to move internationally to seek the highest possible real rate of return, the real interest rate is determined in a global market.
- The equilibrium real interest rate makes global saving equal to global investment.

3 **Explain how government influences the real interest rate, investment, and saving.**

- National saving equals private saving plus government saving.
- Government saving equals net taxes minus government expenditure.
- A government budget deficit might increase the real interest rate and crowd out private investment.
- A government budget deficit might also increase private saving supply because it decreases expected future disposable income.

Key Terms

Bond, 203	Financial capital, 200	Net investment, 200	Stock, 202
Bond market, 203	Financial markets, 202	Physical capital, 200	Stock market, 203
Crowding-out effect, 217	Gross investment, 200	Saving, 202	Wealth, 202
Disposable income, 208	Investment demand, 205	Saving supply, 208	

Exercises

1. On January 1, 2000, Terry's Towing Service owned four tow trucks valued at $300,000. During 2000, Terry's bought two new trucks that cost $180,000, and at the end of the year, the market value of all the firm's trucks was $400,000.
   a. What was Terry's gross investment during 2000?
   b. What was its depreciation?
   c. What was its net investment?

2. Mike takes a summer job washing cars. During the summer, he earns an after-tax income of $3,000 and he spends $1,000 on goods and services.
   a. What was Mike's saving during the summer?
   b. What was the change, if any, to Mike's wealth?

3. What is a financial market? What gets traded in a financial market? What is the price that a financial market determines?

4. Use the link on your Foundations Web site to visit the Toronto Stock Exchange and the London Stock Exchange, and use the additional link to obtain today's exchange rate between the Canadian dollar and the U.K. pound.
   a. Find a stock that trades on both exchanges and obtain its current price in Toronto and London.
   b. Use today's exchange rate to convert the London price to Canadian dollars.
   c. What is the difference in the two prices? Could you earn a profit by buying in one market and selling in the other?
   d. Why do you think the prices are so similar in the two stock markets?

5. Use the links on your Foundations Web site to obtain data on saving rates in Canada and the new industrial economies of East Asia.
   a. Which of the countries has the highest saving rate and which has the lowest?
   b. Of the factors that influence saving, do you think the differences across these economies represent a difference in saving supply or a difference in the quantity of saving supplied? Explain your answer.
   c. Of the influences on saving supply, which do you think might account for the differences in saving rates that you've found?

6. Explain why each of the following items changes the private saving supply:
   a. An increase in the buying power of net assets.
   b. An increase in expected future disposable income.
   c. A cut in current income taxes.

7. Explain why when the real interest rate rises, investment demand does not change but the quantity of investment demanded decreases.

8. Explain how a new technology that increases firms' expected profit influences the financial market. Draw a diagram to show the effect on the real interest rate.

9. The government eliminates its budget deficit and creates a budget surplus. Explain the effects of this change in the government's budget on the financial market.

Economic Growth

CHAPTER CHECKLIST

When you have completed your study of this chapter,
you will be able to:

1 Define and calculate the economic growth rate and explain the implications of sustained growth.

2 Identify the main sources of economic growth.

3 Review the theories of economic growth that explain why growth rates vary over time and across countries.

4 Describe policies that might promote faster economic growth.

In this chapter, we study the trends in real GDP and the standard of living. Will we have a higher standard of living than our parents did? And will our children have a higher standard of living than we do? Do all countries and regions share in rising living standards, or do some perform better than others? These are among the questions that we'll answer in this chapter.

You learned in Chapter 8 what determines the quantity of labour employed and real GDP when there is full employment. And you learned in Chapter 9 how saving and investment bring an increase in the quantity of capital. This chapter combines the lessons of those two chapters and explains how advancing technology and growing population, labour, and capital expand production possibilities and bring sustained growth in real GDP and the standard of living.

10.1 THE BASICS OF ECONOMIC GROWTH

Economic growth is a sustained expansion of production possibilities measured as the increase in real GDP over a given period. Rapid economic growth maintained over a number of years can transform a poor nation into a rich one. Such has been the experience of Hong Kong, South Korea, Taiwan, and some other Asian economies. Slow economic growth or the absence of growth can condemn a nation to devastating poverty. Such has been the fate of Sierra Leone, Somalia, Zambia, and much of the rest of Africa.

The main goal of this chapter is to help you to understand why some economies expand rapidly and others stagnate. We'll begin by learning how to calculate the economic growth rate and by discovering the magic of sustained growth.

■ Calculating Growth Rates

Economic growth rate
The rate of change of real GDP expressed as a percentage per year.

We express the **economic growth rate** as the annual percentage change of real GDP. To calculate this growth rate, we use the formula:

$$\text{Growth rate of real GDP} = \frac{\text{Real GDP in current year} - \text{Real GDP in previous year}}{\text{Real GDP in previous year}} \times 100.$$

For example, if real GDP in the current year is $840 billion and if real GDP in the previous year was $800 billion, then the growth rate of real GDP is:

$$\text{Growth rate of real GDP} = \frac{\$840 \text{ billion} - \$800 \text{ billion}}{\$800 \text{ billion}} \times 100 = 5 \text{ percent}.$$

The growth rate of real GDP tells us how rapidly the total economy is expanding. This measure is useful for telling us about potential changes in the balance of power among nations. But it does not tell us about changes in the standard of living.

Real GDP per person
Real GDP divided by the population.

The standard of living depends on **real GDP per person**, which is real GDP divided by the population. So the contribution of real GDP growth to the change in the *standard of living* depends on the growth rate of real GDP per person. We use the above formula to calculate this growth rate, replacing real GDP with real GDP per person.

Suppose, for example, that in the current year, when real GDP is $840 billion, the population is 30.3 million. Then real GDP per person is $840 billion divided by 30.3 million, which equals $27,723. And suppose that in the previous year, when real GDP was $800 billion, the population was 30 million. Then real GDP per person in that year was $800 billion divided by 30 million, which equals $26,667.

Use these two real GDP per person values with the growth formula to calculate the growth rate of real GDP per person. That is,

$$\text{Growth rate of real GDP per person} = \frac{\$27,723 - \$26,667}{\$26,667} \times 100 = 4 \text{ percent}.$$

The growth rate of real GDP per person can also be calculated using the formula:

$$\text{Growth rate of real GDP per person} = \text{Growth rate of real GDP} - \text{Growth rate of population.}$$

In the example you've just worked through, the growth rate of real GDP is 5 percent. The population changes from 30.0 million to 30.3 million, so the growth rate of the population is:

$$\text{Growth rate of population} = \frac{30.3 - 30.0}{30.0} \times 100 = 1 \text{ percent,}$$

and

$$\text{Growth rate of real GDP per person} = 5 \text{ percent} - 1 \text{ percent} = 4 \text{ percent.}$$

This formula makes it clear that real GDP per person grows only if real GDP grows faster than the population grows. If the growth rate of the population exceeds the growth of real GDP, real GDP per person falls.

■ The Magic of Sustained Growth

Sustained growth of real GDP per person can transform a poor society into a wealthy one. The reason is that economic growth is like compound interest. Suppose that you put $100 in the bank and earn 5 percent a year interest on it. After one year, you have $105. If you leave that money in the bank for another year, you earn 5 percent interest on the original $100 and on the $5 interest that you earned last year. You are now earning interest on interest! Next year, things get even better. Then you earn 5 percent on the original $100 and on the interest earned in the first year and the second year. Your money in the bank is *growing* at a rate of 5 percent a year. Before too many years have passed, you'll have $200 in the bank. But after *how many* years?

The answer is provided by a powerful and general formula known as the **Rule of 70**, which states that the number of years it takes for the level of any variable to double equals 70 divided by the annual percentage growth rate of the variable. Using the Rule of 70, you can now calculate how many years it takes your $100 to become $200. It is 70 divided by 5, which is 14 years.

The Rule of 70 applies to any variable, so it applies to real GDP per person. Table 10.1 shows the doubling time for a selection of other growth rates. You can see that real GDP per person doubles in 70 years (70 divided by 1)—an average human life span—if the growth rate is 1 percent a year. It doubles in 35 years if the growth rate is 2 percent a year and in just 10 years if the growth rate is 7 percent a year.

We can use the Rule of 70 to answer other questions about economic growth. For example, in 2000, Canada's real GDP per person was almost 8 times that of China. China's recent growth rate of real GDP per person was 7 percent a year. If this growth rate were maintained, how long would it take China's real GDP per person to reach that of Canada in 2000? The answer provided by the Rule of 70 is 30 years. China's real GDP per person doubles in 10 (70 divided by 7) years. It doubles again to 4 times its current level in another 10 years. And it doubles yet again to 8 times its current level in another 10 years. So after 30 years of growth at 7 percent a year, China's real GDP per person would be 8 times its current level and would equal that of Canada in 2000.

Rule of 70
The number of years it takes for the level of any variable to double is approximately 70 divided by the annual percentage growth rate of the variable.

TABLE 10.1 GROWTH RATES

Growth rate (percent per year)	Years for level to double
1	70
2	35
3	23
4	18
5	14
6	12
7	10
8	9
9	8
10	7

How Fast Has Real GDP per Person Grown?

Professor Michael Kremer of Harvard University and Professor J. Bradford DeLong of the University of California, Berkeley, have constructed an extraordinary picture of real GDP in the global economy going back one million years. According to their numbers, most human societies lived for almost a million years with no economic growth.

The top figure shows the numbers using the value of the dollar in 2000 as the measuring rod. Real GDP hovered around $100 per person per year from 1,000,000 B.C. until 1350! There were some wiggles and wobbles along the way. When Aristotle and Plato were teaching in Athens, around 500 B.C., real GDP per person climbed to $175. But it slipped back over the next thousand years, and as the Roman Empire collapsed around 400, it was $120. Even when Samuel de Champlain was exploring Canada in the early 1600s, real GDP per person was similar to that of Ancient Greece!

Then, beginning around 1750, first in England and then in Europe and the United States, an astonishing change known as the *Industrial Revolution* occurred. Real GDP per person began to increase, and apparently without limit. By 1850, real GDP per person was twice its 1650 level. By 1950, it was more than *five* times its 1850 level and by 2000, it was *four* times its 1950 level.

The bottom figure gives you a close-up view of real GDP per person in Canada over the past 100 years. In

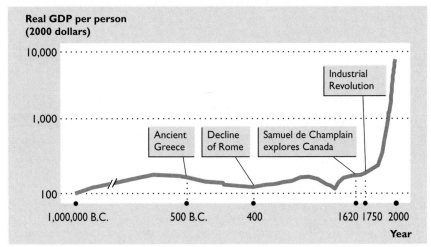

SOURCE: J. Bradford DeLong, *"Estimating World GDP, One Million B.C.–Present."*

2000, real GDP per person was almost 9 times its level in 1900. Over that century, it grew by 2.2 percent a year. But the growth rate has been uneven. The 1910s and the Great Depression years of the 1930s saw no growth. The 1900s, 1920s, and 1960s saw the fastest growth. Since the 1960s, the growth rate has fallen each decade. But if we divide the 1990s into two periods— before and after the Internet (1994)— we see a speedup in the growth rate again. Some people have talked about the current information age as bringing a new economy in which growth will be permanently faster. As the world went into a slowdown in 2001, this view looks less and less likely.

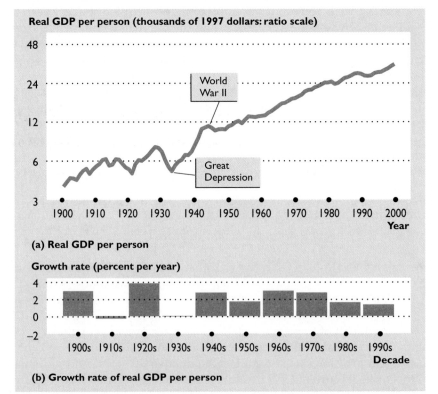

(a) Real GDP per person

(b) Growth rate of real GDP per person

SOURCE: Statistics Canada.

CHECKPOINT 10.1

1 **Define and calculate the economic growth rate and explain the implications of sustained growth.**

Study Guide pp. 149–151

*e*Foundations 10.1

Practice Problem 10.1

Mexico's real GDP was 1,448 billion pesos in 1998 and 1,501 billion pesos in 1999. Mexico's population growth rate in 1999 was 1.8 percent. Calculate:

a. Mexico's economic growth rate in 1999.
b. The growth rate of real GDP per person in Mexico in 1999.
c. The approximate number of years it takes for real GDP per person in Mexico to double if the 1999 economic growth rate and population growth rate are maintained.
d. The approximate number of years it takes for real GDP per person in Mexico to double if the 1999 economic growth rate is maintained but the population growth rate slows to 1 percent a year.

Exercise 10.1

U.S. real GDP was $8,856.5 billion in 1999 and $9,224.0 billion in 2000. U.S. population growth rate in 2000 was 0.9 percent. Calculate:

a. The U.S. economic growth rate in 2000.
b. The growth rate of real GDP per person in the United States in 2000.
c. The approximate number of years it takes for real GDP per person in the United States to double if the 2000 economic growth rate and population growth rate are maintained.
d. The approximate number of years it takes for real GDP per person in the United States to double if the economic growth rate rises to 6 percent a year but the population growth rate remains the same as it was in 2000.

Solution to Practice Problem 10.1

a. Mexico's economic growth rate in 1999 was 3.7 percent. The economic growth rate equals the percentage change in real GDP:
[(Real GDP in 1999 − Real GDP in 1998) ÷ Real GDP in 1998] ×100.
When we substitute the numbers, Mexico's economic growth rate equals
[(1,501 billion − 1,448 billion) ÷ 1,448 billion] × 100, which is 3.7 percent.
b. The growth rate of real GDP per person in Mexico in 1999 was 1.9 percent. The growth rate of real GDP per person equals the growth rate of real GDP minus the population growth rate. When we substitute the numbers, the growth rate of real GDP per person equals 3.7 − 1.8, which equals 1.9 percent.
c. It will take approximately 37 years for real GDP per person in Mexico to double. The Rule of 70 tells us that the value of a variable that grows at 1.9 percent a year will double in 70/1.9 years, which is approximately 37 years.
d. If Mexico's population growth rate falls to 1.0 percent a year, real GDP per person in Mexico will increase to 2.7 percent a year. The Rule of 70 tells us that real GDP in Mexico will double in 70/2.7, which is approximately 26 years.

10.2 THE SOURCES OF ECONOMIC GROWTH

Real GDP grows when the quantities of the factors of production grow or when persistent advances in technology make them increasingly productive. To understand what determines the growth rate of real GDP, we must understand what determines the growth rates of the factors of production and rate of increase in their productivity. We've already seen that saving and investment determine the growth rate of physical capital. We're now going to see how the growth of physical capital and human capital and advances in technology interact to determine the economic growth rate.

Because the standard of living increases only if real GDP *per person* increases, we also want to understand what makes real GDP growth exceed population growth. For this reason, we focus on a classification of the sources of growth that emphasizes the separate contribution of labour growth.

All the influences on real GDP growth can be divided into those that increase:

- Aggregate hours
- Labour productivity

■ Aggregate Hours

Over time, aggregate hours increase. This growth in aggregate hours comes from growth in the labour force rather than from growth in average hours per worker. As you saw in Chapter 6 (pp. 138–139), average hours per worker have *decreased* over the past decades. This decrease—and an associated *increase* in average leisure hours—is one of the benefits of economic growth.

The labour force depends on the population and the *labour force participation rate* (see Chapter 6, pp. 136–137). While the participation rate has increased over the past few decades, it has an upper limit and most of the growth of aggregate hours comes from population growth. So population growth is the only source of growth in aggregate labour hours that can be sustained over long periods.

Population growth brings economic growth, but it does not bring growth in real GDP per person unless labour hours become more productive.

■ Labour Productivity

Labour productivity
The quantity of real GDP per hour of labour.

The quantity of real GDP produced by one hour of labour is called **labour productivity**. It is calculated by using the formula:

$$\text{Labour productivity} = \frac{\text{Real GDP}}{\text{Aggregate hours}}.$$

For example, if real GDP is $800 billion and if aggregate hours are 20 billion, then we can calculate labour productivity as:

$$\text{Labour productivity} = \frac{\$800 \text{ billion}}{20 \text{ billion hours}} = \$40 \text{ an hour}.$$

You can turn this formula around and see that:

$$\text{Real GDP} = \text{Aggregate hours} \times \text{Labour productivity}.$$

When labour productivity grows, real GDP per person grows. So the growth in labour productivity is the basis of rising living standards. The growth of labour productivity depends on three things:

- Saving and investment in physical capital
- Expansion of human capital
- Discovery of new technologies

These three sources of growth in labour productivity interact and are the primary sources of the extraordinary growth in productivity during the past 200 years. Let's look at each in turn.

Saving and Investment in Physical Capital

Saving and investment in physical capital increase the amount of capital per worker and increase labour productivity. Labour productivity took a dramatic upturn when the amount of capital per worker increased during the Industrial Revolution. Production processes that use hand tools can create beautiful objects, but production methods that use large amounts of capital per worker, such as auto plant assembly lines, enable workers to be much more productive. The accumulation of capital on farms, in textile factories, in iron foundries and steel mills, in coal mines, on building sites, in chemical plants, in auto plants, in banks and insurance companies has added incredibly to the productivity of our labour.

A strong and experienced farm worker of 1830, using a scythe, could harvest about 1 hectare of wheat in a day. A farm worker of 1831, using a mechanical reaper, could harvest 6 hectares in a day. And a farm worker of today, using a combine harvester, can harvest and thresh 40 hectares in a day.

The next time you see a movie set in the Old West, look carefully at the small amount of capital around. Try to imagine how productive you would be in such circumstances compared with your productivity today.

Expansion of Human Capital

Human capital—the accumulated skill and knowledge of human beings—comes from two sources:

- Education and training
- Job experience

A hundred years ago, most people attended school for around eight years. A hundred years before that, most people had no formal education at all. Today, 71 percent of Canadians of working age are high school graduates and 43 percent have a post-secondary certificate, diploma, or degree. Our ability to read, write, and communicate effectively contributes enormously to our productivity.

While formal education is productive, school is not the only place where people acquire human capital. We also learn from on-the-job experience—from *learning by doing*. One carefully studied example illustrates the importance of learning by doing. Between 1941 and 1944 (during World War II), U.S. shipyards produced 2,500 Liberty Ships—a cargo ship built to a standardized design. In 1941, it took 1.2 million person-hours to build a ship. By 1942, it took 600,000, and by 1943, it took only 500,000. Not much change occurred in the physical capital employed during these years. But an enormous amount of human capital was accumulated. Thousands of workers and managers learned from experience and more than doubled their productivity in two years.

ECONOMICS *in the* **NEWS**

September 7, 2001

Retiring Boomers Will Leave Labour Shortage

Canada's growth potential could be seriously hampered when the first wave of Baby Boomers—about one-third of Canada's population—reaches the age of 65 in 2011.

NATIONAL POST

Questions
1. How would the retirement of a large number of workers in a short period of time affect potential GDP?
2. What measures could be taken to reduce these effects?

 *e*Foundations **10.2**

The expansion of human capital is the most fundamental source of economic growth because it directly increases labour productivity and is the source of the discovery of new technologies.

Discovery of New Technologies

The growth of physical capital and human capital has made a large contribution to economic growth. But the discovery and application of new technologies has made an even greater contribution.

The development of writing, one of the most basic human skills, was the source of some of the earliest productivity gains. The ability to keep written records made it possible to reap ever-larger gains from specialization and trade. Imagine how hard it would be to do any kind of business if all the accounts, invoices, and agreements existed only in people's memories.

Later, the development of mathematics laid the foundation for the eventual extension of knowledge in physics, chemistry, and biology. This base of scientific knowledge was the foundation for the technological advances of the Industrial Revolution 200 years ago and of today's Information Revolution.

Since the Industrial Revolution, technological change has become a part of everyday life. Firms routinely conduct research to develop technologies that are more productive, and partnerships between business and universities are commonplace in fields such as biotechnology and electronics.

To reap the benefits of technological change, capital *must* increase. Some of the most powerful and far-reaching technologies are embodied in human capital—for example, language, writing, and mathematics. But most technologies are embodied in physical capital. For example, to reap the benefits of the internal combustion engine, millions of horse-drawn carriages had to be replaced by automobiles and trucks; more recently, to reap the benefits of computerized word processing, millions of typewriters had to be replaced by PCs and printers.

■ Sources of Growth: A Summary

Figure 10.1 summarizes the sources of economic growth. Your next task is to learn how these sources combine and how we identify the separate contributions of capital growth and the other influences on labour productivity.

FIGURE 10.1

The Sources of Economic Growth

Real GDP depends on aggregate hours and labour productivity. Labour productivity depends on the amount of capital and human capital and the state of technology. Growth in aggregate hours and labour productivity bring real GDP growth.

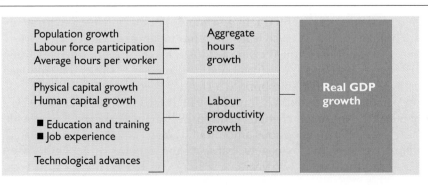

■ The Productivity Curve

The **productivity curve** is a relationship that shows how labour productivity changes as the amount of physical capital per hour of labour changes with a given state of technology. Figure 10.2 illustrates the productivity curve. Capital per hour of labour, measured on the x-axis, is physical capital valued in 1997 dollars. (Remember that even though we use dollar values to measure capital, we are talking about *physical capital*.) Labour productivity (real GDP per hour of labour) is measured on the y-axis. The figure shows two productivity curves, one labelled PC_0 and the other labelled PC_1.

An increase in the quantity of capital per hour of labour increases labour productivity, which is shown by a movement along a productivity curve. For example, on PC_0, when capital per hour of labour is $30, labour productivity is $20 an hour. If capital per hour of labour increases to $60, labour productivity increases to $25 an hour.

At a given amount of capital per hour of labour, labour productivity increases if human capital increases or technology advances. An upward shift of the productivity curve illustrates these influences on labour productivity. For example, if capital per hour of labour is $30 and a technological change increases labour productivity from $20 to $25, the productivity curve shifts upward from PC_0 to PC_1. Similarly, if capital per hour of labour is $60, the same technological change increases labour productivity from $25 to $32 and shifts the productivity curve upward from PC_0 to PC_1.

Productivity curve
The relationship between real GDP per hour of labour and the quantity of capital per hour of labour with a given state of technology.

■ **FIGURE 10.2**
How Labour Productivity Grows

*e*Foundations **10.2**

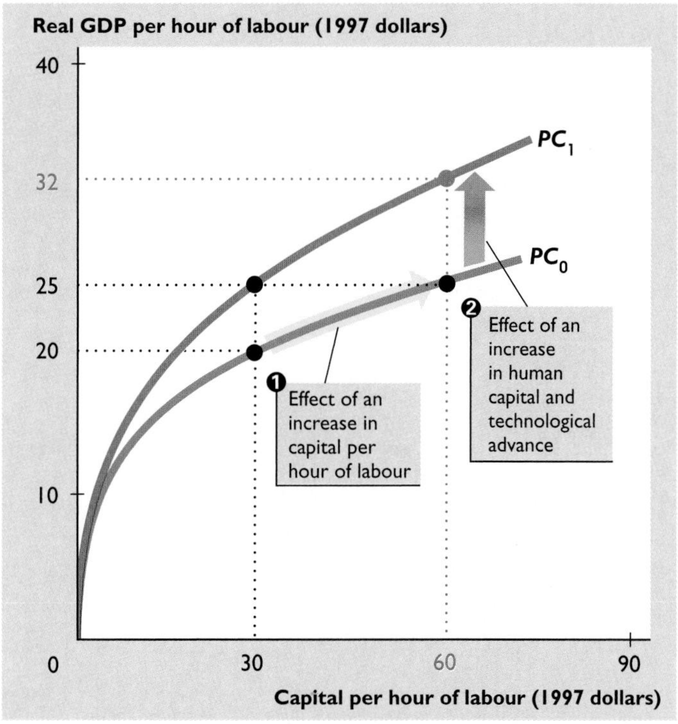

Real GDP per hour of labour (1997 dollars)

Effect of an increase in capital per hour of labour ❶

Effect of an increase in human capital and technological advance ❷

Capital per hour of labour (1997 dollars)

Labour productivity, which is measured by real GDP per hour of labour, can grow for two reasons:

❶ An increase in capital per hour of labour brings a movement along the productivity curve. When capital per hour of labour increases from $30 to $60, real GDP per hour of labour increases along PC_0 from $20 to $25.

❷ An increase in human capital and a technological advance shift the productivity curve upward from PC_0 to PC_1. With this increase in human capital and technological advance, real GDP per hour of labour increases from $20 to $25 when there is $30 of capital per hour of labour and from $25 to $32 when there is $60 of capital per hour of labour.

With constant average hours per worker and a constant labour force participation rate, aggregate hours grow at the same rate as the population. The capital stock grows at a rate determined by saving and investment. If the capital stock grows faster than the population, capital per hour of labour increases. If the capital stock grows slower than the population, capital per hour of labour decreases. And if the capital stock grows at the same rate as the population, capital per hour of labour is constant. The faster the growth rate of capital per hour of labour, the higher is the growth rate of real GDP per person.

But growth from capital alone is limited by diminishing returns.

Diminishing Returns

The shape of the productivity curve reflects a fundamental economic law that you met in Chapter 8 (see p. 182): the law of diminishing returns. The *law of diminishing returns* states that as the quantity of one input increases with the quantities of all other inputs remaining the same, output increases but by ever smaller increments. For example, in a factory that has a given amount of capital, as more labour is hired, output increases. But each additional hour of labour produces less additional output than the previous hour produced. Two dentists sharing one drill fill fewer than twice as many teeth per day as one dentist working alone with one drill.

Applied to capital, the law of diminishing returns states that if a given number of hours of labour use more capital (with the same technology), the additional output that results from the additional capital gets smaller as the amount of capital increases. One

Eye On The CANADIAN ECONOMY

Labour Productivity and Economic Growth since 1960

The figure on this page shows that labour productivity growth was most rapid during the 1960s. It slowed after 1974 in what has been called a "productivity slowdown."

The productivity growth rate edged up again after 1994 but, despite the spread of the personal computer and the expansion of the Internet, the growth rate of the late 1990s remained a long way below that of the 1960s.

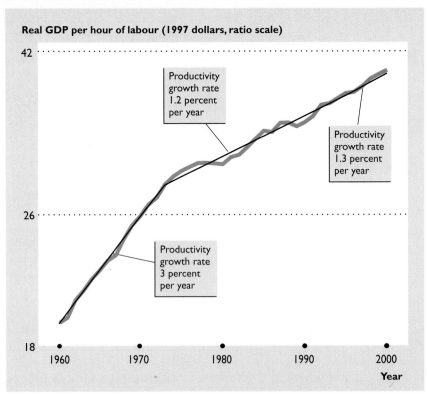

SOURCE: Statistics Canada.

dentist working with two drills fills fewer than twice as many teeth per day as one dentist working with one drill. More generally, one hour of labour working with $40-worth of capital produces less than twice the output of one hour of labour working with $20-worth of capital. But how much less? The answer is given by the one-third rule.

The One-Third Rule

To identify the contribution of capital growth to labour productivity growth, we use a feature of the productivity curve discovered by Robert Solow of MIT. By studying economic growth, Solow noticed a **one-third rule**: On the average, with no change in human capital and technology, a *one percent* increase in capital per hour of labour brings a *one-third percent* increase in labour productivity.

We can use the one-third rule to identify the contribution of capital growth to labour productivity growth. Suppose, for example, that in a year, capital per hour of labour grows by 3 percent and labour productivity grows by 2.5 percent. The one-third rule tells us that capital growth has increased labour productivity by one-third of 3 percent, which is 1 percent.

Labour productivity growth that is not attributed to capital growth arises from human capital growth and technological change. In the above example in which labour productivity grows by 2.5 percent and capital growth contributed 1.0 percent, the remaining 1.5 percent growth of labour productivity comes from human capital growth and technological change.

One-third rule

The observation that on the average, with no change in human capital and technology, a *one percent* increase in capital per hour of labour brings a *one-third percent* increase in labour productivity.

Why did productivity growth slow down after 1974? The figure on this page provides a first look at the answer. First, you can see that the contribution of the growth of capital per hour of labour is remarkably constant. It has been around 0.75 percent per year on the average for the entire 40 year period covered by the figure.

Second, you can see that the contribution of human capital growth and technological change decreased after 1974 and picked up slightly after 1994.

The decrease of the 1970s occurred because:

(1) The focus of technological change shifted from increasing productivity to coping with energy price increases. Oil price hikes in 1973–1974 and 1979–1980 diverted research towards saving energy rather than increasing labour productivity. Airplanes became more fuel efficient, but they didn't operate with smaller crews. Real GDP per litre of fuel increased faster, but real GDP per hour of labour increased more slowly.

(2) More resources were devoted to protecting the environment and improving the quality of the workplace. The benefits of these activities—a cleaner environment and safer factories—are not counted as part of GDP. So the growth of these benefits was not counted as part of productivity growth.

(3) Taxes increased during the 1970s, so incentives were weakened and growth slowed.

(4) The rapid inflation that distorted saving and investment decisions also impacted human capital investment decisions.

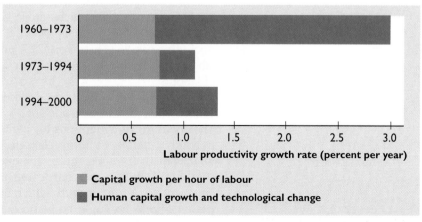

SOURCE: Statistics Canada.

Study Guide pp. 151–154

𝓮Foundations 10.2

2 **Identify the main sources of economic growth.**

Practice Problem 10.2

The table provides some data on the Canadian economy in 1995 and 1996.

Item	1995	1996
Aggregate hours (billions)	22.7	23.0
Real GDP (billions of 1997 dollars)	834.5	848.7
Capital per hour of labour (1997 dollars)	80.25	80.62

a. Calculate the growth rate of real GDP in 1996.
b. Calculate labour productivity in 1995 and 1996.
c. Calculate the growth rate of labour productivity in 1996.
d. If the one-third rule applies in Canada, what were the sources of labour productivity growth in 1996? Explain your answer.

Exercise 10.2

The table provides some data on the U.S. economy in 1990 and 1991.

Item	1990	1991
Aggregate hours (billions)	203.4	200.4
Real GDP (billions of 1996 dollars)	6,684	6,669
Capital per hour of labour (1996 dollars)	92.85	95.77

a. Calculate the growth rate of real GDP in 1991.
b. Calculate labour productivity in 1990 and 1991.
c. Calculate the growth rate of labour productivity in 1991.
d. If the one-third rule applies in the United States, what were the sources of labour productivity growth in 1991? Explain your answer.

Solution to Practice Problem 10.2

a. The growth rate of real GDP in 1996 was [($848.7 billion − $834.5 billion) ÷ $834.5 billion] × 100, which equals 1.7 percent.
b. Labour productivity equals real GDP per hour of labour. In 1995, labour productivity was $834.5 billion/22.7 billion, which equals $36.76 per hour of labour. In 1996, it was $848.7 billion/23.0 billion, which equals $36.90 per hour of labour.
c. The growth rate of labour productivity in 1996 is [($36.90 − $36.76) ÷ $36.76] × 100, which equals 0.38 percent.
d. The one-third rule identifies the contribution of capital growth to labour productivity. Capital per hour of labour grew by [($80.62 − $80.25)/$80.25] ×100, which equals 0.46 percent. So the one-third rule tells us that 1/3 of 0.46 percent, which is 0.15 percent, came from capital growth. The remainder of labour productivity growth, which is 0.21 percent, came from human capital growth and technological advance.

10.3 THEORIES OF ECONOMIC GROWTH

We've seen that real GDP grows when the quantities of labour, capital, and human capital grow and when technology advances. Does this mean that all these factors *cause* economic growth? It might. But there are other possibilities. One of these factors might be the cause of real GDP growth and the others the effect. We must try to discover how the influences on economic growth interact with each other to make some economies grow quickly and others grow slowly. And we must probe the reasons why a country's long-term growth rate sometimes speeds up and sometimes slows.

Growth theories are designed to study the interactions among the several factors that contribute to growth and to disentangle cause and effect. They are also designed to enable us to study how the various factors influence each other.

Growth theories are also designed to be universal. They are not theories about the growth of poor countries only or rich countries only. They are theories about why and how poor countries become rich and rich countries become richer.

We're going to study three theories of economic growth, each of which gives some insights about the process of economic growth. But none provides a definite answer to the basic questions: what causes economic growth and why do growth rates vary? Economics has some way to go before it can provide a definite answer to these most important of questions.

The three growth theories that we will study are:

- Classical growth theory
- Neoclassical growth theory
- New growth theory

■ Classical Growth Theory

Classical growth theory predicts that the clash between an exploding population and limited resources will eventually bring economic growth to an end. According to classical growth theory, labour productivity growth is temporary. When labour productivity rises and lifts real GDP per person above the subsistence level, which is the minimum real income needed to maintain life, a population explosion occurs. Eventually, the population grows so large that labour productivity falls and returns real GDP per person back to the subsistence level.

Adam Smith, Thomas Robert Malthus, and David Ricardo, the leading economists of the late eighteenth and early nineteenth centuries, proposed this theory. But the view is most closely associated with Malthus and is sometimes called the **Malthusian theory**. It is also sometimes called the Doomsday theory.

Many people today are Malthusians. They say that if today's global population of 6 billion explodes to 11 billion by 2200, we will run out of resources and return to a primitive standard of living. We must act, say the Malthusians, to contain the population growth.

The Basic Idea

To understand the basic idea of classical growth theory, let's transport ourselves back to the world of 1776. Adam Smith's *Wealth of Nations* has just been published, the Industrial Revolution is underway in Britain, and Canada is still a colony, nearly a century away from becoming a country. Its main economic activities are

Classical growth theory
The theory that the clash between an exploding population and limited resources will eventually bring economic growth to an end.

Malthusian theory
Another name for classical growth theory—named for Thomas Robert Malthus.

fur trading and farming. Farm work is performed with simple tools and animal power by people who earn less than 2 shillings (roughly $20 in today's money) for working a ten-hour day.

Then advances in farming technology bring new types of ploughs and seeds that increase farm productivity. As farm productivity increases, farm production increases and some farm workers move from the land to the cities, where they get work producing and selling the expanding range of farm equipment. Real GDP per person rises, and people are prospering. But will the prosperity last? Classical growth theory says it will not. The prosperity will induce a population explosion and the population explosion will decrease real GDP per person.

Classical Theory of Population Growth

When the classical economists were developing their ideas about population growth, an unprecedented population explosion was under way. In Britain and other Western European countries, improvements in diet and hygiene had lowered the death rate while the birth rate remained high. For several decades, population growth was extremely rapid.

For example, after being relatively stable for several centuries, the population of Britain increased by 40 percent between 1750 and 1800 and by another 50 percent between 1800 and 1830. At the same time, an estimated 1 million people (about 20 percent of the 1750 population) left Britain for North America and Australia before 1800, and outward migration continued on a similar scale through the nineteenth century. This historical population explosion was the basis for the classical theory of population growth.

To explain the high rate of population growth, the classical economists used the idea of a subsistence real income. If the actual real income is less than the subsistence real income, some people cannot survive and the population decreases. In classical theory, when real income exceeds the subsistence real income, the population grows. But a rising population decreases the amount of capital per hour of labour. So labour productivity and real GDP per person eventually decrease. And no matter how much technological change occurs, real GDP per person is always pushed back towards the subsistence level. This pessimistic conclusion led to economics being called the dismal science.

Productivity Curve Illustration

Figure 10.3 illustrates the classical growth theory using the labour productivity curve. Initially the productivity curve is PC_0. The economy is producing at point A and real GDP per hour is just high enough for people to earn a subsistence real income—real income equals real GDP.

Now capital per hour increases, which moves the economy along the productivity curve to point B. And technology advances, which shifts the productivity curve to PC_1 and moves the economy to point C. Real GDP per hour is now much above the level that provides a subsistence level of real income. So the population and labour hours grow. Capital per hour of labour decreases and real GDP per hour decreases as the economy moves down along productivity curve PC_1. As long as real GDP per hour exceeds the subsistence level, population growth brings a decrease in capital per hour of labour. Eventually, real GDP per hour returns to the subsistence level at point D.

The economy has grown—real GDP has increased—but a larger population is earning only the subsistence real GDP per person.

■ **FIGURE 10.3**
Classical Growth Theory

*e*Foundations **10.3**

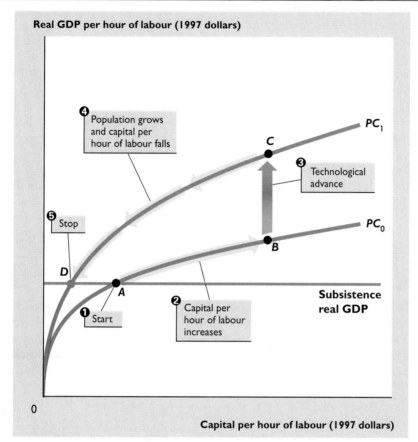

❶ The economy starts out at point *A* on productivity curve PC_0 with real GDP at the subsistence level and the population constant.

❷ The economy moves to point *B* as capital per hour of labour increases and real GDP per person increases above the subsistence level.

❸ The economy moves to point *C* as technological advance (and the accumulation of human capital) increase productivity and the productivity curve shifts upward to PC_1.

❹ With real GDP above the subsistence level, the economy moves towards point *D* as the population grows and capital per hour of labour decreases.

❺ At point *D*, the economy is back at the subsistence level of real GDP per hour of labour.

■ Neoclassical Growth Theory

Neoclassical growth theory (developed by Robert Solow of MIT during the 1960s) predicts that real GDP per person will increase as long as technology keeps advancing. Real GDP will grow at a rate equal to the population growth rate plus the rate of productivity growth induced by technological change and the accumulation of human capital. So according to the neoclassical theory, growth will persist.

Neoclassical growth theory asserts that population growth and the pace of technological change determine, but are not themselves influenced by, the growth rate of real GDP. Let's briefly examine the neoclassical view of population growth and technological change.

Neoclassical growth theory
The theory that real GDP per person will increase as long as technology keeps advancing.

Population Growth

The population explosion of eighteenth century Europe that created the classical theory eventually ended. The birth rate fell and the population growth rate slowed. This slowdown in population growth seemed to make the classical theory

September 11, 2001

No Risk of Crowded Planet, UN Says

The UN has backtracked on warnings that runaway population growth threatens a world crisis, in a report praising technology for preventing many of the dire consequences earlier UN studies predicted....

While the world's population has grown almost fourfold since 1900—from 1.6 billion to 6.1 billion—global production has increased between 20 and 40 times.

NATIONAL POST

Questions

1. Which growth theory does this report support?

2. What are some examples of the kinds of developments that have made such a large expansion of production possible?

3. Do you think it likely that because of these developments, world population will increase more rapidly or less rapidly in the future?

 e Foundations 10.3

increasingly less relevant. And the slowdown in population growth eventually led to the development of a new economic theory of population growth.

Economists began to realize that although the population growth rate is influenced by economic factors, that influence is not the one identified by the classical economists. Key among the economic influences on population growth is the opportunity cost of a woman's time. As women's wage rates increase and their job opportunities expand, the opportunity cost of having children increases. Faced with a higher opportunity cost, families choose to have fewer children and the birth rate falls.

A second economic influence works on the death rate. The technological advances that increase labour productivity also bring advances in health care that extend lives.

So two opposing economic forces influence population growth. As incomes increase, the birth rate decreases and the death rate decreases. It turns out that these opposing forces are offsetting, so the rate of population growth is independent of the rate of economic growth.

The historical population trends contradict the views of the classical economists and call into question the contemporary Doomsday conclusion that one day we will be swamped with too many people for the planet to feed.

Technological Change

In the neoclassical theory, the rate of technological change influences the rate of economic growth, but economic growth does not influence the pace of technological change. It is assumed that technological change results from chance. When we are lucky, we have rapid technological change; and when bad luck strikes, the pace of technological advance slows.

The Basic Idea

To understand the basic idea of neoclassical growth theory, imagine the world of the mid-1950s. Canadians are enjoying post-World War II prosperity, and real GDP per person is around $10,000 a year in today's money. The population is growing at about 2.5 percent a year, and there is enough investment to make capital grow at a similar rate. So real GDP per person is not growing much.

Then technology advances at a more rapid pace across a range of activities. The transistor revolutionizes an emerging electronics industry. New plastics revolutionize the manufacture of household appliances. Jet airliners start to replace piston-engine airplanes and speed transportation. And Elvis and the Beatles change the face of popular music!

These technological advances bring new profit opportunities. Businesses expand and new businesses are created to exploit the new technologies. Investment and saving increase so capital per hour of labour increases. The economy enjoys new levels of prosperity and growth. But will the prosperity last? And will the growth last? Neoclassical growth theory says the prosperity will last but the growth will not unless technology keeps advancing.

The prosperity persists because no population explosion occurs to lower real GDP per person. But growth stops if technology stops advancing because capital accumulation brings diminishing returns, which slow the growth rate of real GDP and reduce the level of saving and investment. Eventually the growth rate of capital slows to that of the population and real GDP per person stops growing.

A Problem with Neoclassical Growth Theory

Neoclassical growth theory predicts that real GDP will grow at a rate that is determined by the pace of technological change. But the theory does not explain what determines technological change. In the neoclassical theory, technological change is like the weather—it rains down on us at a pace that we must simply accept. In reality, the pace of technological change results from choices. The new growth theory, which we'll now study, emphasizes the role of these choices.

■ New Growth Theory

New growth theory predicts that our unlimited wants will lead us to ever-greater productivity and perpetual economic growth. According to new growth theory, real GDP per person grows because of the choices people make in the pursuit of profit. Paul Romer of the University of California at Berkeley developed this theory during the 1980s, but the new theory builds on ideas developed by Joseph Schumpeter during the 1930s and 1940s.

New growth theory
The theory that our unlimited wants will lead us to ever greater productivity and perpetual economic growth.

Choices and Innovation

The new theory of economic growth emphasizes three facts about market economies:

- Human capital grows because of choices.
- Discoveries result from choices.
- Discoveries bring profit, and competition destroys profit.

Human Capital Growth and Choices People decide how long to remain in school, what to study, and how hard to study. And when they graduate from school, people make more choices about job training and on-the-job learning. All these choices govern the speed at which human capital grows.

Discoveries and Choices When people discover a new product or technique, they consider themselves lucky. They are right. But the pace at which new discoveries are made—and at which technology advances—is not determined by chance. It depends on how many people are looking for a new technology and how intensively they are looking.

Discoveries and Profits Profit is the spur to technological change. The forces of competition squeeze profits, so to increase profit, people constantly seek either lower-cost methods of production or new and better products for which people are willing to pay a higher price. Inventors can maintain a profit for several years by taking out a patent or copyright. But eventually, a new discovery is copied, and profits disappear.

Two other facts that play a key role in the new growth theory are:

- Many people can use discoveries at the same time.
- Physical activities can be replicated.

Discoveries Used by All Once a profitable new discovery has been made, everyone can use it. For example, when Marc Andreeson created Mosaic, the Web browser that led to the creation of Netscape Navigator and Microsoft's Internet Explorer, everyone who was interested in navigating the Internet had access to a new and more efficient tool. One person's use of a Web browser does not prevent others from using it. This fact means that as the benefits of a new discovery spread, socially free resources become available. These resources are free because nothing is given up when an additional person uses them. They have a zero opportunity cost.

Replicating Activities Production activities can be replicated. For example, there might be two, three, or fifty-three identical firms making fibre-optic cable using an identical assembly line and production technique. If one firm increases its capital and output, that *firm* experiences diminishing returns. But the economy can increase its capital and output by adding another identical fibre cable factory, and the *economy* does not experience diminishing returns.

The assumption that capital does not experience diminishing returns is the central novel proposition of the new growth theory. And the implication of this simple and appealing idea is astonishing. As capital accumulates, labour productivity grows indefinitely as long as people devote resources to expanding human capital and introducing new technologies.

Perpetual Motion

Figure 10.4 illustrates new growth theory in terms of a perpetual motion machine. Economic growth is driven by insatiable wants that lead us to pursue profit and innovate. New and better products result from this process, which lead to new firms starting up and old firms going out of business. As firms start up and die,

---

FIGURE 10.4

A Perpetual Motion Machine

❶ People want a higher standard of living and are spurred by ❷ profit incentives to make the ❸ innovations that lead to ❹ new and better techniques and new and better products, which in turn lead to ❺ the birth of new firms and the death of some old firms, ❻ new and better jobs, and ❼ more leisure and more consumption goods and services. The result is ❽ a higher standard of living. But people want a yet higher standard of living, and the growth process continues.

Based on a similar figure in *These Are the Good Old Days: A Report on U.S. Living Standards*, Federal Reserve Bank of Dallas 1993 Annual Report.

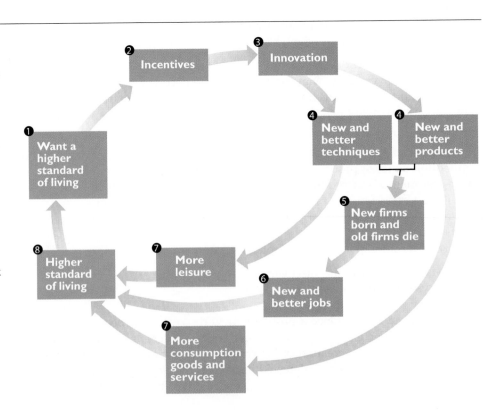

jobs are created and destroyed. New and better jobs lead to more leisure and more consumption. But our insatiable wants are still there, so the process continues, going round and round a circle of wants, profit incentives, innovation, and new products. The growth rate depends on people's ability to innovate and the incentives to do so. Over the years, the ability to innovate has changed. The invention of language and writing (the two most basic human capital tools), and later the development of the scientific method and the establishment of universities and research institutions, brought a huge increase in profit opportunities. Today, a deeper understanding of genes is bringing profit in a growing biotechnology industry. And astonishing advances in computer technology are creating an explosion of profit opportunities in a wide range of new information-age industries.

Productivity Curve and New Growth Theory

Figure 10.5 illustrates new growth theory using the productivity curve. According to this theory, as capital increases technology advances to bring unending growth. The economy starts out on productivity curve PC_0 at point A. Capital per hour of labour increases, which brings a movement along the productivity curve and increases labour productivity. At the same time, technology advances and human capital grows, which shifts the productivity curve upward to PC_1. So, for a second reason, labour productivity increases. The economy moves to point B. This process repeats indefinitely and takes the economy next to point C and then beyond.

FIGURE 10.5
New Growth Theory

 e Foundations **10.3**

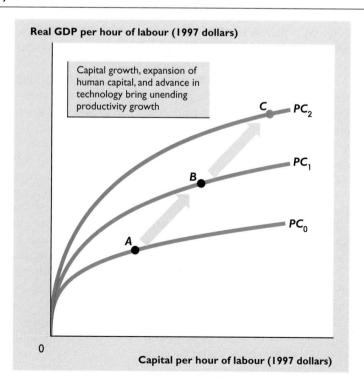

Real GDP per hour of labour (1997 dollars)

Capital growth, expansion of human capital, and advance in technology bring unending productivity growth

Capital per hour of labour (1997 dollars)

The economy starts out at point A on productivity curve PC_0. An increase in capital per hour of labour brings a movement along the productivity curve PC_0 and the expansion of human capital and technological change increase labour productivity and shift the productivity curve upward to PC_1. The economy moves to point B.

The process repeats. The economy moves to point C and then to points of yet greater capital per hour of labour and labour productivity.

Labour Productivity and Capital per Hour: 1960–2000

New growth theory is supported by the performance of the Canadian economy. Each dot in the figure represents a year between 1960 and 2000 and shows the Canadian data on labour productivity and capital per hour of labour. The two curves are the productivity curves of 1960 and 2000 based on the one-third rule.

You can see that advances in technology and the expansion of human capital have shifted the productivity curve upward and overcome diminishing returns.

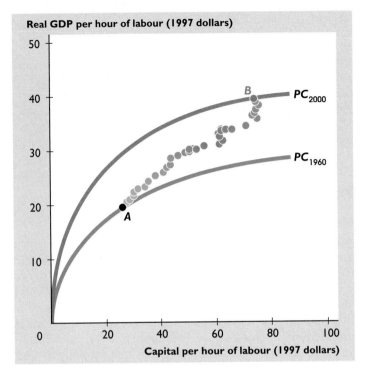

SOURCE: Statistics Canada.

■ Growth in the Global Economy

Economic growth is a global phenomenon, not just a national one. And the three growth theories make strikingly different predictions about the growth patterns that we should find in the global economy.

Classical growth theory predicts that the global economy will stagnate under the pressure of population growth. It also implies that the richest nations will be the ones with the fastest population growth and therefore they will be the first to stagnate. These predictions are resoundingly rejected by the experience of the world economy over the past few decades.

Neoclassical growth theory predicts that the global economy will grow and at a rate that is determined by the pace of technological change. All economies have access to the same technologies, and capital is free to roam the globe seeking the highest available profits. So neoclassical theory predicts that national levels of real GDP and national growth rates will converge. There is some sign of convergence among the rich countries. But convergence is slow and it does not appear to be imminent for all countries (see Eye on the Global Economy).

New growth theory predicts that national growth rates depend on national incentives to save, invest, accumulate human capital, and innovate. Because these incentives depend on factors that are special to each country, national growth rates will not necessarily converge. Some real GDP gaps among rich countries and gaps between rich and poor countries might persist. Other gaps might close as poorer nations create better incentives to boost capital accumulation and technological change. New growth theory fits the facts more closely than do the other two theories.

Eye On The GLOBAL ECONOMY

Persistent Gaps or Convergence?

The figure shows real GDP per person in Canada and other countries and regions from 1960 to 1999.

Part (a) shows some persistent gaps in real GDP per person. The United States has the highest real GDP per person, and growth rates in Canada and Europe's Big 4 (France, Germany, Italy, and the United Kingdom), have been similar to that of the United States, so the gaps between these countries haven't changed much.

Other Western European countries grew faster than the United States before 1975, slowed to the U.S. growth rate during the 1980s, and fell behind during the 1990s. After a brief period of catch-up, former Communist countries of Central Europe fell increasingly behind the United States.

Africa and Central and South America persistently grew more slowly than the world leaders in real GDP per person, so the gaps between these regions and the leaders widened.

Part (b) tells a different story. It shows how the economies of East Asia have converged on the United States.

In 1960, Hong Kong, Singapore, Taiwan, and South Korea had levels of real GDP per person that ranged from 10 percent to 25 percent of that in the United States. By 2000, real GDP per person in Hong Kong and Singapore had moved up to 80 percent of the United States and the two others were close behind. These four small Asian countries are like fast trains running on the same track at similar speeds and with a roughly constant gap between

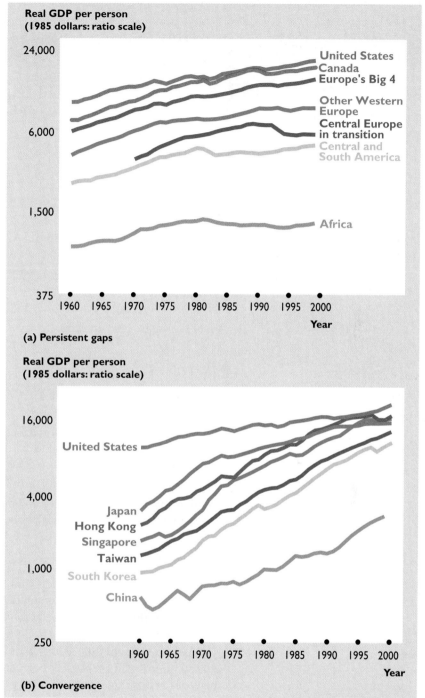

them. Hong Kong is the lead train and runs about 10 years in front of South Korea, which is the last train. Real GDP per person in South Korea in 1990 was similar to that in Hong Kong in 1980, ten years earlier. Between 1960 and

SOURCE: Alan Heston and Robert Summers, *Penn World Tables* 5.6 and *World Economic Outlook*.

2000, Hong Kong transformed itself from a poor developing country into one of the world's richest countries.

Part (b) also shows that China is catching up, but more slowly and from a very long way behind.

241

Study Guide pp. 154–157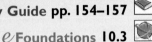

*e*Foundations 10.3

3 **Review the theories of economic growth that explain why growth rates vary over time and across countries.**

Practice Problems 10.3

1. What does classical growth theory say will eventually end economic growth? Does the evidence of history support the prediction of the classical theory?
2. What does neoclassical growth theory say about the source of persistent growth in real GDP per person?
3. Why does neoclassical growth theory predict that national levels of real GDP and national growth rates will converge?
4. What is the driving force of growth, according to new growth theory?
5. What does new growth theory imply about growth in the global economy?

Exercises 10.3

1. Contrast the modern theory of population growth with the classical theory.
2. What is the main limitation of neoclassical growth theory?
3. What are the three facts about market economies that new growth theory emphasizes and how do those facts influence the economic growth rate? Provide examples of each.
4. Why don't diminishing returns limit growth in the new growth theory?
5. Families in China are permitted to have only one child. Predict the effects of this policy according to classical, neoclassical, and new growth theories.

Solutions to Practice Problems 10.3

1. Classical growth theory predicts that real GDP per person will be persistently pulled towards the subsistence level. When real GDP per person exceeds the subsistence level, the population grows and real GDP per person decreases.
2. Neoclassical growth theory says that technological advance is the source of persistent growth in real GDP per person. Technological advances lead to increases in both the quantity of capital per hour of labour and real GDP per hour of labour.
3. Neoclassical growth theory predicts convergence because all countries have access to the same technology and capital is free to roam the globe.
4. The driving force of growth according to the new growth theory is a persistent incentive to innovate and an absence of diminishing returns to new knowledge.
5. New growth theory implies that national growth rates depend on national incentives to save, invest, and innovate. So gaps between rich and poor nations might persist.

10.4 ACHIEVING FASTER GROWTH

Why did it take more than a million years of human life before economic growth began? Why are some countries even today still barely growing? Why don't *all* societies save and invest in new capital, expand human capital, and discover and apply new technologies on a scale that brings rapid economic growth? What actions can governments take to stimulate growth?

■ Preconditions for Economic Growth

The key reason why economic growth is either absent or slow is that some societies lack the incentive system that encourages growth-producing activities. And economic freedom is the fundamental precondition for creating the incentives that lead to economic growth.

Economic Freedom

Economic freedom is present when people are able to make personal choices, their private property is protected, and they are free to buy and sell in markets. The rule of law, an efficient legal system, and the ability to enforce contracts are essential foundations for creating economic freedom. Impediments to economic freedom are corruption in the courts and government bureaucracy; barriers to trade, such as import bans; high tax rates; intrusive regulations on business such as health, safety, and environmental regulation; restrictions on banks; labour market regulations that limit a firm's ability to hire and fire workers; and illegal markets such as those that violate intellectual property rights.

No unique political system is necessary to deliver economic freedom. Democratic systems do a good job. But the rule of law, not democracy, is the key requirement for creating economic freedom. Non-democratic political systems that respect the rule of law do a good job too. Hong Kong is the best example of a country with little democracy but a lot of economic freedom—and a lot of economic growth. No country with a high level of economic freedom is economically poor. But many countries with low levels of economic freedom stagnate.

Economic freedom
A condition in which people are able to make personal choices, their private property is protected, and they are free to buy and sell in markets.

Property Rights

Economic freedom requires the protection of private property—the factors of production and goods that people own. The social arrangements that govern the protection of private property are called **property rights**. They include the rights to physical property (land, buildings, and capital equipment), to financial property (claims by one person against another), and to intellectual property (such as inventions). Clearly established and enforced property rights provide people with the incentive to work and save. If someone attempts to steal their property, a legal system will protect them. Such property rights also assure people that government itself will not confiscate their income or savings.

Property rights
The social arrangements that govern the protection of private property.

Markets

Economic freedom also requires free markets. Buyers and sellers get information and do business with each other in *markets*. And market prices send signals to buyers and sellers that create incentives to increase or decrease the quantities demanded and supplied. Markets enable people to trade and to save and invest. But markets cannot operate without property rights.

Property rights and markets create incentives for people to specialize and trade, to save and invest, to expand their human capital, and to discover and apply new technologies. Early human societies based on hunting and gathering did not experience economic growth because they lacked property rights and markets. Economic growth began when societies evolved the institutions that create incentives. But the presence of an incentive system and the institutions that create it do not guarantee that economic growth will occur. They permit economic growth but do not make it inevitable.

Growth begins when the appropriate incentive system exists because people can specialize in the activities at which they have a comparative advantage and trade with each other. You saw in Chapter 3 how everyone gains from such activity. By specializing and trading, everyone can acquire goods and services at the lowest possible cost. Consequently, people can obtain a greater volume of goods and services from their labour.

As an economy moves from one with little specialization to one that reaps the gains from specialization and trade, its production and consumption grows. Real GDP per person increases and the standard of living rises.

But for growth to be persistent, people must face incentives that encourage them to pursue the three activities that generate *ongoing* economic growth: saving and investment, expansion of human capital, and the discovery and application of new technologies.

■ Policies to Achieve Faster Growth

To achieve faster economic growth, we must either increase the growth rate of capital per hour of labour or increase the growth rate of human capital or the pace of technological advance. The main actions that governments can take to achieve these objectives are:

- Create the incentive mechanisms
- Encourage saving
- Encourage research and development
- Encourage international trade
- Improve the quality of education

Create Incentive Mechanisms

Economic growth occurs when the incentive to save, invest, and innovate is strong enough. And these incentives require property rights enforced by a well-functioning legal system. Property rights and a legal system are key missing ingredients in many societies. For example, they are absent throughout much of Africa. The first priority for growth policy is to establish these institutions so that incentives to save, invest, and innovate exist. Russia is a leading example of a country that is striving to take this step towards establishing the conditions in which economic growth can occur.

Encourage Saving

Saving finances investment, which brings capital accumulation. So encouraging saving can increase the growth of capital and stimulate economic growth. The East Asian economies have the highest saving rates and growth rates. Some African economies have the lowest saving rates and the lowest growth rates.

Tax incentives can increase saving. Registered Retirement Saving Plans (RRSPs) are an example of a tax incentive to save. Economists claim that a tax on consumption rather than on income provides the best incentive to save.

Encourage Research and Development

Everyone can use the fruits of basic research and development efforts. For example, all biotechnology firms can use advances in gene-splicing technology. Because basic inventions can be copied, the inventor's profit is limited and so the market allocates too few resources to this activity.

Governments can direct public funds towards financing basic research but this solution is not foolproof. It requires a mechanism for allocating public funds to their highest-valued use. The National Sciences and Engineering Research Council of Canada is one possibly efficient channel for allocating public funds to universities and public research facilities to finance and encourage basic research. Government programs such as national defence and space exploration also lead to innovations that have wide use. Laptop computers and Teflon coatings are two prominent examples of innovations that came from the U.S. space program.

Encourage International Trade

Free international trade encourages growth by extracting all the available gains from specialization and exchange. The fastest-growing nations today are those with the fastest-growing exports and imports. The creation of the North American Free Trade Agreement and the integration of the economies of Europe through the formation of the European Union are examples of successful actions that governments have taken to stimulate growth through trade.

Improve the Quality of Education

The free market would produce too little education because it brings social benefits beyond the benefits to the people who receive the education. By funding basic education and by ensuring high standards in skills such as language, mathematics, and science, governments can contribute enormously to a nation's growth potential. Education can also be expanded and improved by using tax incentives to encourage improved private provision. Singapore's Information Technology in Education program is one of the best examples of a successful attempt to stimulate growth through education.

■ How Much Difference Can Policy Make?

It is easy to make a list of policy actions that could increase a nation's economic growth rate. It is hard to convert that list into acceptable actions that make a big difference.

Societies are the way they are because they balance the interests of one group against the interests of another group. Change brings gains for some and losses for others. So change is slow. And even when change occurs, if the growth rate can be increased by even as much as a half percentage point, it takes many years for the full benefits to accrue.

A well-intentioned government cannot dial up a big increase in the growth rate. But it can pursue policies that will nudge the growth rate upward. And over time, the benefits from these policies will be large.

Study Guide pp. 157–159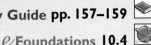

*e*Foundations 10.4

4 **Describe policies that might promote faster economic growth.**

Practice Problems 10.4

1. What are the preconditions for economic growth?

2. Why does much of Africa experience slow economic growth?

3. Why is economic freedom crucial for achieving economic growth?

4. What role do property rights play in encouraging economic growth?

5. Explain why, other things remaining the same, a country with a well-educated population has a faster economic growth rate than a country that has a poorly educated population.

Exercises 10.4

1. What is the key reason why economic growth is either absent or slow in some societies?

2. Why does Russia experience slow economic growth?

3. Is economic freedom the same as democracy? Can you think of a country that enjoys economic freedom and achieves rapid economic growth but does not have democracy?

4. Why are markets a necessary precondition for economic growth?

5. Explain why, other things remaining the same, a country that adopts free international trade (for example, Hong Kong) has a faster economic growth rate than a country that restricts trade internationally (for example, Myanmar).

Solutions to Practice Problems 10.4

1. The preconditions for economic growth are economic freedom, private property rights, and markets. Without these preconditions, people have little incentive to undertake the actions that lead to economic growth.

2. Some African countries experience slow economic growth because they lack economic freedom, private property rights are not enforced, and markets do not function well. People in these countries have little incentive to specialize and trade or to accumulate both physical and human capital.

3. Economic freedom is crucial for achieving economic growth because economic freedom allows people to make choices and gives them the incentives to pursue growth-producing activities.

4. Clearly defined private property rights and a legal system to enforce them gives people the incentives to work, save, invest, and accumulate human capital.

5. A well-educated population has more skills and greater labour productivity than does a poorly educated population. A well-educated population can contribute to research and development that creates new technology.

CHAPTER CHECKPOINT

Key Points

1 **Define and calculate the economic growth rate and explain the implications of sustained growth.**

- Economic growth is the sustained expansion of production possibilities. The annual percentage change in real GDP measures the economic growth rate.
- Real GDP per person must grow if the standard of living is to rise.
- Sustained economic growth transforms poor nations into rich ones.
- The Rule of 70 tells us the number of years in which real GDP doubles— 70 divided by the percentage growth rate of real GDP.

2 **Identify the main sources of economic growth.**

- Real GDP grows when aggregate hours and labour productivity grow.
- Real GDP per person grows when labour productivity grows.
- Saving, investment in physical capital and human capital, and technological advance bring labour productivity growth.
- The productivity curve shows how labour productivity changes when capital per hour of labour changes, other things remaining the same.
- The productivity curve shifts when human capital expands and technology advances.

3 **Review the theories of economic growth that explain why growth rates vary over time and across countries.**

- Classical theory predicts that economic growth will end because a population explosion will lower real GDP per person to its subsistence level.
- Neoclassical theory predicts that economic growth will persist at a rate determined by the pace of technological change.
- New growth theory predicts that capital accumulation, human capital growth, and technological change respond to incentives and can bring persistent growth in labour productivity.

4 **Describe policies that might promote faster economic growth.**

- Economic growth requires an incentive system created by economic freedom, property rights, and markets.
- It might be possible to achieve faster growth by encouraging saving, subsidizing research and education, and encouraging international trade.

Key Terms

Exercises

1. Explain why sustained growth of real GDP per person can transform a poor country into a rich one.

2. In Ireland, the growth rate of real GDP per person averaged 10 percent a year during the 1990s. If this growth rate were to continue, in what year would real GDP per person be twice what it was in 2000?

3. In Russia during the 1990s, the growth rate of real GDP averaged −4.9 percent a year and its population growth rate was 0.3 percent a year. If these growth rates were to continue, in what year would real GDP per person be half what it was in 2000?

4. Describe how Canada's real GDP per person has changed over the last 100 years.

5. Explain how the amount of capital increases, how human capital increases, and how technology advances.

6. What is the link between labour hours, labour productivity, and real GDP?

7. What is a productivity curve? Sketch one.

8. Explain how saving and investment in new capital, increases in human capital, and advances in technology change labour productivity. Use the productivity curve to illustrate your answer.

9. What is the one-third rule? Who discovered the one-third rule?

10. If labour productivity grows by 5 percent when capital per hour of labour grows by 6 percent, what is capital's contribution to growth? What else contributes to growth and what is its contribution?

11. What does classical growth theory imply about growth in the global economy and about the population growth rates of rich and poor countries?

12. What does neoclassical growth theory imply about economic growth in the global economy?

13. New growth theory predicts that economic growth will persist. Does this prediction imply that growth has no opportunity cost? Explain why or why not.

14. Which growth theory best fits the facts? Explain with examples.

15. Why do you think living standards in Asian economies have increased in the last decade by so much more than in Canada?

16. What are the ingredients of economic freedom and how does each make growth more likely?

17. What can governments in poor African countries do to encourage economic growth and raise their living standards?

18. Provide examples of nations that do not enjoy political freedom and that have a low economic growth rate.

19. How does international trade bring economic growth?

20. List five actions that governments can take to encourage economic growth and provide an example of each.

The Money Economy

Part
4

Money and the Monetary System

11

When you have completed your study of this chapter,
you will be able to:

1 Define money and describe its functions.

2 Describe the monetary system and explain the functions of banks and
other monetary institutions.

3 Describe the functions of the Bank of Canada.

You are now going to study the role of money in
the economy. In this chapter and in Chapters 12
and 13, we address two main questions. First,
what brings a persistent rise in the cost of living?
Second, how does the Bank of Canada control
the quantity of money and how do the Bank of
Canada's actions influence interest rates and
spending? This second question sets the scene
for your study of economic fluctuations and stabilization policy in Part 5.

The quick answer to the first question is that many factors cause changes in the cost of living. But one factor dominates in the long run. The cost of living rises when the
quantity of money grows more quickly than real GDP. But
what exactly *is* money? Chapter 11 answers this question and
describes the institutions of the monetary system. How does
money get "created" so that its quantity grows? And how is
the quantity of money controlled? Chapter 12 answers these
questions. What happens when the quantity of money increases? And how does the creation of too much money bring a
rising cost of living? Chapter 13 answers these questions.

11.1 WHAT IS MONEY?

Money, like fire and the wheel, has been around for a very long time. An incredible array of items has served as money. North American Indians used wampum (beads made from shells), Fijians used whales' teeth, and early American colonists used tobacco. Cakes of salt served as money in Ethiopia and Tibet. What do wampum, whales' teeth, tobacco, and salt have in common? Why are they examples of money? Today, when we want to buy something, we use coins or notes (dollar bills), write a cheque, send an e-cheque, present a credit or debit card, or use a "smart card." Are all these things that we use today money? To answer these questions, we need a definition of money.

■ Definition of Money

Money
Any commodity or token that is generally accepted as a means of payment.

Money is any commodity or token that is generally accepted as a *means of payment*. This definition has three parts that we'll examine in turn.

A Commodity or Token

Money is always something that can be recognized and that can be divided up into small parts. So money might be an actual commodity, such as a bar of silver or gold. But it might also be a token, such as a quarter or a $10 bill. Money might also be a virtual token, such as an electronic record in a bank's database (more about this type of money later).

Generally Accepted

Money is *generally* accepted, which means that it can be used to buy anything and everything. Some tokens can be used to buy some things but not others. For example, a phone card is accepted as payment for a phone call. But you can't use your phone card to buy toothpaste. So a phone card is not money. In contrast, you can use a $5 bill to buy either a phone call or toothpaste—or anything else that costs $5 or less. So a $5 bill is money.

Means of Payment

Means of payment
A method of settling a debt.

A **means of payment** is a method of settling a debt. When a payment has been made, there is no remaining obligation between the parties to a transaction. The deal is complete. Suppose that Gus buys a car from his friend Ann. Gus doesn't have enough money to pay for the car right now, but he will have enough three months from now, when he gets paid. Ann agrees that Gus may pay for the car in three months' time. Gus buys the car with a loan from Ann and then pays off the loan. The loan that Ann made to Gus isn't money. Money is what Gus uses to pay off the loan.

So what wampum, whales' teeth, tobacco, and salt have in common is that they have served as a generally accepted means of payment, and that is why they are examples of money.

Money performs three vital functions. It serves as a:

- Medium of exchange
- Unit of account
- Store of value

■ Medium of Exchange

A **medium of exchange** is an object that is generally accepted in return for goods and services. Money is a medium of exchange. Without money, you would have to exchange goods and services directly for other goods and services—an exchange called **barter**. Barter requires a *double coincidence of wants*. For example, if you want a soda and have only a paperback novel to offer in exchange for it, you must find someone who is selling soda and who also wants your paperback novel. Money guarantees that there is a double coincidence of wants because people with something to sell will always accept money in exchange for it. So money acts as a lubricant that smoothes the mechanism of exchange. It enables you to specialize in the activity at which you have a comparative advantage (see pp. 68–70) instead of searching for a double coincidence.

Medium of exchange
An object that is generally accepted in return for goods and services.

Barter
The direct exchange of goods and services for other goods and services, which requires a double coincidence of wants.

■ Unit of Account

A **unit of account** is an agreed-upon measure for stating the prices of goods and services. To get the most out of your budget, you have to figure out whether going to a rock concert is worth its opportunity cost. But that cost is not dollars and cents. It is the number of movies, cappuccinos, ice-cream cones, or local phone calls that you must give up to attend the concert. It's easy to do such calculations when all these goods have prices in terms of dollars and cents (see Table 11.1). If a rock concert costs $32 and movie costs $8, you know right away that going to the concert costs you 4 movies. If a cappuccino costs $2, going to the concert costs 16 cappuccinos. You need only one calculation to figure out the opportunity cost of any pair of goods and services. For example, the opportunity cost of the rock concert is 128 local phone calls ($32.00 ÷ 25¢ = 128).

Now imagine how troublesome it would be if the rock concert ticket agent posted its price as 4 movies, and if the movie theatre posted its price as 4 cappuccinos, and if the coffee shop posted the price of a cappuccino as 2 ice-cream cones, and if the ice-cream shop posted its price as 4 local phone calls! Now how much running around and calculating do you have to do to figure out how much that rock concert is going to cost you in terms of the movies, cappuccinos, ice cream, or phone calls that you must give up to attend it? You get the answer for movies right away from the sign posted by the ticket agent. But for all the other goods, you're going to have to visit many different places to establish the price of each commodity in terms of another and then calculate prices in units that are relevant for your own decision. Cover up the column labelled "price in money units" in Table 11.1 and see how hard it is to figure out the number of local phone calls it costs to attend a rock concert. It's enough to make a person swear off rock! How much simpler it is using dollars and cents.

Unit of account
An agreed-upon measure for stating the prices of goods and services.

TABLE 11.1 A UNIT OF ACCOUNT SIMPLIFIES PRICE COMPARISONS

Good	Price in money units	Price in units of another good
Rock concert	$32.00	4 movies
Movie	$8.00	4 cappuccinos
Cappuccino	$2.00	2 ice-cream cones
Ice-cream cone	$1.00	4 local phone calls
Local phone call	$0.25	

■ Store of Value

Any commodity or token that can be held and exchanged later for goods and services is called a **store of value.** Money acts as a store of value. If it did not, it would not be accepted in exchange for goods and services. The more stable the value of a commodity or token, the better it can act as a store of value and the more useful it is as money. No store of value is completely stable. The value of a physical object, such as a house, a car, or a work of art, fluctuates over time. The value of the commodities and tokens that we use as money also fluctuates, and when there is inflation, money persistently falls in value.

Store of value
Any commodity or token that can be held and exchanged later for goods and services.

■ Money Today

Fiat money
Objects that are money because the law decrees or orders them to be money.

Money in the world today is called **fiat money**. *Fiat* is a Latin word that means "Let it be done." The modern word "fiat" means decree or order. So today's money is money because the law decrees or orders it to be money. The objects that we use as money today are:

- Currency
- Deposits at banks and other financial institutions

Currency

Currency
Bank notes (dollar bills) and coins.

The bank notes and coins that we use in Canada today are known as **currency**. Bank notes are money because the government declares them to be with the words printed on every bank note, "This note is legal tender."

Deposits

Deposits at banks, credit unions, and caisse populaires (savings banks in Quebec) are also money. Deposits are money because people can use them directly to make payments.

Currency in a Bank Is Not Money

Bank deposits are one form of money, and currency *outside the banks* is another form. Currency *inside* the banks is not money. When you get some cash from the ATM, you convert your bank deposit into currency. You change the *form* of your money, but there is no change in the *quantity* of money. Deposits decrease, and currency outside the banks increases. If we counted both bank deposits and currency inside the banks as money, then when you get cash at the ATM, the quantity of money would *appear* to decrease—your currency would increase, but *both* deposits *and* currency inside the banks would decrease. You can see that counting both deposits *and* currency inside the banks as money would be counting the same thing twice—called double counting.

Deposits Are Money but Cheques Are Not

Cheques are not money. To see why, think about what happens when Colleen buys some inline skates from Rocky's Rollers. Colleen has $500 in her deposit account, and Rocky has $3,000 in his deposit account. Both of them bank at the Laser Bank. The total bank deposits of Colleen and Rocky are $3,500.

To pay for her skates, Colleen writes a cheque for $200. Rocky takes the cheque to the bank and deposits it. The Laser Bank now credits Rocky's account and debits Colleen's account. Rocky's deposit increases from $3,000 to $3,200, and Colleen's deposit decreases from $500 to $300. The total deposits of Colleen and Rocky are still the same as before: $3,500. Rocky now has $200 more, and Colleen has $200 less than before.

This transaction has transferred money from Colleen to Rocky. The cheque itself was never money. There wasn't an extra $200 worth of money while the cheque was in circulation. The cheque only instructs the bank to transfer money from Colleen to Rocky. Figure 11.1 shows these transactions.

FIGURE 11.1

Paying by Cheque

LASER BANK *2210 College Avenue, Regina, SK S4P 1C6*

Date	Item	Debit	Credit	Balance
June 1 2001	Opening balance			$500.00
June 11 2001	Rocky's Rollers	$200.00		$300.00

(a) Colleen's account

LASER BANK *2210 College Avenue, Regina, SK S4P 1C6*

Date	Item	Debit	Credit	Balance
June 1 2001	Opening balance			$3,000.00
June 11 2001	Colleen's cheque		$200.00	$3,200.00

(b) Rocky's Rollers account

When you pay by cheque, you tell your bank to take some money from your deposit and put it into someone else's deposit. The deposit is money, but the cheque is not money.

In the example, Colleen and Rocky use the same bank. The same story, but with additional steps, describes what happens if Colleen and Rocky use different banks. In that case, the cheque must be cleared and a payment made by Colleen's bank to Rocky's bank. We explain the details of the process of cheque clearing in Chapter 12, pp. 279–280. This process can take a few days, but the principles are the same as when two people use the same bank.

■ Credit Cards, Debit Cards, E-Cheques, and E-Cash

We've seen that cheques are not money, but what about credit cards, debit cards, e-cheques, and e-cash? Are they money?

Credit Cards

A credit card is not money. It is a special type of ID card. To see why, suppose that Colleen uses her credit card to buy her inline skates. Colleen signs a credit card slip and leaves the store with her new skates. But she has not yet *paid* for the skates. She has taken a loan from the bank that issued her credit card. Rocky's bank credits his account with $200 (minus the bank's charge) and sends a charge to the bank that issued Colleen's credit card. Colleen eventually gets her credit card bill, which she pays, using money.

If you pay by cheque, you are often asked to show your driver's licence. Your driver's licence is obviously not money. It's just an ID card. A credit card is also an

ID card but one that enables you to get a loan at the instant you buy something. So when you use a credit card to buy something, the bank that issued your credit card pays for the goods and you pay later. The credit card is not the means of payment, and it is not money.

Debit Cards

A debit card is not money. To see why, think about what happens if Colleen uses her debit card to buy her inline skates. When the sales clerk swipes Colleen's card in Rocky's store, the Laser Bank's computer gets a message: Take $200 from Colleen's account and put it in the account of Rocky's Rollers. The transactions shown in Figure 11.1 are done in a flash. But again, the bank deposits are the money and the debit card is the tool that causes money to move from Colleen to Rocky.

E-Cheques

An **electronic cheque** (or **e-cheque**) is an electronic equivalent of a paper cheque. It is an instruction to a bank to transfer funds (deposits) to someone, but the instruction is conveyed by e-mail rather than on a piece of paper. Like a paper cheque, an e-cheque is not money. The deposit that is transferred is money.

E-Cash

Electronic cash (or **e-cash**) is an electronic equivalent of paper notes and coins. It is an electronic currency, and for people to be willing to use it, e-cash has to work like money. People use physical currency because it is portable, recognizable, transferable, untraceable, and anonymous and can be used to make change. The designers of e-cash aim to reproduce all of these features of notes and coins. Today's e-cash is portable, untraceable, and anonymous. But it has not yet reached the level of recognition that makes it universally accepted as a means of payment, so it doesn't meet the definition of money.

Like notes and coins, e-cash can be used in shops. It can also be used over the Internet. To use e-cash in a shop, the buyer uses a smart card that stores some e-cash and the shop uses a smart card reader. When a transaction is made, e-cash is transferred from the smart card directly to the shop's bank account. Smart cards receive their e-cash by withdrawing it from a bank account by using a special ATM or a special cell phone.

A handy advantage of e-cash over paper notes arises when you lose your wallet. If it is stuffed with dollar bills, you're out of luck. If it contains e-cash recorded on your smart card, your bank can cancel the e-cash stored in the card and issue you replacement e-cash.

E-cash is in the early stages of development, and is not sufficiently widely accepted to serve as money today. In some experiments with e-cash, people have not found it sufficiently convenient and universally acceptable to make it attractive. Also, many people are still fond of the idea of physically seeing and feeling the money in their pocket, purse, or wallet. But many people view e-cash as the next logical step in the evolution of money and expect that its use will grow and that it will gradually replace physical forms of currency.

**Electronic cheque
(or e-cheque)**
An electronic equivalent of a paper cheque.

Electronic cash (or e-cash)
An electronic equivalent of paper notes and coins.

ECONOMICS
in the **NEWS**

June 28, 2001

Cell Phone Credit Card Proposed

Europe's leading banks will move a step closer to a cashless society today when they unveil plans to turn mobile phones into credit cards.

Once local wireless technology becomes commonplace, the banks hope to provide links to shops so all transactions can be carried out on the phone.

NATIONAL POST

Questions
1. How much extra (as a percentage of your purchases) would you pay for such a service?
2. Do you believe that such a service will eventually replace cash? Why or why not?

 *e*Foundations **4.3**

■ Official Measures of Money: M1 and M2+

Figure 11.2 shows the items that make up two official measures of money. **M1** consists of currency held outside the banks plus chequable deposits owned by individuals and businesses at chartered banks. M1 does not include currency inside the banks, and it does not include currency and bank deposits owned by the government of Canada. **M2+** consists of M1 plus personal savings deposits and nonpersonal notice deposits at chartered banks plus all types of deposits at credit unions, caisse populaires, trust and mortgage companies, and other deposit-taking financial institutions.

M1
Currency outside the banks plus chequable deposits owned by individuals and businesses at chartered banks.

M2+
M1 plus personal savings deposits and nonpersonal notice deposits at banks plus deposits at credit unions, caisses populaires, and other depository institutions.

Are M1 and M2+ Really Money?

Money is a generally accepted means of payment. So the test of whether something is money is whether it serves this purpose. Currency passes the test. Chequable deposits also pass the test because they can be transferred from one person to another electronically or by writing a cheque. Because M1 consists of currency plus chequable deposits and each is a means of payment, M1 is money.

But what about M2+? Some of the savings deposits in M2+ are just as much a means of payment as the chequable deposits in M1. You can use the ATM at the grocery store checkout or gas station to transfer funds from your savings account to pay for your purchase. But other savings deposits such as term deposits *cannot* be transferred in this manner, so they are not means of payment. Technically, they are not money. So all of M1 is money, but only part of M2+ is money.

FIGURE 11.2
Two Measures of Money: June 2001

*e*Foundations 11.1

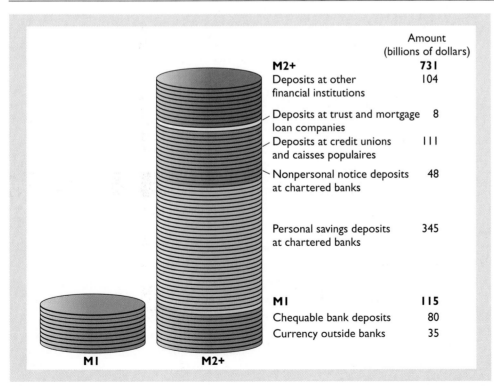

	Amount (billions of dollars)
M2+	**731**
Deposits at other financial institutions	104
Deposits at trust and mortgage loan companies	8
Deposits at credit unions and caisses populaires	111
Nonpersonal notice deposits at chartered banks	48
Personal savings deposits at chartered banks	345
M1	**115**
Chequable bank deposits	80
Currency outside banks	35

M1   Currency held outside banks
Chequable deposits owned by individuals and businesses at chartered banks

M2+   M1
Personal savings deposits at chartered banks
Nonpersonal notice deposits at chartered banks
Deposits at credit unions and caisses populaires
Deposits at trust and mortgage loan companies
Deposits at other financial institutions

SOURCE: Bank of Canada.

Eye On The GLOBAL ECONOMY

Dollarization

The nations of Europe have abolished their national currencies and adopted the euro. Some economists have suggested that Canada would be better off if it got rid of the Canadian dollar and used the U.S. dollar instead. Jeffrey Frankel of Harvard University and Andrew K. Rose of the University of California at Berkeley (a Canadian) have measured the gains from dollarization for Canada and Mexico. The figure shows their staggering numbers. Trade between Canada and the United States more than doubles and Canadian real GDP increases by 36 percent.

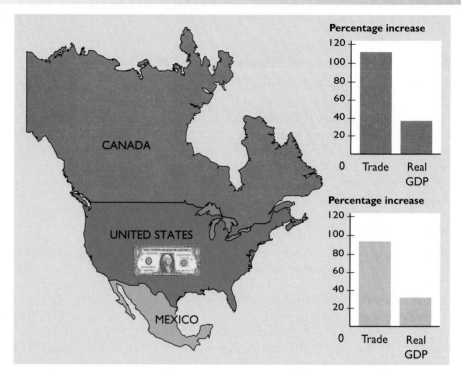

SOURCE: Jeffrey A. Frankel and Andrew K. Rose, "Estimating the Effect of Currency Unions on Trade and Output" NBER Working Paper No. W7857, August 2000.

Figure 11.3 shows the changing composition of money in Canada. Currency and chequable deposits decreased in relative importance in the 1970s and 1980s, but they made a comeback during the 1990s.

FIGURE 11.3

The Changing Face of Money in Canada   *e*Foundations 11.1

Currency has gradually become a smaller proportion of the money that we use. During the inflationary 1970s and 1980s, a declining proportion of money was kept in chequable accounts. But the proportion increased in the 1990s as inflation fell.

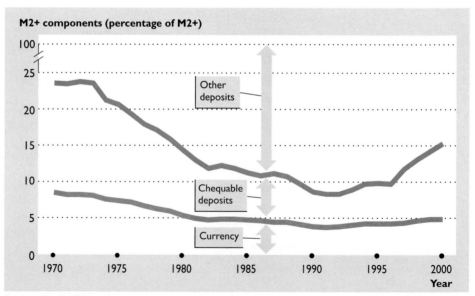

SOURCE: Bank of Canada.

CHECKPOINT 11.1

1 **Define money and describe its functions.**

Study Guide pp. 164–167

*e*Foundations 11.1

Practice Problems 11.1

1. In Canada today, money includes which of the following items?
   a. Your Visa card
   b. The quarters inside public phones
   c. The $20 bills in your wallet
   d. The cheque that you have just written to pay for your rent
   e. The loan you took out last August to pay for your school fees

2. In July 2001, currency held outside the banks was $36 billion; chequable deposits owned by individuals and businesses at chartered banks were $80 billion; personal savings deposits at banks were $345 billion; nonpersonal notice deposits at banks were $50 billion; and deposits at institutions other than banks were $223 billion.
   a. What was M1 in July 2001?
   b. What was M2+ in July 2001?

Exercises 11.1

1. Which of the following items are money?
   a. Chequable deposits at the CIBC
   b. Stelco stock held by individuals
   c. Your MasterCard card
   d. Canada Savings Bonds
   e. Canadian Tire money

2. Sara has a $5,000 term deposit at Scotiabank. She withdraws $1,000 from her term deposit, keeps $50 in cash, and deposits the balance in her chequable account at Scotiabank. What are the immediate changes in M1 and M2+?

3. In February 2001, currency held outside the banks was $34 billion; chequable deposits owned by individuals and businesses at chartered banks were $78 billion; personal savings deposits at banks were $343 billion; nonpersonal notice deposits at banks were $47 billion; and deposits at institutions other than banks were $215 billion.
   a. What was M1 in February 2001?
   b. What was M2+ in February 2001?

Solutions to Practice Problems 11.1

1. Money is defined as a means of payment. Only items b and c (the quarters inside public phones and the $20 bills in your wallet) are money.

2a. M1 is the sum of currency outside the banks, $36 billion, and chequable bank deposits owned by individuals and businesses, $80 billion. M1 is $116 billion.

2b. M2+ is the sum of M1 ($116 billion), personal savings deposits ($345 billion), nonpersonal notice deposits ($50 billion), and deposits at institutions other than banks ($223 billion). M2+ is $734 billion.

11.2 THE MONETARY SYSTEM

Monetary system
The Bank of Canada and the banks and other institutions that accept deposits and provide the services that enable people and businesses to make and receive payments.

The **monetary system** consists of the Bank of Canada and the banks and other monetary institutions that accept deposits and make loans and that provide the services that enable people and businesses to make and receive payments. Figure 11.4 illustrates the institutions of the monetary system. Sitting at the top of the figure, the Bank of Canada sets the rules and regulates and influences the activities of the banks and other institutions. Three types of monetary institutions accept the deposits that are part of the nation's money:

- Chartered banks
- Credit unions and caisses populaires
- Other depository institutions

In this section, we describe the functions of these institutions, and in the final section of the chapter, we describe the structure and functions of the Bank of Canada.

■ Chartered Banks

Chartered bank
A private firm that is chartered by the federal government to receive deposits and make loans.

A **chartered bank** is a private firm that is chartered by the federal government under the Bank Act of 1992 to receive deposits and make loans. In 2001, 13 Canadian-owned chartered banks and 41 foreign-owned chartered banks operated in Canada. The foreign banks deal mostly with businesses rather than with the public. The essence of a bank's business is to take in deposits, make loans, and operate a payments system.

Types of Deposit

A chartered bank accepts three broad types of deposit: chequable deposits, savings deposits, and term deposits. A bank pays a low interest rate (sometimes zero) on chequable deposits and it pays the highest interest rate on term deposits.

■ FIGURE 11.4

The Institutions of the Monetary System   *e*Foundations 11.2

The Bank of Canada regulates and influences the activities of the chartered banks, credit unions and caisses populaires, and other depository institutions whose deposits make up the nation's money.

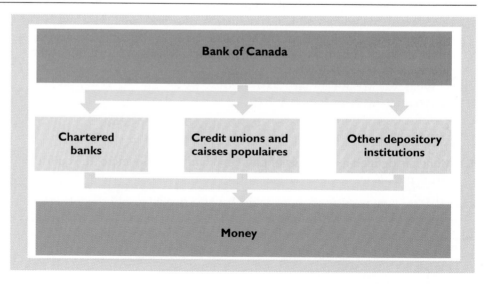

Profit and Prudence: A Balancing Act

The goal of a chartered bank is to maximize its stockholders' long-term wealth. To achieve this goal, a bank makes loans at a higher interest rate than the interest rate it pays on deposits. But lending is risky. The more a bank ties up its deposits in high-risk, high-interest rate loans, the bigger is the risk that it will not be able to pay its depositors when they want to withdraw funds. And if depositors perceive this risk, mass withdrawals might create a crisis for the bank. So a bank must perform a balancing act. It must be prudent in the way it uses the depositors' funds and balance security for the depositors against profit for its stockholders. To achieve security for its depositors, a bank divides its assets into three parts: cash assets, bonds, and loans.

Cash Assets

A bank's *cash assets* consist of its reserves and funds that can be converted into reserves very quickly. **Reserves** are the currency (bank notes and coins) in a bank's vaults plus the bank's deposit at the Bank of Canada. The cash in the bank's vaults is a reserve that the bank keeps for meeting its depositors' withdrawals of cash. These reserves are the source of the cash that a bank teller hands you or you get from the ATM. A bank's deposit at the Bank of Canada is similar to your own bank deposit. Chartered banks use their reserve accounts at the Bank of Canada to make payments and receive payments and to obtain currency.

Reserves
The currency in a bank's vaults plus its deposit at the Bank of Canada.

Funds that can be converted into reserves very quickly include overnight loans, Treasury bills, and other short-term loans. Overnight loans are the banks' first cushion in the event that they have a shortage of reserves. The interest rate on overnight loans between banks and other large financial institutions is called the **overnight rate**.

Overnight rate
The interest rate on overnight loans between banks and other large financial institutions.

Bonds

Bonds are securities issued by the government of Canada and by other large, safe organizations. These bonds are traded every day on the bond market. A bank earns a moderate interest rate on bonds, but it can sell them quickly if it needs cash. But a bank would normally not sell bonds to obtain cash. Instead, it would sell some of its cash assets (described above).

Loans

Loans are the provision of funds to businesses and individuals. Banks earn a high interest rate on loans but they cannot be called in before the agreed date. Banks earn the highest interest rate on unpaid credit card balances, which are loans to their credit card holders.

Bank Deposits and Assets: The Relative Magnitudes

In Canada, chequable deposits are about 31 percent of chartered banks' total deposits. After performing their profit versus prudence balancing acts, the banks on the average keep reserves of less than 1 percent of total deposits as reserves and another 8 percent as other cash assets. Banks use about 28 percent of total deposits to buy government bonds and 63 percent of total deposits to make loans. Figure 11.5 summarizes the dollar values in June 2001.

FIGURE 11.5

Chartered Banks' Deposits and Assets

*e*Foundations **11.2**

In June 2001, the chartered banks had $191 billion in chequable deposits and $418 billion in other deposits. They loaned $382 billion of these deposits, placed $171 billion in bonds, and kept $56 billion as cash assets.

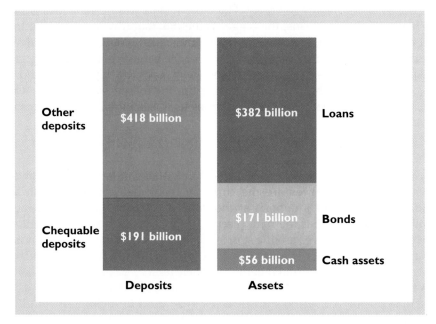

SOURCE: Bank of Canada.

Credit Unions and Caisses Populaires

Credit union

A cooperative organization, owned by a social or economic group such as a firm's employees, that accepts deposits from and makes loans to its members.

A **credit union** is a cooperative organization that operates under the Cooperative Credit Association Act of 1992. A credit union receives deposits from and makes loans to its members, who form a social or economic group, such as the employees of a firm.

A **caisse populaire** is financial institution that operates in Quebec and that is similar in its structure and operations to a credit union.

Caisse populaire

A financial institution that operates in Quebec and that is similar to a credit union.

Like a chartered bank, a credit union and a caisse populaire must perform a balancing act between profit and prudence and so hold some of their deposits as cash assets and some as bonds as well as loans.

In June 2001, credit unions and caisses populaires had total deposits included in M2+ of $111 billion.

Other Depository Institutions

Money market mutual fund

A fund managed by a financial institution that sells shares to people and uses these funds to buy assets.

The main other depository institutions are money market mutual funds and trust and mortgage loan companies. A **money market mutual fund** is a fund managed by a financial institution that obtains funds by selling shares and uses these funds to buy assets such as Treasury bills and other securities. Money market shares act like bank deposits. Shareholders can write cheques on their money market fund accounts. But there are restrictions on most of these accounts. A **trust and mortgage loan company** is a privately owned depository institution that operates under the Trust and Loan Companies Act, 1992. In June 2001, the deposits in other depository institutions, which are part of M2+, were $104 billion.

Trust and mortgage loan company
A privately owned depository institution that operates under the Trust and Loan Companies Act, 1992.

■ Relative Size of Monetary Institutions

Chartered banks provide most of the nation's bank deposits. In Figure 11.6, we show the relative contributions of chartered banks, credit unions and caisses populaires, and other depository institutions in June 2001. Part (a) shows that chequable deposits at chartered banks are 70 percent of M1. Currency represents the other 30 percent of M1.

Part (b) shows that M1 is 16 percent of M2+. The personal savings deposits and nonpersonal notice deposits at chartered banks account for 55 percent of M2+. Deposits at credit unions and caisses populaires account for about 15 percent of M2+, and deposits at other depository institutions make up the remaining 14 percent.

On the basis of these numbers, you can see that the chartered banks are the dominant financial institutions in Canada's monetary system.

■ FIGURE 11.6
The Deposits Behind M1 and M2+

*e*Foundations **11.2**

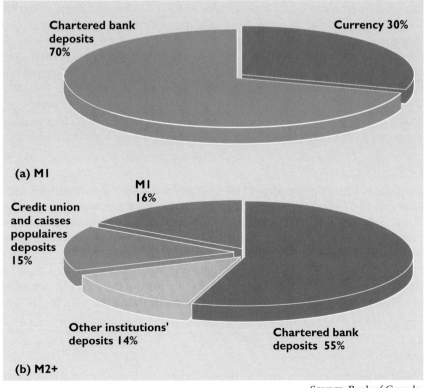

Deposits in chartered banks account for a much larger percentage of the nation's money than do the deposits in other financial institutions.

SOURCE: Bank of Canada.

■ The Economic Functions of Monetary Institutions

The institutions of the monetary system earn their incomes by performing four economic functions that people are willing to pay for:

- Create liquidity
- Lower the costs of lending and borrowing
- Pool risks
- Make payments

Create Liquidity

Liquid asset
An asset that can be easily, and with certainty, converted into money.

A **liquid asset** is an asset that can be easily and with certainty converted into money. Some bank* deposits *are* money. Other deposits are almost money and can be converted into money instantly and safely—they are liquid assets.

A bank creates liquid assets by borrowing short and lending long. Borrowing short means accepting deposits and standing ready to repay them whenever the depositor requests the funds. Lending long means making loan commitments for a long term.

For example, a bank might have accepted $1 million in chequable deposits that could be withdrawn at any time and loaned $1 million to a startup Coffee Shop business for an agreed-upon 5 years. The bank earns part of its income by being able to charge a higher interest rate on a 5-year loan than the interest rate it must pay on a chequable account.

Lower Costs

Banks lower the cost of lending and borrowing funds. People with funds to lend can easily find a bank and make a deposit. Because banks offer a range of types of deposit, it is easy to find the type of deposit that best matches the plans of the depositor.

People who want to borrow can do so by using the facilities offered by banks. Business and personal loans can be tailored to match the cash flows of borrowers. And consumers can obtain instant loans by using credit card facilities.

Again, banks make profits because people are willing to make deposits at much lower interest rates than those available to the banks on their loans. Interest rates on credit card loans are especially high and so are profitable for the banks.

Pool Risks

Lending funds, as banks do, is risky. Some loans don't get repaid. By lending to a large number of businesses and individuals, a bank lowers the average risk it faces. The bank knows the odds of a loan not being repaid like a lottery operator knows the odds of having to pay out on a winning number. The lottery operator offers odds that ensure it ends up with a profit. Similarly, the market for bank loans determines an interest rate that ensures that the amount earned on the loans that do get repaid is sufficiently high to pay for the losses on the ones that don't get repaid. Pooling risks is good not only for the bank but also for its depositors.

---

* We'll use the term "bank" to mean any institution that accepts deposits when there is no gain from distinguishing among these institutions.

Make Payments

Bank deposits are money because they can be transferred from one person or business to another at low cost. The banks provide the payments system that enables these transfers of ownership to occur.

The cheque-clearing system is the main mechanism provided by the banks. Think of this system as a giant delivery service like Purolator that, instead of moving packages overnight to anywhere in the nation, moves cheques and calculates the amounts that each bank must pay or receive based on the totals of the cheques paid by and received by their customers. The banks collect a fee for these cheque-clearing activities.

The credit card payments system is another major payments mechanism operated by the banks. When you buy a new pair of jeans and the checkout clerk swipes your Visa card, a signal goes to the bank that issued your card to get approval for and place a hold on the amount that you are about to spend. Later that day, when the jeans store has some spare time, it transmits the accumulated day's credit card information from its card reader to its own bank and gets its account credited for the day's takings. At that same moment, a message goes from the jeans store's bank to your card-issuing bank (and the banks of all its other customers) that places the charge for your purchase on your credit card account (and likewise for the other customers). All these electronic transactions are performed automatically. The banks collect fees for all these credit card payment activities.

Big Banks

The global banking scene is dominated by European and Japanese banks. Even the United States has only one bank in the world's top ten. The largest Canadian banks are tiny by international standards—less than 40 percent of the size of the tenth-ranked bank on the list in the figure.

Canadian banks say that they must merge in order to become large enough to be competitive on a global scale. But the government of Canada has blocked bank mergers.

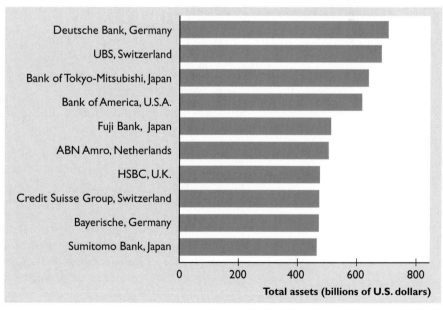

SOURCE: *The Wall Street Journal*, September 27, 1999.

Study Guide pp. 167–169

*e*Foundations 11.2

2 **Describe the monetary system and explain the functions of banks and other monetary institutions.**

Practice Problems 11.2

1. What are the institutions that make up Canada's monetary system?

2. What is a bank's "balancing act"?

3. A bank has the following deposits and assets: $320 in chequable deposits, $896 in savings deposits, $840 in term deposits, $990 in loans to businesses, $400 in outstanding credit card balances, $634 in government bonds and Treasury bills, $2 in currency, and $30 in its deposit account at the Bank of Canada. Calculate the bank's:
   a. Total deposits
   b. Deposits that are part of M1
   c. Deposits that are part of M2+
   d. Loans
   e. Securities
   f. Reserves

Exercises 11.2

1. Explain how a bank makes a profit.

2. A credit union has $400 in chequable deposits, $1,390 in home loans, $856 in savings deposits, $634 in government bonds, $806 in term deposits, $38 in currency, and no deposit at the Bank of Canada. Calculate:
   a. Total deposits
   b. Deposits that are part of M1
   c. Deposits that are part of M2+
   d. Loans
   e. Reserves

3. On which items does the credit union in Exercise 2 pay interest and on which items does it receive interest?

Solutions to Practice Problems 11.2

1. Canada's monetary system consists of the Bank of Canada, chartered banks, credit unions, caisses populaires, and other depository institutions.

2. A bank makes a profit by borrowing from depositors at a low interest rate and lending at a higher interest rate. The bank holds enough reserves to meet withdrawals. The bank's "balancing act" is to balance the profit for its stockholders against security for its depositors.

3a. Total deposits are $320 + $896 + $840 = $2,056.
3b. Deposits that are part of M1 are chequable deposits, $320.
3c. Deposits that are part of M2+ include all deposits, $2,056.
3d. Loans are $990 + $400 = $1,390
3e. Securities are $634—government bonds and Treasury bills.
3f. Reserves are $30 + $2 = $32.

11.3 THE BANK OF CANADA

The **Bank of Canada** is Canada's central bank. A **central bank** is a public authority that provides banking services to banks and regulates financial institutions and markets.

A central bank does not provide banking services to businesses and individual citizens. The Bank of Canada's main customers are chartered banks such as the Royal Bank, the Bank of Montreal, and the CIBC, and the government of Canada. Parliament created the Bank of Canada in 1935, at a time when the economic and financial turmoil of the Great Depression generated pressure for a central agency to regulate and oversee financial markets.

■ Monetary Policy Goals

The Bank of Canada conducts the nation's **monetary policy,** which means that it adjusts the quantity of money in the economy and influences interest rates. The next two chapters explain how monetary policy works. Here, we introduce this large topic by describing the way in which the Bank of Canada formulates and conducts its monetary policy.

The goals of monetary policy can be broken into two parts:

- Ultimate monetary policy objective
- Daily monetary policy target

Ultimate Monetary Policy Objective

An **ultimate monetary policy objective** is a final goal of monetary policy. The Bank of Canada's ultimate monetary policy objective is to keep the inflation rate inside a target range of between 1 percent and 3 percent a year. By keeping the inflation rate steady and low, the Bank seeks to maintain full employment, moderate the business cycle, and contribute towards achieving faster and sustained economic growth.

Complete success in the pursuit of its policy target is impossible, and the Bank of Canada's more modest goal is to improve the performance of the economy and to move it closer to the goals than a hands-off approach would achieve.

The Bank of Canada's policy target is controversial because it places primary emphasis on inflation and secondary emphasis on unemployment, fluctuations, and growth. Some economists would prefer to see the Bank target the unemployment rate or some other real economic variable and be less concerned about the inflation rate. We explore this debate in Chapter 18 (see pp. 438–443).

Actions taken by the Bank of Canada influence the inflation rate with a time lag of around two years. So the inflation rate in 2002 is the result of the Bank's monetary policy actions during 2000. But the Bank needs to know in 2002 whether it is on track to achieve its inflation objective in 2004. To provide information about whether policy is on track, the Bank sets a target that it can check every day.

Daily Monetary Policy Target

A **daily monetary policy target** is a target that the Bank of Canada sets and achieves each day in pursuit of its ultimate inflation target. The daily monetary policy target has changed over the years, and today it is an interest rate called the overnight rate.

Bank of Canada
The central bank of Canada.

Central bank
A public authority that provides banking services to banks and regulates financial institutions and markets.

Monetary policy
Adjusting the quantity of money in the economy.

Ultimate monetary policy objective
The final goal of monetary policy—an inflation rate inside the target range of 1 percent to 3 percent a year.

Daily monetary policy target
A target that the Bank of Canada sets and achieves each day in pursuit of its ultimate inflation target—a target overnight rate.

The Bank of Canada on the World Wide Web

For many years, the Bank of Canada operated behind a veil of secrecy. Monetary policy was considered to be too technical for public discussion and best left to "experts," who conducted their analysis in private and announced their decisions with little explanation. The Bank of Canada was not alone in its secrecy. Central banks around the world behaved in a similar way.

During the 1990s, attitudes changed and central banks around the world became much more engaged with the public. The Bank of Canada played a leading role in this movement towards "openness and transparency."

There was a growing opinion that central bank policies would be more effective if the public and the traders in financial markets understood the economic situation and were well informed about the reasons for the central bank's actions.

The increased openness of central banks coincided with the explosion of the World Wide Web, which provided an ideal means for central banks to communicate directly with the public.

The Bank of Canada launched its Web site (http://www.bankofcanada.ca)

The *overnight rate* is the interest rate on overnight loans between banks and other large financial institutions. These loans arise from the daily operations of the payments system known as the Large Value Transfer System or LVTS.

Large Value Transfer System

Canada's national electronic payments system for very large transactions between the chartered banks, the Bank of Canada, and a few other big financial institutions.

Large Value Transfer System The **Large Value Transfer System** (LVTS) is Canada's national electronic payments system for very large transactions between the chartered banks, the Bank of Canada, and a few other big financial institutions. These payments include those made to settle debts among the banks as cheques are cleared throughout each business day. The LVTS processes payments of more than $100 billion a day—some 20 times the Gross Domestic Product. When a bank sends a payment through the LVTS, that payment is final, just like the payment that you make when you pay by cash.

Banks move funds among themselves throughout each day and, at the end of the day, all the receipts and payments are added up. Some banks have paid more than they've received and are short of funds. Other banks have received more than they have paid and have a surplus of funds. Banks with a surplus make overnight loans to banks with a shortage and the overnight rate is the interest rate on these loans.

The Bank of Canada sets a target for the overnight rate that is consistent with its ultimate target for the inflation rate. To achieve its daily monetary policy target, the Bank uses the policy tools at its disposal. We now describe those tools.

in 1995, originally as an additional means of distributing research papers and other documents. Since that limited start, the site has developed into an outstanding source of data and information. The Bank's Web site is so well designed that it has been rated by London's Lombard Street Research as one of the best. Lombard Street Research says, "…the most impressive aspect of this site is its accessible and educational approach. Whenever an economic or financial term is broached, an explanation is given as to its meaning. Also a wide array of links through the site and to other relevant sites makes it easy to navigate…".

By mid-2001, the Bank's Web site had 95,000 visitors a week. By far the most popular section is the one on foreign exchange rates, which allows the visitor to convert any amount of one currency to its equivalent in another currency at the current exchange rate.

Other popular sections are those on interest rates, government securities, and monetary policy. The site provides a wealth of information on monetary policy with well-written articles that explain policy as well as speeches by the governor and press releases that describe the latest policy actions.

The site also has a popular "Inflation Calculator," which permits quick comparisons of the value of money in different years. Use it to find how much you'd need today to buy what $10 bought in the year you were born.

■ The Bank of Canada's Policy Tools

The Bank of Canada targets the overnight rate by adjusting the reserves of the banking system. This action not only changes the overnight rate but also changes other interest rates as well as the quantity of money floating around the economy. These changes influence the amount of borrowing done by consumers and businesses, which in turn influence expenditure plans and ultimately the inflation rate.

The Bank of Canada can use four policy tools to achieve its objectives:

- Open market operations
- Government deposit shifting
- Bank rate and bankers' deposit rate
- Required reserve ratios

Open Market Operations

An **open market operation** is the purchase or sale of government securities—Government of Canada Treasury bills and bonds—in the open market by the Bank of Canada. These transactions by the Bank of Canada change the reserves of the banks. A change in reserves immediately impacts the amount of overnight borrowing and lending and enables the Bank to hit its overnight rate target. A permanent change in bank reserves has long drawn-out effects on the amount of lending that banks can do and on the spending plans of the banks' customers.

Open market operation
The purchase or sale of Government of Canada securities—Treasury bills and bonds—in the open market by the Bank of Canada.

269

Government Deposit Shifting

The Bank of Canada can shift government deposits between the government's account at the Bank of Canada and its accounts at the various chartered banks. This shifting of deposits affects the banks' reserves, and therefore their ability to make overnight loans. This tool is used on a small scale and only to smooth daily fluctuations in the amount of overnight loans.

Bank Rate and Bankers' Deposit Rate

The **bank rate** is the interest rate at which the Bank of Canada stands ready to lend reserves to chartered banks. The **bankers' deposit rate** is the interest rate that the Bank of Canada pays banks on their deposits at the Bank of Canada. Changes to these rates by the Bank of Canada tend to spread to other interest rates and so influence the amount of lending done by the banks.

Bank rate
The interest rate at which the Bank of Canada stands ready to lend reserves to chartered banks.

Bankers' deposit rate
The interest rate that the Bank of Canada pays banks on their deposits at the Bank of Canada

Required Reserve Ratios

Banks hold reserves so that they can meet the demands of their customers for cash withdrawals and for making payments to other banks when cheques are cleared. These reserves are in the form of currency plus deposits at the Bank of Canada. In many countries, the central bank requires banks to hold reserves amounting to a minimum percentage of their deposits, which is known as the *required reserve ratio*. By increasing or decreasing the required reserve ratio, the central bank can change the amount of lending the banks can do, and therefore change the quantity of money in the economy.

Before 1992, chartered banks in Canada were required to hold a minimum amount of reserves. But today, the Bank of Canada does not use this monetary policy tool—the required reserve ratio is zero.

All of the Bank of Canada's policy tools work by changing the quantity of money in the economy. And they change the quantity of money by changing the monetary base.

■ The Monetary Base

Monetary base
The sum of chartered banks' deposits at the Bank of Canada plus coins and Bank of Canada notes.

The **monetary base** is the sum of the chartered banks' deposits at the Bank of Canada plus coins and Bank of Canada notes. The monetary base is so called because it acts like a base that supports the nation's money. The larger the monetary base, the greater is the quantity of money that it can support. Chapter 12 explains how a change in the monetary base leads to a change in the quantity of money.

In June 2001, the monetary base was $39.5 billion. Figure 11.7 shows how this amount was distributed among its three components: banks' deposits (reserves) at the Bank of Canada were $0.5 billion, Bank of Canada notes were $35.2 billion, and coins were $3.8 billion.

The Bank of Canada's Assets and Liabilities

Bank of Canada notes are the main *liabilities* of the Bank of Canada. Banks' reserves on deposit at the Bank of Canada are another, much smaller, liability. The Bank of Canada's main *assets* are Government of Canada securities; other much smaller assets are the loans that the Bank of Canada makes to the banks.

Why Are Dollar Notes a Liability of the Bank of Canada?

You might be wondering why Bank of Canada notes (dollar bills) are a liability of

■ **FIGURE 11.7**

The Monetary Base and Its Composition   *e*/**Foundations 11.3**

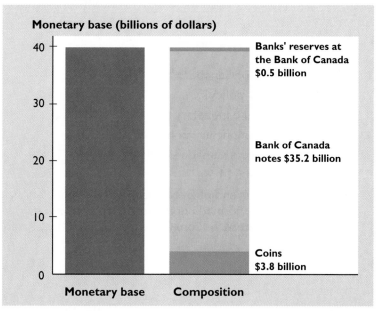

The monetary base is the sum of banks' deposits at the Bank of Canada, Bank of Canada notes, and coins.

SOURCE: Bank of Canada.

the Bank of Canada. When bank notes were invented, they gave their owner a claim on the gold reserves of the issuing bank. These notes were *convertible paper money* and their holders could convert them into gold. So when a bank issued a note, it held itself liable to convert it into gold. The notes were "backed" by gold.

Bank of Canada notes are nonconvertible. A *nonconvertible note* is a bank note that is not convertible into a commodity and that obtains its value by government fiat—hence the term *fiat money*. These notes are the legal liability of the Bank of Canada, and they are "backed" by the Bank of Canada's assets.

■ How the Bank of Canada's Policy Tools Work: A Quick First Look

The next chapter explains how the Bank of Canada's policy tools work and how they change the quantity of money. Here, we'll take a quick first look at the basic ideas.

By selling securities in the open market, the Bank of Canada can mop up bank reserves and decrease the monetary base. The Bank of Canada can also decrease bank reserves and the monetary base by switching some Government of Canada deposits from a chartered bank to itself. By raising the bank rate, the Bank of Canada can make it more costly for the banks to borrow reserves—borrow monetary base—and by raising the interest rate it pays the banks on their own deposits at the Bank of Canada, it can induce the banks to want to hold larger reserves. All of these actions decrease the quantity of money, other things remaining the same.

Similarly, by buying securities in the open market, the Bank of Canada can provide the banks with additional reserves and increase the monetary base. The Bank can also reverse all the other actions described in the previous paragraph to increase bank reserves, the monetary base, and the quantity of money.

Study Guide pp. 169–171

*e*Foundations 11.3

3 **Describe the functions of the Bank of Canada.**

Practice Problems 11.3

1. What is the Bank of Canada?
2. What is monetary policy?
3. What is the ultimate monetary policy objective?
4. What is the daily monetary policy target?
5. What are the Bank of Canada's policy tools?
6. What is the monetary base?
7. Suppose that at the end of December 2005, the monetary base in Canada is $70 billion, Bank of Canada notes are $65 billion, and banks' reserves at the Bank of Canada are $2 billion. Calculate the quantity of coins.

Exercises 11.3

1. What is a central bank?
2. Suppose that at the end of December 2004, the monetary base in Canada is $65 billion, Bank of Canada notes are $60 billion, and coins are $2 billion. What are the chartered banks' reserve deposits at the Bank of Canada?
3. Suppose that at the end of December 2005, the monetary base in Canada is $60 billion, Bank of Canada notes are $55 billion, and there is $2 billion in coins. What are the deposits of the Canadian banks at the Bank of Canada?

Solutions to Practice Problems 11.3

1. The Bank of Canada is the central bank in Canada. A central bank is a public authority that provides banking services to banks and the Canadian government and that regulates the quantity of money and the monetary system.
2. Monetary policy is the adjustment of the quantity of money in the economy.
3. The ultimate objective of monetary policy is to keep the inflation rate inside a target range of 1 percent a year to 3 percent a year.
4. The daily target of monetary policy is the overnight rate, the interest rate on overnight loans among the banks and other large financial institutions.
5. The Bank of Canada's policy tools are open market operations, shifting of government deposits, bank rate, and bankers' deposit rate. Required reserve ratios are a potential tool that is not presently used in Canada.
6. The monetary base is the sum of chartered banks' deposits at the Bank of Canada, Bank of Canada notes, and coins.
7. To calculate the quantity of coin we use the definition of the monetary base: coins plus Bank of Canada notes plus chartered banks' reserves with the Bank of Canada. So coins equal monetary base ($70 billion) minus Bank of Canada notes ($65 billion) minus chartered banks' reserves with the Bank of Canada ($2 billion). At the end of December 2005, the quantity of coins is $3 billion.

CHAPTER CHECKPOINT

Key Points

1 **Define money and describe its functions.**

- Money is anything that serves as a generally accepted means of payment.
- Money serves as a medium of exchange, a unit of account, and a store of value.
- M1 consists of chequable deposits owned by individuals and businesses at the chartered banks plus currency outside the banks. M2+ consists of M1 plus personal savings and notice deposits and deposits at depository institutions other than chartered banks.

2 **Describe the monetary system and explain the functions of banks and other monetary institutions.**

- Chartered banks are by far the largest financial institutions that take deposits and make loans in Canada. The other major depository institutions are credit unions and caisses populaires.
- Banks borrow at a low interest rate, lend at a higher interest rate, and make a profit on the spread between the interest rates that they pay and receive.
- Banks lend most of the funds they receive as deposits and hold only a small amount as reserves to cover withdrawals of cash.

3 **Describe the functions of the Bank of Canada.**

- The Bank of Canada is the central bank of Canada.
- The Bank of Canada targets the inflation rate by setting a daily target for the overnight rate and hitting that target by using open market operations, government deposit switching, and changes in bank rate and the bankers' deposit rate to adjust the monetary base.

Key Terms

Exercises

1. What are the functions of money? Do any of the following items perform any of the functions of money?
    a. Store coupons
    b. A $100 Amazon.com gift certificate
    c. A credit union savings deposit
    d. Frequent flier miles
    e. Credit available on your Visa card
    f. The dollar coins that a coin collector owns
    g. Postage stamps issued to commemorate the 1992 World Series

2. Monica takes $10,000 from her savings account at the Bank of Montreal and puts the funds in a money market mutual fund. What are the immediate changes in M1 and M2+?

3. Terry takes $100 from his chequable account and deposits the $100 in his savings account. What are the immediate changes in M1 and M2+?

4. In December 2000, banks in Australia had deposits of $407 billion and had a reserve ratio of 4 percent. The banks had $4.2 billion in currency. How much did the banks have in reserves at the Reserve Bank of Australia (the Australian central bank)?

5. In December 2005, the Bank of Canada had issued $11 billion in currency and had:
    > Chartered banks' deposits, $3 billion
    > Government bonds, $10 billion
    > Treasury bills, $4 billion

    The Canadian banks had chequable deposits owned by individuals and businesses of $400 billion, personal savings deposits and term deposits of $600 billion, and currency of $1 billion. Calculate:
    a. The chartered banks' reserves
    b. The monetary base
    c. M1
    d. M2+

6. In Mexico in January 2001, the Banco de México (the central bank of Mexico) reported that notes and coins were 175 billion pesos. The Mexican banks had chequable deposits owned by individuals and businesses of 418 billion pesos, personal savings deposits and term deposits of 1,782 billion pesos, and currency of 28 billion pesos. The Mexican banks had deposits at the Banco de México of 186 billion pesos. Calculate:
    a. Banks' reserves
    b. The monetary base
    c. M1
    d. M2+

 7. Use the link on your Foundations Web site to visit the Web site of the Bank of Canada. What was the most recent change that the Bank of Canada made to the bank rate and what were the reasons for that change?

Money Creation and Control

When you have completed your study of this chapter, you will be able to:

1. Explain how banks create money by making loans.

2. Explain how the Bank of Canada influences the quantity of money.

Making imitation dollar bills is a serious crime. But creating billions of dollars' worth of money is a perfectly legal activity that banks perform every day. In this chapter, you're going to learn how banks create money by making loans.

This chapter builds on what you learned in Chapter 11. There, you saw that most of the money in Canada today consists of deposits in chartered banks and other depository institutions. You also learned about the structure of the Bank of Canada and the tools it uses to control the quantity of money that circulates in Canada.

You're now going to see exactly how money gets created and how the Bank of Canada controls its quantity. Understanding these processes is crucial to understanding how inflation occurs and how it can be kept under control. It is also crucial to understanding how the Bank of Canada tries to smooth the business cycle.

First, we'll study the links between the banks' reserves, the quantity of loans that banks make, and the quantity of deposits that they create. Then we'll learn how the Bank of Canada uses open market operations and other tools to influence the quantity of money.

12.1 HOW BANKS CREATE MONEY

Banks[*] create money out of thin air! But this doesn't mean that they have smoke-filled back rooms in which counterfeiters are busily working. Remember, most money is bank deposits, not currency. Banks create these deposits, and they do so by making loans. But they cannot create any amount of money they wish. The amount of deposits they can create is limited by their reserves.

■ Creating a Bank

The easiest way to see how banks create money is to work through the process of creating a bank. Suppose that you and your friends decide to create the Virtual College Bank, an Internet bank that specializes in banking services for college students. You will need to go through the following eight steps:

- Obtain a charter to operate a bank
- Raise some financial capital
- Buy some equipment and computer programs
- Accept deposits
- Establish a reserve account at the Bank of Canada
- Clear cheques
- Buy government securities
- Make loans

Obtaining a Charter

Your first task is to obtain a charter from Parliament to operate a bank. Obtaining a charter to set up a bank is not a quick and simple matter in Canada. You will need the assistance of legal and public relations experts as well as a solid business plan and substantial powers of persuasion. We'll assume that you've obtained your charter and are now ready to start your banking business.

Raising Financial Capital

Balance sheet
A statement that summarizes assets (amounts owned) and liabilities (amounts owed).

Your next task is to get some funds. You figure that you can open your bank with $200,000, so Virtual College Bank creates 2,000 shares, each worth $100, and sells these shares in your local community. Your bank now has a **balance sheet**—a statement that summarizes its assets and liabilities. The bank's assets are what it owns, and its liabilities are the claims against it, or what it owes, and its owners' equity. Table 12.1 shows your new bank's first balance sheet.

■ **TABLE 12.1**
Virtual College Bank's Balance Sheet #1

Assets		Liabilities	
Cash	$200,000	Owners' equity	$200,000

You are now ready to take your third step.

---

[*]In this chapter, we'll use the term "bank" to include chartered banks and financial institutions whose deposits are part of the money supply.

Eye On The PAST

The "Invention" of Banking

Goldsmiths and their customers stumbled upon a brilliant idea that led to the creation of the first banks. You will gain useful insights into modern banks and the way they create money by looking at these early banks.

Because gold is valuable and easy to steal, the goldsmiths of sixteenth-century Europe had well-guarded safes in which to keep their own gold. They also rented space in their safes to artisans and others who wanted to put their gold in safekeeping. The goldsmiths issued a receipt to the owners of the gold entitling them to reclaim their "deposits" on demand. These receipts were similar to the coat check token you get at a theatre or museum.

Isabella has a gold receipt that shows that she has deposited 100 ounces of gold with Samuel Goldsmith. She is going to use her gold to buy some land from Henry.

Isabella can make this transaction in one of two ways: She can visit Samuel, collect her gold, and hand the gold to Henry. Or she can give Henry her gold receipt, which will then enable Henry to claim the 100 ounces of gold from Samuel Goldsmith.

It is obviously much more convenient to pass the receipt to Henry. It is a simpler and safer transaction. When Henry wants to use the gold to buy something, he too can pass the receipt on to someone else.

So Samuel Goldsmith's gold receipt is circulating as a means of payment. It is money!

After some years, Samuel notices that the gold that people have placed in his safe-keeping never leaves his vault. The receipts circulate, and the gold simply sits in the safe.

Samuel realizes that he can lend people gold receipts and charge them interest on the receipts. So he writes some receipts for gold that he does-

n't have and lends these receipts.

After some further years, when many goldsmiths are doing what Samuel is doing, they begin to compete with each other for gold deposits, and instead of charging rent to gold owners, they start to pay interest on gold deposits.

Samuel and his fellow goldsmiths have made the transition from being goldsmiths to being bankers.

As long as they don't issue too many gold receipts, they will always be able to honour requests from depositors who wish to reclaim their gold.

Buying Equipment

You buy some office equipment, a server, banking database software, and a high-speed Internet connection. These items cost you $200,000. Table 12.2 shows your bank's new balance sheet.

■ TABLE 12.2
Virtual College Bank's Balance Sheet #2

Assets		Liabilities	
Cash	$0		
Equipment	$200,000	Owners' equity	$200,000

Accepting Deposits

You are now ready to start accepting deposits. You pass the word around that you are offering the best terms available and the lowest charges on chequable deposits. Deposits begin to roll in. After a hectic day, you have accepted $120,000 of deposits. Table 12.3 shows Virtual College Bank's new balance sheet.

■ **TABLE 12.3**

Virtual College Bank's Balance Sheet #3

Assets		Liabilities	
Cash	$120,000	Chequable deposits	$120,000
Equipment	$200,000	Owners' equity	$200,000

The deposits at Virtual College Bank are now part of the money supply. But the quantity of money in the economy has not increased. People have deposited either currency or cheques drawn on other banks. To keep the story simple, we'll suppose that all the deposits are currency. So currency outside the banks has decreased by $120,000, and chequable deposits have increased by $120,000.

Establishing a Reserve Account

Now that Virtual College Bank has deposits, it needs a reserve account at the Bank of Canada. So Virtual College Bank now opens an account at the Bank of Canada and deposits in that account all its cash. Table 12.4 shows Virtual College Bank's new balance sheet.

■ **TABLE 12.4**

Virtual College Bank's Balance Sheet #4

Assets		Liabilities	
Cash	$0		
Reserves at Bank of Canada	$120,000	Chequable deposits	$120,000
Equipment	$200,000	Owners' equity	$200,000

Reserve ratio
The proportion of a bank's total deposits that are held in reserves.

Desired reserve ratio
The ratio of reserves to deposits that banks wish to hold so that they are sure to have enough cash to cover withdrawals by their customers.

Reserves: Actual and Desired You saw in Chapter 11 that banks don't keep $100 in bills for every $100 that people have deposited with them. In fact, a typical bank today has reserves of a bit less than $2 for every $100 of deposits. But there's no need for panic. These reserve levels are adequate for ordinary business needs.

The proportion of a bank's total deposits that are held in reserves is called the **reserve ratio.** Virtual College Bank has reserves of $120,000 and deposits of $120,000, so its reserve ratio is 100 percent.

The **desired reserve ratio** is the ratio of reserves to deposits that banks wish to hold so that they are sure to have enough cash to cover withdrawals by their customers. We'll suppose that the desired reserve ratio of Virtual College Bank is 25 percent, a much higher percentage than banks actually keep (see Chapter 11, p. 261).

A bank's *desired reserves* are equal to its deposits multiplied by its desired reserve ratio. So Virtual College Bank's desired reserves are:

Desired reserves = $120,000 × 25 ÷ 100 = $30,000.

Actual reserves minus desired reserves are **excess reserves.** Virtual College Bank's excess reserves are:

Excess reserves
Actual reserves minus desired reserves.

Excess reserves = $120,000 − $30,000 = $90,000.

Whenever banks have excess reserves, they are able to make loans. But before Virtual College Bank takes that step, it needs to learn how to clear cheques.

Clearing Cheques

Virtual College Bank's depositors want to be able to make and receive payments by cheque. So when Virtual College depositor Jay writes a cheque for $20,000 to buy some computers from Hal's PCs, which has a chequable deposit at the CIBC, funds must move from Jay's account at your bank to Hal's account at CIBC. In the process, Virtual College loses reserves and CIBC gains reserves. Figure 12.1 tracks the balance sheet changes that occur.

When Hal's PCs banks Jay's cheque at CIBC, CIBC sends the cheque to the Bank of Canada for collection. The Bank of Canada increases CIBC's reserves and decreases Virtual College's reserves by $20,000—see Figure 12.1(a). CIBC now has an extra $20,000 in its reserves at the Bank of Canada, and it increases Hal's PCs' chequable deposit by $20,000. CIBC's assets and liabilities have both increased by $20,000 in Figure 12.1(b). The Bank of Canada returns the cleared cheque to Virtual College. Virtual College now has $20,000 less in its reserve account, and it decreases Jay's chequable deposit by $20,000. Virtual College's assets and liabilities have both decreased by $20,000 in Figure 12.1(c).

■ FIGURE 12.1
Clearing a Cheque

*e*Foundations **12.1**

Bank of Canada

Assets		Liabilities	
		CIBC reserves	+$20,000
		Virtual College reserves	−$20,000

(a) Change in Bank of Canada's balance sheet

CIBC

Assets		Liabilities	
Reserves at the Bank of Canada	+$20,000	Chequable deposits	+$20,000

(b) Change in CIBC's balance sheet

Virtual College Bank

Assets		Liabilities	
Reserves at the Bank of Canada	−$20,000	Chequable deposits	−$20,000

(c) Change in Virtual College Bank's balance sheet

(a) CIBC sends a $20,000 cheque for collection to the Bank of Canada. The Bank of Canada increases CIBC's reserves and decreases Virtual College's reserves by $20,000.

(b) CIBC increases Hal's PCs chequable deposit by $20,000. CIBC's assets and liabilities have both increased by $20,000.

(c) Virtual College decreases Jay's chequable deposit by $20,000. Virtual College's assets and liabilities have both decreased by $20,000.

The quantity of money is unaffected by these transactions. Chequable deposits have increased at CIBC and decreased at Virtual College, but total deposits are unchanged. Total bank reserves are also unaffected. CIBC's reserves have increased and Virtual College's reserves have decreased by the same amount.

Virtual College Bank is now ready to use some of its reserves to earn an income. It buys some government securities—government bonds and Treasury bills.

Buying Government Securities

Government securities provide Virtual College with an income and a safe asset that is easily converted back into reserves when necessary. Suppose that Virtual College decides to buy $60,000 worth of government securities. On the same day, CIBC decides to sell $60,000 of government securities. In reality, a bond broker will match CIBC's sale with Virtual College's purchase.

Figure 12.2 tracks the effects of this transaction on the balance sheets of the two banks and the Bank of Canada. Virtual College gives CIBC a cheque for $60,000, and CIBC transfers the government bonds to Virtual College. CIBC sends the cheque to the Bank of Canada for collection. The Bank of Canada increases

---

FIGURE 12.2
Buying Government Securities

*e*Foundations 12.1

(a) Virtual College buys $60,000 worth of government bonds from CIBC and pays by cheque. The Bank of Canada increases CIBC's reserves by $60,000 and decreases Virtual College's reserves by the same amount.

(b) CIBC's reserves have increased and its government securities have decreased by $60,000.

(c) Virtual College's reserves have decreased and its government securities have increased by the $60,000.

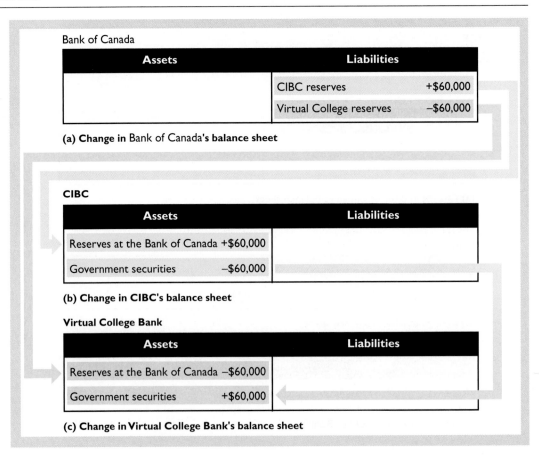

Bank of Canada

Assets	Liabilities	
	CIBC reserves	+$60,000
	Virtual College reserves	−$60,000

(a) Change in Bank of Canada's balance sheet

CIBC

Assets		Liabilities
Reserves at the Bank of Canada	+$60,000	
Government securities	−$60,000	

(b) Change in CIBC's balance sheet

Virtual College Bank

Assets		Liabilities
Reserves at the Bank of Canada	−$60,000	
Government securities	+$60,000	

(c) Change in Virtual College Bank's balance sheet

CIBC's reserves by $60,000 and decreases Virtual College's reserves by the same amount in Figure 12.2(a).

CIBC's reserves have increased and its government securities have decreased by the same $60,000 in Figure 12.2(b). Virtual College's reserves have decreased and its government securities have increased by the same $60,000 in Figure 12.2(c).

After all the transactions we've just followed in Figures 12.1 and 12.2, Virtual College's balance sheet looks like that in Table 12.5.

■ **TABLE 12.5**

Virtual College Bank's Balance Sheet #5

Assets		Liabilities	
Reserves at the Bank of Canada	$40,000	Chequable deposits	$100,000
Government securities	$60,000	Owners' equity	$200,000
Equipment	$200,000		
Total assets	$300,000	Total liabilities	$300,000

With deposits of $100,000 and a desired reserve ratio of 25 percent, Virtual College's desired reserves are $25,000. Because it currently has $40,000 in reserves, Virtual College can make some loans.

Making Loans

With reserves of $40,000 and desired reserves of $25,000, Virtual College has excess reserves of $15,000. So the bank decides to make loans of this amount. Table 12.6 shows the bank's balance sheet on the day the bank makes these loans. Loans of $15,000 are added to the bank's assets. Loans are an asset to the bank because the borrower is committed to repaying the loan on an agreed-upon schedule. The bank places the $15,000 loaned in the chequable deposit accounts of the borrowers. So the bank's chequable deposits increase by $15,000 to $115,000.

■ **TABLE 12.6**

Virtual College Bank's Balance Sheet #6

Assets		Liabilities	
Reserves at the Bank of Canada	$40,000	Chequable deposits	$115,000
Government securities	$60,000	Owners' equity	$200,000
Loans	$15,000		
Equipment	$200,000		
Total assets	$315,000	Total liabilities	$315,000

The bank has now created some money. Chequable deposits have increased by the amount of the loans, so the quantity of money has increased by $15,000. And although Virtual College has made loans equal to its excess reserves of $15,000, it still has those reserves! Because its deposits have increased, its desired reserves have also increased. They are now 25 percent of $115,000, or $28,750. So the bank now has excess reserves of $11,250.

Before you get too excited and decide to lend another $11,250, let's see what happens when the borrowers of $15,000 that you've just loaned start to spend their loans.

Spending a Loan To spend their loans, the borrowers write cheques on their chequable deposits at Virtual College. Let's assume that they spend the entire $15,000. Most likely, the people to whom these cheques are paid do not bank at Virtual College. That's what we'll assume. So when these cheques are cleared, transactions like those that we described above take place. The receiving banks send the cheques to the Bank of Canada for collection. The Bank of Canada increases the reserves of the receiving banks by $15,000 and decreases the reserves of Virtual College by $15,000. Virtual College's balance sheet now looks like that in Table 12.7.

■ **TABLE 12.7**

Virtual College Bank's Balance Sheet #7

Assets		Liabilities	
Reserves at the Bank of Canada $25,000		Chequable deposits	$100,000
Government securities	$60,000	Owners' equity	$200,000
Loans	$15,000		
Equipment	$200,000		
Total assets	$300,000	Total liabilities	$300,000

Both reserves and deposits have decreased by $15,000 because this amount has been paid to people with accounts in other banks. If some of the cheques drawn were paid to customers of Virtual College, deposits and reserves would have fallen by less than the full $15,000 and the bank would still have some excess reserves. But in the situation shown in Table 12.7, the bank is fully loaned—its reserves are just sufficient to meet its desired reserve ratio.

But the banks that received the deposits that Virtual College has lost have also received reserves. These banks now have excess reserves, so they can make some loans. And these loans will create some more money. Also, when Virtual College bought government securities from the CIBC, the reserves of the CIBC increased by $60,000. So other banks now have reserves of $75,000 that they didn't have before that they could now lend. So yet more money can be created.

If you told the loan officer at your own bank that she creates money, she wouldn't believe you. People who work in banks see themselves as lending the money they receive from others, but (unless they've studied economics) they don't see the entire process, so they don't realize that they create money. But in fact, even though *each bank* lends only what it receives, *the banking system* creates money. To see how, let's see what happens in the entire banking system when one bank receives some new reserves.

■ **The Limits to Money Creation**

Figure 12.3 is going to keep track of what is happening in the process of money creation by a banking system in which each bank has a desired reserve ratio of 25 percent. We'll start the process off with every bank holding exactly its desired reserves. Then Harry Potter, after years of wizardry, decides to go to school in Canada. He takes $100,000 of bank notes from under his mattress and deposits them at Virtual College Bank. Virtual College now has $100,000 of new deposits and $100,000 of new reserves. With a desired reserve ratio of 25 percent, the bank's desired reserves are $25,000. So the bank makes a loan of $75,000 to Amy. Then Amy writes a cheque for $75,000 to buy a copy-shop franchise from Barb. At this point, Virtual College has a new deposit of $100,000, a new loan of $75,000, and new reserves of $25,000. You can see this situation in Figure 12.3.

For Virtual College, that is the end of the story. But it's not the end of the story for the banking system. Barb deposits her cheque for $75,000 in the CIBC, where deposits and reserves increase by $75,000. The CIBC puts 25 percent of its increase in deposits ($18,750) into reserves and lends $56,250 to Bob. And Bob writes a cheque to Carl to pay off a business loan.

Figure 12.3 shows the state of play at the end of round 2. Total bank reserves have increased by $43,750 ($25,000 plus $18,750), total loans have increased by $131,250 ($75,000 plus $56,250), and total deposits have increased by $175,000 ($100,000 plus $75,000).

When Carl takes his cheque to the Bank of Montreal, its deposits and reserves increase by $56,250. The Bank of Montreal keeps $14,063 in reserves and lends $42,187. This process continues until there are no excess reserves in the banking

---

◼ FIGURE 12.3
The Multiple Creation of Bank Deposits

*e*Foundations 12.1

Round	The sequence	The running tally — Reserves	Loans	Deposits
	Deposit $100,000			
1. Virtual college	Reserve $25,000 — Loan $75,000	$25,000	$75,000	$100,000
	Deposit $75,000			
2. CIBC	Reserve $18,750 — Loan $56,250	$43,750	$131,250	$175,000
	Deposit $56,250			
3. Bank of Montreal	Reserve $14,063 — Loan $42,187	$57,813	$173,437	$231,250
	Deposit $42,187			
4. First e-bank	Reserve $10,547 — Loan $31,640	$68,360	$205,077	$273,437
	and so on ...	• • • ▼ $100,000	• • • ▼ $300,000	• • • ▼ $400,000

When a bank receives deposits, it keeps 25 percent in reserves and lends 75 percent. The amount loaned becomes a new deposit at another bank. The next bank in the sequence keeps 25 percent and lends 75 percent, and the process continues until the banking system has created enough deposits to eliminate its excess reserves. The running tally tells us the deposits and loans created at each stage. At the end of the process, an additional $100,000 of reserves creates an additional $400,000 of deposits.

system. But the process takes a lot of further steps. Figure 12.3 shows one additional step. The figure also shows the final tallies: Reserves increase by $100,000, loans increase by $300,000, and deposits increase by $400,000.

The sequence in Figure 12.3 is the first four rounds of the process. To work out the entire process, look closely at the numbers in the figure. At each stage, the loan is 75 percent (0.75) of the previous loan and the deposit is 0.75 of the previous deposit. Let's call that proportion L ($L = 0.75$). The complete sequence is:

$$1; L; L^2; L^3; L^4; \text{ and so on.}$$

Remember, L is a fraction, so at each stage in this sequence, the amount of new loans and new deposits gets smaller. The total increase in deposits when the process ends is the sum of the above sequence, which is

$$\frac{1}{1 - L} \times \text{Initial increase in reserves.}$$

If we use the numbers from the example, the total increase in deposits is

$$\$100,000 + 75,000 + 56,250 + 42,187 + \ldots$$

$$= \$100,000 \times (1 + 0.75 + 0.5625 + 0.42187 + \ldots)$$

$$= \$100,000 \times (1 + 0.75 + 0.75^2 + 0.75^3 + \ldots)$$

$$= \$100,000 \times \frac{1}{(1 - 0.75)}$$

$$= \$100,000 \times \frac{1}{0.25}$$

$$= \$100,000 \times 4.$$

$$= \$400,000.$$

So even though each bank lends only the money it receives, the banking system as a whole does create money by making loans.

■ The Deposit Multiplier

The **deposit multiplier** is the number by which an increase in bank reserves is multiplied to find the resulting increase in bank deposits. That is,

$$\text{Change in deposits} = \text{Deposit multiplier} \times \text{Change in reserves.}$$

In the example that we've just worked through, the deposit multiplier is 4. The $100,000 increase in reserves brought a $400,000 increase in deposits. The deposit multiplier is linked to the desired reserve ratio by the following equation:

$$\text{Deposit multiplier} = \frac{1}{\text{Desired reserve ratio}}.$$

In the example, the desired reserve ratio is 25 percent, or 0.25. That is,

$$\text{Deposit multiplier} = \frac{1}{0.25} = 4.$$

CHECKPOINT 12.1

1 Explain how banks create money by making loans.

Study Guide pp. 176–179

*e*Foundations 12.1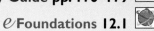

Practice Problems 12.1

1. How do banks create new deposits by making loans, and what factors limit the amount of deposits and loans they can create?

2. The desired reserve ratio is 0.1, and banks have no excess reserves. Jamie deposits $100 in his bank. Calculate:
    a. The bank's excess reserves as soon as Jamie makes the deposit.
    b. The deposit multiplier.
    c. The maximum increase in deposits.

Exercises 12.1

1. Your bank manager tells you that he does not create money. He just lends the money that people deposit in the bank. Explain to him how he does create money.

2. If the banking system receives new deposits of $100 million, what determines the maximum amount of new money that the banks can create?

3. If banks have a desired reserve ratio of 0.2 and Erin deposits $50 of cash in her bank deposit, calculate:
    a. The bank's excess reserves as soon as Erin makes her deposit.
    b. The deposit multiplier.
    c. The maximum increase in deposits.

Solutions to Practice Problems 12.1

1. Banks can make loans when they have excess reserves—reserves in excess of those desired. When a bank makes a loan, it creates a new deposit for the person who receives the loan. The bank uses its excess reserves to create new deposits. The amount of loans that the bank can make, and therefore the amount of new deposits that it can create, is limited by two things: the amount of excess reserves and the desired reserve ratio.

2a. The bank's excess reserves are $90. When deposits increase by $100, the bank desires to keep 10 percent of the deposit as reserves. That is, desired reserves increase by $10 and the bank has $90 of excess reserves.

2b. The deposit multiplier equals 1/Desired reserve ratio, which is 1/0.1 or 10.

2c. The maximum increase in deposits is $1,000. When reserves increase by $100, the deposit multiplier determines the maximum increase in deposits of the banking system. Increase in deposits = Deposit multiplier × Increase in reserves. The deposit multiplier is 10. So with the $100 increase in reserves, deposits can increase by $1,000.

12.2 INFLUENCING THE QUANTITY OF MONEY

The monetary policy actions of the Bank of Canada influence the quantity of money in the economy. The Bank of Canada uses three of the monetary policy tools that we described in Chapter 11 (see pp. 269–270):

- Government deposit shifting
- Changes in bank rate and the bankers' deposit rate
- Open market operations

The tools work by changing the ability or the willingness of the banks to make the loans that create money. Let's see how these three tools work.

■ How Government Deposit Shifting Works

The Government of Canada has deposits in both the Bank of Canada and the chartered banks. The Bank of Canada can shift these funds between itself and the chartered banks. If the Bank of Canada shifts government funds from itself to the banks, the banks' reserves and ability to make loans increase. If the Bank of Canada shifts government funds from the banks to itself, the banks' reserves and ability to make loans decrease. The Bank of Canada uses this policy tool on a small scale to fine-tune the quantity of bank reserves from one day to another.

■ How the Bank Rate and Bankers' Deposit Rate Work

The Bank of Canada sets the bank rate (the interest rate that the Bank of Canada charges chartered banks when it lends them reserves) and the bankers' deposit rate (the rate that the Bank of Canada pays the chartered banks on their reserves deposited at the Bank of Canada). The bankers' deposit rate is set at one-half of a percentage point below the bank rate. The *overnight rate* lies between these two interest rates because a chartered bank would borrow from the Bank of Canada rather than from another bank if the bank rate was below the overnight rate and would add to its reserves at the Bank of Canada rather than lend them to another bank if the bankers' deposit rate was above the overnight rate.

If the Bank of Canada raises these interest rates, the banks increase their reserves and decrease loans. And if the Bank of Canada lowers these interest rates, the banks decrease their reserves and increase loans.

■ How Open Market Operations Work

When the Bank of Canada *buys* government of Canada securities in an open market operation, it pays for them with newly created bank reserves. With more reserves in the banks, the supply of overnight loans increases, the demand for overnight loans decreases, and the overnight rate falls. When the Bank of Canada *sells* securities in an open market operation, buyers pay for the securities with bank reserves. With smaller reserves in the banks, the supply of overnight loans decreases, the demand for overnight loans increases, and the overnight rate rises. The Bank of Canada sets a target for the overnight rate and conducts open market operations on the scale needed to hit its target.

A change in the overnight rate is the first effect of an open market operation. With increased reserves, the banks can increase their lending and create even more money. With decreased reserves, the banks must decrease their lending, which decreases the quantity of money. We'll now study these other effects.

The Bank of Canada Buys Securities

Suppose the Bank of Canada buys $100 million of government of Canada securities in the open market. There are two cases to consider, depending on who sells the securities. A chartered bank might sell some of its securities, or a person or business that is not a bank—the general public—might sell. The outcome is essentially the same in the two cases, but you might need to be convinced of this fact. So we'll study the two cases, starting with the simpler case in which a chartered bank sells securities. (The seller will be someone who believes that the Bank of Canada is offering a good price for securities so that it is profitable to make the sale.)

A Chartered Bank Sells   When the Bank of Canada buys $100 million of securities from the Royal Bank, two things happen:

1. The Royal Bank has $100 million less in securities, and the Bank of Canada has $100 million more in securities.
2. To pay for the securities, the Bank of Canada increases the Royal Bank's reserve account at the Bank of Canada by $100 million.

Figure 12.4 shows the effects of these actions on the balance sheets of the Bank of Canada and the Royal Bank. Ownership of the securities passes to the Bank of Canada, so the Royal Bank's securities decrease by $100 million and the Bank of Canada's securities increase by $100 million, as shown by the red-to-blue arrow running from the Royal Bank to the Bank of Canada. The Bank of Canada increases the Royal Bank's reserves by $100 million, as shown by the green arrow running from the Bank of Canada to the Royal Bank. This action increases the monetary base and increases the reserves of the banking system.

The chartered bank's total assets remain constant, but the composition of them changes. Its holdings of government securities decrease by $100 million, and its reserves increase by $100 million. The bank can use these additional reserves to make loans. When the bank makes loans, the quantity of money increases by the process that we described in the previous section.

FIGURE 12.4
The Bank of Canada Buys Securities from a Chartered Bank

e Foundations **12.2**

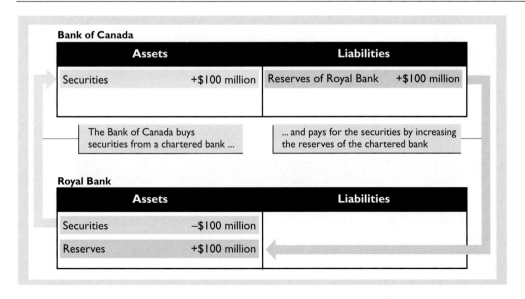

We've just seen that when the Bank of Canada buys government securities from a bank, the bank's reserves increase. What happens if the Bank of Canada buys government securities from the public—say, from London Life, an insurance company?

The Non-bank Public Sells   When the Bank of Canada buys $100 million of securities from London Life, three things happen:

1. London Life has $100 million less in securities, and the Bank of Canada has $100 million more in securities.
2. The Bank of Canada pays for the securities with a cheque for $100 million drawn on itself, which London Life deposits in its account at the Royal Bank.
3. The Royal Bank collects payment of this cheque from the Bank of Canada, and the Royal Bank's reserves increase by $100 million.

Figure 12.5 shows the effects of these actions on the balance sheets of the Bank of Canada, London Life, and the Royal Bank. Ownership of the securities passes from London Life to the Bank of Canada, so London Life's securities decrease by $100 million and the Bank of Canada's securities increase by $100 million (red-to-blue arrow). The Bank of Canada pays for the securities with a cheque payable to London Life, which London Life deposits in the Royal Bank. This payment increases the Royal Bank's reserves by $100 million (green arrow). It also increases

---

■ **FIGURE 12.5**

The Bank of Canada Buys Securities from the Public

e/**Foundations 12.2**

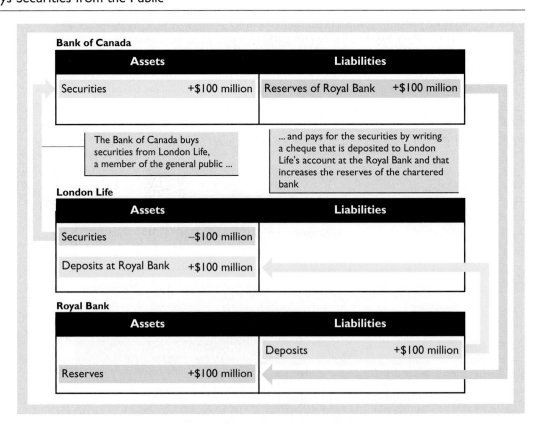

London Life's deposit at the Royal Bank by $100 million (blue arrow). Just as when the Bank of Canada buys securities from a bank, this action increases the monetary base and increases the reserves of the banking system.

London Life has the same total assets as before, but the composition of them has changed. It now has more money and fewer securities. The Royal Bank's reserves increase, and so do its deposits—both by $100 million. Because bank reserves and deposits have increased by the same amount, the bank has excess reserves, which it can use to make loans. When it makes loans, the quantity of money increases, as in the previous section.

We've worked through what happens when the Bank of Canada buys government securities from either a bank or the public. When the Bank of Canada sells securities, the transactions that we've just traced operate in reverse.

The Bank of Canada Sells Securities

If the Bank of Canada sells $100 million of government of Canada securities in the open market, the most likely buyer is a person or business other than a bank. (A bank would buy them only if it had excess reserves and it couldn't find a better use for its funds.)

When the Bank of Canada sells $100 million of securities to London Life:

1. London Life has $100 million more in securities, and the Bank of Canada has $100 million less in securities.
2. London Life pays for the securities with a cheque for $100 million drawn on its deposit account at the Royal Bank.
3. The Bank of Canada collects payment of this cheque from the Royal Bank by decreasing its reserves by $100 million.

These actions decrease the monetary base and decrease the reserves of the banking system. The Royal Bank now has fewer reserves than it desires, so it borrows reserves in the overnight loans market to meet its desired reserve ratio.

The changes in the balance sheets of the Bank of Canada and the banks that we've just described are not the end of the story about the effects of an open market operation; they are just the beginning. A multiplier effect on the quantity of money now begins. To study this multiplier effect of an open market operation on the quantity of money, we will build on the link between bank reserves and bank deposits that you studied in the previous section.

■ The Multiplier Effect of an Open Market Operation

An open market purchase that increases bank reserves also increases the *monetary base*. The increase in the monetary base equals the amount of the open market purchase, and initially, it equals the increase in bank reserves. To see why, recall that the monetary base is the sum of the chartered banks' deposits at the Bank of Canada plus coins and bank notes outside the Bank of Canada. An open market purchase increases the monetary base, by increasing the banks' reserves at the Bank of Canada by the amount of the open market purchase. Nothing else changes, so the monetary base increases by the amount of the open market purchase.

If the Bank of Canada buys securities from the chartered banks, the quantity of deposits (and the quantity of money) does not change. If the Bank of Canada buys securities from the public, the quantity of deposits (and the quantity of money) increases by the same amount as the increase in bank reserves. Either way, the banks have excess reserves that they now start to lend.

November 8, 2001

Governor's Address Suggests More Rate Cuts to Come

Governor David Dodge said that the Bank of Canada would be following "policies that are fairly aggressive about supporting economic growth." He added that "there's lots of room to move [on interest rates]."

NATIONAL POST

Questions
1. What would the Bank of Canada do if it wanted to increase the quantity of money?
2. What would the Bank of Canada do if it wanted to decrease the quantity of money?
3. In the conditions of November 2001, do you think the Bank of Canada would want to increase or decrease the quantity of money? Provide your reasons.

 *e*Foundations **12.2**

Figure 12.6 illustrates the multiplier effect of an open market purchase of securities from the banks. The following sequence of events takes place:

- An open market purchase creates excess reserves.
- Banks lend excess reserves.
- Bank deposits increase.
- The quantity of money increases.
- New money is used to make payments.
- Some of the new money remains in deposits in banks.
- Some of the new money is held as currency—a currency drain.
- Banks' desired reserves increase.
- Excess reserves decrease but remain positive.

This sequence is similar to the one you studied in the previous section of this chapter but with one addition: the currency drain. When banks use excess reserves to make loans, bank deposits increase but currency held outside the banks also increases. An increase in currency held outside the banks is called the **currency drain.** The currency drain does not change the monetary base. Bank reserves decrease, currency increases, and the monetary base remains the same. But a currency drain decreases the amount of money that banks can create from a given increase in the monetary base because currency drains from their reserves and decreases the excess reserves available.

The sequence of rounds described in Figure 12.6 repeats, but each round begins with a smaller quantity of excess reserves than did the previous one. The process ends when excess reserves have been eliminated.

Currency drain
An increase in currency held outside the banks.

■ **FIGURE 12.6**

A Round in the Multiplier Process Following an Open Market Purchase

*e*Foundations **12.2**

❶ An open market operation increases bank reserves and ❷ creates excess reserves. ❸ Banks lend the excess reserves, ❹ new deposits are created, and ❺ the quantity of money increases. ❻ New money is used to make payments. ❼ Households and firms receive payments, keep some on deposit in banks, and keep some in the form of currency— ❽ a currency drain. The increase in bank deposits increases banks' reserves but also ❾ increases banks' desired reserves.

Desired reserves increase by less than actual reserves, so the banks still have some excess reserves, though less than before. The process repeats until excess reserves have been eliminated.

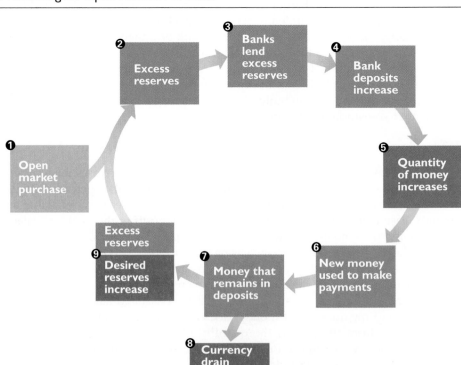

Figure 12.7 keeps track of the magnitudes of the increases in reserves, loans, deposits, currency, and money that result from an open market purchase of $100,000. In this figure, the currency drain is 33.33 percent of money and the desired reserve ratio is 10 percent of deposits. These numbers are assumed in order to keep the arithmetic simple.

The Bank of Canada buys $100,000 of securities from the banks. The banks' reserves increase by this amount, but deposits do not change. The banks have excess reserves of $100,000, and they lend those reserves. When the banks lend $100,000 of excess reserves, $66,667 remains in the banks as deposits and $33,333 drains off and is held outside the banks as currency. The quantity of money has now increased by $100,000—the increase in deposits plus the increase in currency holdings.

The increased bank deposits of $66,667 generate an increase in desired reserves of 10 percent of that amount, which is $6,667. Actual reserves have increased by the same amount as the increase in deposits—$66,667. So the banks now have excess reserves of $60,000. At this stage, we have gone around the circle shown in Figure 12.6 once. The process that we've just described repeats but begins with excess reserves of $60,000. Figure 12.7 shows the next two rounds. At the end of the process, the quantity of money has increased by a multiple of the increase in the monetary base. In this case, the increase is $250,000, which is 2.5 times the increase in the monetary base.

An open market *sale* works similarly to an open market *purchase*, but the sale *decreases* the quantity of money. (Trace the process again but with the Bank of Canada *selling* and the banks or public *buying* securities.)

FIGURE 12.7
The Multiplier Effect of an Open Market Purchase

*e*Foundations 12.2

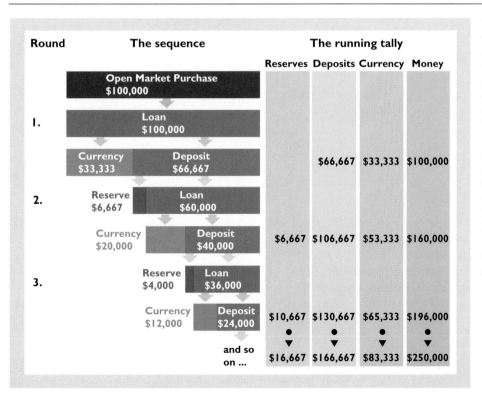

When the Bank of Canada provides the banks with $100,000 of additional reserves in an open market purchase, the banks lend those reserves. Of the amount loaned, $33,333 (33.33 percent) leaves the banks in a currency drain and $66,667 remains on deposit. With additional deposits, desired reserves increase by $6,667 (10 percent desired reserve ratio) and the banks lend $60,000. Of this amount, $20,000 leaves the banks in a currency drain and $40,000 remains on deposit. The process repeats until the banks have created enough deposits to eliminate their excess reserves. An additional $100,000 of reserves creates $250,000 of money.

■ The Money Multiplier

In the example we've just worked through, the quantity of money increases by 2.5 times the increase in the monetary base. The **money multiplier** is the number by which a change in the monetary base is multiplied to find the resulting change in the quantity of money. That is,

Money multiplier
The number by which a change in the monetary base is multiplied to find the resulting change in the quantity of money.

Change in quantity of money = Money multiplier × Change in monetary base.

In the example, the change in monetary base is the size of the open market purchase, which is $100,000, so:

Change in quantity of money = 2.5 × $100,000 = $250,000.

The money multiplier is determined by the banks' desired reserve ratio and by the currency drain. In the above example, the desired reserve ratio is 10 percent of deposits and the currency drain is 33.33 percent of money. So when the banks lend their initial $100,000 of excess reserves, $33,333 drains off as currency and $66,667 remains in the banks as reserves and deposits.

With an additional $66,667 of deposits and a 10 percent desired reserve ratio, the banks' desired reserves increase by $6,667, so their excess reserves are $60,000. Notice that $60,000 is 0.6 of the original $100,000 of excess reserves. That is, in the second round of lending, the banks lend 0.6 of the amount they loaned in the first round. Call this proportion L, ($L = 0.6$). In the third round, the banks lend $0.6^2 = 0.36$ of the original amount ($36,000 in Figure 12.7).

Because L is a fraction, at each stage in this sequence the amount of new loans and new money created get smaller. The total amount of new money created at the end of the process is:

$$\text{Quantity of money created} = \frac{1}{1 - L} \times \text{Open market purchase.}$$

If we use the numbers from the example, the total increase in the quantity of money is:

$$\text{Quantity of money created} = \$100,000 \times \frac{1}{(1 - 0.6)}$$

$$= \$100,000 \times \frac{1}{0.4}$$

$$= \$100,000 \times 2.5$$

$$= \$250,000.$$

The proportion L can be calculated from the currency drain and desired reserve ratio. Call the currency drain C and the desired reserve ratio R. So $C = 0.33$ and $R = 0.1$.

When the banks lend $1, C is held as currency and $(1 - C)$ remains on deposit. Banks must hold R of reserves for each $1 of deposits, so they are free to lend $(1 - R)$ of each dollar on deposit. When $(1 - C)$ remains on deposit, banks can lend $(1 - C) \times (1 - R)$. That is, the proportion L is:

$$L = (1 - C) \times (1 - R).$$

The Money Multiplier

We can measure the money multiplier in Canada by using the following formula:

Money multiplier = Quantity of money ÷ Monetary base.

Because there are two main definitions of money, M1 and M2+, there are two money multipliers: the M1 multiplier and the M2+ multiplier. Also, there are two measures of the currency drain and bank reserve ratios.

Part (a) shows the currency drain measures: the ratio of currency to M1 and the ratio of currency to M2+. Notice the increase in the ratio of currency to M1 before the 1990s and the decrease during the 1990s.

In part (b), you can see that the reserve ratios have fallen. The fall was steep after the Bank of Canada lowered the required reserve ratio during the early 1980s and again after the Bank eliminated required reserves in 1992.

In part (c), you can see the two money multipliers. The M2+ multiplier increased through the 1980s because the required reserve ratio decreased.

This multiplier levelled off during the 1990s because the banks' desired reserve ratio had fallen about as far as it could go.

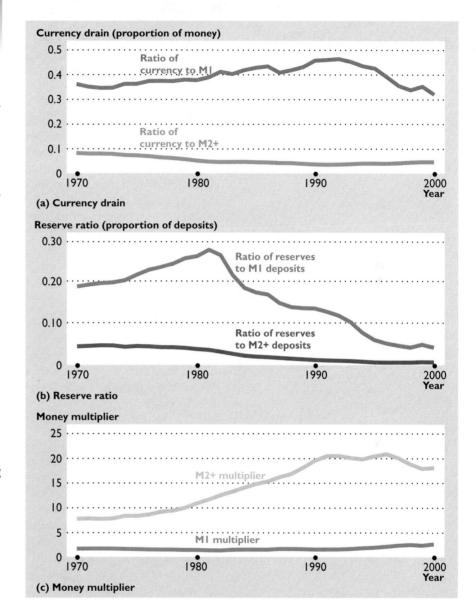

(a) Currency drain

(b) Reserve ratio

(c) Money multiplier

In terms of the numbers in our example,

$$L = (1 - 0.33) \times (1 - 0.1)$$

$$= (0.67) \times (0.9) = 0.6.$$

The larger the currency drain and the larger the desired reserve ratio, the smaller is the money multiplier.

Study Guide pp. 179–183

eFoundations 12.2

2 **Explain how the Bank of Canada influences the quantity of money.**

Practice Problems 12.2

1. What are the Bank of Canada's policy tools?
2. What is the money multiplier? What determines its magnitude?
3. If the Bank of Canada makes an open market purchase of $1 million:
   a. Who can sell the securities to the Bank of Canada in an open market operation? Does it matter from whom the Bank of Canada buys the securities?
   b. What initial changes occur in the economy if the Bank of Canada buys from a bank?
   c. What is the process by which the quantity of money changes?
   d. What determines how much the quantity of money changes?

Exercises 12.2

1. What is an open market operation? How do open market operations influence the monetary base?
2. Explain how the banking system creates money when the Bank of Canada conducts an open market operation.
3. If the Bank of Canada makes an open market sale of $1 million of securities:
   a. What initial changes occur in the economy?
   b. What is the process by which the quantity of money in the economy changes?
   c. By how much does the quantity of money change?
   d. What is the magnitude of the money multiplier?

Solutions to Practice Problems 12.2

1. The Bank of Canada's policy tools are open market operations, bank rate and bankers' deposit rate, and switching government deposits.
2. The money multiplier is the number by which a change in the monetary base is multiplied to find the resulting change in the quantity of money. The currency drain and the banks' desired reserve ratio determine its magnitude.
3a. In an open market operation, the Bank of Canada buys securities from banks or the public but the Bank does *not* buy securities from the government. It does not matter whether banks or the public sells the securities because the change in the monetary base is the same.
3b. The monetary base increases by $1 million. Ownership of the securities passes from the bank to the Bank of Canada. Bank of Canada's assets increase by $1 million and it pays for the securities by increasing the bank's deposit with the Bank of Canada by $1 million. The Bank of Canada's liabilities increase by $1 million. The bank's assets are the same, but their composition has changed. The bank has $1 million more in reserves and $1 million less in securities.
3c. The bank's reserves have increased by $1 million and its deposits have not changed, so it has excess reserves of $1 million. The bank makes loans and creates new deposits. The new deposits are new money.
3d. The desired reserve ratio and the currency drain determine the increase in the quantity of money. The larger the desired reserve ratio or the currency drain, the smaller is the increase in the quantity of money.

CHAPTER CHECKPOINT

Key Points

1 **Explain how banks create money by making loans.**

- Banks create money by making loans.
- Banks hold a proportion of their deposits as reserves to meet their desired reserve ratio.
- Reserves that exceed the desired reserve ratio are *excess reserves*, which banks can loan.
- The quantity of reserves and the desired reserve ratio limit the total quantity of deposits that the banks can create.
- The deposit multiplier is the number by which an increase in bank reserves is multiplied to give the increase in bank deposits.
- The deposit multiplier equals one divided by the desired reserve ratio.

2 **Explain how the Bank of Canada influences the quantity of money.**

- The Bank of Canada uses three tools to influence the quantity of money: government deposit shifting, changes in the bank rate and bankers' deposit rate, and open market operations.
- An increase in the bank rate increases the overnight rate, which makes the banks pay more for borrowed reserves, makes them less willing to borrow reserves, and decreases the quantity of money.
- When the Bank of Canada *buys* securities in an open market operation, it pays for them with newly created bank reserves and money. When the Bank of Canada *sells* securities in an open market operation, people pay for them with money and reserves.
- An open market purchase increases the monetary base and creates the following sequence of events: banks lend excess reserves; the quantity of money increases; new money is used to make payments; some of the new money remains on deposit in banks; some of the new money is held as currency—a currency drain; banks' desired reserves increase; excess reserves decrease. This sequence repeats until excess reserves are eliminated.
- The money multiplier determines the amount of money that banks can create from a given increase in the monetary base.
- The money multiplier is determined by the banks' desired reserve ratio and by the currency drain.

Key Terms

Balance sheet, 276	Desired reserve ratio, 278	Reserve ratio, 278
Currency drain, 290	Excess reserves, 279	
Deposit multiplier, 284	Money multiplier, 292	

Exercises

1. If the banking system receives new deposits of $2 million and the desired reserve ratio is 0.1, calculate:
   a. The bank's excess reserves as soon as the deposit is made.
   b. The maximum amount of loans that the banking system can make.
   c. The maximum amount of new money that the banking system can create.

2. If deposits of $3 million are withdrawn from the banking system and the desired reserve ratio is 0.1, calculate:
   a. The bank's excess reserves as soon as the withdrawal of deposits occurs.
   b. The amount of loans that the banking system calls in.
   c. The amount of money that the banking system destroys.

3. The desired reserve ratio is 5 percent, and the currency drain is 20 percent. If the Bank of Canada makes an open market purchase of $1 million of securities:
   a. What is the change in the monetary base?
   b. Which components of the monetary base change?
   c. By how much does the quantity of money change?
   d. How much of the new money is currency and how much is bank deposits?

4. Initially, the banking system has $200 billion of deposits and no excess reserves. If banks become nervous about the future and raise their desired reserve ratio from 0.1 to 0.5, calculate the change in:
   a. Reserves.
   b. Deposits.
   c. The quantity of money.

5. If the Bank of Canada wants to decrease the quantity of money, what type of open market operation might it undertake? Explain the process by which the quantity of money decreases.

6. Suppose that the currency drain is 10 percent of money and the desired reserve ratio is 1 percent of deposits. If the Bank of Canada sells $100,000 of securities on the open market, calculate the first-round change in:
   a. Excess reserves.
   b. Deposits.
   c. Currency in circulation.

7. To increase the quantity of money without changing the monetary base, explain how the Bank of Canada might:
   a. Switch government deposits.
   b. Change the bank rate.
   c. Conduct an open market operation.
   For any item that the Bank of Canada would not use, explain why not.

 8. Use the link on your Foundations Web site to visit the Bank of Canada. Obtain the most recent data on the bank rate, overnight rate, M1 and M2+.
   a. Do you see a pattern in the statistics that indicates the direction of the Bank of Canada's monetary policy?
   b. What do you think might be the goal of the Bank of Canada's actions?

Money, Interest, and Inflation

CHAPTER CHECKLIST

When you have completed your study of this chapter,
you will be able to:

1 Explain what determines the demand for money and how the demand for money and the supply of money determine the nominal interest rate.

2 Explain how in the long run, the quantity of money determines the price level and money growth brings inflation.

3 Identify the costs of inflation and the benefits of a stable value of money.

You know what money is, how banks create it, and how the Bank of Canada controls its quantity. In this chapter, you are going to learn about the effects of money on the economy.

First, you'll see how, on any given day, the quantity of money determines the interest rate. The effect of money on the interest rate is one of the channels through which the Bank of Canada influences expenditure plans and the business cycle. You'll learn more about these aspects of money in subsequent chapters.

Second, you'll see how, when we smooth out the influence of the business cycle and look only at the long-term trends, the quantity of money determines the price level and money growth in excess of potential GDP growth brings inflation.

Finally, you'll see why inflation matters. Adding a few zeroes to the numbers on all the notes and coins and price tags in the economy is not a big deal. So the price *level* doesn't matter. But ongoing *changes* in the price level— inflation—can have a big influence on people's lives.

WHERE WE ARE AND WHERE WE'RE HEADING

Before we explore the effects of money on the interest rate and the inflation rate, let's take stock of what we've learned, and preview where we are heading.

■ The Real Economy

Real factors that are independent of the price level determine potential GDP and the natural unemployment rate (Chapter 8). The demand for labour and supply of labour determine the quantity of labour employed and the real wage rate at full employment. The full-employment equilibrium quantity of labour and the production function determine potential GDP. At full employment, real GDP equals potential GDP and the unemployment rate equals the natural unemployment rate.

Real GDP and the unemployment rate are independent of the price level only at full employment. Away from potential GDP, aggregate supply and aggregate demand determine equilibrium real GDP and the price level, and fluctuations in aggregate supply and aggregate demand bring fluctuations around full employment (Chapter 8).

Investment demand and saving supply determine the levels of investment and saving and the real interest rate (Chapter 9). Investment and saving along with population growth, human capital growth, and technological change determine the growth rate of real GDP (Chapter 10).

■ The Money Economy

Money—the economy's means of payment—consists of currency and bank deposits (Chapter 11). Banks create deposits by making loans, and the Bank of Canada influences the quantity of money through its open market operations and other monetary policy actions (Chapter 12).

The effects of money on the economy, which we explore in this chapter, are complex and to explain and understand them, we proceed in three steps. We take these steps in an order that might seem strange but that turns out to be the most effective.

Step one looks at the immediate effect of the Bank of Canada's actions. This effect is on the short-term nominal interest rate. The Bank of Canada raises and lowers the short-term nominal interest rate by changing the quantity of money.

Step two looks at the long-term effects of the Bank of Canada's actions. These effects are on the price level and the inflation rate. The Bank of Canada lowers or raises the price level by decreasing or increasing the quantity of money. And the Bank of Canada lowers or raises the inflation rate by slowing down or speeding up the rate at which the quantity of money grows. We take these two steps in the current chapter.

Step three fills in the details between the initial change in the interest rate and the ultimate change in the price level or the inflation rate. This part of the story is a long one that needs to be broken down into manageable bites, and we explore it in the chapters of Part 5.

Some people approach a novel in this order: first, read the introduction, then the conclusion, and then the steps in between. Try it! It sometimes helps to know where you are going.

13.1 MONEY AND THE INTEREST RATE

To understand the Bank of Canada's short-run influence on the interest rate, we must understand what determines the demand for money, the supply of money, and the forces that bring equilibrium in the market for money. We'll begin by studying the demand for money.

■ The Demand for Money

The inventory of money that households and firms choose to hold is the **quantity of money demanded**. What determines the quantity of money demanded? The answer is a benefit–opportunity cost calculation. The quantity of money that households and firms choose to hold is the quantity that balances the benefit of holding an additional dollar of money against the opportunity cost of doing so. But just what are the benefit and opportunity cost of holding money?

Quantity of money demanded
The inventory of money that households and firms choose to hold.

Benefit of Holding Money

You've seen that money is the means of payment and that it serves as a medium of exchange, unit of account, and store of value (Chapter 11, pp. 252–253). You don't need any money to use it as a unit of account. You can keep financial records in dollars and cents even if you don't have any money. You don't need money to store your wealth. You can store it in the form of bonds, stocks, and mutual funds. Money and other financial assets are substitute stores of value. But you do need money to make payments and do transactions. These two features of money are the sources of benefit from holding money. The more money you hold, the easier it is for you to make payments and transactions.

The marginal benefit of holding money is the change in total benefit that results from holding one more dollar as money. The marginal benefit of holding money diminishes as the quantity of money held increases. If you hold only a few dollars in money, holding one more dollar brings large benefits—you can buy a coffee, take a bus ride, or use a pay phone. If you hold enough money to make your normal weekly payments, holding one more dollar brings only a small benefit because you're not very likely to want to spend it. Holding even more money brings only a small additional benefit. You barely notice the difference in the benefit of having $1,000 versus $1,001 in your bank account.

To get the most out of your assets, you hold money only up to the point at which its marginal benefit equals its opportunity cost. But what is the opportunity cost of holding money?

Opportunity Cost of Holding Money

The opportunity cost of holding money is the interest rate forgone on an alternative asset. If you can earn 8 percent a year on a bond, then holding an additional $100 in money costs you $8 a year. Your opportunity cost of holding $100 in money is the goods and services worth $8 that you must forgo.

A fundamental principle of economics is that if the opportunity cost of something increases, people seek substitutes for it. Money is no exception. Other assets such as a bond are substitutes for money. And the higher the opportunity cost of holding money—the higher the interest income forgone by not holding other assets—the smaller is the quantity of money demanded.

Opportunity Cost: *Nominal* Interest is a *Real* Cost

The opportunity cost of holding money is the nominal interest rate. In Chapter 7, you learned the distinction between the *nominal* interest rate and the *real* interest rate and that:

$$\text{Nominal interest rate} = \text{Real interest rate} + \text{Expected inflation rate}.$$

We can use this equation to find the real interest rate for a given nominal interest rate and expected inflation rate. For example, if the nominal interest rate on a bond is 8 percent a year and the inflation rate and expected inflation rate are 2 percent a year, the real interest rate is 6 percent a year. Money loses value because of inflation. So why isn't the real interest rate of 6 percent a year the opportunity cost of holding money? That is, why isn't the opportunity cost of holding $100 in money only $6 worth of goods and services forgone?

The answer is that if you hold $100 in money rather than in a bond, your buying power decreases by $8, not by $6. With inflation running at 2 percent a year, on each $100 that you hold as money and that earns no interest, you lose $2 worth of buying power a year. On each $100 that you put into bonds, you gain $6 worth of buying power a year. So if you hold money rather than bonds, you lose the buying power of $6 plus $2, or $8—equivalent to the nominal interest rate on the bond, not the real interest rate.

Because the opportunity cost of holding money is the nominal interest rate on an alternative asset:

Other things remaining the same, the higher the nominal interest rate, the smaller is the quantity of money demanded.

This relationship describes the money-holding decisions of individuals and firms. It also describes money-holding decisions for the economy—the sum of the decisions of every individual and firm.

We summarize the influence of the nominal interest rate on money-holding decisions in a demand for money schedule and curve.

The Demand for Money Schedule and Curve

Demand for money
The relationship between the quantity of money demanded and the nominal interest rate, when all other influences on the amount of money that people wish to hold remain the same.

The **demand for money** is the relationship between the quantity of money demanded and the nominal interest rate, when all other influences on the amount of money that people wish to hold remain the same. We illustrate the demand for money with a demand for money schedule and a demand for money curve, such as those in Figure 13.1. If the interest rate is 5 percent a year, the quantity of money demanded is $100 billion. The quantity of money demanded decreases to $98 billion if the interest rate rises to 6 percent a year and increases to $102 billion if the interest rate falls to 4 percent a year.

The demand for money curve is *MD*. When the interest rate rises, other things remaining the same, the opportunity cost of holding money rises and the quantity of money demanded decreases—there is a movement up along the demand for money curve. When the interest rate falls, the opportunity cost of holding money falls and the quantity of money demanded increases—there is a movement down along the demand for money curve.

FIGURE 13.1
The Demand for Money

*e*Foundations **13.1**

	Nominal interest rate (percent per year)	Quantity of money (billions of dollars)
A	6	98
B	5	100
C	4	102

Nominal interest rate (percent per year)

❶ Effect of a rise in the interest rate

❷ Effect of a fall in the interest rate

MD

Quantity of money (billions of dollars)

The demand for money schedule is graphed as the demand for money curve, *MD*. Rows *A*, *B*, and *C* in the table correspond to points *A*, *B*, and *C* on the curve. The nominal interest rate is the opportunity cost of holding money.

❶ Other things remaining the same, an increase in the nominal interest rate decreases the quantity of money demanded, and **❷** a decrease in the nominal interest rate increases the quantity of money demanded.

■ Changes in the Demand for Money

A change in the nominal interest rate brings a change in the quantity of money demanded and a movement along the demand for money curve. A change in any other influence on money holding changes the demand for money. The three main influences on the demand for money are:

- The price level
- Real GDP
- Financial technology

The Price Level

The demand for money is proportional to the price level—an *x* percent rise in the price level brings an *x* percent increase in the quantity of money demanded at each interest rate. The reason is that we hold money to make payments: If the price level changes, the dollars that we need to make payments changes in the same proportion.

Real GDP

The demand for money increases as real GDP increases. The reason is that expenditures and incomes increase when real GDP increases. So households and firms must hold larger average inventories of money to make the increased expenditures and income payments.

Financial Technology

Changes in financial technology change the demand for money. Most changes in financial technology come from advances in computing and record keeping. Some advances increase the demand for money, and some decrease it.

Daily interest chequing deposits and automatic transfers between chequing and savings deposits enable people to earn interest on money, lower the opportunity cost of holding money, and increase the demand for money. Automatic teller machines, debit cards, and smart cards, which have made money easier to obtain and use, have increased the marginal benefit of money and increased the demand for money.

Credit cards have made it easier for people to buy goods and services on credit and pay for them when their credit card account becomes due. This development has decreased the demand for money.

■ Shifts in the Demand for Money Curve

A change in any influence on money holdings other than the interest rate changes the demand for money and shifts the demand for money curve, as you can see in Figure 13.2. A rise in the price level, an increase in real GDP, or an advance in financial technology that lowers the opportunity cost of holding money or makes money more useful increases the demand for money and shifts the demand for money curve rightward from MD_0 to MD_1. A fall in the price level, a decrease in real GDP, or a technological advance that creates a substitute for money has the opposite effect. It decreases the demand for money and shifts the demand for money curve leftward from MD_0 to MD_2.

■ **FIGURE 13.2**

Changes in the Demand for Money

*e*Foundations **13.1**

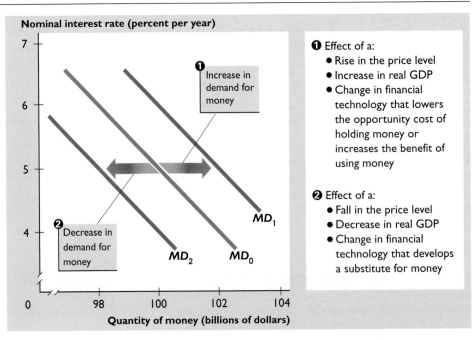

■ The Nominal Interest Rate

People hold some of their financial wealth as money and some in the form of other financial assets. You have seen that the amount that people hold as money depends on the nominal interest rate that they can earn on other financial assets. Demand and supply determine the nominal interest rate. We can study the forces of demand and supply in either the market for financial assets or the market for money. Because the Bank of Canada influences the quantity of money, we focus on the market for money.

Figure 13.3 shows the market for money. The quantity of money is determined by the actions of the banking system and the Bank of Canada. On any given day, there is a fixed quantity of money. The **supply of money**, which is the relationship between the quantity of money supplied and the nominal interest rate, is a fixed quantity. In Figure 13.3, the quantity of money supplied is $100 billion, so the supply of money curve is vertical line *MS*.

Also, on any given day, the price level, real GDP, and the state of financial technology are fixed. Because these influences on the demand for money are fixed, the demand for money curve is given and in Figure 13.3 is the curve *MD*.

The interest rate is the only influence on the quantity of money demanded that is free to fluctuate. And every day, the interest rate adjusts to make the quantity of money demanded equal the quantity of money supplied—to achieve money market equilibrium. In Figure 13.3, the equilibrium interest rate is 5 percent a year. At any interest rate above 5 percent a year, the quantity of money demanded is less than the quantity of money supplied. At any interest rate below 5 percent a year, the quantity of money demanded exceeds the quantity of money supplied.

Supply of money
The relationship between the quantity of money supplied and the nominal interest rate.

■ **FIGURE 13.3**
Money Market Equilibrium

*e*Foundations **13.1**

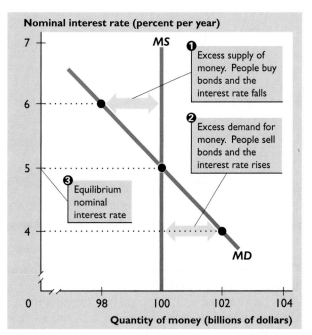

The supply of money curve is *MS*, and the demand for money curve is *MD*.

❶ If the interest rate is 6 percent a year, the quantity of money supplied exceeds the quantity demanded. People buy bonds, the price of a bond rises, and the interest rate falls.

❷ If the interest rate is 4 percent a year, the quantity of money supplied falls short of the quantity demanded. People sell bonds, the price of a bond falls, and the interest rate rises.

❸ If the interest rate is 5 percent a year, the quantity of money supplied equals the quantity demanded. The money market is in equilibrium.

The Fluctuating Demand for Money

The quantity of money that people and businesses hold has fluctuated as a percentage of GDP. Figure (a) shows that M1 fell from 11 percent of GDP in 1972 to 6 percent in 1990 and then climbed back to 10 percent of GDP in 2000. Figure (b) shows that M2+ increased from 42 percent of GDP in 1970 to almost 80 percent in 1992 and then decreased to 65 percent of GDP in 2000.

Several influences on money holding brought these fluctuations. One of them is changes in the interest rate, which brings movements along the demand for money curve. Figures (c) and (d) show some of these movements. In figure (c), as the interest rate fell during the 1990s, there was a movement down along the demand curve for M1. Figure (d) shows a similar movement down along the demand curve for M2+.

But the demand for money curve has shifted. During the 1970s and 1980s, the demand for M1 decreased and during the late 1990s, the demand for M1 increased. The demand for M2+ increased through the 1970s and 1980s and decreased after 1992.

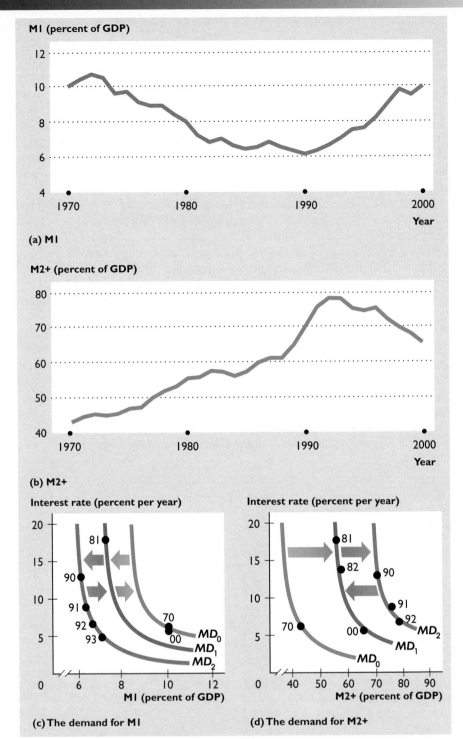

(a) M1

(b) M2+

(c) The demand for M1

(d) The demand for M2+

SOURCES: Statistics Canada and the Bank of Canada.

The Interest Rate and Bond Price Move in Opposite Directions When the government issues a bond, it specifies the dollar amount of interest that it will pay each year on the bond. Suppose that the government issues a bond that pays $100 of interest a year. The interest *rate* that you receive on this bond depends on the price that you pay for it. If the price is $1,000, the interest rate is 10 percent a year—$100 is 10 percent of $1,000.

If the price of the bond *falls* to $500, the interest rate *rises* to 20 percent a year. The reason is that you still receive an interest payment of $100, but this amount is 20 percent of the $500 price of the bond. If the price of the bond *rises* to $2,000, the interest rate *falls* to 5 percent a year. Again, you still receive an interest payment of $100, but this amount is 5 percent of the $2,000 price of the bond.

Interest Rate Adjustment   If the interest rate is above its equilibrium level, people would like to hold less money than they are actually holding. So they try to get rid of money by buying other financial assets such as bonds. The demand for financial assets increases, the prices of these assets rise, and the interest rate falls. The interest rate keeps falling until the quantity of money that people want to hold increases to equal the quantity of money supplied.

Conversely, when the interest rate is below its equilibrium level, people are holding less money than they would like to hold. So they try to get more money by selling other financial assets. The demand for financial assets decreases, the prices of these assets fall, and the interest rate rises. The interest rate keeps rising until the quantity of money that people want to hold decreases to equal the quantity of money supplied.

■ Changing the Interest Rate

To change the interest rate, the Bank of Canada changes the quantity of money. Figure 13.4 illustrates two changes. The demand for money curve is *MD*. If the Bank of Canada increases the quantity of money to $102 billion, the supply of money curve shifts rightward from MS_0 to MS_1 and the interest rate falls to 4 percent a year. If the Bank of Canada decreases the quantity of money to $98 billion, the supply of money curve shifts leftward from MS_0 to MS_2 and the interest rate rises to 6 percent a year.

■ **FIGURE 13.4**
Interest Rate Changes

 *e*/**Foundations 13.1**

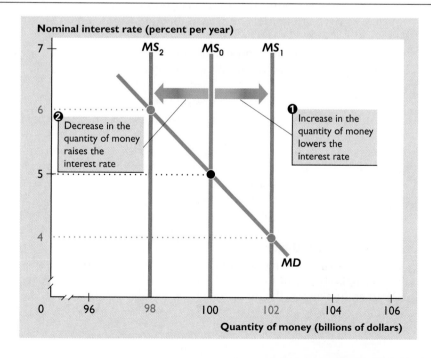

The demand for money curve is *MD*, and initially, the supply of money curve is MS_0. The interest rate is 5 percent a year.

❶ The Bank of Canada increases the quantity of money to $102 billion and the supply of money curve shifts rightward to MS_1. The interest rate falls to 4 percent a year.

❷ The Bank of Canada decreases the quantity of money to $98 billion and the supply of money curve shifts leftward to MS_2. The interest rate rises to 6 percent a year.

Study Guide pp. 188–191

*e*Foundations 13.1

1 **Explain what determines the demand for money and how the demand for money and the supply of money determine the nominal interest rate.**

Practice Problems 13.1

1. Figure 1 shows the demand for money curve.
   a. If the quantity of money is $99 billion, what is the nominal interest rate?
   b. If real GDP increases, how will the interest rate change? Explain the process that brings about the change in the interest rate.
   c. In part (a), the Bank of Canada decreases the quantity of money to $98 billion. Will bond prices rise or fall? Why? What happens to the nominal interest rate?

2. Suppose that the banks increase the fee they charge for credit cards, introduce a user fee on every credit card purchase, and increase the interest rate on outstanding credit card balances.
   a. How would the demand for money change?
   b. How would the nominal interest rate change?

Exercises 13.1

1. Figure 1 shows the demand for money curve.
   a. If the quantity of money is $98 billion, what is the nominal interest rate?
   b. If real GDP decreases, how will the interest rate change? Explain what happens in the market for bonds as the market returns to equilibrium.
   c. In part (a), the Bank of Canada increases the quantity of money to $100 billion. What is the change in the nominal interest rate? What happens to the price of bonds?

2. Suppose that the banks launch an aggressive marketing campaign to get everyone to use credit cards for every conceivable transaction. They offer prizes to new cardholders and slash the interest rate on outstanding credit card balances.
   a. How would the demand for money change?
   b. How would the nominal interest rate change?

Solutions to Practice Problems 13.1

1a. The interest rate is 4 percent a year at the intersection of MD_1 and MS in Figure 2.

1b. The demand for money increases. At an interest rate of 4 percent a year, people want to hold more money so they sell bonds. The price of a bond falls and the interest rate rises (Figure 2).

1c. At an interest rate at 4 percent a year, people would like to hold $99 billion. With only $98 billion of money available, they sell bonds, the price of a bond falls, and the interest rate rises. The new equilibrium nominal interest rate is 6 percent a year (Figure 3).

2a. The demand for money would increase as people used their credit cards less and used money for more transactions.

2b. With an increase in the demand for money, the nominal interest rate would rise.

FIGURE 1

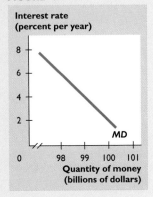

FIGURE 2

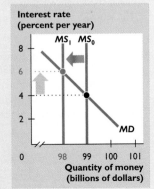

FIGURE 3

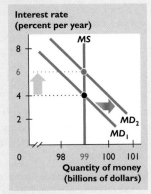

13.2 MONEY, THE PRICE LEVEL, AND INFLATION

Each day, the price level and real GDP are at levels that have resulted from previous decisions. When the Bank of Canada conducts an open market operation to change the quantity of money, the nominal interest rate is the only variable that is free to adjust to make the quantity of money demanded equal the quantity of money supplied. You've seen that the interest rate rises when the quantity of money decreases and falls when the quantity of money increases.

Changes in the nominal interest rate also change the real interest rate. The reason is that the inflation rate and the expected inflation rate adjust slowly and do not change every time the Bank of Canada changes the quantity of money.

Changes in the real interest rate influence spending plans. If the real interest rate falls, firms borrow and invest more and households borrow and spend more on consumption goods, especially on big-ticket items such as homes and automobiles. Similarly, if the real interest rate rises, firms borrow and invest less and households borrow and spend less on consumption goods.

These changes in spending change production and prices. The details of the adjustment process are complex, and we explore them in the next two chapters. But the place where the adjustment process comes to rest is easier to describe. We're now going to explain the long-run outcome of a change in the quantity of money and a change in the growth rate of money.

■ The Money Market in the Long Run

The *long run* refers to the economy at full employment or when we smooth out the effects of the business cycle. Potential GDP, the current state of financial technology, the price level, and the nominal interest rate determine the quantity of money demanded at full employment. The Bank of Canada determines the quantity of money supplied. In the short run, the nominal interest rate adjusts to bring equilibrium in the market for money. But in the long run, the price level does the adjusting. To see why, let's see what determines the other influences on the quantity of money demanded.

Potential GDP and Financial Technology

Potential GDP and the state of financial technology, two influences on the quantity of money demanded, are determined by real factors and are independent of the price level. You studied the forces that determine potential GDP in Chapter 8. Potential GDP is the real GDP produced by the full-employment quantity of labour. This quantity is determined by the equilibrium real wage rate at which the quantity of labour demanded equals the quantity of labour supplied. Potential GDP is independent of the price level.

Financial technology is determined by the state of knowledge and the quantity of capital (computers, ATMs, and so on) that banks have installed. Like potential GDP, financial technology is independent of the price level.

The Nominal Interest Rate in the Long Run

At the end of 2001, businesses in Canada could borrow at a nominal interest rate of around 3 percent a year. Businesses in Russia paid a nominal interest rate of 60 percent a year, and businesses in Turkey paid 80 percent a year. Although the Canadian nominal interest rate has never been as high as these two cases, Canadian businesses paid a nominal interest rate of 16 percent a year in the early 1980s.

Nominal interest rates vary across countries and over time for many reasons, but the dominant one is differences in inflation rates. The equilibrium nominal interest rate equals the equilibrium real interest rate plus the expected inflation rate. That is, the nominal interest rate exceeds the real interest rate by the expected inflation rate.

You studied the global financial market, which determines investment, saving, and the equilibrium real interest rate in Chapter 9. The real interest rate, like potential GDP, is independent of the price level. It is also independent of the inflation rate in the long run.

But the nominal interest rate depends directly on the expected inflation rate. Borrowers are willing to pay a high nominal interest rate when there is inflation because the real value of loans decreases over time. And lenders will insist on receiving a high nominal interest rate because the money with which they are repaid buys less than what the money they loaned would have bought.

An Example Suppose that when there is no inflation, investment equals saving at a real interest rate of 3 percent a year. The Second Cup is willing to pay an interest rate of 3 percent a year to get the funds it needs to open new cafes. Sue is saving to buy a new car. Sue (along with millions of others) is willing to save and lend Second Cup the amount it needs for its new cafes for a real interest rate of 3 percent a year.

Now imagine that the inflation rate is steady at 2 percent a year. All dollar amounts, including companies' prices and profits and car prices, are rising by 2 percent a year. If Second Cup was willing to pay 3 percent a year in interest when there was no inflation, it is now willing to pay 5 percent a year. Its profits are rising by 2 percent a year, so it is really paying only 3 percent a year. Similarly, if Sue was willing to lend at 3 percent a year when there was no inflation, she is now willing to lend only if the interest rate is 5 percent a year. The price of the car that Sue is planning to buy is rising by 2 percent a year, so she is really getting an interest rate of only 3 percent a year.

Because borrowers are willing to pay the higher interest rate and lenders are willing to lend only if they receive the higher interest rate when inflation is present, the nominal interest rate increases by an amount equal to the inflation rate.

We'll explain how the inflation rate is determined later in this chapter.

Money Market Equilibrium in the Long Run

You've seen how all of the influences on the quantity of money demanded except the price level are determined. Money market equilibrium in the long run determines the price level. Figure 13.5 illustrates how.

Part (a) emphasizes the idea that the demand for money depends on the price level and, for a given quantity of money, the equilibrium nominal interest rate depends on the price level. It looks at three *possible* short-run situations. Real GDP equals potential GDP in each of them. First, if the price level were 100, the demand for money curve would be MD_0. In this case, the equilibrium nominal interest rate would be 5 percent a year. Second, if the price level were 102, the demand for money curve would be MD_1 and the equilibrium nominal interest rate would be 6 percent a year. Finally, if the price level were 98, the demand for money curve would be MD_2 and the equilibrium nominal interest rate would be 4 percent a year.

Which of these three *possible* short-run situations describes the long run? Part (b) provides the answer. Saving and investment decisions determine the long-run equilibrium real interest rate. We'll assume this interest rate is 3 percent a year.

FIGURE 13.5

Long-Run Equilibrium

*e*Foundations **13.2**

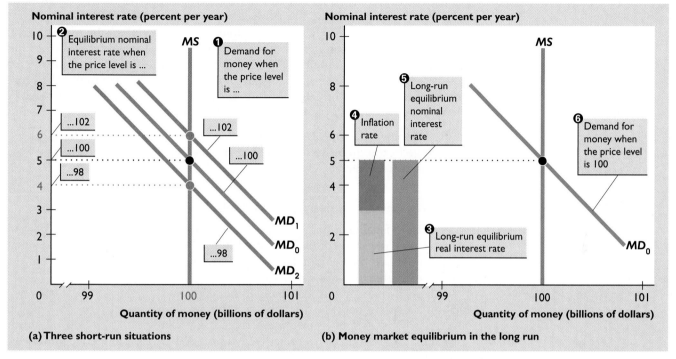

(a) Three short-run situations

(b) Money market equilibrium in the long run

❶ The demand for money depends on the price level, so ❷ the equilibrium nominal interest rate also depends on the price level.

❸ The long-run equilibrium real interest rate (determined in the global financial market) plus ❹ the inflation rate (actual and

expected) determines the ❺ long-run equilibrium nominal interest rate.

❻ The price level adjusts to 100 to achieve money market equilibrium at the long-run equilibrium interest rate.

The nominal interest rate is the real interest rate plus the expected inflation rate. We'll assume that the inflation rate (and expected inflation rate) is 2 percent a year. So the long-run equilibrium nominal interest rate is 5 percent a year. Only one of the *possible* equilibrium situations shown in part (a) is consistent with the long-run equilibrium nominal interest rate. It is the situation in which the price level is 100, the demand for money curve is MD_0, and the nominal interest rate is 5 percent a year.

You will see how this long-run equilibrium comes about by considering what happens if the Bank of Canada changes the quantity of money.

■ A Change in the Quantity of Money

Suppose that the quantity of money is initially $100 billion and then the Bank of Canada increases it by 2 percent to $102 billion. In the short run, the greater quantity of money lowers the nominal interest rate. With a lower interest rate, aggregate demand increases and the price level rises. Eventually, a new long-run equilibrium is reached at which the price level has increased in proportion to the increase in the quantity of money.

Because the quantity of money increased by 2 percent from $100 billion to $102 billion, the price level rises by 2 percent from 100 to 102.

Figure 13.6 illustrates these events. Initially, the supply of money curve is MS_0, the demand for money curve is MD_0, the nominal interest rate is at its long-run equilibrium level of 5 percent a year, and the price level that lies behind MD_0 is 100.

Now the quantity of money increases and the supply of money curve shifts rightward to MS_1. Initially, the price level remains at 100, so the demand for money curve remains at MD_0. The nominal interest rate falls below its long-run equilibrium level to 4 percent a year. With a lower interest rate, aggregate demand increases, which eventually raises the price level to 102. The demand for money increases as the price level rises, and the interest rate rises. Eventually, the economy is back at its long-run equilibrium interest rate but at a higher price level.

You've just seen a key proposition about money and the price level:

In the long run, other things remaining the same, a given percentage change in the quantity of money brings an equal percentage change in the price level.

The Price Level in a Baby-Sitting Club

It is hard to visualize a long-run equilibrium and even harder to visualize and compare two long-run equilibrium situations. So an example of a simpler situation might help to make the relationship between the quantity of money and the price level clearer.

Parents in a neighbourhood have formed a baby-sitting club. The deal is that each time a parent baby-sits for someone else, he or she receives a token that can be used to buy one sit from another member of the club. The club organizer notices that the club is not very active. Every member has a few unspent tokens,

---

■ **FIGURE 13.6**

A Change in the Price Level

e/Foundations 13.2

❶ The quantity of money increases by 2 percent from $100 billion to $102 billion and the supply curve shifts from MS_0 to MS_1.

❷ In the short run, the interest rate falls to 4 percent a year.

❸ In the long run, the price level rises by 2 percent from 100 to 102, the demand for money curve shifts rightward from MD_0 to MD_1, and the nominal interest rate returns to its long-run equilibrium level.

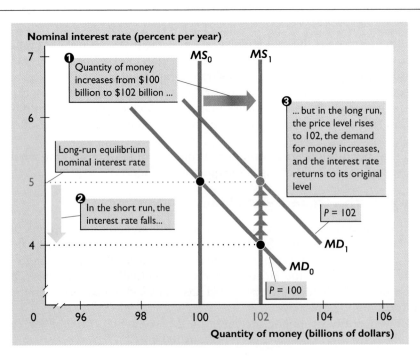

but they spend them infrequently. To make the club more active, the organizer decides to issue every member one token for each token that is currently held, so the quantity of tokens doubles.

With more tokens to spend, parents start to plan more evenings out. Suddenly, the phones are ringing as parents seek baby-sitters. Every member of the club wants a sitter. But there are no more sitters than before. After making a few calls and finding no sitters available, anxious parents who really do need a sitter start to offer a higher price: two tokens per session. That does the trick. At the higher price, the quantity of baby-sitting services demanded decreases and the quantity supplied increases. Equilibrium is restored. Nothing real has changed, but the quantity of tokens and the price level have doubled.

Think of the equilibrium quantity of baby-sitting services as potential GDP, the quantity of tokens as the quantity of money, and the price of a baby-sitting session as the price level. You can then see how a given percentage change in the quantity of money at full employment brings an equal percentage change in the price level.

■ Money Growth and Inflation

So far, we've studied the effects of a one-time increase in the quantity of money at a given inflation rate and expected inflation rate. Let's now see how the inflation rate is determined. You are going to discover how the Bank of Canada influences the inflation rate and how the Bank of Canada does, after all, influence the nominal interest rate in the long run. But you're also going to discover a paradox about the interest rate. To lower the interest rate in the long run, the Bank of Canada must slow the rate at which it increases the quantity of money and raise the interest rate in the short run. If the Bank of Canada speeds up the rate at which it increases the quantity of money and lowers the interest rate in the short run, it will end up raising the interest rate in the long run. Let's see how we can make sense of these propositions.

Steady Inflation

We defined the inflation rate in Chapter 7 as the percentage change in the price level from one year to the next (see Chapter 7, p. 155). Inflation is a process—an ongoing rate of increase in the price level.

We can think of inflation as a persistent repeating of the one-shot increase in the price level shown in Figure 13.6. There, the quantity of money increased from $100 billion to $102 billion—a 2 percent increase. Suppose that this increase occurred over a period of a year. And also suppose that the quantity of money has been increasing by 2 percent a year, on the average, for many years.

For now, we'll suppose that potential GDP is constant. (We'll look at the influence of real GDP growth on inflation later.) We'll also suppose that financial technology doesn't change. With constant potential GDP and no change in financial technology, the price level is the only influence on the demand for money that changes.

An ongoing increase in the quantity of money brings an ongoing increase in the price level. Because, other things remaining the same, an increase in the quantity of money brings an equal percentage increase in the price level, an ongoing increase in the quantity of money of 2 percent a year brings an ongoing rise in the price level of 2 percent a year—an inflation rate of 2 percent a year.

Figure 13.7 illustrates inflation. It also shows what happens when the inflation rate changes.

■ **FIGURE 13.7**

Inflation

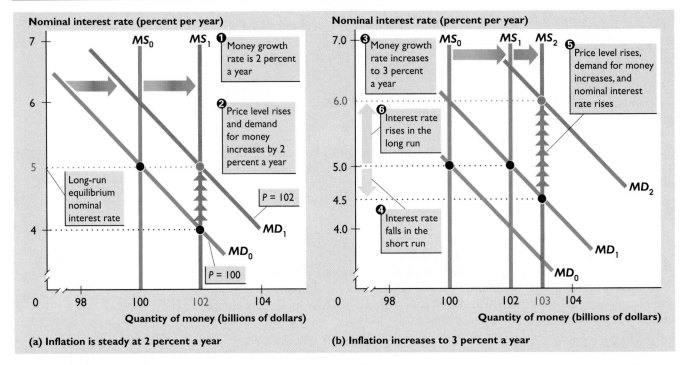

(a) Inflation is steady at 2 percent a year

(b) Inflation increases to 3 percent a year

❶ The quantity of money is growing by 2 percent a year and ❷ the price level is rising by 2 percent a year, so the demand for money increases at the same rate as the quantity of money and the nominal interest rate remains at its long-run equilibrium level.

❸ The money growth rate increases to 3 percent a year. ❹ Initially, the nominal interest rate falls, but eventually, ❺ the price level rises, the demand for money increases, and ❻ the nominal interest rate rises to 6 percent a year.

Part (a) looks at one year of the many years in which the quantity of money is growing by 2 percent a year. (Potential GDP is still assumed to be constant.) During the year, the money growth rate increases by 2 percent from $100 billion to $102 billion. The supply of money curve shifts rightward from MS_0 to MS_1. The price level rises by 2 percent a year, so the demand for money curve shifts rightward at the same pace as the supply of money curve. The demand for money curve shifts from MD_0, with a price level of 100, to MD_1, with a price level of 102. Because the supply of money and the demand for money increase together at the same rate, the interest rate remains constant at its long-run equilibrium level of 5 percent a year.

Increase in the Inflation Rate

Now suppose that the money growth rate increases from 2 percent a year to 3 percent a year and remains at the higher rate for many years. Figure 13.7(b) shows the consequences. First, when the faster money growth begins, the interest rate falls. The reason is that the demand for money curve is shifting rightward at 2 percent a year, but the supply of money curve now shifts rightward by 3 percent a year. The lower interest rate increases spending. Aggregate demand increases and the price level begins to increase more rapidly.

As the higher inflation rate persists, it comes to be expected and the long-run equilibrium nominal interest rate rises. Because the new money supply growth is 3 percent a year, the new equilibrium inflation rate is 3 percent a year and the long-run equilibrium nominal interest rate rises to 6 percent a year.

Potential GDP Growth

So far, we've assumed that potential GDP is constant. But growth of potential GDP increases the demand for money. If the Bank of Canada makes the quantity of money grow at the same rate as the growth rate of potential GDP, the growth rate of the quantity of money demanded will equal the growth rate of the quantity of money supplied and the price level will remain constant. But if the Bank of Canada makes the quantity of money grow more rapidly than the growth rate of potential GDP, the inflation rate will equal the percentage growth rate of the quantity of money minus the percentage growth rate of potential GDP.

■ The Quantity Theory of Money

The proposition that the inflation rate equals the percentage growth rate of the quantity of money minus the percentage growth rate of potential GDP is known as the **quantity theory of money**. An alternative way of looking at the quantity theory of money uses the concept of the velocity of circulation. Velocity means speed. So the **velocity of circulation** means the speed of circulation of money—the number of times in a year that the average dollar of money gets used to buy final goods and services. To calculate the velocity of circulation, we divide nominal GDP by the quantity of money. Let's call the velocity of circulation V, the quantity of money M, the price level P, and real GDP Y. Then nominal GDP is $P \times Y$, and the velocity of circulation is:

$$V = (P \times Y) \div M.$$

Quantity theory of money
The proposition that in the long run, an increase in the quantity of money brings an equal percentage increase in the price level (other things remaining the same).

Velocity of circulation
The average speed with which a dollar circulates in the economy as people use it to buy goods and services; calculated by dividing nominal GDP by the quantity of money.

The Nominal Interest Rate and the Inflation Rate

The figure shows the nominal interest rate and inflation rate in Canada from 1980 to 2000. You can see that most of the fluctuations in the nominal interest rate line up with fluctuations in the inflation rate. The nominal interest rate was at its highest during the early 1980s when the inflation rate exceeded 10 percent a year. As the inflation rate fell during the 1980s and 1990s, so did the nominal interest rate.

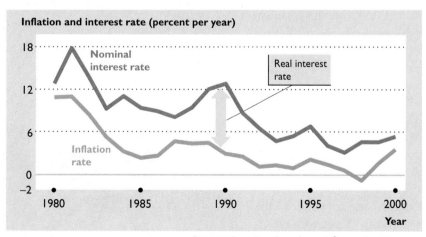

SOURCE: Statistics Canada and the Bank of Canada.

To understand this equation, think about an economy in which the amount spent on goods and services—nominal GDP—is $1,000 a year. Suppose that the quantity of money is $100. Then each dollar is used, on the average, 10 times in a year. The velocity of circulation is 10. Check this value with the formula:

$$V = \$1{,}000 \div \$100 = 10.$$

Equation of exchange
An equation that states that the quantity of money multiplied by the velocity of circulation equals nominal GDP.

Multiply both sides of the equation that defines the velocity of circulation by M. You will then arrive at the **equation of exchange,** which states that the quantity of money multiplied by the velocity of circulation equals nominal GDP. That is:

$$M \times V = P \times Y.$$

It is just one step from the equation of exchange to the quantity theory of money. Divide both sides of the above equation by Y to obtain:

$$P = (M \times V) \div Y.$$

Eye On The CANADIAN ECONOMY

The Quantity Theory of Money in Action

Part (a) shows the ratio of M2+ to real GDP, the velocity of circulation, and the price level between 1960 and 2000. Part (b) shows the decade-by-decade percentage changes in these variables. You can see that the quantity theory of money does a good job, but not a perfect job, of predicting the price level (and the inflation rate).

During each decade, the percentage increase in the price level is similar to the percentage increase in M2+ minus the percentage increase in real GDP. More important, the changes in the inflation rate are similar to the changes in the M2+ growth rate.

But the velocity of circulation does change and on the average, it has fallen during the period shown in these figures.

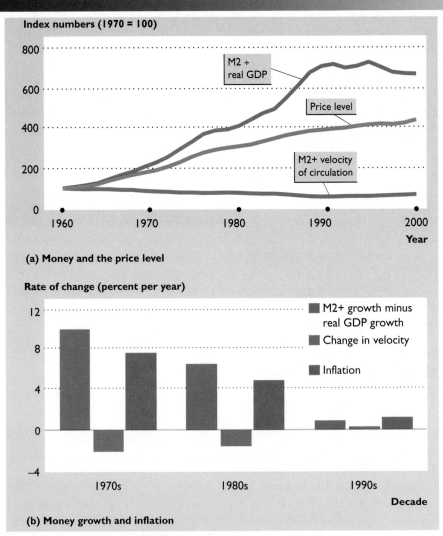

Index numbers (1970 = 100)

(a) Money and the price level

Rate of change (percent per year)

(b) Money growth and inflation

SOURCES: Statistics Canada and the Bank of Canada.

On the left is the price level. And on the right are all the things that influence the price level. The idea behind the quantity theory of money is that the velocity of circulation is relatively stable. Furthermore, velocity does not change when the quantity of money changes. Also, real GDP is determined by real factors and grows at a pace that is independent of the changes in the quantity of money. So if M increases when Y is constant, P must increase, and by the same percentage.

But real GDP grows, so if M grows at the same rate as Y, then $M \div Y$ is constant and (with constant velocity) the price level is also constant. So the price level rises only when $M \div Y$ rises, which means that the price level rises when the quantity of money grows more rapidly than real GDP grows.

Compared with some other countries, inflation in Canada has been moderate. Big inflations are called **hyperinflation**—inflation rates that exceed 50 percent per month. Hyperinflation occurs when the quantity of money increases at an extraordinarily rapid rate.

Hyperinflation
Inflation at a rate that exceeds 50 percent per month.

Eye On The PAST

Hyperinflation in Germany in the 1920s

An international treaty signed in 1919 required Germany to pay large amounts as compensation for war damage to other countries in Europe. To meet its obligations, Germany started to print money. Germany increased the quantity of money by 24 percent in 1921, by 220 percent in 1922, and by 43 *billion* percent in 1923!

Not surprisingly, the price level increased rapidly. The figure shows you how rapidly. In November 1923, when the hyperinflation reached its peak, the price level was more than doubling every day. Wages were paid twice a day, and people spent their morning's wages at lunchtime to avoid the loss in the value of money that the afternoon would bring.

In 1923, bank notes were more valuable as fire kindling than as money, and the sight of people burning Reichmarks (the name of Germany's money at that time) was a common one.

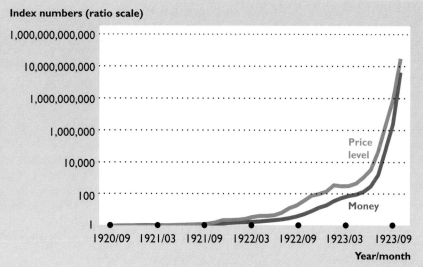

SOURCE: Phillip Cagan, "The Monetary Dynamics of Hyperinflation," in Milton Friedman (editor), *Studies in the Quantity Theory of Money*, University of Chicago Press, 1956.

Study Guide pp. 191–194

*e*Foundations 13.2

2 Explain how in the long run, the quantity of money determines the price level and money growth brings inflation.

Practice Problems 13.2

1. In 1999, the Canadian economy was at full employment. Real GDP was $886 billion, nominal GDP was $975 billion, the nominal interest rate was around 6 percent per year, the inflation rate was 2 percent a year, and the price level was 110.
   a. Calculate the real interest rate.
   b. If the real interest rate remains unchanged when the inflation rate increases to 4 percent a year, explain how the nominal interest rate changes.
   c. If the velocity of circulation was 10, what was the quantity of money in Canada?

2. If the quantity of money grows at a rate of 10 percent a year and potential GDP grows at 3 percent a year, what is the inflation rate in the long run?

Exercises 13.2

1. In 2000, the United Kingdom was close to full employment. Nominal GDP was £800 billion, the real interest rate was around 4 percent per year, the inflation rate was 6 percent a year, and the price level was 120.
   a. Calculate the nominal interest rate.
   b. If the real interest rate remains unchanged when the inflation rate in the long run decreases to 3 percent a year, explain how the nominal interest rate changes.

2. In 2000, the United Kingdom was at full employment. Nominal GDP was £800 billion, the nominal interest rate was 7 percent per year, the price level was 120, and the velocity of circulation was 2. What was the quantity of money in the United Kingdom?

3. In Exercise 2, if the velocity of circulation is 1.5, money grows at 8 percent a year, and potential GDP grows at 5 percent a year in the long run, what is the inflation rate in the long run?

Solutions to Practice Problems 13.2

1a. The real interest rate equals the nominal interest rate minus the inflation rate. That is, the real interest rate equals 6 percent a year minus 2 percent a year, which equals 4 percent a year.

1b. The nominal interest rate rises from 6 percent a year to 8 percent a year.

1c. Velocity of circulation (V) = Nominal GDP ($P \times Y$) ÷ Quantity of money (M). Rewrite this equation as: Quantity of money (M) = Nominal GDP ($P \times Y$) ÷ Velocity of circulation (V). Quantity of money is $975 billion ÷ 10, which equals $97.5 billion.

2. The inflation rate in the long run equals the growth rate of the quantity of money minus the growth rate of real GDP, which is 10 percent a year minus 3 percent a year, or 7 percent a year.

13.3 THE COST OF INFLATION

Inflation decreases potential GDP, slows economic growth, and consumes leisure time. These outcomes occur for four reasons that we classify as the four costs of inflation. They are:

- Tax costs
- Shoe-leather costs
- Confusion costs
- Uncertainty costs

■ Tax Costs

We've seen that inflation occurs when the quantity of money grows more rapidly than real GDP. But why would we ever want to make this happen? Why don't we keep the quantity of money growing at the same pace as real GDP grows? One part of the answer is that the government gets revenue from inflation.

Inflation Is a Tax

The government covers a budget deficit by selling securities. If the Bank of Canada buys some of these securities (in the open market), the monetary base increases and the government spends newly created money. If the Bank buys enough government securities to make the money supply increase 10 percent a year faster than the growth of real GDP, inflation is 10 percent a year.

If the government is spending new money, and if there are no more new goods and services to spend it on, people must be spending less (to make room for the government's spending). How does that happen? It happens because we pay a tax on our money holding.

Suppose that a business holds $100,000 in money on the average. With inflation at 10 percent a year, that money will buy only $90,000 of goods and services after one year. So the business has "lost" $10,000. In effect, it has paid a tax of this amount to the government. And the government has used the inflation tax, in the form of the newly created money that it spends, to buy goods and services.

So inflation is a tax. If this were the end of the story, the inflation tax would not be a problem. It would be just one more way for the government to collect revenue—an alternative to the income tax or the sales tax. Inflation would transfer resources from households and businesses to the government, but it would not be a cost to society. Some would pay and others would benefit, and the two actions would cancel each other out.

Inflation Tax, Saving, and Investment

The inflation tax is bigger than the tax on money holding, and it interacts with the income tax to lower saving and investment. The core of the problem is that inflation increases the nominal interest rate, and because income taxes are paid on nominal interest income, the true income tax rate rises with inflation. Let's consider an example.

Suppose the real interest rate is 4 percent a year and the income tax rate is 50 percent. With no inflation, the nominal interest rate is also 4 percent a year and 50 percent of this rate is taxed. The real after-tax interest rate is 2 percent a year (50 percent of 4 percent). Now suppose the inflation rate is 4 percent a year, so the nominal interest rate is 8 percent a year. The after-tax nominal rate is 4 percent a year (50 percent of 8 percent). Now subtract the 4 percent inflation rate from this amount, and you see that the after-tax real interest rate is zero! The true income tax rate is 100 percent.

The higher the inflation rate, the higher is the true income tax rate on income from capital. And the higher the tax rate, the higher is the interest rate paid by borrowers and the lower is the after-tax interest rate received by lenders.

With a low after-tax real interest rate, the incentive to save is weakened and the supply of saving decreases. With a high cost of borrowing, the amount of investment decreases. And with a fall in saving and investment, the pace of capital accumulation slows and so does the long-term growth rate of real GDP.

■ Shoe-Leather Costs

The "shoe-leather costs" of inflation are costs that arise from an increase in the velocity of circulation of money and an increase in the amount of running around that people do to try to avoid incurring losses from the falling value of money.

When money loses value at a rapid anticipated rate, it does not function well as a store of value and people try to avoid holding it. They spend their incomes as soon as they receive them, and firms pay out incomes—wages and dividends—as soon as they receive revenue from their sales. The velocity of circulation increases.

During the 1990s, when inflation in Brazil was around 80 percent a year, people would end a taxi ride at the ATM closest to their destination, get some cash, pay the driver, and finish their journey on foot. The driver would deposit the cash in his bank account before looking for the next customer.

During the 1920s when inflation in Germany exceeded 50 percent a month—hyperinflation—wages were paid and spent twice in a single day!

Imagine the inconvenience of spending most of your time figuring out how to keep your money holdings close to zero.

One way of keeping money holdings low is to find other means of payment such as tokens, commodities, or even barter. All of these are less efficient than money as a means of payment. For example, in Israel during the 1980s, when inflation reached 1,000 percent a year, the U.S. dollar started to replace the increasingly worthless shekel. Consequently, people had to keep track of the exchange rate between the shekel and the U.S. dollar hour by hour and had to engage in many additional and costly transactions in the foreign exchange market.

■ Confusion Costs

We make economic decisions by comparing marginal cost and marginal benefit. Marginal cost is a real cost—an opportunity forgone. Marginal benefit is a real benefit—a willingness to forgo an opportunity. Although costs and benefits are real, we use money as our unit of account and standard of value to calculate them. Money is our measuring rod of value. Borrowers and lenders, workers and employers, all make agreements in terms of money. Inflation makes the value of money change, so it changes the units on our measuring rod.

Does it matter that our units of value keep changing? Some economists think it matters a lot. Others think it matters only a little.

Economists who think it matters a lot point to the obvious benefits of stable units of measurement in other areas of life.

For example, suppose that we had not invented an accurate time-keeping technology and clocks and watches gained 5 to 15 minutes a day. Imagine the hassle you would have arriving at class on time or catching the start of the ball game.

For another example, suppose that a tailor used an elastic tape measure. You would end up with a jacket that was either too tight or too sloppy, depending on how tightly the tape was stretched.

For a third example, recall the crash of the Mars Climate Orbiter.

> "Mars Climate Orbiter … failed to achieve Mars orbit because of a navigation error. … Spacecraft operating data needed for navigation were provided … in English units rather than the specified metric units. This was the direct cause of the failure." (Mars Program Independent Assessment Team Summary Report, March 14, 2000)

If rocket scientists can't make correct calculations that use just two units of measurement, what chance do ordinary people and business decision-makers have of making correct calculations that involve money when its value keeps changing?

These examples of confusion and error that can arise from units of measurement don't automatically mean that a changing value of money is a big problem. But they raise the possibility that it might be.

■ Uncertainty Costs

A high inflation rate brings increased uncertainty about the long-term inflation rate. Will inflation remain high for a long time or will price stability be restored? This increased uncertainty makes long-term planning difficult and gives people a shorter-term focus. Investment falls, and so the growth rate of real GDP slows.

But this increased uncertainty also misallocates resources. Instead of concentrating on the activities at which they have a comparative advantage, people find it more profitable to search for ways of avoiding the losses that inflation inflicts. As a result, inventive talent that might otherwise work on productive innovations works on finding ways of profiting from the inflation instead.

Uncertainty about inflation makes the economy behave a bit like a casino in which some people gain and some lose and no one can predict where the gains and losses will fall. Gains and losses occur because of unpredictable changes in the value of money. In a period of rapid, unpredictable inflation, resources get diverted from productive activities to forecasting inflation. It becomes more profitable to forecast the inflation rate correctly than to invent a new product. Doctors, lawyers, accountants, farmers—just about everyone—can make themselves better off, not by specializing in the profession for which they have been trained but by spending more of their time dabbling as amateur economists and inflation forecasters and managing their investment portfolios.

From a social perspective, this diversion of talent resulting from inflation is like throwing scarce resources onto the garbage heap. This waste of resources is a cost of inflation.

ECONOMICS *in the* **NEWS**

May 29, 2001

Scotiabank's Mexican Unit Slashes Rates on Mortgages and Auto Loans to 19.9%

Grupo Financiero Scotiabank Inverlat SA, the Mexican unit of Bank of Nova Scotia, cut its interest rates on both auto loans and mortgages to 19.9% as benchmark interest rates are at a seven-year low. "Clients are the winners in this interest-rate reduction," said Peter Cardinal, the bank's chairman, at a news conference. The rates on car loans dropped from 25%, while mortgage rates declined from between 21% and 25%.

NATIONAL POST

Questions
1. What does this article suggest about the inflation rate in Mexico at the time?
2. What negative effects could such an inflation rate have upon the Mexican economy?
3. Would you say that the inflation rate was rising or falling at the time?

 e **Foundations** **13.3**

■ How Big Is the Cost of Inflation?

The cost of inflation depends on its rate and its predictability. The higher the rate, the greater is the cost. And the more unpredictable the rate, the greater is the cost. Canadian economist Peter Howitt of Brown University, building on work by Robert Barro of Harvard University, has estimated that if inflation is lowered from 3 percent a year to zero, the growth rate of real GDP will rise by between 0.06 and 0.09 percentage points a year. These numbers might seem small. But they are growth rates. After 30 years, real GDP would be 2.3 percent higher and the accumulated value of all the additional future output would be worth 85 percent of current GDP, or about $850 billion!

In hyperinflation, the costs are much greater. Hyperinflation is rare, but there have been some spectacular examples of it. Several European countries experienced hyperinflation during the 1920s after World War I and again during the 1940s after World War II. But hyperinflation is more than just a historical curiosity. It occurs in today's world. In 1994, the African nation of Zaire had a hyperinflation that peaked at a monthly inflation rate of 76 percent. Also in 1994, Brazil almost reached the hyperinflation stratosphere with a monthly inflation rate of 40 percent. A cup of coffee that cost 15 cruzeiros in 1980 cost 22 billion cruzeiros in 1994. And Russia has had a near hyperinflation experience in recent years.

CHECKPOINT 13.3

Study Guide pp. 194–197

*e*Foundations 13.3

3 **Identify the costs of inflation and the benefits of a stable value of money.**

Practice Problem 13.3

Suppose that you have $1,000 in your saving account and the bank pays an interest rate of 5 percent a year. The inflation rate is 3 percent a year. The government taxes the interest that you earn on your deposit at 20 percent.
a. Calculate the nominal after-tax interest rate that you earn.
b. Calculate the real after-tax interest rate that you earn.

Exercise 13.3

Sally has a credit card balance of $3,000. The company that issued the credit card charges a nominal interest rate of 15 percent a year on unpaid balances. The inflation rate is 3 percent a year.
a. Calculate the real interest rate that Sally pays the credit card company.
b. If the inflation rate falls to 2 percent a year and the credit card company keeps the nominal interest rate at 15 percent a year, calculate the real interest rate that Sally pays.

Solution to Practice Problem 13.3

a. You earn $50 of interest and the government takes $10 of the interest in tax, so the interest income you earn after tax is $40. The nominal after-tax interest rate is 4 percent a year.
b. The real after-tax interest rate equals the nominal after-tax interest rate minus the inflation rate, which is 1 percent a year.

CHAPTER CHECKPOINT

Key Points

1 **Explain what determines the demand for money and how the demand for money and the supply of money determine the nominal interest rate.**

- The demand for money is the relationship between the quantity of money demanded and the nominal interest rate, other things remaining the same—the higher the nominal interest rate, the smaller is the quantity of money demanded.

- Increases in real GDP and the price level increase the demand for money. Some advances in financial technology increase the demand for money, and some decrease it.

- Each day, the price level, real GDP, and financial technology are given and money market equilibrium determines the nominal interest rate.

- To lower the nominal interest rate, the Bank of Canada increases the quantity of money. To raise the nominal interest rate, the Bank of Canada decreases the quantity of money.

2 **Explain how in the long run, the quantity of money determines the price level and money growth brings inflation.**

- In the long run, real GDP equals potential GDP and the real interest rate is the level that makes the quantity of investment demanded equal the quantity of saving supplied in the global financial market.

- The nominal interest rate equals the equilibrium real interest rate plus the expected inflation rate.

- Money market equilibrium in the long run determines the price level.

- An increase in the quantity of money, other things remaining the same, increases the price level by the same percentage in the long run.

- The inflation rate in the long run equals the growth rate of the quantity of money minus the growth rate of potential GDP.

- The equation of exchange and the velocity of circulation provide an alternative way of viewing the relationship between the quantity of money and the price level (and money growth and inflation).

3 **Identify the costs of inflation and the benefits of a stable value of money.**

- Inflation has four costs: tax costs, shoe-leather costs, confusion costs, and uncertainty costs.

- The higher the inflation rate, the greater are these four costs.

Key Terms

Exercises

1. The Bank of Canada decreases the quantity of money, once and for all. Explain the effects of this action in the short run and the long run on:
   a. The quantity of money demanded.
   b. The nominal interest rate.
   c. The real interest rate.
   d. Real GDP.
   e. The price level.
   f. The inflation rate.

2. In 2000, the United States was at full employment. The quantity of money was growing at 8.3 percent a year, the nominal interest rate was 9.5 percent a year, real GDP grew at 5 percent a year, and the inflation rate was 3.1 percent a year.
   a. Calculate the real interest rate.
   b. Use the information given along with the quantity theory of money to see whether the velocity of circulation was constant. If it was not constant, how did it change? And if it changed, why might it have changed?

3. Use the links on your Foundations Web site to visit the Bank of Canada and Statistics Canada and obtain the latest data on the quantity of M1 and M2+, real GDP, and the price level.
   a. Calculate the inflation rate, the growth rate of the two money aggregates, and the growth rate of real GDP.
   b. Use the information you calculated in part (a) to determine whether the velocity of circulation was constant. If it was not constant, how did it change? If it changed, why might it have changed?
   c. Given the information that you obtained in part (a), do you think the Bank of Canada is trying to slow inflation, speed up inflation, or neither? If neither, what do you think the Bank of Canada is trying to do?

4. Suppose the government passes a new law that sets a limit on the interest rate that credit card companies can charge on unpaid balances. As a result, the nominal interest rate charged by credit card companies falls from 15 percent a year to 7 percent a year. If the average income tax rate is 30 percent, explain how the real after-tax interest rate on unpaid credit card balances changes.

5. Explain what the costs of inflation were for Brazilians when inflation hit 40 percent a month in Brazil.

6. Explain why businesses paid workers twice a day during the hyperinflation in Germany after World War I and why workers spent their incomes as soon as they were paid.

7. Use the link on your Foundations Web site to visit the International Monetary Fund's World Economic Outlook pages.
   a. Obtain data on money supply growth rates and inflation rates for the 10 countries with the highest inflation and the 10 with the lowest inflation.
   b. Use a spreadsheet program (Excel or Lotus 1-2-3) to make a scatter diagram of the data, placing money growth on the *x*-axis and inflation on the *y*-axis.
   c. Do these data support or contradict the quantity theory of money?

Economic Fluctuations

Part 5

CHAPTER CHECKLIST

When you have completed your study of this chapter,
you will be able to:

1 Distinguish between autonomous expenditure and induced expenditure and explain how real **GDP** influences expenditure plans.

2 Explain how real **GDP** adjusts to achieve equilibrium expenditure.

3 Describe and explain the expenditure multiplier.

Our economy grows, bringing ever-higher living standards, and inflation persists, bringing an ever-rising cost of living. But economic growth and inflation don't proceed at a constant pace. Instead, they ebb and flow in a business cycle. For example, we had a recession in 1990–1991 when real GDP shrank for almost a year. The rest of the 1990s brought expansion but at a pace that was sluggish until 1997. Real GDP growth slowed again during 2001, and another recession was widely expected. Firms began to lay off workers and the Bank of Canada repeatedly cut the interest rate in an attempt to keep spending growing and avoid recession.

This chapter begins your exploration of the business cycle by studying the aggregate expenditure model—a model of the forces that make aggregate expenditure and real GDP fluctuate. In Chapter 15, you will explore the connection between aggregate expenditure and aggregate demand and use the *AS-AD* model to explain the business cycle.

A QUICK REVIEW AND PREVIEW

Before we begin our exploration of the aggregate expenditure model, let's take stock of what we've learned and preview where we are heading.

■ The Economy at Full Employment

At full employment, real GDP equals potential GDP and the unemployment rate equals the natural unemployment rate. Potential GDP and the natural unemployment rate are determined by *real* factors and are independent of the price level.

The quantity of money and potential GDP determine the price level. Changes in the quantity of money change the price level but have no effect on potential GDP.

This description of the forces that determine real GDP and the price level applies only to the full-employment economy. Away from potential GDP, real and monetary factors interact to determine real GDP and the price level. But potential GDP is like an anchor around which the economy fluctuates in the business cycle.

■ Departures from Full Employment

We previewed the concepts of aggregate supply and aggregate demand and the *AS-AD* model in Chapter 8. Aggregate supply and aggregate demand determine equilibrium real GDP and the price level. And fluctuations in aggregate supply and aggregate demand bring fluctuations around full employment.

Our economy is like an ocean. Movements in the full-employment economy are the tides, and fluctuations around full employment are the waves. The forces that make the tides—the position of the moon and its gravitational pull—are like the real and money forces that determine potential GDP and the price level. The forces that make the waves—the interaction of the moon and wind—are like the interactions of real and money forces that make the economy fluctuate.

We're now going to learn more about the forces that make our economy fluctuate by using the *AS-AD* model. We begin this process in this chapter by isolating and focusing on aggregate demand fluctuations.

■ Fixed Price Level

The interaction of aggregate demand and aggregate supply determine equilibrium real GDP and the price level simultaneously. But the forces that we want to isolate and put in clear view are hard to see if we consider the *simultaneous* adjustment of real GDP and the price level. So in the aggregate expenditure model, the price level is fixed. The model explains what determines the quantity of real GDP demanded and changes in that quantity *at a given price level*.

The aggregate expenditure model was originally designed to explain what happens in an economy in deep recession when firms can't cut their prices any further but can increase production without raising their prices, so the price level is actually fixed. But you can also think about this model as telling us about the forces that determine the quantity of real GDP demanded at any given price level.

14.1 EXPENDITURE PLANS AND REAL GDP

You've seen from the circular flow of expenditure and income (Chapter 5, p. 111) that aggregate expenditure equals the sum of:

- Consumption expenditure, C
- Investment, I
- Government expenditure on goods and services, G
- Net exports, $X - M$

That is:

$$\text{Aggregate expenditure} = C + I + G + X - M.$$

■ Planned and Unplanned Expenditures

Honda Canada decides to produce 250,000 cars in 2001. The factors of production that it hires to produce these cars cost $5 billion. So the incomes generated and the value of production was $5 billion. Households, other firms, governments, and people in the rest of the world made their expenditure plans. Suppose they decided to buy 200,000 Honda cars. Their total expenditure on cars is $4 billion. Honda had planned to sell 225,000 cars and add 25,000 cars to its inventory. (Firms need inventories to smooth out short-term fluctuations in production and sales.) But Honda is left with 50,000 cars in inventory. Valuing this inventory at the cost of production, Honda Canada has invested $1 billion in an inventory of cars. Total expenditure on cars, including Honda's investment in inventories, equals the value of cars produced and equals the incomes paid to produce the cars—$5 billion. But *planned* expenditure on cars is less than the value of the cars produced because Honda planned to invest only $0.5 billion in new inventory.

This account of a year in the life of Honda Canada can be extended to the economy as a whole. Aggregate expenditure equals income and GDP. But aggregate *planned* expenditure might not equal real GDP because firms can end up with larger or smaller inventories than they had intended. Firms make their production plans, the aggregate value of which is real GDP. They pay incomes that equal the value of production, so aggregate income equals real GDP. Households and governments make their planned purchases of goods and services, and net exports are as planned. Firms make their planned purchases of new buildings, plant, and equipment, and their *planned* inventory changes. The total of all these spending plans is **aggregate planned expenditure.**

If aggregate planned expenditure equals real GDP, the change in firms' inventories is the planned change. But if aggregate planned expenditure exceeds real GDP, firms' inventories are smaller than planned; and if aggregate planned expenditure is less than real GDP, firms' inventories are larger than planned. Notice that *actual* expenditure, which equals *planned* expenditure plus the *unplanned* change in firms' inventories, always equals real GDP and aggregate income.

Unplanned changes in firms' inventories lead to changes in production and incomes. If unwanted inventories have piled up, firms decrease production, which decreases real GDP. If inventories have fallen below their target levels, firms increase production, which increases real GDP.

Aggregate planned expenditure
Planned consumption expenditure plus planned investment plus planned government expenditure plus planned exports minus planned imports.

■ Autonomous Expenditure and Induced Expenditure

Continuing the story of Honda, when the firm decreases production in 2002, the incomes of its workers and suppliers of other factors of production decrease. If most firms share Honda's experience, aggregate incomes fall, and with lower incomes, people decrease their expenditures on all types of goods and services—including cars. So in 2002, Honda sells even fewer cars than it sold in 2001. Where does this process end?

Autonomous expenditure
The components of aggregate expenditure that do not change when real GDP changes.

Induced expenditure
The components of aggregate expenditure that change when real GDP changes.

To begin to answer this question, we must again extend the Honda story to the economy as a whole. Just as lower incomes bring a decrease in expenditure on cars, so lower *aggregate* income—lower real GDP—brings a decrease in expenditure on a wide range of goods and services. We divide aggregate expenditure into two components: autonomous expenditure and induced expenditure. **Autonomous expenditure** is the part of aggregate expenditure that does not respond to changes in real GDP. It equals investment plus government expenditure, plus exports, plus the components of consumption expenditure and imports that are not influenced by real GDP. **Induced expenditure** is the part of aggregate expenditure that changes in response to a change in real GDP. It equals consumption expenditure minus imports (excluding the elements of consumption and imports that are part of autonomous expenditure).

Your next task is to learn more about the influence of real GDP on induced expenditure. We start with its influence on consumption expenditure.

■ The Consumption Function

Consumption function
The relationship between consumption expenditure and disposable income, other things remaining the same.

The **consumption function** is the relationship between consumption expenditure and disposable income, other things remaining the same. *Disposable income* is aggregate income—GDP—minus net taxes. (Net taxes are taxes paid to the government minus transfer payments received from the government.)

Households must either spend their disposable income on consumption or save it. A decision to spend a dollar on consumption is a decision not to save a dollar. The consumption decision and the saving decision is one decision.

Consumption Plans

For households and the economy as a whole, as disposable income increases, planned consumption expenditure increases. But the increase in planned consumption is less than the increase in disposable income. The table in Figure 14.1 shows a consumption schedule. It lists the consumption expenditure that people plan to undertake at each level of disposable income.

Figure 14.1 shows a consumption function based on the consumption schedule. Along the consumption function, the points labelled A through F correspond to the rows of the table. For example, point E shows that when disposable income is $800 billion, consumption expenditure is $750 billion. Along the consumption function, as disposable income increases, consumption expenditure increases.

At point A on the consumption function, consumption expenditure is $150 billion even though disposable income is zero. This consumption expenditure is called *autonomous consumption,* and it is the amount of consumption expenditure that would take place in the short run, even if people had no current income. This consumption expenditure would be financed either by spending past savings or by borrowing.

■ FIGURE 14.1
The Consumption Function

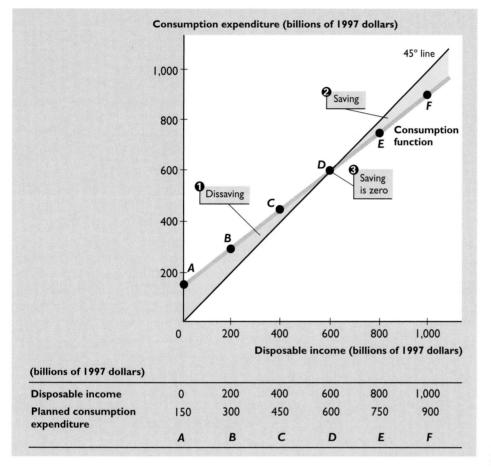

(billions of 1997 dollars)						
Disposable income	0	200	400	600	800	1,000
Planned consumption expenditure	150	300	450	600	750	900
	A	*B*	*C*	*D*	*E*	*F*

The table shows consumption expenditure (and saving) plans at various levels of disposable income. The figure graphs these data as the consumption function. The figure also shows a 45° line along which consumption expenditure equals disposable income.

❶ When the consumption function is above the 45° line, saving is negative (dissaving occurs).

❷ When the consumption function is below the 45° line, saving is positive.

❸ At the point where the consumption function intersects the 45° line, all disposable income is consumed and saving is zero.

Figure 14.1 also shows a 45° line. Because the scale on the *x*-axis measures disposable income and the scale on the *y*-axis measures consumption expenditure, and because the two scales are equal, the 45° line serves as a reference line for comparing consumption expenditure and disposable income. Between *A* and *D*, consumption expenditure exceeds disposable income; between *D* and *F*, disposable income exceeds consumption expenditure; and at point *D*, consumption expenditure equals disposable income.

You can see saving in Figure 14.1. When consumption expenditure exceeds disposable income (and the consumption function is above the 45° line), saving is negative—called *dissaving*. When consumption expenditure is less than disposable income (and the consumption function is below the 45° line), saving is positive. And when consumption expenditure equals disposable income (the consumption function intersects the 45° line), saving is zero.

When consumption expenditure exceeds disposable income, past savings are used to pay for current consumption. Such a situation cannot last forever, but it can and does occur if disposable income falls temporarily.

Marginal Propensity to Consume

Marginal propensity to consume
The fraction of a change in disposable income that is spent on consumption—the change in consumption expenditure divided by the change in disposable income that brought it about.

The **marginal propensity to consume** (*MPC*) is the fraction of a change in disposable income that is spent on consumption. It is calculated as the change in consumption expenditure divided by the change in disposable income that brought it about. That is:

$$MPC = \frac{\text{Change in consumption expenditure}}{\text{Change in disposable income}}.$$

Suppose that when disposable income increases from $600 billion to $800 billion, consumption expenditure increases from $600 billion to $750 billion. The $200 billion increase in disposable income increases consumption expenditure by $150 billion. Using these numbers in the formula to calculate the *MPC*, it is:

$$MPC = \frac{\$150 \text{ billion}}{\$200 \text{ billion}} = 0.75.$$

The marginal propensity to consume tells us that when disposable income increases by $1, consumption expenditure increases by 75¢.

Figure 14.2 shows that the *MPC* equals the slope of the consumption function. A $200 billion increase in disposable income from $400 billion to $600 billion is the base of the red triangle. The increase in consumption expenditure that results from this increase in income is $150 billion and is the height of the triangle. The slope of the consumption function is given by the formula "slope equals rise over run" and is $150 billion divided by $200 billion, which equals 0.75—the *MPC*.

■ **FIGURE 14.2**
Marginal Propensity to Consume

e/**Foundations 14.1**

The marginal propensity to consume, *MPC*, is equal to the change in consumption expenditure divided by the change in disposable income, other things remaining the same. The slope of the consumption function measures the *MPC*.

In the figure, ❶ a $200 billion change in disposable income brings ❷ a $150 billion change in consumption expenditure, so ❸ the *MPC* is $150 billion ÷ $200 billion = 0.75.

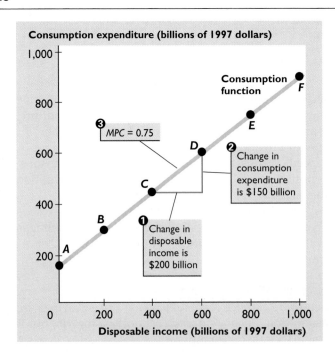

Other Influences on Consumption

Chapter 9 lists the factors that influence saving plans (see p. 208), and these same factors influence planned consumption expenditure. They are:

- Disposable income
- Real interest rate
- The buying power of net assets
- Expected future disposable income

A change in disposable income leads to a change in consumption expenditure and a movement along the consumption function. A change in any of the other influences *shifts* the consumption function. For example, when the real interest rate falls or when the buying power of net assets or expected future income increases, consumption expenditure increases. Figure 14.3 shows the effects of these changes on the consumption function, which shifts upward from CF_0 to CF_1. Such a shift commonly occurs during the expansion phase of the business cycle because a stock market boom increases the buying power of net assets and expected future income increases. A shift such as this occurred during the strong expansion of the late 1990s.

When the real interest rate rises or when the buying power of assets or expected future income decreases, consumption expenditure decreases. Figure 14.3 also shows the effects of these changes on the consumption function, which shifts downward from CF_0 to CF_2. Such a shift often occurs when a recession begins because the stock market crashes and expected future income decreases. A shift such as this occurred during the Great Depression of the 1930s.

■ **FIGURE 14.3**

Shifts in the Consumption Function

*e*Foundations **14.1**

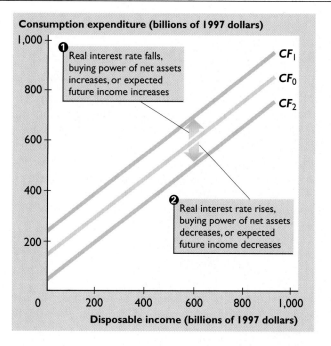

❶ A fall in the real interest rate or an increase in either the buying power of net assets or expected future income increases consumption expenditure and shifts the consumption function upward from CF_0 to CF_1.

❷ A rise in the real interest rate or a decrease in either the buying power of net assets or expected future income decreases consumption expenditure and shifts the consumption function downward from CF_0 to CF_2.

Eye On The CANADIAN ECONOMY

The Canadian Consumption Function

The figure shows data on consumption expenditure and disposable income in Canada. Each blue dot represents consumption expenditure and disposable income in Canada for a year between 1970 and 2000 (labelled at five-year intervals).

The orange line is an estimate of the Canadian consumption function for the period from 1970 to 2000.

The slope of this Canadian consumption function—the marginal propensity to consume—is 0.67, which means that on the average, a $1 increase in disposable income brings a 67¢ increase in consumption expenditure.

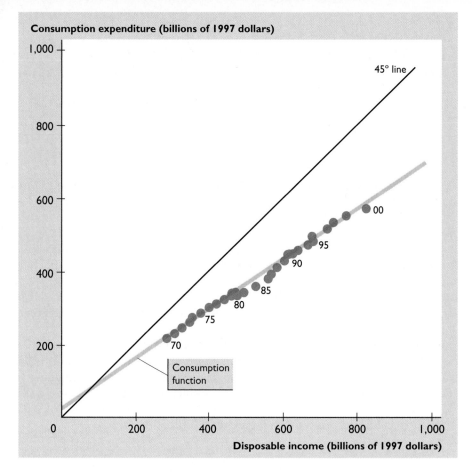

■ Imports and GDP

Imports are the other major component of induced expenditure. Many factors influence Canadian imports, but in the short run, one factor dominates: Canada's real GDP. Other things remaining the same, an increase in Canada's real GDP brings an increase in Canadian imports. The reason for this influence is that an increase in real GDP is also an increase in income. As incomes increase, people increase their expenditures on most goods and services. Because many goods and services are imported, an increase in incomes brings an increase in imports.

The relationship between imports and real GDP is described by the **marginal propensity to import,** which is the fraction of an increase in real GDP that is spent on imports.

Marginal propensity to import
The fraction of an increase in real GDP that is spent on imports—the change in imports divided by the change in real GDP.

$$\text{Marginal propensity to import} = \frac{\text{Change in imports}}{\text{Change in real GDP}}.$$

For example, if, with other things remaining the same, a $100 billion increase in real GDP increases imports by $25 billion, then the marginal propensity to import is 0.25.

CHECKPOINT 14.1

1 Distinguish between autonomous expenditure and induced expenditure and explain how real **GDP** influences expenditure plans.

Study Guide pp. 202–206

e/**Foundations 14.1**

Practice Problems 14.1

1. If the marginal propensity to consume is 0.8 and if disposable income increases by $50 billion, by how much will consumption expenditure change?
2. If Canadians decrease the fraction of each dollar of disposable income they spend on consumption, how will the Canadian consumption function change?
3. If Canadians decide to decrease consumption expenditure by a fixed number of dollars, how will the Canadian consumption function change?
4. Suppose that expected future disposable income increases. Explain how this change in expectation will influence the consumption function.
5. Figure 1 illustrates a consumption function. Calculate the marginal propensity to consume and autonomous consumption.

FIGURE 1

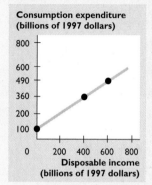

Exercises 14.1

1. The marginal propensity to consume in Japan is less than that in Canada, and for any amount of real GDP, Canadians spend more on consumption than do the Japanese. Compare the consumption functions in Japan and Canada.
2. As China becomes richer, we expect that the marginal propensity to consume in China will decrease. What effect will this decrease have on the consumption function in China?
3. Suppose that the Japanese real interest rate rises. Explain how this change influences the Japanese consumption function.
4. In 2000, autonomous consumption in the United Kingdom was £150 billion and the marginal propensity to consume was 0.9. Plot the U.K. consumption function.
5. The marginal propensity to import is higher in Singapore than it is in Canada. With the growth rate of real GDP in Singapore exceeding that in Canada, which country's imports are growing more quickly and why?

Solutions to Practice Problems 14.1

1. Consumption expenditure will increase by $40 billion, which is 0.8 multiplied by the change in disposable income of $50 billion.
2. The marginal propensity to consume will decrease, so the slope of the consumption function will become less steep.
3. Autonomous consumption decreases, so the consumption function shifts downward.
4. Consumption expenditure will increase, and the consumption function will shift upward.
5. When disposable income increases by $200 billion, consumption expenditure increases by $130 billion. The *MPC* is $130 billion ÷ $200 billion = 0.65. Autonomous consumption (consumption expenditure that is independent of disposable income) equals the *y*-axis intercept and is $100 billion (Figure 2).

FIGURE 2

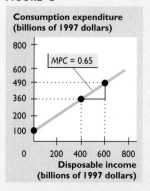

14.2 EQUILIBRIUM EXPENDITURE

You are now going to discover how aggregate expenditure plans interact to determine real GDP. First we will study the relationship between aggregate planned expenditure and real GDP. Then we'll study the forces that make aggregate planned expenditure and actual expenditure equal.

An aggregate expenditure schedule and an aggregate expenditure curve describe the relationship between aggregate planned expenditure and real GDP.

■ Aggregate Planned Expenditure and GDP

You've seen that consumption expenditure increases when disposable income increases. Disposable income equals aggregate income—real GDP—minus net taxes, so disposable income and consumption expenditure increase when real GDP increases. We use this link between consumption expenditure and real GDP to determine equilibrium expenditure.

The table in Figure 14.4 sets out an aggregate expenditure schedule together with the components of aggregate planned expenditure. All the variables are measured in real (constant dollar) values. To calculate aggregate planned expenditure at a given real GDP, we add the various components together.

The first column of the table shows real GDP, and the second column shows the consumption expenditure generated by each level of real GDP. A $300 billion increase in real GDP generates a $225 billion increase in consumption expenditure—the MPC is 0.75. The next three columns show investment, government expenditure on goods and services, and exports. These items do not depend on real GDP. They are autonomous expenditure. Investment is $200 billion, government expenditure is $100 billion, and exports are $150 billion. The next column shows imports, which increase as real GDP increases. A $300 billion increase in real GDP generates a $75 billion increase in imports. The marginal propensity to import is 0.25.

The final column shows aggregate planned expenditure—the sum of planned consumption expenditure, investment, government expenditure on goods and services, and exports minus imports.

Figure 14.4 plots an aggregate expenditure curve. Real GDP is shown on the *x*-axis, and aggregate planned expenditure is shown on the *y*-axis. The aggregate expenditure curve is the red line *AE*. Points *A* through *F* on that curve correspond to the rows of the table. The *AE* curve is a graph of aggregate planned expenditure (last column) plotted against real GDP (first column).

Figure 14.4 also shows the components of aggregate expenditure. The horizontal lines in the figure show the constant components of aggregate expenditure—investment (*I*), government expenditure (*G*), and exports (*X*). The line labelled *C* + *I* + *G* + *X* adds consumption expenditure to the constant components.

Finally, to construct the *AE* curve, subtract imports (*M*) from the *C* + *I* + *G* + *X* line. Aggregate expenditure is expenditure on Canadian-made goods and services. But *C* + *I* + *G* + *X* includes expenditure on imported goods and services. For example, if a student buys a Honda motorbike that is made in Japan, the student's expenditure is part of *C*, but it is not an expenditure on a Canadian-made good. To find the expenditure on Canadian-made goods, we subtract the value of the imported motorbike.

Figure 14.4 shows that aggregate planned expenditure increases as real GDP increases. But notice that for each $1 increase in real GDP, aggregate planned

■ **FIGURE 14.4**

Aggregate Expenditure

*e*Foundations **14.2**

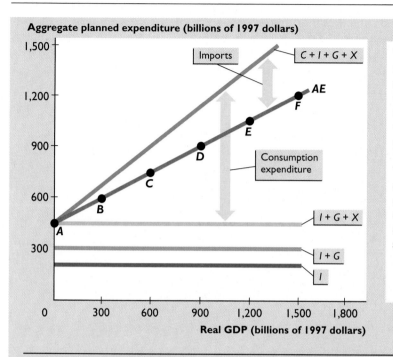

The aggregate expenditure schedule shows the relationship between aggregate planned expenditure and real GDP. For example, in row B of the table, when real GDP is $300 billion, aggregate planned expenditure is $600 billion ($225 + $200 + $100 + $150 − $75). As real GDP increases, aggregate planned expenditure increases.

This relationship is graphed as the aggregate expenditure curve AE. The components of aggregate expenditure that increase with real GDP are consumption expenditure and imports. The other components—investment, government expenditure, and exports—do not vary with real GDP.

	Real GDP (Y)	Consumption expenditure (C)	Investment (I)	Government expenditure (G)	Exports (X)	Imports (M)	Aggregate planned expenditure (AE = C + I + G + X − M)
				Planned expenditure			
				(billions of 1997 dollars)			
A	0	0	200	100	150	0	450
B	300	225	200	100	150	75	600
C	600	450	200	100	150	150	750
D	900	675	200	100	150	225	900
E	1,200	900	200	100	150	300	1,050
F	1,500	1,125	200	100	150	375	1,200

expenditure increases by less than $1. For example, when real GDP increases from $900 billion to $1,200 billion (row *D* to row *E* of the table), aggregate planned expenditure increases from $900 billion to $1,050 billion. A $300 billion increase in real GDP brings a $150 billion increase in aggregate planned expenditure. So a $1 increase in real GDP brings a 50¢ increase in aggregate planned expenditure. This feature of the *AE* curve is important and plays a big role in determining equilibrium expenditure and the effect of a change in autonomous expenditure.

The *AE* curve summarizes the relationship between aggregate planned expenditure and real GDP. But what determines the point on the *AE* curve at which the economy operates? What determines actual aggregate expenditure?

■ Equilibrium Expenditure

Equilibrium expenditure
The level of aggregate expenditure that occurs when aggregate planned expenditure equals real GDP.

Equilibrium expenditure occurs when aggregate *planned* expenditure equals real GDP. In Figure 14.5(a) aggregate planned expenditure equals real GDP at all the points on the 45° line. Equilibrium occurs where the *AE* curve intersects the 45° line at point *D* with real GDP at $900 billion. If real GDP is less than $900 billion, aggregate planned expenditure exceeds real GDP; and if real GDP exceeds $900 billion, aggregate planned expenditure is less than real GDP.

■ **FIGURE 14.5**
Equilibrium Expenditure

e/**Foundations 14.2**

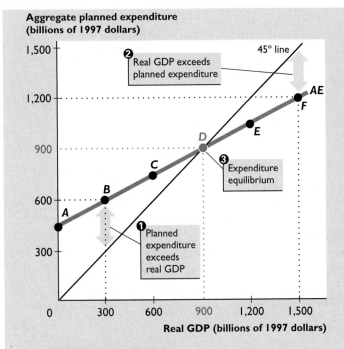

(a) Equilibrium expenditure

	Real GDP	Aggregate planned expenditure	Unplanned inventory change
		(billions of 1997 dollars)	
A	0	450	−450
B	300	600	−300
C	600	750	−150
D	900	900	0
E	1,200	1,050	150
F	1,500	1,200	300

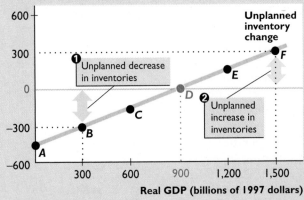

(b) Unplanned inventory change

The table shows expenditure plans and unplanned changes in inventories at different levels of real GDP. Part (a) illustrates equilibrium expenditure, and part (b) shows the unplanned inventory changes that bring changes in real GDP.

❶ When aggregate planned expenditure exceeds real GDP, an unplanned decrease in inventories occurs. Firms increase production, and real GDP increases.

❷ When real GDP exceeds aggregate planned expenditure, an unplanned increase in inventories occurs. Firms decrease production, and real GDP decreases.

❸ When aggregate planned expenditure equals real GDP, there are no unplanned inventory changes and real GDP remains at its equilibrium level.

■ Convergence to Equilibrium

At equilibrium expenditure, production plans and spending plans agree, and there is no reason for production or spending to change. But when aggregate planned expenditure and actual aggregate expenditure are unequal, production plans and spending plans are misaligned, and a process of convergence towards equilibrium expenditure occurs. Throughout this process, real GDP adjusts.

What are the forces that move aggregate expenditure towards equilibrium? To answer this question, we look at a situation in which aggregate expenditure is away from equilibrium. Suppose that in Figure 14.5, real GDP is $300 billion. With real GDP at $300 billion, actual aggregate expenditure is also $300 billion. But aggregate planned expenditure is $600 billion (point B in Figure 14.5a). Aggregate planned expenditure exceeds actual expenditure. When people spend $600 billion and firms produce goods and services worth $300 billion (point B in Figure 14.5b), firms' inventories decrease by $300 billion. Because the change in inventories is part of investment, actual investment is $300 billion less than planned investment.

Real GDP doesn't remain at $300 billion for long. Firms have inventory targets based on their sales. When inventories fall below target, firms increase production. Suppose that they increase production by $300 billion. Real GDP increases by $300 billion to $600 billion. At this real GDP, aggregate planned expenditure rises to $750 billion (point C in Figure 14.5a). The unplanned decrease in inventories is now $150 billion, so firms increase production yet again. Suppose that they increase production by another $300 billion to $900 billion. At this real GDP, aggregate planned expenditure rises to $900 billion (point D in Figure 14.5a). The unplanned inventory change is zero, and firms have no reason to change production. Real GDP and aggregate expenditure are in equilibrium.

You can do a thought experiment similar to the one we've just done but starting with a level of real GDP greater than equilibrium expenditure. In this case, planned expenditure is less than actual expenditure, inventories pile up, and firms cut production. Real GDP decreases, and it will continue to decrease until it reaches its equilibrium level of $900 billion.

Back at Honda Canada

You can now answer the question about Honda that we left dangling earlier in this chapter. Recall that faced with unwanted inventories, Honda and most other firms cut production in 2002. So Honda sells even fewer cars in 2002 than in 2001. We asked: Where does this process end? It ends when expenditure equilibrium is reached. The economy arrives at an expenditure equilibrium because a $1 increase in real GDP brings a less than $1 increase in aggregate planned expenditure (and a $1 decrease in real GDP brings a less than $1 decrease in aggregate planned expenditure).

When aggregate planned expenditure exceeds real GDP, firms increase production and real GDP increases. Aggregate planned expenditure increases, but real GDP increases by more than planned expenditure, so eventually the gap between planned expenditure and actual expenditure closes. Similarly, when aggregate planned expenditure is less than real GDP, firms cut production and real GDP decreases. Aggregate planned expenditure decreases, but real GDP decreases by more than planned expenditure, so again, eventually, the gap between planned expenditure and actual expenditure is closed.

ECONOMICS *in the* NEWS

October 18, 2001

Inventories Remain High

Finished-product inventories stood at $20 billion in August, just short of the record level reported in May 2001.

Finished-product inventories in some industries have remained high in recent months, despite manufacturers' efforts to clear inventories by curtailing production.

STATISTICS CANADA, *THE DAILY*

Questions
1. Inventories can increase for two reasons. What are they?
2. Why do you think inventories remained high in August 2001?
3. What effect would the manufacturers' actions have on equilibrium expenditure?
4. Does this article tell us anything about the likelihood of a recession in the near future?

 *e*Foundations **14.2**

Say's Law and Keynes' Principle of Effective Demand

During the Industrial Revolution, which began around 1760 and lasted for 70 years, technological change was rapid. People have talked about the "new economy" of the 1990s. But the 1990s was just another phase of a process that began in the truly new economy of the early 1800s. The pace of change in economic life during those years was unprecedented. Never before had old jobs been destroyed and new jobs created on such a scale. In this environment of rapid economic change, people began to wonder whether the economy could create enough jobs and a high enough level of demand to ensure that people would buy all the things that the new industrial economy could produce.

A French economist, Jean-Baptiste Say, provided the assurance that people were looking for.

Born in 1767 (he was 9 years old when Adam Smith's *Wealth of Nations* was published—see p. 12), Say suffered the wrath of Napoleon for his conservative call for smaller and leaner government and was the most famous economist of his era. His book *A Treatise on Political Economy (Traité d'économie politique),* published in 1803, became the best-selling university economics textbook in both Europe and North America.

In this book, Say reasoned that *supply creates its own demand*—an idea that came to be called *Say's Law.*

You've seen Say's Law at work in the full-employment economy. The real wage rate adjusts to ensure that the quantity of labour demanded equals the quantity of labour supplied and real GDP equals potential GDP. The real interest rate adjusts to ensure that the quantity of investment demanded equals the quantity of saving supplied. Because saving equals disposable income minus consumption expenditure, the equilibrium real interest rate ensures that consumption expenditure plus investment exactly equals potential GDP.

Say's Law came under attack at various times during the nineteenth century. But it came under an onslaught during the Great Depression of the 1930s. With about a quarter of the labour force unemployed and real GDP at around three-quarters of potential GDP, it seemed like a stretch to argue that supply creates its own demand. But there was no simple principle or slogan with which to replace Say's Law.

In the midst of the Great Depression, in 1936, a British economist, John Maynard Keynes, provided the catchphrase that the world was looking for: *effective demand.*

Born in England in 1883, Keynes was one of the outstanding people of the twentieth century. He was a prolific writer on economic issues, represented Britain at the Versailles peace conference at the end of World War I, and played a prominent role in creating the International Monetary Fund, which monitors the global macroeconomy today.

Keynes revolutionized macroeconomic thinking by turning Say's Law on its head. Supply does *not* create its own demand, and *effective demand* determines real GDP. If businesses fail to spend on new capital the amount that people plan to save, aggregate demand will be less than potential GDP. Prices and wages are sticky, and resources can become unemployed and remain unemployed indefinitely.

The aggregate expenditure model that you're studying in this chapter is the modern distillation of Keynes' idea.

Jean-Baptiste Say

John Maynard Keynes

CHECKPOINT 14.2

2 **Explain how real GDP adjusts to achieve equilibrium expenditure.**

Study Guide pp. 206–209

*e*Foundations 14.2

Practice Problem 14.2

Table 1 is a spreadsheet that gives the components of real GDP in billions of dollars.
a. Calculate aggregate planned expenditure when real GDP is $200 billion.
b. Calculate aggregate planned expenditure when real GDP is $600 billion.
c. Calculate equilibrium expenditure.
d. If real GDP is $200 billion, explain the process that moves the economy towards equilibrium expenditure.
e. If real GDP is $600 billion, explain the process that moves the economy towards equilibrium expenditure.

TABLE 1

	A	B	C	D	E	F	G
1		Y	C	I	G	X	M
2	A	100	110	50	60	60	15
3	B	200	170	50	60	60	30
4	C	300	230	50	60	60	45
5	D	400	290	50	60	60	60
6	E	500	350	50	60	60	75
7	F	600	410	50	60	60	90

Exercise 14.2

Figure 1 shows aggregate planned expenditure.
a. Calculate aggregate planned expenditure when real GDP is $8 billion.
b. Calculate aggregate planned expenditure when real GDP is $2 billion.
c. Calculate equilibrium expenditure.
d. If real GDP is $8 billion, explain the process that moves the economy towards equilibrium expenditure.
e. If real GDP is $2 billion, explain the process that moves the economy towards equilibrium expenditure.

FIGURE 1

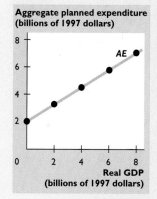

Solution to Practice Problem 14.2

a. Aggregate planned expenditure equals $C + G + I + X - M$. When real GDP is $200 billion, aggregate planned expenditure equals $170 + $50 + $60 + $60 − $30, which equals $310 billion (row *B* of Table 1).
b. Aggregate planned expenditure equals $C + G + I + X - M$. When real GDP is $600 billion, aggregate planned expenditure equals $410 + $50 + $60 + $60 − $90, which equals $490 billion (row *F* of Table 1).
c. Equilibrium expenditure occurs when aggregate planned expenditure equals real GDP. Equilibrium expenditure is $400 billion (row *D* of Table 1).
d. If real GDP is $200 billion, aggregate planned expenditure is $310 billion. Aggregate planned expenditure exceeds real GDP, so firms' inventories decrease. Expenditure plans are not fulfilled. Firms increase production to restore their inventories, and real GDP increases. As long as aggregate planned expenditure exceeds real GDP, firms will increase production to restore their inventories to their target level and real GDP will increase.
e. If real GDP is $600 billion, aggregate planned expenditure is $490 billion. Aggregate planned expenditure is less than real GDP, so firms' inventories increase. Firms cut production and try to reduce their inventories. Real GDP decreases. As long as aggregate planned expenditure is less than real GDP, firms' inventories will increase. Firms will cut production and try to reduce their inventories to their target level. Real GDP decreases.

14.3 THE EXPENDITURE MULTIPLIER

Multiplier
The amount by which a change in any component of autonomous expenditure is magnified or multiplied to determine the change that it generates in equilibrium expenditure and real GDP.

When investment increases, aggregate expenditure and real GDP also increase. But the increase in real GDP is larger than the increase in investment. The **multiplier** is the amount by which a change in investment (or any other component of autonomous expenditure) is magnified or multiplied to determine the change that it generates in equilibrium expenditure and real GDP.

■ The Basic Idea of the Multiplier

The growth of the Internet during the 1990s brought a large increase in investment in personal computers, servers, fibre-optic cables, satellites, and other communication and computing equipment. These investment expenditures increased aggregate expenditure and real GDP.

The increase in real GDP increased disposable income. The increase in disposable income increased consumption expenditure. And the increased consumption expenditure added even more to aggregate expenditure. Real GDP and disposable income increased further, and so did consumption expenditure.

The initial increase in investment brought an even bigger increase in aggregate expenditure because it induced an increase in consumption expenditure.

The multiplier determines the magnitude of the increase in aggregate expenditure that results from an increase in investment or another component of autonomous expenditure.

Consumption expenditure decisions, imports, and income taxes that open a gap between disposable income and real GDP all influence the multiplier. But we can understand the basic idea of the multiplier more clearly if we temporarily ignore the effects of imports and income taxes and focus on the role of consumption expenditure.

Figure 14.6 illustrates the multiplier. The table shows an initial aggregate expenditure schedule, and the initial AE curve is AE_0. With this AE schedule and curve, equilibrium expenditure and real GDP are $900 billion. You can see this equilibrium in row B of the table and where the curve AE_0 intersects the 45° line at point B in the figure.

Now suppose that investment increases by $50 billion. What happens to equilibrium expenditure? Figure 14.6 shows the answer. When this increase in investment is added to the initial aggregate planned expenditure, aggregate planned expenditure increases by $50 billion at each level of real GDP. The new AE curve is AE_1. The new equilibrium expenditure, highlighted in the table (row D'), occurs where AE_1 intersects the 45° line and is $1,100 billion (point D'). At this real GDP, aggregate planned expenditure equals real GDP. The increase in equilibrium expenditure ($200 billion) is larger than the increase in investment that brought it about ($50 billion).

We've just analyzed the effects of an *increase* in investment. The same analysis applies to a *decrease* in investment. If initially the AE curve is AE_1, equilibrium expenditure and real GDP are $1,100 billion. A decrease in investment of $50 billion shifts the AE curve downward by $50 billion to AE_0. Equilibrium expenditure decreases from $1,100 billion to $900 billion. The decrease in equilibrium expenditure ($200 billion) is larger than the decrease in investment that brought it about ($50 billion).

FIGURE 14.6
The Multiplier

e/**Foundations 14.3**

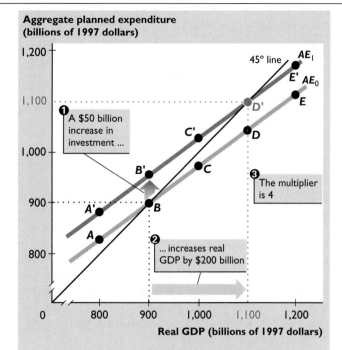

❶ A $50 billion increase in investment shifts the *AE* curve upward by $50 billion from AE_0 to AE_1.

❷ Equilibrium expenditure increases by $200 billion from $900 billion to $1,100 billion.

❸ The increase in equilibrium expenditure is 4 times the increase in autonomous expenditure, so the multiplier is 4.

Real GDP (Y)	Aggregate planned expenditure			
		Original (AE₀)		New (AE₁)
		(billions of 1997 dollars)		
800	A	825	A'	875
900	B	900	B'	950
1,000	C	975	C'	1,025
1,100	D	1,050	D'	1,100
1,200	E	1,125	E'	1,175

■ The Size of the Multiplier

The multiplier is the amount by which a change in autonomous expenditure is multiplied to determine the change in equilibrium expenditure that it generates. To calculate the multiplier, we divide the change in equilibrium expenditure by the change in autonomous expenditure that generated it. That is:

$$\text{Multiplier} = \frac{\text{Change in equilibrium expenditure}}{\text{Change in autonomous expenditure}}.$$

The change in equilibrium expenditure also equals the change in real GDP, which we'll call ΔY. In Figure 14.6, the change in autonomous expenditure is a change in investment, which we'll call ΔI. The multiplier is:

$$\text{Multiplier} = \frac{\Delta Y}{\Delta I}.$$

In Figure 14.6, equilibrium expenditure increases by \$200 billion (ΔY = \$200 billion) and investment increases by \$50 billion (ΔI = \$50 billion), so the multiplier is

$$\text{Multiplier} = \frac{\Delta Y}{\Delta I} = \frac{\$200 \text{ billion}}{\$50 \text{ billion}} = 4.$$

The multiplier is 4—real GDP changes by 4 times the change in investment.

■ Why Is the Multiplier Greater Than 1?

The multiplier is greater than 1 because an increase in autonomous expenditure induces further increases in aggregate expenditure—induced expenditure increases. If Bell Canada spends \$10 million on new telephone equipment, aggregate expenditure and real GDP immediately increase by \$10 million. Telephone engineers and other workers now have more income, and they spend part of the extra income on cars, microwave ovens, vacations, and a host of other goods and services. Real GDP now increases by the initial \$10 million plus the extra consumption expenditure induced by the \$10 million increase in income. The producers of cars, microwave ovens, vacations, and other goods now have increased incomes, and they in turn spend part of the increase in their incomes on consumption goods and services. Additional income induces additional expenditure, which creates additional income.

■ The Multiplier and the MPC

The greater the marginal propensity to consume, the larger is the multiplier. To see why, let's do a calculation. Remember that we are temporarily ignoring imports and income taxes. The change in real GDP (ΔY) equals the change in consumption expenditure (ΔC) plus the change in investment (ΔI). That is:

$$\Delta Y = \Delta C + \Delta I.$$

But the change in consumption expenditure is determined by the change in real GDP and the marginal propensity to consume. It is:

$$\Delta C = MPC \times \Delta Y.$$

Now substitute $MPC \times \Delta Y$ for ΔC in the previous equation:

$$\Delta Y = MPC \times \Delta Y + \Delta I.$$

Now solve for ΔY as

$$(1 - MPC) \times \Delta Y = \Delta I,$$

and rearrange the equation:

$$\Delta Y = \frac{1}{(1 - MPC)}\Delta I.$$

Finally, divide both sides of the previous equation by ΔI to give

$$\text{Multiplier} = \frac{\Delta Y}{\Delta I} = \frac{1}{(1 - MPC)}.$$

If we use the numbers in Figure 14.6, the *MPC* is 0.75, so the multiplier is

$$\text{Multiplier} = \frac{\Delta Y}{\Delta I} = \frac{1}{(1 - 0.75)} = \frac{1}{0.25} = 4.$$

So far, we've ignored the effects of imports and income taxes on the multiplier. Let's now look at the influence of these two factors.

■ Imports and Income Taxes

The size of the multiplier depends, in general, not only on consumption decisions but also on imports and income taxes. Imports make the multiplier smaller than it otherwise would be. To see why, think about what happens following an increase in investment. The increase in investment increases real GDP, which in turn increases consumption expenditure. But part of the increase in expenditure is on imported goods and services, not on Canadian-made goods and services. Only expenditure on Canadian-made goods and services increases Canada's real GDP. The larger the marginal propensity to import, the smaller is the change in Canada's real GDP that results from a change in autonomous expenditure.

Income taxes also make the multiplier smaller than it otherwise would be. Again, think about what happens following an increase in investment. The increase in investment increases real GDP. But with increased incomes, income tax payments increase and disposable income increases by less than the increase in real GDP. Because disposable income influences consumption expenditure, the increase in consumption expenditure is less than it would be if income tax payments had not changed.

The marginal tax rate determines the extent to which income tax payments change when real GDP changes. The **marginal tax rate** is the fraction of a change in real GDP that is paid in income taxes. The larger is the marginal tax rate, the smaller is the change in disposable income and real GDP that results from a given change in autonomous expenditure.

The marginal propensity to import and the marginal tax rate together with the marginal propensity to consume determine the multiplier. And their combined influence determines the slope of the *AE* curve.

The general formula for the multiplier is:

$$\text{Multiplier} = \frac{\Delta Y}{\Delta I} = \frac{1}{(1 - \text{Slope of } AE \text{ curve})}.$$

Figure 14.7 compares two situations. In Figure 14.7(a), there are no imports and no taxes. The slope of the *AE* curve equals the *MPC*, which is 0.75, so the multiplier is 4 (as we calculated above).

In Figure 14.7(b), imports and income taxes decrease the slope of the *AE* curve to 0.5. So in this case, the multiplier is:

$$\text{Multiplier} = \frac{\Delta Y}{\Delta I} = \frac{1}{(1 - 0.5)} = 2.$$

Over time, the value of the multiplier changes as the marginal tax rate, the marginal propensity to consume, and the marginal propensity to import change. These ongoing changes make the multiplier hard to predict. But they do not change the fundamental fact that an initial change in autonomous expenditure leads to a *magnified* change in equilibrium expenditure.

Marginal tax rate
The fraction of a change in real GDP that is paid in income taxes—the change in tax payments divided by the change in real GDP.

The Multiplier and the Slope of the AE Curve   *e*Foundations **14.3**

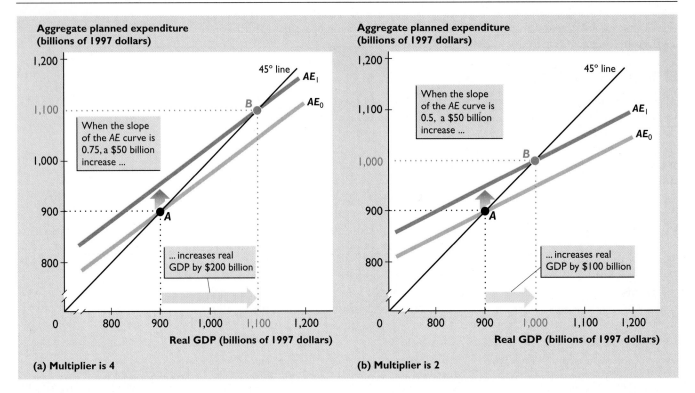

(a) Multiplier is 4   **(b) Multiplier is 2**

In part (a), with no imports and income taxes, the slope of the AE curve equals the marginal propensity to consume, which in this example is 0.75. The multiplier is 4.

In part (b), with imports and income taxes, the slope of the AE curve is less than the marginal propensity to consume. In this example, the slope of the AE curve is 0.5 and the multiplier is 2.

■ Business-Cycle Turning Points

Let's use what we've learned to gain some insights into what happens as the economy moves from expansion to recession and from recession to expansion. Economists understand business-cycle turning points as well as seismologists understand earthquakes. They understand the forces and mechanisms that produce them, but they can't predict them. The forces that bring business-cycle turning points are the swings in autonomous expenditure such as investment and exports. The mechanism that gives momentum to the economy's new direction is the multiplier.

An expansion is triggered by an increase in autonomous expenditure that increases aggregate planned expenditure. At the moment the economy turns the corner into expansion, aggregate planned expenditure exceeds real GDP. In this situation, firms see their inventories taking an unplanned dive. The expansion now begins. To meet their inventory targets, firms increase production, and real GDP begins to increase. This initial increase in real GDP brings higher incomes, and the higher incomes stimulate consumption expenditure. The multiplier process kicks in, and the expansion picks up speed.

The process works in reverse at a business cycle peak. A recession is triggered by a decrease in autonomous expenditure that decreases aggregate planned expenditure. At the moment the economy turns the corner into recession, real GDP exceeds aggregate planned expenditure. In this situation, firms see unplanned inventories piling up. The recession now begins. To reduce their inventories, firms cut production, and real GDP begins to decrease. This initial decrease in real GDP brings lower incomes, which cut consumption expenditure. The multiplier process reinforces the initial cut in autonomous expenditure, and the recession takes hold.

Eye On The CANADIAN ECONOMY
Recent Fluctuations

Figure (a) shows some key facts about real GDP growth in the Canadian economy during the 1990s and 2000.

Figure (b) shows that during the recession and recovery of the early 1990s, fluctuations in the growth of autonomous expenditure (the red line) were similar to the fluctuations in consumption expenditure (the blue line). The aggregate expenditure model predicts these similar fluctuations.

Through the second half of the 1990s, consumption expenditure kept growing despite three dips in the growth of autonomous expenditure. This strong growth of consumption expenditure arose from expectations of continued rapid income growth and was reflected in a rapid growth of stock market prices.

In 2001, the growth rate of autonomous expenditure plunged amidst fears that a recession was around the corner.

Despite a slowing of the growth rate, growth in the first quarter of 2001 was close to the average growth rate of the 1990s.

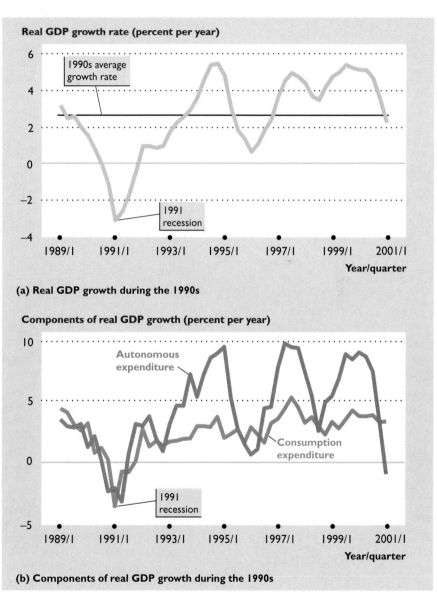

(a) Real GDP growth during the 1990s

(b) Components of real GDP growth during the 1990s

SOURCE: Statistics Canada.

Study Guide pp. 209–212

*e*Foundations 14.3

3 **Describe and explain the expenditure multiplier.**

Practice Problems 14.3

1. An economy has no imports or taxes, the *MPC* is 0.80, and real GDP is $150 billion. If businesses increase investment by $5 billion:
   a. Calculate the multiplier.
   b. Calculate the change in real GDP.
   c. Calculate the new level of real GDP.
   d. Explain why real GDP increases by more than $5 billion.

2. An economy has no imports or taxes. An increase in autonomous expenditure of $2 trillion increases equilibrium expenditure by $8 trillion.
   a. Calculate the multiplier.
   b. Calculate the marginal propensity to consume.
   c. What happens to the multiplier if an income tax is introduced?

Exercises 14.3

1. In a closed economy with no income taxes, the marginal propensity to consume is 0.60 and real GDP is $100 billion. If investment decreases by $10 billion:
   a. Calculate the multiplier.
   b. Calculate the change in real GDP.
   c. Calculate the new level of real GDP.
   d. Explain why real GDP decreases by more than $10 billion.

2. In a closed economy with no income taxes, the multiplier is 1.25. Autonomous expenditure increases by $2 trillion.
   a. Calculate the change in real GDP.
   b. Calculate the marginal propensity to consume.
   c. If the government decides to open the country up to international trade, explain how international trade influences the multiplier.

Solutions to Practice Problems 14.3

1a. The multiplier equals $1/(1 - MPC)$. *MPC* is 0.8, so the multiplier is 5.
1b. Real GDP increases by $25 billion. The increase in investment increases real GDP by the multiplier (5) times the change in investment ($5 billion).
1c. Real GDP increases from $150 billion to $175 billion.
1d. Real GDP increases by more than $5 billion because the increase in investment induces an increase in consumption expenditure.

2a. The multiplier is the increase in equilibrium expenditure ($8 trillion) divided by the increase in autonomous expenditure ($2 trillion). The multiplier is 4.
2b. The marginal propensity to consume is 0.75. The multiplier = $1/(1 - MPC)$. So $4 = 1/(1 - MPC)$, and *MPC* is 0.75.
2c. If the government introduces an income tax, the slope of the *AE* curve becomes smaller. The multiplier equals $1/(1 - \text{Slope of the } AE \text{ curve})$. So with an income tax, the multiplier becomes smaller.

CHAPTER CHECKPOINT

Key Points

1 **Distinguish between autonomous expenditure and induced expenditure and explain how real GDP influences expenditure plans.**

- Investment plus government expenditure plus exports, which real GDP does *not* influence directly, plus the components of consumption expenditure and imports that are not influenced by real GDP is called *autonomous expenditure*.
- Consumption expenditure minus imports, which real GDP influences, is called *induced expenditure*.
- Consumption expenditure varies with disposable income and depends on the marginal propensity to consume.
- Imports vary with real GDP and depend on the marginal propensity to import.

2 **Explain how real GDP adjusts to achieve equilibrium expenditure.**

- Actual aggregate expenditure equals real GDP and differs from planned expenditure when firms have unplanned inventory changes.
- If aggregate planned expenditure exceeds real GDP, firms increase production and real GDP increases. If real GDP exceeds aggregate planned expenditure, firms decrease production and real GDP decreases.
- Real GDP changes until aggregate planned expenditure equals real GDP.

3 **Describe and explain the expenditure multiplier.**

- When autonomous expenditure changes, equilibrium expenditure changes by a larger amount: There is a multiplier.
- The multiplier is greater than 1 because a change in autonomous expenditure changes induced expenditure.
- The larger the marginal propensity to consume, the larger is the multiplier.
- Income taxes and imports make the multiplier smaller.

Key Terms

Aggregate planned expenditure, 327
Autonomous expenditure, 328
Consumption function, 328
Equilibrium expenditure, 336
Induced expenditure, 328

Marginal propensity to consume, 330
Marginal propensity to import, 332
Marginal tax rate, 343
Multiplier, 340

Exercises

1. In the world economy (a closed economy), autonomous consumption is $1 trillion, the marginal propensity to consume is 0.8, investment is $5 trillion, and government expenditure on goods and services are $4 trillion. Taxes are $4 trillion and do not vary with real GDP.
   a. Calculate disposable income when real GDP is $30 trillion.
   b. Calculate consumption expenditure when real GDP is $30 trillion.
   c. Calculate aggregate planned expenditure when real GDP is $30 trillion.
   d. Calculate equilibrium expenditure.
   e. If real GDP is $30 trillion, explain the process that takes the economy to equilibrium expenditure.
   f. If real GDP is $40 trillion, explain the process that takes the economy to equilibrium expenditure.

2. In Exercise 1, investment increases by $0.5 trillion. Calculate:
   a. The size of the shift of the *AE* curve.
   b. The size of the multiplier.
   c. The change in equilibrium expenditure.

3. The Mexican government has just cut the marginal income tax rate. Explain how this cut will change:
   a. Consumption expenditure in Mexico.
   b. Equilibrium expenditure in Mexico.
   c. The multiplier in Mexico.

4. The Japanese economy is in a recession, and economists have suggested that the Japanese government increase its expenditure on goods and services but not change taxes. Explain how such a policy change will influence equilibrium expenditure. Would such a policy change help to turn the economy from recession to expansion?

5. It is 2002, and the U.S. economy is experiencing a slowdown in the growth of real GDP. The pace at which consumption and other components of aggregate expenditure are growing is slowing. Explain how these events will influence:
   a. The U.S. consumption function.
   b. The U.S. aggregate expenditure curve.
   c. Equilibrium expenditure in the United States.
   d. Autonomous expenditure in Mexico and Canada.
   e. The consumption functions of Mexico and Canada.
   f. The aggregate expenditure curves of Mexico and Canada.
   g. Equilibrium expenditure in Mexico and Canada.

6. Throughout the 1990s, the economy of Russia has been depressed. Use the aggregate expenditure model to illustrate the state of the Russian economy during its depression. Then explain how the following events might have influenced aggregate expenditure and equilibrium expenditure in Russia:
   a. The booming economy in the rest of the world.
   b. Tax increases in Russia.
   c. Cuts in government expenditure on goods and services in Russia.

AS–AD and the Business Cycle

When you have completed your study of this chapter, you will be able to:

1 Provide a technical definition of recession and describe the history of the Canadian business cycle.

2 Explain the influences on aggregate supply.

3 Explain the influences on aggregate demand.

4 Explain how fluctuations in aggregate demand and aggregate supply create the business cycle.

The last recession of the twentieth century was in 1990-91. A long expansion followed that became rapid during 1999 and 2000. But by late 2001, the growth of the economy had slowed and the optimism of the "new economy" had turned to the pessimism of recession.

In this chapter, we're going to use the aggregate supply–aggregate demand, or *AS-AD*, model to study recessions and expansions.

You had a sneak preview of the *AS-AD* model in Chapter 8. There, you met the concepts of aggregate supply, aggregate demand, and macroeconomic equilibrium. You saw that the expansion of potential GDP increases aggregate supply and brings economic growth; and that growth in the quantity of money increases aggregate demand and brings inflation. You've filled in a lot of the details about economic growth (in Chapters 9 and 10) and inflation (in Chapters 11–13). Now we're filling in the details on the business cycle. We begin with a bit of business-cycle history.

15.1 BUSINESS-CYCLE DEFINITIONS AND FACTS

We defined the *business cycle* in Chapter 1 (p. 7) as a periodic but irregular up-and-down movement in production and jobs. A business cycle has two phases, expansion and recession, and two turning points, a peak and a trough. An expansion runs from a trough to a peak, and a recession runs from a peak to a trough.

Over the business cycle, real GDP fluctuates around potential GDP. When real GDP is below potential GDP, resources are *under*used—some labour is unemployed and capital is underemployed. When real GDP is above potential GDP, resources are *over*used—people work longer hours than they are willing to put up with in the long run, capital is worked so intensively that it is not maintained in prime condition, delivery times lengthen, bottlenecks occur, and backorders increase.

■ Dating Business-Cycle Turning Points

The task of identifying and dating business-cycle phases and turning points is performed not by Statistics Canada but by a private research organization called the Economic Cycle Research Institute (ECRI). The ECRI uses a business-cycle dating method developed by the National Bureau of Economic Research (NBER) in the United States to date the business cycles of 18 countries, including Canada. The ECRI dates the last completed Canadian recession as running from a peak in July 1990 to a trough in March 1991.

Recession
A decrease in real GDP that lasts for at least two quarters (six months) or a period of significant decline in total output, income, employment, and trade, usually lasting from six months to a year, and marked by widespread contractions in many sectors of the economy.

To date the cycle turning points, the ECRI needs a definition of recession. A standard definition of **recession** is a decrease in real GDP that lasts for at least two quarters (six months). The ECRI uses a broader definition. It defines a recession as "a period of significant decline in total output, income, employment, and trade, usually lasting from six months to a year, and marked by widespread contractions in many sectors of the economy."

In this definition of recession, total output and income are the same thing as real GDP. You've seen that employment fluctuations closely match fluctuations in real GDP. And because real GDP measures production in all sectors of the economy, a decrease in real GDP means that many sectors of the economy are experiencing declining production. So although the ECRI looks beyond real GDP to date the turning points precisely, a two-quarter decrease in real GDP is a good practical indicator of recession and gives almost the same dating as the more refined method of the ECRI.

■ Canadian Business-Cycle History

Canada has experienced 11 complete cycles since 1895. (In 2001, we were in the 12th expansion). Over all 11 complete cycles, the average length of an expansion is 87 months (a bit more than 7 years), the average length of a recession is 21 months, and the average time from trough to trough is 108 months (9 years). So over the 106 years since 1895, the Canadian economy has been in recession for about one-fifth of the time and in expansion for about four-fifths of the time.

The 106-year averages that we've just reviewed hide significant changes that have occurred in the relative length of the recession and expansion phases. Figure 15.1 shows these changes by dividing Canadian business-cycle history into three periods: 1895–1921; 1921–1946; and 1946–2001.

FIGURE 15.1
Recession, Expansion, and Cycle Length: A Summary

*e*Foundations 15.1

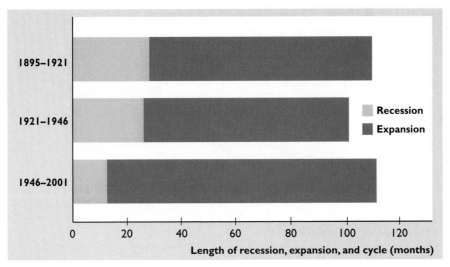

During the late nineteenth century and through World War II, recessions lasted for more than two years on the average. During the twentieth century, recessions have shortened and expansions have lengthened.

SOURCE: Morris Altman, *Review of Income and Wealth*, 1992, Economic Cycle Research Institute.

The figure shows that before 1921, recessions lasted for 28 months and expansions for 80 months on the average. So during this period, recession was a relatively common experience.

From the start of the 1920s to just after World War II, the average recession shortened slightly to 26 months and the average expansion also shortened to 74 months. One recession during this period, the Great Depression, was enormous and lasted for 48 months.

During the years since World War II, the average recession has shortened yet again to 13 months and the average expansion has lengthened to 93 months (almost 8 years) for completed cycles and to 98 months if we include the incomplete expansion that began in April 1991 and was still in place in mid–2001.

■ The Current Cycle

The current cycle began at a trough that followed a recession that ran from April 1990 to March 1991. After March 1991, the economy expanded. This expansion, which in September 2001 had lasted for 126 months, is the second longest in Canadian history. (The record expansion occurred between 1958 and 1974. On the ECRI business-cycle dating method, the economy expanded for 195 months beginning in March 1958 and ending in June 1974.)

Figure 15.2 shows three features of the current cycle: real GDP fluctuations around potential GDP, the unemployment rate, and the inflation rate. The dates in the three parts of the figure are aligned above each other so that you can see the relationship between the three variables. The recession is highlighted in all three parts and runs from the first quarter of 1990 to the first quarter of 1991.

In part (a), you can see that real GDP decreased from a peak in the first quarter of 1990 to a trough in the first quarter of 1991. In the recession, real GDP moves from above to below potential GDP. From the trough, real GDP begins its long

■ **FIGURE 15.2**

The Current Cycle

A recession (highlighted in all three parts) ran from the first quarter of 1990 to the first quarter of 1991. It was followed by the second-longest expansion in Canadian history. When real GDP decreases in the recession (part a), the unemployment rate increases (part b) and keeps increasing for several quarters. The inflation rate decreases (part c).

As real GDP increases towards potential GDP, the unemployment rate falls towards the natural unemployment rate and the inflation rate falls. When real GDP climbs above potential GDP, the unemployment rate falls below the natural unemployment rate, and the inflation rate increases.

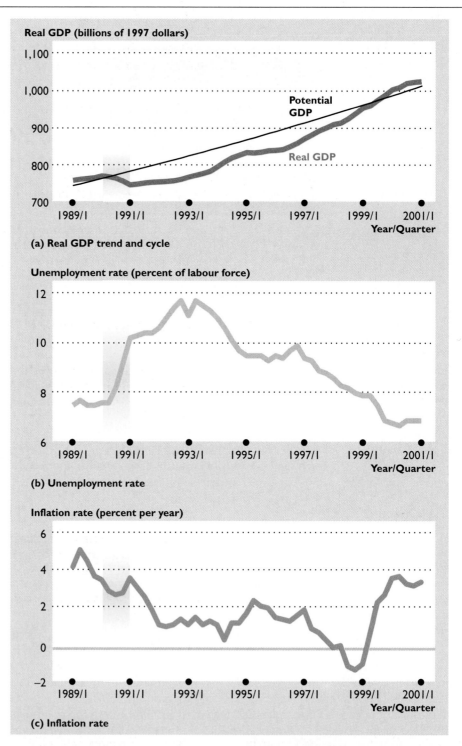

(a) Real GDP trend and cycle

(b) Unemployment rate

(c) Inflation rate

SOURCE: Statistics Canada.

expansion. But it remains below potential GDP until the late 1990s. No one knows for sure when real GDP reached potential GDP, but in the figure, we assume that full employment was reached by the third quarter of 1999. Rapid productivity growth kept potential GDP growing through this period.

In part (b), you can see that the unemployment rate increased during the recession. It kept increasing for another year after the recession, but then began a long and steady decline. At its peak, the unemployment rate exceeded the natural unemployment rate. This tendency for the unemployment rate to increase after the recession is over is normal. It occurs because firms are producing below potential and seeking cost-cutting measures.

It is likely that the natural unemployment rate decreased during the 1990s. But during 1999, when real GDP surpassed potential GDP, the unemployment rate fell below the natural unemployment rate.

In part (c), the inflation rate fell as the economy went into recession in 1990. It reached its lowest level in 1998 and it then began to increase as real GDP moved above potential GDP. So the business cycle is not confined to the real economy. The money economy cycles alongside the real economy. The inflation rate tends to decrease when real GDP is below potential GDP and to increase when real GDP is above potential GDP.

CHECKPOINT 15.1

1 **Provide a technical definition of recession and describe the history of the Canadian business cycle.**

Study Guide pp. 218–220

e/**Foundations 15.1**

Practice Problem 15.1

Table 1 shows U.S. real GDP each quarter from 1989 through 1993. In these years:
a. When was the United States at a business-cycle peak?
b. When was the United States at a business-cycle trough?
c. Did the United States experience a recession? If so, when?
d. Did the United States experience an expansion? If so, when?

Exercise 15.1

Table 2 shows real GDP in Mexico in each quarter of 1994, 1995, and 1996.
a. In which quarter was Mexico at a business-cycle peak?
b. In which quarter was Mexico at a business-cycle trough?
c. Did Mexico experience a recession during these years? If so, when?
d. In what quarters did Mexico experience an expansion?

Solution to Practice Problem 15.1

a. The United States was at a business-cycle peak in the second quarter of 1990.
b. The United States was at a business-cycle trough in the first quarter of 1991.
c. Yes—in the third and fourth quarters of 1990 and the first quarter of 1991.
d. Yes—from the end of the first quarter of 1989 to the second quarter of 1990 and from the end of the first quarter of 1991 to the fourth quarter of 1993.

TABLE 1

Billions of 1996 dollars

Year	Quarter			
	1	2	3	4
1989	6,544	6,579	6,611	6,634
1990	6,716	6,732	6,719	6,664
1991	6,631	6,669	6,685	6,721
1992	6,783	6,847	6,900	6,991
1993	6,989	7,031	7,062	7,169

TABLE 2

Trillions of 1993 pesos

Year	Quarter			
	1	2	3	4
1994	1.25	1.19	1.29	1.27
1995	1.21	1.16	1.28	1.27
1996	1.27	1.29	1.25	1.37

15.2 AGGREGATE SUPPLY

We introduced the concept of *aggregate supply* in Chapter 8 (pp. 175–176). You learned that aggregate supply is the relationship between the quantity of real GDP supplied and the price level when all other influences on production plans remain the same. Other things remaining the same, the higher the price level, the greater is the quantity of real GDP supplied, and the lower the price level, the smaller is the quantity of real GDP supplied. We illustrate aggregate supply with an upward-sloping aggregate supply curve.

In Chapter 8, we described how the price level influences the quantity of real GDP supplied, but we didn't explain *why* it occurs. Here, we'll explain the reasons. We'll also explore the link between aggregate supply and potential GDP, and we'll study the factors that make aggregate supply change.

■ Aggregate Supply Basics

The *quantity of real GDP supplied* depends on:

* The quantity of labour employed
* The quantities of capital and human capital and the technologies they embody
* The quantities of land and natural resources used
* The amount of entrepreneurial talent available

At full employment, the real wage rate makes the quantity of labour demanded equal the quantity of labour supplied, and the quantity of real GDP supplied equals potential GDP. Over the business cycle, the quantity of real GDP supplied fluctuates around potential GDP and the quantity of labour employed fluctuates. The quantities of capital and human capital grow, technology advances, and the amount of entrepreneurial talent increases as the population increases. These changes are the source of economic growth, but they occur gradually and do not fluctuate much over the business cycle.

■ Aggregate Supply and Potential GDP

Figure 15.3 shows an aggregate supply curve, *AS*, and a potential GDP line. Along the aggregate supply curve, the only influence on production plans that changes is the price level. A rise in the price level brings an increase in the quantity of real GDP supplied and a movement up along the aggregate supply curve; a fall in the price level brings a decrease in the quantity of real GDP supplied and a movement down along the aggregate supply curve. All the other influences on production plans remain constant. Among these other influences are:

* The money wage rate
* The money prices of other resources

In contrast, along the potential GDP line, when the price level changes, the money wage rate and the money prices of other resources change by the same percentage as the change in the price level to keep the real wage rate (and other real prices) at the full-employment equilibrium level.

FIGURE 15.3

A Change in the Quantity of Real GDP Supplied

e/**Foundations** 15.2

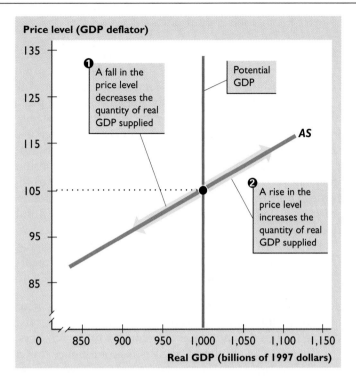

The aggregate supply (*AS*) curve shows the relationship between the quantity of real GDP supplied and the price level when the money wage rate, other resource prices, and potential GDP remain the same. The quantity of real GDP supplied ❶ decreases when the price level falls and ❷ increases when the price level rises.

Why the *AS* Curve Slopes Upward

Why does the quantity of real GDP supplied increase when the price level rises and decrease when the price level falls? The answer is that a movement along the *AS* curve brings a change in the real wage rate (and changes in the real cost of other resources whose money prices are fixed). If the price level rises, the real wage rate falls, and if the price level falls, the real wage rate rises.

Think about a concrete example. Suppose Microsoft has a contract with its programmers to pay them $200 an hour. Microsoft sells copies of Windows Me to computer makers (such as Dell Computer Corporation) for $100 a copy. The real wage rate of a programmer is 2 copies of Windows Me. That is, Microsoft must sell 2 copies of Windows Me to buy one hour of programming labour. Now suppose the price of a copy of Windows Me falls to $50. The real wage rate of a programmer has increased to 4 copies of Windows Me—Microsoft must now sell 4 copies of the program to buy one hour of programming labour.

If the price of a copy of Windows Me increased, the real wage of a programmer would fall. For example, if the price increased to $200 a copy, the real wage rate would be one copy of Windows Me—Microsoft would need to sell only one copy of the software to buy one hour of programmer time.

A change in the real wage rate means that the cost of labour changes relative to the revenue that an hour of labour can produce, and it changes a firm's profit. A rise in the real wage rate cuts into a firm's profit, and a fall in the real wage rate boosts a firm's profit. Firms respond to a change in the real wage rate and its profit in one of three possible ways:

- Go out of business or start up in business.
- Shut down temporarily or restart production.
- Change their output rate.

Business Failure and Startup   New businesses are born and some existing businesses die every day. Real GDP changes when the number of firms in business changes. And the price level influences this number in the short run.

People create businesses in the hope of earning a profit. When profits are generally high, more firms start up and fewer existing firms fail. So the number of firms in business increases. When profits are squeezed or when losses arise, fewer new firms start up and more existing firms fail. So the number of firms in business decreases.

The price level relative to wage and other costs influences the number of firms in business. If the price level rises relative to costs, profits increase, the number of firms in business increases, and the quantity of real GDP supplied increases. If the price level falls relative to costs, profits fall, the number of firms in business decreases, and the quantity of real GDP supplied decreases.

In a severe recession, business failure can be contagious. The failure of one firm puts pressure on both its suppliers and its customers and can bring a flood of failures and a large decrease in the quantity of real GDP supplied.

Temporary Shutdowns and Restarts   A firm that is incurring a loss might foresee a profit in the future. So rather than going out of business, such a firm might decide to shut down temporarily and lay off its workers.

The price level relative to costs is an influence on temporary shutdown decisions. If the price level rises relative to costs, fewer firms will decide to shut down temporarily, so more firms operate and the quantity of real GDP supplied increases. If the price level falls relative to costs, a larger number of firms find that they cannot earn enough to pay the wage bill and so temporarily shut down. The quantity of real GDP supplied decreases.

Changes in Output Rate   The price level relative to costs influences even those firms that remain profitable and keep producing. You know that to produce more output, a firm must hire more labour. It is profitable to hire more labour if the additional labour brings in more revenue than it costs. If the price level rises and the money wage rate doesn't change, an extra hour of labour that was previously unprofitable becomes profitable. So when the price level rises and the money wage rate doesn't change, the quantity of labour demanded increases and production increases. For the economy as a whole, the quantity of real GDP supplied increases.

Production at a Pepsi Plant

A Pepsi bottling plant produces the quantity of Pepsi that maximizes profit. The production plant is fixed, but Pepsi can increase production by hiring more labour and working the plant harder. But each additional hour of labour hired produces fewer additional bottles of Pepsi than the previous hour produces. So Pepsi increases the quantity of labour hired and increases production only if the real wage rate falls. But if the price of Pepsi rises and wage rates and other costs don't change, the real wage rate *does* fall. Similarly, if the price of Pepsi falls and wage rates and other costs don't change, the real wage rate *rises*. In this situation, Pepsi decreases the quantity of labour demanded and decreases production.

What is true for Pepsi bottlers is true for the producers of all goods and services. So when the price level rises and the money wage rate and other resource prices remain constant, the quantity of labour demanded increases and the quantity of real GDP supplied increases.

■ Changes in Aggregate Supply

You saw in Figure 15.3 that a change in the price level changes the quantity of real GDP supplied and brings a movement along the aggregate supply curve. But it does not change aggregate supply.

Aggregate supply changes when any influence on production plans other than the price level changes. In particular, aggregate supply changes when:

- Potential GDP changes
- The money wage rate changes
- The money prices of other resources change

Changes in Potential GDP

Anything that changes potential GDP—real GDP at full employment—changes aggregate supply and shifts the aggregate supply curve. Figure 15.4 shows these changes. You can think of point C as an anchor point. The AS curve and potential GDP line are anchored at this point, and when potential GDP changes, AS changes along with it. Point C shifts to point C', and the aggregate supply curve and potential GDP line shift rightward together. When potential GDP increases from $1,000 billion to $1,100 billion, the AS curve shifts from AS_0 to AS_1.

■ **FIGURE 15.4**

An Increase in Potential GDP

*e*Foundations **15.2**

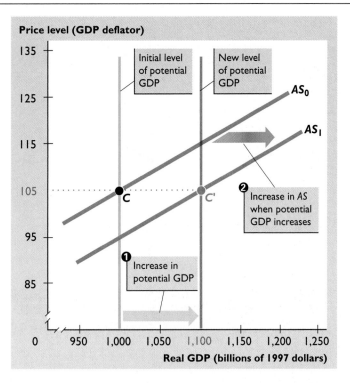

❶ An increase in potential GDP increases aggregate supply. ❷ The aggregate supply curve shifts rightward from AS_0 to AS_1.

Changes in Money Wage Rate and Other Resource Prices

A change in the money wage rate or in the money price of another resource changes aggregate supply because it changes firms' costs. The higher the money wage rate, the higher are firms' costs and the smaller is the quantity that firms are willing to supply at each price level. So an increase in the money wage rate decreases aggregate supply.

Suppose that the money wage rate is $21 an hour and the price level is 105. Then the real wage rate is $20 an hour ($21 × 100 ÷ 105 = $20). If the full-employment equilibrium real wage rate is $20 an hour, the economy is at full employment and real GDP equals potential GDP. In Figure 15.5, the economy is at point C on the aggregate supply curve AS_0. The money wage rate is $21 an hour at all points on AS_0.

Now suppose the money wage rate rises to $23 an hour but the full-employment equilibrium real wage rate remains at $20 an hour. Real GDP now equals potential GDP when the price level is 115, at point D on the aggregate supply curve AS_2. (If the money wage rate is $23 an hour and the price level is 115, the real wage rate is $23 × 100 ÷ 115 = $20 an hour.) The money wage rate is $23 an hour at all points on AS_2. The rise in the money wage rate *decreases* aggregate supply and shifts the aggregate supply curve leftward from AS_0 to AS_2.

A change in the money wage rate does not change potential GDP. The reason is that potential GDP depends only on the economy's real ability to produce and on the full employment quantity of labour, which occurs at the equilibrium *real* wage rate. The equilibrium real wage rate can occur at any money wage rate.

▩ FIGURE 15.5

A Change in the Money Wage Rate

e **Foundations 15.2**

A rise in the money wage rate decreases aggregate supply. The aggregate supply curve shifts leftward from AS_0 to AS_2. A rise in the money wage rate does not change potential GDP.

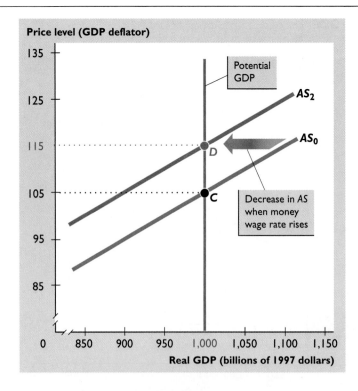

CHECKPOINT 15.2

2 **Explain the influences on aggregate supply.**

Study Guide pp. 220–223
*e*Foundations 15.2

Practice Problem 15.2

In May 2000, armed men took over the Parliament in Fiji and held the Prime Minister and other people as hostages. This action led to many other events. Explain the effect of each of the following events on Fiji's aggregate supply:

a. Downtown Suva (the capital of Fiji) was heavily looted, and businesses were destroyed.
b. Dock workers in Australia refused to handle cargo to and from Fiji, including raw material going to Fiji's garment industry and clothing going to Australia.
c. The number of tourists fell and many hotels closed.
d. As unemployment increased, the workweek was shortened.
e. The fresh tuna industry boomed with increased sales to Japan and the United States.
f. With widespread shortages, suppose that the unionized workers demanded higher wage rates and got them.

Exercise 15.2

Many events followed the ending of apartheid in South Africa. Explain the effect of each of the following events on South Africa's aggregate supply:

a. Businesses around the world established branches in South Africa.
b. More South Africans have access to education.
c. Trade sanctions ended.
d. Unemployment decreased.
e. Tourism increased and many new hotels were built.
f. AIDS became more prevalent.

Solution to Practice Problem 15.2

a. As businesses closed, real GDP supplied at the current price level decreased. The AS curve shifted leftward (from AS_0 to AS_1 in Figure 1).
b. As Fiji's garment industry ran out of raw materials, production in the garment industry decreased and the quantity of real GDP supplied at the current price level decreased. The AS curve shifted leftward (from AS_0 to AS_1 in Figure 1).
c. As many hotels closed, the quantity of tourist services supplied decreased and the quantity of real GDP supplied at the current price level decreased. The AS curve shifted leftward (from AS_0 to AS_1 in Figure 1).
d. As employers cut the workweek and shared jobs among workers, production decreased and the AS curve shifted leftward (from AS_0 to AS_1 in Figure 1).
e. As the tuna industry continued to expand, production increased. In isolation, its effect shifted the AS curve rightward (from AS_0 to AS_2 in Figure 1).
f. As the wage rate increased, businesses that became unprofitable closed and real GDP produced at the current price level decreased. The AS curve shifted leftward (from AS_0 to AS_1 in Figure 1).

FIGURE 1

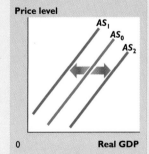

Price level

AS_1
AS_0
AS_2

0   Real GDP

15.3 AGGREGATE DEMAND

We introduced the concept of *aggregate demand* in Chapter 8 (pp. 176–177). Aggregate demand is the relationship between the quantity of real GDP demanded and the price level when all other influences on expenditure plans remain the same: The higher the price level, the smaller is the quantity of real GDP demanded, and the lower the price level, the greater is the quantity of real GDP demanded. We illustrate aggregate demand with a downward-sloping aggregate demand curve.

In Chapter 8, we described the influence of the price level on the quantity of real GDP demanded, but we didn't explain *why* it occurs. Here, we'll explain the reasons. (If you studied Chapter 14, you can learn about the link between aggregate expenditure and aggregate demand in the Appendix on pp. 374–376.)

■ Aggregate Demand Basics

The *quantity of real GDP demanded* is the total amount of final goods and services produced in Canada that people, businesses, governments, and foreigners plan to buy. This quantity is the sum of the real consumption expenditure (C), investment (I), government expenditure (G), and exports (X) minus imports (M). That is,

$$Y = C + I + G + X - M.$$

Many factors influence expenditure plans; to study aggregate demand, we divide them into two groups: the price level and everything else. We'll first consider the influence of the price level on expenditure plans and then consider the other influences.

■ Aggregate Demand and the *AD* curve

Figure 15.6 shows an aggregate demand curve, *AD*. Along the aggregate demand curve, the only influence on expenditure plans that changes is the price level. A rise in the price level decreases the quantity of real GDP demanded and brings a movement up along the aggregate demand curve; a fall in the price level increases the quantity of real GDP demanded and brings a movement down along the aggregate demand curve.

The price level influences the quantity of real GDP demanded because a change in the price level brings changes in:

- The buying power of money
- The real interest rate
- The real prices of exports and imports

The Buying Power of Money

A rise in the price level lowers the buying power of money and decreases the quantity of real GDP demanded. To see why, think about the buying plans of Anna, who lives in Moscow, Russia. She has worked hard all summer and saved 20,000 rubles (the ruble is the currency of Russia), which she plans to spend attending graduate school when she has finished her economics degree. So Anna's money holding is 20,000 rubles. Anna has a part-time job, and her income from this job pays her expenses. The price level in Russia rises by 100 percent. Now

FIGURE 15.6
A Change in the Quantity of Real GDP Demanded

e/**Foundations 15.3**

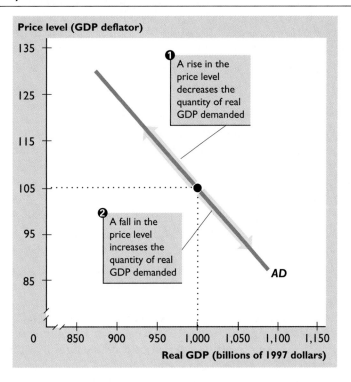

The aggregate demand curve (*AD*) shows the relationship between the quantity of real GDP demanded and the price level when all other influences on expenditure plans remain the same. The quantity of real GDP demanded ❶ decreases when the price level rises and ❷ increases when the price level falls.

Anna needs 40,000 rubles to buy what 20,000 rubles once bought. To make up some of the fall in the buying power of her money, Anna buys fewer goods.

Similarly, a fall in the price level, other things remaining the same, brings an increase in the quantity of real GDP demanded. To see why, think about the buying plans of Mika, who lives in Tokyo, Japan. She too has worked hard all summer and saved 200,000 yen (the yen is the currency of Japan), which she plans to spend attending school next year. The price level in Japan falls by 10 percent; now Mika needs only 180,000 yen to buy what 200,000 yen once bought. With a rise in what her money buys, Mika decides to buy a DVD player.

The Real Interest Rate

When the price level rises, the real interest rate rises. You saw in Chapter 13 (pp. 301–302) that an increase in the price level increases the amount of money that people want to hold at each interest rate—increases the demand for money. When the demand for money increases, the nominal interest rate rises. In the short run, the inflation rate doesn't change, so a rise in the nominal interest rate brings a rise in the real interest rate. Faced with a higher real interest rate, businesses and people delay plans to buy new capital and consumer durable goods and cut back on spending. So the quantity of real GDP demanded decreases.

Anna and Mika Again   Think about Anna and Mika again. Both of them want to buy a computer. In Moscow, a rise in the price level increases the demand for money and raises the real interest rate. At a real interest rate of 5 percent a year,

Anna was willing to borrow to buy the new computer. But at a real interest rate of 10 percent a year, she finds the payments too high, so she delays buying it. The rise in the price level decreases the quantity of real GDP demanded.

In Tokyo, a fall in the price level lowers the real interest rate. At a real interest rate of 5 percent a year, Mika was willing to borrow to buy a low-performance computer. But at a real interest rate of close to zero, she decides to buy a fancier computer that costs more: The fall in the price level increases the quantity of real GDP demanded.

The Real Prices of Exports and Imports

When the Canadian price level rises and other things remain the same, the prices in other countries do not change. So a rise in the Canadian price level makes Canadian-made goods and services more expensive relative to foreign-made goods and services. This change in real prices encourages people to spend less on Canadian-made items and more on foreign-made items. For example, if the Canadian price level rises relative to the foreign price level, foreigners buy fewer Canadian-made cars (Canadian exports decrease) and Canadians buy more foreign-made cars (Canadian imports increase).

Anna's and Mika's Imports   In Moscow, Anna is buying some new shoes. With a sharp rise in the Russian price level, the Russian-made shoes that she planned to buy are too expensive, so she buys a less expensive pair imported from Brazil. In Tokyo, Mika is buying a CD player. With the fall in the Japanese price level, a Sony player made in Japan looks like a better buy than one made in Taiwan.

In the long run, when the price level changes by more in one country than in other countries, the exchange rate changes. The exchange rate change neutralizes the price level change, so this international price effect on buying plans is a short-run effect only. But in the short run, it is a powerful effect.

■ Changes in Aggregate Demand

A change in any factor that influences expenditure plans other than the price level brings a change in aggregate demand. When aggregate demand increases, the aggregate demand curve shifts rightward, which Figure 15.7 illustrates as the rightward shift of the AD curve from AD_0 to AD_1. When aggregate demand decreases, the aggregate demand curve shifts leftward, which Figure 15.7 illustrates as the leftward shift of the AD curve from AD_0 to AD_2. The factors that change aggregate demand are:

- Expectations about the future
- Fiscal policy and monetary policy
- The state of the world economy

Expectations

An increase in expected future income increases the amount of consumption goods (especially big-ticket items such as cars) that people plan to buy now and increases aggregate demand.

An increase in expected future inflation increases aggregate demand because people decide to buy more goods and services now before their prices rise.

An increase in expected future profit increases the investment that firms plan to undertake now and increases aggregate demand.

FIGURE 15.7
Changes in Aggregate Demand

*e*Foundations **15.3**

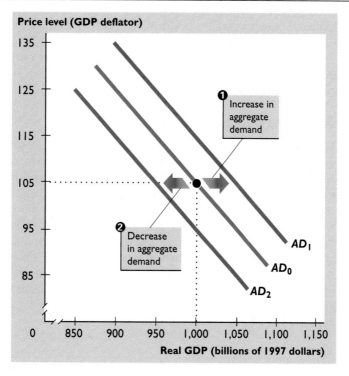

Aggregate demand:

❶ *Increases if:*

- Expected future income, inflation, or profits increase.
- The government or the Bank of Canada takes steps to increase planned expenditure.
- The exchange rate falls or the global economy expands.

❷ *Decreases if:*

- Expected future income, inflation, or profits decrease.
- The government or the Bank of Canada takes steps to decrease planned expenditure.
- The exchange rate rises or the global economy contracts.

Fiscal Policy and Monetary Policy

We study the effects of policy actions on aggregate demand in Chapter 16. Here, we'll just briefly note that the government can influence aggregate demand by setting and changing taxes, transfer payments, and government expenditure on goods and services. And the Bank of Canada can influence aggregate demand by changing the quantity of money and the interest rate.

A tax cut or an increase in either transfer payments or government expenditure increases aggregate demand. A cut in the interest rate or an increase in the quantity of money increases aggregate demand.

The World Economy

Two main influences that the world economy has on Canadian aggregate demand are the foreign exchange rate and foreign real income. The foreign exchange rate is the amount of a foreign currency that you can buy with a Canadian dollar. Other things remaining the same, a rise in the foreign exchange rate decreases aggregate demand. To see how the foreign exchange rate influences aggregate demand, suppose that $1 exchanges for 100 Japanese yen. A Fujitsu phone made in Japan costs 12,500 yen, and an equivalent Nortel phone made in Canada costs $110. In Canadian dollars, the Fujitsu phone costs $125, so people around the world buy the cheaper Canadian phone. Now suppose the exchange rate rises to 125 yen per dollar. At 125 yen per dollar, the Fujitsu phone costs $100 and is now cheaper than the Nortel phone. People will switch from the Canadian phone to the

Japanese phone. Canadian exports will decrease and Canadian imports will increase, so aggregate demand in the Canadian economy will decrease.

An increase in foreign real income increases Canadian exports and increases aggregate demand in Canada. For example, an increase in real income in the United States increases American consumers' and producers' planned expenditures on Canadian-made goods and services.

Because Canada exports a high percentage of its output, economic conditions in the world (and especially the United States) have a strong influence on aggregate demand in Canada.

■ The Aggregate Demand Multiplier

The aggregate demand multiplier is an effect that magnifies changes in expenditure plans and brings potentially large fluctuations in aggregate demand. When any influence on aggregate demand changes expenditure plans, the change in expenditure changes income; and the change in income induces a change in consumption expenditure. The increase in aggregate demand is the initial increase in expenditure plus the induced increase in consumption expenditure.

Figure 15.8 illustrates this multiplier effect. Initially, the aggregate demand curve is AD_0. Investment then increases by \$40 billion (ΔI) and the purple curve $AD_0 + \Delta I$ now describes aggregate spending plans at each price level. An increase in income induces an increase in consumption expenditure of \$60 billion, and the aggregate demand curve shifts rightward to AD_1. Chapter 14 (pp. 340–345) explains the expenditure multiplier in detail.

■ **FIGURE 15.8**
The Aggregate Demand Multiplier

*e*Foundations **15.3**

❶ An increase in investment increases aggregate demand and increases income. ❷ The increase in income induces an increase in consumption expenditure, so ❸ aggregate demand increases by more than the initial increase in investment.

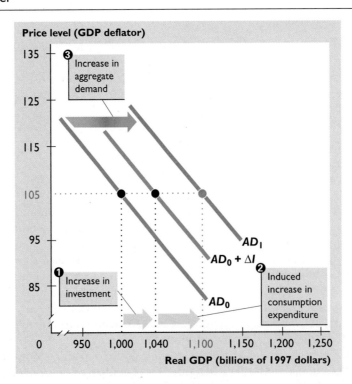

CHECKPOINT 15.3

3 **Explain the influences on aggregate demand.**

Study Guide pp. 223–225

e Foundations 15.3

Practice Problem 15.3

Mexico has signed free trade agreements with many countries, including the United States, Canada, and the European Union. Explain the effect of each of the following events on Mexico's aggregate demand in the short run:
a. The price level in Mexico rises.
b. Mexico's real interest rate rises in the short run.
c. The United States and Canada experienced strong economic growth.
d. The European Union goes into a recession.
e. The Mexican government sets new environmental standards that require factories to upgrade their production facilities.
f. Mexico adopts an expansionary monetary policy and increases the quantity of money.

Exercise 15.3

Explain the effect on Japan's aggregate demand in the short run of each of the following events, one at a time:
a. The price level in Japan is constant, and the price level in its trading partners increases.
b. The real interest rate in Japan is negative in the short run.
c. The rest of Asia goes into recession.
d. The Asian economies experience very strong growth.
e. The yen strengthens against world currencies.
f. Japan adopts an expansionary fiscal policy and cuts taxes.

Solution to Practice Problem 15.3

a. As Mexico's price level increases faster than that of its trading partners, its exports become relatively more expensive. The quantity demanded of Mexican real GDP by its trading partners decreases. Mexico's aggregate demand does not change—there is a movement up along the *AD* curve (see Figure 1).
b. A rise in the real interest rate decreases the quantity of Mexican real GDP demanded—there is a movement up along the *AD* curve (see Figure 1).
c. Strong economic growth in Canada and the United States increases the demand for Mexican real GDP and increases aggregate demand in Mexico. The *AD* curve shifts rightward (from AD_0 to AD_1 in Figure 2).
d. If recession occurs in the European Union next year, European demand for goods and services from Mexico will decrease. So Mexico's exports will decrease, and its aggregate demand will decrease. The *AD* curve will shift leftward (from AD_0 to AD_2 in Figure 2).
e. As factories upgrade their production facilities, investment increases. Aggregate demand in Mexico will increase, and the *AD* curve will shift rightward (from AD_0 to AD_1 in Figure 2).
f. An increase in the quantity of money will increase aggregate demand, and the *AD* curve will shift rightward (from AD_0 to AD_1 in Figure 2).

FIGURE 1

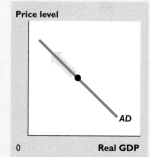

FIGURE 2

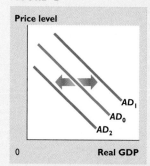

15.4 UNDERSTANDING THE BUSINESS CYCLE

Aggregate supply and aggregate demand determine real GDP and the price level (see Chapter 8, p. 178). And changes in aggregate demand and aggregate supply bring changes in real GDP and the price level. These changes generate the business cycle.

The business cycle is an irregular cycle because the changes in aggregate demand and aggregate supply occur at irregular intervals and are of variable magnitude. And these changes initiate adjustments that are spread out over time.

To study the business cycle, we're first going to consider the effects of fluctuations in aggregate demand. Then we'll examine the effects of fluctuations in aggregate supply. Finally, we'll look at the adjustments that keep real GDP returning towards potential GDP when aggregate demand or aggregate supply shocks occur.

■ Aggregate Demand Fluctuations

We're going to describe a business cycle that results from fluctuations in aggregate demand with no changes in aggregate supply. In the Canadian economy, potential GDP grows and the full-employment price level rises over a business cycle. To focus on the cycle, we'll ignore economic growth and inflation. We'll suppose that potential GDP remains constant and that the full-employment price level is also constant.

Figure 15.9 illustrates the sequence of events. Throughout the cycle, potential GDP is $1,000 billion and the full-employment price level is 105. Aggregate supply is shown by the AS curve, which does not change. Part (a) shows the changes in aggregate demand that bring an expansion, and part (c) tracks real GDP.

The economy starts out at a trough at point A at the intersection of AD_0 and AS. Real GDP is $950 billion and the price level is 100. Expecting high future profits, firms increase investment and aggregate demand. The AD curve shifts rightward to AD_1, and the economy moves to point B. There is now full employment. Investment and consumption increase again, the AD curve shifts further rightward to AD_2, and the economy moves to a business-cycle peak at point C. The economy is now at an above full-employment equilibrium.

Figure 15.9(b) shows the changes in aggregate demand that bring a recession, and part (c) continues to track real GDP. The economy is at a peak at point C at the intersection of AD_2 and AS. Real GDP is $1,050 billion and the price level is 110. Now, expecting low future profits, firms decrease investment and aggregate demand decreases. The AD curve shifts leftward to AD_3, and the economy moves to point D. There is full employment again. Investment and consumption expenditure decrease again, the AD curve shifts further leftward to AD_4, and the economy moves to a new business-cycle trough at point E.

Here, changes in profit expectations drive changes in investment and aggregate demand to create the business cycle. This factor is frequently the one at work. But sometimes other factors initiate a change in aggregate demand, and any of the factors that influence expenditure plans that we reviewed above (on pp. 362–364) could be at work. For smaller countries, a change in exports is frequently the initiating factor and the source of an international business cycle.

ECONOMICS *in the* **NEWS**

November 2, 2001

Unemployment Higher

Employment was unchanged in October, leaving it down 13,000 since May, when labour market conditions began to weaken. The unemployment rate edged up 0.1 percentage points to 7.3%.

While overall employment was little changed, an increase in part-time work (+28,000) was offset by a similar decline in full-time employment (−26,000).

STATISTICS CANADA, *THE DAILY*

Questions
1. What are three signs in this article that the economy is slowing down and perhaps slipping into a recession?
2. What other data would you look at to determine if we are entering a recession?

 *e*Foundations 15.4

■ FIGURE 15.9
An Aggregate Demand Cycle

*e***Foundations 15.4**

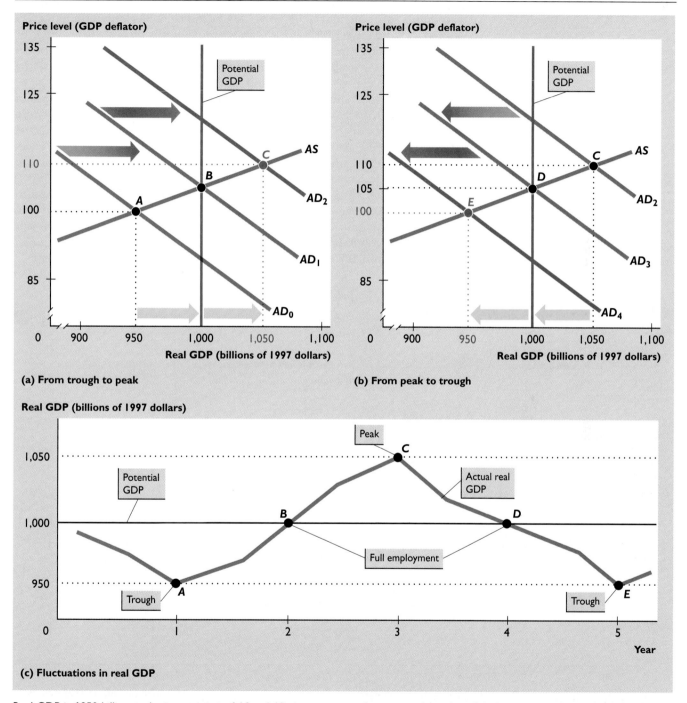

(a) From trough to peak

(b) From peak to trough

(c) Fluctuations in real GDP

Real GDP is $950 billion at the intersection of *AS* and *AD*₀ in part (a), and the economy is at a trough at point *A* in part (c). An increase in investment increases aggregate demand through *AD*₁ to *AD*₂. The economy moves from *A* through full employment at *B* to a business-cycle peak at *C*. A decrease in investment decreases aggregate demand through *AD*₃ to *AD*₄ in part (b). The economy moves from *C* through full employment at *D* to a new business-cycle trough at *E*.

■ Aggregate Supply Fluctuations

Aggregate supply can fluctuate for two types of reasons. First, potential GDP grows at an uneven pace. During a period of slow technological change and capital accumulation, potential GDP grows slowly and below its long-term trend. The productivity slowdown of the 1970s is an example of this type of event.

Second, a change in the money price of a major resource, such as crude oil, might change. Oil is used so widely throughout the economy that a large change in its price affects almost every firm and impacts the aggregate economy.

Figure 15.10 shows how a large change in the price of oil can bring recession and expansion. In part (a), the aggregate demand curve is AD and initially, the aggregate supply curve is AS_0. Equilibrium real GDP is $1,000 billion, which equals potential GDP, and the price level is 105. Then the price of oil rises. Faced with higher energy and transportation costs, firms decrease production. Aggregate supply decreases, and the aggregate supply curve shifts leftward to AS_1. The price level rises to 110, and real GDP decreases to $975 billion. Because real GDP decreases, the economy experiences recession. Because the price level increases, the economy experiences inflation. A combination of recession and inflation, called **stagflation**, actually occurred in North America and the global economy in the mid-1970s and early 1980s. But events like this are infrequent.

Stagflation
A combination of recession (decreasing real GDP) and inflation (rising price level).

■ **FIGURE 15.10**
An Oil Price Cycle

*e*Foundations **15.4**

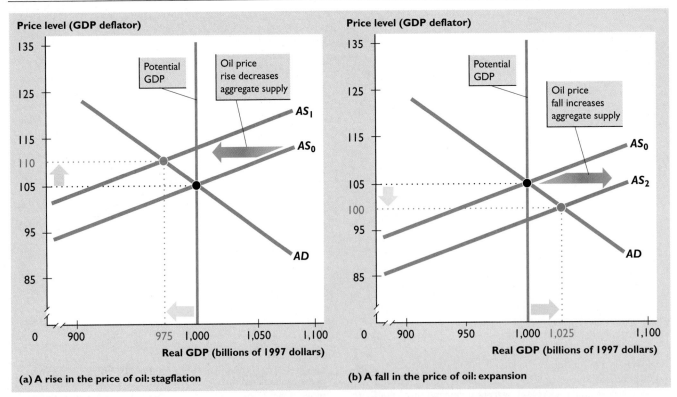

(a) A rise in the price of oil: stagflation

(b) A fall in the price of oil: expansion

In part (a), a decrease in aggregate supply shifts the AS curve leftward to AS_1. Real GDP decreases, and the price level rises.

In part (b), an increase in aggregate supply shifts the AS curve rightward to AS_2. Real GDP increases, and the price level falls.

In Figure 15.10(b), starting from the same full-employment equilibrium as before, the price of oil falls. With lower energy and transportation costs, firms increase production and the aggregate supply curve shifts rightward to AS_2. The price level falls to 100, and real GDP increases to $1,025 billion. The economy experiences expansion and moves above full employment, but the price level falls. Similar events occurred in the North American and global economies during the mid-1980s, bringing strong economic expansion. The price level didn't fall, but inflation slowed, so the price level was lower than it otherwise would have been.

Eye On The PAST

Oil Price Cycles in the Global Economy

In 1973, a barrel of crude oil cost around $3.50—a bit more than $12 in the dollars of 2001 (see figure). Most of the world's crude oil came from a handful of nations mainly located in the Persian Gulf region, and the large producer nations were (and still are) members of an international cartel known as OPEC—the Organization of Petroleum Exporting Countries. (A cartel is an organization that seeks to control the production and price of a commodity and is illegal in most countries.)

In September 1973, OPEC cut the production of crude oil and raised its price to $10 a barrel—about $30 in today's money. This near tripling of the price of crude oil sent the global economy into a tailspin. Real GDP in the United States, Europe, Japan, and the developing nations fell for the next two years in an oil price recession.

Through the rest of the 1970s, the price of oil drifted upward slightly. Then, in 1980, OPEC delivered its second jolt to the global economy by again cutting

production and then raising the price to $37 a barrel—$70 in today's money.

The global economy experienced another recession. But this recession was much more severe than that of the mid-1970s because the oil price shock was accompanied by a large decrease in aggregate demand that resulted from the monetary policy of the world's central banks.

With the very high price of oil, it did not take long for non-OPEC producers to increase production. Canada and the United States intensified exploration

and increased North American oil production. Britain and Norway developed oil resources in the North Sea. And Mexico stepped up its production.

As these additional sources of supply came on stream, the price of oil tumbled. By 1988, it had fallen to $16 a barrel—only $21 in today's money. This gradual fall in the price of oil aided the expansion of the global economy during the 1980s.

During the late 1990s, the price of oil again increased and, by 2001, it was back at its 1974 level in real terms.

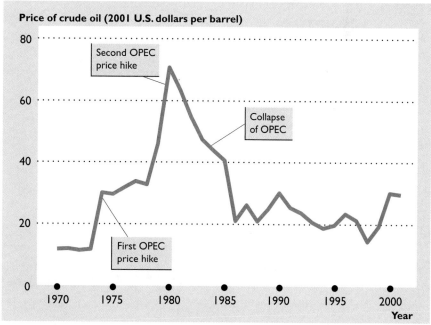

SOURCES: *International Financial Statistics*, International Monetary Fund, and Bureau of Economic Analysis.

■ Adjustment Towards Full Employment

When the economy is away from full employment, forces begin to operate that move it back towards full employment. In Figure 15.11(a), aggregate supply is AS_0 and an increase in aggregate demand from AD_0 to AD_1 moves real GDP to above potential GDP. There is now an **inflationary gap**—a gap that brings a rising price level. Workers have experienced a fall in the buying power of their wages, and firms' profits have increased. Workers demand higher wage rates, and firms, anxious to maintain their employment and output levels in the face of a labour shortage, meet those demands. As the money wage rate rises, aggregate supply decreases and the aggregate supply curve shifts leftward. Eventually, it will reach AS_1, where real GDP is back at potential GDP.

In Figure 15.11(b), aggregate supply is AS_1 and a decrease in aggregate demand from AD_1 to AD_2 moves real GDP to below potential GDP. There is a **deflationary gap**—a gap that brings a falling price level. The people who are lucky enough to have jobs see the buying power of their wages rise and firms' profits shrink. In these circumstances, and with a labour surplus, the money wage rate gradually falls and the aggregate supply curve shifts rightward. Eventually, it reaches AS_2, where real GDP is back at potential GDP.

Inflationary gap
A gap that exists when real GDP exceeds potential GDP and that brings a rising price level.

Deflationary gap
A gap that exists when potential GDP exceeds real GDP and that brings a falling price level.

■ **FIGURE 15.11**
Adjustments Towards Full Employment

𝑒Foundations **15.4**

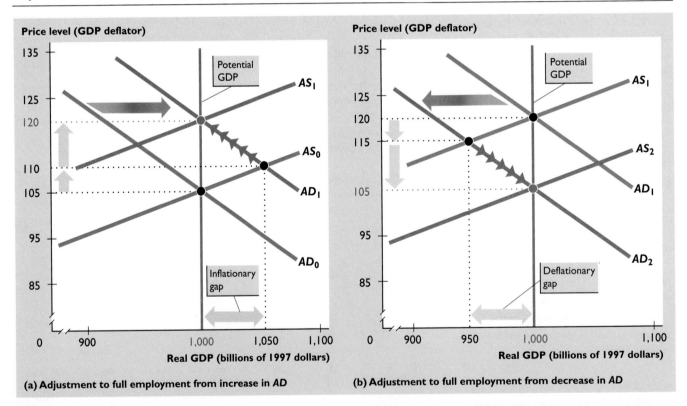

(a) Adjustment to full employment from increase in AD

(b) Adjustment to full employment from decrease in AD

In part (a), real GDP exceeds potential GDP—there is an inflationary gap. The money wage rate rises, aggregate supply decreases, real GDP decreases, and the price level rises.

In part (b), potential GDP exceeds real GDP—there is a deflationary gap. The money wage rate falls, aggregate supply increases, real GDP increases, and the price level falls.

CHECKPOINT 15.4

4 Explain how fluctuations in aggregate demand and aggregate supply create the business cycle.

Study Guide pp. 225–228

e **Foundations 15.4**

Practice Problem 15.4

The Canadian economy is in long-run equilibrium. Then the following events occur one at a time:

- The world economy goes into a strong expansion.
- World oil price tumbles.
- Canadian businesses expect future profits to rise.

a. Explain the effect of each event on aggregate demand and aggregate supply in Canada.
b. Explain the effect of each event separately on Canadian real GDP and price level.
c. Explain the combined effect of all the events together on Canadian real GDP and price level.

Exercise 15.4

In the U.S economy, real GDP equals potential GDP. Then the following events occur one at a time:

- A deep recession hits the world economy.
- The world oil price rises by a large amount.
- U.S. businesses expect future profits to fall.

a. Explain the effect of each event on aggregate demand and aggregate supply in the United States.
b. Explain the effect of each event separately on the U.S. real GDP and price level.
c. Explain the combined effect of all the events together on the U.S. real GDP and price level.
d. Which event, if any, brings stagflation?

Solution to Practice Problem 15.4

a. The boom in the world economy increases Canadian aggregate demand (for example, from AD_0 to AD_1 in Figure 1). The fall in the world oil price increases Canadian aggregate supply (for example, from AS_0 to AS_1 in Figure 1). Canadian businesses' expectation of higher future profits increases investment and aggregate demand (for example, from AD_0 to AD_1 in Figure 1).
b. When the world economy goes into a strong boom, real GDP increases and the price level rises. When the world oil price tumbles, real GDP increases and the price level falls. When Canadian businesses expect future profits to rise, real GDP increases and the price level rises (Figure 1).
c. All three events increase Canadian real GDP, but the price level might rise, fall, or remain unchanged (Figure 1). The strong expansion in the world economy and the rise in expected future profits increase the price level but the fall in the world oil price decreases the price level.

FIGURE 1

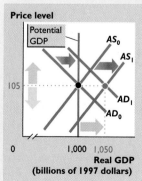

Key Points

1 **Provide a technical definition of recession and describe the history of the Canadian business cycle.**

- A recession is a decrease in real GDP that lasts for at least two quarters.
- Canadian recessions have been getting shorter, and expansions have been getting longer.

2 **Explain the influences on aggregate supply.**

- With a constant money wage rate, a rise in the price level lowers the real wage rate, increases the quantity of labour demanded, and increases the quantity of real GDP supplied.
- A change in potential GDP, a change in the money wage rate, or a change in the money price of other resources changes aggregate supply.

3 **Explain the influences on aggregate demand.**

- A rise in the price level decreases the quantity of real GDP demanded, other things remaining the same.
- The reason is that the higher price level decreases the buying power of money, raises the real interest rate, and raises the real price of domestic goods compared with foreign goods.
- Changes in expected future income, inflation, and profits, changes in fiscal policy and monetary policy, and changes in the foreign exchange rate and foreign real GDP change aggregate demand.

4 **Explain how fluctuations in aggregate demand and aggregate supply create the business cycle.**

- Aggregate demand and aggregate supply determine real GDP and the price level.
- The business cycle occurs because aggregate demand and aggregate supply fluctuate.
- Away from full employment, gradual adjustment of the money wage rate moves real GDP towards potential GDP.

Key Terms

Deflationary gap, 370
Inflationary gap, 370

Recession, 350
Stagflation, 368

Exercises

1. Figure 1 shows real GDP in Germany from the first quarter of 1991 to the last quarter of 1994.
   a. In which quarter was Germany at a business-cycle peak?
   b. In which quarter was Germany at a business-cycle trough?
   c. Did Germany experience a recession during these years?
   d. In what years did Germany experience an expansion?

2. The Canadian economy is at full employment.
   a. Suppose that next year, the money wage rate rises and all other influences on aggregate supply remain the same. Explain the effect of the rise in the money wage rate on aggregate supply.
   b. Suppose that next year, the price level rises and all other influences on aggregate supply remain the same. Explain the effect of the rise in the price level on aggregate supply.
   c. Over time, potential GDP grows. Explain the effect of the increase in potential GDP on aggregate supply.

3. In 2001, Canada entered a recession.
   a. The Bank of Canada responded by increasing the quantity of money. Ignoring all other influences on aggregate demand, explain the effect of the increase in the quantity of money.
   b. The federal government responded by cutting taxes. Ignoring all other influences on aggregate demand, explain the effect of the tax cut.
   c. The world economy goes into recession. Explain the effect of the world recession on the Canadian economy.
   d. Inflation in Canada made the Canadian price level rise faster than the price level in the rest of the world. Explain the effect of Canadian inflation.

4. In 2001, the Japanese economy is at a below full-employment equilibrium.
   a. Compare the unemployment rate in Japan with Japan's natural unemployment rate.
   b. Compare Japan's real GDP with its potential GDP.
   c. What policies could Japan adopt to restore full employment?
   d. In your answer to Exercise 4(c), would any of the policies create inflation? Explain.

5. Table 1 gives U.K. aggregate demand and aggregate supply schedules in 2001.
   a. Plot the aggregate demand curve.
   b. Plot the aggregate supply curve.
   c. What is the macroeconomic equilibrium?
   d. If potential GDP in the United Kingdom was 750 pounds, what is the type of macroeconomic equilibrium?

FIGURE 1

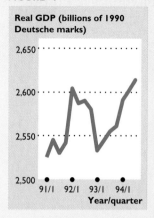

Real GDP (billions of 1990 Deutsche marks)

TABLE 1

Price level (GDP deflator)	Real GDP demanded	Real GDP supplied
	(billions of 1995 pounds)	
90	900	600
100	850	700
110	800	800
120	750	900
130	700	1,000

When you have completed your study of this appendix, you will be able to:

1 Derive the *AD* curve from equilibrium expenditure.

In Chapter 14, we studied the aggregate expenditure model, in which firms change production when sales and inventories change but they don't change their prices. The aggregate expenditure model determines real GDP and equilibrium expenditure at a given price level. In the current chapter, we've studied the simultaneous determination of real GDP and the price level using the *AS-AD* model. The aggregate demand curve and equilibrium expenditure are related, and this appendix shows you how.

■ **Deriving the *AD* Curve from Equilibrium Expenditure**

The *AE* curve is the relationship between aggregate planned expenditure and real GDP when all other influences on expenditure plans remain the same. A movement along the *AE* curve arises from a change in real GDP.

The *AD* curve is the relationship between the quantity of real GDP demanded and the price level when all other influences on expenditure plans remain the same. A movement along the *AD* curve arises from a *change* in the price level.

Equilibrium expenditure depends on the price level. When the price level rises, other things remaining the same, aggregate planned expenditure decreases and equilibrium expenditure decreases. And when the price level falls, other things remaining the same, aggregate planned expenditure increases and equilibrium expenditure increases. The reason is that a change in the price level changes the buying power of money, the real interest rate, and the real prices of exports and imports (see pp. 360–362).

When the price level rises, each of these effects decreases aggregate planned expenditure at each level of real GDP. So the *AE* curve shifts downward. A fall in the price level has the opposite effect. When the price level falls, the *AE* curve shifts upward.

Figure A15.1(a) shows the shifts of the *AE* curve. When the price level is 105, the *AE* curve intersects the 45° line at point *B*. Equilibrium expenditure is $1,000 billion. If the price level rises to 125, the *AE* curve shifts downward and equilibrium expenditure is $900 billion at point *A*. If the price level falls to 85, the *AE* curve shifts upward and equilibrium expenditure is $1,100 billion at point *C*.

The price level changes that shift the *AE* curve and change equilibrium expenditure bring movements along the *AD* curve. Figure A15.1(b) shows these movements. At a price level of 105, the quantity of real GDP demanded is $1,000 billion—point *B* on the *AD* curve. If the price level rises to 125, the quantity of real GDP demanded decreases to $900 billion at point *A*. If the price level falls to 85, the quantity of real GDP demanded increases to $1,100 billion at point *C*.

The two parts of Figure A15.1 are connected and illustrate the relationship between the *AE* curve and the *AD* curve. Each point of equilibrium expenditure corresponds to a point on the *AD* curve. The equilibrium expenditure points *A*, *B*, and *C* (part a) correspond to the points *A*, *B*, and *C* on the *AD* curve (part b).

FIGURE A15.1
Equilibrium Expenditure and Aggregate Demand

*e*Foundations **A15.1**

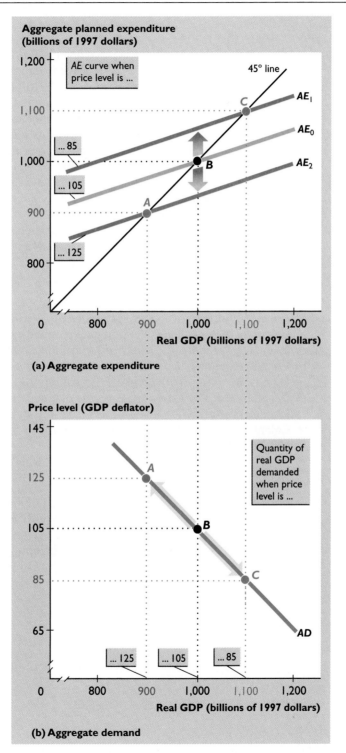

A change in the price level shifts the *AE* curve and results in a movement along the *AD* curve. When the price level is 105, equilibrium expenditure is $1,000 billion at point *B*. When the price level is 125, equilibrium expenditure is $900 billion at point *A*. When the price level is 85, equilibrium expenditure is $1,100 billion at point *C*. Points *A*, *B*, and *C* on the *AD* curve in part (b) correspond to the equilibrium expenditure points *A*, *B*, and *C* in part (a).

(a) Aggregate expenditure

(b) Aggregate demand

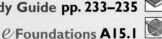
Study Guide pp. 233–235

e **Foundations A15.1**

Exercises

1. In the global economy, when the price level is 100, aggregate planned expenditure would be $10 trillion if real GDP were zero; when the price level is 90, aggregate planned expenditure would be $11 trillion if real GDP were zero; and when the price level is 110, aggregate planned expenditure would be $9 trillion if real GDP were zero. For each $1 increase in real GDP, aggregate planned expenditure increases by 75¢, and this relationship between expenditure plans and real GDP is the same at every price level.
   a. Calculate aggregate planned expenditure when the price level is 100 at real GDP levels of $35 trillion, $40 trillion, and $45 trillion.
   b. Calculate aggregate planned expenditure when the price level is 110 at real GDP levels of $35 trillion, $40 trillion, and $45 trillion.
   c. Calculate aggregate planned expenditure when the price level is 90 at real GDP levels of $35 trillion, $40 trillion, and $45 trillion.
   d. Calculate equilibrium expenditure at price levels of 90, 100, and 100.
   e. Make graphs of the *AE* curve at price levels of 90, 100, and 110, and the *AD* curve.

2. In Exercise 1, global investment increases by $1 trillion.
   a. Calculate the new levels of aggregate planned expenditure when the price level is 100 at real GDP levels of $35 trillion, $40 trillion, and $45 trillion.
   b. Calculate the new levels of aggregate planned expenditure when the price level is 110 at real GDP levels of $35 trillion, $40 trillion, and $45 trillion.
   c. Calculate the new levels of aggregate planned expenditure when the price level is 90 at real GDP levels of $35 trillion, $40 trillion, and $45 trillion.
   d. Calculate the new levels of equilibrium expenditure at price levels of 90, 100, and 110.
   e. Make graphs of the new *AE* curve at price levels of 90, 100, and 110 and the *AD* curve.

3. Compare the *AD* curve of Exercise 1 with that of Exercise 2.
   a. Does the *AD* curve shift leftward or rightward? Explain the direction of the shift.
   b. Does the *AD* curve shift by the same $1 trillion increase in investment, by more than that amount, or by less than that amount? Explain the magnitude of the shift.

Fiscal and Monetary Policy Effects

CHAPTER CHECKLIST

When you have completed your study of this chapter,
you will be able to:

1 Describe the federal budget process and explain the effects of fiscal policy.

2 Describe the Bank of Canada's monetary policy process and explain the effects of monetary policy.

In 2000, Canadian governments spent $430 billion or 41 cents of every dollar that Canadians earned. In a sharp reversal of past years, governments had a budget surplus—they collected about $38 billion more in taxes than they spent. What are the effects of government spending, taxes, and the government budget surplus (or deficit) on the economy?

Eight times a year, on dates fixed in advance, the Bank of Canada announces how it will change interest rates. These announcements are preceded by considerable discussion, speculation, and second-guessing about what the Bank should do or will do. What are the effects of the Bank of Canada's actions on the economy?

In this chapter, we build on what you have learned about aggregate demand and aggregate supply, aggregate expenditures, and money to explore the tools used by the federal government and the Bank of Canada to influence aggregate demand and counteract the forces that push the economy away from full employment. Our focus in this chapter is on the effects of these tools. The next two chapters examine questions about priorities and strategies in using these tools.

16.1 THE FEDERAL BUDGET AND FISCAL POLICY

Fiscal policy
Adjusting the federal budget to influence employment and production.

The federal government makes Canada's **fiscal policy**, which means that it adjusts the federal budget to influence employment and production.

■ The Federal Budget

Federal budget
An annual statement of the expenditures, tax receipts, and surplus or deficit of the government of Canada.

Budget surplus
The budget balance when tax receipts exceed expenditures.

Budget deficit
The budget balance when expenditures exceed tax receipts.

Balanced budget
The budget balance when tax receipts equal expenditures.

National debt
The total amount of debt outstanding that arises from past budget deficits.

The **federal budget** is an annual statement of the expenditures, tax receipts, and the surplus or deficit of the government of Canada. The government's surplus or deficit is equal to its tax receipts minus its expenditures. That is,

Budget surplus (+) or deficit (−) = Tax receipts − Expenditures.

The government has a **budget surplus** if tax receipts exceed expenditures, a **budget deficit** if expenditures exceed tax receipts, and a **balanced budget** if tax receipts equal expenditures. The total amount of debt outstanding that has accumulated from past budget deficits is called the **national debt**.

A Personal Analogy   The government's budget and the national debt are like a student's budget and debt—only bigger. If you take a student loan each year to go to school, you have a budget deficit and a growing debt. If after graduating and getting a job, you repay some of your loan each year, you have a budget surplus and a shrinking debt.

Figure 16.1 illustrates the relationship between a government's budget and its debt. The key thing to note is that the budget is an annual event that changes the national debt, and the national debt outstanding is the result of past budgets.

■ **FIGURE 16.1**
Government Budget Deficits, Surpluses, and Debt   *e*Foundations **16.1**

In 1998 (before the figure begins), the national debt was $50 billion. In 1999, the government had a budget deficit of $10 billion and the national debt increased to $60 billion.

In 2000, a $20 billion budget deficit increased the national debt to $80 billion.

In 2001, a $10 billion budget surplus decreased the national debt to $70 billion and a $20 billion surplus in 2002 decreased the national debt to $50 billion.

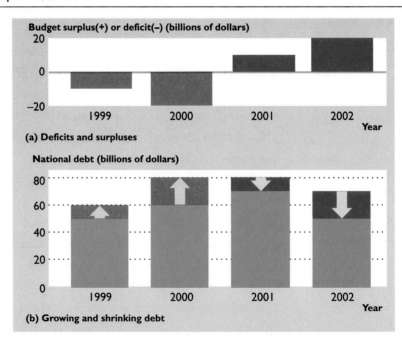

Eye On The PAST

The Federal Budget

In 1926, the government of Canada collected $400 million in taxes, spent $400 million, and had a balanced budget. In 2000, tax receipts were $193 billion, expenditures, $182 billion, and the budget surplus, $11 billion.

To make these numbers easier to compare, we'll express them as percentages of GDP—or cents of each dollar earned. Tax receipts increased from 7 percent of GDP in 1926 to 19 percent of GDP in 2000. Expenditures grew from 7 percent of GDP in 1926 to 18 percent of GDP in 2000.

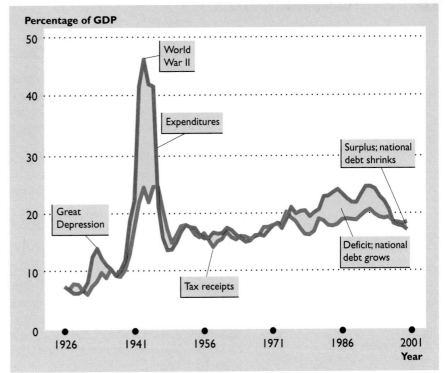

SOURCE: Statistics Canada.

Eye On The GLOBAL ECONOMY

Canada's Budget in Global Perspective

In 2000, summing the budgets of all the governments in the world, the IMF estimated that budgets were in deficit by a bit more than 1 percent of world GDP.

Japan had the biggest deficit at more than 7 percent of GDP. But the developing countries of Asia, which include China and India, had large deficits.

Norway and the United States had the largest budget surpluses. Canada also had a surplus.

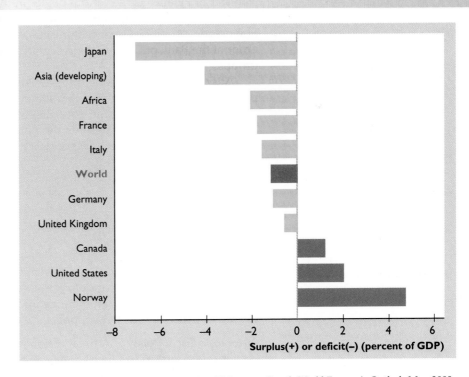

SOURCE: International Monetary Fund, *World Economic Outlook*, May 2000.

■ Fiscal Policy: Background and Objectives

The Great Depression of the 1930s strengthened the resolve of governments to take a more active role in trying to manage the business cycle. And the then new macroeconomics of John Maynard Keynes (which in essence is the model that you studied in Chapter 14) gave governments the tools they needed to pursue their new policy goal.

In 1945, the federal government published a White Paper entitled *Employment and Incomes* that expressed this policy change. Asserting its responsibility for maintaining a "high and stable level of employment," the government stated that it

> ... will be prepared, in periods when unemployment
> threatens, to incur the deficits ... [either] ... through
> increased expenditures or reduced taxation.

This statement set the stage for the federal government to actively change its expenditure and taxes to manage the level of aggregate demand. The 1945 White Paper focused on combating recessions and unemployment, which would require increasing its expenditure on goods and services and decreasing taxes to stimulate aggregate demand. Later, during the 1960s, it became accepted that fiscal policy could also be used to curb inflation, by decreasing government expenditure and increasing taxes to restrain aggregate demand.

Budget Making

The budget-making process is a lengthy and complex one that involves many players. Parliament has the responsibility to determine fiscal policy and the Minister of Finance is the central player in the process.

Budget making begins with extensive consultations between the Minister of Finance, the provincial finance ministers, Department of Finance officials, the governor of the Bank of Canada, representatives of Canadian business, and consumer groups.

After these consultations, the Minister of Finance develops a set of budget proposals, which are presented to Cabinet. After Cabinet discussion and approval, the budget proposals become government policy.

Finally, the Minister presents the budget plan to Parliament, which debates the budget and enacts the laws necessary to implement it.

Types of Fiscal Policy

Fiscal policy can be either:

- Discretionary, or
- Automatic

Discretionary fiscal policy
A fiscal policy action that is initiated by an act of Parliament.

Automatic fiscal policy
A fiscal policy action that is triggered by the state of the economy, such as an increase in payments to the unemployed and a decrease in tax receipts triggered by recession.

Discretionary Fiscal Policy   A fiscal action that is initiated by an act of Parliament is called **discretionary fiscal policy**. It requires a change in a spending program or in a tax law. For example, an increase in defence spending or a cut in the income tax rate is a discretionary fiscal policy.

Automatic Fiscal Policy   A fiscal action that is triggered by the state of the economy is called **automatic fiscal policy**. For example, an increase in unemployment induces an increase in payments to the unemployed. And a fall in incomes induces a decrease in tax receipts.

■ Discretionary Fiscal Policy: Demand-Side Effects

Discretionary fiscal policy influences both aggregate demand and aggregate supply. We'll look first at the demand-side effects. Changes in government expenditure and changes in taxes have multiplier effects on aggregate demand similar to the multiplier that you studied in Chapters 14 and 15.

The Government Expenditure Multiplier

The **government expenditure multiplier** is the magnification effect of a change in government expenditure on goods and services on aggregate demand. Government expenditure is a component of aggregate expenditure, so when government expenditure changes, aggregate demand changes. The increase in aggregate demand increases real GDP, which induces an increase in consumption expenditure. And the increase in consumption expenditure brings a further increase in aggregate expenditure. A multiplier process ensues. This process is like the one described in Chapter 14 (pp. 340–344) and Chapter 15 (p. 364).

A Health-Care Multiplier   In 2000, the federal government increased its expenditure on health-care facilities and services. Initially, every $100 million of such spending became $100 million of additional income for the construction workers and contractors who were hired to build the new health-care facilities and for health-care workers who were hired to supply the additional health-care services. With larger incomes, these workers increased their consumption expenditures. With increasing revenues, other businesses boomed and expanded their payrolls. A second round of increased consumption expenditures increased incomes yet further. The increase in government expenditure and its multiplier increased aggregate demand. Eventually, expenditures and incomes stopped rising.

Changing its expenditure on goods and services is one way in which the government can change aggregate demand. A second way is to change taxes. Let's see how this action works.

The Tax Multiplier

The **tax multiplier** is the magnification effect of a change in taxes on aggregate demand. A *decrease* in taxes *increases* disposable income. And an increase in disposable income increases consumption expenditure. With increased consumption expenditure, employment and incomes rise and consumption expenditure rises yet further. So a decrease in taxes works like an increase in government expenditure. Both actions increase aggregate demand and have a multiplier effect.

The magnitude of the tax multiplier is smaller than the government expenditure multiplier. The reason is that a $1 tax cut generates *less than* $1 of expenditure. In contrast, a $1 increase in government expenditure generates exactly $1 of expenditure. Why the difference?

A $1 tax cut increases disposable income by $1 and increases expenditure—consumption expenditure—by an amount that depends on the marginal propensity to consume. If, for example, the marginal propensity to consume is 0.75, then a $1 increase in disposable income increases consumption expenditure initially by 75 cents. A multiplier just like the government expenditure multiplier magnifies this initial change in expenditure. But because the initial increase in expenditure is smaller, the outcome is also smaller.

Government expenditure multiplier
The magnification effect of a change in government expenditure on goods and services on aggregate demand.

Tax multiplier
The magnification effect of a change in taxes on aggregate demand.

A Canadian Tax Cut Multiplier   In 2001, Canadians' disposable income grew as a result of the first stage of a five-year reduction in the federal personal income tax rates. These tax cuts will have a multiplier effect. Each year through 2005, with billions of dollars of extra money in their pockets, people will increase consumption expenditure. This spending will increase incomes, which will spur yet more consumption expenditure. Through 2005, these tax cuts will add a cumulative total of $90 billion to Canadians' disposable income. Eventually, expenditures and incomes will reach new equilibriums and, other things remaining unchanged, will remain there.

The Balanced Budget Multiplier

Balanced budget multiplier
The magnification effect on aggregate demand of *simultaneous* changes in government expenditure and taxes that leave the budget balance unchanged.

The **balanced budget multiplier** is the magnification effect on aggregate demand of *simultaneous* changes in government expenditure and taxes that leave the budget balance unchanged. The size of the balanced budget multiplier is smaller than either the government expenditure multiplier or the tax multiplier, because to achieve a balanced budget, both government expenditure and taxes must change in the same direction and so have opposing effects on aggregate demand.

The balanced budget multiplier is not zero—it is positive—because the size of the government expenditure multiplier is larger than the size of the tax multiplier. That is, a $1 increase in government expenditure increases aggregate demand by more than a $1 increase in taxes decreases aggregate demand. So when both government expenditure and taxes increase by $1, aggregate demand still increases.

Eye On The CANADIAN ECONOMY

Federal Tax Cuts

In January 2001, Canadians received their first tax cut under the federal government's five-year tax reduction plan. The average tax cut was 21 percent. For families with children, the cut was larger and meant an extra $1,000 a year.

The figure shows the size and components of the tax cuts through 2005.

In the short run, the tax cuts will boost aggregate demand in a slowing economy. In the long run, the tax cuts will improve incentives to work, save, and invest.

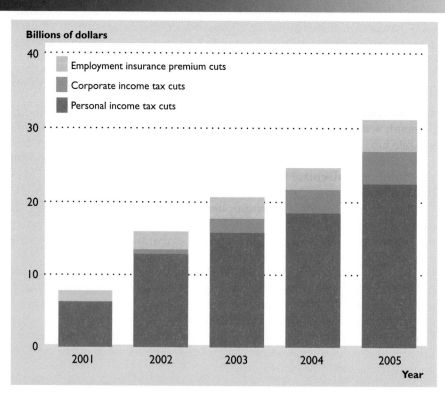

SOURCE: Department of Finance, *Economic Statement and Budget Update*, October 18, 2000.

Discretionary Fiscal Stabilization

If real GDP is below potential GDP, discretionary fiscal policy might be used in an attempt to restore full employment. The government might increase its expenditure on goods and services, cut taxes, or do some of both. These actions would increase aggregate demand. If they were timed correctly and were of the correct magnitude, they could restore full employment. Figure 16.2 shows how.

In Figure 16.2(a), potential GDP is $1,000 billion. Real GDP is $900 billion and the price level is 100. There is a $100 billion *deflationary gap* (p. 370).

To eliminate the deflationary gap and restore full employment, the government takes a discretionary fiscal policy action. An increase in government expenditure or a cut in taxes increases aggregate expenditure by ΔE. If this were the only change in spending plans, the AD curve would become $AD_0 + \Delta E$ in Figure 16.2(b). But the increase in government expenditure or tax cut sets off a multiplier process, which increases consumption expenditure. As the multiplier process plays out, aggregate demand increases and the AD curve shifts rightward to AD_1.

With no change in the price level, the economy would move from the initial equilibrium point A to point B on AD_1. But the increase in aggregate demand combined with the upward-sloping aggregate supply curve brings a rise in the price level. So the economy moves to a new equilibrium at point C. The price level rises to 105, and real GDP increases to $1,000 billion. Full employment is restored.

FIGURE 16.2
Expansionary Fiscal Policy

*e*Foundations **16.1**

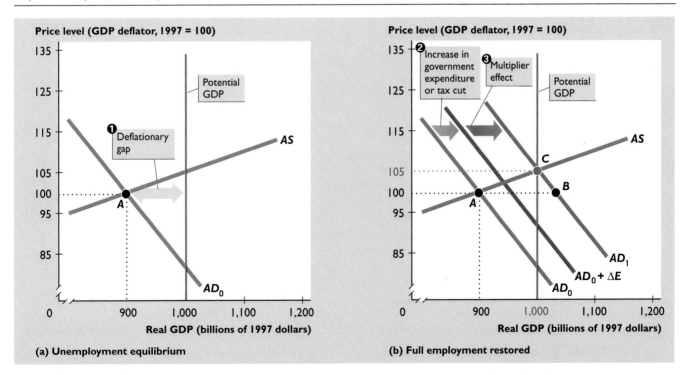

(a) Unemployment equilibrium

(b) Full employment restored

Potential GDP is $1,000 billion, real GDP is $900 billion, and ❶ there is a $100 billion deflationary gap (part a). ❷ An increase in government expenditure or a tax cut increases expenditure by ΔE.

❸ The multiplier increases induced expenditure and shifts the AD curve rightward to AD_1, the price level rises to 105, real GDP increases to $1,000 billion, and the deflationary gap is eliminated.

If an inflationary gap exists, discretionary fiscal policy can be used to decrease aggregate demand, restore full employment, and eliminate inflationary pressure. In this case, the government decreases its expenditure on goods and services, raises taxes, or does some of both. These actions decrease aggregate demand, decrease real GDP, and lower the price level. Figure 16.3 illustrates these effects.

In Figure 16.3(a), potential GDP is $1,000 billion. Real GDP is $1,100 billion and the price level is 110. There is a $100 billion *inflationary gap* (p. 370).

To eliminate the inflationary gap and restore full employment, the government takes a discretionary fiscal policy action. A decrease in government expenditure or a tax increase decreases aggregate expenditure by ΔE. If this were the only change in spending plans, the AD curve would become $AD_0 - \Delta E$. But the initial decrease in aggregate expenditure sets off a multiplier process, which decreases consumption expenditure. As the multiplier process plays out, aggregate demand decreases and the AD curve shifts leftward to AD_1.

With no change in the price level, the economy would move from the initial equilibrium point A to point B on AD_1. But the decrease in aggregate demand combined with the upward-sloping AS curve brings a fall in the price level. So the economy moves to a new equilibrium at point C. The price level falls to 105, and real GDP decreases to $1,000 billion. The inflationary gap has been eliminated, inflation has been avoided, and the economy is back at full employment.

FIGURE 16.3
Contractionary Fiscal Policy

e/**Foundations 16.1**

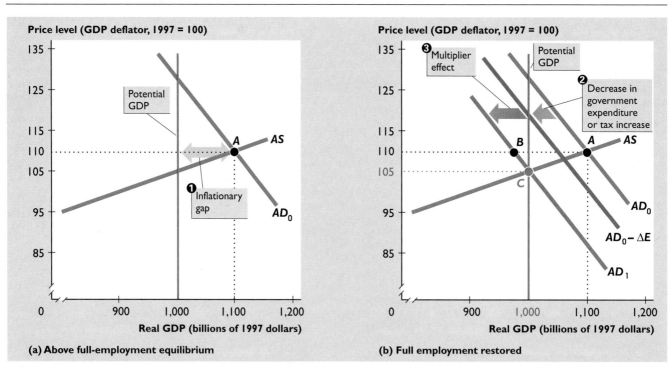

(a) Above full-employment equilibrium   **(b) Full employment restored**

Potential GDP is $1,000 billion, real GDP is $1,100 billion, and ❶ there is a $100 billion inflationary gap (part a). ❷ A decrease in government expenditure or tax increase decreases expenditure by

ΔE. ❸ The multiplier decreases induced expenditure and shifts the AD curve leftward to AD_1. The price level falls to 105, real GDP decreases to $1,000 billion, and the inflationary gap is eliminated.

■ Discretionary Fiscal Policy: Supply-Side Effects

We'll now look at the supply-side effects of fiscal policy. Government provides services such as law and order, public education, and public health that increase production possibilities. Government also provides capital such as highways, bridges, tunnels, and dams that increase our production possibilities. But government services and capital can be overprovided to the point that they no longer increase production possibilities. So long as we have not reached this point of overprovision, an increase in government expenditure that increases the quantities of productive services and capital increases aggregate supply and a decrease in government expenditure decreases aggregate supply.

To pay for the productive services and capital that the government provides, it collects taxes. All taxes create disincentives to work and save. So taxes decrease the supply of labour and decrease the supply of saving. A decrease in the supply of labour increases the equilibrium real wage rate and decreases the equilibrium quantity of labour employed. Similarly, a decrease in the supply of saving increases the equilibrium real interest rate and decreases the equilibrium quantity of investment and capital employed. With smaller quantities of labour and capital, potential GDP decreases, and so does aggregate supply. So an increase in taxes decreases aggregate supply.

Figure 16.4 illustrates the effects of fiscal policy on aggregate supply. An increase in government expenditure on productive services and capital or a tax cut increases aggregate supply and shifts the AS curve rightward from AS_0 to AS_1. A decrease in government expenditure on productive services and capital or a tax increase decreases aggregate supply and shifts the AS curve leftward from AS_0 to AS_2.

■ FIGURE 16.4
The Supply-Side Effects of Fiscal Policy

$\mathcal{e}$Foundations **16.1**

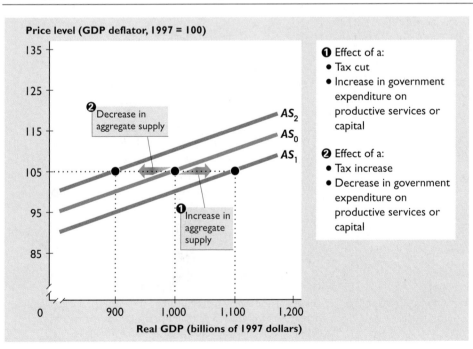

Combined Demand and Supply Effects

When we combine the supply-side and demand-side effects, we see that an increase in government expenditure or a tax cut increases equilibrium real GDP but might raise, lower, or have no effect on the price level. Figure 16.5 illustrates two cases for an expansionary fiscal policy.

In Figure 16.5(a), which shows the conventional view, an expansionary fiscal policy increases aggregate demand by a large amount and the AD curve shifts from AD_0 to AD_1. The same fiscal actions also increase aggregate supply, but this effect is small, so the AS curve shifts by a small amount, from AS_0 to AS_1. The combination of a large increase in aggregate demand and a small increase in aggregate supply increases real GDP and *raises* the price level.

In Figure 16.5(b), which shows the supply-side view, an expansionary fiscal policy increases aggregate supply by a large amount, so the AS curve shifts from AS_0 to AS_1. The same fiscal actions increase aggregate demand but by a smaller amount and the AD curve shifts from AD_0 to AD_1. The combination of a large increase in aggregate supply and a small increase in aggregate demand increases real GDP and *lowers* the price level.

If the increases in aggregate demand and aggregate supply were equal, real GDP would increase and the price level would remain constant. The outcome that actually occurs depends on the fiscal policy. But it is easy to think of tax-cut packages that would have a much larger supply-side effect than demand-side effect.

■ **FIGURE 16.5**

Two Views of the Supply-Side Effects of Fiscal Policy   *e* **Foundations 16.1**

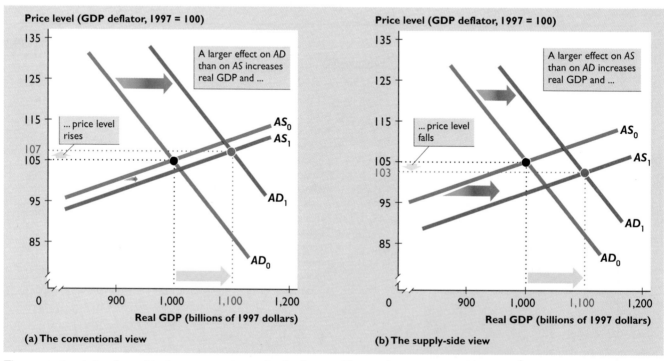

(a) The conventional view

(b) The supply-side view

The conventional view (part a) is that an expansionary fiscal policy increases aggregate demand by more than it increases aggregate supply. Real GDP increases and the price level rises.

The supply-side view (part b) is that an expansionary fiscal policy increases aggregate supply by more than it increases aggregate demand. Real GDP increases and the price level falls.

■ Limitations of Discretionary Fiscal Policy

Figures 16.2 and 16.3 make fiscal policy look easy. Calculate the deflationary gap or the inflationary gap, calculate the multiplier, and determine the magnitude of the change in government expenditure or taxes that, with the multiplier effect, will eliminate the gap. In reality, things are not that easy. The use of discretionary fiscal policy is seriously hampered by three factors:

- Law-making time lag
- Estimating potential GDP
- Economic forecasting

Law-Making Time Lag

The law-making time lag is the amount of time it takes Parliament to pass the laws needed to change taxes or spending. The process takes time because the members of Parliament have different ideas about what is the best tax or spending program to change, so long debates are needed to present conflicting views. The economy might benefit from fiscal stimulation today, but by the time Parliament acts, a different fiscal medicine might be needed.

Estimating Potential GDP

It is not easy to tell whether real GDP is below, above, or at potential GDP. So a discretionary fiscal action might move real GDP *away* from potential GDP instead of towards it. This problem is a serious one because too much fiscal stimulation brings inflation and too little might bring recession.

Economic Forecasting

Fiscal policy changes take a long time to enact in Parliament and yet more time to become effective. So fiscal policy must target forecasts of where the economy will be in the future. Economic forecasting has improved enormously in recent years, but it remains inexact and subject to error. So for a second reason, discretionary fiscal action might move real GDP *away* from potential GDP and create the very problems it seeks to correct.

Let's now look at automatic fiscal policy.

■ Automatic Fiscal Policy

Automatic fiscal policy is a consequence of tax receipts and expenditures that fluctuate with real GDP. These features of fiscal policy are called **automatic stabilizers** because they work to stabilize real GDP without explicit action by the government. Their name is borrowed from engineering and conjures up images of shock absorbers, thermostats, and sophisticated devices that keep airplanes and ships steady in turbulent air and seas.

Automatic stabilizers
Features of fiscal policy that stabilize real GDP without explicit action by the government.

Induced Taxes

On the receipts side of the budget, tax laws define tax *rates*, not tax *dollars*. Tax dollars paid depend on tax rates and incomes. But incomes vary with real GDP, so tax receipts depend on real GDP. Taxes that vary with real GDP are called **induced taxes**. When real GDP increases in an expansion, wages and profits rise, so the taxes on these incomes—induced taxes—rise. When real GDP decreases in a recession, wages and profits fall, so the induced taxes on these incomes fall.

Induced taxes
Taxes that vary with real GDP.

Automatic Stabilizers in Action

The budget deficit increases in a recession and decreases in an expansion because induced taxes and induced transfer payments work as automatic stabilizers.

The figure shows the relationship between the business cycle and the budget deficit in Canada between 1975 and 2000. Part (a) shows the fluctuations of real GDP around potential GDP. Part (b) shows the federal budget balance. Both parts highlight the 1982 and 1990–1991 recessions by shading those periods.

By comparing the two parts of the figure, you can see how the budget moved into a larger deficit in each recession.

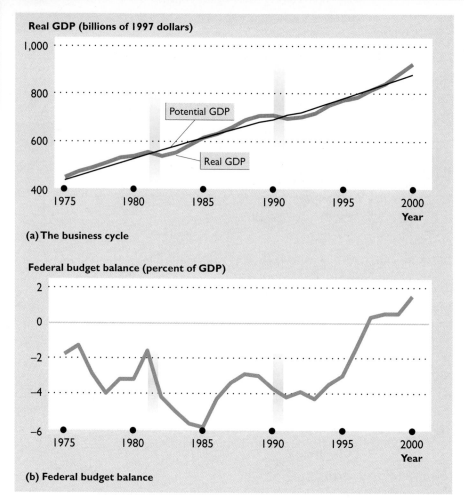

(a) The business cycle

(b) Federal budget balance

SOURCE: Statistics Canada.

Induced transfer payments
Payments made under social programs such as unemployment benefits and welfare benefits, the size of which depends on the state of the economy.

Induced Transfer Payments

On the spending side of the budget, the government creates social programs that pay unemployment benefits and welfare benefits to suitably qualified people and businesses. Government spending on such programs is called **induced transfer payments** because the size of these transfer payments depends on the state of the economy. In a recession, the number of people experiencing economic hardship increases, and induced transfer payments increase. In an expansion, the number of people experiencing economic hardship decreases, and induced transfer payments decrease.

Induced taxes and induced transfer payments decrease the multiplier effect of a change in autonomous expenditure (such as investment or exports). So they moderate both expansions and recessions and make real GDP more stable. They achieve this outcome by weakening the link between real GDP and disposable income and so reduce the effect of a change in real GDP on consumption expenditure. When real GDP increases, induced taxes increase and induced transfer payments decrease, so disposable income does not increase by as much as the increase in real GDP. As a result, consumption expenditure does not increase by as much as it otherwise would have and the multiplier effect is reduced.

CHECKPOINT 16.1

1 **Describe the federal budget process and explain the effects of fiscal policy.**

Practice Problems 16.1

1. Classify each of the following as discretionary fiscal policy or automatic fiscal policy or neither:
   a. A decrease in tax receipts in a recession.
   b. Additional expenditure to upgrade highways.
   c. An increase in the public education budget.
   d. A purchase of $10 million of medicines to treat AIDS sufferers in Africa.
   e. A cut in funding for national defence during an expansion.

2. Explain the change in aggregate demand when:
   a. Government expenditure on goods and services increases by $100 billion.
   b. Taxes are increased by $100 billion.
   c. Both (a) and (b) occur simultaneously.

Exercises 16.1

1. Classify each of the following as discretionary fiscal policy or automatic fiscal policy or neither:
   a. Huge fines imposed on the tobacco companies.
   b. A cut in the gas tax.
   c. A cut in cross-border (customs) taxes.
   d. The cost of refurnishing the Prime Minister's office.
   e. An increase in payments to unemployed people.

2. Illustrate, using an *AS-AD* diagram, the effects of:
   a. A $100 billion decrease in government expenditure on goods and services.
   b. A $100 billion decrease in taxes.
   c. Both (a) and (b) occurring simultaneously.

Solutions to Practice Problems 16.1

1a. A decrease in tax receipts in a recession is an automatic fiscal policy.
1b. Expenditure to upgrade highways is a discretionary fiscal policy.
1c. An increase in the public education budget is discretionary fiscal policy.
1d. A purchase of $10 million of medicines is a discretionary fiscal policy.
1e. A cut in funding for national defence is a discretionary fiscal policy.

2a. Aggregate demand increases by more than $100 billion because the increase in government expenditure has a multiplier effect that increases induced expenditure.
2b. Aggregate demand decreases by more than $100 billion because the tax increase has a multiplier effect that decreases induced expenditure.
2c. Aggregate demand increases because the increase in 2(a) is larger than the decrease in 2(b).

16.2 BANK OF CANADA AND MONETARY POLICY

You learned about the structure of the Bank of Canada in Chapter 11, how the Bank of Canada controls the quantity of money in Chapter 12, and how the quantity of money influences interest rates in Chapter 13. Here, we're going to see how the Bank of Canada monitors the economy and examine the effects of its policy actions on aggregate demand and how those effects ripple through the economy to influence real GDP and the price level.

■ The Monetary Policy Process

The Bank of Canada makes monetary policy, and it does so in an open and transparent process that involves three main elements:

- Monitoring economic conditions
- Meetings of the Board of Directors and Executive Committee
- *The Monetary Policy Report* and *Update*

Monitoring Economic Conditions

The Bank of Canada monitors economic conditions in three main ways. First, it tracks and analyzes conditions in Canadian and global financial markets. Second, it analyzes the data compiled by Statistics Canada on the Consumer Price Index, real GDP, employment, and other indicators of macroeconomic performance. Third, it monitors economic conditions across Canada directly through its regional offices and from the direct experience of its Board members.

The Bank of Canada provides a running commentary on the state of the economy in the form of the data that it publishes on its Web site and less formally in the speeches made, from time to time, by the Governor and other senior officials of the Bank.

David Dodge
Governor of Bank of Canada

Meetings of the Board of Directors and Executive Committee

The Bank of Canada's Board of Directors consists of the Governor and Senior Deputy Governor, the Deputy Minister of Finance, and twelve prominent Canadians with varied backgrounds and interests who live in all regions of the country. The Board meets eight times a year and formally approves interest rate decisions.

A smaller group that consists of the Governor and Senior Deputy Governor, the Deputy Minister of Finance, and four of the other Board members forms the Bank's Executive Committee, which meets more frequently and as needed to review the Bank's policy.

The Monetary Policy Report and *Update*

Twice a year, in May and November, the Bank of Canada prepares a *Monetary Policy Report*. And at other times of the year, as needed, the Bank publishes a *Monetary Policy Report Update*. These reports provide a detailed summary of the Bank's policies and of the Bank's strategic thinking. They also provide a detailed description of the current state of the economy and the outlook for future inflation.

These reports are the main way in which the Bank communicates its analysis of the current and projected future state of the economy to the Canadian business and financial community.

■ Influencing the Interest Rate

When the Bank of Canada announces a policy change, its press release talks about the overnight rate, the interest rate at which banks borrow reserves from each other, or the bank rate, the interest rate at which banks borrow reserves from the Bank of Canada. The press release does not talk about the quantity of money or the size of the open market operation it plans. This focus on interest rates makes it appear as though the Bank sets interest rates rather than the quantity of money. But this impression is misleading for two reasons: a long-run reason and a short-run reason.

In the Long Run

In the long run, saving supply and investment demand determine the real interest rate in global financial markets (see Chapter 9, pp. 205–211). The expected inflation rate, along with the real interest rate, determines the nominal interest rate (Chapter 13, p. 300). The expected inflation rate is determined by actual inflation experience, which in turn depends on the growth rate of the quantity of money that results from the Bank of Canada's actions.

So in the long run, the Bank of Canada *influences* the nominal interest rate by the effects of its policies on the inflation rate. But it does not directly control the nominal interest rate, and it has no control over the real interest rate.

In the Short Run

In the short run, the Bank of Canada can determine the nominal interest rate and take actions to set the overnight rate. But to do so, the Bank must undertake open market operations that change the quantity of money. It is by changing the quantity of money that the Bank of Canada achieves its target for the nominal interest rate.

Also, in the short run, the expected inflation rate is determined by recent monetary policy and inflation experience. So when the Bank of Canada changes the nominal interest rate, the real interest rate also changes, temporarily.

How the Bank of Canada Raises the Interest Rate

Suppose that the Bank of Canada fears inflation and decides to take action to decrease aggregate demand. The Bank of Canada announces that it will raise the short-term interest rate. How does the Bank of Canada achieve this goal?

The Bank of Canada sells government securities in the open market. This action mops up bank reserves. Some banks are short of reserves and seek to borrow reserves from other banks. The overnight rate rises. With fewer reserves, the banks make a smaller quantity of new loans each day until the quantity of loans outstanding has fallen to a level that is consistent with the new lower level of reserves. The quantity of money decreases.

The demand for money determines the quantity of money that will achieve the Bank of Canada's interest rate target. The Bank of Canada could, if it chose, fix the quantity of money and let the interest rate adjust to its equilibrium level. Or the Bank can, and does, fix the interest rate and adjust the quantity of money to the level that makes the chosen interest rate the equilibrium rate.

Suppose, for example, that the Bank of Canada decides to increase the short-term nominal interest rate from 5 to 6 percent a year. Figure 16.6(a) shows what the Bank must do. The demand for money curve is *MD*, so when the quantity of money is $100 billion, the interest rate is 5 percent a year. The Bank of Canada

FIGURE 16.6
Interest Rate Changes

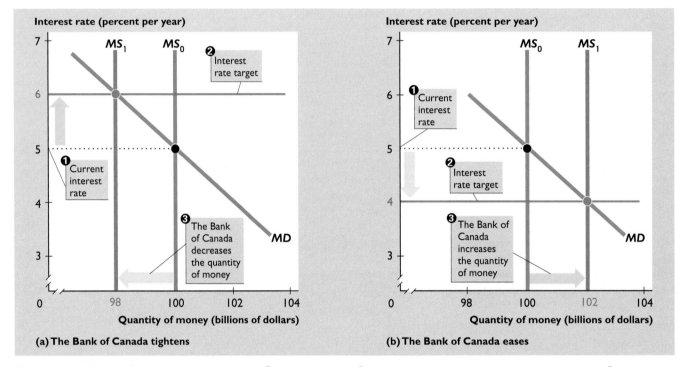

(a) The Bank of Canada tightens

(b) The Bank of Canada eases

❶ The current interest rate is 5 percent a year, and ❷ the Bank of Canada's target is 6 percent a year. To raise the interest rate to the target, the Bank of Canada must sell securities in the open market and ❸ decrease the quantity of money to $98 billion.

❶ The current interest rate is 5 percent a year, and ❷ the Bank of Canada's target is 4 percent a year. To lower the interest rate to the target, the Bank of Canada must buy securities in the open market and ❸ increase the quantity of money to $102 billion.

conducts an open market sale on a large enough scale to decrease the quantity of money from $100 billion to $98 billion. When the quantity of money is $98 billion, the nominal interest rate is 6 percent a year, the Bank's target level.

How the Bank of Canada Lowers the Interest Rate

If the Bank of Canada fears recession, it acts to increase aggregate demand. The Bank of Canada announces that it will lower the short-term interest rate. To achieve this goal, the Bank of Canada buys securities in the open market. This action increases bank reserves. Flush with reserves, banks now seek to lend reserves to other banks. The overnight rate falls. With more reserves, the banks increase their lending and the quantity of money increases.

Again, the demand for money determines the change in the quantity of money that achieves the Bank of Canada's interest rate target. Suppose the Bank of Canada wants to lower the interest rate from 5 percent a year to 4 percent a year. Figure 16.6(b) shows what it must do. When the quantity of money is $100 billion, the interest rate is 5 percent a year. The Bank of Canada conducts an open market purchase on a large enough scale to increase the quantity of money from $100 billion to $102 billion. When the quantity of money is $102 billion, the nominal interest rate is 4 percent a year, the Bank's target level.

■ The Ripple Effects of the Bank of Canada's Actions

Suppose that the Bank of Canada increases the interest rate. What happens next? Three main events follow:

- Investment and consumption expenditure decrease.
- The Canadian dollar rises, and net exports decrease.
- A multiplier process induces a further decrease in consumption expenditure and aggregate demand.

Investment and Consumption Expenditure

The interest rate influences investment and consumption expenditure. When the Bank of Canada increases the nominal interest rate, the real interest rate rises temporarily, and investment and expenditure on consumer durables decrease. The reason is that the interest rate is the *opportunity cost* of the funds used to finance investment and the purchase of big-ticket consumer items. So when the opportunity costs of buying capital and consumer goods rise, the quantities bought and expenditures on these items decrease.

The Dollar and Net Exports

A rise in the interest rate, other things remaining the same, means that the Canadian interest rate rises relative to the interest rates in other countries. Some people will want to move funds into Canada from other countries to take advantage of the higher interest rate that they can now earn on Canadian bank deposits and bonds. When people move money into Canada, they buy Canadian dollars and sell other currencies, such as U.S. dollars or Japanese yen. With more Canadian dollars demanded, the price of the Canadian dollar rises on the foreign exchange market.

The higher price of the Canadian dollar means that foreigners must now pay more for Canadian-made goods and services. So the quantity demanded and the expenditure on Canadian-made items decreases. Canada's exports decrease. Similarly, the higher price of the Canadian dollar means that Canadians now pay less for foreign-made goods and services. So the quantity demanded and the expenditure on foreign-made items increases. Canadian imports increase.

The Multiplier Process

Taking these effects together, investment, consumption expenditure, and net exports are all interest-sensitive components of expenditure. So a rise in the interest rate brings a decrease in aggregate expenditure.

You already know the rest of the story because it is the same as that of the fiscal policy multipliers. The decrease in expenditure decreases incomes, and the decrease in income induces a decrease in consumption expenditure. The decreased consumption expenditure lowers aggregate expenditure. Real GDP and disposable income decrease further, and so does consumption expenditure. Real GDP growth slows, and the inflation rate slows.

If the Bank of Canada lowers the nominal interest rate, the events that we've just described occur in the opposite directions, so real GDP growth and the inflation rate speed up.

Figure 16.7 summarizes the process that we've just described. It begins with the Bank of Canada's open market operations that change the quantity of money and the interest rate and ends with the effects on real GDP and the price level.

July 18, 2001
Bank Rate Drops by 25 Points

The Bank of Canada cut its benchmark interest rate by a quarter of a percentage point yesterday. The Bank has now cut rates five times over the past 6 months by a total of 1.5 percentage points in hopes of staving off a recession, but such cuts usually take 9 to 12 months to trickle down and have a substantial impact on the economy.

NATIONAL POST

Questions
1. Why would the Bank of Canada cut interest rates for the fifth time in six months?
2. Why does a cut in interest rates take about a year to have a substantial effect on the economy?
3. What might lessen the effect of the interest rate cuts on the economy?

 *e*Foundations **16.2**

■ **FIGURE 16.7**

Ripple Effects of the Bank of Canada's Actions

*e*Foundations 16.2

The Bank of Canada's open market operations change the quantity of money and the interest rate. Expenditure plans eventually change, and so does aggregate demand. Eventually, the Bank of Canada's open market operation has ripple effects that change real GDP and the price level.

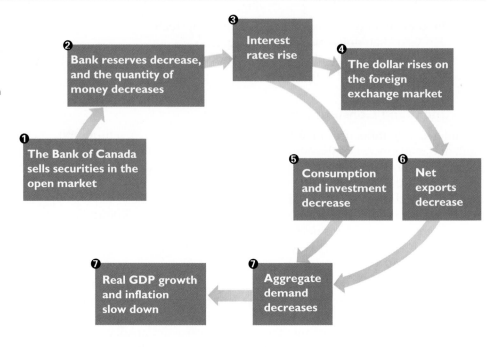

(a) The Bank of Canada tightens

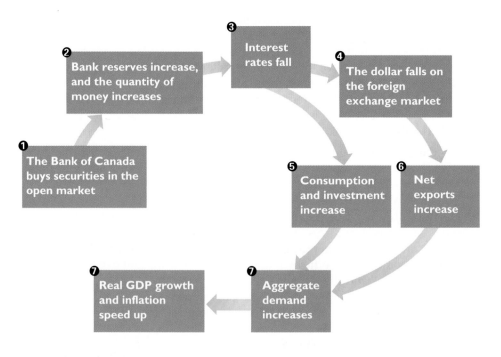

(b) The Bank of Canada eases

■ Monetary Stabilization in the *AS-AD* Model

We've described the broad outline of how the Bank of Canada's actions influence the economy. Let's now see how monetary policy might be used to stabilize real GDP.

The Bank of Canada Tightens to Fight Inflation

In Figure 16.8, part (a) shows investment demand and part (b) shows aggregate demand and aggregate supply. Initially, the interest rate is 5 percent a year and the quantity of investment is $200 billion. At this level of investment (and given the other components of aggregate expenditure not shown in the figure), aggregate demand is AD_0 in part (b). The aggregate supply curve is AS, so equilibrium real GDP is $1,100 billion, which exceeds potential GDP.

The Bank of Canada now conducts an open market sale that increases the interest rate to 6 percent a year. The quantity of investment decreases to $150 billion. If this were the only change in aggregate expenditure, aggregate demand would be $AD_0 - \Delta I$. But the multiplier decreases aggregate demand and the aggregate demand curve shifts leftward to AD_1.

The Bank of Canada's actions have removed the inflation threat, brought real GDP back to potential GDP, and lowered the price level. In reality, real GDP is growing and the price level is rising, so the Bank's actions would slow real GDP growth and reduce inflation rather than decrease real GDP and the price level.

■ **FIGURE 16.8**
Monetary Stabilization: Avoiding Inflation

e/**Foundations 16.2**

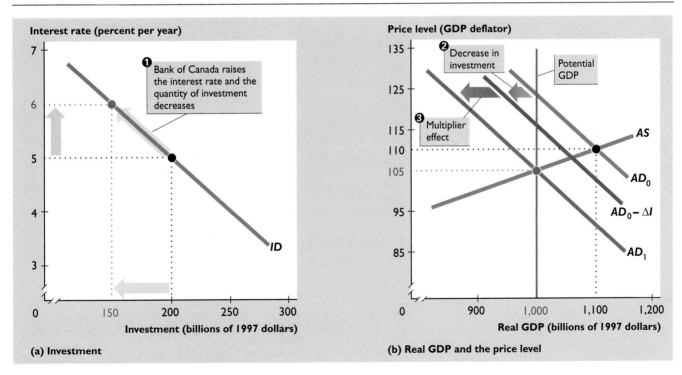

(a) Investment

(b) Real GDP and the price level

Real GDP exceeds potential GDP (part b). To avoid inflation, ❶ the Bank of Canada raises the interest rate (part a). ❷ Expenditure decreases by ΔI, and ❸ the multiplier induces additional expenditure cuts. The aggregate demand curve shifts to AD_1. Real GDP decreases to potential GDP, and inflation is avoided.

The Bank of Canada Eases to Fight Recession

Figure 16.9 is similar to Figure 16.8. The starting point in part (a) is the same. The interest rate is 5 percent a year, and the quantity of investment demanded is $200 billion. But the starting point in part (b) is different. Now, at the equilibrium level of investment (and other components of aggregate expenditure), aggregate demand is AD_0 in part (b). The aggregate supply curve is AS, so equilibrium real GDP is $900 billion, which is less than potential GDP.

The Bank of Canada now conducts an open market purchase that lowers the interest rate to 4 percent a year. The quantity of investment increases to $250 billion. Other interest-sensitive expenditure items (not shown in the figure) also increase. If this were the only change, aggregate demand would increase to $AD_0 + \Delta I$.

With an increase in aggregate expenditure, the multiplier increases aggregate demand. The aggregate demand curve shifts to AD_1. The Bank's actions have eliminated a recession and brought real GDP to equal potential GDP at $1,000 billion and the price level to 105.

The Size of the Multiplier Effect

The size of the multiplier effect of monetary policy depends on the sensitivity of expenditure plans to the interest rate The larger the effect of a change in the interest rate on aggregate expenditure, the greater is the multiplier effect and the smaller is the change in the interest rate needed to achieve the Bank of Canada's objective.

■ **FIGURE 16.9**

Monetary Stabilization: Avoiding Recession   *e*/**Foundations 16.2**

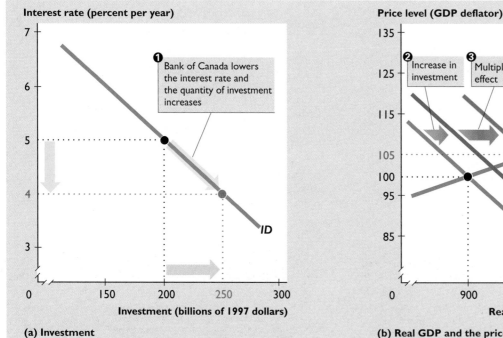

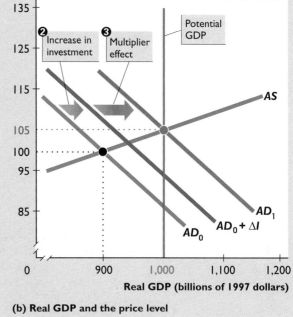

(a) Investment

(b) Real GDP and the price level

Real GDP is less than potential GDP (part b). To avoid a recession, ❶ the Bank of Canada lowers the interest rate (part a). ❷ Expenditure increases by ΔI, and ❸ the multiplier induces additional expenditure.

The aggregate demand curve shifts to AD_1. Real GDP increases to potential GDP, and the recession is avoided.

■ Limitations of Monetary Stabilization Policy

Monetary policy has an advantage over fiscal policy because it cuts out the law-making time lags. The Bank of Canada sets eight dates each year on which it announces any change in the interest rate, but it can announce a change between those dates if necessary. The actual actions that change the quantity of money are taken daily by the Bank of Canada. So monetary policy is a continuous policy process and is not subject to the long decision lag associated with the legislative process required for discretionary fiscal policy.

But monetary policy shares the other two limitations of fiscal policy: Estimating potential GDP is hard, and economic forecasting is error-prone. Monetary policy suffers an additional limitation: Its effects are indirect and depend on how private decisions respond to a change in the interest rate. These responses are themselves hard to forecast and vary from one situation to another in unpredictable ways. A related problem is that the time lags in the operation of monetary policy are longer than those for fiscal policy. So the forecasting horizon must be longer.

In this chapter, we've described the fiscal and monetary policy processes and explained the effects of stabilization policies on real GDP and the price level. In the next two chapters, we study policy tradeoffs and alternative policy strategies.

Eye On The CANADIAN ECONOMY

The Bank of Canada in Action

The figure shows the overnight rate and the 3 month Treasury bill rate between 1970 and 2000. The 3 month Treasury bill rate is a good general indicator of the cost of short-term loans to the federal government and large firms.

Notice how closely these interest rates move together. The overnight rate, which the Bank of Canada directly targets, is the main influence on the short-term interest rate at which the government and businesses borrow.

The figure shows how the Bank of Canada increases interest rates to fight inflation and reduces interest

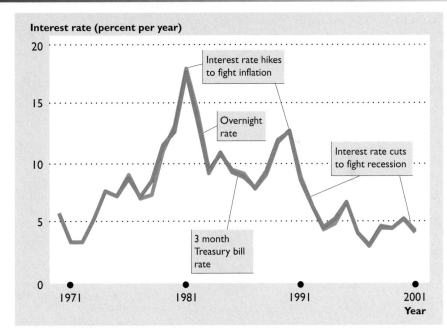

SOURCE: Bank of Canada.

rates to combat recessions. The interest rate increases of the early 1980s and early 1990s were especially severe, and resulted in recessions. After the 1990–1991 recession, low inflation rates and the economy's slow recovery

kept interest rates at the lowest level in years. By the late 1990s, inflation concerns led to increases in interest rates, but in 2001 fears of a recession led the Bank of Canada to reduce short-term interest rates again.

Study Guide pp. 242–245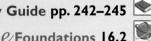

e Foundations 16.2

2 **Describe the Bank of Canada's monetary policy process and explain the effects of monetary policy.**

Practice Problems 16.2

1. If the Bank of Canada reduces the quantity of money, explain how each of the following items changes:
   a. Businesses' purchases of new capital equipment.
   b. Households' purchases of new cars and houses.
   c. Foreigners' purchases of Canadian-made goods and services.
   d. Canadians' purchases of imported goods and services.

2. What is the multiplier effect of monetary policy? How does it work? How does the size of the autonomous expenditure multiplier influence the size of the multiplier effect of monetary policy?

Exercises 16.2

1. If the Bank of Canada lowers the interest rate, explain how each of the following items changes:
   a. Canadian exports.
   b. Canadian imports.
   c. Investment.
   d. The value of the Canadian dollar on the foreign exchange market.

2. Explain the process by which the Bank of Canada's monetary policy influences aggregate demand in the Canadian economy.

3. Compare the effectiveness of monetary policy and fiscal policy for stabilizing Canada's real GDP and employment.

Solutions to Practice Problems 16.2

1a. When the Bank of Canada cuts the quantity of money, the interest rate rises and businesses delay their purchases of new capital equipment.

1b. Households will delay their purchases of new cars and houses.

1c. As the Canadian interest rate rises and foreign interest rates remain the same, the foreign exchange value of the Canadian dollar rises. Canadian-made goods become relatively more expensive for foreigners to buy. Foreigners' purchases of Canadian-made goods decrease.

1d. As the Canadian dollar rises, imported goods become relatively cheaper for Canadians to buy. Canadians' purchases of imported goods increase.

2. When the Bank of Canada increases the quantity of money, interest rates fall and the foreign exchange value of the dollar falls. As interest rates fall, aggregate expenditure increases because investment, consumption expenditure, and net exports increase. The multiplier effect of monetary policy is the increase in aggregate expenditure divided by the increases in the quantity of money.

    When the interest rate changes, part of autonomous expenditure changes and the autonomous expenditure multiplier determines the change in aggregate demand. The larger the autonomous expenditure multiplier, the larger is the multiplier effect of monetary policy.

CHAPTER CHECKPOINT

Key Points

1 **Describe the federal budget process and explain the effects of fiscal policy.**

- The federal budget is an annual statement of the expenditures, tax receipts, and surplus or deficit of the government of Canada.
- The purposes of the federal budget are to finance federal government expenditures and to stabilize the economy.
- Fiscal policy can be either discretionary or automatic.
- Changes in government expenditure and changes in taxes have multiplier effects on aggregate demand and can be used to try to keep real GDP at the level of potential GDP.
- In practice, law-making lags, the difficulty of estimating potential GDP, and the limitations of economic forecasting seriously hamper discretionary fiscal policy.
- Automatic stabilizers arise because tax receipts and expenditures fluctuate with real GDP.

2 **Describe the Bank of Canada's monetary policy process and explain the effects of monetary policy.**

- The Bank of Canada constantly monitors the condition of the economy and monetary conditions. On eight prescheduled dates each year, it announces any change in its monetary policy.
- When the Bank of Canada announces a policy change, it is in terms of the interest rate, not the quantity of money.
- In the long run, the Bank of Canada influences the nominal interest rate by the effects of its policies on the inflation rate. But it does not directly control the nominal interest rate, and it has no control over the real interest rate.
- In the short run, the Bank of Canada can determine the nominal interest rate but, to do so, it must undertake open market operations that change the quantity of money.
- When the Bank of Canada changes the interest rate, the effects ripple through the economy by changing aggregate demand.
- The size of the multiplier effect of monetary policy depends on the sensitivity of expenditure plans to the interest rate.
- Monetary policy has no law-making time lag, but its effects are indirect and depend on how the interest rate influences private borrowing decisions.

Key Terms

Automatic fiscal policy, 380
Automatic stabilizers, 387
Balanced budget, 378
Balanced budget multiplier, 382
Budget deficit, 378

Budget surplus, 378
Discretionary fiscal policy, 380
Federal budget, 378
Fiscal policy, 378
Government expenditure multiplier, 381

Induced taxes, 387
Induced transfer payments, 388
National debt, 378
Tax multiplier, 381

Exercises

1. Suppose that the government of Canada increases its expenditure on high-ways and bridges by $5 billion in 2002. Explain the effect that this expenditure would have on:
   a. Autonomous expenditure.
   b. Aggregate demand.
   c. Real GDP.
   d. Induced transfer payments.
   e. The government's budget surplus.

2. Suppose that the Bank of Canada forecasts a recession in the near future. What change in monetary policy will avoid a recession? Explain the effect of the Bank of Canada's policy on:
   a. Interest rates.
   b. The quantity of money.
   c. Investment.
   d. The foreign exchange value of the Canadian dollar.
   e. Aggregate demand.
   f. The price level.

3. Explain why monetary policy is used more often than fiscal policy to stabilize the economy.

4. Explain the effect of a decrease in the quantity of money on aggregate demand. What determines how big the change in aggregate demand will be?

5. If the government of Canada wanted to increase investment, would the government change its own fiscal policy or encourage the Bank of Canada to change its monetary policy? Explain why. What effect would the policy change have on the price level?

6. If the government of Canada wanted to increase exports, would it change its own fiscal policy or encourage the Bank of Canada to change its monetary policy? Explain why. What effect would the policy change have on the composition of aggregate expenditure?

7. Use the links on your Foundations Web site to review the current state of the Canadian economy. In light of what you've discovered about real GDP, inflation, and the unemployment rate, set out your policy recommendations to:
   a. The Bank of Canada.
   b. The Department of Finance.

8. Use the links on your Foundations Web site to review the current state of the global economy. In light of what you discover about real GDP growth and inflation, set out your policy advice to the governments of the major countries.

9. In 2001, the growth of the Canadian economy slowed and there was concern that the economy would go into recession. Use the links on your Foundations Web site to determine:
   a. The extent of the slowdown (compare the real GDP growth rate in 2000 with that in the years that follow).
   b. How the federal government's budget responded to the situation (compare the rate of growth of federal government spending to the rate of growth of tax revenues in each year, and compare the size of federal surpluses or deficits).
   c. How the Bank of Canada responded to the situation (compare short-term interest rates in 2000 with that in the years that follow).

The Short-Run Policy Tradeoff

When you have completed your study of this chapter,
you will be able to:

1 Describe the short-run tradeoff between inflation and unemployment.

2 Distinguish between the short-run and the long-run Phillips curves and describe the shifting tradeoff between inflation and unemployment.

3 Explain how the Bank of Canada can influence the expected inflation rate and how expected inflation influences the short-run tradeoff.

The task of this chapter is to explore a tradeoff that we face in implementing fiscal and monetary stabilization policies.

We want low unemployment and low inflation. But can we have both at the same time? Must we pay the price of a bit more inflation to obtain the benefits of a bit less unemployment— or the price of a bit more unemployment to obtain the benefits of a bit less inflation? That is, do we face a tradeoff between unemployment and inflation?

If we do face a tradeoff, what is it like? Is it a permanent or a temporary tradeoff? That is, must we pay the price of a permanently higher unemployment rate to obtain the benefits of permanently lower inflation? Or do we have to pay for a limited time to secure a permanent benefit?

And how harsh is the tradeoff? Must we pay a high price in terms of unemployment for a small gain in lower inflation? Or can we get a big drop in inflation at a small unemployment cost?

17.1 THE SHORT-RUN PHILLIPS CURVE

Short-run Phillips curve
A curve that shows the relationship between the inflation rate and the unemployment rate when the natural unemployment rate and the expected inflation rate remain constant.

The **short-run Phillips curve** is a curve that shows the relationship between the inflation rate and the unemployment rate when the natural unemployment rate and the expected inflation rate remain constant. The short-run Phillips curve is a downward-sloping curve along which an increase in the unemployment rate is associated with a decrease in the inflation rate.

Figure 17.1 illustrates a short-run Phillips curve. In this example, the natural unemployment rate is 6 percent and the expected inflation rate is 3 percent a year. If the economy were at full employment, the unemployment rate would equal the natural unemployment rate and the inflation rate would equal the expected inflation rate at point *B*. This point is the anchor point for the short-run Phillips curve.

An expansion that takes the economy above full-employment decreases the unemployment rate and increases the inflation rate. In an expansion, the economy might move to a point such as *A*, where the unemployment rate is 5 percent and the inflation rate is 4 percent a year. A recession that takes the economy below full-employment increases the unemployment rate and lowers the inflation rate. In a recession, the economy might move to a point such as *C*, where the unemployment rate is 7 percent and the inflation rate is 2 percent a year.

The short-run Phillips curve presents a *tradeoff* between inflation and unemployment because, along a given curve, a lower unemployment rate can be achieved only by paying the price of a higher inflation rate, and a lower inflation rate can be achieved only by paying the price of a higher unemployment rate. For example, in Figure 17.1, a decrease in the unemployment rate from 6 percent to 5

■ **FIGURE 17.1**
A Short-Run Phillips Curve

e/**Foundations 17.1**

The short-run Phillips curve (*SRPC*) shows the relationship between inflation and unemployment at a particular natural unemployment rate and expected inflation rate. Here, if the natural unemployment rate is 6 percent, the inflation rate is 3 percent a year.

Higher unemployment rates bring lower inflation rates, and lower unemployment rates bring higher inflation rates.

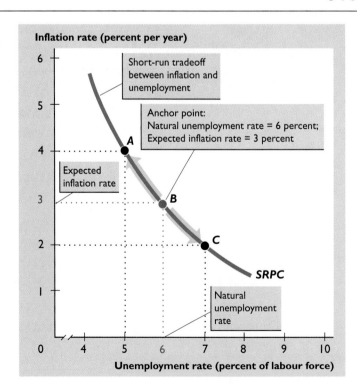

percent costs a 1-percentage point increase in the inflation rate from 3 percent a year to 4 percent a year.

The short-run Phillips curve describes a *short-run* tradeoff because the tradeoff changes when the expected inflation rate or the natural unemployment rate changes. We'll explore the effects of these changes later in this chapter.

■ Aggregate Supply and the Short-Run Phillips Curve

The *AS-AD* model explains the negative relationship between unemployment and inflation along the short-run Phillips curve. The short-run Phillips curve is another way of looking at the upward-sloping aggregate supply curve. Both curves arise because the money wage rate is sticky in the short run. When the price level changes but the money wage rate doesn't change, the real wage rate changes and so does the quantity of labour demanded and the quantity of real GDP supplied. (Chapter 8, pp. 175–176, provides a brief account of this process and Chapter 15, pp. 354–356, provides a detailed account.) A change in real GDP also changes the unemployment rate, and a change in the price level also changes the inflation rate. Let's explore the connections between the variables used in the *AS-AD* model and the short-run Phillips curve a bit more closely.

Unemployment and Real GDP

In a given period, with a fixed amount of capital and given state of technology, real GDP depends on the quantity of labour employed. At full employment, the quantity of real GDP is *potential GDP* and the unemployment rate is the natural unemployment rate. If real GDP is less than potential GDP, employment is less than its full employment level and the unemployment rate is greater than the natural unemployment rate. Similarly, if real GDP exceeds potential GDP, employment exceeds its full-employment level, and the unemployment rate is less than the natural unemployment rate.

The quantitative relationship between the unemployment rate and real GDP was first estimated by economist Arthur M. Okun and is called **Okun's Law**. Okun's Law states that for each percentage point that the unemployment rate is above the natural unemployment rate, there is a 2 percent gap between real GDP and potential GDP. If the natural unemployment rate is 6 percent and potential GDP is $1,000 billion, then when the actual unemployment rate is 7 percent, real GDP is $980 billion—98 percent of potential GDP or 2 percent below potential GDP. When the actual unemployment rate is 5 percent, real GDP is $1,020 billion—102 percent of potential GDP or 2 percent above potential GDP. Table 17.1 summarizes this relationship.

Inflation and the Price Level

The inflation rate is defined as the percentage change in the price level. So starting from any given price level, the higher the inflation rate, the higher is the current period's price level. Suppose that last year, the price level was 100. If in the current year, the inflation rate is 2 percent, the price level rises to 102; if the inflation rate is 3 percent, the price level rises to 103; and if the inflation rate is 4 percent a year, the price level rises to 104.

With these relationships between the unemployment rate and real GDP and between the inflation rate and the price level, we can establish the connection between the short-run Phillips curve and the aggregate supply curve. Figure 17.2 shows this connection.

Okun's Law
For each percentage point that the unemployment rate is above the natural unemployment rate, there is a 2 percent gap between real GDP and potential GDP.

TABLE 17.1

	Unemployment rate (percent)	Real GDP (billions of dollars)
A	5	1,020
B	6	1,000
C	7	980

If in the current year, the economy expands along its full-employment path, real GDP equals potential GDP of $1,000 billion and the unemployment rate equals the natural unemployment rate of 6 percent in Figure 17.2. Point *B* on the short-run Phillips curve in part (a) and point *B* on the aggregate supply curve in part (b) show this situation. The inflation rate is 3 percent a year (its expected rate) in part (a) and the price level is 103 (also its expected level) in part (b).

If instead of expanding along its full-employment path, the economy expands more strongly, real GDP might be $1,020 billion at point *A* on the aggregate supply curve in part (b). In this case, the unemployment rate is 5 percent at point *A* in part (a). The inflation rate is 4 percent a year (higher than expected) in part (a), and the price level is 104 (also higher than expected) in part (b).

Finally, if instead the economy expands by less than potential GDP, real GDP might be $980 billion at point *C* on the aggregate supply curve in part (b). In this case, the unemployment rate is 7 percent at point *C* in part (a). The inflation rate is 2 percent a year (lower than expected) in part (a), and the price level is 102 (also lower than expected) in part (b).

FIGURE 17.2

The Short-Run Phillips Curve and the Aggregate Supply Curve

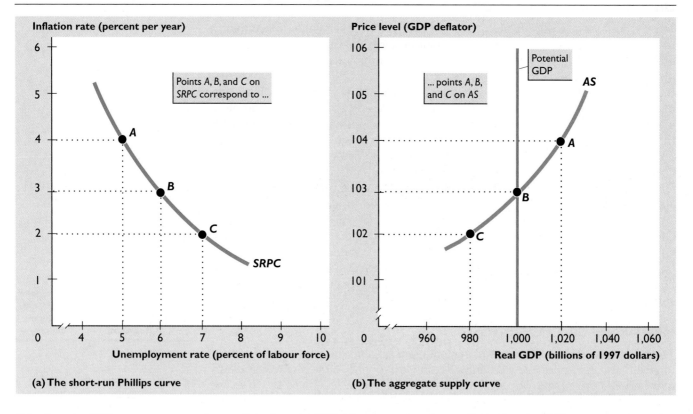

(a) The short-run Phillips curve

(b) The aggregate supply curve

Point *A* on the Phillips curve corresponds to point *A* on the aggregate supply curve: The unemployment rate is 5 percent and the inflation rate is 4 percent a year (in part a), and real GDP is $1,020 billion and the price level is 104 (in part b).	Point *B* on the Phillips curve corresponds to point *B* on the aggregate supply curve: The unemployment rate is 6 percent and the inflation rate is 3 percent a year (in part a), and real GDP is $1,000 billion and the price level is 103 (in part b).	Point *C* on the Phillips curve corresponds to point *C* on the aggregate supply curve: The unemployment rate is 7 percent and the inflation rate is 2 percent a year (in part a), and real GDP is $980 billion and the price level is 102 (in part b).

Aggregate Demand Fluctuations

Aggregate demand fluctuations bring movements along the aggregate supply curve and equivalent movements along the short-run Phillips curve. A decrease in aggregate demand that brings a movement along the aggregate supply curve from point B to point C lowers the price level and decreases real GDP relative to what they would have been. That same decrease in aggregate demand brings a movement along the Phillips curve from point B to point C. The inflation rate falls, and the unemployment rate increases.

Similarly, an increase in aggregate demand that brings a movement along the aggregate supply curve from point B to point A raises the price level and increases real GDP relative to what they would have been. That same increase in aggregate demand brings a movement along the Phillips curve from point B to point A. The inflation rate rises, and the unemployment rate decreases.

John Vanderkamp

Eye On The
PAST

The Canadian Phillips Curve

The Phillips curve is so named because New Zealand economist A. W. (Bill) Phillips discovered the relationship in about 100 years of unemployment and wage inflation data for the United Kingdom.

Phillips made his discovery in 1958. Very soon thereafter, economists looked for Phillips curves in the unemployment and inflation data of other countries.

The figure shows what John Vanderkamp of the University of Guelph found in the Canadian unemployment and inflation data.

From the early 1960s to the mid-1960s, the Canadian data showed the same type of curve that Phillips had found in the United Kingdom data. This discovery raised the hope that a stable and predictable relationship had been discovered between these two key targets for economic policy. And it led to the optimistic belief that an

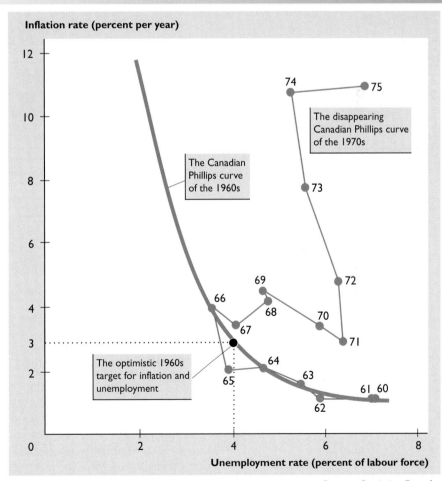

SOURCE: Statistics Canada.

unemployment rate of 4 percent could be achieved with an inflation rate of only 3 percent a year.

But, after 1967, the Canadian Phillips curve began to disappear as both inflation and unemployment increased.

Eye On The GLOBAL ECONOMY

Inflation and Unemployment

The figures show data on inflation and unemployment in the United Kingdom and the United States over most of the twentieth century. Like the Canadian

data, these data reveal no clear, single tradeoff that can be used to predict events reliably. Rather, the short-run tradeoff shifts around a great deal.

The highest inflation rates have *not* occurred at the lowest unemployment rate. And the highest unemployment during the Great Depression of the 1930s did *not* bring the lowest inflation rates, although prices did fall rapidly in the United States during the recession years of 1931 and 1932, as they did in Canada.

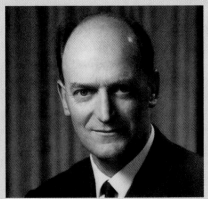

Bill Phillips

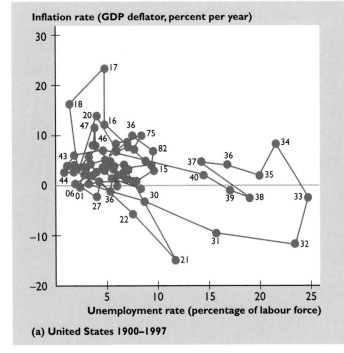

(a) United States 1900–1997

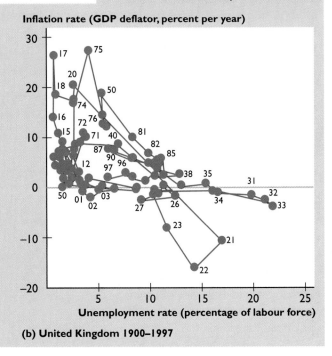

(b) United Kingdom 1900–1997

Source: Michael Parkin, "Unemployment, Inflation, and Monetary Policy," *Canadian Journal of Economics*, November 1998.

■ Why Bother with the Phillips Curve?

You've seen that the short-run Phillips curve is another way of looking at the aggregate supply curve. And you might be wondering, why bother with the short-run Phillips curve? Isn't the aggregate supply curve adequate for describing the short-run tradeoff?

There are two reasons for using the Phillips curve. First, it focuses directly on two policy targets: the inflation rate and the unemployment rate. Second, the aggregate supply curve shifts whenever the money wage rate or potential GDP changes. Such changes occur every day. So the aggregate supply curve is not a stable tradeoff. The short-run Phillips curve isn't a stable tradeoff either, but it is more stable than the aggregate supply curve. It shifts only when the natural unemployment rate changes or when the expected inflation rate changes.

CHECKPOINT 17.1

1 **Describe the short-run tradeoff between inflation and unemployment.**   **Study Guide pp. 250–254**

e/**Foundations 17.1**

Practice Problem 17.1

Table 1 describes five possible situations that might arise in 2003, depending on the level of aggregate demand in that year. Potential GDP is $700 billion, and the natural unemployment rate is 5 percent.

a. Calculate the inflation rate for each possible outcome.
b. Use Okun's Law to find the real GDP associated with each unemployment rate in Table 1.
c. What is the expected inflation rate in 2003?
d. What is the expected price level in 2003?
e. Plot the short-run Phillips curve for 2003.
f. Plot the aggregate supply curve for 2003.
g. Mark the points *A, B, C, D*, and *E* on each curve that correspond to the data provided in the table and the data that you have calculated.

Exercises 17.1

1. In the economy in the Practice Problem, the outcome in 2003 turned out to be row *B* of Table 1. Table 2 shows five possible outcomes for 2004 depending on the level of aggregate demand in that year. Potential GDP has grown to $735 billion, but the natural unemployment rate has remained at 5 percent.
    a. Plot the short-run Phillips curve for 2004.
    b. Use Okun's Law to find the real GDP associated with each unemployment rate in Table 2.
    c. What is the expected inflation rate in 2004?
    d. What is the expected price level in 2004?
    e. Plot the aggregate supply curve for 2004.
    f. Mark the points *A, B, C, D*, and *E* on each curve that correspond to the data provided in Table 2 and the data you have calculated.

2. Compare the short-run Phillips curves and aggregate supply curves of 2004 with those of 2003. Thinking about the definitions of the short-run Phillips curve and the aggregate supply curve, what might have changed between the two years to make the curves shift?

Solution to Practice Problem 17.1

a. and b. The inflation rate is the (Price level − 100) ÷ 100; real GDP equals potential GDP minus *x* percent of potential GDP, where *x* = 2 × (unemployment rate − natural unemployment rate)—Okun's Law.
c. The expected inflation rate in 2003 is 6 percent a year.
d. The expected price level in 2003 is 106.
e. Figure 1 shows the short-run Phillips curve for 2003.
f. Figure 2 shows the aggregate supply curve for 2003.
g. The points are *A, B, C, D*, and *E* on each curve in Figures 1 and 2.

TABLE 1

	Price level (2002 = 100)	Unemployment rate (percentage)
A	102.5	9
B	105.0	6
C	106.0	5
D	107.5	4
E	110.0	3

TABLE 2

	Price level (2002 = 100)	Unemployment rate (percentage)
A	108	9
B	113	6
C	115	5
D	118	4
E	123	3

FIGURE 1

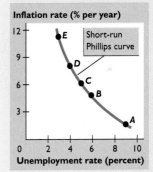

FIGURE 2

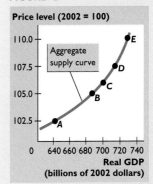

17.2 SHORT-RUN AND LONG-RUN PHILLIPS CURVES

The short-run Phillips curve that you've just studied is the *short-run* tradeoff between inflation and unemployment when aggregate demand changes and the natural unemployment rate and expected inflation rate remain the same. Over time, these two factors do not remain the same. And you've seen in the data that the actual fluctuations in inflation and unemployment do not fall along a neat Phillips curve.

Changes in the expected inflation rate influence the short-run tradeoff most. And changes in expected inflation create a long-run Phillips curve. Let's look at the properties of the long-run Phillips curve.

■ The Long-Run Phillips Curve

Long-run Phillips curve
The vertical line that shows the relationship between inflation and unemployment when the economy is at full employment.

The **long-run Phillips curve** shows the relationship between inflation and unemployment when the economy is at full employment. You learned in Chapter 8 that at full employment, the unemployment rate is the *natural unemployment rate*. So on the long-run Phillips curve, there is only one possible unemployment rate: the natural unemployment rate.

In contrast, the inflation rate can take on any value at full employment. You learned in Chapter 13 (pp. 311–315) that at full employment, for a given real GDP growth rate, the greater the growth rate of the quantity of money, the greater is the inflation rate.

This description of the economy in the long run tells us the properties of the long-run Phillips curve. The long-run Phillips curve is a vertical line located at the natural unemployment rate. In Figure 17.3, it is the vertical line *LRPC*. The long-run Phillips curve tells us that any inflation rate is possible at the natural unemployment rate.

■ **FIGURE 17.3**
The Long-Run Phillips Curve

*e*Foundations **17.2**

The long-run Phillips curve is a vertical line at the natural unemployment rate. There is no unemployment-inflation tradeoff in the long run.

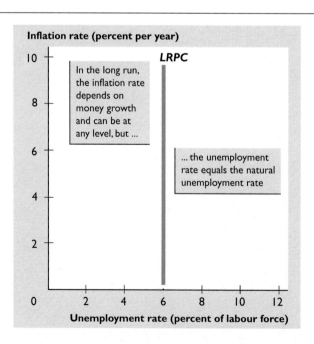

No Long-Run Tradeoff

Because the long-run Phillips curve is vertical, there is no long-run tradeoff between unemployment and inflation. In the long run, the only unemployment rate available is the natural unemployment rate. But any inflation rate can occur.

You can think of the long-run Phillips curve as another way of looking at the potential GDP line in the *AS-AD* model. Let's examine this parallel.

■ Long-Run Adjustment in the *AS-AD* Model

The *AS-AD* model explains both the short-run and long-run effects of a change in aggregate demand. Figure 17.4 shows the long-run effect. Last year, aggregate demand was AD_0 and aggregate supply was AS_0. The price level was 100, and real GDP was $1,000 billion—potential GDP. (To simplify the story, suppose there is no economic growth, so potential GDP remains at $1,000 billion.)

Case 1: In the current year, aggregate demand increases from AD_0 to AD_1. The money wage rate rises to keep the real wage rate at its full-employment level. So the aggregate supply curve shifts to AS_1. The price level rises to 103—the inflation rate is 3 percent—and real GDP remains at potential GDP.

Case 2: In the current year, aggregate demand increases from AD_0 to AD_2. The money wage rate rises to keep the real wage rate at its full-employment level. So the aggregate supply curve shifts to AS_2. The price level rises to 107—the inflation rate is 7 percent—and real GDP remains at potential GDP.

The *AS-AD* model predicts that in the long run, any price level is possible but only one level of real GDP can occur—potential GDP. Aggregate demand and aggregate supply determine the price level.

■ FIGURE 17.4
Long-Run Adjustment in the *AS-AD* Model

e/Foundations **17.2**

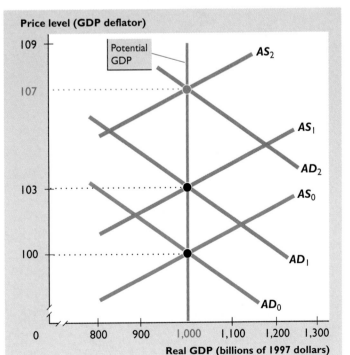

Last year, aggregate demand was AD_0, aggregate supply was AS_0, the price level was 100, and real GDP was $1,000 billion (at full employment).

If aggregate demand increases to AD_1 and aggregate supply changes to AS_1, the price level rises by 3 percent to 103.

But if aggregate demand increases to AD_2 and aggregate supply changes to AS_2, the price level rises by 7 percent to 107.

In both cases, real GDP remains at $1,000 billion, and because the economy is at full employment, unemployment remains at the natural unemployment rate.

■ Expected Inflation

Expected inflation rate
The inflation rate that people forecast and use to set the money wage rate and other money prices.

Full employment occurs when the *AD* and *AS* curves intersect at potential GDP. We're going to see that at full employment, the inflation rate equals the expected inflation rate. The **expected inflation rate** is the inflation rate that people forecast and use to set the money wage rate and other money prices.

Suppose there is full employment and Harveys' servers earn $7 an hour. With no inflation, a money wage rate of $7 an hour keeps the market for servers in equilibrium. But with 10 percent inflation, a constant money wage rate means a falling real wage rate and a shortage of servers. Now, a 10 percent rise in the money wage rate to $7.70 is needed to keep the market for servers in equilibrium. If Harvey's and everyone else expect 10 percent inflation, the money wage rate will rise by 10 percent to prevent a labour shortage from arising.

If expectations about the inflation rate turn out to be correct, the price level rises by the 10 percent expected and the real wage rate remains constant at its full-employment equilibrium level. Real GDP remains at potential GDP and unemployment remains at the natural unemployment rate.

Because the actual inflation rate equals the expected inflation rate at full employment, we can interpret the long-run Phillips curve as the relationship between inflation and unemployment when the inflation rate equals the expected inflation rate.

Figure 17.5 shows short-run Phillips curves for two expected inflation rates. A short-run Phillips curve shows the tradeoff between inflation and unemployment at *a particular expected inflation rate*. When the expected inflation rate changes, the

---

■ **FIGURE 17.5**
Short-Run and Long-Run Phillips Curves

*e*Foundations **17.2**

If the natural unemployment rate is 6 percent, the long-run Phillips curve is *LRPC*. If the expected inflation rate is 3 percent a year, the short-run Phillips curve is $SRPC_0$. If the expected inflation rate is 7 percent a year, the short-run Phillips curve is $SRPC_1$.

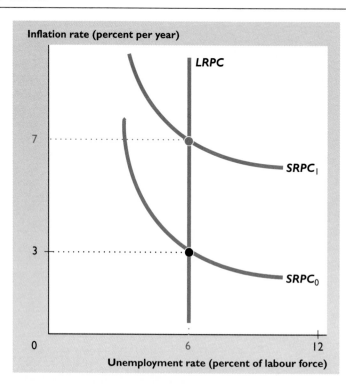

short-run Phillips curve shifts to intersect the long-run Phillips curve at the expected inflation rate.

In Figure 17.5, when the expected inflation rate is 3 percent a year, the short-run Phillips curve is $SRPC_0$, and when the expected inflation rate is 7 percent a year, the short-run Phillips curve is $SRPC_1$.

■ The Natural Rate Hypothesis

The **natural rate hypothesis** is the proposition that when the growth rate of the quantity of money changes (and the aggregate demand growth rate changes), the unemployment rate changes *temporarily* and eventually returns to the natural unemployment rate.

Figure 17.6 illustrates the natural rate hypothesis. Initially, aggregate demand growth generates inflation at 3 percent a year and the economy is at full employment, at point A. Then aggregate demand grows more rapidly, at a rate that will eventually generate inflation at 7 percent a year. But in the short run, with a sticky money wage rate, the increase in aggregate demand brings an increase in real GDP and a decrease in the unemployment rate. The inflation rate increases to 5 percent a year, and the economy moves from point A to point B. Eventually, the higher inflation rate is expected and the money wage rate increases. As the expected inflation rate increases from 3 percent to 7 percent, the short-run Phillips curve shifts upward from $SRPC_0$ to $SRPC_1$. Inflation speeds up, real GDP moves back to its full-employment level, and the unemployment rate returns to the natural unemployment rate. In Figure 17.6, the economy moves from point B to point C.

Natural rate hypothesis
The proposition that when the growth rate of the quantity of money changes, the unemployment rate changes temporarily and eventually returns to the natural unemployment rate.

■ **FIGURE 17.6**
The Natural Rate Hypothesis

e/**Foundations 17.2**

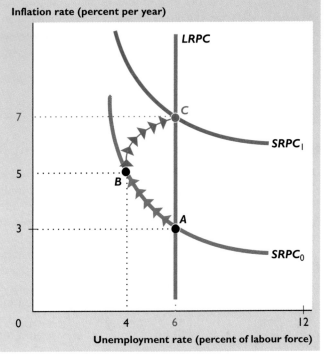

The inflation rate is 3 percent a year and the economy is at full employment, at point A. Then the inflation rate increases. In the short run, the increase in inflation brings a decrease in the unemployment rate—a movement along $SRPC_0$ to point B.

Eventually, the higher inflation rate is expected and the short-run Phillips curve shifts upward to $SRPC_1$. At the higher expected inflation rate, unemployment returns to the natural rate—the natural rate hypothesis.

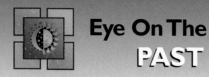

Eye On The PAST

A Live Test of the Natural Rate Hypothesis

The figure describes the Canadian economy during the 11 years from 1960 to 1971 and shows that the natural rate hypothesis provides a good description of reality during these years.

The natural unemployment rate was around 5 percent, so the long-run Phillips curve, *LRPC*, was located at that unemployment rate.

At the beginning of the period, the inflation rate and the expected inflation rate were around 1.5 percent a year. So the short-run Phillips curve was $SRPC_0$.

Through 1965, the expected inflation rate remained at 1.5 percent a year but the actual inflation rate edged upward and the unemployment rate decreased below the natural unemployment rate. The economy moved upward along $SRPC_0$ from point A to point B.

Then, from 1966 through 1969, the inflation rate increased and so did the expected inflation rate. In 1966, the economy moved to point C. By 1969, the expected inflation rate was around 4 percent a year and the short-run Phillips curve had shifted upward to $SRPC_1$. As the higher inflation rate came to be expected, the unemployment rate increased; by 1971, it had moved above the natural unemployment rate

and the economy was at point D.

Notice the similarity between the actual events of this period and the natural rate hypotheses in Figure 17.6.

Interestingly, Edmund S. Phelps of Columbia University and Milton Friedman of the University of Chicago suggested the natural rate hypothesis, which is an implication of the classical dichotomy that you learned about in Chapter 8, *before* these events occurred.

■ Changes in the Natural Unemployment Rate

If the natural unemployment rate changes, both the long-run Phillips curve and the short-run Phillips curve shift. When the natural unemployment rate increases, both the long-run Phillips curve and the short-run Phillips curve shift rightward; and when the natural unemployment rate decreases, both the long-run Phillips curve and the short-run Phillips curve shift leftward.

Figure 17.7 illustrates these changes. When the natural unemployment rate is 6 percent, the long-run Phillips curve is $LRPC_0$. If the expected inflation rate is 3 percent a year, the short-run Phillips curve is $SRPC_0$. An increase in the natural unemployment rate, with no change in the expected inflation rate, shifts the two Phillips curves rightward to $LRPC_1$ and $SRPC_1$. And a decrease in the natural unemployment rate, with no change in the expected inflation rate, shifts the two Phillips curves leftward to $LRPC_2$ and $SRPC_2$.

FIGURE 17.7

Changes in the Natural Unemployment Rate

*e*Foundations **17.2**

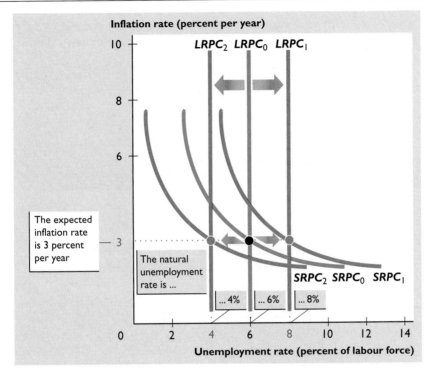

The natural unemployment rate is 6 percent, and the long-run Phillips curve is $LRPC_0$. The expected inflation rate is 3 percent a year, and the short-run Phillips curve is $SRPC_0$. An increase in the natural unemployment rate shifts the two Phillips curves rightward to $LRPC_1$ and $SRPC_1$. And a decrease in the natural unemployment rate shifts them leftward to $LRPC_2$ and $SRPC_2$.

■ Does the Natural Unemployment Rate Change?

You learned in Chapter 6 (p. 146) that economists don't agree about the size of the natural unemployment rate or the extent to which it fluctuates. During the 1960s, the belief (or hope) was that the natural unemployment rate was constant and at about 5 percent. But during the 1970s and 1980s, an increasing number of economists came to the view that the natural unemployment rate was increasing. Most economists now accept the view that the natural unemployment rate did increase during the 1970s and 1980s and that it decreased during the 1990s.

Changes in frictional and structural unemployment bring changes in the natural unemployment rate. These changes increased the natural unemployment rate during the 1980s to perhaps as high as 10 percent and decreased the natural rate in the 1990s to around 7.5 percent. These numbers are subject to a large margin of uncertainty (and controversy) because economists do not yet have a definite way of measuring the natural unemployment rate.

You learned about the factors that determine the natural unemployment rate in Chapter 8 (pp. 190–195). Those factors divide into two groups: influences on job search and influences on job rationing. Job search is influenced by demographic change, unemployment benefits, and structural change. And job rationing arises from efficiency wages, the minimum wage, and union wages.

No one is sure how important these factors are in changing the natural unemployment rate. But to the extent that they do have an influence, they probably increased the natural unemployment rate during the 1970s. The sharp increase in the birth rate (known as the "baby boom") that occurred after World War II in the late 1940s and early 1950s brought a bulge in the number of young people entering the labour force during the late 1960s and early 1970s. This bulge in the number of new entrants probably increased the natural unemployment rate. Also during the 1970s, unemployment benefits became more generous, which probably increased the natural unemployment rate.

Structural change during the 1970s and 1980s, much of it a response to massive hikes in the world price of oil, probably increased the natural unemployment rate further during the later 1970s and early 1980s. In the early 1990s, there was also evidence of rising structural unemployment, this time as the economy

The Shifting Short-Run Tradeoff

The short-run tradeoff becomes less favourable—more inflation and more

unemployment—if either the expected inflation rate or the natural unemployment rate increases. And the short-run tradeoff becomes more favourable—less inflation and less unemployment—if either the expected inflation rate or the natural unemployment rate decreases. When the tradeoff becomes less favourable, the short-run Phillips curve shifts

rightward and upward. When the tradeoff becomes more favourable, the short-run Phillips curve shifts leftward and downward.

The figures describe the shifting tradeoff in Canada. During the late 1960s and 1970s, the expected inflation rate increased from 1.5 percent a year to more than 10 percent a year and the natural unemployment rate

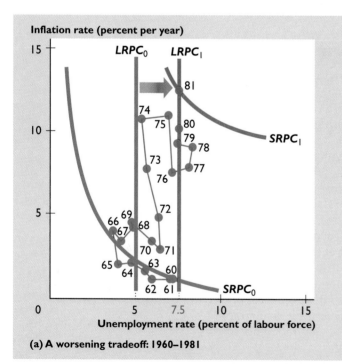

(a) A worsening tradeoff: 1960–1981

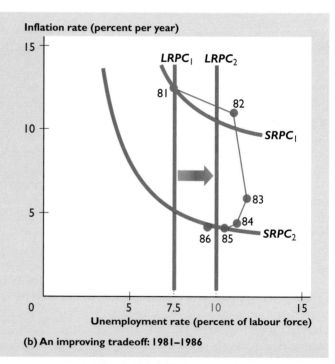

(b) An improving tradeoff: 1981–1986

restructured in response to the rapid increase in both imports and exports that resulted from the Canada-U.S. Free Trade Agreement of 1989.

By the late 1990s, there was reason to believe that the natural unemployment rate was falling. One reason was that cuts to welfare and unemployment benefits had increased the incentive to find a job. Also, a fall in the birth rate during the 1970s lowered the number of new labour market entrants. These factors, combined with an increased pace of technological change in the "new economy" made job search faster and lowered the natural unemployment rate.

This description of the changing natural unemployment rate is consistent with the data and consistent with the shifting short-run tradeoff between inflation and unemployment. But it remains speculation rather than solid knowledge.

increased from 5 percent to 7.5 percent. The Phillips curves shifted from $SRPC_0$ and $LRPC_0$ to $SRPC_1$ and $LRPC_1$ in Figure (a). The tradeoff worsened.

Between 1981 and 1986, the expected inflation rate decreased from more than 10 percent a year to 4 percent a year but the natural unemployment rate increased from 7.5 percent to about 10 percent. The

Phillips curves shifted from $LRPC_1$ and $SRPC_1$ to $LRPC_2$ and $SRPC_2$ in Figure (b). The tradeoff improved.

Between 1986 and 1993, the expected inflation rate decreased from 4 percent a year to 3 percent a year but the natural unemployment rate didn't change. The short-run Phillips curve shifted to $SRPC_3$ in Figure (c). The tradeoff improved

again.

Finally, between 1993 and 2000, the expected inflation rate remained constant but the natural unemployment rate fell from 10 percent to 7.5 percent. The Phillips curves shifted from $LRPC_2$ and $SRPC_3$ to $LRPC_3$ and $SRPC_4$ in Figure (d). The tradeoff improved (slightly) yet again.

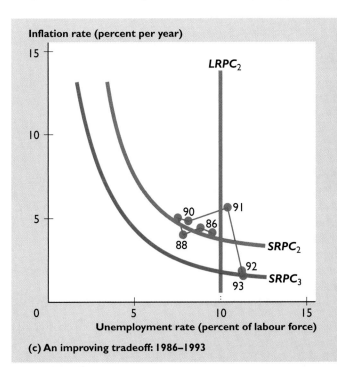

(c) An improving tradeoff: 1986–1993

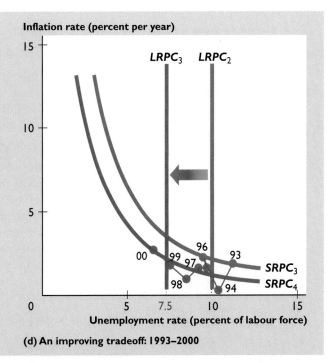

(d) An improving tradeoff: 1993–2000

Study Guide pp. 254–258

*e*Foundations 17.2

2 Distinguish between the short-run and the long-run Phillips curves and describe the shifting tradeoff between inflation and unemployment.

FIGURE 1

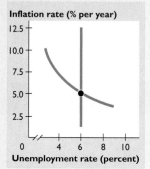

FIGURE 2

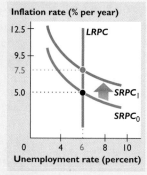

FIGURE 3

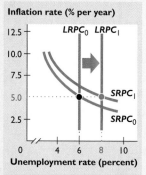

FIGURE 4

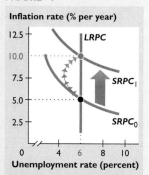

Practice Problems 17.2

1. Figure 1 shows a short-run Phillips curve and a long-run Phillips curve.
   a. Label the two curves to identify which is the long-run curve and which is the short-run curve.
   b. What is the expected inflation rate?
   c. What is the natural unemployment rate?
   d. If the expected inflation rate increases to 7.5 percent a year, show the new short-run and long-run Phillips curves.
   e. If the natural unemployment rate increases to 8 percent, show the new short-run and long-run Phillips curves.

2. In the economy illustrated in Figure 1, aggregate demand starts to grow more rapidly, and eventually, the inflation rate rises to 10 percent a year. Explain the course of unemployment and inflation in this economy.

Exercises 17.2

1a. Draw a figure to show the short-run Phillips curve and the long-run Phillips curve in an economy in which the natural unemployment rate is 7 percent and the expected inflation rate is 4 percent a year.

1b. If the expected inflation rate changes to 3 percent a year, show the new short-run and long-run Phillips curves.

1c. If the natural unemployment rate becomes 6 percent, show the new short-run and long-run Phillips curves.

2. In Exercise 1, aggregate demand starts to grow more slowly, and eventually, the inflation rate will fall to 2 percent a year. Explain the course of unemployment and inflation in this economy.

Solutions to Practice Problems 17.2

1a. The long-run Phillips curve is the vertical curve, *LRPC*, and the short-run Phillips curve is the downward-sloping curve, *SRPC₀* (Figure 2).

1b. The expected inflation rate is 5 percent a year. The expected inflation rate is the inflation rate at which *LRPC* and *SRPC₀* intersect.

1c. The natural unemployment rate is 6 percent. The long-run Phillips curve is vertical at the natural unemployment rate.

1d. The short-run Phillips curve shifts upward, but the long-run Phillips curve does not change (see Figure 2).

1e. Both the short-run and long-run Phillips curves shift rightward (see Figure 3).

2. Figure 4 shows the course of unemployment and inflation. As the change in the inflation rate becomes expected, the short-run Phillips curve shifts upward and eventually intersects the long-run Phillips curve at an inflation rate of 10 percent a year. The unemployment rate falls below the natural unemployment rate but gradually returns to the natural unemployment rate.

17.3 EXPECTED INFLATION

You've seen that expected inflation plays a big role in determining the position of the short-run tradeoff. When the expected inflation rate is low, as it was in 2000, the tradeoff is more favourable than when the expected inflation rate is high, as it was in 1980. The effect of expected inflation on the short-run tradeoff raises three questions:

- What determines the expected inflation rate?
- How responsive is the short-run tradeoff to a change in expected inflation?
- What can policy do to lower expected inflation?

■ What Determines the Expected Inflation Rate?

The *expected inflation rate* is the inflation rate that people forecast and use to set the money wage rate and other money prices. To forecast the inflation rate, people use the same basic method that they use to forecast other variables that affect their lives.

Data make up the first ingredient in forecasting—data about the past behaviour of the phenomenon that we want to forecast. When people bet that Tiger Woods would win the British Open in 2000, they based their forecast on the performance of Tiger and the other golfers in the months prior to that event.

Science is the second ingredient in forecasting—the specific science that seeks to understand the phenomenon that we wish to forecast. If we want to know whether it is likely to rain tomorrow, we turn to the science of meteorology. Science is not a substitute for data. It is knowledge that tells people how to interpret data.

So to forecast inflation, people use data about past inflation and other relevant variables and the science of economics, which seeks to understand the forces that cause inflation.

You already know the relevant economics: the *AS–AD* model. You know that the growth rate of the quantity of money determines the growth of aggregate demand and that the trend growth rate of real GDP is the growth rate of aggregate supply. So the trend growth rate of the quantity of money minus the trend growth rate of real GDP determines the trend inflation rate.

The inflation rate fluctuates around its trend as the state of the economy changes over the business cycle. In an expansion, the inflation rate rises above trend, and in a recession, the inflation rate falls below trend as aggregate demand fluctuates to bring movements along the aggregate supply curve. And you know that the growth rate of the quantity of money is one of the influences on these aggregate demand fluctuations.

The Bank of Canada determines the growth rate of the quantity of money, so the major ingredient in a forecast of inflation is a forecast of the Bank of Canada's actions. Economic forecasters use these ideas along with a lot of data and elaborate statistical models of the economy to forecast the inflation rate.

When all the relevant data and economic science are used to forecast inflation, the resulting forecast is called a **rational expectation.** The rational expectation of the inflation rate is a forecast based on the Bank of Canada's forecasted monetary policy along with forecasts of the other forces that influence aggregate demand and aggregate supply. But the dominant factor is the Bank's monetary policy.

Rational expectation
The inflation forecast resulting from use of all the relevant data and economic science.

■ How Responsive is the Tradeoff to a Change in Expected Inflation?

A change in the expected inflation rate shifts the short-run tradeoff gradually. The reason is that the tradeoff depends on the rate of increase in the money wage rate. The tradeoff changes only when the rate of increase in the money wage rate changes in response to a change in the expected inflation rate.

Some money wage rates respond quickly to a changed expectation about inflation. But many money wage rates are determined by long-term contracts. Contracts in place in the current year were agreed upon as long as three years ago. And the inflation forecasts that were used to set those wage rates were the rational expectations of the past, not the present. So even if people now change their forecast of future inflation, many of them can't use their new forecast right away. They must wait until they negotiate a new long-term contract.

The presence of long-term labour contracts means that the short-run tradeoff responds gradually to a change in the expected inflation rate. If the Bank of Canada increases the trend inflation rate, it will take several years before the tradeoff shifts upward to reflect that change.

The gradual response of the tradeoff to a change in the expected inflation rate leads to fluctuations around full employment. For example, during the 1970s when inflation increased, the tradeoff shifted upward and became less favourable, but the actual inflation rate exceeded the expected inflation rate for several years and the unemployment rate was below the natural unemployment rate. Similarly, during the 1980s when inflation decreased, the tradeoff shifted downward and became more favourable, but the actual inflation rate decreased below the expected inflation rate for several years and the unemployment rate was above the natural unemployment rate.

■ What Can Policy Do to Lower Expected Inflation?

If the Bank of Canada wants to lower the inflation rate, it can pursue two alternative lines of attack:

- A surprise inflation reduction
- A credible announced inflation reduction

A Surprise Inflation Reduction

Figure 17.8 illustrates the economy at full employment with inflation raging at 10 percent a year. The inflation rate of 10 percent a year is expected, so unemployment is at the natural unemployment rate, which is 6 percent. The economy is on its long-run Phillips curve, $LRPC$, and its short-run Phillips curve, $SRPC_0$.

No one is expecting the Bank of Canada to change its policy. The expected inflation rate seems stubbornly set at 10 percent a year. But suppose that the Bank does change its policy and slows inflation. The Bank raises interest rates and slows money growth. With no change in the expected inflation rate, the money wage rate continues to rise by the same amount as before but aggregate demand growth slows, and the economy moves along the short-run Phillips curve $SRPC_0$. The unemployment rate rises to 8 percent, and the inflation rate falls. The Bank of Canada's policy has succeeded in slowing inflation but at the cost of recession. Real GDP is below potential GDP, and unemployment is above the natural unemployment rate.

FIGURE 17.8
Slowing Inflation

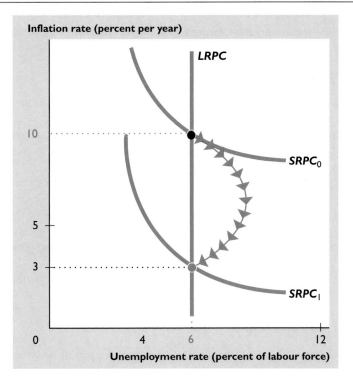

The economy is on the short-run Phillips curve $SRPC_0$ and on the long-run Phillips curve $LRPC$. The inflation rate is 10 percent a year and the unemployment rate equals the natural unemployment rate of 6 percent.

An unexpected slowdown in aggregate demand growth slows inflation to 9 percent and increases the unemployment rate to 8 percent as the economy slides down along $SRPC_0$. Eventually, the expected inflation rate falls and the short-run Phillips curve shifts to $SRPC_1$. The unemployment rate remains above 6 percent through the adjustment.

Alternatively, a credible, announced slowdown in aggregate demand growth lowers the expected inflation rate and shifts the short-run Phillips curve downward to $SRPC_1$. Inflation slows to 3 percent a year, and unemployment remains at 6 percent.

A Credible Announced Inflation Reduction

Suppose that instead of unexpectedly slowing the growth of aggregate demand, the Bank of Canada announces its intention ahead of its action in a credible manner so that its announcement is believed. That is, the Bank convincingly announces its plan to slow the growth rate of the quantity of money and aggregate demand so as to bring the inflation rate down along a specified path.

If the Bank of Canada's announced policy is credible, the expected inflation rate falls. With a lower expected inflation rate, the money wage rate increases more slowly.

The lower expected inflation rate shifts the short-run Phillips curve in Figure 17.8 downward to $SRPC_1$, and the inflation rate falls to 3 percent a year and the unemployment rate remains at the natural unemployment rate of 6 percent.

This announced inflation reduction lowers the inflation rate but with no increase in unemployment or accompanying loss of output.

Inflation Reduction in Practice

When the Bank of Canada slowed inflation in 1981, we paid a high price. The Bank's policy action was unexpected. It occurred in the face of money wage rates that had been set at too high a level to be consistent with the growth of aggregate demand that the Bank subsequently allowed. The consequence was recession—a decrease in real GDP and a rise in unemployment.

Whether policy can lower inflation without a deep recession is a controversial question. We'll return to it in the next chapter, where we review policy debates.

Study Guide pp. 258–260

𝑒**Foundations 17.3**

3 **Explain how the Bank of Canada can influence the expected inflation rate and how expected inflation influences the short-run tradeoff.**

FIGURE 1

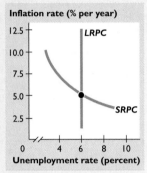

FIGURE 2

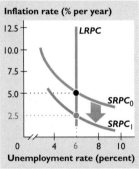

FIGURE 3

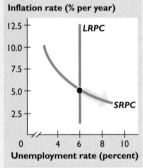

FIGURE 4

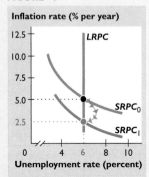

Practice Problem 17.3

Figure 1 shows the short-run and long-run Phillips curves. The current inflation rate is 5 percent a year.

a. Inflation is expected to remain at 5 percent next year. If the Bank of Canada slows the growth rate of the quantity of money, explain the effect of the Bank's action on inflation and unemployment.

b. If the Bank of Canada announces that it will slow the growth rate of the quantity of money such that inflation will fall to 2.5 percent a year and everyone believes the Bank of Canada, explain the effect of the Bank's action on inflation and unemployment.

c. Inflation is expected to remain at 5 percent next year. If the Bank of Canada slows the growth rate of the quantity of money such that inflation will fall to 2.5 percent a year and keeps it there for many years, explain the effect of the Bank's action on inflation and unemployment.

Exercise 17.3

In Figure 1, the current inflation rate is 5 percent a year.

a. If the Bank of Canada announces that it will increase the growth rate of the quantity of money such that the inflation rate will rise to 6 percent a year and everyone believes the Bank of Canada, explain the effect of the Bank's action on inflation and unemployment.

b. Inflation is expected to remain at 5 percent next year. If the Bank of Canada speeds up the growth rate of the quantity of money, explain the effect of the Bank's action on inflation and unemployment.

c. In part (b), if the Bank of Canada keeps the growth rate of the quantity of money constant for many years, explain the effect of the Bank's action on inflation and unemployment.

Solution to Practice Problem 17.3

a. The inflation rate will fall below 5 percent a year and the unemployment rate will rise above 6 percent as the economy moves down along its short-run Phillips curve (Figure 2).

b. The inflation rate falls to 2.5 percent a year, and unemployment remains at 6 percent. If people believe the Bank's policy announcement, the expected inflation rate falls to 2.5 percent a year. The short-run Phillips curve shifts downward (Figure 3).

c. Initially, inflation falls below 5 percent a year and unemployment rises above 6 percent. The longer the Bank of Canada maintains the slower growth rate of the quantity of money, the more people will start to expect lower inflation and the short-run Phillips curve will start to shift downward. As the short-run Phillips curve shifts downward, the unemployment rate decreases. Eventually, the inflation rate falls to 2.5 percent a year and the unemployment rate returns to 6 percent (Figure 4).

CHAPTER CHECKPOINT

Key Points

1 **Describe the short-run tradeoff between inflation and unemployment.**

- The short-run Phillips curve is the downward-sloping relationship between the inflation rate and the unemployment rate when all other influences on these two variables remain the same.
- The short-run Phillips curve presents a *tradeoff* between inflation and unemployment.
- The short-run Phillips curve is another way of looking at the aggregate supply curve.

2 **Distinguish between the short-run and long-run Phillips curves and describe the shifting tradeoff between inflation and unemployment.**

- The long-run Phillips curve shows the relationship between inflation and unemployment when the unemployment rate equals the natural unemployment rate and the inflation rate equals the expected inflation rate.
- The long-run Phillips curve is vertical at the *natural unemployment rate,* and there is no long-run tradeoff between unemployment and inflation.
- When the expected inflation rate changes, the short-run Phillips curve shifts to intersect the long-run Phillips curve at the expected inflation rate.
- When the growth rate of the quantity of money changes, the unemployment rate changes temporarily and eventually returns to the natural unemployment rate—the natural rate hypothesis.
- Changes in the natural unemployment rate shift both the short-run Phillips curve and the long-run Phillips curve.

3 **Explain how the Bank of Canada can influence the expected inflation rate and how expected inflation influences the short-run tradeoff.**

- The rational expectation of the inflation rate is based on the forecasted actions of the Bank of Canada's monetary policy and the other forces that influence aggregate demand and aggregate supply.
- A change in the expected inflation rate changes the short-run tradeoff gradually because the money wage rate responds only gradually to a change in the expected inflation rate.
- To lower the expected inflation rate, the Bank of Canada must take actions that will slow the actual inflation rate.

Key Terms

Expected inflation rate, 410
Long-run Phillips curve, 408
Natural rate hypothesis, 411

Okun's Law, 403
Rational expectation, 417
Short-run Phillips curve, 402

Exercises

1. Table 1 describes five possible situations that might arise in 2002, depending on the level of aggregate demand in that year.

TABLE I

	Price level (2001 = 100)	Real GDP (billions of dollars)	Unemployment rate (percent of labour force)
A	102	700	9
B	104	710	7
C	106	720	5
D	108	730	4
E	110	740	3

   a. Plot the short-run Phillips curve and the aggregate supply curve for 2002.
   b. Mark the points $A, B, C, D,$ and E on each curve that correspond to the data provided in Table 1.

2. In the economy in Exercise 1, the outcome in 2002 turned out to be row C of Table 1. Five possible outcomes for 2003 are shown in Table 2:

TABLE 2

	Price level (2001 = 100)	Real GDP (billions of dollars)	Unemployment rate (percent of labour force)
A	108	710	9
B	110	720	7
C	112	730	5
D	114	740	4
E	116	750	3

   a. Plot the short-run Phillips curve and the aggregate supply curve for 2003.
   b. Mark the points $A, B, C, D,$ and E on each curve that correspond to the data provided in Table 2.
   c. Compare the short-run Phillips curves and aggregate supply curves of 2003 with those of 2002.

3. Refer to the data in Exercise 1.
   a. The natural unemployment rate is 6 percent in 2001. What is the expected inflation rate?
   b. If in 2002, the natural unemployment rate increases to 7 percent, explain how the short-run and long-run Phillips curves change.
   c. If in 2002, the natural unemployment rate remains at 6 percent but the expected inflation rate is 4 percent a year, explain how the short-run and long-run Phillips curves change.

4. Currently, the inflation rate is 3 percent a year and the economy is at full employment. The unemployment rate is 4 percent. Explain the natural rate hypothesis.

5. The inflation rate is 3 percent a year, and the economy is at full employment. The unemployment rate is 4 percent. If the Bank of Canada expectedly slows the growth rate of the quantity of money and keeps it at the lower rate for a long time, explain how unemployment and inflation change in:
   a. The short run.
   b. The long run.

Fiscal and Monetary Policy Debates

When you have completed your study of this chapter,
you will be able to:

1 Compare fiscal policy and monetary policy as stabilization tools.

2 Explain and contrast a monetarist fixed-rule and a Keynesian feedback-rule for targeting real GDP.

3 Assess the case for targeting inflation or the price level rather than real GDP.

Should macroeconomic stability be left to the Bank of Canada and monetary policy or should the government use fiscal policy to maintain stability? Should policy respond to the state of the economy or should policy set a steady course that does not respond to every twist and turn in the economy? Should we strive to keep real GDP close to potential GDP and not worry about inflation? Or should we target the inflation rate rather than real GDP and employment?

You've seen the *effects* of monetary and fiscal policy, and you've seen the *short-run tradeoff* that stabilization policy faces. These aspects of stabilization policy define the constraints. They tell us "what if," but they don't tell us "what" monetary or fiscal policy to pursue or what its goals should be.

This chapter studies some hard "should" questions about fiscal and monetary policy. How should stabilization policy be conducted? Surprisingly, economists are agreed on most of the answers. But there are no simple answers, and some disputes remain, as you're about to discover.

18.1 FISCAL POLICY VERSUS MONETARY POLICY

Should short-run economic fluctuations be stabilized with monetary policy or fiscal policy? Which policy tool does the better job? These questions have been debated for many decades and were at the core of a controversy that raged during the 1960s. That old debate has been settled, but the lessons that we learn from it are important and remain relevant today. We will examine the monetary policy versus fiscal policy debate by considering its three aspects:

- Policy effects
- Goal conflicts
- Timing and flexibility

■ Policy Effects

Which policy action has the larger and more predictable effect on aggregate demand: a change in the quantity of money or a change in government expenditure or taxes? The answer to this question was once controversial, and the question lay at the heart of the original 1960s debate.

Investment demand (Chapter 9, pp. 205–207) and the demand for money Chapter 13, pp. 299–301) influence the effects of monetary policy and fiscal policy. Let's look first at the effects of monetary policy, using an expansionary monetary policy as our example.

The Effects of Monetary Policy

Three steps in the transmission of monetary policy are:

Step 1 An increase in the quantity of money lowers the interest rate.

Step 2 A fall in the interest rate increases investment and other interest-sensitive components of domestic expenditure.

Step 3 A fall in the interest rate lowers the exchange rate, which in turn increases net exports.

Let's look at each step.

Step 1 Whether a given increase in the quantity of money lowers the interest rate by a lot or a little depends on the sensitivity of the demand for money to the interest rate. Suppose that the quantity of money demanded is relatively insensitive to the interest rate, so a given change in the interest rate brings a small change in the quantity of money demanded. Then, when the quantity of money increases by a given amount, the decrease in the interest rate is large. In contrast, suppose that the quantity of money demanded is highly sensitive to the interest rate, so even a small change in the interest rate brings a large change in the quantity of money demanded. Then, when the quantity of money increases by a given amount, the decrease in the interest rate is small.

Step 2 Whether a given decrease in the interest rate increases aggregate expenditure by a lot or a little depends on the sensitivity of investment demand and other components of aggregate expenditure to the interest rate. If aggregate expenditure is highly sensitive to the interest rate, then a given change in the interest rate brings a large change in aggregate expenditure. If aggregate expenditure is insensitive to the interest rate, then a given change in the interest rate brings a small change in aggregate expenditure.

Figure 18.1 illustrates the two cases. In part (a), when the quantity of money increases from $100 billion to $102 billion, the interest rate falls from 6 percent to 4 percent a year and investment increases from $200 billion to $400 billion. In contrast, in part (b), the same change in the quantity of money lowers the interest rate from 6 percent to 5 percent a year and investment increases only slightly, from $200 billion to $225 billion. In part (a), monetary policy is powerful; in part (b) it is weak.

FIGURE 18.1
The Effectiveness of Monetary Policy   *e*Foundations 18.1

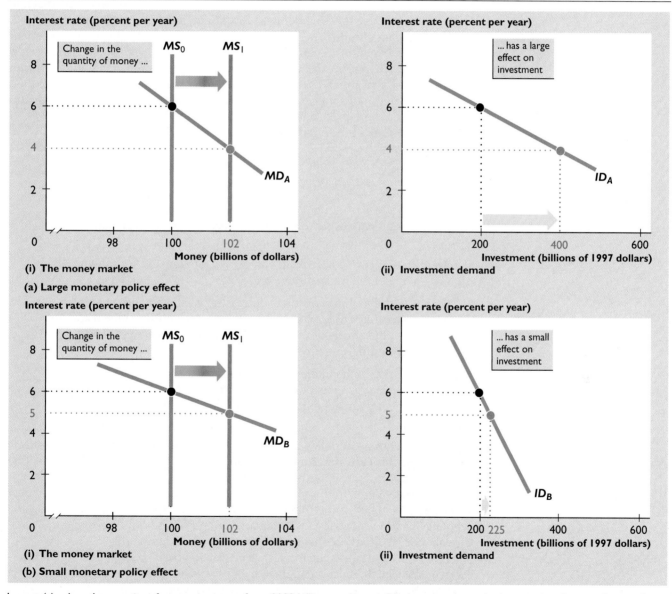

(a) Large monetary policy effect
(i) The money market
(ii) Investment demand

(b) Small monetary policy effect
(i) The money market
(ii) Investment demand

In part (a), when the quantity of money increases from $100 billion to $102 billion, the interest rate falls from 6 percent to 4 percent a year and investment increases from $200 billion to $400 billion.

In part (b), the same change in the quantity of money lowers the interest rate from 6 percent to 5 percent a year and increases investment from $200 billion to only $225 billion. Monetary policy is more powerful in the conditions shown in part (a).

Step 3 The effect of monetary policy on the exchange rate reinforces the effects you've just studied. The larger the fall in the interest rate, the greater is the fall in the exchange rate. But whether a given decrease in the exchange rate increases net exports by a lot or a little depends on the sensitivity of exports and imports to their prices. If exports and imports are highly sensitive to their prices, then a given change in the exchange rate brings a large change in net exports. If exports and imports are insensitive to their prices, then a given change in the exchange rate brings a small change in net exports.

The Predictability of Monetary Policy The three steps in the transmission of monetary policy determine the predictability of monetary policy.

At step 1, for a given change in the quantity of money to have a predictable effect on the interest rate, the demand for money must be predictable. At step 2, for a given change in the interest rate to have a predictable effect on investment and aggregate expenditure, investment demand must be predictable. And at step 3, for a given change in the exchange rate to have a predictable effect on net exports, net exports must respond predictably to the exchange rate.

So the more predictable are the demand for money, investment demand, and net exports, the more predictable is the effect of monetary policy.

Let's now look at the effects of an expansionary fiscal policy.

The Effects of Fiscal Policy

Four steps in the transmission of fiscal policy are:

Step 1 An increase in government expenditure or a tax cut increases aggregate expenditure and increases aggregate demand with a multiplier.

Step 2 An increase in real GDP increases the demand for money, which raises the interest rate.

Step 3 A rise in the interest rate decreases investment and other interest-sensitive components of aggregate expenditure, which counter-act the effects of the initial increase in aggregate expenditure—a crowding-out effect.

Step 4 A rise in the interest rate raises the exchange rate, which decreases net exports and counteracts the effects of the initial increase in aggregate expenditure —an international crowding-out effect.

The power of fiscal policy depends on the strength of the crowding-out effects that counteract it. If in step 2 the rise in the interest rate is large and if in step 3 the higher interest rate has a large effect on aggregate expenditure, then the crowding-out effect is large. If in step 4 the change in the exchange rate has a large effect on net exports, then the international crowding-out effect is large. In this case, fiscal policy has a weak effect on aggregate demand. These conditions that make fiscal policy weak are those that make monetary policy powerful.

If in step 2 the rise in the interest rate is small and if in step 3 the higher interest rate has a small effect on aggregate expenditure, then the crowding-out effect is small. If in step 4 the change in the exchange rate has a small effect on net exports, then the international crowding-out effect is small. In this case, fiscal policy has a strong effect on aggregate demand. These conditions that make fiscal policy powerful are those that make monetary policy weak.

Fiscal policy is strongest and monetary policy is weakest if the demand for money curve is horizontal at some low interest rate at which people are willing to hold *any* quantity of money. This situation is called a **liquidity trap**. In a liquidity trap, a change in the quantity of money changes the quantity of money held but has no effect on the interest rate. So a change in the quantity of money has no effect on aggregate expenditure. But a change in government expenditure leaves the interest rate unchanged, so there is no crowding out and fiscal policy has a large multiplier effect on aggregate expenditure. Some people have suggested that Japan was in a liquidity trap in 2001, but this view is not supported by any evidence.

Liquidity trap
An interest rate at which people are willing to hold any quantity of money.

Reality

During the 1960s, monetarists and Keynesians argued about the relative potency of monetary and fiscal policy. Keynesian economists believed that a liquidity trap rendered monetary policy useless and fiscal policy all-powerful. Monetarist economists believed the opposite. We now know, as a result of a huge amount of research, that neither extreme occurs in real economies. A government that seeks to manipulate aggregate demand can do so by using either monetary policy or fiscal policy.

■ Goal Conflicts

You've seen that both monetary policy and fiscal policy influence aggregate demand, so either policy can be used in the attempt to stabilize aggregate demand. But stabilization policy actions have side effects—effects on factors other than the stabilization goals. These side effects can create a conflict between stabilization and some other goals.

Fiscal Policy Goal Conflicts

Fiscal policy has three goals: to provide public goods and services, to redistribute income, and to stabilize aggregate demand. These goals can come into conflict.

One aspect of the government's budget that does not create conflict is its *automatic stabilizer* effect. We described these features in Chapter 16 (pp. 387–388). The income tax and induced transfer payments, such as unemployment benefits, that automatically adjust expenditure and tax receipts in response to the state of the economy help to achieve the government's goals of redistributing income and, at the same time, improve economic stability.

In contrast, *discretionary* fiscal actions—actions that require changes in spending or taxes to be legislated—create goal conflicts. The main source of conflict is the very large number of spending programs and tax arrangements in place and the difficulty (impossibility perhaps) of changing all of them to balance the costs and benefits of one against the costs and benefits of others.

For example, suppose that fiscal stimulation is called for in a recession. Should the government spend more on security and national defence, or on health care, or education, or the environment? Or should it cut the income tax? And whose income tax should it cut? Should all Canadians benefit proportionately, or should the tax cuts change how income is distributed among the people? Or should the government cut the excise tax on alcohol, or tobacco, or gasoline?

The government must make a very large number of detailed decisions about what to produce more of, who to benefit, which industries to benefit, and which regions to benefit.

If the government wants to meet its goals in the provision of public goods and services, and achieve its income redistribution goals, fiscal policy must be freed up from the additional task of helping to stabilize the economy.

Monetary Policy Goal Conflicts

Monetary policy has three main goals: price level stability, real GDP stability, and stability of the financial system. There is less conflict among these goals than among those of fiscal policy.

First, stability of aggregate demand contributes to the stability of the financial system by minimizing the dangers of both recession and inflation. Second, stability of aggregate demand contributes to the stability of real GDP and the price level. So there is no goal conflict here.

But like fiscal policy, monetary policy does not affect all sectors of the economy evenly. Because monetary policy operates through changes in interest rates and the exchange rate, it has especially strong effects on the housing and construction industries and on export producers.

■ Timing and Flexibility

The ability to forecast the future state of the economy and to act promptly to counteract recession or inflation is a crucial part of a successful stabilization policy. Both the direction and the timing of policy actions are vitally important. How do fiscal policy and monetary policy stack up on this dimension?

Inflexible Fiscal Policy

Fiscal policy is political. In deciding both the direction and timing of changes in government expenditure and taxes, governments are little influenced by economic forecasts and heavily influenced by political considerations.

Competition among the political parties makes fiscal policy a game of short-term political expediency rather than one of the pursuit of economic stability. Governments are slow to take policy actions that decrease aggregate demand and fast to take actions that increase aggregate demand, regardless of the state of the economy.

Flexible Monetary Policy

In contrast, stabilization is the purpose of monetary policy. The Bank of Canada was created to enable policy actions to be taken quickly and on the basis of a careful, professional evaluation of the current and likely future state of the economy. Every day, the Bank of Canada monitors the financial markets and watches for signs that its policy needs to be tweaked to keep the economy on course.

Monetary policy *effects*, on the other hand, are long and drawn out. So although monetary policy actions can be taken quickly and be well timed, monetary policy actions need to be taken with a long forecast horizon in view.

■ And the Winner Is?

There is no clear winner. Automatic fiscal stabilizers do an important part of the job of maintaining macroeconomic stability. Discretionary fiscal policy is sometimes a vital part of the policy mix, especially if the economy is in a deep recession or in a seriously overheated condition. But for dealing with normal fluctuations, monetary policy is the preferred stabilization tool because it is more flexible in its timing.

What should monetary policy try to achieve? Should it try to maintain full employment? Or should it try to stabilize the inflation rate (or price level) rather than real GDP and employment? We study these questions in the next section.

CHECKPOINT 18.1

1 **Compare fiscal policy and monetary policy as stabilization tools.**

Study Guide pp. 266–270

*e*Foundations **18.1**

Practice Problems 18.1

1. The Bank of Canada decreases the quantity of money. Use a figure similar to Figure 18.1 to work out:
   a. The effects of the Bank of Canada's policy on the interest rate, the quantity of money demanded, and investment.
   b. The effects of the Bank of Canada's policy on aggregate expenditure and aggregate demand.
   c. The conditions that make the Bank of Canada's policy powerful.

2. If a change in the quantity of money leads to a large change in the interest rate and investment is very sensitive to the interest rate, would a decrease in government expenditure be powerful fiscal policy? Explain why or why not.

Exercises 18.1

1. If the government decreases its expenditure on goods and services, explain:
   a. The effects of the government's policy on the interest rate, the quantity of money demanded, and investment.
   b. The effects of the government's policy on aggregate expenditure and aggregate demand.
   c. The conditions that make the government's policy powerful.

2. If a change in the quantity of money leads to a small change in the interest rate and investment is not very sensitive to the interest rate, would an increase in government expenditure on goods and services be powerful fiscal policy? Explain why or why not.

3. Explain why monetary policy might be a better tool than fiscal policy for stabilizing aggregate demand.

Solutions to Practice Problems 18.1

1a. When the Bank of Canada decreases the quantity of money, the interest rate rises. The quantity of money demanded decreases and investment decreases.

1b. The decrease in investment decreases aggregate expenditure. Aggregate demand decreases.

1c. The Bank of Canada's policy is powerful, the larger is the resulting change in aggregate demand. The reduction in aggregate demand will be larger, the bigger the reduction in investment resulting from a given increase in the interest rate. And the increase in the interest rate will be larger, the less sensitive is the demand for money to the interest rate. Figure 18.1(a) illustrates these conditions. Also, the reduction in aggregate demand will be larger, the higher the exchange rate moves in response to the higher interest rate.

2. A decrease in government expenditure on goods and services decreases aggregate demand, which decreases real GDP. The decrease in real GDP decreases the demand for money, and the interest rate falls by a large amount. With investment highly sensitive to the interest rate, investment increases by a large amount. The increase in investment works against the decrease in government expenditure to limit the effect of the fiscal policy action.

18.2 TARGETING REAL GDP

We've seen that both monetary policy and fiscal policy are capable of influencing aggregate demand in an attempt to stabilize the economy. But *what* should stabilization policy seek to stabilize? When the Bank of Canada and the federal government made their first attempt at stabilization policy during the 1950s, the answer was that stabilization policy should keep real GDP as close as possible to potential GDP. By this means, the horrors of the Great Depression were to be avoided. More recently, the emphasis of stabilization policy has shifted to targeting inflation. We'll look at inflation targeting and the more general problem of selecting the appropriate target for stabilization policy in the next section. Here, we'll focus on the task of targeting real GDP and the debate about how best to do it.

Economists have proposed two broad approaches to the task of stabilizing real GDP:

- Fixed-rule policies
- Feedback-rule and discretionary policies

■ Fixed-Rule Policies

Fixed-rule policy
A policy that is pursued independently of the state of the economy.

A **fixed-rule policy** specifies an action to be pursued independently of the state of the economy. A stop sign is an everyday life example of a fixed rule. It says, "Stop regardless of the state of the road ahead, even if no other vehicle is trying to use the road." The best-known fixed-rule policy is one proposed as long ago as 1948 by Nobel prize-winning economist Milton Friedman. Friedman proposed that policy maintain a constant growth rate of the quantity of money year in and year out, regardless of the state of the economy. He argued that this policy would stabilize real GDP more effectively than any other policy and at the same time would maintain low and stable inflation. Fixed rules are rarely followed in practice, but they have some merits in principle. In the following pages, we study how they would work if they were pursued.

■ Feedback-Rule and Discretionary Policies

Feedback-rule policy
A policy that specifies how policy actions respond to changes in the state of the economy.

A **feedback-rule policy** specifies how policy actions respond to changes in the state of the economy. A yield sign is an everyday feedback rule. It says, "Stop if another vehicle is attempting to use the road ahead, but otherwise, proceed." A feedback rule for monetary policy is one that changes the quantity of money or interest rate in response to the state of the economy. The Bank of Canada used a feedback rule when it lowered interest rates during 2000 and 2001.

Discretionary policy
A policy that is based on the judgments of policy makers about the current needs of the economy.

Discretionary policy is a policy that is based on the judgments of the policy makers about the current needs of the economy. Discretionary monetary policy is setting the overnight rate and determining open market operations by the Bank of Canada based on the expert opinion of the governor and his advisors. Examples of discretionary policy occur every minute on our highways. Each driver uses discretionary policy in deciding how fast and how close to the vehicle in front to travel.

An example of discretionary monetary policy occurred during 1998 in the face of a sagging Asian economy. The Bank of Canada cut the interest rate to prevent the crisis from spreading here. The Bank might have delayed cutting interest rates until it was sure that lower rates were needed but instead used discretion based on lessons it had learned from earlier episodes. The line between feedback-rule policies and discretionary policies is a fine one. Both types of policy respond to the current and the forecasted future state of the economy and because history never exactly repeats, there is almost always an element of discretion in whatever actions the Bank of Canada and government take.

We'll study the effects of stabilization policy rules by comparing the performance of real GDP and the price level under a fixed rule and a feedback rule. Because fluctuations can result from demand shocks or supply shocks, we need to consider these two cases. We'll begin by studying demand shocks.

■ Stabilizing Aggregate Demand Shocks

We'll study an economy that starts out at full employment and has no inflation. Figure 18.2 illustrates this situation. The economy is on aggregate demand curve AD_0 and aggregate supply curve AS. The price level is 105, and real GDP is $1,000 billion, which is also potential GDP.

Investment decreases because of a wave of pessimism about future profits and aggregate demand decreases. The aggregate demand curve shifts leftward to AD_1 in Figure 18.2. Aggregate demand curve AD_1 intersects the aggregate supply curve AS at a price level of 102 and a real GDP of $980 billion. The economy is in a recession. Real GDP is less than potential GDP, and unemployment is above the natural unemployment rate.

At some later time, when profit prospects improve and firms increase investment, aggregate demand will return from AD_1 to AD_0. In the meantime, while aggregate demand is depressed at AD_1, the course of real GDP and the price level depend on the stabilization policy that is pursued. We'll work out how the economy responds under a fixed rule and then under a feedback rule.

■ **FIGURE 18.2**

A Decrease in Aggregate Demand Brings Recession

*e***Foundations 18.2**

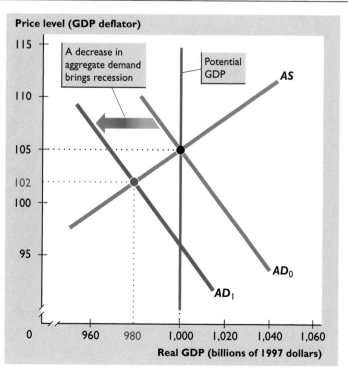

Aggregate demand decreases from AD_0 to AD_1, and the economy goes into recession. Real GDP decreases to $980 billion, and the price level falls to 102.

Fixed Rule: Monetarism

Monetarist
An economist who believes that fluctuations in the quantity of money are the main source of economic fluctuations.

The fixed rule that we'll study here is one in which the quantity of money remains constant. This is the rule advocated by monetarists. A **monetarist** is an economist who believes that fluctuations in the quantity of money are the main source of economic fluctuations.

Figure 18.3(a) illustrates the response of the economy under a fixed rule. A decrease in aggregate demand brings recession as the economy moves from A to B. With a deflationary gap and unemployment above the natural unemployment rate, the money wage rate gradually falls. Aggregate supply increases towards AS_1 to take the economy from B to C and back to full employment.

Eventually aggregate demand returns to its original level, and the aggregate demand curve shifts rightward to AD_0. Real GDP now expands in a move from C to D. With an inflationary gap and unemployment below the natural unemployment rate, the money wage rate gradually rises. Aggregate supply decreases towards AS_0 to take the economy from D to A and to full employment once more.

With a fixed-rule monetary policy, fluctuations in aggregate demand bring fluctuations in real GDP around potential GDP. Let's contrast the performance of the economy under a fixed rule with that under a feedback rule.

FIGURE 18.3
Stabilization Policies: Aggregate Demand Shocks

*e*Foundations 18.2

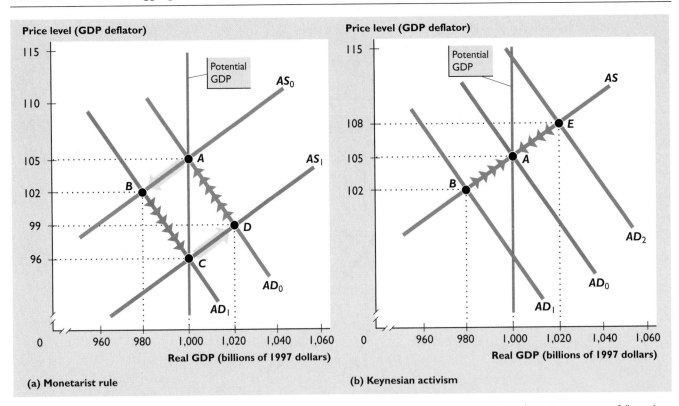

(a) Monetarist rule

(b) Keynesian activism

A monetarist fixed-rule policy leaves real GDP and the price level to fluctuate from A to B, to C, to D and back to A.

A Keynesian activist feedback-rule policy tries to restore full employment as quickly as possible by moving the economy back to A.

Feedback Rule: Keynesian Activism

A **Keynesian activist** is an economist who believes that fluctuations in investment are the main source of economic fluctuations, and who advocates interest rate cuts and fiscal stimulus when real GDP falls below potential GDP and interest rate hikes and fiscal restraint when real GDP exceeds potential GDP.

Figure 18.3(b) illustrates the response of the economy under this feedback-rule policy. When aggregate demand decreases to AD_1, the economy is at point B. There is a deflationary gap to which the Bank of Canada reacts by cutting the interest rate. This policy action increases aggregate demand, but only gradually. The aggregate demand curve shifts towards AD_0. As it does so, real GDP increases and the price level rises. Eventually, the economy is back at point A, its starting point before the recession.

When profit prospects improve and firms increase investment, aggregate demand increases from AD_0 to AD_2, and the economy moves to point E. This expansion brings an inflationary gap to which the Bank of Canada reacts. The Bank now raises the interest rate. This policy action gradually decreases aggregate demand, and the aggregate demand curve shifts leftward towards AD_0. As it does so, real GDP decreases and the price level falls. Again, the economy returns to point A, its starting point before the expansion.

The Two Rules Compared

Under a fixed-rule policy, a decrease in aggregate demand puts real GDP below potential GDP, where it remains until either a fall in the money wage rate or a subsequent increase in aggregate demand restores full employment. Similarly, an increase in aggregate demand puts real GDP above potential GDP, where it remains until either a rise in the money wage rate or a subsequent decrease in aggregate demand restores full employment.

Under a feedback-rule policy, the economy is pulled out of a deflationary gap or an inflationary gap by a policy action. There is no need to wait for an adjustment in the money wage rate—which everyone agrees takes a long time—for full employment to be restored.

Real GDP decreases and increases by the same amounts under the two policies, but real GDP stays below potential GDP and above potential GDP for longer with a fixed rule than it does with the feedback rule.

Are Feedback Rules Better?

Isn't it obvious that a feedback rule is better than a fixed rule? Can't the Bank of Canada use feedback rules to keep the economy close to full employment with a stable price level? Of course, unforecasted events—such as a collapse in business confidence—will hit the economy from time to time. But by responding with a change in the interest rate, can't the Bank minimize the damage from such a shock?

Despite the apparent superiority of a feedback rule, many economists remain convinced that a fixed rule stabilizes aggregate demand more effectively than a feedback rule does. These economists assert that fixed rules are better than feedback rules because:

- Potential GDP is not known.
- Policy lags are longer than the forecast horizon.
- Feedback-rule policies are less predictable than fixed-rule policies.

Keynesian activist
An economist who believes that fluctuations in investment are the main source of economic fluctuations, and who advocates interest rate cuts and fiscal stimulus when real GDP falls below potential GDP and interest rate hikes and fiscal restraint when real GDP exceeds potential GDP.

Let's look at these assertions.

Knowledge of Potential GDP   To decide whether a feedback-rule policy needs to stimulate or retard aggregate demand, it is necessary to determine whether real GDP is currently above or below potential GDP. But potential GDP is not known with certainty. It depends on a large number of factors, one of which is the level of employment when unemployment is at the natural unemployment rate. But uncertainty and disagreement exist about how the labour market works, so we can only estimate the natural unemployment rate. As a result, there is often uncertainty about the direction in which a feedback policy should be pushing the level of aggregate demand.

Policy Lags and the Forecast Horizon   The effects of policy actions taken today are spread out over the following two years or even more. But no one is able to forecast accurately that far ahead. The forecast horizon—the distance into the future that forecasters can see—is less than one year. Further, the Bank of Canada can't predict the precise timing and magnitude of the effects of its policy actions. So a feedback policy that reacts to today's economy might be inappropriate for the economy at that uncertain future date when the policy's effects are felt.

Predictability of Policies   To make decisions about long-term contracts for employment (wage contracts) and for borrowing and lending, people must anticipate the future course of the price level—the future inflation rate. To forecast the inflation rate, it is necessary to forecast aggregate demand. And to forecast aggregate demand, it is necessary to forecast the Bank of Canada's policy actions.

If the Bank of Canada sticks to a rock-steady, fixed rule for the growth rate of the quantity of money, then policy is predictable and it does not contribute to unexpected fluctuations in aggregate demand.

In contrast, if the Bank pursues a feedback rule, there is more scope for the policy actions to be unpredictable. The main reason is that feedback rules are not written down for all to see. Rather, they have to be inferred from the Bank's behaviour. So with a feedback-rule policy, it is necessary to predict the variables to which the Bank reacts and the extent to which it reacts. Consequently, a feedback rule for monetary policy can create more unpredictable fluctuations in aggregate demand than a fixed rule can.

We reviewed three reasons why feedback-rule policies might not be more effective than fixed-rule policies in controlling aggregate demand. But there is a fourth reason why some economists prefer fixed rules: Not all shocks to the economy are shocks to aggregate demand. Advocates of feedback rules generally believe that most fluctuations do come from aggregate demand. Some advocates of fixed rules believe that aggregate supply fluctuations are the dominant ones. Let's now see how aggregate supply fluctuations affect the economy under a fixed rule and a feedback rule. We will also see why those economists who believe that aggregate supply fluctuations are the dominant ones also favour a fixed rule rather than a feedback rule.

■ Stabilizing Aggregate Supply Shocks

Everyone agrees that the economy is sometimes hit by an aggregate supply shock. There is disagreement about how frequent and important these shocks are. But there is no disagreement about the effect on aggregate supply of world oil price changes. In 1974, when the world oil price increased from $2 a barrel to $10 a barrel, the global economy was delivered a severe negative supply shock. A further negative supply shock occurred in 1980 and 1981 when the world oil price jumped first to $26 and then $32 a barrel. Positive supply shocks occurred during the 1980s as the world oil price fell back to around $13 a barrel. A price hike to $24 in 1991 delivered another negative shock, and price cuts through 1994 brought a further positive aggregate supply shock. A sharp rise in the price of oil brought another negative aggregate supply shock in 2000–2001.

Negative aggregate supply shocks are a particularly difficult problem because they cause real GDP to decrease and the price level to rise at the same time. By increasing aggregate demand to prevent real GDP from decreasing, policy actions raise the price level yet further, as you'll now see.

To study the effects of aggregate supply shocks and the policy to stabilize them, we'll again start out at full employment with no inflation. Figure 18.4 illustrates an economy with aggregate demand curve AD and aggregate supply curve AS_0. The price level is 105, and real GDP is $1,000 billion, which is also potential GDP.

The world oil price jumps and aggregate supply decreases. The aggregate supply curve shifts leftward, to AS_1 in Figure 18.4. Aggregate supply curve AS_1 intersects the aggregate demand curve, AD, at a price level of 108 and a real GDP of $990 billion. The economy is in a recession. Real GDP is less than potential GDP, and unemployment exceeds the natural unemployment rate.

At some later time, when world oil production increases, the world price of oil will fall to its original level and aggregate supply will return from AS_1 to AS_0. In the meantime, while aggregate supply is at AS_1, the course of real GDP and the price level depend on the stabilization policy that is pursued. We'll again work out how the economy responds under a fixed rule and a feedback rule.

FIGURE 18.4

A Decrease in Aggregate Supply Brings Recession

*e*Foundations 18.2

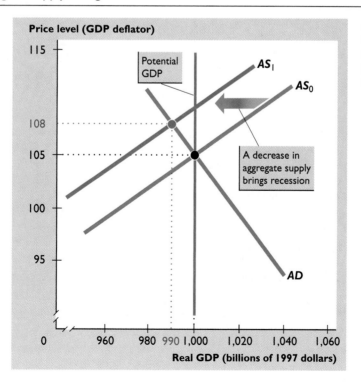

Aggregate supply decreases from AS_0 to AS_1, and the economy goes into recession. Real GDP decreases to $990 billion, and the price level rises to 108.

Fixed Rule

Under a monetarist fixed-rule policy, when aggregate supply decreases, the government does not stimulate aggregate demand. Real GDP decreases as the economy moves from point A to point B in Figure 18.5(a). With a deflationary gap and unemployment exceeding the natural unemployment rate, the money wage rate gradually falls. The falling money wage rate increases aggregate supply from AS_1 towards AS_0. Real GDP gradually returns to potential GDP as the economy moves from point B back to point A.

Feedback Rule

Under a Keynesian activist feedback rule, when the economy is at point B in Figure 18.5(b), the Bank of Canada reacts by cutting the interest rate. This policy action gradually increases aggregate demand from AD_0 towards AD_1. Real GDP increases towards potential GDP but at a higher price level as the economy moves from point B to point C.

So stabilization policies that target real GDP in the face of a mixture of aggregate demand and aggregate supply shocks bring a higher price level. And repeating these actions brings rising inflation.

■ **FIGURE 18.5**
Stabilization Policies: Aggregate Supply Shocks

*e*Foundations **18.2**

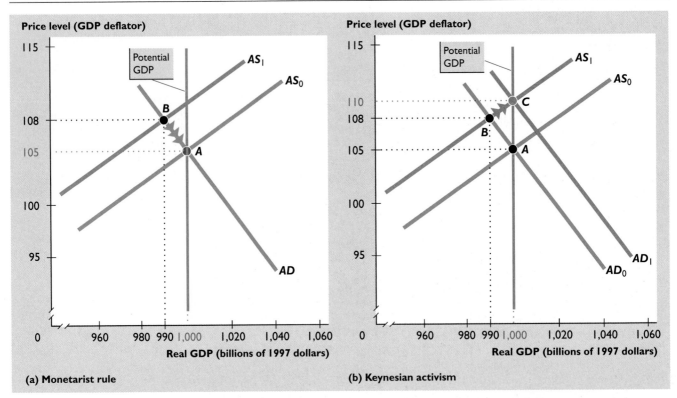

(a) Monetarist rule

(b) Keynesian activism

A monetarist fixed-rule policy leaves real GDP and the price level to gradually return from B to A as the money wage rate falls.

A Keynesian activist feedback-rule policy tries to restore full employment as quickly as possible by moving the economy from B to C.

CHECKPOINT 18.2

2 **Explain and contrast a monetarist fixed-rule and a Keynesian feedback-rule for targeting real GDP.**

Study Guide pp. 270–273

𝑒Foundations 18.2

Practice Problem 18.2

The economy shown in Figure 1 is initially on aggregate demand curve AD_0 and aggregate supply curve AS. Then aggregate demand decreases, and the aggregate demand curve shifts leftward to AD_1.

a. What is the equilibrium real GDP and price level before and after the decrease in aggregate demand?
b. If the goal of stabilization policy is to stabilize real GDP and employment, what will the Bank of Canada's policy response be?
c. If the goal of stabilization policy is to stabilize real GDP and employment, how will fiscal policy respond?
d. If these policies work, what happens to the aggregate demand curve, real GDP, and the price level?
e. Is there any risk of inflation as a side effect of these policies? Why?

FIGURE 1

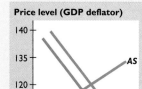

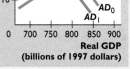

Exercises 18.2

1. The economy shown in Figure 2 is initially on aggregate demand curve AD_0 and aggregate supply curve AS. Then aggregate demand increases, and the aggregate demand curve shifts rightward to AD_2. If the target of stabilization policy is to stabilize real GDP and employment:
    a. What will the Bank of Canada do?
    b. How will the government change its budget?
    c. How will these policies affect the aggregate demand curve?
    d. Is there any risk of inflation as a side effect of these policies? Why?

2. Suppose that in Figure 1, aggregate supply decreased rather than aggregate demand. How does this change your answers to questions **a** through **d** in Practice Problem 18.2?

FIGURE 2

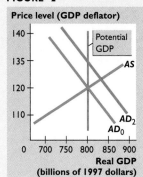

Solution to Practice Problem 18.2

a. Initially, real GDP is $800 billion, and the price level is 120. After the decrease in aggregate demand, real GDP decreases to $780 billion, and the price level falls to 118.
b. The Bank of Canada will try to increase aggregate demand by increasing the quantity of money and reducing interest rates.
c. There will be an increase in government expenditure and/or a reduction in taxes.
d. The aggregate demand curve will shift back to AD_0, and real GDP and the price level will be restored to $800 billion and 120, respectively.
e. A stabilization policy will create inflation if it increases aggregate demand by more than intended and shifts the aggregate demand curve farther rightward than to AD_0.

18.3 TARGETING INFLATION

Everyone agrees that keeping real GDP close to potential GDP is a good thing. When real GDP fluctuates around potential GDP, unemployment fluctuates around the natural unemployment rate. So keeping real GDP equal to potential GDP is the same as keeping unemployment at the natural unemployment rate.

When real GDP is than potential GDP, the economy is in a deflationary gap, output is lost and jobs are hard to find. So if policy can close a deflationary gap, people will be better off. When real GDP exceeds potential GDP, the economy is in an inflationary gap, resources are overworked and inefficient plant break-downs and bottlenecks arise. Also, inflation increases, which brings its own costs. So if policy can close an inflationary gap, people will be better off.

If aggregate demand shocks were the only source of economic fluctuations, the choice of a target for stabilization policy would be easy: stabilize aggregate demand. By stabilizing aggregate demand, real GDP would remain close to potential GDP, and the price level and the inflation rate would be stable.

Two technical questions remain. First, does fiscal policy or monetary policy provide the better tool kit for stabilizing aggregate demand? And second, do a feedback rule and discretion perform better than a fixed rule in stabilizing aggregate demand? But these questions are secondary to that of the target.

Shocks to aggregate supply complicate the stabilization problem. We've just seen in the preceding section that if stabilization policies target real GDP in the face of aggregate supply shocks, then the price level rises. Now imagine repeatedly responding to aggregate supply shocks with an increase in the quantity of money that keeps increasing aggregate demand. Such a policy pursued repeatedly will bring inflation.

Stabilization policy did target real GDP from the 1950s through the 1970s. At first, with few shocks to aggregate supply, the policy worked well. But when monetary policy was used to counteract decreases in aggregate supply, inflation erupted. So the question arises: How should monetary policy try to influence aggregate demand when aggregate supply changes? We'll address this question by first comparing two extreme cases: one in which real GDP is the sole target of monetary policy, and one in which the price level is the sole target.

■ Real GDP Target

When monetary policy targets real GDP, it seeks to neutralize the effects of aggregate supply shocks on real GDP. That is, an increase in aggregate supply is met by a decrease in aggregate demand; and a decrease in aggregate supply is countered by an increase in aggregate demand.

Figure 18.6(a) illustrates real GDP targeting. The blue band is the real GDP target. If the aggregate supply curve is AS_0, monetary policy aims to place the aggregate demand curve (not shown) through point A. Here, real GDP is on target at $1,000 billion and the price level is 105. If aggregate supply increases to AS_1, monetary policy aims to *decrease* aggregate demand and place the aggregate demand curve through point B. Here, real GDP remains on target at $1,000 billion but the price level falls to 102. If aggregate supply decreases to AS_2, monetary policy aims to *increase* aggregate demand and place the aggregate demand curve through point C. Again, real GDP remains on target at $1,000 billion, but the price level now rises to 108.

You can see that in the face of shocks to aggregate supply, stabilizing real GDP means destabilizing the price level.

■ FIGURE 18.6

Alternative Monetary Policy Targets

e Foundations 18.3

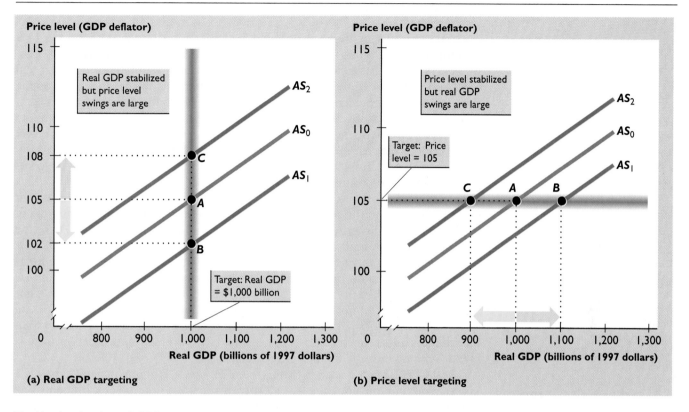

(a) Real GDP targeting

(b) Price level targeting

The blue band is the real GDP target. When aggregate supply increases from AS_0 to AS_1 or decreases from AS_0 to AS_2, monetary policy aims to change aggregate demand to keep real GDP on target at $1,000 billion.

The blue band is the price level target. When aggregate supply increases from AS_0 to AS_1 or decreases from AS_0 to AS_2, monetary policy aims to change aggregate demand to keep the price level on target at 105.

■ Price Level Target

If monetary policy targets the price level, it seeks to neutralize aggregate supply shocks. That is, an increase in aggregate supply is met by an *increase* in aggregate demand. And a decrease in aggregate supply is countered by a *decrease* in aggregate demand.

Figure 18.6(b) shows the outcome if monetary policy targets the price level. The blue band is now the price level target. If aggregate supply is AS_0, monetary policy aims to place the aggregate demand curve (not shown) through point *A*. Here, the price level is on target at 105 and real GDP is $1,000 billion.

If aggregate supply increases to AS_1, monetary policy aims to *increase* aggregate demand and place the aggregate demand curve through point *B*. Here, the price level remains on target at 105 but real GDP increases to $1,100 billion.

If aggregate supply decreases to AS_2, monetary policy aims to *decrease* aggregate demand and place the aggregate demand curve through point *C*. Again, the price level remains on target at 105 but real GDP decreases to $900 billion.

You can see that in the face of shocks to aggregate supply, stabilizing the price level means destabilizing real GDP.

ECONOMICS
in
the
NEWS

October 24, 2001

Rates Dive as Economy Is in "Mess"

The Bank of Canada slashed interest rates to 40-year lows yesterday with an aggressive cut of three-quarters of a percentage point. The last time interest rates were this low was in November 1961.

NATIONAL POST

Questions

1. What is the Bank of Canada's official policy target?
2. How did real GDP change in the fall of 2001?
3. Do you think the Bank of Canada policy target changed in the fall of 2001? Why?

 *e*Foundations **18.3**

■ More General Targets

Monetary policy might target something less extreme than either real GDP or the price level. It might place some weight on fluctuations in both real GDP and the price level.

You can think of the macroeconomic stabilization target as the target in a shooting contest. Figure 18.7 illustrates this idea. In this figure, we represent fluctuations in real GDP as the output gap—the percentage difference between real GDP and potential GDP. And we represent fluctuations in the price level as the inflation rate—the percentage change in the price level in a given period.

The *x*-axis measures the output gap, and the *y*-axis measures the inflation rate centred on zero. Here, the bull's-eye is an output gap and an inflation rate of zero. Let's suppose the score for hitting the bull's-eye is 100. Missing the bull's-eye by 1 percent scores 75; missing by 2 percent scores 50; and missing by 3 percent scores 25. A bigger miss is completely off target!

If the macroeconomic stabilization target was like Figure 18.7(a), equal weight would be placed on the output gap and the inflation rate. Policy would try to get as close to the bull's-eye as possible and would not worry about real GDP or the price level independently of each other. For example, hitting the target at a 2 percent inflation rate and a zero output gap is just as good as hitting it at zero inflation and a 2 percent output gap or at any other point on the circle on which those two points lie. Unlike the target at a shooting competition, the macroeconomic stabilization target need not be round. It might be elliptical, like the targets in Figure 18.7(b) and 18.7(c). In part (b), an output-gap miss is penalized more heavily than an inflation miss. And in part (c), the penalty is reversed—an inflation miss is penalized more heavily than an output-gap miss.

Real GDP targeting is an extreme case of Figure 18.7(b) in which the target is a vertical line running along the *y*-axis. Any inflation rate is acceptable, but only one output gap is acceptable: a zero gap. Price level targeting is an extreme case of Figure 18.7(c) in which the target is a horizontal line running along the *x*-axis. Any output gap is acceptable, but only one inflation rate is acceptable: zero inflation.

FIGURE 18.7
The Shape of the Target

*e*Foundations **18.3**

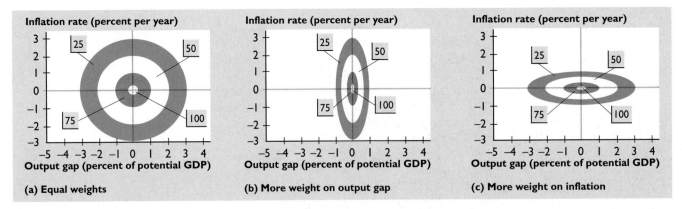

The "bull's-eye" is an output gap and an inflation rate of zero. The bigger the miss, the lower is the score. In part (a), equal weight is placed on fluctuations in real GDP and the inflation rate. In part (b), an output-gap miss is penalized more heavily than an inflation miss, and in part (c), an inflation miss is penalized more heavily than an output-gap miss.

■ A Tradeoff or a Free Lunch?

Both real GDP and price level fluctuations are costly, and policy must trade one off against the other. When aggregate supply changes, a decision must be made about how to divide its effect between a change in the price level and a change in real GDP.

But an interesting complication arises from a connection between the stabilization target that is used and the swings in aggregate supply. And this complication might be the source of a "free lunch." (See Chapter 3, pp. 61–62, for a reminder on the distinction between a tradeoff and a free lunch.)

Aggregate supply changes for three reasons: Potential GDP changes, the money wage rate changes, and the money prices of other resources change (see Chapter 15, p. 357). Monetary policy cannot influence potential GDP. But it can and does influence the money wage rate and the money prices of other resources. These influences operate through the expected price level.

A change in the expected price level changes the money wage rate and the money prices of other resources and so changes aggregate supply. Stabilizing the price level also stabilizes the expected price level (and expected inflation rate) and so also makes aggregate supply more stable.

In contrast, stabilizing real GDP, which destabilizes the price level, also destabilizes the expected price level (and expected inflation rate) and so makes aggregate supply *less* stable.

This connection between the monetary policy target and the stability of aggregate supply tilts the balance against directly targeting real GDP and towards targeting the price level. But directly targeting the price level brings the "free lunch" of a more stable aggregate supply and therefore more stable real GDP.

Eye On The PAST

Price Level Targeting

In September 1931, the Swedish central bank, the Riksbank, began targeting the CPI (reset at 100). The experiment ran until April 1937.

The figure shows what happened during the 67 months of CPI targeting.

The Great Depression was raging through this period and Sweden had a much less severe recession than most countries did. This outcome has been attributed to its decision to target the price level. Sweden eventually abandoned this policy because of concerns (probably misplaced) about the foreign exchange rate.

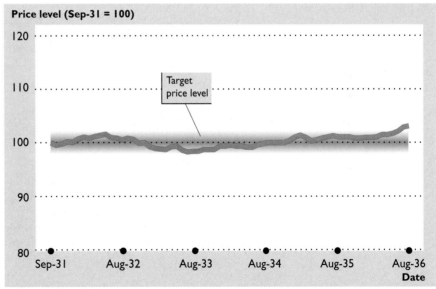

SOURCE: Federal Reserve Bank of St. Louis.

■ Zero Versus Positive Inflation

Should the target be to achieve zero inflation, or is a little inflation beneficial?

Inflation is costly. It slows economic growth and wastes leisure time for four reasons: tax costs, shoe-leather costs, confusion costs, and uncertainty costs (see Chapter 13, p. 317–320). Everyone agrees that these costs arise but that they are hard to measure. Nonetheless, some people believe that the costs are large. Others are sceptical and regard the absence of clearly measured large costs to be a sign that they are probably not present. But even the most sceptical do not claim that inflation is a good thing for its own sake.

People who caution against price level stability assert that the costs of attaining it are too large. Major advances in our knowledge have come in recent years on the cost side of this calculation. The three reasons why a positive inflation might be preferred to zero inflation are:

- The measured inflation rate overstates the true inflation rate.
- Inflation lubricates the labour market.
- The nominal interest rate cannot fall below zero.

Measurement Bias

If measurement bias were the only reason for a positive target inflation rate, the target rate for the currently measured CPI would be less than 1 percent a year. And it would be easy to construct a value-of-money index (VMI) that equals the CPI scaled back for the best available estimate of the upward measurement bias. So this argument for positive inflation does not stand up to a close look.

Labour Market Lubricant

The labour market lubricant view is based on the belief that the natural rate hypothesis is incorrect and that a long-run tradeoff between inflation and unemployment exists—the long-run Phillips curve (see Chapter 17, pp. 408–409) is not vertical.

It is alleged that unemployment increases at a low inflation rate because the real wage rate gets stuck at too high a level. And the real wage rate gets stuck at too high a level because the money wage rate doesn't fall. A little bit of inflation can bring a fall in the real wage rate, even though the money wage rate remains constant.

For example, advances in ATM technology have decreased the demand for bank tellers, and the equilibrium real wage rate of tellers has fallen. The lower real wage rate encourages many former tellers to quit and look for new types of work. The money wage rate of bank tellers has not fallen, but inflation has lowered their real wage rate.

If we had no inflation, it is argued, the real wage rate of bank tellers would not have fallen and many people would be spending time looking for hard-to-find but good jobs as tellers, so the unemployment rate would increase.

Some economists say that this problem can be avoided by maintaining inflation at a rate that is sufficiently high to ensure that almost all the required decreases in the real wage rate can be accomplished with a zero change in the money wage rate.

While there is plenty of evidence that money wage rates are sticky, there is no evidence that they are stickier downward than upward. So while there is plenty of evidence that a short-run tradeoff exists, there is no evidence that a long-run tradeoff exists. The natural rate hypothesis appears to be correct, so this argument for positive inflation is incorrect.

The Zero Lower Bound

Lawrence Summers, a former U.S. Treasury Secretary, suggested some years ago, when he was a Harvard professor, that there is a long-run tradeoff between inflation and unemployment that arises from the fact that the nominal interest rate cannot fall below zero. The claim is that expansionary monetary policy cannot be used to get the economy out of recession if the nominal interest rate is zero, so in such a situation, recession will last longer. Because the nominal interest rate will be zero more frequently the lower is the inflation rate, the economy will spend longer in recession, on the average, the lower is the inflation rate. The experience of Japan during recent years is often cited as an example of an economy that has hit the zero lower bound.

This argument is an old one. It was a subject of much debate before and during the Great Depression and has, for many years, been known to be incorrect. The Bank of Canada can always inject more money into the economy. And even if the nominal interest rate does not fall, more money brings more spending by way of an exchange rate effect and a buying power of money effect.

Eye On The CANADIAN ECONOMY

Inflation Targeting

The Bank of Canada began inflation targeting in 1991. At that time, the inflation rate was almost 6 percent a year and widely regarded as too high.

The Bank set a target path for bringing the inflation rate down from a range of between 3 percent and 5 percent in 1991 to between 1 percent and 3 percent by 1995. The target was renewed twice and was still in place in 2001. The figure shows the target range as the shaded band.

The actual rate of inflation fell as targeted and remained inside the target range through 2001.

Some critics of inflation targeting say that Canada's high unemployment rate during the 1990s was caused by the targets.

But over the period that the inflation rate was lowered, the unemployment rate also decreased. By 2000, the unemployment rate had reached its lowest level in 25 years. The behaviour of unemployment suggests that the inflation targets had the beneficial effect of lowering the expected inflation rate in step with the falling actual inflation rate. The result was a leftward shift of the short-run Phillips curve through the 1990s (see p. 415).

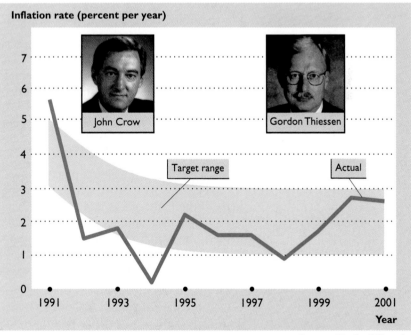

SOURCE: Bank of Canada.

Study Guide pp. 273–276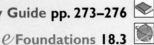

*e*Foundations 18.3

3 Assess the case for targeting inflation or the price level rather than real GDP.

Practice Problems 18.3

1. Suppose that the economy experiences a positive aggregate supply shock and the Bank of Canada reacts to this shock by adjusting its monetary policy. Explain the effect of the Bank of Canada's action on real GDP and the price level if the Bank of Canada places:
   a. No weight on real GDP fluctuations.
   b. No weight on inflation.
   c. Equal weight on inflation and real GDP fluctuations.

2. Suppose that in 2003, the inflation rate is 3 percent a year and potential GDP is $1,200 billion. Faced with a decrease in aggregate supply, the Bank of Canada decides to keep the inflation rate between 1 percent and 5 percent a year and to keep real GDP between $1,190 billion to $1,210 billion.
   a. Is the Bank of Canada placing more weight on inflation or on real GDP?
   b. What actions will the Bank of Canada take?

Exercises 18.3

1. Suppose that the economy experiences a negative aggregate supply shock and the Bank of Canada reacts to this shock by adjusting its monetary policy. Explain the effect of the Bank of Canada's action on real GDP and the price level if the Bank of Canada:
   a. Places more weight on real GDP fluctuations than on inflation.
   b. Places more weight on inflation than on real GDP fluctuations.
   c. Targets the price level.

2. In 2000, the inflation rate is 3 percent a year and the price level is 110. If the Bank of Canada targets the price level and keeps inflation at 3 percent a year but allows the price level to fluctuate between −1 and +1 percent of the target:
   a. Draw a figure to show the Bank of Canada's target range for the price level between 2000 and 2005.
   b. What is the possible range for the price level in 2005?

Solutions to Practice Problems 18.3

1a. If the Bank of Canada places no weight on real GDP fluctuations, then it targets the price level, which will remain steady, and real GDP will increase.

1b. If the Bank of Canada places no weight on inflation, then it targets real GDP. Real GDP remains at potential GDP, and the price level falls.

1c. If the Bank of Canada places equal weight on inflation and real GDP fluctuations, then it targets a combination of the price level and real GDP. The outcome would be somewhere between the outcomes in (1a) and (1b).

2a. The Bank of Canada is placing more weight on real GDP. A deviation from potential GDP of $1,200 billion by $20 billion is less than a 1 percent deviation. The Bank of Canada is willing to tolerate a much larger spread in inflation.

2b. When aggregate supply decreases, the Bank will increase the quantity of money to increase aggregate demand and keep real GDP inside its target range.

CHAPTER CHECKPOINT

Key Points

1 **Compare fiscal policy and monetary policy as stabilization tools.**

- The demand for money and investment demand determine the effects of monetary policy and fiscal policy on aggregate demand. Both policy tools affect aggregate demand.

- Monetary policy has less conflict among its goals than does fiscal policy and is more flexible than fiscal policy.

- Monetary policy and automatic fiscal policy are the preferred tools for stabilizing aggregate demand in normal times.

2 **Explain and contrast a monetarist fixed-rule and a Keynesian feedback-rule for targeting real GDP.**

- In the face of shock to aggregate demand, a fixed-rule policy takes no action. Real GDP and the price level fluctuate.

- In the face of a shock to aggregate demand or aggregate supply, a feedback-rule policy takes offsetting action. An ideal feedback rule keeps the economy at full employment, with a stable price level.

- Some economists say that a feedback rule creates fluctuations because it requires greater knowledge of the economy than we have, operates with time lags that extend beyond the forecast horizon, and introduces unpredictability about policy reactions.

3 **Assess the case for targeting inflation or the price level rather than real GDP.**

- If monetary policy targets real GDP, it offsets shocks to aggregate supply and destabilizes the price level.

- If monetary policy targets the price level, it neutralizes shocks to aggregate supply and destabilizes real GDP.

- Stabilizing real GDP destabilizes the price level and destabilizes the expected price level, so it makes aggregate supply *less* stable. So price level targeting might deliver more stable real GDP than real GDP targeting.

- The case for positive inflation is weak.

Key Terms

Discretionary policy, 430
Feedback-rule policy, 430
Fixed-rule policy, 430

Keynesian activist, 433
Liquidity trap, 427
Monetarist, 432

Exercises

1. Draw graphs to illustrate the conditions under which:
   a. Fiscal policy is effective and monetary policy is ineffective.
   b. Monetary policy is effective and fiscal policy is ineffective.
   c. Monetary policy and fiscal policy are equally effective.

2. For the Bank of Canada to stabilize aggregate demand, what does the Bank of Canada have to be able to accurately predict?

3. What are the goals of discretionary fiscal policy? Does discretionary fiscal policy create goal conflicts? Explain why or why not.

4. Which industries and sectors of the economy are most strongly affected by monetary policy? Why?

5. "Canadians buy 60 percent of Canadian GDP and foreigners buy the other 40 percent. Fiscal policy influences only the Canadian demand, while monetary policy influences both the Canadian and foreign demand." Is this statement true? Explain why or why not.

6. Use the link on your Foundations Web site to visit the Bank of Canada and Statistics Canada.
   a. Draw a graph showing the target range for the inflation rate and the actual inflation rate for the last few years.
   b. Has the inflation rate stayed within the target range?
   c. If not, what action has the Bank of Canada taken to correct the situation?
   d. What events might force the Bank of Canada to abandon its inflation target?

7. Use the link on your Foundations Web site to visit the Bank of Canada and Statistics Canada.
   a. Has Canada had a recession recently?
   b. If so, what was the policy response of the Bank of Canada?
   c. If so, what changes occurred in the budget of the federal government?
   d. Did the foreign exchange value of the Canadian dollar fall? Why would a fall in the foreign exchange value of the Canadian dollar be considered desirable under recession conditions?

8. In 2000, the Canadian and U.S. economies were both operating close to potential GDP and full employment. Then there was an aggregate supply shock in the form of a sharp increase in the world price of oil. Make an argument that for Canada, this aggregate supply shock was:
   a. A very negative development.
   b. Not such a negative development, and maybe even a positive one.

9. As the U.S. economy continued to expand and its stock market soared to new record levels during 2000, the U.S. central bank raised interest rates.
   a. What was the objective of the U.S. central bank in raising interest rates?
   b. How would you expect this policy to affect real U.S. GDP and the price level?

10. During 2001, the Bank of Canada and the U.S. central bank implemented a series of reductions in interest rates that amounted in total to the sharpest decline in interest rates in history.
    a. What led to such a dramatic reversal of monetary policy?
    b. What do you think the Bank's policy objective was?
    c. Was the policy successful?

International Trade

When you have completed your study of this chapter,
you will be able to:

1 Describe the patterns and trends in international trade.

2 Explain why nations engage in international trade and why trade
benefits all nations.

3 Explain how trade barriers reduce international trade.

4 Explain the arguments used to justify trade barriers and show why they
are incorrect but also why some barriers are hard to remove.

Canada is an integral part of the North American
economy and a large player in the global economy. Our exports bring employment and prosperity, but they also bring macroeconomic
disturbances such as recessions from other
countries. International trade also forces
Canadian producers to compete with low-wage
Asian and Mexican producers. Do we benefit
from our international trade? And can we compete with
countries like Mexico that pay their workers a fraction of
Canadian wages?

In this chapter, you are going to learn about international
trade. You will discover how all nations can gain by specializing in producing the goods and services in which they have a
comparative advantage and trading with other countries. You
will discover that all countries can compete, no matter how
high their wages. And you'll learn why, despite the fact that
international trade brings benefits to all countries, they
nevertheless restrict trade.

19.1 TRADE PATTERNS AND TRENDS

The goods and services that we buy from people in other countries are called *imports*. The goods and services that we sell to people in other countries are called *exports*. What are the most important things that we import and export? Most people would probably guess that Canada exports mostly natural resources and resource products and imports manufactured goods. This guess would be wrong! Today, only about one-quarter of Canada's exports are resource products. Canada's largest single export is automobiles, and nearly half of all the exports that we sell to foreigners consist of manufactured goods such as cars, machinery, and consumer goods. In return, we buy manufactured items—televisions, VCRs, household appliances, blue jeans, and T-shirts—from foreign producers. We also import and export a huge volume of services.

■ Trade in Goods

Manufactured goods account for almost one-half of Canadian exports and for more than one-half of Canadian imports. Resource products, such as forest products, energy, and agricultural products, account for only one-quarter of Canada's exports and one-tenth of Canada's imports. Trade in agriculture is small, at around one-twentieth of total imports and exports.

Total trade in goods accounts for 88 percent of Canadian exports and 85 percent of Canadian imports. The rest of Canada's international trade is in services.

■ Trade in Services

You might be wondering how a country can export and import services. Here are some examples.

If you take a vacation in France and travel there on an Air France flight from Montreal, Canada imports transportation services from France. The money you spend in France on hotel bills and restaurant meals is also classified as a Canadian import of services. Similarly, the vacation taken by a French student in Canada counts as a Canadian export of services to France.

When we import TV sets from South Korea, the owner of the ship that transports them might be Greek and the company that insures them might be British. The payments that we make for the transportation and insurance are Canadian imports of services. Similarly, when a Canadian shipping company transports Canadian lumber to Tokyo, the transportation cost is a Canadian export of a service to Japan. Canadian international trade in these types of services is large and growing.

■ Trends in the Volume of Trade

Canada participates more heavily in international trade than most nations. In 1960, exports were about 17 percent of Canada's GDP and imports were 18 percent of GDP. By 2000, these numbers had increased dramatically to 45 percent of GDP exported and more than 40 percent of GDP imported. The composition of exports has changed. Canada's exports of manufactured goods have increased more rapidly than its exports of agricultural and resource products. The composition of Canada's imports has changed little. Automobiles, machinery and equipment, and electrical products have remained the dominant items for many years.

Eye On The GLOBAL ECONOMY

The Major Items That We Trade with Other Nations

The figure shows Canada's volume of trade and balance of trade for the 25 largest items traded. If a bar has more blue (exports) than red (imports), Canada has a trade surplus in that category.

Motor vehicles and parts; machinery and equipment; and electrical products are the largest items. The combined exports of agricultural, energy, and forest products are smaller than exports of motor vehicles and parts.

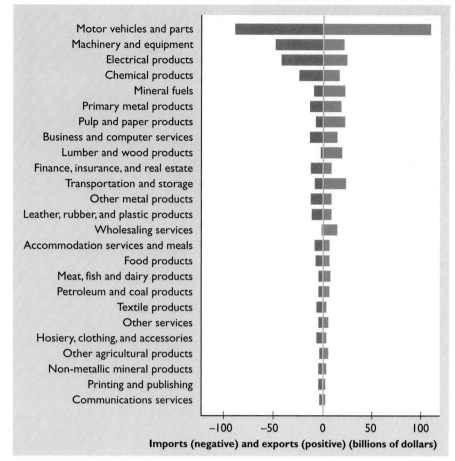

SOURCE: Statistics Canada.

■ Trading Partners and Trading Blocs

Canada has trading links with every part of the world and is a member of several international organizations that seek to promote both regional and international trade.

Canada's Trading Partners

The United States is Canada's biggest trading partner by a huge margin. Our trade with the United States makes Canada an integral part of the North American economy. Trade with the European Union (EU), Japan, China, and Mexico is significant but on a much smaller scale than trade with the United States. The Eye on the Global Economy on p. 452 shows the data for our largest trading partners.

Trading Blocs

Trading blocs are groupings of nations into an international trading organization. The world today divides into three major geographical blocs, and Canada is a member of two of them. The two blocs of which Canada is a member are the North American Free Trade Agreement and Asia-Pacific Economic Cooperation. The other large bloc is the European Union. We'll provide a brief description of each of these trading blocs.

Canada's Major Trading Partners and Volumes of Trade

The figure shows Canada's volume of trade and balance of trade with its major trading partners. If a bar has more red (imports) than blue (exports), Canada has a trade deficit with that country.

The United States is by far Canada's largest trading partner—the destination of over 85 percent of our exports and the source of 76 percent of our imports. The European Union (EU), Japan, and China come next. Our other NAFTA trading partner, Mexico, comes a distant fifth.

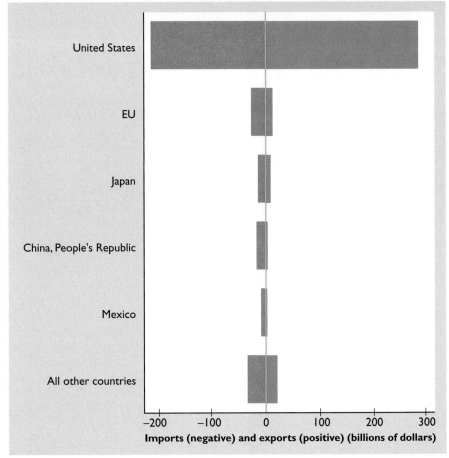

Imports (negative) and exports (positive) (billions of dollars)

SOURCE: Statistics Canada.

North American Free Trade Agreement The North American Free Trade Agreement, or NAFTA, is an agreement between the United States, Canada, and Mexico to make trade among the three countries easier and freer. The Agreement came into effect in 1994. During the years since then, trade among the three nations has expanded rapidly.

North and South America consist of 35 nations, and the governments of the 34 democracies (which excludes Cuba) have entered into a Free Trade of the Americas process. The objective of this process is to achieve free international trade among all the nations of the Americas by 2005.

Asia-Pacific Economic Cooperation Asia-Pacific Economic Cooperation, or APEC, is a group of 21 nations that border the Pacific Ocean. The largest of these are the United States, China, Japan, and Canada. But other significant members are Australia, Indonesia, and the dynamic new industrial Asian economies. In 1999, APEC nations conducted 44 percent of the world's international trade.

APEC was established in 1989 as an informal discussion group, but it has developed into an organization with the goal of promoting freer trade and cooperation among its member nations.

European Union The European Union, or EU, is a group of 15 nations of Western Europe. The EU began as the European Common Market when six countries (Belgium, Germany, France, Italy, Luxembourg, and the Netherlands) embarked on a process of economic integration in 1951. The EU is developing institutions of government that are more like those of a federal state than a group of independent states. On January 1, 1999, the EU introduced its own currency, the euro.

■ Balance of Trade and International Borrowing

The value of exports minus the value of imports is called the **balance of trade**. In 2000, Canada exported $53 billion more than it imported. When a country exports more than it imports, it has a trade surplus and lends to other countries or buys more foreign assets to enable the rest of the world to pay its deficit. When a country imports more than it exports, it has a trade deficit and pays by borrowing from foreigners or selling some of its assets.

Balance of trade
The value of exports minus the value of imports.

CHECKPOINT 19.1

1 **Describe the patterns and trends in international trade.**

Study Guide pp. 282–284

*e*Foundations 19.1

Practice Problem 19.1

Use the link on your Foundations Web site to answer the following questions:
a. In 1990, what percentage of Canadian production was exported to the United States and what percentage of total goods and services bought by Canadians was imported from the United States?
b. In 2000, what percentage of Canadian production was exported to the United States and what percentage of total goods and services bought by Canadians was imported from the United States?

Exercise 19.1

Use the link on your Foundations Web site to answer the following questions:
a. In 1990, what percentage of Mexican production was exported to Canada and what percentage of total goods and services bought by Mexicans was imported from Canada?
b. In 1998, what percentage of Mexican production was exported to Canada and what percentage of total goods and services bought by Mexicans was imported from Canada?

Solution to Practice Problem 19.1

a. In 1990, Canada exported 16.5 percent of total production to the United States and imported 14.4 percent of total goods and services purchased from the United States.

b. In 2000, Canada exported 34.6 percent of total production to the United States and imported 27 percent of goods and services purchased from the United States.

19.2 THE GAINS FROM INTERNATIONAL TRADE

Comparative advantage is the fundamental force that generates international trade. And comparative advantage arises from differences in opportunity costs. You met this idea in Chapter 3 (pp. 68–70), but we're now going to put some flesh on the bones of the basic idea. We'll begin by looking at an item that we export.

■ Why Canada Exports Locomotives

General Motors in London, Ontario produces many more locomotives each year than CP and CN in Canada buy. Most of GM's production goes to railways in other parts of the world. Canada is an exporter of locomotives. Why?

The answer is that Canada has a comparative advantage in the production of locomotives. The opportunity cost of producing a locomotive is lower in Canada than in most other countries. So buyers can obtain locomotives from Canada for a lower price than the price at which they could buy them from other potential suppliers. And GM can sell locomotives to foreigners for a higher price than it could obtain from an additional Canadian buyer.

So both countries gain. Foreign buyers gain from lower-priced locomotives. And GM's stockholders, managers, and workers gain from higher-priced locomotives. A win-win situation!

Figure 19.1 illustrates the effects of international trade in locomotives. The demand curve *D* shows the demand for locomotives in Canada. This curve tells us the quantity of locomotives that Canadian railways are willing to buy at various prices. The demand curve also tells us the most that an additional locomotive is worth to a Canadian railway at each quantity.

The supply curve *S* shows the supply of locomotives in Canada. This curve tells us the quantity of locomotives that Canadian producers are willing to sell at various prices. The supply curve also tells us the opportunity cost of producing an additional locomotive at each quantity.

No Trade

First, let's see what happens in the market for locomotives if there is no international trade. Figure 19.1(a) shows the situation. The locomotive market is in equilibrium when 40 locomotives are produced in Canada and bought by Canadian railways. The price is $1 million a locomotive.

Trade

Second, let's see what happens in the market for locomotives if international trade takes place. Figure 19.1(b) shows the situation. The price of a locomotive is determined in the world market, not the Canadian domestic market. World demand and world supply determine a world price. Suppose that price is $1.3 million per locomotive. In Figure 19.1(b), the world price line shows this price.

The Canadian demand curve, *D*, tells us that at $1.3 million per locomotive, Canadian railways will buy 30 locomotives a year. The Canadian supply curve, *S*, tells us that at $1.3 million per locomotive, Canadian firms will produce 80 locomotives a year. So Canadian production at 80 locomotives a year exceeds Canadian purchases at 30 a year.

The quantity produced in Canada minus the quantity purchased by Canadian railways is the quantity of Canadian exports, which are 50 locomotives a year.

FIGURE 19.1

An Export

e **Foundations 19.2**

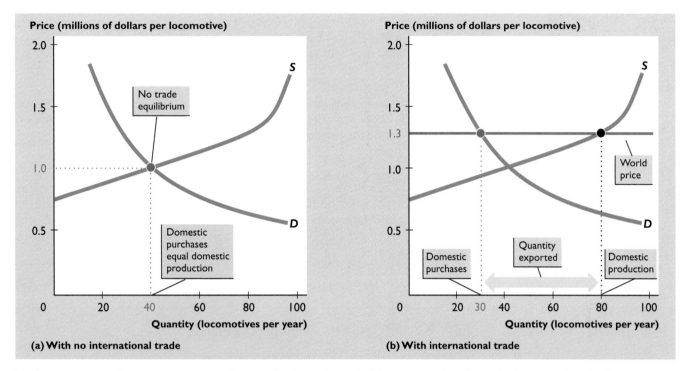

(a) With no international trade

(b) With international trade

With no international trade in locomotives, the Canadian demand and supply curves determine the price ($1 million per locomotive) and the quantity produced and purchased (40 locomotives a year).

With international trade, world demand and supply determine the price, which is $1.3 million per locomotive. Canadian purchases decrease to 30 locomotives a year, Canadian production increases to 80 locomotives a year, and 50 locomotives a year are exported.

Comparative Advantage

You can see that Canadian producers have a comparative advantage in producing locomotives by comparing the Canadian supply curve and the world price line. At the equilibrium quantity of 80 locomotives a year, the world opportunity cost of producing a locomotive is $1.3 million. But the Canadian supply curve tells us that only the 80th locomotive has an opportunity cost of $1.3 million. Each of the other 79 locomotives has an opportunity cost of less than $1.3 million.

■ Why Canada Imports T-Shirts

Canadians spend more than twice as much on clothing as the value of Canadian apparel production. That is, more than half of the clothing that we buy is manufactured in other countries and imported into Canada. Why?

The answer is that the rest of the world (mainly Asia) has a comparative advantage in the production of clothes. The opportunity cost of producing a T-shirt is lower in Asia than in Canada. So Canadian buyers can obtain T-shirts from Asia for a lower price than the price at which they could buy them from Canadian garment makers. And Asian garment makers can sell T-shirts to Canadians for a higher price than they could obtain from an additional Asian buyer.

So again, both countries gain. The Canadian buyer gains from lower-priced T-shirts, and Asian garment makers gain from higher-priced T-shirts. Another win-win situation!

Figure 19.2 illustrates the effects of international trade in T-shirts. Again, the demand curve *D* and the supply curve *S* show the demand and supply in the Canadian domestic market only.

The demand curve tells us the quantity of T-shirts that Canadians are willing to buy at various prices. The demand curve also tells us the most that an additional T-shirt is worth to a Canadian at each quantity.

The supply curve tells us the quantity of T-shirts that Canadian garment makers are willing to sell at various prices. The supply curve also tells us the opportunity cost of producing an additional T-shirt in Canada at each quantity.

No Trade

We'll first look at a market with no international trade, shown in Figure 19.2(a). The T-shirt market is in equilibrium when 4 million T-shirts a year are produced by Canadian garment makers and bought by Canadians. The price is $8 a shirt.

■ **FIGURE 19.2**
An Import

*e***Foundations 19.2**

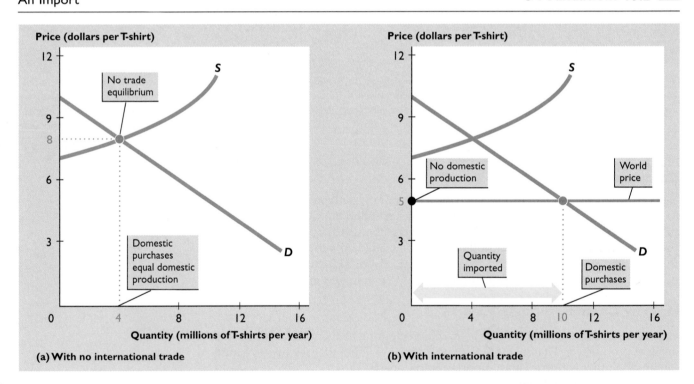

(a) With no international trade

(b) With international trade

With no international trade in T-shirts, the Canadian demand and supply curves determine the price ($8 per shirt) and the quantity produced and purchased (4 million shirts a year).

With international trade, world demand and supply determine the price, which is $5 per shirt. Canadian purchases increase to 10 million a year, and Canadian production decreases to zero. The entire 10 million shirts a year are imported.

Trade

Figure 19.2(b) shows what happens in the market for T-shirts if international trade takes place. Now the price of a T-shirt is determined in the world market, not the Canadian domestic market. Suppose that world demand and world supply determine a world equilibrium price of $5 per shirt. In Figure 19.2(b), the world price line shows this price.

The Canadian demand curve, *D*, tells us that at $5 per shirt, Canadians buy 10 million shirts a year. The Canadian supply curve, *S*, tells us that at $5 per shirt, Canadian garment makers produce no T-shirts. So there is no Canadian production, and Canadian purchases are 10 million T-shirts a year. The entire quantity of T-shirts purchased in Canada is the quantity imported.

Comparative Advantage

Now you can see that Asian garment makers have a comparative advantage in producing T-shirts by comparing the Canadian supply curve and the world price line. At the equilibrium quantity of 10 million T-shirts a year, the world opportunity cost of producing a T-shirt is $5. But the Canadian supply curve tells us that no Canadian garment maker has such a low opportunity cost, not even at smaller outputs. So Asian garment makers have a comparative advantage in producing T-shirts.

■ Gains from Trade and the *PPF*

The demand and supply model that you've just studied makes it clear why we export some goods and import others. But it doesn't show directly the gains from international trade. Another way of looking at comparative advantage uses the production possibilities frontier (*PPF*) that you learned about in Chapter 3. This approach shows the gains from trade in a powerful way, as you're about to discover.

Let's explore comparative advantage by looking at production possibilities in Canada and China.

Production Possibilities in Canada and China

To focus on the essential idea, suppose that Canada can produce only two goods: regional jets and sports shoes. China can also produce only these same two goods. But production possibilities are different in the two countries.

If Canada uses all of its resources to produce regional jets, its output is 100 jets per year and no sports shoes. If it uses all of its resources to produce sports shoes, its output is 100 million pairs of shoes per year and no jets. We'll assume that the Canadian opportunity cost of producing a jet is constant. To produce 100 jets, Canada must forgo 100 million pairs of shoes, which means that to produce 1 jet, Canada must forgo 1 million pairs of shoes. That is:

The Canadian opportunity cost of producing 1 jet is 1 million pairs of shoes.

In contrast, if China uses all of its resources to make regional jets, it can produce 20 jets per year and no sports shoes. And if it uses all of its resources to make sports shoes, it can produce 100 million pairs of shoes per year and no jets. We'll assume that China's opportunity cost of producing a jet is constant. To produce 20 jets, China must forgo 100 million pairs of shoes, which means that to produce 1 jet, China must forgo 5 million pairs of shoes. That is:

China's opportunity cost of producing 1 jet is 5 million pairs of shoes.

The assumption that the opportunity costs of producing a regional jet in Canada and in China are constant makes the point that we're illustrating in the simplest and cleanest way. We could assume increasing opportunity costs. We would reach the same conclusion that we'll reach here, but the story would be a bit more complicated and the point wouldn't jump out as clearly as it does by making the assumption of constant opportunity costs.

Figure 19.3(a) shows the production possibilities for Canada, and Figure 19.3(b) shows the production possibilities for China. The assumption that the opportunity costs are constant means that the two *PPF*s are linear. Along Canada's *PPF*, 1 jet costs 1 million pairs of shoes. And along China's *PPF*, 1 jet costs 5 million pairs of shoes.

FIGURE 19.3
Production Possibilities in Canada and China

*e*Foundations **19.2**

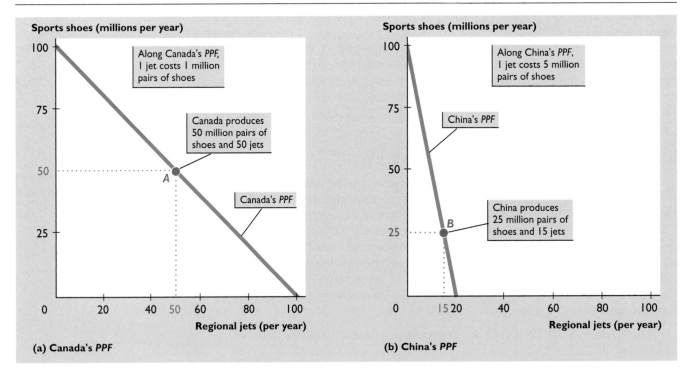

Canada produces at point *A* on its *PPF* (part a), and China produces at point *B* on its *PPF* (part b). The opportunity cost of a regional jet is lower in Canada, so it has a comparative advantage in producing regional jets. The opportunity cost of a pair of shoes is lower in China, so it has a comparative advantage in producing shoes.

No Trade

With no international trade, we'll suppose that Canada produces 50 jets and 50 million pairs of shoes at point *A* on its *PPF*. And we'll suppose that China produces 15 jets and 25 million pairs of shoes at point *B* on its *PPF*.

Comparative Advantage

In which of the two goods does China have a comparative advantage? Recall that comparative advantage is a situation in which one nation's opportunity cost of producing a good is lower than another nation's opportunity cost of producing that same good. China has a comparative advantage in producing shoes. China's opportunity cost of a pair of shoes is 1/5,000,000 of a jet, whereas Canada's opportunity cost of a pair of shoes is 1/1,000,000 of a jet.

You can see China's comparative advantage by looking at the *PPF*s for China and Canada in Figure 19.3. China's *PPF* is steeper than Canada's *PPF*. To produce an additional 1 million pairs of shoes, China must give up fewer jets than does Canada. So China's opportunity cost of a pair of shoes is less than Canada's opportunity cost of a pair of shoes. This means that China has a comparative advantage in producing shoes.

Canada has a comparative advantage in producing regional jets. In Figure 19.3, Canada's *PPF* is less steep than China's *PPF*. This means that Canada must give up fewer shoes to produce an additional jet than does China. Canada's opportunity cost of producing a jet is 1 million pairs of shoes, which is less than China's 5 million pairs. So Canada has a comparative advantage in producing regional jets.

Because China has a comparative advantage in producing shoes and Canada has a comparative advantage in producing jets, both China and Canada can gain from specialization and trade. China specializes in shoes, and Canada specializes in regional jets.

Achieving the Gains from Trade

If Canada, which has a comparative advantage in producing jets, allocates all of its resources to that activity, it can produce 100 jets a year. If China, which has a comparative advantage in producing shoes, allocates all of its resources to that activity, it can produce 100 million pairs a year. By specializing, Canada and China together can produce 100 million pairs of shoes and 100 jets. With no trade, their total production had been 65 jets (50 produced by Canada and 15 by China) and 75 million pairs of shoes (50 million produced by Canada and 25 million by China).

So with specialization and trade, Canada and China can consume outside their production possibilities frontiers. But to achieve the gains from specialization, Canada and China must trade with each other.

Suppose that Canada and China agree to the following deal: China agrees to pay Canada 2 million pairs of shoes per jet; Canada agrees to sell China 30 jets a year at this price.

With this deal in place, Canada has 60 million pairs of shoes and 70 jets—a gain of 10 million pairs of shoes and 20 jets. China now has 40 million pairs of shoes and 30 jets—a gain of 15 million pairs of shoes and 15 jets.

Figure 19.4 shows these gains from trade. Canada originally produced and consumed at point *A*. It now produces at point *P* and consumes at point *A'*, a point outside its *PPF*. China originally produced and consumed at point *B*. It now produces at point *Q* and consumes at point *B'*, a point outside its *PPF*. As a result of specialization and trade, both countries can consume outside their production possibilities frontiers. Both countries gain from trade.

In this example, Canada can out-produce China and has an *absolute advantage* (see Chapter 3, p. 70), but it can get shoes at a lower cost by trading regional jets for shoes with China. Gains from specialization and trade are always available when opportunity costs diverge.

Dynamic Comparative Advantage

Learning-by-doing
Repeatedly performing the same task and becoming more productive at producing a particular good or service.

Dynamic comparative advantage
A comparative advantage that a person (or country) obtains by specializing in an activity, resulting from learning-by-doing.

Resources and technology determine comparative advantage. But just by repeatedly producing a particular good or service, people become more productive in that activity, a phenomenon called **learning-by-doing**. **Dynamic comparative advantage**, a comparative advantage that a person (or country) obtains by specializing in an activity, results from learning-by-doing.

Hong Kong, South Korea, and Taiwan are examples of countries that have pursued dynamic comparative advantage vigorously. They have developed electronics and biotechnology industries in which initially they did not have a comparative advantage, but through learning-by-doing, they have become low opportunity cost producers in those industries.

■ FIGURE 19.4
The Gains from Trade

*e***Foundations 19.2**

If Canada specializes in regional jets, it produces 100 a year at point *P*. If China specializes in shoes, it produces 100 million pairs a year at point *Q*.

If shoes and aircraft are traded at 2 million pairs of shoes per regional jet, both countries can increase their consumption of both goods and consume at points *A'* and *B'*. The gains from trade are the increases in consumption of the two countries.

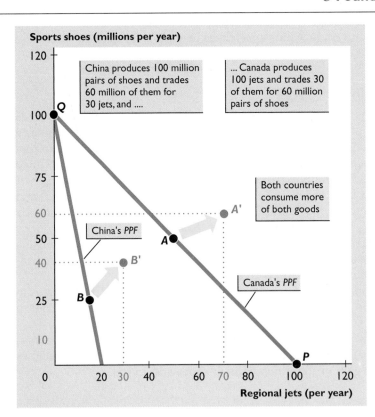

CHECKPOINT 19.2

2 Explain why nations engage in international trade and why trade benefits all nations.

Study Guide **pp. 284–288**

*e*Foundations **19.2**

Practice Problem 19.2

During most of the Cold War, North America and Russia did not trade with each other. North America produced manufactured goods and farm produce. Russia produced manufactured goods and farm produce. Suppose that in the last year of the Cold War, North America could produce 100 million units of manufactured goods or 50 million units of farm produce and Russia could produce 30 million units of manufactured goods or 10 million units of farm produce.

a. What was the opportunity cost of 1 unit of farm produce in North America?
b. What was the opportunity cost of 1 unit of farm produce in Russia?
c. Which country had a comparative advantage in producing farm produce?
d. With the end of the Cold War and the opening up of trade between Russia and North America, which good did North America import from Russia?
e. Did North America gain from this trade? Explain why or why not.
f. Did Russia gain from this trade? Explain why or why not.

Exercise 19.2

In 2001, the United States does not trade with Cuba. Suppose that the United States can produce 1,000 million units of manufactured goods or 500 million units of food. Suppose that Cuba can produce 2 million units of manufactured goods or 5 million units of food.

a. What was the opportunity cost of 1 unit of food in the United States?
b. What was the opportunity cost of 1 unit of food in Cuba?
c. Which country had a comparative advantage in producing food?
d. Suppose that the United States opens up trade with Cuba. Which good will the United States import from Cuba?
e. Will the United States gain from this trade? Explain why or why not.
f. Will Cuba gain from this trade? Explain why or why not.

Solution to Practice Problem 19.2

a. The North American opportunity cost of 1 unit of farm produce was 2 units of manufactured goods.
b. The Russian opportunity cost of 1 unit of farm produce was 3 units of manufactured goods.
c. North America had a comparative advantage in producing farm produce because the North American opportunity cost of a unit of farm produce was less than the Russian opportunity cost of farm produce.
d. North America imported from Russia the good in which Russia had a comparative advantage. North America imported manufactured goods.
e. and f. Both North America and Russia gained because each country ended up with more of both goods. When countries specialize in producing the good in which they have a comparative advantage and then trade with each other, both countries gain.

Governments restrict international trade to protect domestic industries from foreign competition. The two main tools that governments use are:

- Tariffs
- Non-tariff barriers

Tariff
A tax on a good that is imposed by the importing country when an imported good crosses its international boundary.

Nontariff barrier
Any action other than a tariff that restricts international trade.

A **tariff** is a tax on a good that is imposed by the importing country when an imported good crosses its international boundary. A **nontariff barrier** is any action other than a tariff that restricts international trade. Examples of nontariff barriers are quantitative restrictions and health and safety standards.

■ Tariffs

The temptation for governments to impose tariffs is a strong one. First, tariffs provide revenue to the government. Second, they enable the government to satisfy special interest groups in import-competing industries. But as we will see, free international trade brings enormous benefits that are reduced when tariffs are imposed. Let's see how.

Eye On The PAST

The History of the Canadian Tariff

Canada's tariffs today are modest in comparison with their historical levels. The figure shows the average tariff rate—total tariffs as a percentage of total imports. Tariffs increased sharply in the 1870s, then decreased slowly until the 1930s, when they increased again during an international trade war, which began when the U.S. Congress passed the Smoot-Hawley Act that increased U.S. tariffs.

In 1947, the General Agreement on Tariffs and Trade (GATT), an international agreement to eliminate trade restrictions, was established. Under the GATT, a series of rounds of nego-

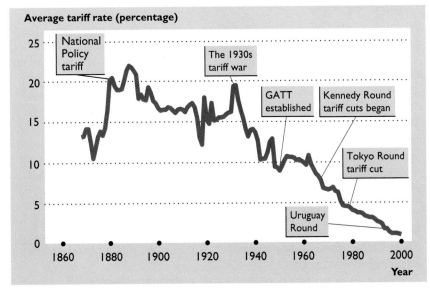

SOURCE: Statistics Canada.

tiations brought widespread tariff cuts. Today, the World Trade Organization (WTO) continues the work of GATT.

Canada is a party to the North American Free Trade Agreement

(NAFTA), which came into effect in 1994 and under which barriers to trade between Canada, Mexico, and the United States will be virtually eliminated over a 15-year period.

To analyze how tariffs work, let's return to the example of T-shirt imports into Canada. Figure 19.5 shows the market for T-shirts in Canada. Part (a) is the same as Figure 19.2(b) and shows the situation with free international trade. Canada produces no T-shirts, and imports 10 million shirts a year at the world market price of $5 a shirt.

Now suppose that under pressure from Canadian garment makers, the Canadian government imposes a 50 percent tariff on imported T-shirts. What happens?

- The price of a T-shirt in Canada rises.
- The quantity of T-shirts bought in Canada decreases.
- The quantity of T-shirts produced in Canada increases.
- The quantity of T-shirts imported by Canada decreases.
- The Canadian government collects the tariff revenue.
- Canadian consumers lose.

FIGURE 19.5
The Effects of a Tariff   *e*Foundations **19.3**

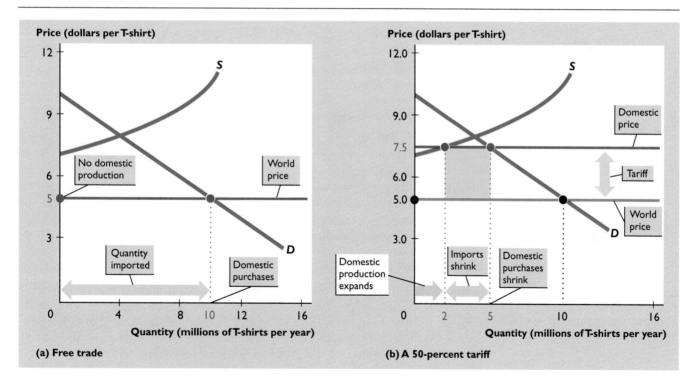

(a) Free trade

(b) A 50-percent tariff

With free trade (part a), Canada produces no T-shirts and imports 10 million T-shirts a year.

In part (b), Canada imposes a tariff on imports of T-shirts. The price in Canada equals the world price plus the tariff, so the tariff raises the price that Canadians pay for a T-shirt.

The quantity of T-shirts that Canadians buy decreases, the quantity produced in Canada increases, and the quantity imported into Canada decreases. The Canadian government collects tariff revenue (the purple rectangle).

Rise in Price of a T-Shirt

To buy a T-shirt, Canadians must pay the world market price plus the tariff. So the price of a T-shirt in Canada rises by 50 percent to $7.50. Figure 19.5(b) shows the domestic price, which is 50 percent (or $2.50) above the world price.

Decrease in Purchases

The higher price of a T-shirt brings a decrease in the quantity demanded, which Figure 19.5(b) shows as a movement along the demand curve for T-shirts from 10 million a year at $5 a shirt to 5 million a year at $7.50 a shirt.

Increase in Domestic Production

The higher price of a T-shirt stimulates domestic production, which increases from zero to 2 million shirts a year—a movement along the supply curve in Figure 19.5(b).

Decrease in Imports

T-shirt imports decrease by 7 million a year—from 10 million to 3 million a year. Both the decrease in purchases and the increase in domestic production contribute to this decrease in imports.

Tariff Revenue

The government collects tariff revenue of $2.50 per shirt on the 3 million shirts imported each year, a total of $7.5 million, as shown by the purple rectangle.

Canadian Consumers Lose

A T-shirt costs only $5 to produce—the opportunity cost of that shirt is $5. But the Canadian consumer pays $7.50—$2.50 a shirt more than its opportunity cost. Consumers are willing to buy up to 10 million shirts a year at a price that equals the opportunity cost. The tariff makes people pay more than the opportunity cost and deprives them of items they are willing to buy at a price that exceeds the opportunity cost.

Let's now look at the other tools for restricting trade: nontariff barriers.

■ Nontariff Barriers

Quota
A specified maximum amount of a good that may be imported in a given period of time.

A **quota** is a quantitative restriction on the import of a good that specifies the maximum amount of the good that may be imported in a given period. Canada imposes quotas on imports on textiles and clothing. Canada is gradually eliminating these quotas, but some remain. For example, the quota on swimwear will be eliminated on January 1, 2002, but the quota on corduroy will remain.

How a Quota Works

Figure 19.6 shows how a quota works. Begin by identifying the situation with free international trade. Canada produces no T-shirts and imports 10 million shirts a year at the world market price of $5 a shirt.

Now suppose that Canada imposes a quota that restricts imports to 3 million T-shirts a year. The imports permitted under the quota plus the quantity produced in Canada is the market supply in Canada. This market supply curve is the one labelled *S + quota* in Figure 19.6.

FIGURE 19.6

The Effects of a Quota

*e*Foundations 19.3

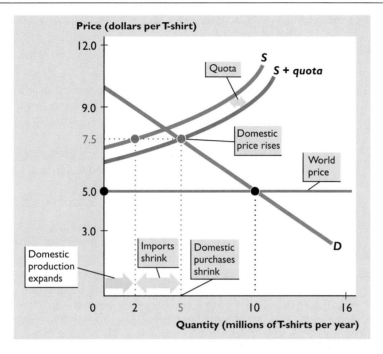

A quota of 3 million shirts a year restricts imports. This quota is added to Canadian supply to give the market supply curve, *S + quota*. At the equilibrium price of $7.50 a shirt, Canada produces 2 million shirts a year and Canadian imports equal the quota of 3 million a year.

With this new supply curve, the price in Canada rises to $7.50—the price that makes the quantity demanded by Canadians equal the quantity supplied by Canadian producers plus imports. This quantity is 5 million shirts a year.

At a price of $7.50, Canadian garment makers produce 2 million shirts a year and Canadian imports equal the quota of 3 million a year.

We've made the outcome with a quota in Figure 19.6 the same as that with a tariff in Figure 19.5(b). But there is a difference between a tariff and a quota. In the case of a tariff, the Canadian government collects tariff revenue. In the case of a quota, there is no tariff revenue and the difference between the world price and the Canadian price goes to the person who has the right to import T-shirts under the import quota regulations.

Health, Safety, and Other Nontariff Barriers

Thousands of detailed health, safety, and other regulations restrict international trade. Here are just a few examples. Goods imported into Canada for retail sale have to comply with labelling laws; motor vehicles have to meet emission control standards; food and agricultural products have to pass health and sanitary checks; and importers of steel, cheese, and wine must obtain permits. The European Union has banned imports of most genetically modified foods, such as Canadian granola. Australia has banned the import of U.S. grapes to protect its domestic grapes from a virus that is present in California. In 2001, the scare of foot and mouth disease virtually closed down international trade in live cattle and beef. Restrictions also apply to many non-food items. Although such nontariff barriers are not usually designed to limit international trade, they have that effect.

Study Guide pp. 288–290

*e*Foundations 19.3

3 **Explain how trade barriers reduce international trade.**

Practice Problems 19.3

1. Before 1995, Canada imposed tariffs on goods imported from Mexico. In 1995, Mexico joined NAFTA. Canadian tariffs on imports from Mexico and Mexican tariffs on imports from Canada are gradually being removed. Explain how the removal of tariffs will change:
   a. The price that Canadian consumers pay for goods imported from Mexico.
   b. The quantity of imports from Mexico into Canada.
   c. The quantity of Canadian exports to Mexico.
   d. The Canadian government's tariff revenue from trade with Mexico.

2. Almost all U.S. imports of potatoes come from Canada. In 1999–2000, the U.S. government banned potato imports from Prince Edward Island. Explain how this ban would have influenced:
   a. The price that U.S. consumers paid for potatoes.
   b. The quantity of potatoes consumed in the United States.
   c. The price received by Canadian potato growers.
   d. The U.S. and Canadian gains from trade.

Exercises 19.3

1. The United States imposes a tariff on imports of softwood lumber from Canada. Explain the effect of this tariff on:
   a. The price that American buyers pay for softwood lumber.
   b. The quantity of softwood lumber exported from Canada to the United States.
   c. The quantity of softwood lumber produced in Canada.
   d. The Canadian and American gains from trade.

2. China has a comparative advantage in producing textiles, but Canada sets a quota on textile imports from China. Explain how the quota influences:
   a. The price that Canadian consumers pay for textiles.
   b. The quantity of textiles produced in Canada.
   c. The Canadian and Chinese gains from trade.

Solutions to Practice Problems 19.3

1a. The price that Canadian consumers pay for goods imported from Mexico will fall.
1.b The quantity of Canadian imports from Mexico will increase.
1c. The quantity of Canadian exports to Mexico will increase.
1d. The Canadian government's tariff revenue from trade with Mexico will fall.

2a. The ban increased the price that U.S. consumers paid for potatoes.
2b. The quantity of potatoes consumed in the United States fell.
2c. The price received by Canadian potato growers fell.
2d. Both the U.S. and Canadian gains from trade decreased.

19.4 THE CASE AGAINST PROTECTION

For as long as nations and international trade have existed, people have debated whether a country is better off with free international trade or with protection from foreign competition. The debate continues, but for most economists, a verdict has been delivered and it is the one you have just seen. Free trade promotes prosperity for all countries: Protection reduces the potential gains from trade. We've seen the most powerful case for free trade: All countries benefit from their comparative advantage. But there is a broader range of issues in the free trade versus protection debate. Let's review these issues.

■ Three Main Arguments for Protection

The three main arguments for protection and restricting international trade are:

- The employment argument
- The infant-industry argument
- The dumping argument

Let's look at each in turn.

The Employment Argument

The employment argument is: When we buy shoes from Brazil or shirts from Taiwan, Canadian workers lose their jobs. With no earnings and poor prospects, these workers become a drain on welfare and spend less, causing a ripple effect of further job losses. The proposed solution to this problem is to ban imports of cheap foreign goods and to protect Canadian jobs. The proposal is flawed for the following reasons.

First, free trade does cost some jobs, but it also creates other jobs. It brings about a global rationalization of labour and allocates resources to their highest-valued activities. In the five years following the signing of NAFTA, 800 textile plants in Canada's clothing industry have closed and 33,000 jobs have been lost. But tens of thousands of workers in developing countries, such as Sri Lanka and China, have gotten jobs because textile mills have opened there. And tens of thousands of Canadian workers have gotten jobs that are better-paying jobs than those lost in the textile industry because export industries have expanded and created more jobs than have been destroyed.

Second, imports create jobs. They create jobs for retailers that sell imported goods and for firms that service those goods. They also create jobs by creating incomes in the rest of the world, some of which are spent on imports of Canadian-made goods and services.

The Infant-Industry Argument

The **infant-industry argument** for protection is that it is necessary to protect a new industry to enable it to grow into a mature industry that can compete in world markets. The argument is based on the idea of dynamic comparative advantage, which can arise from learning-by-doing.

Learning-by-doing is a powerful engine of productivity growth, and comparative advantage evolves and changes because of on-the-job experience. But these facts do not justify protection.

Infant-industry argument
The argument that it is necessary to protect a new industry to enable it to grow into a mature industry that can compete in world markets.

Dumping
When a foreign firm sells its exports at a lower price than the price in the foreign firm's domestic market.

ECONOMICS *in* *the* NEWS

November 2, 2001

Lumber Duty Leaves Entire Sector in Red

The antidumping penalty the United States is slapping on Canadian lumber ensures that almost every major Canadian forest products company will lose money next year.

Combined with a 19.3% countervail penalty imposed last August, the new antidumping charge raises the total duty on Canadian lumber to about 32%.

The countervail is supposed to punish Canada for unfairly subsidizing its lumber industry. The antidumping penalty is supposed to punish Canadian producers for selling wood in the United States at below cost.

NATIONAL POST

Questions
1. What are the two complaints that the United States has against imports of Canadian lumber?
2. Why might Canada and the United States gain from free trade in lumber?
3. Who benefits and who loses from limiting Canadian exports of lumber to the United States?

 e Foundations **19.4**

The infant-industry argument is valid only if the benefits of learning-by-doing accrue not only to the owners and workers of the firms in the infant industry but also spill over to other industries and parts of the economy. For example, there are huge productivity gains from learning-by-doing in the manufacture of aircraft. But almost all of these gains benefit the stockholders and workers of aircraft producers. Because the people making the decisions, bearing the risk, and doing the work are the ones who benefit, they take the dynamic gains into account when they decide on the scale of their activities. In this case, almost no benefits spill over to other parts of the economy, so there is no need for government assistance to achieve an efficient outcome.

The Dumping Argument

Dumping occurs when a foreign firm sells its exports at a lower price than the price at which the product is normally sold in the foreign firm's domestic market. A firm that wants to gain a global monopoly might use dumping. In this case, the foreign firm sells its output in the domestic market at a price that is low enough to drive domestic firms out of business. When the domestic firms have gone, the foreign firm takes advantage of its monopoly position and charges a higher price for its product. Dumping is usually regarded as a justification for antidumping tariffs. For example, Canada has imposed antidumping tariffs on steel from 11 countries and the United States has imposed antidumping tariffs on softwood lumber from Canada.

But there are powerful reasons to resist the dumping argument for protection. First, it is virtually impossible to detect dumping. The test for dumping is whether a firm's export price is below the price it charges in its domestic market. But this test is a weak one because it can be rational for a firm to charge a lower price in markets in which the quantity demanded is highly sensitive to price and a higher price in a market in which demand is less price-sensitive.

Second, it is hard to think of a good that is produced by a natural global monopoly. So even if all the domestic firms in some industry were driven out of business, it would always be possible to find many alternative foreign sources of supply and to buy at prices determined in competitive markets.

Third, if a good or service were a truly global natural monopoly, the best way to deal with it would be by regulation—just as in the case of domestic monopolies. Such regulation would require international cooperation.

The three arguments for protection that we've just examined have an element of credibility. The counterarguments are in general stronger, so these three arguments do not make the case for protection. But they are not the only arguments that you might encounter. The many other arguments that are commonly heard are quite simply wrong. They are fatally flawed.

■ Other Arguments for Protection

Six other arguments for restricting international trade are that protection:

- Maintains national security
- Allows us to compete with cheap foreign labour
- Brings diversity and stability
- Penalizes lax environmental standards
- Protects national culture
- Prevents rich countries from exploiting developing countries

Maintains National Security

To maintain our national security, a country must protect its vital industries, such as food, water, and energy. In addition, it must protect those industries on which the vital industries rely for their raw materials and other intermediate inputs. This argument for protection does not withstand close scrutiny.

First, this argument is one for international isolation. A country can set health and safety standards without setting quotas or tariffs on imports. Second, if the case is made for boosting the production of vital goods and services, it is more efficient to achieve this outcome with a subsidy to the firms in the industries, which is financed out of taxes, than with a tariff or quota. A subsidy would keep the industries operating at the scale judged appropriate, and free international trade would keep the prices faced by consumers at their world market levels.

Allows Us to Compete with Cheap Foreign Labour

With the removal of protective tariffs in North America, prominent Texan Ross Perot said that free trade with Mexico under NAFTA would result in a "giant sucking sound" as jobs rushed from Canada and the United States into Mexico. (see the cartoon). Let's see what's wrong with this view.

The labour cost of a unit of output equals the wage rate divided by labour productivity. For example, if a Canadian autoworker earns $30 an hour and produces 15 units of output an hour, the average labour cost of a unit of output is $2. If a Mexican autoworker earns $3 an hour and produces 1 unit of output an hour, the average labour cost of a unit of output is $3. Other things remaining the same, the higher a worker's productivity, the higher is the worker's wage rate. High-wage workers have high productivity. Low-wage workers have low productivity.

"I don't know what the hell happened—one minute I'm at work in Flint, Michigan, then there's a giant sucking sound and suddenly here I am in Mexico."

SOURCE: © The New Yorker Collection 1993
Mick Stevens from cartoonbank.com. All rights reserved.

Although high-wage Canadian workers are more productive, on the average, than lower-wage Mexican workers, there are differences across industries. Canadian labour is relatively more productive in some activities than in others. For example, the productivity of Canadian workers in producing transportation equipment, telecommunication systems, and financial services is relatively higher than their productivity in the production of footwear and clothing. The activities in which Canadian workers are relatively more productive than their Mexican counterparts are those in which Canada has a comparative advantage. By engaging in free trade, increasing our production and increasing our exports of the goods and services in which we have a comparative advantage and decreasing our production and increasing our imports of the goods and services in which our trading partners have a comparative advantage, we can make both ourselves and the citizens of other countries better off.

Brings Diversity and Stability

A diversified investment portfolio is less risky than one that has all of its eggs in one basket. The same is true for an economy's production. A diversified economy fluctuates less than an economy that produces only one or two goods.

But big, rich, diversified economies like those of Canada, the United States, Japan, and Europe do not have this type of stability problem. Even a country such as Saudi Arabia that produces almost only one good (in this case, oil) can benefit from specializing in the activity at which it has a comparative advantage and then investing in a wide range of other countries to bring greater stability to its income and consumption.

Penalizes Lax Environmental Standards

A new argument for protection is that many poorer countries, such as Mexico, do not have the same environmental standards that we have, and because they are willing to pollute and we are not, we cannot compete with them without tariffs. So if they want free trade with the richer and "greener" countries, they must clean up their environments to our standards.

This argument for trade restrictions is weak. While everyone wants a clean environment, a poor country is less able than a rich one to devote resources to achieving this goal. The best hope for a better environment in the developing countries is rapid income growth through free trade. As their incomes grow, developing countries will have the means to match their desires to improve their environment. Also, because poor countries are willing to accept "dirty" activities (such as iron ore smelting and chemical production), it is easier for rich countries to achieve the high environmental standards that they seek.

Protects National Culture

In Canada, we frequently hear the national culture argument for protection. The expressed fear is that free trade in books, magazines, movies, and television programs means U.S. domination and the end of local culture. So, the reasoning continues, it is necessary to protect domestic "culture" industries from free international trade to ensure the survival of a national cultural identity.

Protection of these industries is common and takes the form of nontariff barriers. For example, regulations often require local content on radio and television broadcasting and in magazines.

The cultural identity argument for protection has no merit, and it is just one more example of rent seeking (see p. 472). Writers, publishers, and broadcasters want to limit foreign competition so that they can earn larger economic profits. There is no actual danger to national culture. In fact, many of the creators of so-called American cultural products are not Americans, but the talented citizens of other countries including Canadians, ensuring the survival of their national cultural identities in Hollywood! Also, if national culture is in danger, there is no surer way of helping it on its way out than by impoverishing the nation whose culture it is. And protection is an effective way of doing just that.

Prevents Rich Countries from Exploiting Developing Countries

Another new argument for protection is that international trade must be restricted to prevent the people of the rich industrial world from exploiting the poorer people of the developing countries, forcing them to work for slave wages.

Wage rates in some developing countries are indeed very low. But by trading with developing countries, we increase the demand for the goods that these countries produce, and, more significantly, we increase the demand for their labour. When the demand for labour in developing countries increases, the wage rate also increases. So far from exploiting people in developing countries, trade improves their opportunities and increases their incomes.

We have reviewed the arguments that are commonly heard in favour of protection and the counterarguments against them. There is one counterargument to protection that is general and quite overwhelming. Protection invites retaliation and can trigger a trade war. The best example of a trade war occurred during the Great Depression of the 1930s when the United States erected high barriers to trade. Country after country retaliated with its own tariff, and in a short period, world trade had almost disappeared. The costs to all countries were large and led to a renewed international resolve to avoid such self-defeating moves in the future. They also led to the creation of the General Agreement on Tariffs and Trade, and are the impetus behind the free-trade efforts of NAFTA, the European Union, and APEC.

■ Why Do Nations Restrict International Trade?

Why, despite all the arguments against protection, is trade restricted? There are two key reasons:

- Tariff revenue
- Rent seeking

Tariff Revenue

Government revenue is costly to collect. In developed countries, such as Canada, well-organized tax collection systems exist that can generate billions of dollars of income tax and sales tax revenues. These tax collection systems are made possible by the fact that most transactions are done by firms that are required by law to keep properly audited financial records. Without such records, the revenue collection agencies such as Revenue Canada would be severely hampered in their work. Even with audited financial accounts, some proportion of potential tax revenue is lost. Nonetheless, for industrialized countries, the income tax and sales taxes are the major sources of revenue and the tariff plays a very small role.

June 21, 2001

Pop Icons Bring Wealth into Canada

A new federal study shows a multi-million-dollar surge in Canadian cultural exports to the United States due to the success of artists such as Shania Twain, Alanis Morissette, Celine Dion, and Bryan Adams.

NATIONAL POST

Questions

1. Who benefits from restrictions on cultural imports?

2. Is the evidence that Canadian performers do not need protection likely to lead to a reduction in federal government restrictions on cultural imports?

 *e*Foundations **19.4**

But governments in developing countries have a difficult time collecting taxes from their citizens. Much economic activity takes place in an informal economy with few financial records. So these countries collect only a small amount of revenue from income taxes and sales taxes. The one area in which economic transactions are well recorded and audited is international trade. So this activity is an attractive base for tax collection in these countries and is used much more extensively than in the developed countries.

Rent Seeking

The major reason why international trade is restricted is because of rent seeking. **Rent seeking** is lobbying and other political activity that seeks to capture the gains from trade. Free trade increases consumption possibilities on the average, but not everyone shares in the gain and some people even lose. Free trade brings benefits to some and imposes costs on others, with total benefits exceeding total costs. It is the uneven distribution of costs and benefits that is the principal source of impediment to achieving more liberal international trade.

Suppose that we had a tariff on T-shirts, as in the example that you studied earlier in this chapter, and the tariff is removed. A few thousand (perhaps a few hundred) garment makers and their employees who must switch to some other activity would bear the cost of Canada moving to free trade. The millions of T-shirt buyers would reap the benefits of moving to free trade. The number of people who gain will, in general, be enormous in comparison with the number who lose. The gain per person will therefore be small. The loss per person to those who bear the loss will be large. Because the loss that falls on those who bear it is large, it will pay people who lose to incur considerable expense to lobby against free trade. On the other hand, it will not pay those who gain to organize to achieve free trade. The gain from trade for any one individual is too small for that individual to spend much time or money on a political organization to lobby for free trade. The loss from free trade will be seen as being so great by those bearing that loss that they will find it profitable to join a political organization to prevent free trade. Each group is weighing benefits against costs and choosing the best action for themselves. But the anti-free-trade group will undertake a larger quantity of political lobbying than the pro-free-trade group.

Compensating Losers

If, in total, the gains from free international trade exceed the losses, why don't those who gain compensate those who lose so that everyone will be in favour of free trade?

The main answer is that there are serious obstacles to providing direct and correctly calculated compensation. First, the cost of identifying the losers from free trade and of estimating the value of their losses would be enormous.

Second, it would never be clear whether a person who has fallen on hard times is suffering because of free trade or for other reasons, perhaps reasons that are largely under the control of the individual.

Third, some people who look like losers at one point in time may, in fact, end up gaining. A young garment worker who loses her job in Montreal and becomes a computer assembly worker in Ottawa resents the loss of work and the need to move. But a year or two later, looking back on events, she counts herself fortunate. She has made a move that has increased her income and given her greater job security.

Rent seeking
Lobbying and other political activity that seeks to capture the gains from trade.

Despite the absence of explicit compensation, those who lose from a change in protection do receive some compensation. But compensation is not restricted to the losers from changes in trade policy. Employment insurance provides substantial compensation to workers who lose their jobs regardless of the reason for the job loss. Inter-provincial transfers result in tax dollars collected in the rich and expanding provinces being spent in the poorer provinces.

Because we do not explicitly compensate the losers from free trade, protectionism remains a popular and permanent feature of our national economic and political life.

Eye On The GLOBAL ECONOMY

Competing with Low-Wage Nations

New Balance athletic shoes are made in two ways:

At a New Balance factory in Norridgewock, Maine, skilled workers who earn $14 an hour operate "see-and-sew" machines—$100,000 automated sewing machines guided by cameras. It costs $4 to make a pair of shoes in Maine.

At a subcontractor's factory in China, low-skilled women in their teens and early twenties who earn 40 cents an hour operate ordinary sewing machines. It costs $1.30 to make a pair of shoes in China.

New Balance is willing to pay the additional $2.70, which is about 4 percent of the retail price of a shoe, to produce shoes in the United States.

New Balance produces 25 percent of its output in the United States and the rest in Asia.

Nike, Reebok, and all the other makers of athletic shoes produce their entire output in Asia.

The Asian economies have a comparative advantage at making athletic shoes. Even when New Balance has invested heavily in equipment to make its U.S. work force much more productive than the Chinese work force, the labour cost alone of a pair of shoes is more than three times the cost in China. Add the capital cost to the equation, and New Balance pays much more for its shoes than do its competitors.

You would predict, and you'd be correct, that New Balance is not the most profitable shoemaker.

Study Guide pp. 291–292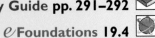

*e*Foundations 19.4

4 **Explain the arguments used to justify trade barriers and show why they are incorrect but also why some barriers are hard to remove.**

Practice Problems 19.4

1. Japan sets quotas on imports of rice. California rice growers would like to export more rice to Japan. What are Japan's arguments for restricting imports of Californian rice? Are these arguments correct? Who loses from this restriction in trade?

2. In June 2001, Canada imposed tariffs as high as 45 percent on steel imports from nine countries that allegedly had been exporting steel to Canada at prices below their cost of production. What is the argument that Canada would use to justify this action? Who wins from this restriction? Who loses?

3. The United States maintains a quota on imports of textiles. What is the argument for this quota? Is this argument flawed? If so, explain why.

Exercises 19.4

1. Labour unions argued against NAFTA. What was their argument against a free trade zone in North America? What was wrong with their argument? Whom did the unions see as the loser from NAFTA?

2. The Summit of the Americas in April 2001 decided to extend NAFTA to cover all of the Americas. Why would Canada and the United States support this extension? Who will be the winners? Who will be the losers?

3. Hong Kong has never restricted trade. What gains has Hong Kong reaped by unilaterally adopting free trade with all nations? Is there any argument for restricted trade that might have benefited Hong Kong?

Solutions to Practice Problems 19.4

1. Japan has used a number of arguments for low quotas on rice imports. Some of these are that Japanese consumers can get a better quality of rice from Japanese producers and that the quota limits competition faced by Japanese producers. The arguments are not correct. If Japanese consumers do not like the quality of Californian rice, they will not buy it. The quota does limit competition, but the Japanese quota allows Japanese farmers to use their land less efficiently. The big losers are the Japanese consumers because the price of rice in Japan is about three times the price paid by U.S. consumers.

2. The argument for a tariff on steel imports is that foreign producers dump steel on the Canadian market. With antidumping tariffs, Canadian producers will face less competition and Canadian jobs will be saved. Workers in the Canadian steel industry and owners of steel companies will win at the expense of Canadian buyers of steel and products containing steel.

3. The argument for a quota on U.S. imports of textiles is that textile workers in developing countries are paid low wages and so U.S. textile jobs would be lost if the quota was removed. This employment argument is flawed because the United States does not have a comparative advantage in the manufacture of textiles. A quota allows the U.S. textile industry to continue producing. With free trade in textiles, the U.S. textile industry would be smaller.

CHAPTER CHECKPOINT

Key Points

1 **Describe the patterns and trends in international trade.**

- Large flows of trade take place between countries, most of which is in manufactured goods exchanged among rich industrialized countries.
- Since 1960, the volume of Canada's international trade has increased dramatically.

2 **Explain why nations engage in international trade and why trade benefits all nations.**

- When opportunity costs between countries diverge, comparative advantage enables countries to gain from international trade.
- By increasing production of goods and services in which it has a comparative advantage and then trading some of the increased output, a country can consume at points outside its production possibility frontier.

3 **Explain how trade barriers reduce international trade.**

- Countries restrict international trade by imposing tariffs and nontariff barriers such as quotas.
- Trade restrictions raise the domestic price of imported goods and lower the volume of imports.

4 **Explain the arguments used to justify trade barriers and show why they are incorrect but also why some barriers are hard to remove.**

- The arguments that protection is necessary to maintain employment, for infant industries, and to prevent dumping are weak.
- Arguments that protection maintains national security, allows us to compete with cheap foreign labour, makes the economy diversified and stable, is needed to offset the costs of environmental policies, and protects national culture are fatally flawed.
- Trade is restricted because tariffs raise government revenue and because protection brings a small loss to a large number of people and a large gain per person to a small number of people.

Key Terms

Balance of trade, 453
Dumping, 468
Dynamic comparative advantage, 460
Infant-industry argument, 467
Learning-by-doing, 460
Nontariff barrier, 462
Quota, 464
Rent seeking, 472
Tariff, 462

FIGURE I

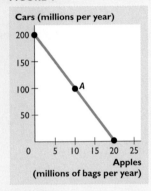

FIGURE I

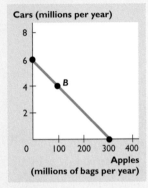

FIGURE 2

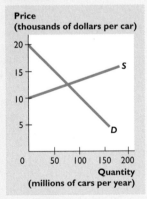

FIGURE 3

Exercises

1. Suppose that with no international trade between Canada and Brazil, Figure 1 shows Canada's production possibilities and the quantities of apples and cars produced (point *A*). Figure 2 shows Brazil's production possibilities and the quantities of coffee and cars produced (point *B*).
    a. What is the opportunity cost of a bag of apples in Canada?
    b. What is the opportunity cost of a bag of apples in Brazil?
    c. Which country has a comparative advantage in producing apples?
    d. Which country has a comparative advantage in producing cars?
    e. With free trade between Brazil and Canada, what does Canada import from Brazil and what does it export to Brazil? Explain your answer.
    f. Does Brazil gain from trade with Canada? Why or why not?

2. When free trade occurs in Exercise 1, the world price of a bag of apples is 1/25th of a car. If Brazil completely specializes in apples and exports half of it to Canada:
    a. Show on Figure 2 the quantities of the two goods that Brazil consumes.
    b. Show on Figure 1 the quantities of the two goods that Canada consumes.

3. Figure 3 shows the car market in Brazil when Brazil places no restriction on imports of cars. The world price of a car is $10,000. If the government of Brazil introduces a 20 percent tariff on car imports, what will be:
    a. The price of a car in Brazil?
    b. The quantity of cars imported into Brazil?
    c. The quantity of cars produced in Brazil?
    d. The government's tariff revenue?

4. Suppose that in Exercise 3, the Brazilian government introduces a quota of 50 million cars a year. Show on the figure:
    a. The price of a car in Brazil.
    b. The quantity of cars imported into Brazil.
    c. The quantity of cars produced in Brazil.

5. In the 1950s, Ford and General Motors established a small car-producing industry in Australia and argued for a high tariff on car imports. The tariff has remained through the years. In 2000, the tariff was cut from 22.5 percent to 15 percent. What would supporters of the high tariff argue that it was intended to achieve? Is the tariff the best way to achieve these goals?

6. The Canadian government argues against free trade in magazines and movies. Why is the Canadian government concerned about the quantity of U.S. magazines and movies that Canadians see? What is wrong with the Canadian government's argument? Who in Canada gains from the government's argument?

7. The U.S. government imposes a quota on lamb imports from New Zealand and Australia. New Zealand and Australia have lobbied the U.S. government for an increase in the quota. What is the argument put forward by the New Zealand and Australian governments? What is the counterargument put forward by the U.S. government? Which argument is really an example of rent seeking?

International Finance

CHAPTER CHECKLIST

When you have completed your study of this chapter,
you will be able to:

1 Describe a country's balance of payments accounts and explain what determines the amount of international borrowing and lending.

2 Explain how the exchange rate is determined and why it fluctuates.

In 2000, Canada's exports to the rest of the world exceeded imports by more than $50 billion. But for more than 15 years during the 1980s and 1990s, Canada paid more for imported goods and services than it earned from exporting goods and services. How can a nation spend more than it earns? What determines the balance of international payments?

From 1970 through 1986, the Canadian dollar fell from equality with the U.S. dollar to 72 U.S. cents. The Canadian dollar then rose to 87 U.S. cents in 1991. But since 1991, the Canadian dollar has fallen and in the fall of 2001, it was worth only 63 U.S. cents. Why is the value of our dollar so volatile? Is there anything we can do or should do to stabilize its value?

In this chapter, you are going to learn about international finance. You will discover how nations keep their international accounts, what determines the balance of payments, and how the value of the dollar is determined in the foreign exchange market.

20.1 FINANCING INTERNATIONAL TRADE

When Sony Stores in Canada imports CD players from Japan, it does not pay for them with Canadian dollars—it uses Japanese yen. When an Irish railroad company buys a locomotive from GM in London, Ontario, it uses Canadian dollars. Whenever we buy things from another country, we use the currency of that country to make the transaction. It doesn't make any difference what the item being traded is—it might be a consumption good, a capital good, a building, or a firm.

We'll study the markets in which money—different types of currency—is bought and sold. But first we'll look at the scale of international trading and borrowing and lending and at the way in which we keep our records of these transactions. Such records are called the balance of payments accounts.

■ Balance of Payments Accounts

Balance of payments accounts
The accounts in which a nation records its international trading, borrowing, and lending.

A country's **balance of payments accounts** record its international trading, borrowing, and lending. There are in fact three balance of payments accounts:

- Current account
- Capital account
- Official settlements account

Current account
Record of international receipts and payments—current account balance equals exports minus imports, plus net interest and transfers received from abroad.

Capital account
Record of foreign investment in Canada minus Canadian investment going abroad.

Official settlements account
Record of the change in Canadian official reserves.

Canadian official reserves
The government's holdings of foreign currency.

The **current account** records receipts from the sale of goods and services to other countries (exports), minus payments for goods and services bought from other countries (imports), plus the net amount of interest and transfers (such as foreign aid payments) received from and paid to other countries. The **capital account** records foreign investment in Canada minus Canadian investment abroad. The **official settlements account** records the change in Canada's official reserves. **Canadian official reserves** are the government's holdings of foreign currency. If Canadian official reserves increase, the official settlements account balance is negative. The reason is that holding foreign money is like investing abroad. Canadian investment abroad is a minus item in the capital account and in the official settlements account. (By the same reasoning, if Canadian official reserves decrease, the official settlements account balance is positive.)

The sum of the balances on the three accounts always equals zero. That is, a country with a current account deficit must either borrow more from abroad than it lends abroad or use its official reserves to cover the deficit.

Table 20.1 shows the Canadian balance of payments accounts in 2000. Items in the current account and capital account that provide foreign currency to Canada have a plus sign; items that cost Canada foreign currency have a minus sign. The table shows that in 2000, Canada's exports exceeded its imports by $53 billion and the current account surplus was $27 billion. This surplus provided us with the funds to lend to the rest of the world. The rest of the world paid for its imports of Canadian goods and services in excess of Canada's imports from the rest of the world by borrowing from Canada. The capital account tells us how much we lent. We lent $129 billion (Canadian investment abroad) but we borrowed $114 billion abroad (foreign investment in Canada). Our measured net lending to the rest of the world was $29 billion. Measurement error (recorded in the balance of payments accounts as a statistical discrepancy) was –$7 billion, and our official reserves increased by $5 billion.

Eye On The PAST

Canada's Balance of Payments

The numbers in Table 20.1 provide a snapshot of Canada's balance of payments in 2000. The figure puts this snapshot into perspective by showing how the balance of payments evolved from 1980 to 2000.

(Because the economy grows and the price level rises, changes in the dollar value of the balance of payments do not convey much information. To remove the influences of growth and inflation, the figure shows the balance of payments as a percentage of nominal GDP.)

The capital account balance is almost a mirror image of the current account balance because the official settlements balance is very small in comparison with the balances on

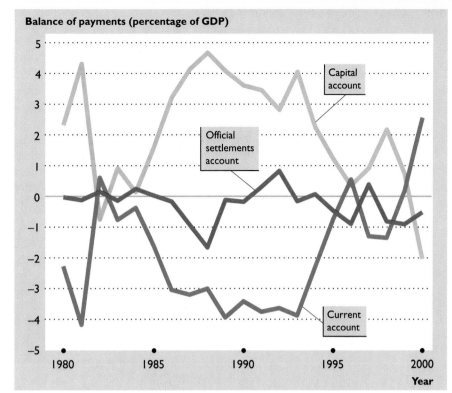

SOURCE: Bank of Canada.

these other two accounts. A large current account deficit emerged from 1985 to 1993. But it decreased after

that and turned into a current account surplus in 2000—the first surplus in nearly 20 years.

TABLE 20.1

Canada's Balance of Payments Accounts in 2000

Current account	(billions of dollars)
Exports of goods and services	+478
Imports of goods and services	−425
Net transfers	+1
Net interest payments	−27
Current account balance	+27
Capital account	
Foreign investment in Canada	+114
Canadian investment abroad	−129
Statistical discrepancy	−7
Capital account balance	−22
Official settlements account	
Official settlements account balance	−5

SOURCE: Bank of Canada.

You might better understand the balance of payments accounts and the way in which they are linked together if you think about the income and expenditure, borrowing and lending, and bank account of an individual.

Individual Analogy

An individual's current account records the income from supplying the services of factors of production and the expenditure on goods and services. Consider, for example, Joanne. She worked in 2000 and earned an income of $25,000. Joanne has $10,000 worth of investments that earned her interest income of $1,000. Joanne's current account shows an income of $26,000. Joanne spent $18,000 buying goods and services for consumption. She also bought a new house, which cost her $60,000. So Joanne's total expenditure was $78,000. The difference between her expenditure and income is $52,000 ($78,000 minus $26,000). This amount is Joanne's current account deficit.

To pay for expenditure of $52,000 in excess of her income, Joanne has to use the money that she has in the bank or she has to take out a loan. In fact, Joanne took a mortgage of $50,000 to help buy her house. This mortgage was the only borrowing that Joanne did, so her capital account surplus was $50,000. With a current account deficit of $52,000 and a capital account surplus of $50,000, Joanne is still $2,000 short. She got that $2,000 from her own bank account. Her cash holdings decreased by $2,000.

Joanne's income from her work is analogous to a country's income from its exports. Her income from her investments is analogous to a country's interest from foreigners. Her purchases of goods and services, including her house, are analogous to a country's imports. Joanne's mortgage—borrowing from someone else—is analogous to a country's borrowing from the rest of the world. The change in her bank account is analogous to the change in the country's official reserves.

■ Borrowers and Lenders, Debtors and Creditors

A country that is borrowing more from the rest of the world than it is lending to it is called a **net borrower.** Similarly, a **net lender** is a country that is lending more to the rest of the world than it is borrowing from it.

Canada is a net borrower and has been one for most of the past 55 years. During the 55 years between the end of World War II and 2000, Canada was a net lender in only 14 years when it had a surplus on its current account and a deficit on its capital account. Most of these years were during the late 1940s and in 1982, 1996, 1999, and 2000.

Most countries are net borrowers like Canada usually has been. But a small number of countries, including Japan and oil-rich Saudi Arabia, are net lenders. These countries' exports exceed their imports, providing them with the funds to lend to and invest in other nations.

A net borrower might be reducing its net assets held in the rest of the world, or it might be going deeper into debt. A nation's total stock of foreign investment determines whether the nation is a debtor or creditor. A **debtor nation** is a country that during its entire history has borrowed more from the rest of the world than it has lent to it. It has a stock of outstanding debt to the rest of the world that exceeds the stock of its own claims on the rest of the world. A **creditor nation** is a country that has invested more in the rest of the world than other countries have invested in it.

Net borrower
A country that is borrowing more from the rest of the world than it is lending to the rest of the world.

Net lender
A country that is lending more to the rest of the world than it is borrowing from the rest of the world.

Debtor nation
A country that during its entire history has borrowed more from the rest of the world than it has lent to it.

Creditor nation
A country that during its entire history has invested more in the rest of the world than other countries have invested in it.

Flows and Stocks

At the heart of the distinction between a net borrower and a net lender on the one hand and between a debtor nation and a creditor nation on the other hand is the distinction between flows and stocks, which you have encountered many times in your study of macroeconomics. Borrowing and lending are flows—amounts borrowed or lent per unit of time. Debts are stocks—total amounts owed at a point in time. The flow of borrowing and lending changes the stock of debt.

Canada is a debtor nation. Through the nineteenth century, we borrowed from Europe to finance our westward expansion, the building of our railroads, and the development of our industries. We paid off our debt and became a creditor nation for most of the twentieth century. But following a string of current account deficits, we became a debtor nation again in 1989.

The total stock of Canadian borrowing from the rest of the world has exceeded Canadian lending to the rest of the world. The largest debtor nations are the capital-hungry developing countries (as Canada was during the nineteenth century). The international debt of these countries grew from less than a third to more than a half of their Gross Domestic Product during the 1980s and created what was called the "Third World debt crisis."

Should we be concerned that Canada is a net borrower? The answer to this question depends mainly on what the net borrower is doing with the borrowed money. If borrowing is financing investment that in turn is generating economic growth and higher income, then borrowing is not a problem. If the borrowed money is being used to finance consumption, then higher interest payments are being incurred, and consequently, consumption will eventually have to be reduced. In this case, the more a country borrows and the longer the borrowing goes on, the greater is the reduction in consumption that will eventually be necessary. We'll see below whether Canada is borrowing for investment or for consumption.

■ Current Account Balance

What determines a country's current account balance and net foreign borrowing? You've seen that net exports (NX) is the main item in the current account. We can define the current account balance (CAB) as:

$$CAB = NX + \text{Net interest and transfers from abroad.}$$

Fluctuations in net exports are the main source of fluctuations in the current account balance. Net interest and transfers from abroad are small and have trends but do not fluctuate much. So we can study the current account balance by looking at what determines net exports.

■ Net Exports

The government budget and private saving and investment determine net exports. To see how they determine net exports, we need to recall some of the things that we learned about the National Accounts in Chapter 5. Table 20.2 will refresh your memory and summarize some calculations.

■ **TABLE 20.2**

Net Exports, the Government Budget, Saving, and Investment

	Symbols and equations	Canada in 2000 (billions of dollars)
(a) Variables		
Exports	X	479
Imports	M	426
Investment	I	191
Saving	S	207
Government expenditure	G	218
Net taxes	T	255
(b) Balances		
Net exports	$X - M$	479 − 426 = 53
Private sector balance	$S - I$	207 − 191 = 16
Government sector balance	$T - G$	255 − 218 = 37
(c) Relation among balances		
National accounts	$Y = C + I + G + X - M = C + S + T$	
Rearranging:	$X - M = S - I + T - G$	
Net exports	$X - M$	53
Equals:		
Private sector balance	$S - I$	16
Plus		
Government sector balance	$T - G$	37

SOURCE: Statistics Canada.

Private sector balance
Saving minus investment.

Government sector balance
Net taxes minus government expenditure on goods and services.

Part (a) of Table 20.2 lists the national income variables that are needed, with their symbols. Part (b) defines three balances. *Net exports* are exports of goods and services minus imports of goods and services.

The **private sector balance** is saving minus investment. If saving exceeds investment, a private sector surplus is lent to other sectors. If investment exceeds saving, borrowing from other sectors finances a private sector deficit.

The **government sector balance** is equal to net taxes minus government expenditure on goods and services for all levels of government. If that number is positive, a government sector surplus is lent to other sectors; if that number is negative, borrowing from other sectors finances a government deficit.

Part (b) of Table 20.2 shows the values of these balances for Canada in 2000. As you can see, exports of $479 billion and imports of $426 billion generated a surplus of $53 billion. The private sector saved $207 billion and invested $191 billion, so its balance was a $16 billion surplus. The government sector's revenue from net taxes was $255 billion, and it purchased $218 billion worth of goods and services. The government sector balance was a $37 billion surplus.

Part (c) of Table 20.2 shows the relationship among the three balances. From the national accounts, we know that real GDP, Y, is the sum of consumption expenditure, C; investment, I; government expenditure, G; and net exports, $X - M$. Real GDP also equals the sum of consumption expenditure; saving, S; and net taxes, T. Rearranging these equations tells us that net exports equals $(S - I)$, the private sector balance, plus $(T - G)$, the government sector balance. In 2000, net exports were $53 billion, which is the sum of two surpluses: $(S - I)$ of $16 billion and $(T - G)$ of $37 billion.

■ Has Canada Borrowed for Consumption or Investment?

During the 1980s and 1990s, net exports accumulated to minus $300 billion and we borrowed this amount from abroad. Did we borrow for consumption or investment? In 2000, private investment in buildings, plant, and equipment was $191 billion. Government investment in public structures such as highways and schools was $25 billion. All this investment added to the nation's capital and much of it increased productivity. Governments also spent on education and health care services, which increased human capital.

Our international borrowing is financing private and public investment, not consumption.

Eye On The GLOBAL ECONOMY

Current Account Balances Around the World

The outstanding feature of the global current account situation is the massive U.S. current account deficit. No other country has a deficit remotely similar to that of the United States.

The next largest deficits are those of developing countries in the Western Hemisphere—the nations of Latin America.

Canada has usually had a current account deficit that was relatively small by global standards. In 2000, Canada had a surplus.

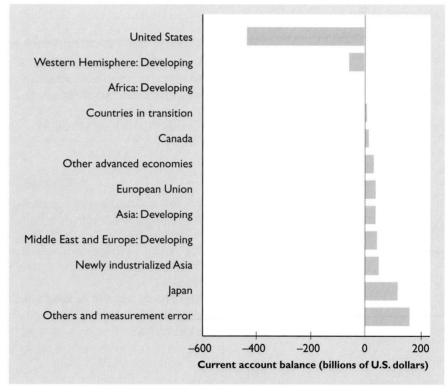

SOURCE: International Monetary Fund, *World Economic Outlook*, October 2000.

Japan and the newly industrialized Asian economies have current account surpluses, as do all other groups of countries.

Study Guide pp. 298–302

*e*Foundations **20.1**

1 Describe a country's balance of payments accounts and explain what determines the amount of international borrowing and lending.

Practice Problem 20.1

It is 2004 and the Canadian economy records the following transactions: Imports of goods and services, $200 billion; interest paid to the rest of the world, $50 billion; interest received from the rest of the world, $40 billion; decrease in Canadian official reserves, $1 billion; government sector balance, $20 billion; saving, $180 billion; investment, $200 billion; net transfers, zero.

a. Calculate the current account balance, the capital account balance, the official settlements account balance, and exports of goods and services.

b. Is Canada a debtor or a creditor nation in 2004?

c. If government expenditure increases by $10 billion, what happens to the current account balance?

Exercise 20.1

It is 2005 and the Canadian economy records the following transactions: Exports of goods and services, $180 billion; interest paid to the rest of the world, $55 billion; interest received from the rest of the world, $35 billion; decrease in Canadian official reserves, $1 billion; government sector balance, $20 billion; saving, $180 billion; investment, $200 billion; net transfers, zero.

a. Calculate the current account balance, the capital account balance, the official settlements account balance, and imports of goods and services.

b. Has Canada become a larger or smaller debtor or creditor nation in 2005?

c. If net taxes increase by $10 billion, what happens to the capital account balance?

Solution to Practice Problem 20.1

a. The current account balance equals net exports plus net interest income (–$10 billion) plus net transfers (zero). Net exports equal the government sector balance ($20 billion) plus the private sector balance. The private sector balance equals saving ($180 billion) minus investment ($200 billion), which is –$20 billion. So net exports are zero, and the current account balance is –$10 billion.

   The capital account balance is the negative of the sum of the current account and official settlements accounts balances, which is $9 billion.

   The official settlements account balance is a surplus of $1 billion. Exports of goods and services equal net exports (zero) plus imports ($200 billion) and so are $200 billion.

b. Canada is a debtor nation in 2004. You can determine this fact because it pays out more in interest to the rest of the world than it receives from the rest of the world.

c. If government expenditure increases by $10 billion, the government sector balance decreases. Net exports decrease, and the current account deficit increases.

20.2 THE EXCHANGE RATE

When we buy foreign goods or invest in another country, we have to obtain some of that country's currency to make the transaction. When foreigners buy Canadian-produced goods or invest in Canada, they have to obtain some Canadian dollars. We get foreign currency, and foreigners get Canadian dollars in the foreign exchange market. The **foreign exchange market** is the market in which the currency of one country is exchanged for the currency of another. The foreign exchange market is not a place like a downtown flea market or produce market. The market is made up of thousands of people: importers and exporters, banks, and specialists in the buying and selling of foreign exchange, called foreign exchange brokers. The foreign exchange market opens on Monday morning in Hong Kong, which is still Sunday evening in Toronto. As the day advances, markets open in Singapore, Tokyo, Bahrain, Frankfurt, London, New York, Toronto, and San Francisco. As the West Coast markets close, Hong Kong is only an hour away from opening for the next day of business. Dealers around the world are in continual contact, and on a typical day in 2000, $1.5 trillion U.S. changed hands.

The price at which one currency exchanges for another is called a **foreign exchange rate.** For example, in October 2001, one Canadian dollar bought 65 U.S. cents. The exchange rate was 65 U.S. cents per Canadian dollar. We can also express the exchange rate in terms of Canadian dollars per U.S. dollar, which in October 2001 was $1.54 Canadian per U.S. dollar.

Currency appreciation is the rise in the value of one currency in terms of another currency. For example, if the value of the Canadian dollar rises from 65 to 67 U.S. cents, the Canadian dollar appreciates by a bit more than 3 percent.

Foreign exchange market
The market in which the currency of one country is exchanged for the currency of another.

Foreign exchange rate
The price at which one currency exchanges for another.

Currency appreciation
The rise in the value of one currency in terms of another currency.

Eye On The PAST

The Canadian Dollar Since 1970

The figure shows the exchange rate of the Canadian dollar in terms of the U.S. dollar from 1970 to 2000. The Canadian dollar has depreciated from one U.S. dollar to 63 U.S. cents over this period. But the Canadian dollar appreciated from 1986 to 1991.

The low Canadian dollar makes Canadian exports cheaper but it makes the prices that Canadians pay for imports higher.

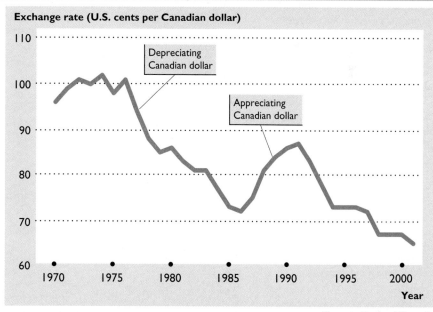

SOURCE: Bank of Canada.

Currency depreciation
The fall in the value of one currency in terms of another currency.

Currency depreciation is the fall in the value of one currency in terms of another currency. For example, if the Canadian dollar falls from 65 to 63 U.S. cents, the Canadian dollar depreciates by about 3 percent. When the Canadian dollar depreciates, the U.S. dollar appreciates against the Canadian dollar.

Why does the Canadian dollar fluctuate in value? To answer this question, we need to understand the forces that determine the exchange rate.

The exchange rate is a price—the price of one country's money in terms of another country's money. And like all prices, demand and supply determine the exchange rate. So to understand the forces that determine the exchange rate, we need to study demand and supply in the foreign exchange market.

■ Demand in the Foreign Exchange Market

The quantity of Canadian dollars demanded in the foreign exchange market is the amount that traders plan to buy during a given time period at a given exchange rate. This quantity depends on many factors but the main ones are:

- The exchange rate
- Interest rates in Canada and other countries
- The expected future exchange rate

Let's look first at the relationship between the quantity of Canadian dollars demanded in the foreign exchange market and the exchange rate.

■ The Law of Demand for Foreign Exchange

People do not buy Canadian dollars because they enjoy having them. The demand for dollars is a *derived demand*. People demand Canadian dollars so that they can buy Canadian-made goods and services (Canadian exports). They also demand Canadian dollars so that they can buy Canadian assets such as bank accounts, bonds, stocks, businesses, and real estate. Nevertheless, the law of demand applies to dollars just as it does to anything else that people value.

Other things remaining the same, the higher the exchange rate, the smaller is the quantity of Canadian dollars demanded. For example, if the price of the Canadian dollar rises from 65 U.S. cents to 70 U.S. cents but nothing else changes, the quantity of dollars that people plan to buy decreases. Why does the exchange rate influence the quantity of dollars demanded? There are two separate reasons, both related to the two sources of the derived demand for dollars:

- Exports effect
- Expected profit effect

Exports Effect

The larger the value of Canadian exports, the larger is the quantity of dollars demanded. But the value of Canadian exports depends on the exchange rate. The lower the exchange rate, other things remaining the same, the cheaper are Canadian-made goods and services to people in the rest of the world, the more Canada exports, and the greater is the quantity of dollars demanded to pay for them.

Expected Profit Effect

The larger the expected profit from holding Canadian dollars, the greater is the quantity of dollars demanded in the foreign exchange market. But expected profit depends on the exchange rate. The lower the exchange rate, other things remaining the same, the larger is the expected profit from buying dollars and the greater

June 20, 2001

Weak Dollar Main Boost to Economy, Study Says

OTTAWA—The weak dollar has done more to boost exports to the United States than the free trade agreement, a new Industry Canada study says, but it warns against becoming too dependent on the weak dollar.

It states: "We cannot continue to rely upon a weak Canadian dollar for maintaining our cost competitiveness in the U.S. market."

Instead, it argues, Canada must increase its competitiveness in New Economy industries in order to close the large income gap between it and the United States and not to lose ground there to increasing competition from Mexico and China.

NATIONAL POST

Questions
1. How would the weak Canadian dollar account for Canada's high exports to the United States?
2. How could relying on the weak Canadian dollar work to the disadvantage of Canadian firms and industries over the longer term?

 *e*Foundations **20.2**

FIGURE 20.1
The Demand for Dollars

*e*Foundations **20.2**

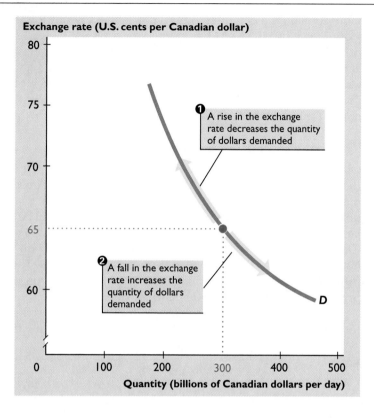

Other things remaining the same, the quantity of dollars that people plan to buy depends on the exchange rate.

❶ If the exchange rate rises, the quantity of dollars demanded decreases and there is a movement up along the demand curve for dollars.

❷ If the exchange rate falls, the quantity of dollars demanded increases and there is a movement down along the demand curve for dollars.

is the quantity of dollars demanded on the foreign exchange market.

To understand this effect, suppose that people think the Canadian dollar will be worth 70 U.S. cents by the end of the month. If a Canadian dollar costs 65 U.S. cents today, people with U.S. dollars will buy Canadian dollars. But a person who thinks that the Canadian dollar will still be worth 65 U.S. cents at the end of the month does not buy dollars. Now suppose that the exchange rate falls to 60 U.S. cents per Canadian dollar. More people think that they can profit from buying Canadian dollars, so the quantity of dollars demanded increases.

Figure 20.1 shows the demand curve for Canadian dollars in the foreign exchange market. Other things remaining the same, when the foreign exchange rate rises, the quantity of dollars demanded decreases and there is a movement up along the demand curve, as shown by the arrow. And when the exchange rate falls, the quantity of dollars demanded increases and there is movement down along the demand curve, as shown by the arrow.

■ Changes in the Demand for Dollars

A change in any other influence on the quantity of Canadian dollars that people plan to buy in the foreign exchange market brings a change in the demand for dollars and the demand curve for dollars shifts. Demand either increases or decreases. These other influences are:

- Interest rates in Canada and other countries
- The expected future exchange rate

Interest Rates in Canada and Other Countries

People and businesses buy financial assets to make a return. The higher the interest rate that people can earn on Canadian assets compared with foreign assets, the more Canadian assets they buy. What matters is not the level of the Canadian interest rate but the Canadian interest rate minus the foreign interest rate, a gap called the **Canadian interest rate differential.** If the Canadian interest rate rises and the foreign interest rate remains constant, the Canadian interest rate differential increases. The larger the Canadian interest rate differential, the greater is the demand for Canadian assets and the greater is the demand for Canadian dollars on the foreign exchange market.

Canadian interest rate differential
The Canadian interest rate minus the foreign interest rate.

The Expected Future Exchange Rate

Other things remaining the same, the higher the expected future exchange rate, the greater is the demand for dollars. To see why, suppose you are the finance manager for a multinational corporation. The exchange rate is 65 U.S. cents per dollar, and you think that by the end of the month, it will be 70 U.S. cents per dollar. You use $US 650,000 today to buy $C 1,000,000. At the end of the month, the Canadian dollar is 70 U.S. cents, as you predicted and you sell the $C 1,000,000. You get $US 700,000. You've made a profit of $US 50,000. The higher the expected future exchange rate, other things remaining the same, the greater is the expected profit and the greater is the demand for dollars.

Figure 20.2 summarizes the above discussion of the influences on the demand for Canadian dollars. A rise in the Canadian interest rate differential or a rise in

---

■ **FIGURE 20.2**

Changes in the Demand for Dollars

*e*Foundations **20.2**

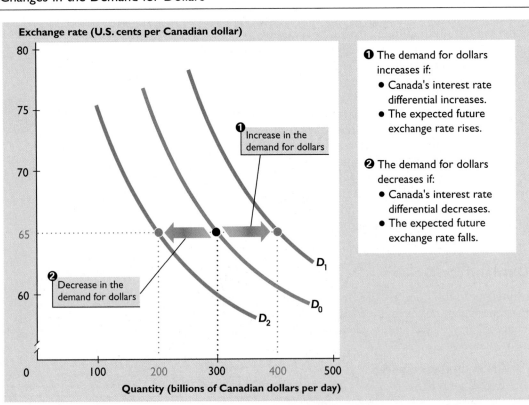

The demand for dollars increases if:
- Canada's interest rate differential increases.
- The expected future exchange rate rises.

The demand for dollars decreases if:
- Canada's interest rate differential decreases.
- The expected future exchange rate falls.

the expected future exchange rate increases the demand for dollars and shifts the demand curve rightward from D_0 to D_1. A fall in the Canadian interest rate differential or a fall in the expected future exchange rate decreases the demand for dollars and shifts the demand curve leftward from D_0 to D_2.

■ Supply in the Foreign Exchange Market

The quantity of Canadian dollars supplied in the foreign exchange market is the amount that traders plan to sell during a given time period at a given exchange rate. This quantity depends on many factors but the main ones are:

- The exchange rate
- Interest rates in Canada and other countries
- The expected future exchange rate

Let's look first at the relationship between the quantity of Canadian dollars supplied in the foreign exchange market and the exchange rate.

■ The Law of Supply of Foreign Exchange

Traders supply dollars in the foreign exchange market when people and businesses buy other currencies. And they buy other currencies so that they can buy foreign-made goods and services (Canadian imports). They also supply dollars and buy foreign currencies so that they can buy foreign assets such as bank accounts, bonds, stocks, businesses, and real estate. The law of supply applies to dollars just as it does to anything else that people plan to sell.

Other things remaining the same, the higher the exchange rate, the greater is the quantity of Canadian dollars supplied in the foreign exchange market. For example, if the price of the Canadian dollar rises from 65 U.S. cents to 70 U.S. cents but nothing else changes, the quantity of Canadian dollars that people plan to sell in the foreign exchange market increases. Why does the exchange rate influence the quantity of dollars supplied?

There are two reasons, and they parallel the two reasons on the demand side of the market:

- Imports effect
- Expected profit effect

Imports Effect

The larger the value of Canadian imports, the larger is the quantity of foreign currency demanded to pay for these imports. And when people buy foreign currency, they supply Canadian dollars. So the larger the value of Canadian imports, the greater is the quantity of Canadian dollars supplied on the foreign exchange market. But the value of Canadian imports depends on the exchange rate. The higher the exchange rate, with everything else the same, the cheaper are foreign-produced goods and services to Canadians, the more Canada imports, and the greater is the quantity of Canadian dollars supplied on the foreign exchange market.

Expected Profit Effect

The larger the expected profit from holding a foreign currency, the greater is the quantity of that currency demanded and the greater is the quantity of Canadian dollars supplied in the foreign exchange market. But the expected profit from holding a foreign currency depends on the exchange rate. The higher the

Other things remaining the same, the quantity of dollars that people plan to sell depends on the exchange rate.

❶ If the exchange rate rises, the quantity of dollars supplied increases and there is a movement up along the supply curve for dollars.

❷ If the exchange rate falls, the quantity of dollars supplied decreases and there is a movement down along the supply curve for dollars.

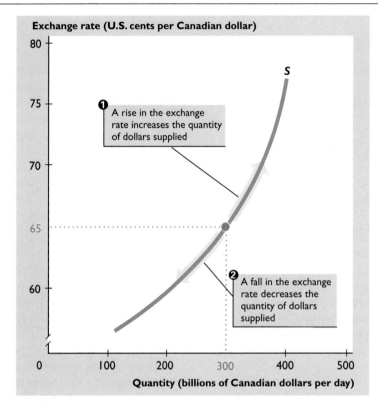

exchange rate, other things remaining the same, the larger is the expected profit from selling Canadian dollars and the greater is the quantity of dollars supplied on the foreign exchange market.

For the two reasons we've just reviewed, other things remaining the same, when the foreign exchange rate rises, the quantity of dollars supplied increases and when the foreign exchange rate falls, the quantity of dollars supplied decreases. Figure 20.3 shows the supply curve for Canadian dollars in the foreign exchange market. When the foreign exchange rate rises, other things remaining the same, there is an increase in the quantity of dollars supplied and a movement up along the supply curve, as shown by the arrow. When the exchange rate falls, other things remaining the same, there is a decrease in the quantity of dollars supplied and a movement down along the supply curve, as shown by the arrow.

■ Changes in the Supply of Dollars

A change in any other influence on the quantity of Canadian dollars that people plan to sell in the foreign exchange market brings a change in the supply of dollars and the supply curve for dollars shifts. Supply either increases or decreases. These other influences on supply parallel the other influences on demand but have exactly the opposite effects. These influences are:

- Interest rates in Canada and other countries
- The expected future exchange rate

Interest Rates in Canada and Other Countries

The larger the Canadian interest rate differential, the smaller is the demand for foreign assets and the smaller is the supply of Canadian dollars on the foreign exchange market.

The Expected Future Exchange Rate

Other things remaining the same, the higher the expected future exchange rate, the smaller is the supply of dollars. To see why, suppose that the Canadian dollar is trading at 65 U.S. cents per dollar today and you think that by the end of the month, the dollar will trade at 70 U.S. cents per dollar. You were planning on selling Canadian dollars today, but you decide to hold off and wait until the end of the month. If you supply dollars today, you get only 65 U.S. cents per dollar. But at the end of the month, if the dollar is worth 70 U.S. cents as you predict, you'll get 70 U.S. cents for each dollar you supply. You'll make a profit of 5 U.S. cents per dollar. So the higher the expected future exchange rate, other things remaining the same, the smaller is the expected profit from selling Canadian dollars today and the smaller is the supply of Canadian dollars today.

Figure 20.4 summarizes the above discussion of the influences on the supply of Canadian dollars. A fall in the Canadian interest rate differential or a fall in the expected future exchange rate increases the supply of Canadian dollars and shifts the supply curve rightward from S_0 to S_2. A rise in the Canadian interest rate differential or a rise in the expected future exchange rate decreases the supply of Canadian dollars and shifts the supply curve leftward from S_0 to S_1.

■ FIGURE 20.4
Changes in the Supply of Dollars   *e*Foundations **20.2**

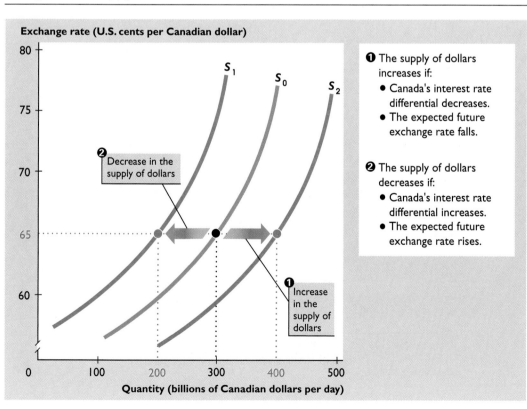

■ Market Equilibrium

Figure 20.5 shows how demand and supply in the foreign exchange market determine the exchange rate. The demand curve is *D*, and the supply curve is *S*. Just like all the other markets you've studied, the price (the exchange rate) acts as a regulator. If the exchange rate is too high, there is a surplus—the quantity supplied exceeds the quantity demanded. For example, in Figure 20.5, if the exchange rate is 70 U.S. cents per Canadian dollar, there is a surplus of Canadian dollars.

If the exchange rate is too low, there is a shortage—the quantity supplied is less than the quantity demanded. For example, in Figure 20.5, if the exchange rate is 60 U.S. cents per Canadian dollar, there is a shortage of Canadian dollars.

At the equilibrium exchange rate, there is neither a shortage nor a surplus. The quantity supplied equals the quantity demanded. In Figure 20.5, the equilibrium exchange rate is 65 U.S. cents per Canadian dollar. At this exchange rate, the quantity demanded equals the quantity supplied and is $300 billion a day.

The foreign exchange market is constantly pulled to its equilibrium by the forces of supply and demand. Foreign exchange dealers are constantly looking for the best price they can get. If they are selling, they want the highest price available. If they are buying, they want the lowest price available. Information flows from dealer to dealer through the worldwide computer network, and the price adjusts second by second to keep buying plans and selling plans in balance. That is, price adjusts second by second to keep the market at its equilibrium.

■ **FIGURE 20.5**
Equilibrium Exchange Rate

*e*Foundations **20.2**

The demand curve for dollars is *D*, and the supply curve is *S*.

❶ If the exchange rate is 70 U.S. cents per Canadian dollar, there is a surplus of dollars and the exchange rate falls.

❷ If the exchange rate is 60 U.S. cents per Canadian dollar, there is a shortage of dollars and the exchange rate rises.

❸ If the exchange rate is 65 U.S. cents per Canadian dollar, there is neither a shortage nor a surplus of dollars and the exchange rate remains constant. The market is in equilibrium.

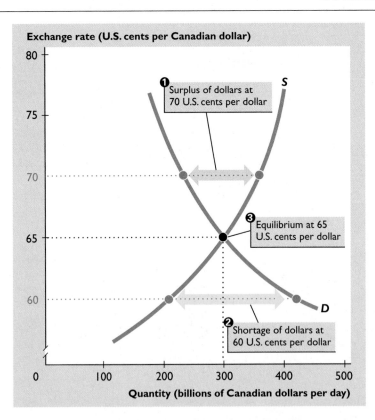

■ Changes in the Exchange Rate

If the demand for dollars increases and the supply of dollars does not change, the exchange rate rises. If the demand for dollars decreases and the supply of dollars does not change, the exchange rate falls. Similarly, if the supply of dollars decreases and the demand for dollars does not change, the exchange rate rises. If the supply of dollars increases and the demand for dollars does not change, the exchange rate falls.

These predictions about the effects of changes in demand and supply are exactly the same as for any other market.

Why the Exchange Rate Is Volatile

Sometimes the Canadian dollar depreciates and at other times it appreciates, but the quantity of dollars traded each day barely changes. Why? The main reason is that supply and demand are not independent of each other in the foreign exchange market.

When we studied the demand for dollars and the supply of dollars, we saw that unlike other markets, the demand side and the supply side of the market have some common influences. A change in the expected future exchange rate or a change in the Canadian interest rate differential changes both demand and supply, and they change in opposite directions. These common influences on both demand and supply explain why the exchange rate can be volatile at times, even though the quantity of dollars traded does not change much.

Everyone in the market is potentially either a demander or a supplier. Each has a price above which he or she will sell and below which he or she will buy. Let's see how these common supply and demand effects work by looking at two episodes: one in which the dollar appreciated and one in which it depreciated.

An Appreciating Dollar: 1986–1991

From 1986 to 1991, the Canadian dollar appreciated from 72 U.S. cents to 87 U.S. cents. Figure 20.6(a) explains this rise. In 1986, the demand and supply curves were those labelled D_{86} and S_{86}. The exchange rate was 72 U.S. cents per Canadian dollar. During the next 5 years, people expected the Canadian dollar to appreciate. They expected a higher exchange rate. As a result, the demand for Canadian dollars increased and the supply of them decreased. The demand curve shifted rightward to D_{91}, and the supply curve shifted leftward to S_{91}. The exchange rate rose by 20 percent, reaching 87 U.S. cents per Canadian dollar.

A Depreciating Dollar: 1991–2000

Between 1991 and 2000, the Canadian dollar depreciated against the U.S. dollar. Its value fell from 87 to 65 U.S. cents per Canadian dollar. Figure 20.6(b) explains why this happened. In 1991, the demand and supply curves were those labelled D_{91} and S_{91} and the exchange rate was 87 U.S. cents per dollar. During the 1990s, traders expected the Canadian dollar to depreciate. They expected a lower exchange rate. The demand for Canadian dollars decreased, and the supply of Canadian dollars increased. The demand curve shifted from D_{91} to D_{00}, and the supply curve shifted from S_{91} to S_{00}. These two shifts reinforced each other, and the exchange rate decreased to 65 U.S. cents per Canadian dollar.

■ FIGURE 20.6

Exchange Rate Fluctuations

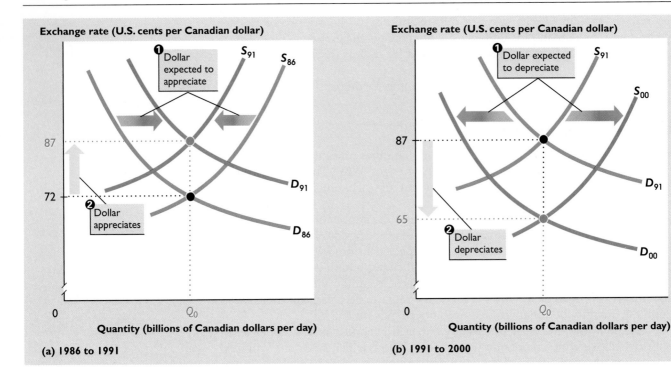

(a) 1986 to 1991

(b) 1991 to 2000

■ Exchange Rate Expectations

The exchange rate changes we've just examined occurred in part because the exchange rate was expected to change. This explanation sounds a bit like a self-fulfilling forecast. But what makes expectations change? The answer is new information about the deeper forces that influence the value of money. These forces are:

- Purchasing power parity
- Interest rate parity

Purchasing Power Parity

Money is worth what it will buy. But two kinds of money, Canadian dollars and U.S. dollars, for example, might buy different amounts of goods and services. Suppose a Big Mac costs $4 (Canadian) in Toronto and $3 (U.S.) in New York. If the Canadian dollar exchange rate is 75 U.S. cents per Canadian dollar, the two monies have the same value. You can buy a Big Mac in either Toronto or New York for either $4 Canadian or $3 U.S.

The situation we've just described is called **purchasing power parity,** which means equal value of money. If purchasing power parity does not prevail, some powerful forces go to work. To understand these forces, let's suppose that the price of a Big Mac in New York rises to $4 U.S., but in Toronto it remains at $4 Canadian. Suppose the exchange rate remains at 75 U.S. cents per Canadian dollar. In this case, a Big Mac in Toronto still costs $4 Canadian or $3 U.S. But in New

Purchasing power parity
Equal value of money—a situation in which money buys the same amount of goods and services in different currencies.

Eye On The GLOBAL ECONOMY

Purchasing Power Parity

Purchasing power parity (PPP) holds in the long run, but in the short run, large deviations from PPP can occur.

The figure shows the range of deviations from PPP in March 2001. The Japanese yen was overvalued by almost 30 percent. The Hungarian forint was the most undervalued currency.

According to PPP, an overvalued currency is one that will depreciate at some time in the future; an undervalued currency is one that will appreciate at some time in the future.

With the Canadian dollar undervalued, many expect that it will appreciate against the U.S. dollar. But if you are thinking of making a quick profit, be warned that PPP does not predict *when* a currency will depreciate or appreciate.

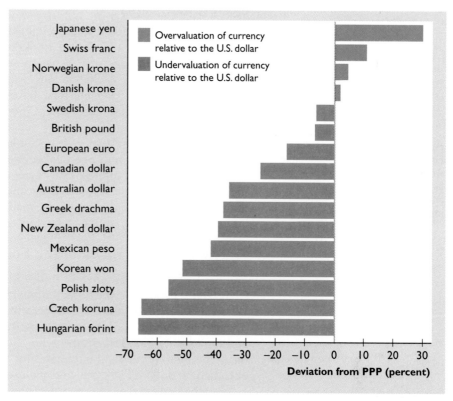

SOURCE: PACIFIC FX Service, University of British Columbia, March 23, 2001.

York, it costs $4.00 U.S. or $5.33 Canadian. Money buys more in Canada than in the United States. Money is not of equal value in both countries.

If all (or most) prices have increased in the United States and not increased in Canada, then people will generally expect that the value of the Canadian dollar on the foreign exchange market must rise. The demand for Canadian dollars increases, and the supply of Canadian dollars decreases. The Canadian dollar exchange rate rises, as expected. If the Canadian dollar rises to $1.00 U.S. and there are no further price changes, purchasing power parity is restored. A Big Mac now costs $4 in either U.S. dollars or Canadian dollars in both New York and Toronto.

If prices increase in Canada but remain constant in the United States, then people will generally expect that the value of the Canadian dollar on the foreign exchange market is too high and that it is going to fall. The demand for Canadian dollars decreases, and the supply of Canadian dollars increases. The Canadian dollar exchange rate falls, as expected.

Ultimately, the value of money is determined by the price level, which in turn is determined by aggregate supply and aggregate demand (see Chapter 8, pp. 175–179, and Chapter 15, pp. 366–370). So the deeper forces that influence the exchange rate have tentacles that spread throughout the economy. If prices in Canada rise faster than those in other countries, the exchange rate falls. If prices in Canada rise more slowly than in other countries, the exchange rate rises.

Interest Rate Parity

Suppose a Canadian dollar deposit in a Toronto bank earns 5 percent a year and a U.S. dollar deposit in a New York bank earns 3 percent a year. Why does anyone deposit money in New York? Why doesn't all the money flow to Toronto? The answer is because of exchange rate expectations. Suppose people expect the Canadian dollar to depreciate by 2 percent a year. This 2 percent depreciation must be subtracted from the 5 percent interest to obtain the net return of 3 percent a year that an American can earn by depositing funds in a Toronto bank. The two returns are equal. This situation is one of **interest rate parity**—equal interest rates when exchange rate changes are taken into account.

Adjusted for risk, interest rate parity always prevails. Funds move to get the highest return available. If for a few seconds a higher return is available in Toronto than in New York, the demand for Canadian dollars rises and the Canadian dollar exchange rate rises until expected interest rates are equal.

Interest rate parity
Equal interest rates—a situation in which the interest rate in one currency equals the interest rate in another currency when exchange rate changes are taken into account.

■ The Bank of Canada in the Foreign Exchange Market

The Bank of Canada's monetary policy influences the Canadian interest rate (see Chapter 13, p. 305). So the Bank's monetary policy influences the exchange rate. When the Canadian interest rate rises relative to those in other countries, the demand for Canadian dollars increases, the supply of Canadian dollars decreases, and the exchange rate rises. And when the Canadian interest rate falls relative to those in other countries, the demand for Canadian dollars decreases, the supply of Canadian dollars increases, and the exchange rate falls.

But the Bank of Canada can intervene directly in the foreign exchange market. It can buy or sell Canadian dollars to try to smooth out fluctuations in the exchange rate. Suppose the Bank of Canada wants the exchange rate to be steady at 65 U.S. cents per dollar. If the exchange rate rises above 65 U.S. cents, the Bank sells Canadian dollars. If the exchange rate falls below 65 U.S. cents, the Bank buys Canadian dollars. By these actions, the Bank of Canada can keep the exchange rate close to its target rate of 65 U.S. cents.

Figure 20.7 shows this Bank of Canada intervention in the foreign exchange market. The supply of dollars is S, and initially, the demand for dollars is D_0. The equilibrium exchange rate is 65 U.S. cents per dollar. This exchange rate is the Bank of Canada's target—the horizontal red line.

When the demand for dollars increases and the demand curve shifts rightward to D_1, the Bank of Canada sells 100 billion Canadian dollars. This action increases the supply of dollars by $100 billion and prevents the exchange rate from rising. When the demand for dollars decreases and the demand curve shifts leftward to D_2, the Bank of Canada buys 100 billion Canadian dollars. This action prevents the exchange rate from falling. If the demand for dollars fluctuates between D_1 and D_2 and, on the average, is D_0, the Bank of Canada sometimes buys and sometimes sells, but on the average, it neither buys nor sells.

But suppose the demand for dollars increases permanently from D_0 to D_1. To maintain the exchange rate at 65 U.S. cents per dollar indefinitely, the Bank of Canada would have to sell dollars every day and buy foreign currency. It would be piling up foreign currency and increasing Canadian official reserves.

Now suppose the demand for Canadian dollars decreases permanently from D_0 to D_2. To maintain the exchange rate at 65 U.S. cents per dollar indefinitely, the Bank of Canada would have to sell official reserves and buy Canadian dollars every day. Eventually, it would run out of foreign currency and have to abandon its attempt to fix the exchange rate.

Eye On The GLOBAL ECONOMY

The Sliding Euro

The euro was launched in January 1999 at 1.00 = $US1.16. The euro has been on a slide for most of its life and by mid-2001 it had fallen to 86 U.S. cents.

Faced with this slide in the euro, the European Central Bank (ECB) based in Frankfurt, Germany, has intervened from time to time in the foreign exchange market to support its currency.

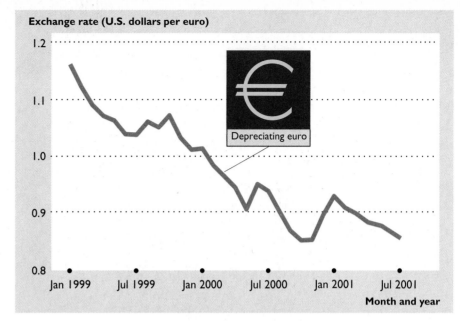

Exchange rate (U.S. dollars per euro)

Depreciating euro

Month and year

SOURCE: PACIFIC FX Service, University of British Columbia.

■ **FIGURE 20.7**
Foreign Exchange Market Intervention

*e*Foundations 20.2

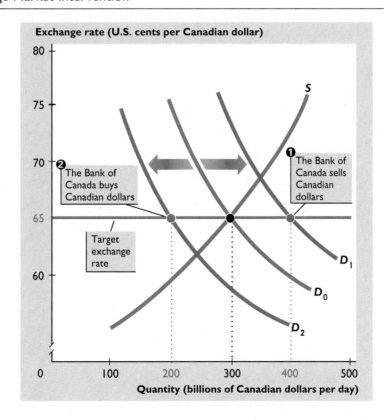

Exchange rate (U.S. cents per Canadian dollar)

2 The Bank of Canada buys Canadian dollars

Target exchange rate

1 The Bank of Canada sells Canadian dollars

Quantity (billions of Canadian dollars per day)

Initially, the demand for dollars is D_0, the supply of dollars is S, and the exchange rate is 65 U.S. cents per Canadian dollar. The Bank of Canada can intervene in the foreign exchange market to keep the exchange rate close to its target rate (65 U.S. cents in this example).

1 If demand increases from D_0 to D_1, the Bank of Canada sells Canadian dollars to increase supply.

2 If demand decreases from D_0 to D_2, the Bank of Canada buys Canadian dollars to decrease supply.

Persistent intervention on one side of the market cannot be sustained.

Study Guide pp. 302–306

*e*Foundations 20.2

2 Explain how the exchange rate is determined and why it fluctuates.

Practice Problem 20.2

Suppose that yesterday, the Canadian dollar was trading on the foreign exchange market at 68 U.S. cents per dollar. Today, the Canadian dollar is trading at 70 U.S. cents per dollar.

a. Which of the two currencies (the Canadian dollar or the U.S. dollar) has appreciated and which has depreciated today?

b. List the events that could have caused today's change in the value of the Canadian dollar on the foreign exchange market.

c. Did the events that you listed in part (b) change the demand for Canadian dollars, the supply of Canadian dollars, or both the demand for and supply of Canadian dollars?

d. If the Bank of Canada had tried to stabilize the value of the Canadian dollar at 68 U.S. cents per dollar, what action would it have taken?

e. In part (d), what effect would the Bank of Canada's actions have had on Canadian official reserves?

Exercise 20.2

Suppose that yesterday, the Canadian dollar was trading on the foreign exchange market at 80 yen per dollar. Today, the Canadian dollar is trading at 75 yen per dollar.

a. Which of the two currencies (the Canadian dollar or the Japanese yen) has appreciated and which has depreciated today?

b. List the events that could have caused today's change in the value of the Canadian dollar on the foreign exchange market.

c. Did the events that you listed in part (b) increase or decrease the demand for Canadian dollars, the supply of Canadian dollars, or both the demand for and supply of Canadian dollars?

d. If the Bank of Canada had tried to stabilize the value of the Canadian dollar at 80 yen, what action would it have taken?

e. In part (d), what effect would the Bank of Canada's actions have had on Canadian official reserves?

Solution to Practice Problem 20.2

a. Because the Canadian dollar costs a larger number of U.S. cents, the Canadian dollar has appreciated. The U.S. dollar has depreciated because it buys fewer Canadian dollars.

b. The main events might be an increase in Canadian interest rates, a decrease in the U.S. interest rate, or an expected rise in the Canadian dollar exchange rate.

c. The events that you listed in part (b) change both the demand for and supply of Canadian dollars. They increase demand and decrease supply.

d. To stabilize the value of the Canadian dollar at 68 U.S. cents, the Bank of Canada would have sold Canadian dollars.

e. When the Bank of Canada sells Canadian dollars, it buys foreign currency. Canadian official reserves would have increased.

CHAPTER CHECKPOINT

Key Points

1 **Describe a country's balance of payments accounts and explain what determines the amount of international borrowing and lending.**

- Foreign currency is used to finance international trade.
- A country's balance of payments accounts record its international transactions.
- Historically, Canada has been a net borrower from the rest of the world.
- Net exports are equal to the private sector balance plus the government sector balance.

2 **Explain how the exchange rate is determined and why it fluctuates.**

- Foreign currency is obtained in exchange for domestic currency in the foreign exchange market.
- The exchange rate is determined by demand for and supply of Canadian dollars in the foreign exchange market.
- The lower the exchange rate, the greater is the quantity of Canadian dollars demanded. A change in the exchange rate brings a movement along the demand curve for Canadian dollars.
- Changes in the expected future exchange rate and the Canadian interest rate differential change the demand for Canadian dollar assets and shift the demand curve for dollars.
- The lower the exchange rate, the smaller is the quantity of Canadian dollars supplied. A change in the exchange rate brings a movement along the supply curve for Canadian dollars.
- Rapid fluctuations in the exchange rate can occur because fluctuations in the demand for and supply of Canadian dollars are not independent.
- The Bank of Canada can intervene in the foreign exchange market to smooth fluctuations in the Canadian dollar exchange rate.

Key Terms

Balance of payments accounts, 478
Canadian interest rate differential, 488
Canadian official reserves, 478
Capital account, 478
Creditor nation, 480
Currency appreciation, 485

Currency depreciation, 486
Current account, 478
Debtor nation, 480
Foreign exchange market, 485
Foreign exchange rate, 485
Government sector balance, 482

Interest rate parity, 496
Net borrower, 480
Net lender, 480
Official settlements account, 478
Private sector balance, 482
Purchasing power parity, 494

Exercises

1. The following data describes the economy of Mexico in 2050:

Item	(millions of new pesos)
GDP	600
Consumption expenditure	360
Net taxes	150
Investment	150
Imports of goods and services	120
Government expenditure	135
Change in Mexican official reserves	−25
Net interest from abroad	−50
Net transfers from abroad	0

Calculate the following for Mexico:
a. Exports of goods and services.
b. Current account balance.
c. Capital account balance.
d. Saving.
e. Private sector balance.
f. Government sector balance.

2. Use the link on your Foundations Web site to visit Statistics Canada's Web site and find data on the exchange rate and international trade.
a. When did Canada last have a current account surplus?
b. Does Canada have a surplus or a deficit in trade in goods?
c. Does Canada have a surplus or a deficit in trade in services?
d. What has happened to foreign investment in Canada over the past 10 years?
e. Do you think Canada's balance of payments record is a matter for concern? Why or why not?

3. The *Eye on the Global Economy* on page 495 explains why in 2000-2001 many people expected the Canadian dollar to rise above 65 U.S. cents per dollar.
a. Explain why the Canadian dollar might have continued to fall despite these expectations.
b. Explain why when the foreign exchange value of the Canadian dollar stopped falling and started to rise, it might continue to rise for a considerable period of time.
c. Use the link on your Foundations Web site to visit Statistics Canada's Web site and find data on the Canadian dollar exchange rate. Has it fallen below 65 U.S. cents, or has it risen? What forces might explain any changes?
d. What information would you need to determine whether the Bank of Canada has intervened in the foreign exchange market to influence the foreign exchange value of the Canadian dollar?

4. Suppose that the Canadian dollar appreciates. State with reasons which of the following events could have caused these changes to occur:
a. The Bank of Canada intervened in the foreign exchange market and sold Canadian dollars.
b. The Bank of Canada conducted an open market operation and sold bonds.
c. People began to expect the Canadian dollar to appreciate.
d. The Canadian interest rate differential narrowed.
e. The Canadian current account went into deficit.

GLOSSARY

Above full-employment equilibrium When equilibrium real GDP exceeds potential GDP. (p. 179)

Absolute advantage When one person is more productive than another person in several or even all activities. (p. 70)

Aggregate demand The relationship between the quantity of real GDP demanded and the price level when all other influences on expenditure plans remain the same. (p. 177)

Aggregate hours The total number of hours worked by all the people employed, both full time and part time, during a year. (p. 133)

Aggregate planned expenditure Planned consumption expenditure plus planned investment plus planned government expenditure plus planned exports minus planned imports. (p. 327)

Aggregate supply The relationship between the quantity of real GDP supplied and the price level when all other influences on production plans remain the same. (p. 175)

Automatic fiscal policy A fiscal policy action that is triggered by the state of the economy such as an increase in payments to the unemployed and a decrease in tax receipts triggered by recession. (p. 380)

Automatic stabilizers Features of fiscal policy that stabilize real GDP without explicit action by the government. (p. 387)

Autonomous expenditure The components of aggregate expenditure that do not change when real GDP changes. (p. 328)

Balance of payments accounts The accounts in which a nation records its international trading, borrowing, and lending. (p. 478)

Balance of trade The value of exports minus the value of imports. (p. 453)

Balance sheet A statement that summarizes assets (amounts owned) and liabilities (amounts owed). (p. 276)

Balanced budget The budget balance when tax receipts equal expenditures. (p. 378)

Balanced budget multiplier The magnification effect on aggregate demand of *simultaneous* changes in government expenditure and taxes that leave the budget balance unchanged. (p. 382)

Bank of Canada The central bank of Canada. (p. 267)

Bank rate The interest rate at which the Bank of Canada stands ready to lend reserves to chartered banks. (p. 270)

Bankers' deposit rate The interest rate that the Bank of Canada pays banks on their deposits at the Bank of Canada. (p. 270)

Barter The direct exchange of goods and services for other goods and services, which requires a double coincidence of wants. (p. 253)

Base period A period for which the CPI is defined to equal 100. Currently, the base period is 1992. (p. 152)

Below full-employment equilibrium When potential GDP exceeds equilibrium real GDP. (p. 179)

Benefit The benefit of something is the gain or pleasure that it brings. (p. 15)

Bond A promise to pay specified sums of money on specified dates; it is a debt for the issuer. (p. 203)

Bond market A financial market in which bonds issued by firms and governments are traded. (p. 203)

Budget deficit The budget balance when expenditures exceed tax receipts. (p. 378)

Budget surplus The budget balance when tax receipts exceed expenditures. (p. 378)

Business cycle A periodic but irregular up-and-down movement in production and jobs. (p. 7)

Caisse populaire A financial institution that operates in Quebec and that is similar to a credit union. (p. 262)

Canadian interest rate differential The Canadian interest rate minus the foreign interest rate. (p. 488)

Canadian official reserves The government's holdings of foreign currency. (p. 478)

Capital Tools, instruments, machines, buildings, and other constructions that have been produced in the past and that businesses now use to produce goods and services. (p. 38)

Capital account Record of foreign investment in Canada minus Canadian investment abroad. (p. 478)

Central bank A public authority that provides banking services to banks and regulates financial institutions and markets. (p. 267)

Ceteris paribus Other things remaining the same (often abbreviated to *cet. par.*). (p. 12)

Change in demand A change in the quantity that people plan to buy when any influence on buying plans other than the price of the good changes. (p. 81)

Change in supply A change in the quantity that suppliers plan to sell when any influence on selling plans other than the price of the good changes. (p. 86)

Change in the quantity demanded A change in the quantity of a good that people plan to buy that results from a change in the price of the good. (p. 81)

Change in the quantity supplied A change in the quantity of a good that suppliers plan to sell that results from a change in the price of the good. (p. 86)

Chartered bank A private firm that is chartered by the federal government to receive deposits and make loans. (p. 260)

Circular flow model A model of the economy that shows the circular flow of expenditure and incomes that result from decision makers' choices, and the way those choices interact to determine what, how, and for whom goods and services are produced. (p. 42)

Classical growth theory The theory that the clash between an exploding population and limited resources will eventually bring economic growth to an end. (p. 233)

Comparative advantage The ability of a person to perform an activity or produce a good or service at a lower opportunity cost than someone else. (p. 68)

Complement A good that is consumed with another good. (p. 81)

Complement in production A good that is produced along with another good. (p. 86)

Consumer Price Index (CPI) A measure of the average of the prices paid by households for a fixed market basket of consumer goods and services. (p. 152)

Consumption expenditure The expenditure by households on consumption goods and services. (p. 109)

Consumption function The relationship between consumption expenditure and disposable income, other things remaining the same. (p. 328)

Consumption goods and services Goods and services that are bought by individuals and used to provide personal enjoyment and contribute to a person's standard of living. (p. 36)

Correlation The tendency for the values of two variables to move in a predictable and related way. (p. 13)

Cost of living The number of dollars it takes to buy the goods and services that achieve a given standard of living. (p. 7)

Cost of living index A measure of changes in the amount of money that people would need to spend to achieve a given standard of living. (p. 158)

Credit union A cooperative organization, owned by a social or economic group such as a firm's employees, that accepts deposits from and makes loans to its members. (p. 262)

Creditor nation A country that during its entire history has invested more in the rest of the world than other countries have invested in it. (p. 480)

Cross-section graph A graph that shows the values of an economic variable for different groups in a population at a point in time. (p. 26)

Crowding-out effect The tendency for a government budget deficit to decrease private investment. (p. 217)

Currency Bank notes (dollar bills) and coins. (p. 254)

Currency appreciation The rise in the value of one currency in terms of another currency. (p. 485)

Currency depreciation The fall in the value of one currency in terms of another currency. (p. 486)

Currency drain An increase in currency held outside the banks. (p. 290)

Current account Record of international receipts and payments—current account balance equals exports minus imports, plus net interest and transfers received from abroad. (p. 478)

Cyclical unemployment The fluctuating unemployment over the business cycle that increases during a recession and decreases during an expansion. (p. 144)

Daily monetary policy target A target that the Bank of Canada sets and achieves each day in pursuit of its ultimate inflation target—a target overnight rate. (p. 267)

Debtor nation A country that during its entire history has borrowed more from the rest of the world than it has lent to it. (p. 480)

Deflationary gap A gap that exists when potential GDP exceeds real GDP and that brings a falling price level. (p. 370)

Demand The relationship between the quantity demanded and the price of a good when all other influences on buying plans remain the same. (p. 79)

Demand curve A graph of the relationship between the quantity demanded of a good and its price when all other influences on buying plans remain the same. (p. 80)

Demand for labour The relationship between the quantity of labour demanded and real wage rate when all other influences on firms' hiring plans remain the same. (p. 183)

Demand for money The relationship between the quantity of money demanded and the nominal interest rate, when all other influences on the amount of money that people wish to hold remain the same. (p. 300)

Demand schedule A list of the quantities demanded at each different price when all other influences on buying plans remain the same. (p. 80)

Deposit multiplier The number by which an increase in bank reserves is multiplied to find the resulting increase in bank deposits. (p. 284)

Depreciation The decrease in the value of capital that results from its use and from obsolescence—also called capital consumption (p. 116)

Desired reserve ratio The ratio of reserves to deposits that banks wish to hold so that they are sure to have enough cash to cover withdrawals by their customers. (p. 278)

Diminishing returns The tendency for each additional hour of labour employed to produce a successively smaller additional amount of real GDP. (p. 182)

Direct relationship A relationship between two variables that move in the same direction. (p. 28)

Discouraged worker A person who does not have a job, is available and willing to work but has not made specific efforts to find a job within the previous four weeks. (p. 132)

Discretionary fiscal policy A fiscal policy action that is initiated by an act of Parliament. (p. 380)

Discretionary policy A policy that is based on the judgments of policy makers about the current needs of the economy. (p. 430)

Disposable income Income earned minus net taxes. (p. 208)

Dumping When a foreign firm sells its exports at a lower price than the price in the firm's domestic market. (p. 468)

Dynamic comparative advantage A comparative advantage that a person (or country) obtains by specializing in an activity, resulting from learning-by-doing. (p. 460)

Econometrics The use of statistical tools in economics. (p. 13)

Economic freedom A condition in which people are able to make personal choices, their private property is protected, and they are free to buy and sell in markets. (p. 243)

Economic growth rate The rate of change of real GDP expressed as a percentage per year. (p. 222)

Economic model A description of some aspect of the economic world that includes only those features that are needed for the purpose at hand. (p. 11)

Economic theory A generalization that summarizes what we understand about the economic choices that people make and the economic performance of industries and nations based on models that have repeatedly passed the test of corresponding well with real-world data. (p. 11)

Economics The social science that studies the choices that individuals, businesses, governments, and entire societies make as they cope with scarcity. (p. 5)

Efficiency wage A real wage rate that is set above the full-employment equilibrium wage rate to induce greater work effort. (p. 193)

Electronic cash (or **e-cash**) An electronic equivalent of paper notes and coins. (p. 256)

Electronic cheque (or **e-cheque**) An electronic equivalent of a paper cheque. (p. 256)

Entrepreneurship The human resource that organizes labour, land, and capital. (p. 39)

Equation of exchange An equation that states that the quantity of money multiplied by the velocity of circulation equals nominal GDP. (p. 314)

Equilibrium expenditure The level of aggregate expenditure that occurs when aggregate planned expenditure equals real GDP. (p. 336)

Equilibrium price The price at which the quantity demanded equals the quantity supplied. (p. 89)

Equilibrium quantity The quantity that is bought and sold at the equilibrium price. (p. 89)

Excess demand A situation in which the quantity demanded exceeds the quantity supplied. (p. 90)

Excess reserves Actual reserves minus desired reserves. (p. 279)

Excess supply A situation in which the quantity supplied exceeds the quantity demanded. (p. 90)

Expected inflation rate The inflation rate that people forecast and use to set the money wage rate and other money prices. (p. 410)

Exports Goods and services produced in Canada and sold in other countries. (p. 36)

Exports of goods and services Items that firms in Canada sell to the rest of the world. (p. 110)

Factor markets Markets in which factors of production are bought and sold. (p. 42)

Factors of production The productive resources used to produce goods and services—land, labour, capital, and entrepreneurship. (p. 37)

Federal budget An annual statement of the expenditures, tax receipts, and surplus or deficit of the government of Canada. (p. 378)

Feedback-rule policy A policy that specifies how policy actions respond to changes in the state of the economy. (p. 430)

Fiat money Objects that are money because the law decrees or orders them to be money. (p. 254)

Final good or service A good or service that is produced for its final user and not as a component of another good or service. (p. 108)

Financial capital The funds that firms use to buy and operate physical capital. (p. 200)

Financial markets The collection of households, firms, governments, banks, and other financial institutions that lend and borrow. (p. 202)

Firms The institutions that organize the production of goods and services. (p. 42)

Fiscal policy Adjusting the federal budget to influence employment and production. (p. 378)

Fixed-rule policy A policy that is pursued independently of the state of the economy. (p. 430)

Foreign exchange market The market in which the currency of one country is exchanged for the currency of another. (p. 485)

Foreign exchange rate The price at which one currency exchanges for another. (p. 485)

Frictional unemployment The unemployment that arises from normal labour turnover—from people entering and leaving the labour force and from the ongoing creation and destruction of jobs. (p. 143)

Full employment When there is no cyclical unemployment or, equivalently, when all the unemployment is frictional, structural, and seasonal. (p. 146)

Full-employment equilibrium When equilibrium real GDP equals potential GDP. (p. 179)

Full-time workers People who usually work 30 hours or more a week. (p. 132)

Functional distribution of income The percentage distribution of income among the factors of production. (p. 39)

GDP deflator An average of current prices expressed as a percentage of base-year prices. (p. 121)

Goods and services The objects that people value and produce to satisfy human wants. Goods are physical objects, and services are work done for people. (p. 6)

Goods markets Markets in which goods and services are bought and sold. (p. 42)

Government expenditure multiplier The magnification effect of a change in government expenditure on goods and services on aggregate demand. (p. 381)

Government expenditure on goods and services The expenditure by all levels of government on goods and services. (p. 110)

Government goods and services Goods and services that are bought by governments. (p. 36)

Government sector balance Net taxes minus government expenditure on goods and services. (p. 482)

Great Depression A period during the 1930s in which the economy experienced its worst-ever recession. (p. 8)

Gross domestic product (GDP) The market value of all the final goods and services produced within a country in a given time period. (p. 108)

Gross investment The total amount spent on new capital goods. (p. 200)

Households Individuals or groups of people living together as decision-making units. (p. 42)

Human capital The knowledge and skill that people obtain from education, on-the-job training, and work experience. (p. 38)

Hyperinflation Inflation at a rate that exceeds 50 percent per month. (p. 315)

Imports of goods and services Items that households, firms, and governments in Canada buy from the rest of the world. (p. 110)

Induced expenditure The components of aggregate expenditure that change when real GDP changes. (p. 328)

Induced taxes Taxes that vary with real GDP. (p. 387)

Induced transfer payments Payments under social programs such as unemployment benefits and welfare benefits, the size of which depends on the state of the economy. (p. 388)

Infant-industry argument The argument that it is necessary to protect a new industry to enable it to grow into a mature industry that can compete in world markets. (p. 467)

Inferior good A good for which the demand decreases when income increases. (p. 81)

Inflation A situation in which the cost of living is rising and the value of money is shrinking. (p. 7)

Inflation rate The percentage change in the price level from one year to the next. (p. 155)

Inflationary gap A gap that exists when real GDP exceeds potential GDP and that brings a rising price level. (p. 370)

Interest Income paid for the use of capital. (p. 39)

Interest rate parity Equal interest rates—a situation in which the interest rate in one currency equals the interest rate in another currency when exchange rate changes are taken into account. (p. 496)

Intermediate good or service A good or service that is produced by one firm, bought by another firm, and used as a component of a final good or service. (p. 108)

Inverse relationship A relationship between two variables that move in the opposite direction. (p. 29)

Investment The purchase of new *capital goods* (tools, instruments, machines, buildings, and other constructions) and additions to inventories. (p. 109)

Investment demand The relationship between investment and the real interest rate, other things remaining the same. (p. 205)

Investment goods Goods that are bought by businesses to increase their productive resources. (p. 36)

Involuntary part-time workers People who work part time but who want a full-time job. (p. 132)

Job rationing A situation that arises when the real wage rate is above the equilibrium level. (p. 192)

Job search The activity of looking for an acceptable vacant job. (p. 191)

Keynesian activist An economist who believes that fluctuations in investment are the main source of economic fluctuations, and who advocates interest rate cuts and fiscal stimulus when real GDP falls below potential GDP and interest rate hikes and fiscal restraint when real GDP exceeds potential GDP. (p. 433)

Labour The work time and work effort that people devote to producing goods and services. (p. 37)

Labour force The number of people employed plus the number unemployed. (p. 130)

Labour force participation rate The percentage of working-age population who are members of the labour force. (p. 132)

Labour productivity The quantity of real GDP per hour of labour. (p. 226)

Land The "gifts of nature," or *natural resources*, that we use to produce goods and services. (p. 37)

Large Value Transfer System Canada's national electronic payments system for very large transactions between the chartered banks, the Bank of Canada, and a few other big financial institutions. (p. 268)

Learning-by-doing Repeatedly performing the same task and becoming more productive at producing a particular good or service. (p. 460)

Linear relationship A relationship that graphs as a straight line. (p. 28)

Liquid asset An asset that can be easily, and with certainty, converted into money. (p. 264)

Liquidity trap An interest rate at which people are willing to hold any quantity of money. (p. 427)

Long-run Phillips curve The vertical line that shows the relationship between inflation and unemployment when the economy is at full employment. (p. 408)

M1 Currency outside the banks plus chequable deposits owned by individuals and businesses at chartered banks. (p. 257)

M2+ M1 plus personal savings deposits and nonpersonal notice deposits at banks plus deposits at credit unions, caisses populaires, and other depository institutions. (p. 257)

Macroeconomic equilibrium When the quantity of real GDP demanded equals the quantity of real GDP supplied at the point of intersection of the *AD* curve and the *AS* curve. (p. 178)

Macroeconomics The study of the aggregate (or total) effects on the national economy and the global economy of the choices that individuals, businesses, and governments make. (p. 5)

Malthusian theory Another name for classical growth theory—named for Thomas Robert Malthus. (p. 233)

Margin A choice at the margin is a choice that is made by comparing *all* the relevant alternatives systematically and incrementally. (p. 16)

Marginal benefit The benefit that arises from a one-unit increase in an activity. The marginal benefit of something is *measured by* what you are *willing to give up* to get *one more* unit of it. (p. 16)

Marginal cost The cost that arises from a one-unit increase in an activity. The marginal cost of

something is what you *must give up* to get *one more* unit of it. (p. 16)

Marginal propensity to consume The fraction of a change in disposable income that is spent on consumption—the change in consumption expenditure divided by the change in disposable income that brought it about. (p. 330)

Marginal propensity to import The fraction of an increase in real GDP that is spent on imports—the change in imports divided by the change in real GDP. (p. 332)

Marginal tax rate The fraction of a change in real GDP that is paid in income taxes—the change in tax payments divided by the change in real GDP. (p. 343)

Market Any arrangement that brings buyers and sellers together and enables them to get information and do business with each other. (p. 42)

Market equilibrium When the quantity demanded equals the quantity supplied—when buyers' and sellers' plans are consistent. (p. 89)

Means of payment A method of settling a debt. (p. 252)

Medium of exchange An object that is generally accepted in return for goods and services. (p. 253)

Microeconomics The study of the choices that individuals and businesses make, the interaction of these choices, and the influence that governments exert on these choices. (p. 5)

Minimum wage law A government regulation that makes hiring labour for less than a specified wage illegal—an example of a

price floor. (p. 99)

Monetarist An economist who believes that fluctuations in the quantity of money are the main source of economic fluctuations. (p. 432)

Monetary base The sum of chartered banks' deposits at the Bank of Canada plus coins and Bank of Canada notes. (p. 270)

Monetary policy Adjusting the quantity of money in the economy. (p. 267)

Monetary system The Bank of Canada and the banks and other institutions that accept deposits and provide the services that enable people and businesses to make and receive payments. (p. 260)

Money Any commodity or token that is generally accepted as a means of payment. (p. 252)

Money market mutual fund A fund managed by a financial institution that sells shares to people and uses these funds to buy assets. (p. 262)

Money multiplier The number by which change in the monetary base is multiplied to find the resulting change in the quantity of money. (p. 292)

Multiplier The amount by which a change in any component of autonomous expenditure is magnified or multiplied to determine the change that it generates in equilibrium expenditure and real GDP. (p. 340)

National debt The total amount that the federal government has borrowed in the past to finance its budget deficits (government payments in excess of receipts). (p. 46)

Natural rate hypothesis The proposition that when the growth rate of the quantity of money changes, the unemployment rate changes temporarily and eventually returns to the natural unemployment rate. (p. 411)

Natural unemployment rate The unemployment rate at full employment. (p. 146)

Negative relationship A relationship between two variables that move in the opposite direction. (p. 29)

Neoclassical growth theory The theory that real GDP per person will increase as long as technology keeps advancing. (p. 235)

Net borrower A country that is borrowing more from the rest of the world than it is lending to the rest of the world. (p. 480)

Net domestic product at factor cost The sum of the four factor incomes—wages, interest, rent, and profit. (p. 116)

Net exports of goods and services The value of exports of goods and services minus the value of imports of goods and services. (p. 110)

Net investment The change in the quantity of capital—equals gross investment minus depreciation. (p. 200)

Net lender A country that is lending more to the rest of the world than it is borrowing from the rest of the world. (p. 480)

New growth theory The theory that our unlimited wants will lead us to ever greater productivity and perpetual economic growth. (p. 237)

Nominal GDP The value of the final goods and services produced in a given year valued at the prices that prevailed in that same year. (p. 119)

Nominal interest rate The interest payable on a loan expressed as a percentage of the loan. (p. 167)

Nominal wage rate The average hourly wage rate measured in *current* dollars. (p. 164)

Nontariff barrier Any action other than a tariff that restricts international trade. (p. 462)

Normal good A good for which the demand increases when income increases. (p. 81)

Official settlements account Record of the change in Canadian official reserves. (p. 478)

Okun's Law For each percentage point that the unemployment rate is above the natural unemployment rate, there is a 2 percent gap between real GDP and potential GDP. (p. 403)

One-third rule The observation that on the average, with no change in human capital and technology, a *one percent* increase in capital per hour of labour brings a *one-third percent* increase in labour productivity. (p. 231)

Open market operation The purchase or sale of Government of Canada securities—Treasury bills and bonds—in the open market by the Bank of Canada. (p. 269)

Opportunity cost The opportunity cost of something is what you must give up to get it. (p. 15)

Overnight rate The interest rate on overnight loans between banks and other large financial institutions. (p. 261)

Part-time workers People who usually work less than 30 hours per week. (p. 132)

Personal distribution of income The percentage distribution of income among households. (p. 40)

Physical capital The tools, instruments, machines, buildings, and other constructions that have been produced in the past and that are used to produce goods and services. (p. 200)

Positive relationship A relationship between two variables that move in the same direction. (p. 28)

Post hoc **fallacy** The error of reasoning that a first event *causes* a second event because the first occurred *before* the second. (p. 13)

Potential GDP The level of real GDP that the economy would produce if it were at full employment. (p. 146)

Price ceiling The highest price at which it is legal to trade a particular good, service, or factor of production. (p. 97)

Price floor The lowest price at which it is legal to trade a particular good, service, or factor of production. (p. 99)

Private sector balance Saving minus investment. (p. 482)

Production function A relationship that shows the maximum quantity of real GDP that can be produced as the quantity of labour employed changes and all other influences on production remain the same. (p. 182)

Production possibilities frontier The boundary between combinations of goods and services that can be produced and combinations that cannot be produced, given the available factors of production and the state of technology. (p. 58)

Productivity curve The relationship between real GDP per hour of labour and the quantity of capital per hour of labour with a given state of technology. (p. 229)

Productivity Total production per person employed. (p. 17)

Profit (or **loss**) Income earned by an entrepreneur for running a business. (p. 39)

Property rights The social arrangements that govern the protection of private property. (p. 243)

Purchasing power parity Equal value of money—a situation in which money buys the same amount of goods and services in different currencies. (p. 494)

Quantity demanded The amount of any good, service, or resource that people are willing and able to buy during a specified period at a specified price. (p. 79)

Quantity of labour demanded The total labour hours that all the firms in the economy plan to hire during a given time period at a given real wage rate. (p. 183)

Quantity of labour supplied The number of labour hours that all the households in the economy plan to work during a given time period and at a given real wage rate. (p. 185)

Quantity of money demanded The inventory of money that households and firms choose to hold. (p. 299)

Quantity supplied The amount of any good, service, or resource that people are willing and able to sell during a specified period at a specified price. (p. 84)

Quantity theory of money The proposition that in the long run, an increase in the quantity of money brings an equal percentage increase in the price level (other things remaining the same). (p. 313)

Quota A specified maximum amount of a good that may be imported in a given period of time. (p. 464)

Rational choice A choice that uses the available resources most effectively to satisfy the wants of the person making the choice. (p. 15)

Rational expectation The inflation forecast resulting from use of all the relevant data and economic science. (p. 417)

Real GDP The value of the final goods and services produced in a given year when valued at constant prices. (p. 119)

Real GDP per person Real GDP divided by the population. (p. 222)

Real interest rate The interest rate payable on the loan expressed in the purchasing power of the interest received—the nominal interest rate adjusted for the effects of inflation. (p. 167)

Real wage rate The average hourly wage rate measured in the dollars of a given base year. (p. 164)

Recession A decrease in real GDP that lasts for at least two quarters (six months) or a period of significant decline in total output, income, employment, and trade, usually lasting from six months to a year, and marked by widespread contractions in many sectors of the economy. (p. 350)

Rent Income paid for the use of land. (p. 39)

Rent ceiling A law that makes it illegal for landlords to charge a rent that exceeds a set limit—an example of a price ceiling. (p. 97)

Rent seeking Lobbying and other political activity that seeks to capture the gains from trade. (p. 472)

Reserve ratio The proportion of a bank's total deposits that are held in reserves. (p. 278)

Reserves The currency in a bank's vaults plus its deposit at the Bank of Canada. (p. 261)

Rule of 70 The number of years it takes for the level of any variable to double is approximately 70 divided by the annual percentage growth rate of the variable. (p. 223)

Saving The amount of income that is not paid in taxes or spent on consumption goods and services—adds to wealth. (p. 202)

Saving supply The relationship between the quantity of saving supplied and the real interest rate, other things remaining the same. (p. 208)

scarcity The condition that arises because the available resources are insufficient to satisfy wants. (p. 4)

Scatter diagram A graph of the value of one variable against the value of another variable. (p. 26)

Seasonal unemployment The unemployment that arises because of seasonal weather patterns. (p. 144)

Shortage or excess demand A situation in which the quantity demanded exceeds the quantity supplied. (p. 90)

Short-run Phillips curve A curve that shows the relationship between the inflation rate and the unemployment rate when the natural unemployment rate and the expected inflation rate remain constant. (p. 402)

Slope The change in the value of the variable measured on the y-axis divided by the change the value of the variable measured on the x-axis. (p. 31)

Stagflation A combination of recession (decreasing real GDP) and inflation (rising price level). (p. 368)

Standard of living The level of consumption of goods and services that people enjoy on the average; it is measured by average income per person. (p. 6)

Stock A certificate of ownership and claim to the profits that a firm makes. (p. 202)

Stock market A financial market in which shares of companies' stocks are traded. (p. 203)

Store of value Any commodity or token that can be held and exchanged later for goods and services. (p. 253)

Structural unemployment The unemployment that arises when changes in technology or international competition change the skills needed to perform jobs or change the locations of jobs. (p. 144)

Substitute A good that can be consumed in place of another good. (p. 81)

Substitute in production A good that can be produced in place of another good. (p. 86)

Supply The relationship between the quantity supplied and the price of a good when all other influences on selling plans remain the same. (p. 84)

Supply curve A graph of the relationship between the quantity supplied of a good and its price when all other influences on selling plans remain the same. (p. 85)

Supply of labour The relationship between the quantity of labour supplied and the real wage rate when all other influences on work plans remain the same. (p. 185)

Supply of money The relationship between the quantity of money supplied and the nominal interest rate. (p. 303)

Supply schedule A list of the quantities supplied at each different price when all other influences on selling plans remain the same. (p. 85)

Surplus or excess supply A situation in which the quantity supplied exceeds the quantity demanded. (p. 90)

Tariff A tax on a good that is imposed by the importing country when an imported good crosses its international boundary. (p. 462)

Tax multiplier The magnification effect of a change in taxes on aggregate demand. (p. 381)

Time-series graph A graph that measures time on the x-axis and the variable or variables in which we are interested on the y-axis. (p. 26)

Tradeoff A constraint or limit to what is possible that forces an exchange or a substitution of one thing for something else. (p. 61)

Trend A general tendency for the value of a variable to rise or fall. (p. 26)

Trust and mortgage loan company A privately owned depository institution that operates under the Trust and Loan Companies Act, 1992. (p. 263)

Ultimate monetary policy objective The final goal of monetary policy—an inflation rate inside the target range of 1 percent to 3 percent a year. (p. 267)

Unemployment The state of being available and willing to work but unable to find suitable work. (p. 6)

Unemployment rate The percentage of the people in the labour force who are unemployed. (p. 131)

Union wage A wage rate that results from collective bargaining between a labour union and an employer. (p. 193)

Unit of account An agreed-upon measure for stating the prices of goods and services. (p. 253)

Value added The value of a firm's production minus the value of the intermediate goods it buys from other firms. (p. 117)

Velocity of circulation The average speed with which a dollar circulates in the economy as people use it to buy goods and services; calculated by dividing nominal GDP by the quantity of money. (p. 313)

Wages Income paid for the services of labour. (p. 39)

Wealth The value of all the things that a person owns. (p. 202)

Working-age population The total number of people aged 15 years and over. (p. 130)

INDEX

CREDITS

(continuation from page vi)

PHOTO CREDITS

Chapter 1: p. 5 left and right: Scott Foresman/Addison Wesley Longman, Focus on Sports; p. 6 left: © CORBIS; p. 6 right: Digital Image © 2001 PhotoDisc, Inc.; p. 8 left: AP/Wide World Photos; p. 8 right: © Bettmann/CORBIS; p. 11: National Museum of Photography, Film & Television/Science & Society Picture Library; p. 12: Bettmann/CORBIS; p. 16 left: Digital Image © 2001/PhotoDisc, Inc.; p. 16 right: Copyright © David Young-Wolf/PhotoEdit; p. 18 left: © Charles E. Rotkin/ CORBIS; p. 18 right: Digital Image © 2001/PhotoDisc, Inc.

Chapter 3: p. 74: Steve Vidler/SuperStock.

Chapter 4: p. 78 left: Roderick Chen/SuperStock; p. 78 centre: AP/Wide World Photos; p. 78 right: © Steve Rubin/The Image Works; p. 93: Digital Image © 2001/PhotoDisc, Inc.

Chapter 5: p. 114: Romilly Lockyer/Getty Images/The Image Bank.

Chapter 6: p. 133: Courtesy of U.S. Census Bureau; p. 136: © CORBIS; p. 143: Copyright © David Young-Wolf/PhotoEdit; p. 144: © James A. Sugar/CORBIS.

Chapter 8: p. 195: Digital Image © 2001/PhotoDisc, Inc.

Chapter 10: p. 228 top: © Minnesota Historical Society/CORBIS; p. 228 bottom: © Bob Rowan, Progressive Image/CORBIS.

Chapter 11: p. 268: Courtesy of the Bank of Canada; p. 269: Courtesy of the Bank of Canada.

Chapter 12: p. 277: © Francis G. Mayer/CORBIS/Magma.

Chapter 13: p. 315: © Bettmann/CORBIS.
Chapter 14: p. 338 top: © Bettmann/CORBIS; p. 338 bottom: Private Collection/Roger Violet, Paris/Bridgeman Art Library.

Chapter 16: p. 390: Courtesy of the Bank of Canada.

Chapter 17: p. 405: Archival and Special Collections, McLaughlin Library, University of Guelph; p. 406: MIT Museum; p. 412 top: © Bettmann/CORBIS/Magma; p. 412 bottom: Courtesy of Edmund S. Phelps.

Chapter 18: p. 443 left: Courtesy of the Bank of Canada; p. 443 right: Courtesy of the Bank of Canada/Andrew Balfour.

Chapter 19: p. 473 left: Jason Grow/SABA; p. 473 right: David G. McIntyre/BLACKSTAR.

FIGURE AND TABLE CREDITS

Figure 2.1: Statistics Canada, *National Income and Expenditure Accounts* (13-001).
Figure 2.2: Statistics Canada, *National Income and Expenditure Accounts* (13-001).
Figure 2.3: Statistics Canada, *Income Distributions by Size in Canada*, 1998 (13-207).
Figure 2.6: Statistics Canada, *National Income and Expenditure Accounts* (13-001).
Figure 2.7: Statistics Canada, *National Income and Expenditure Accounts* (13-001).

Table 5.1: Statistics Canada Web site, CANSIM II, table 380-0002 and Catalogue no. 13-001-XIB.
Table 5.2: CANSIM II, table 380-0001 and Catalogue no. 13-001-XIB.
Figure 6.1: CANSIM II, tables 279-0003, 279-0010, 279-0014, 279-0018, 279-0020 and 279-0023.
Figure 6.2: Statistics Canada, *Historical Labour Force Statistics* (71-201).
Figure 6.3: Statistics Canada, *Historical Labour Force Statistics* (71-201).
Figure 6.4: Statistics Canada, *Canadian Economic Observer* (11-010).

Figure 6.5: For 1976-2000: Statistics Canada, *Canadian Economic Observer* (11-010).
Figure 6.6: Statistics Canada, Catalogue no. 89F0133XIE.
Figure 6.8: Statistics Canada, *Canadian Economic Observer* (11-010) and Bank of Canada, *Banking and Financial Statistics* February 2001.
Figure 6.9: Statistics Canada, *National Income and Expenditure Accounts* (13-001) and the authors' assumptions.

Figure 7.1: Statistics Canada, *The Consumer Price Index* (62-001).
Figure 7.2: Statistics Canada, *The Consumer Price Index* (62-001).
Figure 7.3: Statistics Canada, *The Consumer Price Index* (62-001) and *Canadian Economic Observer, Historical Statistical Supplement 1999-2000* (11-210).
Figure 7.4: Statistics Canada, *National Income and Expenditure Accounts* (13-001), *Canadian Economic Observer, Historical Statistical Supplement 1999-2000* (11-210) and *The Consumer Price Index* (62-001).
Table 7.1: Data collected by E. H. Phelps Brown and Sheila V. Hopkins, "Seven

Centuries of the Prices of Consumables, compared with Builders' Wage-rates," *Economica*, XXII, 87, 1955.

Figure 11.2: Bank of Canada, *Banking and Financial Statistics,* May 2001.
Figure 11.3: Bank of Canada, *Banking and Financial Statistics,* May 2001.
Figure 11.5: Bank of Canada, *Banking and Financial Statistics,* May 2001.
Figure 11.6: Bank of Canada, *Banking and Financial Statistics,* May 2001.
Figure 11.7: Bank of Canada, *Banking and Financial Statistics,* May 2001.

P. 313: Bank of Canada, *Banking and Financial Statistics,* May 2001.

Figure 15.1: Statistics Canada, Catalogue no. 13F0031MIE00005 and 11-516-XIE, F1 13.
Figure 15.2: Statistics Canada, Catalogue no. 9713 GDIF; Catalogue no. 71F0004XCB.

P. 451: Statistics Canada, International Trade Division, 31-532-GIE.

Macroeconomic Data

These macroeconomic data series show some of the trends in GDP and its components, the price level, and other variables that provide information about changes in the standard of living and the cost of living—the central questions of macroeconomics. You will find these data in a spreadsheet that you can download from your Foundations Web site.

		NATIONAL ACCOUNTS	1978	1979	1980	1981	1982	1983	1984	1985	1986	1987
		EXPENDITURE APPROACH										
the sum of	1	Personal consumption expenditure	134.8	150.6	169.1	191.1	204.8	224.9	245.1	267.6	289.6	313.4
	2	Investment	**48.2**	**60.5**	63.0	78.7	61.1	69.4	79.2	86.9	93.5	108.3
	3	Government expenditure	61.5	67.4	76.5	87.4	99.4	105.6	111.4	120.4	126.3	133.4
	4	Exports	61.3	75.2	88.3	97.0	97.6	104.7	128.8	137.4	142.8	149.9
less	5	Imports	60.4	73.6	82.5	94.4	82.8	91.3	112.9	126.1	137.8	143.3
equals	6	Gross domestic product	245.5	280.3	315.2	361.4	380.8	412.4	450.7	486.8	513.8	560.4
		INCOME APPROACH										
the sum of	7	Wages, salaries, and supplementary labour income	134.2	150.9	170.6	196.7	210.1	220.3	237.2	255.8	272.8	296.4
	8	Interest and investment income	18.9	23.2	27.3	33.3	38.0	37.1	39.6	40.8	39.5	38.8
	9	Profits of corporations and government enterprises	29.1	38.8	42.7	40.8	29.2	41.2	50.6	54.7	49.8	63.0
	10	Income of farms and unincorporated businesses	14.6	15.8	16.8	17.5	19.2	22.7	25.6	28.7	32.4	32.8
equals	11	Net domestic product at factor cost	196.8	228.7	257.4	288.3	296.5	321.3	353.0	380.0	394.5	431.0
plus	12	Indirect taxes less subsidies*	20.9	19.4	20.7	30.1	37.6	41.5	44.4	48.5	56.7	63.0
	13	Capital consumption	27.8	32.1	37.2	43.0	46.7	49.6	53.3	58.4	62.6	66.3
equals	14	Gross domestic product	245.5	280.3	315.2	361.4	380.8	412.4	450.7	486.8	513.8	560.4
	15	Real GDP (billions of 1997 dollars)	552.9	576.7	583.7	602.9	585.8	601.7	636.7	666.8	682.9	711.9
	16	Real GDP growth rate (percent per year)	4.1	4.3	1.2	3.3	−2.8	2.7	5.8	4.7	2.4	4.2
		OTHER DATA										
	17	Population (millions)	24.0	24.2	24.5	24.8	25.1	25.4	25.6	25.8	26.1	26.4
	18	Labour force (millions)	11.1	11.5	11.9	12.2	12.3	12.5	12.7	13.0	13.3	13.5
	19	Employment (millions)	10.2	10.6	11.0	11.3	10.9	11.0	11.3	11.6	12.0	12.3
	20	Unemployment (millions)	0.9	0.9	0.9	0.9	1.4	1.5	1.4	1.4	1.3	1.2
	21	Labour force participation rate (percent)	62.6	63.6	64.2	65.0	64.4	64.7	65.0	65.5	66.0	66.4
	22	Unemployment rate (percent of labour force)	8.3	7.5	7.5	7.6	11.0	11.9	11.3	10.7	9.6	8.8
	23	Real GDP per person (1997 dollars per year)	23,038	23,831	23,824	24,310	23,339	23,689	24,871	25,845	26,165	26,966
	24	Growth rate of real GDP per person (percent per year)	2.8	3.4	0	2.0	−4.0	1.5	5.0	3.9	1.2	3.1
	25	Quantity of money (M2+, billions of dollars)	127.3	149.1	174.9	201.1	218.7	235.5	252.1	277.8	306.3	341.7
	26	GDP deflator (1997 = 100)	44.4	48.6	54.0	59.9	65.0	68.5	70.8	73.0	75.3	78.7
	27	GDP deflator inflation rate (percent per year)	6.5	9.5	11.1	10.9	8.5	5.3	3.4	3.1	3.1	4.6
	28	Consumer Price Index (1992 = 100)	43.6	47.6	52.4	58.9	65.3	69.1	72.1	75.0	78.1	81.5
	29	CPI inflation rate (percent per year)	9.0	9.2	10.1	12.4	10.9	5.8	4.3	4.0	4.1	4.4
	30	Current account balance (billions of dollars)	−9.4	−9.8	−7.1	−15.0	2.3	−3.1	−1.7	−7.8	−15.5	−17.8
	31	Short-term interest rate	8.7	11.7	12.7	17.8	13.7	9.3	11.1	9.4	9.0	8.2
	32	Long-term interest rate	9.3	10.2	12.5	15.2	14.3	11.8	12.8	11.0	9.5	10.0

* includes residual error